In tribute to Cardinal Carlo Maria Martini, SJ

whose devoted service to the Word and meticulous scholarship

has inspired my priestly ministry these many years.

—Richard J. Sklba

* * * * *

"All scripture is inspired by God and is useful for teaching, for refutation, for correction, and for training in righteousness, so that one who belongs to God may be competent, equipped for every good work." (2 Timothy 3:16-17)

Contents

Preface

Anyone privileged to be called to leadership at weekday celebrations of the Eucharist in a parish community knows that some of the best of folks gather regularly for Mass. They can represent the prayer power of a community. There are the retired who are finally able to incorporate daily Mass into a more leisurely schedule; others feel the need to include an early morning Eucharist on their way to work. Sometimes possessing a profoundly mature spirituality, they practice their faith by that daily immersion into the mystery of the Lord's death and resurrection sacramentally renewed at the parish altar. They seek spiritual nourishment for the day's activity, whatever it may be.

The following pages represent a collection of possible ideas for the type of short homily usually expected and provided for those who regularly attend the weekday Masses. These brief ideas are called "fire starters," a term familiar to campers and to anyone with scouting experience. One piles the kindling wood lined with more easily flammable paper and then provides the spark to set the little pyre afire. The flickering flame slowly grows to illumine the darkness and give comfort to those gathered around.

The various thoughts gathered into this volume might also provide an initial spark of personal prayer for anyone interested in using the church's Lectionary for the practice of daily *lectio divina*. At their Twelfth World Synod on "The Word of God in the Life and Mission of the Church" (2008) the Catholic bishops strongly reaffirmed that devotion, as did Benedict XVI in his subsequent apostolic exhortation, *Verbum Domini* (September 30, 2010). The benefit of employing the *Lectionary for Mass* for the practice of daily *lectio divina* during Ordinary Time resides in its use of *lectio continua*, or semi-continuous readings. Thus each day's readings follow upon those from the previous day, providing a cumulative awareness of the Scriptures. While the cycle of Gospel readings repeats each year, the reader should be careful to follow the correct cycle for the first reading and responsorial psalm. Odd-numbered years use Year I; even-numbered years use Year II.

In 1943 Pius XII requested that Catholic exegetes and preachers keep historical-critical methodology in mind when studying the Scriptures, and the Second Vatican Council repeated that teaching with the church's highest authority (*Dei Verbum* §12 and 19). This was spelled out more clearly in the 1964 Instruction from the Biblical Commission, which insisted on the three levels of evangelical history: what Christ said and did, what the apostles spoke about concerning the words and deeds of Christ after the resurrection, and finally how the individual gospels chose to present the portrait of Jesus according to theological and literary images. This volume presumes that awareness as background yet recognizes that the liturgical assembly hears the text primarily as an inspired literary proclamation of carefully delineated size, and the presider preaches it as such. It is a post-critical piety that this resource aims to nourish.

This volume provides the biblical citations for each of the day's readings together with the heading provided by the *Lectionary for Mass*, usually drawn from the text itself. This heading serves as the church's hermeneutical lens, typically making connections with the other readings for the day. The minimalism of these headings allows for a variety of homiletical approaches. It is thus in the spirit of such headings that the following "Fire Starters" are offered, taking the headings as initial "sparks." The reading's introductory focus also reminds us that the phrase in the Lectionary should not be easily overlooked or casually dismissed in our use of that text.

Similarly, the *Lectionary for Mass* also includes an antiphonal refrain for each psalm as a communal response to that freshly proclaimed passage. Although probably rare in the practice of Catholic preachers, the antiphon itself, or one of the verses from the proposed psalm response, may become a source for the day's homiletic reflection. Because the psalm is designed for community recitation, however, this portion of God's Word has a different function in our liturgy. It becomes the prayer of the entire assembly, presider and people alike. The fact that the refrain is repeated several times suggests that it could provide an insight into the Word as incorporated into the church's worship that day. The phrase could even become the basis for a recurring meditation within the individual worshiper's subsequent prayer and daily activities.

There are fundamental truths inherent in the way God operates in our world. Returning to them at different times in our life or in new circumstances enhances the richness of our spirituality and maturity. Thus themes will occasionally be repeated in this volume because there are recurring patterns in God's revelation and those patterns will inevitably find voice in the church's liturgy.

Those who use this resource volume are encouraged to select any one of the "fire starters" and linger over it so that it might come alive with further concrete examples for the gathered community. On occasion additional insights and applications will be discovered if one also explores the immediate context before or after the specific text chosen for the Lectionary reading that day. No biblical text exists in isolation, literary or historical, and this is reflected in the church's practice of *lectio continua* as embedded in the weekday readings.

Thus one of the potential hazards of any homiletic resource that focuses on individual readings is the temptation to overlook the larger theological themes of the total text or its literary structure. In an effort to preclude any overly narrow reversion to homiletic "versification" or a proof-texting mentality, I have included a brief introduction to each biblical book when it first appears in the Lectionary cycle of readings. It is my hope that this initial scanning of the forest before looking at the trees will assist a preacher's effort to avoid such an error. To this end I have also provided among the "fire starters" for the Gospel reading a brief notation of "literary links"—namely, a reminder of the passage's location in the structural outline of the gospel as proposed by the New American Bible Revised Edition (NABRE). In using this resource the presumption remains that the individual homilist will spend time with the sacred text each day, personally pondering the words within context, seeking the grace of that inspired divine communication and exploring its implications for the lives of the contemporary congregation. The ideal is that each of us as preachers first be encountered by the Scriptures themselves. Only when we ourselves hear the Word as if for the first time can we break it open for others. Every preacher of the Gospel is first and foremost, like the Apostle Paul, a witness to the grace of God at work. The medieval conviction that we can only hand on what we have first contemplated ourselves is an enduring mandate for all preachers. In our post-Holocaust world every effort must be made to avoid even the slightest hint of anti-Semitism. Pejorative references to first-century Judaism or Pharisaism can never be part of Catholic preaching because God's gift and call are irrevocable (Rom 11:29).[†]

At the end of this volume is a brief litany of citations referring to the Word of God, which an individual preacher might use by way of an introductory prayer before preparing to preach, or as a spiritual reminder of the privileged importance of the ministry of preaching.

Allow me to add a final note of profound thanks to all friends and colleagues, preachers and prayers, who have shaped my understanding of God's Word over the years and contributed thereby to this volume. Only the Lord knows the full extent of my gratitude.

Richard J. Sklba
Milwaukee, Wisconsin
September 30, 2012
The Feast of Saint Jerome, Doctor of the Church

[†] A new resource highly recommended for preachers is *The Jewish Annotated New Testament*, ed. Amy-Jill Levine and Marc Z. Brettler (New York: Oxford University Press, 2011).

Monday of the First Week in Ordinary Time

First Reading (Year I)

Hebrews 1:1-6

God spoke to us through the Son.

The Epistle to the Hebrews

Written in elegant theological prose of a very different character from the writings of the apostle Paul, Hebrews is richly threaded with biblical allusions. Its aim is to encourage enduring fidelity to the profession of faith in Jesus, Redeemer and Lord, and to illustrate how this faith develops and deepens the convictions of Israel. Written after the destruction of the temple, the epistle tries to find theological significance in that tragedy. One should beware of interpreting the epistle's extended comparisons as if Christianity simply superseded or replaced first-century Judaism. That would be contrary to Romans 11:29 and the consequent teaching of the Catholic Church. Perhaps, rather than seeing the contrast as one of historical sequence, it might be helpful to invoke the Platonic view of earthly reality versus heavenly fulfillment. The christological and priestly character of Jesus as Son of God is highlighted.

God's Continuing Action in Every Age

The initial reference to the many and "various ways" (v. 1) in which God has spoken to us over the centuries serves to highlight the reality of divine activity in all of history, including our own day. In every human circumstance and in all situations good and bad, God has been present and indeed addressing us. Our God is a speaking God, who has often chosen to reveal his divinity and purpose through the prism of human experience. The various inspired sayings of Scripture build upon and illumine each other. This historic character of God's presence includes this very moment when God speaks to us as well. History is not only the past; it embraces this precise moment with all the finite circumstances of the day at hand.

The Nature of Speech

To *speak* (v. 1) is to communicate and to presume an implicit anticipation of a response of some kind, whether it be an action or a new understanding or some change in attitude and behavior. Something is always expected from the hearer. In fact, every statement by definition includes three elements: a statement of judgment, an expression of self-revelation, and an invitation to respond with reciprocal revelation. Even to say "It's hot/cold out today" makes a judgment about the weather, reveals one's own condition, and invites a confirming or negating response. Every speech by its very nature seeks to create a bond of unity. God speaks, and speech always reveals something about the speaker.

Jesus the Laser Beam and Privileged Prism of God

For believers and disciples the culminating moment for all divine speech over the centuries is found in the person and message of Jesus of Nazareth who is the *Son* (v. 2). As Son he shares characteristics with his divine Father, and actually embodies in his own human flesh the message/word of God. He speaks it clearly and in a format that all human beings are able to understand. Jesus is everything that could and should be said by God to us as a people on pilgrimage to our eternal destiny. There is a striking similarity of message between these opening verses and those of the prologue to John's gospel.

Antiphon (Year I)

Psalm 97:7c

Let all his angels worship him.

Type of Psalm

This psalm has been called an "enthronement psalm" because it could well have been used for an annual covenant renewal celebration when the Lord, Yhwh,

Monday of the First Week in Ordinary Time

was again recognized as Israel's king forever (v. 1). Every time the eucharistic assembly gathers we likewise again proclaim God as our Sovereign Majesty and Supreme Lord forever. The rest is decoration and commentary. Enthronement psalms protest every form of human idolatry and relativize all human authority, be they pharaohs, kings, presidents, or even the majority of a democratic consensus.

God's Angels

The refrain refers to worshiping "angels" (v. 7). Curiously, the Hebrew version of the psalm has "all gods" and alludes to the pagan deities who tremble before the solemn majesty of Israel's God, but the Greek version, quoted here to echo the passage from Hebrews, reads "*angeloi*/messengers." This refrain obviously reflects a different ancient version of the psalm. All heavenly beings, however, whatever their name, are subordinate to God and praise him constantly. They cannot do otherwise, for God is the source and final destiny of everything.

The World Invisible

We are reminded by the reference to gods or angels, that the Creed proclaimed at Mass every Sunday includes a reference to God, the Creator of "all things, visible and invisible." The world around our individual lives and our small weekday worshiping congregation is far larger and much more extensive than anything we can see or touch or even imagine as we move through the activities of the day. The invisible material forces of nature, known or still to be discovered, and even all the currents of human thought, are places where God's grace is always at work. There is an enduring bond between what we call the church militant and the church triumphant. Heaven and earth are filled with God's glory. There is more to see than what we see.

First Reading (Year II)

1 Samuel 1:1-8

Hannah's rival turned it into a constant reproach to her that the Lord had left her barren.

The First Book of Samuel

This book is part of what is known as the Deuteronomic history, namely, an attempt to describe the beginnings of the Davidic monarchy in light of God's election of Israel and Israel's fidelity to the Mosaic covenant. From the birth and early dedication of the great prophet Samuel to the death and burial of King Saul, the book documents the fundamental temptations, sins, and successes of Israel's first leaders. It lays the ground for its final explanation of the temple's destruction by the Babylonians.

Family Rivalries

Even out of petty family rivalries and human jealousies, as illustrated by this story about Hannah and Peninnah (v. 6), God can bring forth something important for the world's salvation. Therefore we need to seek out honestly the life-giving truth of all our disagreements and relationships. We certainly are called to help heal petty family jealousies and to rise above them in dealing with each other. Individual differences should be acknowledged, respected, and welcomed, not ridiculed. One of the purposes of Elkanah's annual pilgrimage, like all pilgrimages true to their nature, was to restore the human fabric of his family's relationships as well as to honor God. This is also true of every celebration of the Eucharist; hence the sign of peace is an important element in worship. The grace of reconciliation is a gift from the God who desires all human unity.

The Pain of Infertility

The memory of Hannah and her husband Elkanah might be a model for couples who desperately seek fertility and children in their marriage (v. 2). This can become very painful at times, and even playful teasing can be hurtful. The passage provides an opportunity for the entire community to pray for such couples and to offer support to their hopes. Not every method of fertility treatment currently proposed by science, however, can be automatically accepted by Christians. A perennial ethical question remains: Just because we can do something, should we? Why or why not? Adults without children of their own should be encouraged to find a local need to "adopt" in service and leadership.

ANTIPHON (YEAR II)

Psalm 116:17a

To you, Lord, I will offer a sacrifice of praise.

Type of Psalm

This is a psalm of thanksgiving that includes the public fulfillment of vows (repeated word for word in vv. 14 and 18) made during distress or danger. We make many promises to God throughout life, and this psalm reminds us of our countless verbal contracts and our obligation to fulfill whatever we may have promised to God or neighbor. Especially when we stand before God, we should be people of "our word." God is faithful and summons us to the same. In a real sense, every time we celebrate the Eucharist we implicitly renew our baptismal vows. They also were promised once and for all times.

Human Response to Blessings

The refrain is a response to the haunting question regarding how to repay God (v. 12) and how to respond suitably and gratefully for all the blessings given throughout a lifetime. The full focus can never remain simply on the pleasure and satisfaction of the recipient! By definition God is God, lavishly giving without measure. It is we who have the duty, and we remain a subhuman species when we neglect to offer praise and thanks. The refrain is an answer to the prior question: "How can I repay . . . ?" In a fuller sense this psalm prepares for the Eucharist we celebrate, because it is the very best response that is humanly possible.

Praise and Thanksgiving as Sacrifice

Where we sing in the English translation of "praise," the Hebrew has "*todah*/thanksgiving." The psalm presumes that every act of thanksgiving and praise (v. 17) is equivalent to a sacrifice because it summons us to humble submission, emphasizes our utter dependence, places ourselves at God's disposition, and offers our song as worship. We are even transformed in the process, something akin to the eucharistic action itself! Human melody echoes and rises like incense to give honor to God, filling every hidden crack and corner of the church. Song gives a certain special new beauty to material creation.

GOSPEL

Mark 1:14-20

Repent, and believe in the Gospel.

The Gospel of Mark

Generally recognized as the first written of our canonical gospels, Mark highlights the death and resurrection of Christ with an account of his Galilean ministry of proclaiming the kingdom. The title of "Son" stretches from the baptism to the confession of the centurion under the cross. This gospel explains the nature of Christ's sonship. His teaching in parables and his healings illustrate the way in which God is at work in the world.

Literary Link

The brief reference to the arrest of John (v. 14) places the ministry of Jesus in a historical context, and his opening summons to repentance (v. 15) provides theological continuity with John's ministry. The call of the first four disciples turns the dynamic toward the future, and underscores the intent of Jesus to gather partners in the work of the kingdom.

The Kingdom of God

The proclamation of the kingdom (v. 15) by Jesus has nothing to do with geographical

Monday of the First Week in Ordinary Time

borders or political structures but rather points to God's sovereign action in the world. Everything said and done by Jesus is intended to show how God works, and requires the response of new thinking, *metanoia*. What is translated as "repent" (v. 15) is literally aimed at thinking "outside one's mind," not penitential self-denial or Lenten discipline.

Partnership

There are two elements in this passage: Jesus' early Galilean proclamation of the nearness of the kingdom after his baptism (vv. 14, 15) and then his calling of the brothers fishing (vv. 16-20). They are not separate isolated episodes but rather interrelated and thus serve to remind us that God eagerly seeks partners in the unfolding of the kingdom! Each person is invited with his or her unique gifts and personality, for a distinctive purpose that cannot be fulfilled by anyone else! If we choose not to cooperate, we leave a rip in the history of humanity that even God can't fill; God respects our freedom that much. All this happened after the arrest of John the Baptist (v. 14). We can't help but wonder whether Jesus now felt himself in need for other partners in the work of God.

Two by Two

The call comes to these first disciples in pairs, "two by two," as a reminder of the biblical custom (Matt 18:16) that each person's respective individual witness must be legally supported and confirmed by another's, and that the strengths of one can support the weakness of the other. Every call is somehow communal in God's eyes. There may well have been larger groups actually involved in that day's work, but the gospel chooses to recognize the familiar dyad for theological purposes. As Archbishop Desmond Tutu insisted, "The totally self-sufficient person is sub-human."*

Immediacy

Those of us who tend to dither over major decisions and to consider endlessly the pros and cons of any choice are always astonished by Mark's description of the apparent quickness and decisiveness of the response of these early disciples' "immediately" (vv. 18, 20). It may help to recall that the Greek verbs are in the aorist tense, namely, describing an action, not only past, but done decisively once and for all. The team of brothers may well in fact have carefully balanced their options in real life, and at considerable length pondered all the implications of each choice, but once made, the matter was closed and a new age had begun for them and the world.

* "The Truth and Reconciliation Process—Restorative Justice" (Third Longford Lecture, Church House, Westminster, February 16, 2004).

Tuesday of the First Week in Ordinary Time

First Reading (Year I)

Hebrews 2:5-12

He made the one who leads them to their salvation perfect through suffering.

The Value of Suffering in Life

There is no individual and no family without some heartache or something we desperately wish would change . . . but it doesn't, and we suffer in large and small ways. We can learn from our suffering: dependency and need for others, the blessings of small comforts and kindnesses, the importance of never taking anything for granted. A fully mature Christian can sometimes finally come to the ability to say thanks for crosses, even those that hurt, because they are finally understood as moments of grace and growth. Christ's own human suffering actually perfected him (v. 10).

Final Victory through Christ Glorified and Human Dignity

Jesus is called the "leader" to salvation (v. 10) but the word itself suggests a "pioneer/*archegos*." It is a grace of sheer wonder that all things in the world to come are to be subject to a human being in the person of Jesus the Christ! This only emphasizes the inherent dignity of human beings and our need to be respectful of everyone, friends and enemies alike. Whatever is human is precisely what God has chosen to reconcile the world and to bring all things together in perfection. In God's mysterious plan this happens through weakness on the cross, not mere physical power.

The Call to Partnership in Transforming the World

It is all too obvious from the newspapers and television that things are not yet so subject (v. 5). The tragedies and violence of every age bring heartaches to so many people. Our task is to be partners with Christ in achieving that goal. The salvation to which we are called is social, not individualistic, eventually encompassing the entire universe. The communal character of everything is a constant theme running through the biblical witness.

Antiphon (Year I)

Psalm 8:7

You have given your Son rule over the works of your hands.

Human Beings as the Crown of Creation

Amid all the wonders of creation, this psalm celebrates all human beings who serve as the crowning glory of everything that is (v. 7). It is also specifically invoked by the church's liturgy to lift up the human existence of Jesus the Christ, Son of God. The biblical vision, however, always presumes that the greatest of all is the one who serves! The call of human beings therefore is to serve all of material creation, and to exercise good stewardship of the world. Ecology is woven into the very fabric of God's creation, and God is the model. Although some may argue against an anthropocentric view of the universe as too arrogant, the central figure of Christ makes that imperative.

Unpacking the Notion of the "Son of Man"

The original Hebrew wording pays tribute to the "son of man/*ben ʾadam*" (v. 5). This is a Semitic phrase for a human being as human, as related to the mud (*ʾadamah*) of the earth and destined to return to the earth from which he was created. Even this or perhaps especially this, sings the psalmist, is the high point of all creation. The liturgical refrain (v. 7) knows that the expression "son of man" is in the words of the psalm, but replaces the phrase with a more explicit reference, "your," to the Son, who is also the high point of the new creation! That the Son of God should assume the very mud of creation to make it

Tuesday of the First Week in Ordinary Time

his own is a great wonder. Our very being is related to the earth under our feet; the stars of heaven as is that of Jesus the Christ.

FIRST READING (YEAR II)

1 Samuel 1:9-20

The LORD God remembered Hannah, and she gave birth to Samuel.

Grace from Human Pain

God can bring grace and truth, even from a prayer of human bitterness and sorrow. Admitting our utter dependence upon God (as in the first and second "steps" of Alcoholics Anonymous), and acknowledging our limitations, gives space for God's salvation. Like Paul, we are encouraged to boast in our weakness and in God alone (1 Cor 1:31). Only when the seed falls to the ground and dies, does it bring forth fruit (John 12:24). God does not desire that we should suffer, but God brings forth goodness and grace, even from that suffering. From the yearning of Hannah came the great figure of Samuel (v. 20), who anointed the first kings of Israel and laid the foundation for Jesus the Anointed One.

The Danger of Rash Judgment

When the priest Eli saw the external movement of lips, he misjudged Hannah's situation as possibly drunken (v. 13) and out of order, thus providing us with a caution against judging mere externals without knowing the inner truth of a person's heart! We are called to make practical judgments at times, about many mundane things such as what to have for supper or what to wear to work, even the appropriateness of the human actions of others, but judging the inner values of another is what Jesus forbids when he warns, "Stop judging, that you may not be judged" (Matt 7:1).

Response to Those Who Misjudge Us

Being misjudged can be very hurtful, and there is always the temptation to lash back. Violence, however, even verbal, always begets further violence. The best response is one of respectful clarification regarding the real truth of the matter. Hannah's request that Eli "think kindly" of her (v. 15) remains a permanent admonition for each of us in our dealings with those around us. Rash judgment rips a community apart, but truth reunites and charity cements the bond.

ANTIPHON (YEAR II)

1 Samuel 2:1

My heart exults in the Lord, my Savior.

Hannah's "Magnificat"

This refrain is the first verse from the jubilant song of Hannah, who praised God for the gift of her son, Samuel. The words continue the story of the first reading by giving to the congregation the very words of Hannah at the birth of her son. Her words include a sense of joy over the gift of this new relationship and the promise of yet another future generation with whom each of us is bound by God's goodness! We can rightly use the same words for every and any gift of God.

A Song of Salvation across a Thousand Years

The refrain highlights the literary relationship of Hannah's song with the *Magnificat* of Mary, who adds the title of "Savior" (Luke 1:47) to her rendition of Hannah's song. The Divine Benefactor becomes a Savior who enters every human hardship to save us from being slaves to it! Each person and every generation needs to be saved from some difficulty over which they have no control. Surely, it is God, and God alone, who saves us as the contemporary song from Isaiah 12 proclaims.

GOSPEL

Mark 1:21-28

Jesus taught them as one having authority.

Literary Link

Having called the initial disciples, Mark presents two events that characterize the first Sabbath ministry of Jesus at Capernaum: the cure of the demoniac in the synagogue (vv. 21-28) and the cure of Peter's mother-in-law at home after the synagogue service (vv. 29-31). By seeing him at work they become his "apprentices." The chapter includes four healing stories: the demoniac (vv. 21-28), mother-in-law (vv. 29-31), general evening cures (vv. 32-34), and the leper (vv. 40-45).

The Authority of Jesus

It is significant that Jesus would first exhibit his authority in Capernaum (v. 21), a place where Herod's authority for collecting taxes from the passing commercial caravans and where Roman military authority was exercised so relentlessly and ruthlessly at times. By contrast, the authority of Jesus was moral, not military. Some impressive walled ruins from first-century Capernaum have been discovered. Recalling the geographical and political context of a place named in the Scriptures can illumine and focus the message. Jesus speaks with clarity, conviction, and compelling directness. All human authority is rendered relative.

Types of Human Authority

There are many different types of authority. For instance, there is the authority of knowledge (as the doctor who knows all the negative effects of smoking but continues to do so personally), of experience (the person who has gone through the tough struggle to break the habit), and of delegation (the movie theater employee who knows nothing about it and never smoked but has the responsibility of making sure that no one smokes in the theater!). It is helpful to explore the type of authority invoked by Jesus and perceived by his listeners (v. 27). Perhaps Jesus possesses all three types . . . and many more.

The Compelling Power of Holiness

There is a sort of authority, a commanding presence, that is associated with a person's true holiness. The unclean spirit acknowledged Jesus as "the Holy One of God" (v. 24) and submitted to his authority. To be holy, *qadosh*, suggests in Hebrew that the person is somehow different from others. That very distinctiveness can be enough to catch the attention of others and to offer an example of a different response than the normal human flash of anger, disdain, envy, or greed. Although our actions should not be taken merely to be seen and admired, they can have that effect on others when deeply sincere and genuine before God.

Wednesday of the First Week in Ordinary Time

First Reading (Year I)

Hebrews 2:14-18

He had to become like his brothers and sisters in every way, that he might be merciful.

The Solidarity of Jesus with All Human Beings

Sharing in our flesh and blood (v. 14) means sharing in the physical realities of limitation, weakness, and death. The fact of sharing all human sorrows and joys is the point. The article of our faith as expressed in the early Creeds insists that Jesus is "perfectly human," not a perfect human, and that distinction makes all the difference in the world.

Learning Mercy

Perhaps the best way to learn mercy (v. 17) and compassion is to have experienced the same human situation and condition as those who suffer. Those who grieve are best helped by those who have walked that same path. Becoming like brothers and sisters with all their hopes and fears enables a Christian to listen respectfully and reach out appropriately to others. The best classroom for that type of mercy may be the sickroom, the funeral parlor, the courtroom, or the prison. A hospital chaplain who suffers from a disability and uses a wheelchair to visit patients is a powerful instrument of grace.

Death as Slavery

Slavery, that is, the lack of freedom, takes many forms: physical, emotional, financial, and political. The fear of death, for example, is described as a slavery (v. 15), a reality that can restrict our freedom, limit our choices, and cripple our imagination. The gift of life in Christ after death is the gateway to freedom. This places Jesus as the liberator from sin and death within the ancient biblical tradition of freeing from physical slavery (exodus from Egypt) and from cultural and religious slavery (return from exile in Babylon).

Tested by Suffering

To be tested by suffering (v. 18) is to understand that moments of suffering or difficulty of any kind are moments when we reveal our deepest values and our true selves: resentful or retaliating, self-serving or altruistic, honest or manipulative, and so forth. We have the opportunity to look at ourselves squarely in the mirror of suffering. The opportunity to make some attitudinal changes can be the direct result of hard times.

Antiphon (Year I)

Psalm 105:8

The Lord remembers his covenant for ever.

Divine Fidelity

This psalm is an exultant hymn of praise for God's fidelity throughout the ages, and in particular to the chosen people as the extended family of Abraham and Sarah who remain the special object of God's care. The major eras in the history of salvation are rehearsed in this psalm, and our liturgical use of this refrain suggests that we understand ourselves to be yet another generation blessed by God's fidelity. Human beings live and die, sin and repent, laugh and cry . . . and God remains forever.

Covenant

The gift of covenant is a relationship of friendship and concern. More than an agreement or a pact (which is usually about some third reality), a covenant is the bond that unites persons in a mutual relationship that changes everything. Marriage and family are covenants, not mere legal agreements. From the reality of covenant flow the three perennial and fundamental religious categories of Israel's faith: mutual concern for covenantal members (*hesed*), justice (*tzedeqah*, the right relationship to everything), and peace (*shalom*, reconciled relationships).

First Reading (Year II)

1 Samuel 3:1-10, 19-20

Speak, O Lord, for your servant is listening.

Discerning God's Call

The call of God can be confusing at times, and patience is needed for *sorting out* its true origin, authenticity, and purpose. Samuel's repeated response continued until he was finally able to settle down, and wait for a fuller understanding that, in his case, came through the advice of another human being, Eli, the priest of that sanctuary (v. 8). Patience together with the involvement of others seem to be two aspects of the perennial pattern of discernment. This is a lifelong process for everyone!

Those Called Always Live in a Context

In the midst of a description of many details of time, place, and even relationships, little Samuel hears a call and responds (four times), *"Here I am."* Similarly in the midst of our own concrete daily life we also must answer, "Here I am." The fundamental question is, where is the "here" that I claim in answer to that call? Whatever happens always requires a sense of the surrounding currents of thought and the needs of others around us. "Here" is concrete, definite, and circumscribed by geography, human history, and relationships. It can also imply not being somewhere else!

The Task of Listening

A valuable lifelong mantra could be, "Speak, Lord, for your servant is listening" (v. 9). Listening is the stance of a true student/disciple. It is a curious fact that there is no specific word in Hebrew for "obey." The word usually used in Hebrew is to "hear," presuming that if one truly listens carefully, one's attitudes and activity inevitably change. True listening is always transformative.

God of Growth

The Lord was with Samuel in his growing up and becoming an adult (v. 19), just as God is with each of us in our movements of growing, maturing, and unfolding from one stage of life to another. A different manner of describing this type of divinely desired growth is the perfecting of the distinctive and unique individuality of every single human being. Matthew's admonition in the Sermon on the Mount is to be perfected (not perfect) as God is perfected (5:48). Our God loves us into goodness.

The Effective Word

The fact that God did not prevent any word of Samuel to be "without effect" suggests that a sign of an authentic prophet is not merely speaking boldly in God's name, but also speaking in such a way as to make a difference eventually (v. 19)! Prophets do not foretell the future, but they point out what God is doing before most other people can recognize it. Only in this sense do they seem to "make things happen." The actual work itself is God's, and the prophet only points it out, sometimes even paying a price for doing so.

Antiphon (Year II)

Psalm 40:8a, 9a

Here am I, Lord; I come to do your will.

The Grace of This Moment

God's grace always starts wherever we happen to be, emotionally, physically, and spiritually. We only know what we need when we know where we are. Therefore we regularly need to take a moment to clarify, diagnose, and define the "here" so as to know its need. There is an enormous value to the simple act of pausing at the entrance to prayer and "checking in" with God. Sometimes we speak of "the sacrament of the present moment."

The Value of Obedience in Dialogue

One way of describing our entire life's journey is to see us as seeking God for the

Wednesday of the First Week in Ordinary Time

ultimate purpose of being obedient to the divine imperative. The motto of Pope John XXIII was "*obedientia et pax*/obedience and peace." That holy pope then slyly suggested the need to find the true church of Christ in order to focus our obedience and find genuine peace (not complacency); sadly, it may not be identified with the ecclesial structures at hand. Biblical obedience always presumes a dialogue in which human beings speak their worries, fears, and needs as part of the process of accepting the will of God. This relationship is dialogic, not mindless acceptance. Even Mary, model of faith that she is, is described by Luke as expressing her concern at the annunciation (Luke 1:34).

Gospel

Mark 1:29-39

Jesus cured many who were sick with various diseases.

Literary Link

The second Sabbath event, the private cure of Peter's mother-in-law (vv. 29-31), is at home, thus signaling the fact that a Jewish Sabbath includes domestic relationships. This is followed by multiple exorcisms and cures after sunset (the technical end of Sabbath) and an early departure from Capernaum the next morning, which sends Jesus not to private prayer in the desert but to the beginning of his successful preaching tour of towns in Galilee (vv. 32-39).

A Context of Family

The fact that Simon and Andrew shared a single home (v. 29), in which even Simon's mother-in-law lived, suggested the extended family of the ancient Jewish world. Even after marriage, children lived in the home of their parents. The relatives are for the most part unnamed. God, however, never sees anyone as completely isolated and solely individual. The ancient realities of tribal relationship were important, and their absence from contemporary society may represent a human loss if arbitrarily and causally cast off. The radical individualism of our culture is a serious disease in itself! Similarly, as we gather for the Eucharist, we bring unnamed members of our own families. We never show up alone.

Importance of Community

Jesus himself does not show up alone. Jesus enters with his disciples (v. 29) as a social group, which is itself a united entity of individuals bonded together, called to be a social source of blessing for others. Another way of seeing that traveling group is to understand that they are a type of the church itself, a community working together with multiple gifts for the salvation of others. One might say that this gospel passage suggests that the "church" is at work from the beginning! It is a Catholic perspective to see the entire community as the medium for healing, revelation, forgiveness, and grace.

The Disease of Fever

A serious *fever* is not pleasant; it is often experienced with harsh thirst and chills. The ancient world without our modern hygiene or medical knowledge was often exposed to such illness. Clay dinner plates were even inscribed with incantations to protect the user from digestive ailments or food poisoning that produced such fevers. Even beyond the physical, however, the cure of Simon's mother-in-law from this particular ailment (v. 30) can become a type of God's care for all fevers, including our own emotional burning desires and frailties. The Lord heals them all so that we can better serve others (v. 31).

Sabbath for Renewed Work

For the ancient world a new day started at sunset, not sunrise. Consequently after sunset on the evening of Sabbath (v. 32), Jesus is already functioning at the beginning of the first day of the week, which the early church understood as the sacred day of resurrection. Day after day, again and again, creation arises out of primeval darkness. The ancients experienced "night" better than we do today. Illnesses and demon possessions are cured by the power of the new creation and the transcendent light of Christ, even during the earthly ministry of Jesus.

The Work of the Kingdom

Reviewing this fast-paced description of the first day of the week of Jesus, it is clear that three major kinds of work define the concrete activities of Jesus for the kingdom: curing, teaching, and confronting the demonic in our world, whether psychological, emotional, or moral. They are presented for disciples (perhaps better called "apprentices"), so that we can have a sharper focus on the major priorities among all the things we are called to do as partners in the work of the kingdom. The work is always rooted in personal prayer (v. 25).

The Demonic in Life

Demons (*daimonia*) were understood in the ancient world as powerful personal impulses from deep within an individual that drove one to harmful and even destructive behavior. They did not understand compulsions or addictions. Unclean spirits were afflicting not only those who were driven to sexual improprieties but also anyone separated from the community of faith by habits of sin or antisocial behavior. Ritual uncleanliness in particular was very comprehensive and included any forbidden contact with the origins of life and its final end. This was mysterious and therefore dangerous. Jesus expelled demons (v. 34). Removing the inner isolating compulsion restored a person to community life and worship.

Thursday of the First Week in Ordinary Time

First Reading (Year I)

Hebrews 3:7-14

Encourage yourselves daily while it is still "today."

The Holy Spirit

The definitive ascription of the citation from Psalm 95 to the Holy Spirit (v. 7) recognizes the reality of inspiration. Somehow God is the author of all Scripture, working heart and mind with the human poet who seeks to find the right words to say what God wishes to communicate. That same attribution of the psalm to the Holy Spirit also raises the question of which other media might the Holy Spirit use to speak to us each day.

Today

The letter encourages perseverance in faith in spite of contrary pressures and opposition. Each day is enough for itself, and the passage encourages such an immediate focus—similar perhaps to the "one day at a time" goal of sobriety by AA. Every day is presented to each of us by God as a new beginning, a fresh start and an opportunity to embody justice and charity in a new manner of response to the new realities of a new day (v. 8). The past no longer exists and the future is not yet, so all we have is this present moment to do the right thing for the right reason!

Hard-Heartedness

It is a terrible thing to be judged as hardhearted (v. 8), especially in the Jewish Christian tradition, which makes love of God and neighbor so central. The great prayer commands love of God "with all [our] heart" (Deut 6:5). Spiritual *kardiosklerosis*, the deliberate hardening of one's attitude toward the legitimate and necessary needs of others, might therefore be called the ultimate sin because of its radical centrality.

God's Judgment of the Inner Heart

There is sadness in the statement of the psalmist who imagines God concluding that human hearts always go "astray" (see v. 10). Not only are our actions subject to the judgment of the Lord but even our inner attitudes and the dispositions of our hearts, and that is precisely what receives the negative judgment. That seemingly inevitable proclivity toward selfishness and evil points to what we describe as the effects of original sin. Everyone is caught in the tide. The good news is that the same God is open to forgiveness, mercy, and radical redirection by grace.

Antiphon (Year I)

Psalm 95:8

If today you hear his voice, harden not your hearts.

New Year's Psalm

The ancient Mishnah saw this psalm as a "New Year's psalm," which took place at the annual autumn renewal of the covenant. The song begins with joyful worship of the king of Israel (v. 6) but recognizes the sins of the past and the possibility of repeating them again (v. 8). There is a sense in which the ancient cycle of human sin and divine salvation recurs each year, encompassing and welcoming successive new generations into God's work of redemption because they invariably are in need of mercy.

Heart Hardening

Reference to Israel's Lord as king evokes the memory of the ancient king of Egypt whose heart was hardened. The book of Exodus repeatedly spoke of the Pharaoh's response to Moses as hardening his heart in opposition (Exod 7:3). Sometimes the Pharaoh hardened his own heart, and sometimes God was the permissive "cause" by giving the power to say no. Perhaps this can be understood as an ancient attempt to understand the reality of grace and human cooperation, both of which contribute to human responses and behaviors. The leaders of Egypt as well as the people of God in the desert experienced the same resistance to the will of God. So do we today.

Massah and Meribah

The letter to the Hebrews cites this same psalm but translates the names of the places back into their literal meaning, namely, "rebellion." The reference is to the story of discontent over lack of water amid great thirst (Exod 17:1-7). Suddenly forgetful of all God's past blessings, the people complain about lack of water, which God, through the staff of Moses, then provides in abundance. The immediate wants of the people lead them to forget the past all too quickly. Any place that is the occasion for a sudden childish tantrum is a place of "rebellion," even in our own lives.

First Reading (Year II)

1 Samuel 4:1-11

Israel was defeated and the ark of God was captured.

The Dangers of False Security

The presence of God in the ark of the covenant with its tablets of the law was powerful enough to make the gods of the Philistines fall before him in ruin (1 Sam 5:4). God, however, is the true power, not the material object of the ark! Religious activity based upon the possession of a specific material object risks reducing religion to something merely mechanical, magical, and manipulative. That is also idolatry. This would be Jeremiah's complaint about reliance on the physical existence of the temple in Jerusalem (7:4).

God of Defeat

In all situations God must be allowed to be God in our life and in our world. This particular defeat by the Philistines (v. 10) was, however, not the end of Israel's world! The danger of victory is the temptation to presume that God will always do what we think should be done, or that we can assume that any triumph is due to our own abilities. In the weakness of defeat we learn fundamental dependence and humility. The cross itself was an initial sign of defeat, yet we honor that symbol as the source of new life and the occasion for total trust in God.

Antiphon (Year II)

Psalm 44:27b

Redeem us, Lord, because of your mercy.

Redemption

The fundamental notion of redemption (v. 27) is to restore someone or something to its original place or state. The "redeemer/*goʾel*" in Israel was the kinsman who bore the duty of restoring relatives sold into slavery because of the crushing burden of their debts. Likewise land was repurchased and restored by the redeemer to the family patrimony. Our God is one who desires to bring people home—but the question remains, Where is our real home to which God can bring us?

Mercy

In this psalm the "mercy" that is invoked by the psalmist as a motive for the work of redemption is actually *hesed*, the quality that binds covenanted partners together into partnership and makes them mutually concerned about each other's needs. Mutual fidelity is part and parcel of the relationship, and God remains ever faithful and loyal to his word. God brings people home because the obligations of his covenant promised to do so.

Gospel

Mark 1:40-45

The leprosy left him, and he was made clean.

Literary Link

Jesus is summoned by Simon Peter from an intended day of prayer in the desert to the beginning of a successful preaching tour through neighboring towns (vv. 35-39). The frenetic activity of Jesus on this first day of the week finds a dramatic

Thursday of the First Week in Ordinary Time

expression in the fourth cure, namely, that of the leper (vv. 40-45).

Touching the Leper's Wounds

Jesus not only healed the leper but actually reached out and touched him (v. 41), thus contracting the ritual contagion of leprosy and therefore entering the leper's world of isolation. The incarnation includes the belief that Jesus reached out to touch all the alienation and illnesses of humanity, entering into the depths of human misery and identifying with human beings at every level. Until we touch the wounds of our world, we will not understand them or heal them. Unless we allow our wounds to be touched, they cannot be healed. When the risen Lord invited the apostle Thomas in the Upper Room to touch his wounds, Thomas was able to feel the love that inspired the acceptance of those wounds.

The Price of Love and Service

Among the most dramatic passages of the gospels, this story describes the fact that Jesus "put aside" the divine injunction not to touch lepers and placed his entire religious and "professional" reputation on the line out of love for the leper. Perhaps very conscious of the eyes of critics gathered around, Jesus nevertheless deliberately reached out to offer a loving and healing touch to the leper's sores (v. 41). Doing the right thing often carries a price in society and in the church, especially when the loving gesture is viewed as completely countercultural and somehow forbidden!

Rejection and Isolation

The fact of having contracted the ritual penalty of leprosy through his touch meant that Jesus no longer could enter the towns (v. 45), a price he paid for his willingness to identify with the outcasts of his day. Jesus seems to have actually obeyed the law of isolation in order to identify completely with the situation of lepers in the ancient world. The theology of the cross suggests that even there Jesus also became unclean and contemptible in the eyes of the world in order to rise victorious.

The Risks and Courage of Discipleship

The story is a clear call to courage and confidence in service to the needy. Those who are always too cautious to step out of the imaginary line of prudence and safety will never feel the utter freedom of trust in God. In another but very powerful instruction, we learn that the very first group of individuals rejected from the heavenly Jerusalem as unworthy are not adulterers, murderers, or idolaters, but the *deiloi*/cautious (see Rev 21:8).

Friday of the First Week in Ordinary Time

First Reading (Year I)

Hebrews 4:1-5, 11

Let us strive to enter into that rest.

Entering God's Rest

The final day of creation is described as God taking great joy, satisfaction, and delight from the results of creative work. The Sabbath is fundamentally a divine state. Those who enter into it (v. 1) through the successful completion of any human endeavor experience something of God. This is very attractive, especially in moments of weariness when life is burdensome and our daily responsibilities weigh us down. Christianity transferred that divine rest to the first day of the week, the day of resurrection. For us Christians excessive human business, therefore, on that first day of the week precludes sharing that divine rest, and results in the absence of the new creation in our lives: strained relationships untended and gratitude unoffered! Modern secular society has experienced an enormous loss.

Gift and Challenge

God's rest is a gift given to those who share his labors (v. 11). The actual commandment is to work for six days and only then to rest on the seventh (Exod 20:9). The celebration of the Sabbath can only come at the completion of the week's work of perfecting the world. The duty of resting from work presumes that one has in fact done some work! This is never a blessing for the lazy and indolent.

Partnership

Creation is a communal reality, ultimately cocreation. Human beings can only enter God's rest when they have participated in God's work (v. 3). The work of any given day can seem totally individual, but a larger view of things will always keep in mind the fact that the source of energy and planning is God alone who inspires the worker and accomplishes the deed.

Antiphon (Year I)

Psalm 78:7b

Do not forget the works of the Lord!

Forgetting

If to remember something biblically is to make it present "anew" or to make it present "still," with all its power to save and to transform, then to forget is to somehow remove the object or action from existence and render it powerless. A mother's love forgotten loses its power to motivate and inspire. Forgetting all of God's blessings over the years leaves one without any sense of gratitude or any obligation to share those blessings generously with others.

The Works of the Lord

Perhaps the full object of the remembering is that the works are God's, not merely the result of human activity. God alone is the source of the thought or action. God alone brings them to fruition. Everything we do is in some way God's work. That is what we are asked to never forget.

First Reading (Year II)

1 Samuel 8:4-7, 10-22a

You will complain against the king whom you have chosen, but on that day the Lord will not answer you.

The Challenge of Sons and Daughters

It was the elders who came to complain about Samuel's sons as unfit for leadership (v. 5). Perhaps those sons were in fact arrogantly impious and unfit for religious leadership, but perhaps they were still immature and attempting to assimilate Israel's treasured religious traditions into another new and different generation. They may not have been fit because they were not yet ready. The elders themselves moved away from that tradition in their own way by requesting a human king in place of the traditional divine king of Israel (v. 5). Intergenerational transmission of the faith

Friday of the First Week in Ordinary Time

is complicated and not always very clear. Handing on the faith demands the patience as well as the fidelity of those who do so.

The Danger of Unexamined Cultural Imitation

The elders asked for a king like the nations (v. 5). There is a danger in the desire to imitate blindly the surrounding culture and mores because, unfortunately, the new values could become the inappropriate but primary focus of one's life. The summons to be countercultural is clear, but we must first be conscious of the unexamined assumptions of our lives. If something surprises us, it is a signal that we had assumed otherwise. What are the unacceptable things that "everyone else is doing" in our own community these days? What makes them unacceptable?

Learning from History

The biblical text interweaves both positive and negative attitudes toward the royal monarchy of Israel. This passage is called an "antimonarchical" section. The list of negative practices (vv. 11ff.) that a human king would introduce into the domestic and local life of Israel was in fact described in retrospect, namely, from a later age that could clearly see what price that new human institution had cost Israel. We see all things better in retrospect. That demands both prudence and humble discernment.

Samuel as Mediator

The fact that Samuel relayed the sentiments of the people to God (v. 21) momentarily ignores the fact that God was already present to hear all the conversation without need for Samuel's recapitulation. God allowed Samuel to summarize and add his own "take" on the matter. Sometimes God desires human partners; sometimes people need spokespersons. This task of Samuel emphasizes the tradition of mediation between God and his people from the beginning. Any number of daily human enterprises benefit from a mediator to smooth the path of conversation or prepare for action.

Human Freedom

God so respects our human freedom as to allow us to make our own choices and then to live with their consequences. The request of ancient Israel was for a king. God expressed an acceptance of their request (v. 22) because God can make good things come forth, even from the most flawed of human realities. God keeps trying to make things right, even after our poor choices.

Antiphon (Year II)

Psalm 89:2

For ever I will sing the goodness of the Lord.

Singing of God's Goodness

The same Hebrew word, *qara᾽*, means both to read and to call. The presumption of the antiphon's emphasis on singing (Hebrew: *shiyr*) is that all reading would be done aloud. For this reason the Talmud forbids the establishment of a school in a neighborhood without the neighbors' permission because it made so much noise! The traditional rubric for saying the Breviary was a requirement to at least move one's lips. Somehow praise is not real unless it is spoken or sung. "To sing is to pray twice," is the familiar adage of Saint Augustine. Genuine congregational prayer without singing is diminished.

Faithful Goodness

The Hebrew text has *hesed*, that is, covenantal fidelity and mercy, where this English version offers "goodness." Thus, in the Hebrew we hear the echoes of God's reciprocal faithfulness as a result of the covenant that binds God to his people and his people to God. How can one not sing when recalling God's faithful presence in good times and more difficult ones?

Singing Forever

The antiphon promises to offer praise throughout one's entire life . . . "forever!"

Curiously, the word translated as "forever" is *ʿolam*, namely, the world as it unfolds in history. The presumption is that the world around us will change and develop. In every different age, a faithful person sings praise. This is a dynamic reality within which people praise the God of all history, but one day at a time.

GOSPEL

Mark 2:1-12

The Son of Man has authority to forgive sins on earth.

Literary Link

After the dramatic encounter with the leper (vv. 40-45), Jesus returns to Capernaum to heal a paralytic and to demonstrate his authority to forgive sins (vv. 1-12). Portions of verses 5-10 may represent Mark's further reflections from early polemics with the scribes. After the healings, Mark presents five conflict stories (2:1-3, 6a). Each new event, however, adds another piece of mosaic to Mark's portrait of Jesus (1:14–8:26), which concludes just before Peter's confession of Jesus as the Christ (8:27-30).

The Word Preached

As he "preached the word" (v. 2), Jesus proclaimed and heralded that word, not explained it. Jesus, as the successor of the great prophets, had his own "*dabar*/word" that he spoke, namely, both event and oral statement (v. 2). The word proclaimed by Jesus was his pointing out the way of the kingdom of God, that is, the sovereign action of God in human history was unfolding in their midst. In a real sense the presentation of the paralytic was a test of God's action, and an attempt to see how divine action would address the paralytic.

The Crowds

The fact of constant crowds (v. 2) suggested that the word of God proclaimed by Jesus spoke to people's deepest fears and needs and hopes. They came in great numbers because Jesus spoke to their lives and their hearts. The crowds of fathers and sons who are attracted these days to popular "days for men" suggest the need to be addressed as social units, not mere isolated individuals.

The Faith of the Friends

The fact that Jesus saw "their" faith (v. 5) before responding to the plight of the paralytic reminds us of the power of the believing community in God's work for our individual salvation. The paralytic was not alone, and neither are we. There is no record of any complaint about the damaged roof—only admiration for the determination of the friends.

Knowing Their Hearts

When Jesus was able to know what they were thinking in their hearts (v. 8), he showed himself to be like the God who knew the mind and heart of Jeremiah (1:5; 12:3; 20:12) and the inner depths of each of our lives.

Divine Power at Work

The healing miracle of Jesus was an attempt to illustrate the power of God for forgiveness of sin, and the fact that the people responded after the healing with praise for God (v. 12) underscores that in this case Jesus himself was not the primary focal point, but rather it was the action of God that drew praise. Miracles are not isolated ends in themselves but always find focus and purpose beyond themselves, to the glory of God, not the human instrument.

Saturday of the First Week in Ordinary Time

First Reading (Year I)

Hebrews 4:12-16

Let us confidently approach the throne of grace.

God's Word

Every human word addresses something, but if it is truly God's word, it speaks to the very heart of a situation, like a two-edged sword (v. 12, that is, an instrument, not for cutting but for stabbing into the center of things). The image is keenly sharp and powerful, always effective, touching all the way to the heart where the ancient world presumed plans and decisions were made. God's word, in touching us so profoundly, can change history because it affects decisions. As a sword, it opens up everything and reveals the inner reality of every person so addressed.

The Sympathetic High Priest

True empathy can only come from someone "who's been through the same thing, and knows what it feels like." We are often warned, however, about saying too casually, "I know how you feel," because few others really do. Jesus our High Priest, who gains access to God with and for us, experienced everything human except sin, and does indeed approach with sympathy (v. 15) because he knows how it feels.

Antiphon (Year I)

John 6:63c

Your words, Lord, are Spirit and life.

Commanding Words

Although the antiphon is from a different source, the verses of the actual response itself are a portion from Psalm 19 with a series of alternative expressions for "word": law/instruction, decree, precepts, command, ordinances—each somehow seeking a personal response of compliance, acceptance, submission, or obedience. God's speech expects a human response that includes a change in our own thoughts and actions. When God speaks, something should happen. If it doesn't, or if there is no change in our lives, the world is deprived of blessing and grace.

Fear of the Lord

Psalm 19, like all those composed under the influence of the Wisdom tradition of Israel, includes the notion of "fear." This response to the word of God is reverence and respect (v. 15), not the craven fear of one humiliated and frightened of physical abuse or unjust mistreatment. We can have this sort of fear for those we love and venerate, for respected teachers and mentors, and for all who bring us into their confidence and introduce us to the larger world around us. Whom do we revere? Should we bring anything less to the instructions of God?

First Reading (Year II)

1 Samuel 9:1-4, 17-19; 10:1

This is the man of whom the Lord God spoke,
Saul who will rule his people.

Saul the Man

Saul was remembered as a strikingly handsome person (v. 2). This in itself was presumed to be the result of a special gift from God. His physical height enabled people to look up to Saul in every way. Moral, emotional, and intellectual qualities are far more commanding. All of these are considered gifts from God for human leadership. What makes a person attractive and engaging?

Saul the Anointed

The ancient world's manner of designating leadership almost always entailed anointing (10:1). That action indicated a change in the person thus chosen because oil, as it was absorbed into the individual's body, was understood as inherently possessing healing and strengthening properties. Oil changed and transformed the person. When mixed with spices and aromatic elements, the oil made the individual somehow outstanding and attractive. Saul was never the same again, even with his human flaws and imperfections. God was with him, even in his weakness. All of this is background for the church's subsequent sacramental use of Christian anointing at baptism, confirmation, and ordination.

Antiphon (Year II)

Psalm 21:2a

Lord, in your strength the king is glad.

The Strength of God

This is a fascinating antiphon, especially chosen as it is from Psalm 21, which describes the relationship between Israel's God and Israel's human king. Those chosen and anointed for leadership among God's people were understood to have been strengthened (v. 2) and thus to have shared a bit of God's own power and strength through the gift of God's Spirit. The gift was a remarkable mixture of human and divine. The king was promised an answer to his prayers (v. 3), length of days (v. 5), personal majesty (v. 6), and a face-to-face experience of God (v. 7). To be strengthened by God himself, therefore, is to have a sense of personal confidence, no matter what trials one would face.

Gladness

What does it take to make someone happy? Is happiness the same as gladness or joy? Perhaps to be glad, as suggested by this antiphon (v. 2), is to have a sense of purpose and accomplishment, and to be pleased with the situation as it unfolds. The knowledge of God's presence alone (v. 7), with all God's attendant gifts and abilities, can make someone glad. One could be afflicted with illness and even in discomfort, yet be glad! Physical well-being itself does not make a person glad nor give joy.

Gospel

Mark 2:13-17

I did not come to call the righteous but sinners.

Literary Link

Immediately after the healing of the paralytic and the forgiveness of his sins (2:1-12), Jesus calls Levi the tax collector to be a disciple and partner, and immerses himself in the society of those in practical need of repentance and forgiveness (vv. 13-17). This is Mark's second conflict story and offers yet another element in the way his gospel presents the mystery of Jesus (1:14–8:26).

Levi

Curiously, Mark 2:14 and Luke 5:27 both speak of a tax collector by the name of Levi, while Matthew's gospel (9:9) calls him the more familiar name of "Matthew." Perhaps the individual had two given names. Matthew's gospel may have preferred to use a popular name in his community of Torah observant Jews and Gentiles. The name could also emphasize the similarity between the name "Matthew" and the Greek word for a disciple, *mathetes*. Here it is Levi the tax collector, possibly a member of the priestly Levitical tribe. All sorts of representative individuals were eventually summoned into the Twelve! The group even included a zealot, presumably dedicated to the extermination of the Roman occupying army, as well as this Levi/Matthew who worked for the Romans! Jesus was the transforming unity for all of them.

Tax Collector

The person probably was sitting at a table, possibly with some shade from the day's sun, collecting a tax on dried fish being transferred or some other merchandise at Capernaum (2:1), which was a crossroads of commerce. The individual was someone who functioned as a representative of the despised Roman occupation army. Such people were often experienced in Judea as unscrupulously oppressing the poor for self-serving purposes. The call of Jesus was answered, however, and a conversion occurred. Yet Levi remained related to his former "professional" colleagues as the story of the dinner illustrates (v. 15). Levi's call to discipleship somehow included the duty to invite others to new integrity and justice. Levi/Matthew did not abandon his former life but transformed it.

Monday of the Second Week in Ordinary Time

First Reading (Year I)

Hebrews 5:1-10

Son though he was, he learned obedience from what he suffered.

A Human Representative before God

In order to be the "representative" of others (v. 1), one must first share their lives, hopes, and fears completely. The passage begins with the presumption that human priests both experience and model a profound identity with their people in every way, including sin. The contemporary word is "solidarity," which the priests of Israel, as well as those called priests in the new covenant, have always been somehow presumed to share with their people. For that reason, they all experience the need for some type of purification before approaching the utter mystery of God's presence. The passage is an opportunity to think of all the ways in which a person represents others: politically (elected officials), economically (wage earners), and spiritually (intercessors).

The Blessings of Weakness

The experience of human weakness (v. 2) can become an occasion for dealing patiently and compassionately, but also honestly and truthfully, with the weaknesses of others, as every priest must do. Because of one's own weakness, one can know the challenge from the inside, and offer helpful encouragement. Weakness is also an opportunity to be purified and perfected because it enables one to recognize one's complete dependence on God and others. God always uses the weaknesses that we acknowledge as an opportunity for grace and growth. The apostle Paul was able to boast of his weaknesses (2 Cor 12:5) and his afflictions (Rom 5:3). In our Western culture of independent individualism, this demands spiritual maturity.

Antiphon (Year I)

Psalm 110:4b

You are a priest for ever, in the line of Melchizedek.

Enduring Israelite Priesthood

The priesthood in Israel was dynastic and tribal in character. If one was of Levitical lineage, one was automatically a member of a priestly family, and that historical relationship was understood as remaining forever, as expressed in this antiphon (v. 4). In Christianity, priestly character is established by association with Jesus the Christ through baptism into his death and resurrection. Christ is the priest, and we are but his members. That relationship is traditionally distinguished between identification with the general mission of Christ for the transformation of the world through baptism, and a more focused ministry of service through ordination to serve the community itself.

The "Line" of Melchizedek

This phrase (v. 4) has perplexed believers and scholars for centuries. The Hebrew text of Psalm 110 has the word *dabar*, as in "a word," "an oracle," or a historical event brought into being by the word of God. In that sense the figure and history of Melchizedek (Gen 20:18) is suggested as the original pattern provided by that ancient king without family lineage who suddenly appeared in history, offered sacrifice, and received the priestly tithe. The psalm's Greek translation, however, uses the word *taksis*, a group classified as distinct from other social types. In either case the use of the antiphon in Christian liturgy asserts distinctiveness for Jesus and for his ability to mediate and intercede for us with God. Through baptism we share that role for the larger world.

First Reading (Year II)

1 Samuel 15:16-23

Obedience is better than sacrifice. Because you have rejected the command of the Lord, he, too, has rejected you as ruler.

The Ban of Destruction

The theological background to the story was the conviction of the ancient Israelite world that their battles were fought by God, and that the spoils (even human captives) of any victory belonged to God alone. They were sacred and must not be retained for human use in any way. Everything was to be destroyed. The practice was called *herem* in Hebrew, sometimes referred to as "holy war." To modern sensitivities, especially in the light of our developing Catholic moral evaluation of war, this may sound needlessly harsh and brutal. Knowing some of the rationale may make the tales more understandable.

The Sin of Saul

Saul chose to second-guess God's commandment that he had received (15:9) through the voice of the prophet Samuel and to retain some of the captured flock for sacrifice. That decision of Saul's was also in subtle self-interest since he could then enjoy the portion of sacrificial offerings that was traditionally shared with the donor. Saul offered a "plan B" on his own initiative and contrary to the expressed will of God in this matter. The passage offers a cautionary warning against facile choice of easier options that are veiled self-interest.

Priority of Obedient Submission

Humble obedience, especially after honestly presenting the whole picture to one's superiors, is described as more acceptable to God than sacrifice (v. 22). The latter, as we know, can be foolhardy or a subtle quest for praise to the donor. Public sacrifice on our part can also stem from a variety of self-serving motives. Obedience to the commands of the covenant is a major element in the teaching of the Deuteronomic theology expressed in the books of Samuel. The Bible insists on the serious consequences and punishments for those who choose to do otherwise. Jews and Christians share the importance of radical obedience with their Muslim neighbors, for whom obedient submission is the actual meaning of the word "Islam."

Antiphon (Year II)

Psalm 50:23b

To the upright I will show the saving power of God.

A Psalm of Liturgical Judgment

After several verses of stern condemnation for those who sin against their neighbors, Psalm 50 concludes with a promise of salvation for all participants in worship who refuse to be implicated in evil. One should never forget the implied evaluation and judgment of the God who is present for all sacrifices of praise. The human praise we offer is judged by the very God to whom our praise is directed.

Salvation

Again and again we are reminded that the notion of "salvation" (v. 23) as expressed in this antiphon refers to God's willingness to intervene and to extricate human beings from whatever tight spots may occur in life. God's "saving power" is the divine willingness to open paths of escape and provide the freedom for new beginnings in hope. God stands beside those who suffer but also offers fresh starts to the upright in attitude and action.

Gospel

Mark 2:18-22

The bridegroom is with them.

Literary Link

The discussion regarding fasting (vv. 18-22) is Mark's third conflict story within the gospel's account of the Galilean ministry of Jesus.

Fasting

Monday of the Second Week in Ordinary Time

Perhaps more important than the basic physical action of fasting is its motive and the religious meaning it embodies. Pharisees fasted to commemorate the tragic destruction of the temple by the Babylonians in 586 BC. The followers of Jesus have sorrowfully commemorated the death of Jesus (v. 20) and also expressed empathy and solidarity for those less materially blessed. Christian fasting embodies love of God and love of neighbor. Those who may have fasted as Jews prior to becoming disciples of Jesus added new meaning to their practices. Although the notion of fasting is often viewed by Christians as primarily a Lenten consideration, it remains a year-long reality for faithful people desiring to maintain discipline in their lives and actions. After the death of Jesus, the early disciples continued to live in the shadow of that tragedy, even though it quickly preceded his resurrection and vindication by God because they recognized their personal complicity in the tragedy.

New Beginnings

Though clearly rooted in Judaism, there remains something novel in the entire teaching of Jesus who offers new wine and new wineskins (v. 22). While the Gospel of Matthew tends to emphasize continuity with Judaism, Mark's gospel, which seemed to originate from a more completely Gentile community, stresses the new beginning and fresh start of the mission and message of Jesus. Customs and traditions develop and change over time, and every Christian community must always keep them appropriate and meaningful to the age in which they live and the cultures that shape their lives. Every scribe instructed in the kingdom is like the householder who brings forth the new and the old (Matt 13:52).

Tuesday of the Second Week in Ordinary Time

First Reading (Year I)

Hebrews 6:10-20

This hope we have as an anchor sure and firm.

The Promise

Abraham waited for God's promise, and once given, it was sufficient because Abraham knew that God's word was "good as gold." By and of itself, even though not as yet fully fulfilled, the promise was worthy of trust (v. 13). Because it is God who does the promising, we can have hope as well. The question for the recipients of the Letter to the Hebrews (and for us) remains: What do we trust in, and why? Does every promise merit confidence? This passage also insists that we pay close attention to God's promises, and see them as a sort of anchor for our lives. Moreover, those who eagerly await the fulfillment of the promises, particularly the faithful and devout people of Israel, are offered as models (v. 12). This was particularly important for Jews initially converted to the Jesus movement but now experiencing a slackness of spirit or religious enthusiasm.

Swearing

This may be an opportunity to distinguish a few concepts that are often muddled in popular colloquial speech. Technically to swear, for example, is to invoke God's name as testimony to the truth of our statement (v. 16). The passage makes a point that God swears to the truth of his promise by his own name because there is no higher authority (v. 17). *Swearing* has nothing to do with vulgar language that in itself may be impolite or crude but not sinful. *Cursing* is damning someone or something to hell and is an offense against charity as well as justice.

Good Works

The just judgment of God encompasses everything, and therefore it is consoling to remember that God's justice never overlooks or ignores our good works (v. 10). Similarly, every personal examination of conscience should include an acknowledgment of things done well (by God's grace) as well as the less noble aspects of our lives. The specific good works mentioned in the passage are those offered in service to the holy ones (baptized) in our community (v. 10).

Love for God's Name

Initially, in a culture of arranged marriages, the notion of "love" was primarily a political term; it was promised to those with whom one entered a covenant. Such love required care and concern for the interest of others. Love for God's name (v. 10) is demonstrated by the respect given to the Person of God (since in Semitic culture, "name" is a reverential reference to person) and for all the things willed and commanded by God. Far more than merely the avoidance of casual misuse of the divine name in daily speech or oaths, the reference includes respect for everything sacred to God, especially God's holy ones (v. 10), for they are precious in God's sight. Care for their needs is always linked to love of God. Love of God and love of neighbor are once again bound together in a fundamental way of life. One is reminded of the poet Elizabeth Barrett Browning, who mused, "How do I love thee? Let me count the ways."*

The Image of "Anchor"

An anchor provides stability and steadfast security for a boat, preventing mindless drifting or the loss of a location, safe from currents or passing tides. This passage is one of the sources for considering hope as symbolized in an "anchor" (v. 19), with the tines securely buried, not in the sandy bottom of a lake or river, but in this case, in heaven itself, from which we receive assurance and confidence for our daily lives and decisions. Exploring that common image is helpful and its basis for "hope" encouraging.

* Sonnet 43, *Sonnets from the Portuguese* (1850).

Antiphon (Year I)

Psalm 111:5

The Lord will remember his covenant for ever.

Tuesday of the Second Week in Ordinary Time

Remembering

It is simple enough to recall that when one "remembers," she makes the original reality present still or present again. Remembering either the good or the bad brings all the emotions and sentiments back to mind and renders them again active realities in our lives. Kindnesses continue to bless, while unresolved human hurts burn throughout all of life. When it is God who remembers (v. 5), the reality is assured.

God's Fidelity

God's enduring commitment to keep his word forever (v. 5), even when we fallible human beings choose to be less stable or trustworthy, is a fundamental characteristic of our Divine Creator. Knowing all things, even the surging tides of the human heart, God respects our volatile free will when we choose to change our minds and dismiss prior promises. God's fidelity endures forever and therefore human praise for God should also be sung forever, as Psalm 111 recommends (v. 10).

First Reading (Year II)

1 Samuel 16:1-13

Samuel anointed David in the presence of his brothers, and the Spirit of the Lord God rushed upon him.

Samuel's Grief

The aging prophet Samuel had watched King Saul's downward spiral from being a promising young ruler into fearful paranoia that tottered on the edge of violence (1 Sam 19:1). Even God reprimanded Samuel for clinging to his sorrow (v. 1). In God's providence it was time for a fresh start with young David the giant killer. Samuel complied with God's command to anoint the charming lad (v. 12), but rued the changing of the age and the new world being born around him. When the ceremonies were over, Samuel went back home to Ramah (v. 13). The process of aging inevitably brings a deeper appreciation for the successes and failures over past years. Some dreams went sour, and unexpected realities had to be reckoned with. Things never turn out the way we think they will or should. Spiritual maturity includes coming to terms with the changes within and around us. Even Samuel the Elder has much to teach us.

God's Improbable Choices

God's choices are always unlikely from a human point of view. For that reason the successes may be clearly the result of God's action, not that of the human agent. The prophet's selection of young David as a future king (v. 11) startled Jesse and his family, who hadn't even bothered to bring him in from the fields for the sacred festival (v. 12). The choice of the least likely from an initial human standpoint makes it very clear that the true source of success is God and God alone. Human beings merely cooperate with that call.

Anointing

The anointing with oil is an ancient symbol of the gift of the spirit because oil is absorbed into the person's physical being. Exploring the natural qualities of olive oil reveals that oil serves to heal, strengthen, and protect the individual chosen for leadership. The ritual signals and effects a change and transformation in the individual so anointed. The fragrance of such ritual oil remains as a symbol of God's enduring though invisible presence in the action and in the life of the person so designated. Samuel anointed young David (v. 13) and a new age began for Israel. We are anointed at baptism, confirmation, and ordination.

Antiphon (Year II)

Psalm 89:21a

I have found David, my servant.

A Psalm of Lament

In prior verses Psalm 50 acknowledged God's many blessings given to Israel throughout history, including the offering of a covenant to David (v. 4) and the establishment of the Davidic dynasty (v. 21). The responsorial hymn itself also acknowledged that a subsequent disaster had overtaken the chosen people and destroyed the city of Jerusalem as well as its temple (vv. 39-46). The day's liturgy chooses to ignore that tragedy, however, and merely to focus on the fact of God's enduring choice of David, no matter what may happen.

Servant

In the culture of ancient Israel, servants were either indentured or owned. The title also became honorific in court life, and signified obedience, loyalty, attention to wishes, and compliance with requests and given tasks. This usage is even reflected today in major governmental cabinet positions called "secretary" or "minister/ servant." Both meanings of the term are in the background as God acknowledges the obedience initially exhibited by David (v. 21). Even liturgy is called "service" because worship provides the context for all the qualities expected of a good and faithful servant.

Gospel

Mark 2:23-28

The sabbath was made for people, not people for the sabbath.

Literary Link

The fourth conflict story (vv. 23-28) deals with the issue of "work" on the Sabbath. It highlights the flexibility and priority of human needs over narrow literal compliance.

Work

The action of the disciples was more than merely taking a handful of grain in hunger, but was described by Mark as making a path through the fields (v. 23). This came closer to the servile work of harvesters, and gave rise to the concerns of the Pharisees. Curiously, the actual command of the Decalogue is first and foremost to work for six days (Exod 20:9) and only afterwards to rest on the seventh! The rabbinic tradition allowed exceptions for caring for the sick. Jesus did not allow charity to trump the commandment but acknowledged that charity was already part of that commandment. In this matter Jesus followed the school of Rabbi Hillel, who was concerned about the intention of the law as well as its letter. Work always has an element of relativity to the individual involved. Field work for the farmer is different from leisurely tending an urban flower garden!

Sabbath

The fact that the *Sabbath* is made for the benefit of human beings (v. 27) means that the cessation of regular work is also important for human mental and spiritual health. The Sabbath is intended as a time to rest but also to reestablish a renewed right relationship with everyone and everything! One honors God by caring for one's own well being. The assertion is surprising because it focuses on our needs, not on the Sabbath, as something for God's benefit. Worthy of further reading might be a consultation with Rabbi Abraham Joshua Heschel's classic book on *The Sabbath* (1951) or Pope John Paul II's letter on the sacredness of Sundays for Catholics, Day of the Lord/*Dies Domini* (May 31, 1998).

Wednesday of the Second Week in Ordinary Time

FIRST READING (YEAR I)

Hebrews 7:1-3, 15-17

You are a priest forever according to the order of Melchizedek.

Melchizedek

Early Christian preachers combed the Scriptures of Israel to find patterns for God's actions in the world, and to seek human figures who might illustrate that work as seen in the life of Jesus of Nazareth. They quickly found the figure of the mysterious king of Salem who exercised sacrificial ministry as a prerogative of his royal status (v. 1). He was a servant of God Most High, offering bread and wine, who accepted a tithe that acknowledged his legitimate priesthood (Exod 14:18). His superiority over Abraham himself made this figure stand out, and the description of his authority easily became a way to speak of the unique priestly ministry of Jesus as contrasted with the Levitical priesthood in Israel. For all the Gentiles who now gather for daily Eucharist, tribal heritage no longer matters.

Forever

Because Melchizedek is presented without prior family lineage, his enduring presence was projected forward into the future, not backward into history. For that reason the author of Hebrews speaks of the indestructible power of his life (v. 16). Although the Word entered historical time and became subject to its limitations, he also transcended that reality and shares eternal life with God forever. This participation in life forever is communicated to all who enter the Lord's paschal mystery through baptism. We all now live with a future orientation toward the Second Coming and final redemption of the world.

ANTIPHON (YEAR I)

Psalm 110:4b

You are a priest for ever, in the line of Melchizedek.

Priestly-Kingship Psalm

Filled with royal and priestly imagery, Psalm 110 could well have been used as a coronation hymn. Though somewhat violent in the description of the destiny of the kings' enemies, the psalm clearly acknowledges his power and victorious conquest over all hostile opponents. The ancient world used military strength and victory as the primary metaphor for power. We now have additional natural alternatives as the images of nuclear fusion and the force locked into physical atoms.

Priesthood

Since all the patriarchs and heads of families in general were authorized to offer sacrifice to God, the priesthood of Israel had a slightly different function. One became a priest by tribal background, ritual consecration, and becoming so familiar with the nature of the god of a sanctuary as to know with certainty which actions and human attitudes were acceptable to that deity (v. 4). Priests gave *torah*/instruction to worshipers and often provided a liturgical "examination of conscience" for those seeking entrance to the shrine. In this light, the priesthood of the baptized also presumes clear knowledge of the will of our God.

FIRST READING (YEAR II)

1 Samuel 17:32-33, 37, 40-51

David overcame the Philistine with sling and stone.

Utterly Inadequate Weapons

A sling and five smooth stones (v. 40), as contrasted with all the fearful Philistine metal armor, illustrates God's consistent pattern of using inadequate human instruments to demonstrate that the victory is God's alone! Both unlikely youthful servants and foolishly chosen instruments made it very clear that God alone is the source of success. Those who trust in God need not feel inadequate about their own weaknesses.

An Antimilitary Conviction

The fundamental fact that God does not save "by sword or spear" (v. 47) is part of the antimilitary strain that also runs through the biblical history. Especially Isaiah shows contempt for the power of horse and army (31:1) rather than confidence in God's power alone. The paradox remains that beside the countless biblical tales of battles and warfare there also exists a fundamental conviction that rejects all mere human weapons in favor of divine power alone.

Antiphon (Year II)

Psalm 144:1

Blessed be the Lord, my Rock!

A Psalm of Royal Victory

Like Psalm 18, the hymn of Psalm 144 celebrates a military victory and praises the God-given power and strength of the king. In the Greek translation of the psalms, this hymn is explicitly related to David's victory over Goliath. The images may well have come from the ancient tradition of liturgical celebrations for royal conquest.

Shield

The Hebrew word *magen*/"shield" can mean a specific weapon of personal protection against swords; it became a title for God (v. 2) that would certainly fit into this context. When revocalized as *mogen*, however, it meant a supreme royal figure, such as an emperor! Although our text uses the former, both meanings lie hidden in the inspired text. That word would recall the name for a common kosher wine. In any case, the Lord is praised as protector.

Gospel

Mark 3:1-6

Is it lawful on the sabbath to save life rather than to destroy it?

Literary Link

The fifth conflict story (3:1-5) in this series retains the Sabbath context but moves from the question of work to healing. The final verse reports the decision of Pharisees and Herodians to reject Jesus (v. 6).

The Withered Hand

The hand as an object for healing by Jesus has symbolic value in itself (v. 1). A hand is more than merely an anatomical member of the man's body. It is also a symbol of one's human activity that requires God's healing in order to be fully effective. Although the passage does not differentiate between right or left, the cure could also restore the man to social interaction with family and friends because the right hand was traditionally used in the Middle East for communal eating and physical contact with friends, while the left was restricted to personal bodily functions. A left hand could never be used in any social context.

The Initiative of Jesus

Curiously, this is a miracle without request from the individual in need of healing, or from friends. Jesus himself initiates the healing (v. 3) and almost seems to deliberately provoke the debate. Characteristically, we human beings tend to argue over what is important to us. Consequently, we should not be surprised that the Sabbath was the occasion for any number of debates within the Pharisaic tradition (v. 2). Perhaps the question of "Sabbath/Sunday" observance is an issue that contemporary Catholics should discuss more often because it should matter for us too! Jesus invites us, as well as his Pharisee friends, to explore the meaning of the Sabbath together!

Reframing the Issue

Asking a question differently and approaching a challenge from an alternative direction could provide a fresh answer to any number of human dilemmas. Thus, in this case Jesus changes the topic from one of abstention from work to one of "sav[ing] life"/help for a neighbor (v. 4)! Jesus often simply reframes a question, as here, for example, from disobeying a command not to work on the Sabbath to one of doing good on the Sabbath, thus opening up the question to different solutions. God can always see things differently.

Wednesday of the Second Week in Ordinary Time

Thursday of the Second Week in Ordinary Time

FIRST READING (YEAR I)

Hebrews 7:25–8:6

He offered sacrifice once for all when he offered himself.

The Qualities of the Great High Priest

The Lectionary's passage begins with the recitation of the ideal characteristics and qualities of a perfect priest as envisioned by the author: holy, innocent, undefiled, and separated from sinners (v. 26). The list serves as an excellent examination of conscience, not only for anyone presiding over the church's eucharistic assembly, but also for all the members of God's priestly people who are participating in the worship. The biblical notion of "holiness," as understood in the Semitic culture, emphasized a difference and a separation from normal human attitudes and behavior that are inevitably tainted by human sin and selfishness. All who gather for daily Eucharist are humbled by the difference they recognize between themselves and that ideal. Such a list invariably prepares for the initial penitential rites of the liturgical assembly.

Pattern, Copy, and Shadow

The philosophy of Plato, which was very popular in first-century-AD Alexandria, envisioned all our earthly experiences as mere shadows, patterns, or poor replicas of a more perfect heavenly reality. In particular, human worship was explained as only a shabby reflection of the perfect praise of God that fills the heavens with adoration of God's immense and eternal majesty. That idea of a pattern (8:5), however, is also rooted in the Pentateuch itself when God gave Moses a divine *tabnit* or model/"pattern" (Exod 25:9, 40) for constructing the sanctuary and officiating at its worship. Before the utter transcendence of God, everything human is imperfect and deeply flawed, especially our attempts to offer suitable worship. Adding a chronological dimension to imperfection, we acknowledge that we are but rough drafts of future realities.

The High Priesthood of Jesus

In contrast to all human effort, the priesthood of Jesus is described as so perfect, and therefore so effective, as to require but only a single action of sacrificial praise before God. His enduring "once and for all" action of self-sacrifice is recognized as sufficient to achieve the reconciliation of all sinful humanity with God. It allows him to take his place at the heavenly throne forever. The church insists that the daily repetition of the Eucharist does not duplicate or repeat Christ's singular action but only renews it and extends it to a new particular group of humans in need of that transforming presence of God in their midst.

The Offering of Gifts

The Letter to the Hebrews singles out the offering of gifts (v. 3) as an essential activity of priesthood at God's altar, but a deeper reality is the ultimate characteristic of that function, namely, knowing God's instructions so well as to know what and how such an offering might be truly pleasing. It is *Torah* or instruction that marks the priestly ministry in ancient Israel (Jer 18:18). The priest knows what God wishes and sincerely, together with his people, attempts to comply.

ANTIPHON (YEAR I)

Psalm 40:8a, 9a

Here am I, Lord; I come to do your will.

A Psalm of Thanksgiving

Although the latter portion of Psalm 40 is an extended prayer of supplication for deliverance from affliction, the initial dozen verses represent a magnificent expression of true religious sentiments and genuine devotion. To anyone seeking a picture of the ideal worshiper, one could simply recite this hymn of submissive confidence and joy in the reality of God's presence.

Thursday of the Second Week in Ordinary Time

Complete and Total Obedience

The antiphon is a combination of two phrases from the psalm (vv. 8 and 9), and thus collectively represents the perfect response of a creature before God. Called into existence by God, and created for God's purposes, every creature finds its perfection and happiness in complete compliance with the will of God. We Christians celebrate Jesus of Nazareth as having achieved perfect conformity to the will of his heavenly Father. Thus he is the ultimate model for all his disciples. It may be interesting to note that the Muslim ideal of holiness is precisely such submission to the will of the utterly transcendent God; every human plan is qualified by *Inshallah*, "if God wills it."

First Reading (Year II)

1 Samuel 18:6-9; 19:1-7

My father Saul is trying to kill you.

The Gift of Human Friendship

After David was welcomed into King Saul's court, he became a very close friend of Saul's son, Jonathan (19:1). Their relationship deepened and grew to genuine mutual respect and fondness for each other. These bonds of friendship are great gifts in life and blessings that cannot be achieved by any type of pressure, purchase, or manipulation. They are gifts to be included in our sense of stewardship and treasures for which we are also ultimately accountable before God. We should be ever grateful as well.

Jealousy

David was a very attractive figure, and a person to whom people naturally turned in respect and admiration (v. 7). Saul, however, saw David as a threat to his own leadership (v. 8). In an enduring mood of paranoia and personal inadequacy, Saul repeatedly attempted to kill David and thus eliminate him as a potential rival to his own position of leadership and that of his son Jonathan (19:1). The story serves as a powerful warning against the lethal danger of jealousy. Rather, one should appreciate the gifts of those around us, rejoice in their talents, and find ways to be mutually strengthened by cooperation.

Antiphon (Year II)

Psalm 56:5b

In God I trust; I shall not fear.

Trust Twice Repeated

The fundamental reality of trust in God is highlighted in this psalm by the fact that this very antiphon is repeated twice (vv. 5 and 12). In moments of deep anguish and personal anxiety we need to repeat our fundamental stance before God often as a mantra of prayer. Some sentiments are so important and so fundamental that they need frequent renewals in order to become fundamental values in life. The alternative, to travel through life constantly suspicious and distrustful, is a deep stumbling block, a "satan," if you will, to spiritual growth.

The Roots of Fear

A person fears whatever is powerful enough to be harmful or destructive, something over which there is no control. If we live in the total confidence that a truly benevolent God is in control and journeys with us through the hurts and heartaches of life, we can be confident that ultimate victory and final success are with God and that God cares enough to get us through the dangers. That was the attitude that accompanied David, even when threatened and persecuted by Saul. The God of Israel does not preserve us from painful experiences but stays at our side until they are resolved.

Gospel

Mark 3:7-12

The unclean spirits shouted, "You are the Son of God," but Jesus warned them sternly not to make him known.

Literary Link

Immediately after the initial rejection of Jesus by some of the Pharisees and Herodians (3:6), Mark presents two positive scenes. We first learn of the people who continue to come to Jesus and to follow him (vv. 7-12), no matter what the opposition, and then the choice of the Twelve (vv. 13-19a).

Titles of Jesus

The Gospel of Mark uses the titles of Jesus to teach about his person and mission. Although the gospels of Matthew and Luke make the title of "son" the center of the temptation story, in that instance Mark is more generic. The spirits do proclaim him as such; however, in this summary passage (v. 12) and finally the centurion under the cross will solemnly acclaim him by that title (15:39). Sonship may refer to physical relationship and family descent, but it also serves to emphasize shared characteristics and similarity, as when someone comments in playfulness or exasperation, "You certainly are your mother's son." The entire gospel is an effort to explain to often dull and uncomprehending disciples precisely how Jesus is uniquely like his heavenly Father.

Healing

In Mark's gospel the healing ministry of Jesus is often highlighted and emphasized as a significant activity. Mark's account of the very beginning of his public ministry included four different healing references. Healing is a sign of the kingdom of God at work; it is evidence of the way in which the works of Jesus are reflective of the work of his Father who wills the healing of everyone. The crowds flocked from all directions to be healed by him (v. 10). The spirits see it for what it is, even if human disciples and apprentices are less perceptive. Any work we do for the sick and infirm marks us off as disciples of that same Jesus and partners in his work for the kingdom.

Friday of the Second Week in Ordinary Time

First Reading (Year I)

Hebrews 8:6-13

He is mediator of a better covenant.

Mediator

To act as a mediator (v. 6) is to somehow understand and represent at least two sides of an issue or two diverse groups. Jesus, a single individual person who, according to the teaching of the church, shares both the divine and human natures, is eminently qualified to act in that capacity for us. It took several centuries before early Christians could find the most helpful words and phrases to express and communicate this truth. He is perfectly divine and perfectly human, sharing the qualities of both in such a fashion that they are neither intermingled nor confused. Therefore, Jesus is eminently qualified to act as a mediator and advocate on our behalf.

Old and New Covenants

In citing the famous prophecy of Jeremiah (v. 8; citing Jer 31:31-34), Hebrews refers to the prophet's promise of a covenant, not replaced but renewed. The Torah remains the same as the instruction of Moses, but will become so internalized (v. 10) as to make human compliance an instinctive personal and immediate expression of obedience. Over the centuries this text has been cited as if it taught "supersessionism," namely, the replacement of the old by the new. This would, however, contradict both Jeremiah and Paul's teaching on the enduring reality of God's covenant with Israel, which remains "irrevocable" in God's sight (Rom 11:29)! With the destruction of the temple in AD 69, early Christians perceived the former religious order to be changing, and as yet did not know how the future would unfold. Two fundamental convictions must be held by Catholic Christians faithful to the Scriptures: the universal salvation achieved by Christ's death and resurrection, and the enduring validity of Israel as God's chosen people. Precisely how to maintain both truths in tension is still a challenge for Christians in this post-Holocaust (*Shoah*) age.

Antiphon (Year I)

Psalm 85:11a

Kindness and truth shall meet.

Kindness

The Hebrew word that is translated in this liturgical formula from Psalm 85 is *hesed,* namely, the mutual care and concern that characterize members of a covenantal relationship and bind them together (v. 11). More than merely civility or courtesy, the bond and its consequent duties are obligatory and enduring. They bring God and human beings together into a solidarity that constantly seeks each other's best interests and welfare. This type of kindness is true and enduring.

Truth

Although the scholastic philosophers may define "truth" as the correlation of one's ideas with outer external reality, the biblical concept is slightly different. In the Semitic mind truth/*ʾemet*, is something stable enough to lean against and strong enough to support the efforts of human beings. Falsehood would, by contrast, be something insubstantial and flimsy, unable to support the convictions or commitments of any human being. When they meet (v. 11), one's covenantal concern finds something secure enough to support and maintain life's choices and obligations. The fullness of truth includes this type of kindness.

First Reading (Year II)

1 Samuel 24:3-21

I will not raise a hand against my lord,
for he is the Lord's anointed.

Saul's Emotional Breakdown

This sad story, almost of soap opera dimensions, of the relationship between Saul and David illustrates King Saul's spiral into paranoia and his desperate search for David (v. 3). His jealousy turns even against friends and colleagues who demonstrate their refusal to harm (v. 11). In such mental illness anyone who shines and elicits admiration can become an enemy to be persecuted and eliminated. Everything human somehow finds it way into the biblical witness to the flaws and failings of humanity. On the one hand, this story can be a warning against ever being so fearful as to hurt others; on the other hand, this becomes an occasion to pray for those suffering from mental illness of this type, and for family members who struggle daily to deal with such a heartache in their families.

David's Patient Response

Even though David is repeatedly persecuted by his troubled king, he refuses to take advantage of the king's momentary weakness and vulnerability (vv. 10-12). He will not engage in a reciprocal repeat of the same kind of behavior. That would only beget more violence. It may well be that in this case the Deuteronomic historian rinsed a bit of history to make David seem ideally better than the actual full history would have supported; still David became the model of those who refuse to repay violence with violence, and anticipates the teachings of Jesus in the Sermon on the Mount that counseled us to pray for and do good to those who persecute us (Matt 5:38-48).

David the Ideal Servant

The characteristics of David, as illustrated in this episode, are nobility, generosity, largesse, and respect for the dignity of others no matter what their situation (v. 7). The historical reality of David's life may have, in fact, been at times a bit more scheming and less noble, but these were the fundamental God-given qualities that God loved. They were the basis for David's being chosen as king and shepherd for God's people. The challenge is to make sure that all good gifts deepen rather than diminish throughout one's lifetime. David was also a model of penitence when he failed (2 Sam 11). These are the requirements for true leadership in any age.

Antiphon (Year II)

Psalm 57:2a

Have mercy on me, God, have mercy.

Mercy

The Hebrew word translated as "mercy" in this psalm refrain (v. 2) is *hanan*, usually understood as "grace." This grace/*hanan* is a characteristic quality that makes someone attractive in the eyes of others. It is also understood as "favor" in the sense of one's ability, for whatever set of reasons, to find favor in the eyes of someone else. By contrast, the Hebrew word for "mercy," as cited in the last verse of this responsorial from Psalm 57, is *hesed*, covenantal loyalty (v. 11). Imprecise translations, even in liturgy, can be exasperating at times!

The Gift of Being Attractive

This comment flows from the clarification above. As we know, attractiveness can be superficial and physical, or something moral and more deeply rooted in a person's personality and demeanor. By the very fact that it is requested of God, as in this antiphon (v. 2), "mercy"/favor/attractiveness is acknowledged to be a gift from God, requested humbly and cherished gratefully. Although such a quality can become identified with a person's lifelong behavior, it is a gift never to be taken for granted. It is a quality never to be the occasion for pride or arrogance.

Gospel

Mark 3:13-19

Jesus summoned those whom he wanted and they came to him.

Literary Link

The second positive fact reported by Mark after noting the opposition of some of the Pharisees and Herodians is the selection of the Twelve (vv. 13-19). They are destined in God's plan to become his personal extension into time and space once the proposed death of Jesus took place (v. 6).

Friday of the Second Week in Ordinary Time

The Appointment of the Twelve

In selecting these very distinctively unique and individual people to become the inner circle of his disciples (vv. 16-19), Jesus even brought together very contrasting personalities and causes. This is evidenced by the fact that he chose both Matthew, a tax collector who worked for the occupying Roman authorities, and Simon the Cananean, who was also elsewhere called a "Zealot" (Luke 6:15), namely, one who belonged to the party dedicated to overthrowing the Roman oppressors, even by violence if need be. Uniformity of personality is certainly not a quality that Jesus had in mind when choosing this group. The very fact of association and friendship with Jesus refines and perfects each distinctive personality, ourselves included. The same process goes on throughout each generation of human disciples.

Vocation for Mission

Jesus brings the group together for a purpose. They gather not for the sake of being together but rather in order to "be with him" and be sent to preach (v. 14). As a result of being with him, they themselves were transformed into a united force for the mission of transforming the larger world. They were sent to herald the kingdom, namely, God's work within the world, and to confront demons, that is, all evil everywhere. Thus we see in this memorable selection a respect for some very improbable personalities, together with a sense of vocation/calling as well as the task of transforming the community and the larger world. This is precisely the pattern and the larger picture for every community gathered for Mass throughout history. We are ultimately a community on a mission.

Saturday of the Second Week in Ordinary Time

First Reading (Year I)

Hebrews 9:2-3, 11-14

He entered once for all into the Sanctuary with his own Blood.

The Greater and More Perfect Tabernacle

There is an inner dynamism and power that runs through all of the life of Jesus, uniting each separate activity into the single paschal mystery. Given the liturgical character that the Letter to the Hebrews gives to Christ's death and resurrection, he is described as passing very concretely through the bloody sacrifice of his death into a "tabernacle [sanctuary] not made by hands" (v. 11), that is, the heavenly holy of holies. This is the final destination for which he was sent and through which he was called. That final "place" of personal intimacy with God forever is but one way of describing the destiny at the end of every baptized person's life journey. It is the final address to which everyone moves and where she or he lives forever. Just as the temple was distinguished between the holy place and the holy of holies (v. 3), this world is described as a holy place and the next, the holy of holies.

Not By Mere Physical Blood and Ashes

Physical sacrifices in themselves are limited acts of worship for sanctification and purification (v. 13), as the Letter to the Hebrews now sees them. Rather, it is a person's attitude of loving service and personal devotion brought to worship that purifies an individual's heart. This is a gift of grace. Christ, precisely because of the perfect love that he has for his Father, achieves the purification and the salvation of the entire world. So, when we are associated with the mind of Christ through baptism and faith, our consciences are cleansed (v. 14) and we become acceptable to God again.

Antiphon (Year I)

Psalm 47:6

God mounts his throne to shouts of joy: a blare of trumpets for the Lord.

Psalm 47: A Royal God

Scholars suggest that this psalm was used by Israel for the annual New Year's celebration of the kingship of the Lord in Jerusalem. The way in which it refers to God assuming his royal throne in the temple could also serve as a description of Christ assuming his rightful place in glory at the right hand of the Father after his death and resurrection. The specific verses selected by the Lectionary provide a very fitting response to the reading from Hebrews.

Trumpets

Trumpets (v. 6), drums, and cymbals were the musical instruments used in Israel's liturgical celebrations. For that reason, the psalms projected the same instruments into the heavenly realms. Conversely, our earthly celebrations that share the same music can be understood as feeble echoes and anticipations of the heavenly reality. That marvelous interplay between heaven and earth was presumed by the author of Hebrews.

First Reading (Year II)

2 Samuel 1:1-4, 11-12, 19, 23-27

How can the warriors have fallen in battle!

The Second Book of Samuel

Continuing the Deuteronomic theology of First Samuel, this scroll described the history of early Israel from the anointing of David over Judah, his early battles to secure the safety of his people, his sin with Uriah's wife Bathsheba, and his many family problems. The book ends with David's sorrow and penance for the self-satisfying census, which was judged sinful because it was initiated to celebrate human success, while forgetting that God is the ultimate source of everything.

Grief at the Death of Family or Friend

The announcement of the deaths of Saul and Jonathan was a national tragedy because it was the death of Israel's first king and the defeat of an army that considered itself protected by God. It was also a personal tragedy for David, who loved Jonathan dearly (v. 11). Grief at a time of such loss includes many different areas of life, and needs to be expressed as part of the healing. This reading includes portions from David's poignant elegy for Saul and Jonathan (vv. 19-27). Every human emotion finds expression in the literary works of Scripture. Sooner or later everyone loses a loved one. Even in our grief God is at work because we can discover what is truly important and we can learn again how dependent we are upon others.

Saturday of the Second Week in Ordinary Time

Song of Lament

David's poetic response expresses with remarkable skill the emotional pain of the death of such a close friend (vv. 19-27). Ancient Israelite laments often began with the word *how* as a deep expression of personal inability to understand or explain such sorrow before God. It is repeated three times (vv. 5, 19, 27) as a refrain for David's grief. The laments serve to express our effort to understand *how* the God of the covenant could allow such heartache. Inspired laments offer words for our sorrow. An inspired song such as David's can become the shared song of an entire community in time of grief and loss.

ANTIPHON (YEAR II)

Psalm 80:4b

Let us see your face, Lord, and we shall be saved.

Seeing God's Face

The antiphon's petition (v. 4) is surprising because it was generally understood in ancient Israel that no one could see God's face and live, so terrifying and brilliant was that experience. That conviction was Israel's rationale for asking Moses to be their mediator at Sinai (Exod 20:19). Psalm 80 is a lament begging for salvation (v. 3). Its liturgical antiphon suggests that seeing God would be the occasion for salvation, not death, if one is granted the ability to behold such utter majesty. Even as we experience the passing of all things material in our lives, we yearn for the enduring presence of God.

The Transformation of "Seeing"

We are always changed by what we see. If we see someone in need, we become obliged to respond and we are changed. The two blind beggars who asked Jesus to heal them (Matt 9:31) were launched into an entirely new way of life. To be saved from lack of sight/vision is to be confronted with new options and decisions that recognize the power of God and his ability to take our part and bring us new freedom.

GOSPEL

Mark 3:20-21

They said, "He is out of his mind."

Literary Link

After two positive events subsequent to the rejection (v. 6), the presence of crowds (vv. 7-12) and the appointment of the Twelve (vv. 13-18), we are now presented with a series of negative responses. The first comes from the family of Jesus (v. 21).

The Family's Exasperation

One should not miss the ironic, if not slightly amusing, contrast between the relatives' final complaint that Jesus is "out of his mind" (v. 21) and the ritual announcement that immediately follows in its liturgical context: "The Gospel [good news] of the Lord." Those who listen carefully should catch the contradiction, perhaps smile a bit at the incongruity, and be puzzled by it. Curiously, the comment of the family ends up being a sort of translation of the word *metanoia*/"repentance," namely, to "think outside of our mind" and to see things differently. Perhaps the fact that Jesus saw things from the vantage point of God, not from the normal human view of things, suggests that he really was "out of his mind" in an unexpected fashion. The account offers an example of "conversion" for the rest of us!

Seized by One's Family

Kingdom values are profoundly different from the values normally embraced by human beings! They are "holy" in the Semitic sense. As we attempt to sort out life's calling, we may come into conflict with our natural families, who may oppose a vocation and attempt to redirect our lives according to their preferences and values (v. 21). The life of Francis of Assisi is a perfect example of that conflict as his puzzled, and perhaps even enraged, father attempted to call Francis back to "sanity." The fact is that Jesus must have separated himself in some way from his natural human family. This would seem crazy to the ancient world, which valued the human family and tribal relationship as supreme. Family relationships were their social network in times of illness or need. That Jesus would turn in a different direction was inconceivable and, as they saw it, demanded opposition. Discipleship, as Jesus reminded his followers, can sometimes be a source of family division between fathers and sons or mothers and daughters (Matt 10:34ff.). Perhaps Jesus spoke out of painful personal experience.

Monday of the Third Week in Ordinary Time

First Reading (Year I)

Hebrews 9:15, 24-28

Christ who offered once to take away the sins of many, will appear a second time to those who eagerly await him.

Death before Inheritance

This biblical passage and the logical thought behind it simply assume that no one inherits anything until after the death of the benefactor (v. 15). If it is a true inheritance and the fulfilled promise of an eventual gift, then someone must have died. That individual was Jesus so that all would be enriched. As we gather for our weekday Eucharist, it is helpful to remember that Christ died once and for all (v. 26) for our sins and for the very sin of the world. Therefore we have "inherited" a place at the table. Our purpose in gathering for such a daily celebration is not to repeat that sacrifice but to extend the benefits of that inheritance to the lives of those who now gather in a different human time and place.

A True Testament

The shift in Greek terminology from "covenant" to "testament/*diathēkē*" (v. 15), though not immediately evident from the English translation, occurs because of the intervening fact of Christ's death, which then gives way to an inheritance. A covenant is different from a last will and testament. His death removed our sins and provided each and all of us the opportunity for sharing in the riches of the new creation. We seldom think of the implications of the title of "Testament" we give to our Christian Scriptures and its contrast with the biblical term "covenant." The latter speaks of relationships among partners, and the former alludes to the sacrifice that bonds them together.

The Sins of Many

The Letter to the Hebrews speaks of Christ's death as taking away "the sins of many" (v. 28). The Hebrew idiom used this phrase in a universal sense, reflecting Isaiah's description of the Suffering Servant who bore the "guilt of us all" (Isa 53:6) and justified "many" (v. 11) through his suffering. This wording reflects the literal wording of the institution narrative at the Last Supper, namely, the "blood poured out for many" (see Mark 14:24; Matt 26:28). The universalism of God's will is only limited by human rejection. That tragedy demonstrates how much God respects human freedom. This topic may be pastorally useful in light of the recent change in the translation offered by the newly revised Roman Missal.

Antiphon (Year I)

Psalm 98:1a

Sing to the Lord a new song, for he has done marvelous deeds.

A New Song

If the song is "new" (v. 1), as the antiphon suggests, it must be inspired by new actions of God in our history, or at least by a new personal appreciation for those actions of God throughout all of history. A new experience of salvation creates a new people who sing a new song! Every time we gather, we should be conscious and grateful for the most recent actions of God on our behalf, even though some of them may be initially painful from the merely human perspective. Only in retrospect do we see that experiences of difficulty can also be moments of grace and growth.

The Nations

Psalm 98 is clear about the fact that the "new deeds" are not limited to the merely personal but include a more universal social scope. The nations are a witness to God's saving deeds (v. 2). Israel is always encouraged to look beyond its borders and self-interest to see God at work in a larger and more universal context. The headlines of our daily papers and the "breaking news" of TV may provide some insight into those "new deeds" within which God continues to work in our world each day. As Christians we ought to count them, label them, and celebrate them!

FIRST READING (YEAR II)

2 Samuel 5:1-7, 10

You shall shepherd my people Israel.

David as an Agent for Unity

David, for all his human faults, had the skill and charm needed to be a unifier in Israel. In fact, both southern Judah and northern Israel claimed him as king and the result was a united kingdom (v. 5). The choice of the new and different city of Jerusalem as a capital of the united kingdom is a sign of that effort. From the very beginning the city of Jerusalem (v. 7) was a sign of unity among diverse peoples. The contemporary tragedy of the Israeli and Palestinian peoples is that the city of Jerusalem is divided once again after all these centuries. Fidelity to God's will urges us to work and pray for unity among the deeply and bitterly divided inhabitants of the city today. Moreover, it is incumbent upon all Christians to pray for the unity among the major religions of our world, which now share that Holy City.

Leadership of Solidarity

Leadership presumes some type of identity with those who are called to follow. Leadership is rooted within the group of people who recognize that they share the humanity and hopes of their leader just as he shares theirs. The recognition that David is of the same "bone and . . . flesh" (v. 1) remains a concrete image to describe the bond between leaders and partners. To truly lead, one must identify with those summoned as followers. At the same time, true leadership will take followers to a new and sometimes uncomfortable place for their material and spiritual growth. They begin and end united, but the path between the stages may be challenging.

ANTIPHON (YEAR II)

Psalm 89:25a

My faithfulness and my mercy shall be with him.

A Psalm of Lament

Psalm 89 is divided into three parts: an initial hymn of praise for God (vv. 1-19), followed by a recitation of God's promises to David (vv. 20-38), and then a final gasp of sorrow over the apparent rejection of Israel (vv. 39-52). Only the middle section of the psalm, celebrating the divine election of David and the promises given to him and his followers, is used in this particular portion of the Lectionary's response to David's remarkable leadership. Is leadership always tested? Does God always hide when people presume that their success is due solely to their own human efforts? The later section of the psalm's lament remains hidden from those who gather for prayer this day.

Faithfulness and Mercy for David

Scholars often point out the conditional nature of the Mosaic covenant, namely, "If you obey my commands and keep my words . . ." as contrasted with the unconditional character of the Davidic covenant. The latter remains forever, even if individual generations or successors may be punished for their sins. In such an enduring relationship the two divine qualities expressed in the refrain (v. 25) make great sense: *ʾamunah* (sturdy and dependable fidelity) and *hesed* (mutual covenantal concern). That is how God related to David—and to all who promise to love the Lord.

GOSPEL

Mark 3:22-30

It is the end of Satan.

Literary Link

The second negative response after the reference to the rejection by some Pharisees in Galilee is found in the controversy with scribes from Jerusalem over the source of the power of Jesus to drive out demons (vv. 22-30).

Monday of the Third Week in Ordinary Time

Driving Out Demons by Demons

How easy it is to discount, demean, and dismiss anything that might force us to change our thinking. If nothing else, we resort to attacking the person when the ideas are too strong for us! That was the strategy used by this group of scribes from Jerusalem to reject the person and teaching of their "fellow Pharisee" Jesus, claiming that his power came from the "prince of demons" (v. 22). Unfortunately, the pattern is perennial; its remedy is found in clearly restating the truth, and demonstrating the foolishness of the objection. Jesus insists that power against itself would be illusory and utterly ineffective (v. 26). The same dodging precludes any change of heart or conversion on our part, but Jesus will not be put off so easily!

The Debates of Jesus with Scribes and Pharisees

It is important to remember that the harsh rhetoric in the gospels (v. 22) might reflect the acrimonious debates at the time of their composition, rather than the original historical differences between Jesus and religious leaders during his earlier earthly ministry. According to authentic Catholic teaching, the three levels of history reflected in the gospels were (1) what Jesus himself said and did, (2) how the apostles spoke about those events after the resurrection, and (3) the theological portrait chosen by each of the four evangelists to present a clear catechetical picture of the Lord they loved. Debates such as this story of controversy over Beelzebul could well have reflected the latter stages rather than the first. This is true, especially given the fact that Jesus himself stood within the Pharisaic traditions of his day. This account should not be used to give general criticism of the entire Pharisaic tradition of spirituality.

Blasphemy against the Spirit

The concept of blasphemy against the Holy Spirit (v. 29) is difficult to fully understand, and has been the subject of countless discussion among saints and scholars since the beginning. Perhaps its fundamental point is the simple fact that such a sin cannot be forgiven precisely because it is the Spirit who is the source of forgiveness, as the resurrection account of John's gospel suggested (20:22-23). In the Upper Room the risen Lord had breathed his gift of the Holy Breath/Spirit and immediately associated that gift with the forgiveness of sins. To deny the Spirit is to deny the possibility of forgiveness!

Tuesday of the Third Week in Ordinary Time

First Reading (Year I)

Hebrews 10:1-10

Behold, I come to do your will, O God.

The Limitations of Life by the Law

The law is but a shadow (v. 1) of the future because mere compliance does not change or "make perfect" the interior of a person. For that reason the law of annual sacrifice requires regularly repeated actions. Yet the fullness of the Torah/divine instruction also included the gift of the Spirit of God who transforms the inner being of people in Christ (Rom 5:5). One should beware of being held captive by first-century religious debates in which early Christians dismissed the Judaism of their time and did not recognize its enduring reality, contrary to the teaching of the apostle Paul in his Letter to the Romans (11:29).

The Will of God

A repeated prophetic theme throughout the centuries is the superiority of obedience and compliance with God's will over the physical actions of sacrifice (vv. 5ff.; see 1 Sam 15:22; Hos 6:6; Matt 9:13). It is compliance with the will of God that consecrates the inner person (v. 10) and makes any human action of obedience into an unbloody sacrifice acceptable before God.

Antiphon (Year I)

Psalm 40:8a, 9a

Here I am, Lord; I come to do your will.

The Opportunity of the Present Moment

A common biblical phrase in Hebrew for acknowledging one's position before God is simply "*hinneni*/here I am." Wherever we may be, geographically or emotionally, at any given moment, we are precisely and always before God. That place is the opportunity for recognition of God's will and for consequent obedience. Every moment and every place is a *kairos* for obedience. The movement into God's presence is attitudinal. It is often spiritually helpful to pause for a consideration of "where is the 'here'?" and "who is the 'I'?"

Docility

Compliance with God's will, as expressed in this refrain (v. 9), is a final summary of our response, not the whole picture. God is not displeased with any human effort to ask questions and thus to seek understanding when confronted by the will of God. That is clear from Luke's account of the question of Mary to the angel Gabriel at the time of the annunciation (Luke 1:34). In fact, a full human response to obedience presumes some effort on our part to understand and thus to be transformed into one who offers free compliance whenever possible. The final response to divine and legitimate human authority, however, is one of open acceptance and a willingness to be taught.

First Reading (Year II)

2 Samuel 6:12b-15, 17-19

David and all the children of Israel were bringing up the ark of the Lord with shouts of joy.

The Lord amid His People

Once the covenant had been made, with its fundamental phrase establishing that bond, "I will be your God, and you will be my people" (Lev 26:12), God always wishes to be in the midst of his chosen people. The ark was a visible "sacramental" sign of that presence. For that reason it was brought into the City of David (v. 12). That presence was always a source of rejoicing. David was a human instrument in accomplishing that divine desire. It continues to be the desire of individual faithful followers of God to bring that same presence to every place we travel.

Shouts of Joy

The annual ancient covenant renewal ceremony each autumn was always accompanied by singing and shouts of joy

(vv. 14-15). Many biblical accounts reflect or presume that practice, even, for example, the shouting that accompanied the ark when it was paraded around the ancient fortress city of Jericho (Judg 6:20). Worship in song and movement incorporated the whole human person, physically and spiritually, into the joyous celebration of God's presence.

Gifts of Food

Tuesday of the Third Week in Ordinary Time

The gifts of bread, meat, and raisin cakes (v. 19) were more than signs of royal generosity and festivity. They may well have been the final ritual of the sacrifices of Israel, which were called "*Shelamim*/communion sacrifices." Such sacrifices were comprised of gifts offered in sacrifice, not completely destroyed by fire but rather baked with the intention that a portion would be offered to the priests of the temple, and the rest shared by the family that offered the gift. This "communion" ritual signified the shared unity between God and his people, as well as between the people themselves. That ritual provided an ancient pattern for Christian Eucharist. It also served as a constant reminder that the poor should rejoice whenever the church/synagogue celebrates.

ANTIPHON (YEAR II)

Psalm 24:8

Who is this king of glory? It is the Lord!

A Psalm of "Torah Liturgy"

The first verses of Psalm 24, although not quoted in this responsorial hymn, include responses to the question of who can ascend the mountain/stand in God's holy place. Scholars suggest that a sort of examination of conscience and worthiness was needed before entrance into the sanctuary. Only then do we find the triumphant dialogue between the priestly guardians and the entrance of God's ark itself (v. 8) into the temple with jubilant welcome of choirs and sanctuary attendants. Once one sees the psalm as a ritual expression of welcome, its power and its liturgical utility for contemporary worship becomes obvious! Like the people at the time of David, we also welcome God into our worshiping assembly.

King of Glory

The Hebrew word for "glory" is *chabod*, a very rich but elusive concept that resists easy translation. At its root, it suggests something heavy and valuable as well as something shining enough to catch one's eye for a second look. In this sense a large diamond or a bar of gold might be "glorious" in the Semitic sense. To speak of God as the "king of glory" (v. 8) is to acclaim the Person of God as immensely valuable and luminously brilliant for those trained to see clearly. The angels of Bethlehem sing of glory attributed to God (Luke 2:14) for the great gift of a Savior for Israel. In this psalm the city and sanctuary gates are opened to welcome this God as a treasured royal guest and sovereign Lord.

GOSPEL

Mark 3:31-35

Whoever does the will of God is my brother and sister and mother.

Literary Link

Having noted the opposition of the family of Jesus earlier (v. 21), Mark returned to the theme of his immediate natural family in order to create a contrast with his family of the new creation (vv. 31-35), concluding the section of negative response after the rejection of Pharisees (3:6).

Obedience That Unites

Customary human thought suggests that family is created by a shared blood lineage, and intensified by residence in a common location. Those are the folks at the door (v. 31), signaling a desire to speak with him. They may have hoped to convince Jesus to return to Nazareth and to resume a more predictable and proper way of life rather than his peripatetic preaching. His response, however, reframed the issue by highlighting a different type of "family bond," namely, one based on obedience to God's will (v. 35). In the mind of Jesus, doing the will of God is what ultimately creates the familial DNA of the new creation. Such obedience bonds people together more profoundly than natural kinship.

A New Universalism

Pondering the boundaries of such a definition, we see that the effort to obey God's will (v. 35) does in fact cross national borders and erases ethnic and racial differences. Following the logic of Jesus, one cannot help but ask to what degree does that sincere effort to do God's will even go beyond the boundaries and limits of the various world religions to create a very radical sense of God's family? This was suggested by John Paul II when visiting the young Muslims of Morocco (August 19, 1985). This insight, however, is not to suggest a relativism that would hold that all religious are equal; some have a greater share of God's truth than others. It is to acknowledge, however, that the very desire to obey God does create a new bond of unity among peoples everywhere. The violence of religious wars and mutual disdain is incompatible with Christian discipleship.

Wednesday of the Third Week in Ordinary Time

First Reading (Year I)

Hebrews 10:11-18

He has made perfect forever those who are being consecrated.

Lifelong Human Consecration

The once-and-for-all death of Christ continues to have an effect on our lives as they unfold because he has "made perfect forever those who are being consecrated" (v. 14). Although the action of Christ may be once and for all, the effect of that reality in our lives is not; it continues to deepen or diminish. Being "consecrated," like being "perfected," is a lifetime process. Decision after decision, action after action, day after day we are asked to be transformed by the way in which we embrace God's will and are embraced by it. The universal call to holiness is a historical reality that deepens as we mature physically, emotionally, and spiritually.

The Mystery of Forgiveness

Our deep need for forgiveness of sin (vv. 11 and 18), not merely any mistakes or misjudgments on our part, remains part of the human reality. The author of Hebrews insists that such forgiveness, once given by God and received by human beings, precludes the need for additional atoning sacrifice. Have we lost our sense of forgiveness because our secular culture seems to have lost its sense of sin?

Antiphon (Year I)

Psalm 110:4b

You are a priest for ever, in the line of Melchizedek.

Eternal Enthronement

Psalm 110's refrain (v. 4) regarding the eternal priesthood of Jesus fittingly reflects the statement in the reading that Jesus has taken his seat forever at the right hand of God (v. 12). The eternal intercession and mediation of Jesus is an expression of his eternal priesthood. This truth would have been a source of consolation for those who grieved the destruction of the temple by the Romans in AD 69.

(See the refrain of Wednesday of the Second Week in Ordinary Time.)

First Reading (Year II)

2 Samuel 7:4-17

I will raise up your heir after you and I will make his kingdom firm.

David's Temple Building Plan

In the verses immediately preceding the text of the day, David had proposed to build a "house of cedar" for the Lord (v. 2), and the prophet Nathan had initially expressed approval. In a subsequent night vision, however, Nathan learned that the plan was not acceptable to God (v. 13). Perhaps it was the bloodshed or political intrigue that accompanied David's rise to power; the end result, however, was the polite refusal of David's offer by God. Solomon, not David, was to be God's construction manager. Like David, our lives are lived in a constant reassessment and acceptance of "plan B." Our human plans for building or for any other endeavor are always contingent upon God. The Lord of history is the single final determination of what happens in our world. We cooperate by our proposals, but as the ancient adage suggests, it is God alone who disposes. In the last analysis, we are always a people of plan B.

The Pun of "House"

The word "house" can mean a concrete physical dwelling (as David had assumed), but it can also refer to a dynasty of successive family generations. The British speak of the House of Winsor. David proposed the former, but God determined the latter (v. 11). Every family is a gift from God and the interrelated generations are intended by God as a blessing; the family also becomes a "quasi-residence" for God. We propose our wants, but God grants a response to our needs. More important than a material temple is the continuity of a chosen Davidic family that would obey the will of God (v. 14) and thus serve the spiritual unity and security of God's people.

Prophetic Compliance

A true prophet, like any faithful creature of God, must be open to divine correction. Although Nathan had originally accepted and approved David's proposal, he learned that God had other plans (v. 8). The will of God was the ultimate factor, and any prophet claiming to be the spokesperson for God had to be prepared to change a message when it became an obstacle rather than an instrument of God. God doesn't change his mind, but his true servants change in their maturing efforts to be faithful to the full and final will of God.

ANTIPHON (YEAR II)

Psalm 89:29a

For ever I will maintain my love for my servant.

Divine Love

By the very fact that the word "love" is common usage in the political treaties of mutual support among the great empires of the ancient world, we understand that the word connotes care and concern rather than romantic involvement. Borrowing the term from its earlier political context avoids over-anthropomorphizing the divine-human relationship. The central portion of Psalm 89 celebrates God's choice of David and his family. God promises love and concern for each and every chosen servant, especially someone like David (v. 29). That is also the type of "love" that we are commanded to extend toward all our neighbors, whether we happen to like them or not!

Eternal Love

God's fundamental love for his people is eternal (v. 29) and unchanging. It is a fact of Christian spirituality that we do not have to be good for God to love us, because God will love us into goodness if we but love him. It is we, however, who are the fickle and inconstant party in the relationship, and it is we who can choose to ignore or dismiss that divine love and its effects in our lives. God so respects human freedom as to offer, but not impose, friendship and blessings.

GOSPEL

Mark 4:1-20

A sower went out to sow.

Literary Link

After the section of Mark's gospel that contrasts negative and positive reactions to Jesus (3:7-35), we now turn toward a summary of his teachings by way of parables (4:1-34).

The Gift of Parables

The fact that Jesus teaches by parable (v. 2), not by proposition, suggests that he wishes to draw us into the story by inviting us to gradually explore its meaning and to learn its implications. This evokes our free consent, rather than merely obedience to divine commands. It is a means of invitation to discover the import of the teaching for each human being's life. Mark's gospel collects several parables of the kingdom into chapter 4, while Matthew's structure places them in his chapter 13 and Luke scatters them through his description of the public ministry of Jesus. Parables of the kingdom are descriptions about how God operates in our world.

A Parable of Trusting Confidence

Many scholars suggest that the purpose of the original parable of the sower and the seed was to give comfort and confidence because, in spite of all the many obstacles (vv. 3-7), the sowing does eventually produce an extraordinarily abundant harvest (v. 8). We tend to moralize this parable, namely, to focus on the different types of people within hearing range, and, as a matter of fact, the gospel itself includes that element within the inspired text as we now have it (vv. 13-20). Parables, however, are primarily about God, and only secondarily about us. This is a God who is determined to grant the fullest of harvests, no matter what obstacles we may create.

Wednesday of the Third Week in Ordinary Time

Religious Art

This parable is wonderfully illustrated in the bas-relief of white marble on the facade of the great pulpit in the National Shrine to the Immaculate Conception in Washington, DC. The concrete elements inherent in the parables and in so many of the events described in the gospels suggest a periodic review of the artwork in our churches to see if an illustration for our preaching might be found on the altar panels, paintings, or side chapels already existing in our parish churches. It is profoundly Catholic to utilize fine art in our holy places, but so easy for worshipers to take them for granted and no longer notice them anymore due to familiarity.

In Parables So That They May "see but not perceive"

The suggestion of Jesus (quoting Isa 6:9), namely, that parables were chosen to prevent understanding (v. 12) among outsiders rather than to assist it, is a very mysterious and even troublesome statement! The fact is that the parables could have many interpretations, thus encouraging personal efforts at understanding; that fact could also become an excuse for not understanding and for walking away if listeners so chose. Could this be one way of admitting/explaining the lack of response to Jesus while still holding the sovereignty of God's will in creation?

A Later Allegory

The final portion of this reading presents a different approach to the interpretation of the original parable. By explaining each element (vv. 14-20), the teaching is now re-presented, not as a parable with its single focus, but as an allegory. Perhaps Jesus did so on another different occasion. Perhaps the early church chose to use the parable for catechetical purposes. The hearers need to understand that these verses present a different type of religious literature.

Thursday of the Third Week in Ordinary Time

First Reading (Year I)

Hebrews 10:19-25

Let us hold unwaveringly to our confession that gives us hope and consider how to raise one another to love.

Human Confidence before God

Just imagine for a moment the confidence (v. 19) needed to enter the glorious heavenly sanctuary by people like ourselves, burdened by weakness and sin, stained by every sort of selfishness and self-centered justifications! Bold access to heaven, therefore, can only happen because of our identification with the cleansing action of Christ (v. 22). Too much focus on ourselves and the temptation to think that our own efforts can achieve our salvation can lead to discouragement, and perhaps even to absenting ourselves from the Christian assembly (v. 25). Our association with Christ, who freely chooses to make us coworkers and partners, and our sincere good efforts in mutual love for each other (v. 24) remain the source and support for our trust. By good example we encourage each other.

"Confession" as Conviction

We can too easily think of the sacrament of penance when hearing the word "confession" (v. 23), but the ancient usage of the early church first thought of "confession" as a clear public profession of one's Christian faith. Holding on to our confession therefore suggests that the fundamental expression of faith at the time of our baptism must remain the rallying cry of our entire lifelong existence. To confess that "Jesus is Lord" (1 Cor 12:3) and that God is Father, Son, and Spirit is a baptismal conviction, which remains a gift of grace and a transforming reality in our lives. This confession perennially links us to the mystery of God and enables us to enter the fullness of the next age—an eternal sanctuary (v. 19) of God's transforming presence and power.

Regular Eucharistic Participation

The invitation not to stay away from our assembly (v. 25) has a remarkably contemporary tone as we ponder the pastoral reality of so many Catholics who do not see the need or value of regular weekly attendance at the eucharistic celebration. The Letter to the Hebrews recommends mutual encouragement for people wavering in their commitment, tired of the inner struggle for obedience to the commandments in a hostile or contrary pagan world or burdened by their sins. Christians who are "practicing" their faith can find all the elements of mature spirituality in the weekly assemblies to celebrate the resurrection: acknowledgment of sin, instruction from the Word, mutual support in the assembly, community by God's grace, and renewed mission shared by those like ourselves sent to transform their world each week. Weekly practice is good training; the Holy Spirit is our "personal trainer"!

Antiphon (Year I)

Psalm 24:6

Lord, this is the people that longs to see your face.

The "Torah" Psalm

Psalm 24 offers a description of the sentiments needed for communal purification and confident entrance into the sanctuary of God. It includes a self-description of people who truly long to see God's face (v. 6). The ancient faith of Israel included a fundamental conviction that no one could ever see God and live (Judg 13:22). The psalm suggests that the pilgrims, purified by sorrow and forgiveness, may enter the temple sanctuary and may see signs of God's presence. This psalm is both instruction and examination of conscience.

The "Face" of God

Curiously, the Hebrew terminology always uses the plural of the noun "*panim*/faces" of God rather than the singular.

Perhaps this usage communicates the fact that God has multiple presences and varying "emotional" responses to human actions. No one experience or one divine response can ever begin to exhaust God's immense grandeur or transcendence in relating to his people. It is Catholic belief that by God's grace we are created to experience the fullness of divine reality. That destiny is the ultimate goal of our human pilgrimage through life.

Thursday of the Third Week in Ordinary Time

First Reading (Year II)

2 Samuel 7:18-19, 24-29

Who am I, Lord God, and who are the members of my house?

The Prayer of David

On rare occasions the Scriptures allow us to eavesdrop on the personal prayers of key figures such as David (v. 18) in the history of salvation. It is important to remember, however, that these prayers are fashioned by their inspired human authors. They most clearly express, therefore, the theological perspectives and intentions of the inspired writers: the gift and blessing of the Davidic dynasty, the election of Israel by God, and the everlasting nature of that dynasty in some mysterious fashion—even when the prayer is said after the destruction of the temple in 587 BC and the virtual disappearance of Davidic rule in Jerusalem.

The Humility of David

The prayer clearly proclaims David's admission of his nothingness before God (v. 18)! There is no self-promotion or aggrandizement expressed in this recognition of all gifts and blessings as coming from God alone (v. 21). The amazed "Who am I?" of David's prayer (v. 18) will be echoed countless times over the centuries by many other divine servants, including Elizabeth when greeting Mary, her visiting cousin (Luke 1:41). The phrase could well be a constant prayer for anyone conscious of the multiple blessings that fill our days.

Antiphon (Year II)

Luke 1:32b

The Lord God will give him the throne of David, his father.

An Angelic Promise

This antiphon is taken from the message of Gabriel to Mary at the time of the annunciation. As an explanation of the divine plan of salvation and a promise of its universal significance, Gabriel proclaimed continuity between the ancient Davidic dynasty and the destiny of this child yet to be born. By uniting the prayer of David with the message of Gabriel, the liturgy creates bonds across the centuries and insists on a single trajectory of God's eternal plan.

A Pilgrimage Psalm of "Ascents"

Scholars often see Psalm 132, used here as a response to the prayer of David, as having ancient roots even from the time of Solomon, and as reflecting the actual ritual of the temple's dedication. The reference to the ark (v. 8, not included in the responsorial psalm) certainly suggests its composition prior to the Babylonian destruction in 587 BC when the ark disappeared from history! Highlighting the remarkable mutual oaths of God and David to each other (vv. 2 and 11), the psalm celebrates God's choice of both king and location as a holy place for the merging of divine purpose and human destiny. Salvation history is human history is cosmic history!

Gospel

Mark 4:21-25

A lamp is to be placed on a lampstand. The measure with which you measure will be measured out to you.

Literary Link

After the parable of the sower and its later allegorical explanation (vv. 1-20),

Mark adds a collection of different teachings, each aimed at making a particular point, first the importance of public witness and then the fact that we are eventually judged by our own standards.

The Purpose of Light

In a modern world of neon lights and constant electric illumination we forget the very different reality of the ancient world and the preciousness of even the dimmest of light provided by olive oil lamps (v. 21). The image used by Jesus goes to the heart of the matter by stressing the purpose of light, that is, personal vision and social visibility. Just as clothing is for wearing, not for a closet shelf, and food for eating, not decoration, light is for disclosure. The gospel follows the earlier description of the different classes of response to the sown word of God (vv. 14-20), and promises that one's secret response, choked, withered, or flourishing, will eventually be made public (v. 22)!

Criterion for Judgment

It continues to be remarkable that God judges as we do—he allows us to establish the criteria for our own judgment! The very measurements we choose for assessing others around us will be the measuring cup (v. 24) God will use to evaluate our own lives. Those who are hard on others but easy on themselves are in for a big surprise! We set the standards for our own judgment. God has that much respect for our freedom! For that reason, gifts given to us will be taken away if we are not similarly generous with others (v. 25).

Friday of the Third Week in Ordinary Time

First Reading (Year I)

Hebrews 10:32-39

Do not throw away your confidence.
It will have a great reward.

Contest of Suffering

The suffering (v. 32) to which Hebrews refers is probably social stigma and family alienation rather than physical punishment or persecution. In a world where faith and social relationships were tightly intertwined, a move in one sphere inevitably had repercussions and ramifications in the other. This explains the importance of the early Christian communities who then provided both emotional support and belonging as well as care for the sick and hungry. The radical individualism of our contemporary Western society would have made no sense in the ancient world.

Confidence

The Greek word is *parresia*, "boldness, candor, or confident conviction" (see v. 35). It is a quality that marked the testimony given by the apostles immediately after the resurrection. To those who had initially become members of the Jesus movement, but now had second thoughts about that move, the same quality is recommended. Perseverance in living with a decision is often more important (and difficult) than making the decision itself.

Antiphon (Year I)

Psalm 37:39a

The salvation of the just comes from the Lord.

Salvation

If by definition salvation refers to a difficult situation from which we are unable to free ourselves, freedom must come from outside our abilities, and ultimately from God alone. The Christian theology of grace insists that we cannot save ourselves, even if we are asked to freely cooperate with God's gifts—and even if the cooperation is the result of the gift of grace.

Trust

In several verses the psalm recommends a lively sense of trust in the goodness of God who supplies for the needs of the just. This happens, however, not according to our human stipulations and demands, but in God's way and in God's time. From a purely human standpoint we may be justifiably apprehensive when placing our lives on the line in trust, but God will not fail us if we do not act out of presumption. In proceeding with trust, we should also remember the temptation of Jesus to throw himself off the pinnacle of the temple (Luke 4:9), for the same God who invites trust will not save us from our own foolishness!

First Reading (Year II)

2 Samuel 11:1-4a, 5-10a, 13-17

You have despised me and have taken the wife of Uriah to be your wife (see 2 Samuel 12:10).

The Great Sin of David

With all the poignancy of a soap opera, the text is a magnificent literary composition, exposing the sin of David and his repeated devious attempts to avoid detection by arranging the death of Bathsheba's innocent husband Uriah. The Scriptures do not shrink away from either dark human sinfulness or luminous generous holiness. The fact is that God can be at work within each, and in this case God can find a way of using that human love to produce the wisdom of Solomon and, because Solomon, David's second son by Bathsheba, is listed in the genealogy of Jesus (Matt 1:6), the eventual birth of a Messiah Savior. There is always a spark of goodness in our sin, and a spark of sin in our goodness.

The Obedience of Uriah

The military obedience of a well-trained soldier like Uriah was taken advantage of by his king. Scholars note that if Uriah lived close enough to the royal palace so that the king could see the activity on the roof of Uriah's house, he must have been of sufficient social stature and economic prosperity to be a trusted colleague of prominence. That makes the sin of David even more treacherous. One wonders if Uriah ever had a hint of the deviousness of his commanders or the tragedy that was about to engulf him? This story is an admonition to be truthful, and a not so subtle invitation to examine the real motives for all our actions, and to keep both intention and actions noble.

Antiphon (Year II)

Psalm 51:3a

Be merciful, O Lord, for we have sinned.

The Great Penitential Prayer

Psalm 51 is the quintessential prayer of penance and sorrow for one's personal sins. Recited every Friday in the church's Liturgy of the Hours, its verses acknowledge with brutal honesty the depth and pervasiveness of the evil of the human heart from the very beginning of our existence, as well as the need for personal cleansing by divine grace. This psalm is a most appropriate response to the sad tale of Uriah's death because it is explicitly linked to David's sin with Bathsheba (v. 1). The psalm also dreams of a re-created heart (v. 12) as part of God's new creation.

The Plea for Mercy

Curiously enough, the psalm begins with an urgent cry for a special kind of mercy (v. 3). The Hebrew word is *chen*, more properly translated as "grace/favor," which renders a person once again attractive and worthy of positive attention. Rather than a plea for compassion or forgiveness, the petition begs the gift that can transform an individual at the very center of his existence. The God of creation is also the God of forgiveness and new beginnings.

Gospel

Mark 4:26-34

A man scatters seed on the land and would sleep and the seed would sprout and grow, he knows not how.

Literary Link

After the sayings about the purpose of light, Mark adds two more final parables of the kingdom: the way seeds mysteriously grow to maturity without human intervention (vv. 26-29) and the disproportion between the initial mustard seed and its eventual size (vv. 30-32). Both present variations on the theme initiated by the parable of the sower and the seed (vv. 3-8).

The Mystery of Growth

Another explanation for the celebrated phrase "the kingdom of God" is the "sovereign action of God" that often remains hidden in the currents of human history or the experiences of life. The mysterious laws of growth (v. 27), quiet and effective, beyond the scope of immediate human observation except by contrast between one week and another, became a teaching on the way in which God is at work in our lives. God prefers to remain anonymous. Often enough, our own personal changes for better or worse go unnoticed except from a distance or over a longer period of time. To say "this is how it is with the kingdom of God" and to read the parables that illustrate this action is to suggest that the gradual manner in which life unfolds is really God at work. This gradualness could include, for example, the manner in which infatuation develops into affection and then into lifelong commitment, or the way a skill at mechanics unfolds from familiarity with tools to diagnosing auto problems, or any other human experience/skill that unfolds and deepens slowly and almost imperceptibly . . . God at work!

Mustard Seed

God can and does use very insignificant realities for grand purposes. Although the mustard seed isn't really the smallest of all seeds (v. 31), its eventual size is a considerable difference from its beginnings. Moreover, the parable is not merely a contrast in size but also a teaching that true growth is for service, as exemplified by the birds of the air in its branches (v. 32). Growth is not merely for self-satisfied complacency!

Friday of the Third Week in Ordinary Time

Saturday of the Third Week in Ordinary Time

First Reading (Year I)

Hebrews 11:1-2, 8-19

He was looking forward to the city whose architect and maker is God.

The Faith of Abraham

One after the other, Abraham's decisions to leave home (v. 8), seek a promised but foreign land (v. 9), trust in receiving an heir (v. 11), and even to raise the sacrificial knife over his beloved son Isaac (v. 17) all expressed his profound faith in his God. Although we may not be required to take such drastic steps during our lives, our own Christian faith, built in some fashion upon the foundation of Abraham's faith, leads us to make similar acts of confident faith, large and small, frequently every day. True faith is a daily reality, not merely something restricted to major moments in life.

Faith according to the Letter to the Hebrews

This faith is not merely the intellectual acceptance of some proposition revealed by God but the gift of self to a relationship of friendship with the God who directs our lives and eventually leads us to where our home should be. The definition in this text has become classic: "the realization of what is hoped for and evidence of things not seen" (v. 1). There must be enough evidence to make the gift of self reasonable, even if we are not able to find the type of scientific proof that allows no alternative. True faith is also free faith, because it is not forced by scientific or mathematical conclusions.

Antiphon (Year I)

Luke 1:68

Blessed be the Lord the God of Israel;
he has come to his people.

The "Benedictus" of Zechariah as Psalm Response

Surprisingly, the response to the reading's hymn of praise for Abraham's faith in this first reading from Hebrews is a portion of Zechariah's song on the occasion of the circumcision of little John the Baptist. Zechariah's recognition of the way in which God raises leadership for the salvation of Israel is a fitting echo of Abraham's trust that God could provide a child to elderly parents. The connection is made by the hymn's reference to Abraham (v. 73). The church's liturgy, therefore, on this occasion places John after Abraham and invites us to take our places in that same stream of all those remembered for their trust in God's saving actions in history! Abraham was only the beginning!

"Blessed Be the Lord"

The opening words of the Benedictus (Luke 1:68) and the first words of the refrain suggest that we are obliged to praise and bless God's providence in every moment of our lives. Like Job, who responded to his tragic heartaches, we are encouraged to say, "the Lord gives and the Lord takes away; blessed be the Lord forever" (see Job 1:21). In good times and in more painfully troubled ones, we say, "Blessed be God forever!" This was Zechariah's response at the unexpected birth of a son in old age and in his acceptance of a name (John), contrary to the wishes of family and friends, because God had so commanded. How often do we express that prayer? How often should we?

First Reading (Year II)

2 Samuel 12:1-7a, 10-17

I have sinned against the Lord.

David's Judgment and Penance

The remarkable parable of Nathan the court prophet led David to pronounce unwittingly a condemnation upon his own head (v. 5). The story of the poor man's pet lamb (vv. 1-4) outraged David and made him see with utter clarity and horror what he himself had done to Uriah. Sometimes when our choices are reframed by those around us, we can often see them more easily for what they really are, noble or contemptible, as the case may be. We need Nathans in our lives, truth-sayers who love us enough to speak the truth to us, even the truth we would rather not hear. Those who candidly address our misuse of alcohol, our inability to drive an auto, or the devastating effects of our words on others do us a great favor. They should be thanked.

Saturday of the Third Week in Ordinary Time

Painful Consequences of Sin

Every decision and every action has consequences. In this passage David is confronted by the fact of his sin of secret adultery and its final punishment in the death of the child (v. 14). In God's mysterious ways, we are often punished, not for our sins, but by our sins, which turn out to be themselves painful and purifying. To everyone's sorrow and sadness, the child dies. David is confronted and his lust purified by the loss of an heir.

Antiphon (Year II)

Psalm 51:12a

Create a clean heart in me, O God.

The Great Penitential Psalm

Most appropriately, Psalm 51 is once again chosen by the Lectionary as the liturgical response to the reading of the second act of the drama. Its title (v. 3) links the hymn to David's sorrow after his sin with Bathsheba, and hence becomes the ideal response to the story of his judgment by the prophet Nathan! As pointed out yesterday when a different antiphon was taken from this same psalm, it becomes the perfect expression of sorrow for everyone and for all congregations in every age at times of penance.

A Clean Heart

The psalm acknowledges that a clean heart, precisely because it is acknowledged as created by God (v. 12), is not our doing or an accomplishment of our own making. This is the point of the antiphon. Any new beginning in life is the gift of God who alone takes away the sins of the world. All the resolutions in the world, and all the penances we might devise, cannot cleanse us from the guilt of our sins, but only the God of creation and new creation, before whom we stand humbly and sorrowfully.

Gospel

Mark 4:35-41

Then who is this whom even wind and sea obey?

Literary Link

After Mark's collection of parables related to seeds and growth, the gospel presents the first of three miracle stories, namely, the calming of the storm (vv. 36-41).

Jesus, Lord of Creation

Coming immediately after the parables of secret growth and astonishing contrast between the mustard seed and its subsequent large size at maturity, Mark now describes the power of Jesus in the external world, over wind and storm as well. Jesus confronts the storm with power (v. 39). Matters, large or small, simple or destructive, are all presented as subordinate to the power of Jesus. The disciples are astonished by his power (v. 41). Mark the storyteller adds small details that help to humanize the account, such as the little head cushion used by Jesus on the boat (v. 38). This brings the tale alive, and enables the modern reader to understand the enormous power wielded by Jesus, even in his earthly ministry. The account of this same event as told in Luke 5 leaves us wondering if it is a description of a postresurrection experience retroactively told to help us see the continuity of his divine power present in both pre- and postresurrection events in the life of the Lord. One is moved to the confession of "Jesus is Lord" (1 Cor 12:3).

Need for Faith

After the calming of the storm, Jesus challenges the wavering faith of his disciples (v. 40). In Mark's gospel the disciples never seem to quite get it, and become themselves figures like the wavering faith of his readers. In Year I, these disciples provide a contrast with the great faith of Abraham in the first reading of the day. Faith expects from us the assumption that God can be God, and that God can do great things beyond our expectations. One can often find a deliberate contrast or continuity between the day's two readings, intentionally placed next to each other by those who arranged the passages in the weekday Lectionary. A valuable practice is to seek echoes of continuity or contrast from the first and second readings each day.

Monday of the Fourth Week in Ordinary Time

First Reading (Year I)

Hebrews 11:32-40

By faith they conquered kingdoms.
God had foreseen something better for us.

Martyrs and Heroes of Faith

This is an extraordinary litany of saints and martyrs, each important in her or his own day but now only described by some single solitary action by which they are remembered. The list of "all saints" concludes with a summary judgment to the effect that "[t]he world was not worthy of them" (v. 38). They were persons of great faith, and approved by God because of it. They were individuals who had not as yet experienced the fullness of God's promises. One might say that each age has its own heroic list of people who merit an "All Saints' celebration" of their own, and one might add that the assembly at weekday celebrations of the Eucharist is comprised of such individuals! Is there anyone within our experience about whom we might or perhaps should say, "The world [is] not worthy of them"? Earlier, the reader was reminded that "God is not ashamed to be called their God" (v. 16).

Something Better for Us

The Letter to the Hebrews offers a message, repeated in many forms through its chapters, namely, that its own contemporary cast of characters had been blessed as none before with an opportunity for witnessing the fulfillment of those promises (v. 40). Participation in the heavenly liturgy through the sacrifice of Jesus was now uniquely available. Writer and readers alike were created by God and called to be active in the "last age" of salvation history. All were encouraged to persevere in their faith so as to receive the great and final reward of the faithful. This sacred literature is breathtakingly beautiful.

Antiphon (Year I)

Psalm 31:25

Let your hearts take comfort, all who hope in the Lord.

A Psalm of Lament

The refrain is the final verse of the psalm that curiously is not a part of the actual response provided by the Lectionary! Psalm 31 rehearses a series of woes endured by a faithful individual: illness, calumny and opposition, hostility from former friends. Like all such songs, the thread of trust is woven into the text as is a repetition of the importance of trust in God. Scholars suggest that the theme of thanksgiving is offered, almost as if the petition is already effective once promised by the presider at the temple's liturgy. Because of its confident praise, this psalm is a superb prayer for anyone deeply burdened by troubles.

Comfort for the Heart

In the anatomy as known to the ancient Semitic world, the heart is not the place of romantic love, as imagined in more contemporary thinking, but rather the place where plans were fashioned and decisions made. Therefore, it is precisely the heart (v. 25) that is encouraged by the refrain to move forward and make plans for the future in spite of the heartaches of life at the moment. The refrain's insistent invitation to hope in God (repeated six times) is an assurance offered to all God's faithful people who suffer during their lifelong pilgrimage to the final blessings promised by God. It is the perfect response to the litany of holy people described in the day's first reading from Hebrews.

First Reading (Year II)

2 Samuel 15:13-14, 30; 16:5-13

Let us take flight, or none of us will escape from Absalom. Let Shimei alone and let him curse, for the Lord has told him to.

Flight from Absalom

This passage is from a tragic episode in the final years of David's reign when his beloved son Absalom rebelled and attempted to take over the kingdom (v. 13). Perhaps this disruption from within his own family is a punishment for having violated and disrupted the family of Uriah. Sin and punishment always have some correlation in Deuteronomic theology. Any punishment announced by prophets offers a surprising correlation to the sin condemned. The bitterness of intergenerational strife and rivalry afflicts many families, and often becomes the heartache of parents who see their families divided by the wounds of old resentments, mysterious and unhealed. This reading should inspire prayer for all the divided families of the congregation.

David's Response to Hardship and Opposition

Shimei was an embittered relative of the former king Saul, by then long dead after a disastrous defeat in battle (16:5). The family had blamed David for Saul's death and now this individual appeared from the shadows of history to throw stones (v. 6) and to curse David at the low point of his life, almost as if the punishment of stoning was now being ironically decreed against him for the misdeeds of his past. David's humble reaction to the cursing and stone throwing of Shimei offers a lesson in how to deal with those who speak badly of us, falsely judging our actions or speaking untruth about us. David becomes an illustration of the Lord's admonition in the Sermon on the Mount to bless those who curse us and do good to those who persecute us (Matt 5:44). The question remains very contemporary: How do we react to false accusations and hostility? Can we ever come to see such situations as gifts of grace? How can we make amends if we have done the same thing to others?

ANTIPHON (YEAR II)

Psalm 3:8a

Lord, rise up and save me.

A Psalm of Lament

The title for Psalm 3 explicitly links it with the event when David fled for his life from the rebellion of Absalom (v. 1), and therefore is the perfect response to this day's Lectionary reading. The various kinds of hostility and hardship experienced by David during his momentary fall from power are laced with expressions of humble trust (v. 4) in the God who had called him to kingship. Trust, even amid disaster, is the only sentiment that enables a person to endure and survive. Our God does not protect us from heartache but walks with us through pain into the light.

A Plea for Salvation

If ever there was a "tight spot" from which only God could save, it was this tragic moment in David's life. For that reason, the refrain simply begs to be saved (v. 8). Absalom died, a victim of his own vain and proud arrogance (as tomorrow's first reading will report), but for the moment David's prayer for deliverance commands our attention and offers words for any heartache we may experience in our lifetime. Imagine any personal sorrow or family tragedy, and then recite the verses from Psalm 3, making this refrain your own!

GOSPEL

Mark 5:1-20

Unclean spirit, come out of the man!

Literary Link

The exorcism of the demon from the madman of the pagan tombs (vv. 1-20) is the second miracle of Jesus reported after his teachings on the seeds.

Mental Disease

Upon having crossed into pagan Gerasene territory, Jesus and his community of disciples encounter the madman of the cemetery. The symptoms of this Gerasene demoniac seem to point to a case of violent raging psychological anger or guilt that is even capable of self-destruction

(v. 6). Our own day witnesses the tragic phenomenon of adolescent (self) cutters. Our society tends to medicate these urges and to suppress them but often seems unable to discover and to cure the reality behind the symptoms. All of us know the surging emotions of what spiritual writers call the seven capital sins, and their potential harm to our own spirits. We also know the critical value of being confronted by the holy healing of Christ for our holiness, happiness, and health. This is a day to pray for all who suffer from mental disease, and for their professional and family caretakers.

Monday of the Fourth Week in Ordinary Time

The Demoniac's Plea

The demoniac of the Gerasene cemetery was a tortured person who came to Jesus, acknowledging his own powerlessness over the forces within him and begging for help (v. 7). His plea not to be tortured can be paraphrased into something like, "Just please don't hurt me in the process!" We know of our own inner compulsions, our own "demons," if you will, which can be destructive if unchecked and undisciplined. When we beg for help, we also fear being hurt in the process of treatment and cure! Addictions and mental illness is a family tragedy, not only for the individual so afflicted, but also for everyone who knows and cares about that person. We often feel helpless before such dark inner mysteries. Modern treatments and medications may provide comfort and some alleviation of symptoms, but the heartache may never quite go away. With closer inspection we can see so many familiar faces in this haunting account.

The Plea of the Villagers

The astonishment of the villagers and their fear of the power of Jesus, who had cured the demoniac but destroyed the herd of pigs, led them to beg Jesus to go away (v. 17). It is one of the saddest verses of the gospels. Rather than come to faith in the healing power of Jesus and his ability to confront the demonic in all its forms, they shrink in fear and beg him to leave. It is a story of grace offered and refused. If once rejected, however, there may not be another opportunity, no matter how God may try. Rejection out of fear may become its own habit. Sin and mental illness are very disruptive. Curiously, however, healing also changes things, sometimes much to the discomfort of those who had gotten used to things as they were! Sending the healer away is very shortsighted!

Evangelization at Home

Jesus heals and helps the man (v. 15) but declines to allow him to join in the close circle of disciples who traveled with him through the area (v. 19). Rather, the man is told to return to his home and to tell others what God had done for him. Sometimes ordinary and good folks are fearful of the invitation to be evangelizers, thinking that it may mean knocking on neighbors' doors or handing out leaflets. A fundamental aspect of evangelization, however, is the simple willingness to speak honestly and gratefully about all that God has done for each of us. This is more to the point than street-corner preaching or pamphlet distribution. The cured demoniac is a model for various vocations in the work of the kingdom! He is an improbable "patron" of evangelizers.

Tuesday of the Fourth Week in Ordinary Time

First Reading (Year I)

Hebrews 12:1-4

Let us persevere in running the race that lies before us.

A Cloud of Witnesses

Every gathering of Christians, no matter how small or insignificant in number or note, is always surrounded by a "cloud of witnesses"/martyrs (v. 1). The immediate reference is to the powerful list of unnamed heroes described in the prior day's reading from Hebrews, but it also includes all the holy people already participating in the "church triumphant" of heaven above. The invocation of all the saints in each of the eucharistic prayers reminds us of the larger community, seen and unseen, present when Christians gather for prayer. They are all models and cheerleaders for us as we run the race.

Running the Race

The Greek word "*agōn*/race" (v. 1) refers to a more generic athletic competition, but the verb clearly means to run—so all translations choose to refer to a race, which makes contemporary joggers happy. The author of the Second Letter to Timothy also uses athletic imagery to describe all of life's struggles (6:12): effort, practice, discipline, goal, and purpose! In a thoroughly hellenized culture the athletic competition and workouts at the local gymnasia provided a ready reference and helpful image for the struggle involved in lifelong fidelity to God. We could speak of the Holy Spirit as a "personal trainer"! One should not miss acknowledging that Muslim spirituality also uses a similar notion, *jihad*/struggle, for the spiritual discipline of faithfulness, even though recent events have unfortunately (and incorrectly) tended to see that term only in the context of terrorism!

Jesus the "Leader"

There are many images and metaphors for Jesus and his work of redemption. The Letter to the Hebrews uses the title of *archēgos*/pioneer/"leader" for Jesus (v. 2), who goes first through a life of obedience to the will of God, passing through death to the fullness of life. This also offers some further insights into the metaphor of running: a team effort, surrounded by spectators and fans, with a sharply defined objective—and even the implication of a relay race in which something (the faith) is passed from one person to another. The fact that the many witnesses are called a "cloud," rather than merely a crowd, suggests some of those witnesses may be more heavenly and ethereal, including the entire heavenly court of God!

Antiphon (Year I)

Psalm 22:27b

They will praise you, Lord, who long for you.

The Proto-Gospel

Early Christians combed the Scriptures for hints and preshadows of the life and mission of Jesus, and found Psalm 22 to be a magnificent text for that purpose! Beginning with the cry of abandonment (v. 2), later placed on the lips of Jesus on the cross (Mark 15:34 and Matt 27:46), followed by references to being scorned, bones counted, and garments divided. The second portion of the psalm, used here as the response, goes on to describe returning to give praise in the midst of the congregation. This was later applied to a postresurrection appearance of Jesus in the Upper Room.

The Praise of the Assembly

The antiphon picks up the theme of popular praise for God and applies it to the joyful response of heaven as Jesus Triumphant takes his seat at the right hand of God. All of heaven becomes a "welcome home" celebration. The refrain can also offer a prism for viewing the weekday eucharistic assembly itself, perhaps small, but filled with praise for the God of universal salvation.

First Reading (Year II)

2 Samuel 18:9-10, 14b, 24-25a, 30–19:3

My son, Absalom, if only I had died instead of you.

Absalom's Death by Vanity

The judgment oracles of classic Israelite prophets regularly saw a correlation between the sin and the punishment decreed by God. Absalom is no exception. He was remembered for his physical handsomeness, and was very vain about his hair (2 Sam 14:26), so there was irony in the fact that he was rendered immobile and captured when his hair caught in the branches of a tree (v. 9), where he was killed by Joab the general. Arrogant vanity is a danger to body and spirit. All gifts are precisely gifts, never to be assumed as if they were entitled personal qualities of our own making. We show ourselves to be very foolish if we think otherwise.

The Sorrow of David

David shared the enduring love of a parent for his child, no matter what had happened. Even though Absalom had been an arrogant rebel, determined to remove his father from the throne, David still grieved the death and loss bitterly (19:1). By twists and turns of family rivalry, the presumed successors of David are eliminated, leaving Solomon as a major candidate. It remains a great sadness anytime parents are faced with the death of their children. The reading can inspire prayers for all parents of the world who have lost children, no matter what the circumstances.

Antiphon (Year II)

Psalm 86:1a

Listen, Lord, and answer me.

A Psalm of Lament

Although many verses of this psalm echo passages and expressions found elsewhere, Psalm 86 is not necessarily a late composition that simply borrows from earlier songs of sorrow and need. As a liturgical song for people in grief, it expresses a sort of universal sorrow. In terms of our reading, the psalm fits the mood of David as he mourns his beloved son.

A Petition for Hearing

Both the beginning (v. 1) and the end (v. 6) of the portion of this psalm selected for the day's liturgical use repeat an urgent prayer for hearing before God. A plea that is heard can expect some type of response—perhaps not the answer desired, but at least recognition that God has indeed heard and takes seriously the petition. A parent who has experienced a tragic loss such as that of David often prays for understanding, asking, How could this happen? and Why me? Moreover, and more generally, a fundamental element in all our lifelong relationships with family, friends, and neighbors is our communication and our desire to be heard by those around us. In any grief, to know that we have been heard is to begin the journey toward healing and contentment.

Gospel

Mark 5:21-43

Little girl, I say to you, arise!

Literary Link

After the calming of the storm and the exorcism of the demoniac, a third account of miraculous actions on the part of Jesus includes this passage of interwoven cures (vv. 21-43).

Tales of Healing and Communal Restoration

Jesus repeatedly reunites people to their primary community and the forty verses of this chapter provide three illustrations: the mentally ill Gerasene restored to family (v. 19), the woman with the hemorrhage who had been separated from community by her illness restored to society (v. 34), and the synagogue official Jairus reunited with his raised daughter (v. 43). The mission of Jesus has a special focus on community health and social well-being. Modern individualism risks the loss of the social reality that permeated the ancient biblical world and provided a focus for the mission of Jesus and his church.

Two Interwoven Miracles

The events of life are rarely separated neatly into categories; like this passage the plight of the mature woman and the family tragedy of the little girl's death are mixed together as Jesus responds to both in yet another busy and action-packed day. This type of breathless narrative shows the energy of Jesus as well as the many different categories addressed and healed by Jesus. God's healing power is present to everyone, and often in a manner that recognizes the relationship we have to each other—even worldwide—only "six degrees of separation."

The Ridicule of the Crowds

The crowd at the home of Jairus was constrained by the natural law of death that they had witnessed, and refused to see any other possibility or alternative. They mocked Jesus when he announced that the child was merely asleep (v. 40). Although we should not live in foolish presumption as if God intervenes always, and thus trivialize the miraculous, the unexpected can happen. Our secularized world often refuses to accept any possibility of miracles, and mocks the faith of those who think differently. Nothing is impossible for God, as proven by the joy of the girl's parents (v. 42).

Wednesday of the Fourth Week in Ordinary Time

First Reading (Year I)

Hebrews 12:4-7, 11-15

The Lord disciplines those he loves.

Discipline

Whether one understands "discipline/*paideia*" (v. 5) as rigorous daily practice in denying one's inclinations and maintaining order in one's life or as punishment, the letter recommends understanding all the hardships of life through that category. We are told that everything is for our "discipline" (v. 7). Recalling the metaphor of God as a truly loving divine parent, we are reminded that God expects us to learn something from every experience of life. From illness we can learn not to take health for granted; from weakness we can learn to depend on others; from deprivation we can learn generosity. A prayer at the end of each day might well include the question, what did I learn today?

Holiness

A certain level of *holiness* is demanded of anyone who truly desires to see God (v. 14). Although holiness is always a gift from God and not achieved by our own efforts alone, it can be a goal eagerly desired by human beings who prepare themselves diligently to receive that gift. Many definitions and descriptions abound, but one brief summary of "holiness" would suggest that genuine Christian holiness includes three aspects: (1) being so rooted in the Lord's death and resurrection as to be honest even when the truth is embarrassing, (2) being generous even when it may cost something, and (3) being humble before God. God doesn't demand that we be pious but does expect us to be holy.

Antiphon (Year I)

Psalm 103:17

The Lord's kindness is lasting to those who fear him.

The Lord's Kindness

Once again, the "kindness/*hesed*" celebrated in this refrain (v. 17) refers specifically to the mutual concern that should exist between covenantal partners. God's kindness is reciprocal and, once pledged by God, exists for all generations. At the same time God so respects our human freedom that he will never impose his friendship upon an unwilling human partner.

Those Who Fear

The "fear" to which this refrain refers (v. 17) is not some type of servile cowering of the little before the powerful but rather a sense of reverence before someone who is deeply respected for goodness and generosity. This type of fear exists in the heart of a truly humble person who honestly understands his or her own limitations and appreciates the dignity of mutual interdependence with another, namely, God. This notion of fear is frequently found in Wisdom literature; it includes the respect that one should have for a parent, teacher, or mentor.

First Reading (Year II)

2 Samuel 24:2, 9-17

It is I who have sinned, but these are sheep;
what have they done?

Surveying and Counting God's People

At first blush we find it difficult to see sin in David's desire to take a census in order to know the full number of citizens from the twelve tribes of Israel (v. 2). It would seem a morally neutral governmental practice/action for good planning, at least to modern nations. By our Constitution we in the United States are committed to such a count every ten years. The sinfulness, therefore, must be related not to David's action in itself but to his intention and purpose for ordering such a census. David's decision was probably rooted in a self-aggrandizing desire to know his power and wealth. To place the focus on the human person of the king, rather than on God who is the source of life and prosperity for all nations, may be the reason for divine displeasure and punishment as expressed by the prophet Gad (v. 12). It is the inner motive and intention that is judged in this account. The story also serves as a reminder of the fact that our own inner intentions are open to God's scrutiny and judgment as well.

Punishment Offered and Chosen

When David admits the sinfulness in his decision as well as his foolishness (v. 10), the prophet Gad offers a choice of punishment: three years of famine, three months of flight before enemies, or three days of plague. After David had chosen the pestilence (v. 15), and then saw the terrible pain that this entailed for innocent people, it was God who stopped the punishment midway in order to limit the sorrow and protect the city of Jerusalem (v. 16). David begged that the punishment be restricted to the person primarily responsible for the sin, himself (v. 17). The individual and the community need constant counterbalancing.

Communal and Individual

The ancient world was primarily social in seeing blessings and punishments. No matter what the sin, it was perceived as affecting an entire tribe or family. Only slowly, some five hundred years later under the scrutiny of Ezekiel (18:1-31), did the notion of individual responsibility become fully recognized in Israel. Contemporary Western society, on the other hand, has become so radically individualized that the learning curve must go in the other direction, toward perceiving the social character of sin and injustice as well as its individual consequences.

ANTIPHON (YEAR II)

Psalm 32:5c

Lord, forgive the wrong I have done.

A Penitential Psalm

Psalm 32 is counted among the seven great penitential psalms of the early church, namely, 6, 32, 38, 51, 102, 130, and 143. These psalms would have been recited by those temporarily excluded from the worshiping community during their time of atonement for their sins against God and community as they prepared for readmittance. These psalms were the prayer of those who were members of the ancient "order of penitents." That was the name given to the group of acknowledged public sinners who had committed any of the *tria capitalia*, that is, the three most serious sins that separated a person from the community: idolatry, adultery, and murder. We are told that Psalm 32 was Augustine's favorite, perhaps because it included God's favorable response.

The Three Elements in the Antiphon

Studying this brief refrain (v. 5), one quickly sees that it contains three distinctive elements. First, there is the recognition that the issue at hand is morally evil because it is called "the wrong." Second, the sinner acknowledges that he or she has in fact been personally responsible for the evil action. Finally, the offender is led to a realization that God is the one to be approached with a plea for forgiveness. Judaism is firmly clear in teaching that only the one offended can offer forgiveness, but in Christianity God is so identified with humans as to be also offended by our evil actions. God forgives, and the church is called to be the instrument of that gift.

GOSPEL

Mark 6:1-6

A prophet is not without honor except in his native place.

Literary Link

Earlier in the unfolding of Mark's gospel, Jesus had been rejected by some of the religious leadership among the Pharisees and by the political leadership of the Herodians

(3:6). Now, after the initial account of the teaching and healing performed by Jesus in Galilee, he is rejected by his own people (6:1-6). Both events prepare readers for the events surrounding the passion and death of Jesus. The gospels continue to probe the mystery of rejection.

Sabbath Synagogue Services

With considerable frequency we are told that Jesus attended the synagogue on the Sabbath (v. 2). After the destruction of the temple by the Babylonians in 587 BC, the development of alternative places for prayer and worship became more common. Even after the dedication of the rebuilt temple in Jerusalem, synagogues for community affairs and public worship flourished, especially in areas more distant from Jerusalem such as Galilee. It is helpful to pause at this reference (v. 2) in order to be reminded of the Jewishness of Jesus and his disciples. The more we know about Jewish life and practice, ancient as well as contemporary, the more we will understand Jesus and the early Christian church. It is a very valuable experience for contemporary Christians to visit a synagogue for a Friday evening Sabbath service.

Wednesday of the Fourth Week in Ordinary Time

The "Scandal of the Familiar"

Familiarity may not necessarily breed contempt, but it can often induce a certain form of blindness! It is an all too common element in our relationships with family and friends around us. Sometimes knowing their weaknesses and warts can prevent us from seeing the best and brightest in the people we know so well. This would seem to have been the affliction of the former neighbors of Jesus who were astonished by his sense of inner authority, and chose to dismiss him and "took offense" at him (v. 3). They thus chose to avoid the task of searching further for the source of his superiority. Jesus was astonished by their lack of faith (v. 6)—and perhaps at ours as well.

Brothers and Sisters

The reference to the brothers and sisters of Jesus (v. 3) can catch us off guard given the church's teaching regarding the singular conception of Jesus by the Holy Spirit and the perpetual virginity of Mary. Over the centuries there have been many explanations and interpretations offered for these familial relationships. It may be helpful to recall that, although Greek seems to have a special word for everything, the Hebrew languages and general Semitic culture of the ancient world had no common word for those whom we would call "cousins" or other more distant relatives. All those within the immediate family circles were simply called "brothers and sisters." Those who rejected Jesus knew his family and were not able to imagine anything unusual or remarkable about him.

Thursday of the Fourth Week in Ordinary Time

First Reading (Year I)

Hebrews 12:18-19, 21-24

You have approached Mount Zion and the city of the living God.

Sinai and Zion

The Letter to the Hebrews constantly contrasts the first and second covenant, and all the elements that characterized each. The issue is not geography but symbols of respective communities. In this case the fearful transcendence of God at Sinai is compared to a festive celebration on Mount Zion (v. 22), especially as projected into the final heavenly age of divine victory over all sin. This becomes a template for understanding the reality of the final heavenly gathering where the firstborn (v. 23) presides as mediator forever (v. 24). A God who is truly loving and merciful presides over Sinai/covenant and Zion/temple. This passage offers a contrast between differing modes of divine communication, namely, the frightening phenomena of nature designed to inspire awe and obedience, and the heavenly Jerusalem that aims at inviting participation. Both are valuable and even necessary at different times in human growth under grace. The early Christian communities, which included Torah observant Jews as well as Gentiles, strove to maintain a profound unity between these contrasting forms of discipleship. We are invited to appreciate both.

The Utter Transcendence of God

In celebrating the reality of the incarnation, and the abiding presence of the "firstborn" (v. 23) who is also Emanuel, God-with-us, we should never forget the other part of the truth, that is, God as judge of all (v. 23) with total superiority over everything human. The fire and thunder at Sinai are images for that unfathomable distance, and also deserve to be remembered forever. No one image, positive or negative, can exhaust the nature of God; all images deserve to be remembered and cherished.

Antiphon (Year I)

Psalm 48:10

O God, we ponder your mercy within your temple.

Mercy

In our prayer over the antiphonal refrains that are proposed in the church's Lectionary for communal worship, we return frequently to the specific Hebrew word in question. This enables us to have a more precise understanding of the nature and focus of the prayer. In this case (v. 10) the word in question is *hesed*, the reciprocal and mutual care of covenantal partners for each other's welfare and well-being. Therefore the object of the refrain is not merely compassion or kind generosity but a reference to the duty to care for each other, which is accepted by those who enter into covenant, even God!

Temple Worship

The communal liturgy of ancient Israel included songs with chorus and musical instruments as well as various types of sacrifice. The gathering of people, whether pilgrims from afar or nearby neighborhood residents, also provides opportunities for pondering the nature and works of God. There is something powerfully effective when we consider God's deeds of salvation in a setting of being surrounded by others who share the same vision. We become specially united in a shared sense of gratitude and praise. We ponder as well as praise. There is also a cherished place for silence in our worship in order to privately explore the meaning of all these gifts and graces.

Thursday of the Fourth Week in Ordinary Time

First Reading (Year II)

1 Kings 2:1-4, 10-12

I am going the way of all flesh.
Take courage and be a man.

Farewell Speech of David

The biblical witness provided by the lives of most major figures usually concludes with a farewell speech offering a summary of their life and mission. Since the book is a literary composition by the human as well as the divine author, it is worthy of very careful study. In this case David's fundamental admonition refers to obedience to the Mosaic Torah (v. 3) and to the covenant within which his instruction was expressed and transmitted. There is a conditional element to God's promise (v. 4), and each succeeding royal figure will be judged according to the degree of his or her fidelity to that covenant.

The First Book of Kings

The Deuteronomic theology of this extended history of the rise and eventual demise of David's dynasty in Judah continues. A new division in the material now considers the anointing of Solomon and the beginning of his rule, grand and sinful as it was. Covenantal theology, dominated by the shadow of the bond between God and Israel mediated by Moses, judges all people. That same shadow also includes the final sin and destruction of Judah by the Babylonians.

"Take Courage and Be a Man"

Similar but not identical words were used by Moses for the transfer of his leadership authority to Joshua (Deut 31:6, 23; Josh 1:6, 9) at the time of entering the Promised Land. Here Solomon is encouraged to be a true "*ʾish*/man" (v. 2). This instruction of David to his son and successor, Solomon, is a perfect opportunity to offer a true sense of Christian masculinity: strong, principled, generous, devoted to serve and protect those under one's care, decisive, God-fearing, and humble. Although Solomon promised to offer protection to his rebellious brother, Adoniah, a way (pretext?) was eventually found to have him killed. Certainly violence was not presumed particularly masculine, though it occurs with sad frequency in the ancient world of David and Solomon as well as in our own day.

Antiphon (Year II)

1 Chronicles 29:12b

Lord, you are exalted over all.

Final Prayer of David

Although 1 Kings offers David's final instruction to Solomon, it was the First Book of Chronicles that offered David's final prayer before God (29:10-12). The theological perspective of Chronicles is uniquely different from the books of Samuel and Kings, focused completely on David as the source and guiding inspiration for the worship of Israel. David's final prayer is simply and completely a celebration of divine transcendence. Even today, this prayer is a perfect Morning or Evening Prayer for all faithful believers. The antiphon itself, however, is not mentioned in the verses chosen by the Lectionary for the response.

"Blessed Are You"

Like virtually all prayers in contemporary Judaism (and also in the prayers of offering the bread and wine in the renewed Mass of Paul VI), the prayer-hymn begins with a blessing for God. David's prayer also included recognition of God as "father" (v. 10). The books of Chronicles were written after the return from Babylonian exile and aimed at providing the theology for the reconstructed temple. During that time the notion of God as Father became more popular (Isa 63:16). The practice of Jesus, therefore, is not singular or far removed from mainstream Jewish piety and religious devotion.

Gospel

Mark 6:7-13

Jesus summoned the Twelve and began to send them out.

Literary Link

After the rejection of Jesus by his own people (6:3-6), the Gospel of Mark turns to focus on his relationship to his disciples (vv. 7-13), and to illustrate how they also continued to misunderstand his mission.

The Mission of the Twelve

Apparently the mission of the Twelve recorded here was not envisioned by Mark as occurring immediately after their election (3:13-19). Only after a period of initial formation and instruction regarding the true nature of the kingdom of God did Jesus begin to send them out (v. 7), and even then, only two by two. This was in accord with ancient Israelite practice so that their testimony would be mutually corroborated and therefore credible (Deut 19:15). Just as Jesus himself was sent to herald the kingdom (Mark 1:15), so his primary followers/apprentices began with a similar mission of authority and purpose.

Without Food, Luggage, Money, or Extra Clothing

The fact that they were told to take "nothing for the journey" (way/*odos*; v. 8) might remind us that the entire Jesus movement was once called "the way" (Acts 9:2) and that the instructions for the Twelve could be generalized for everyone in some fashion. The lack of material possessions served to underscore their total dependence upon God, not upon their own human resources, however limited or extensive they may have been. Only the walking stick (v. 8) for possible defense against stray dogs (or perhaps like the staff of Moses and Aaron; Exod 4:20) and sandals for physical ease of travel (or like the Passover instructions; Exod 12:11) were permitted to the itinerant preachers in the traditions of Mark's community. Forbidding extra clothing may also reflect the eschatological urgency of the last age. In these minor details regarding supplies and luggage, the variations between the three Synoptics probably reflect different theologies as well as community customs.

"Metanoia"/Repentance

From the very beginning the preaching of the Twelve focused on "repentance/*metanoia*" (v. 12), that is, a change of thinking about God's ways in the world. This should not be a concern merely restricted to the season of Lent but a yearlong and lifelong effort. It is the fundamental command of Christianity (Mark 1:15). It would seem even more basic than the command to love one another (John 13:34) because the command to change our minds also refers to how we deal with those around us.

Anointing

The unusual gospel reference to "anoint[ing] with oil" (v. 13) suggests that our sacramental practice of anointing of the sick has very ancient origins in apostolic activity and in the Jewish practices within which they lived. Scholars suggest that the use of vinegar for cleansing and oil for healing was common medical treatment for wounds in the ancient world. As a concrete sign of the kingdom of God at work, Christ made it a sign of God's inner healing.

Friday of the Fourth Week in Ordinary Time

First Reading (Year I)

Hebrews 13:1-8

Jesus Christ is the same yesterday, today, and forever.

Hospitality

The first example of "brotherly love/ *philadelphia*" (v. 1) that is to continue among Christians is hospitality (v. 2; literally, "*philoxenia*/love of strangers"). It was one of the most important duties of the ancient Semitic world, especially among the people of the desert where existence itself could depend upon food and help in time of need from even the most casual or temporary of neighbors. That virtue remained a constant duty throughout the entire history of the people of the first covenant. The Letter to the Hebrews suggests that some may have entertained "angels" (v. 2); the reference may be either to heavenly messengers or to heads of early churches traveling incognito (Rev 1:20). In the New Testament it was Martha who exemplified the virtue of hospitality in a special manner when welcoming Jesus into the home she shared with her sister Mary (Luke 10:40). The actions of Mary in turn embodied the need to learn from those we welcome.

Prison Ministry

Being mindful of prisoners and anyone ill-treated is another example of extended hospitality (v. 3). It was encouraged on the basis of the fact that believers shared with them in the life of the body. The fact that we share corporeal existence with others gives us a sense of obligatory solidarity with everyone, especially those who suffer. Although some of the early Christians may have already been imprisoned for their faith, this passage does not differentiate between believers and nonbelievers. All in prison, guilty or innocent, are commended to the care of followers of Jesus who identified himself with those in prison (Matt 25:36). From the beginning, this was a mark of Christian discipleship.

Catechists and Teachers

The reading encourages respectful remembrance of all who have taught us over the years (v. 7), especially catechists and religious leaders who have proclaimed the Word in speech and in the example of their lives. Apparently even members of the early church were inclined to forget their initial teachers. Personal prayer for them by name is an expression of gratitude, not only for them personally, but for God's grace, which inspired those teachers to accept their vocation and ministry.

Antiphon (Year I)

Psalm 27:1a

The Lord is my light and my salvation.

The Lord as Light

Any title and attribute applied to God is worthy of sustained reflection, asking first, What does it mean? and then, How is it applied to God? The refrain personifies both light and salvation, and applies them to God. Light (v. 1) illumines the path, reveals potential perils, and helps to disclose the environment within which we travel through life. All material flashlights, torches, or candles pale before the psalm's metaphorical use of light as a quality of the transcendent God. At the Easter Vigil the church also applies the title to the risen Lord.

Dispelling All Fear

Psalm 27 proceeds to list all the major sources of human fear, such as encamped enemies (v. 3), war, and even the absence of a sense of God's presence (v. 5). Prophets who lived with a deep bond of communion with the living God continue to say, "Fear not" (Isa 43:1), as did the angel Gabriel when announcing God's plans for Mary (Luke 1:30). Human fears often come from a presumption that success and victory depend on our strength alone!

First Reading (Year II)

Sirach 47:2-11

With his every deed, David offered thanks to God Most High; in words of praise he loved his Maker.

The Book of Ben Sirach (Ecclesiasticus)
Periodically, especially at the end of a sequence of biblical readings about a major figure in salvation history, the Lectionary pauses to include a final ode of praise for the specific contribution and example given by that personality. Written about two hundred years before Christ by a figure of major import as a religious teacher, the Book of Sirach is a masterpiece of spiritual wisdom, well worthy of a full and thoughtful reading.

David's Primary Qualities Worth Remembering

Even after some seven hundred years, the people of Israel still gave praise for the major attributes of King David: his physical strength in dealing with wild animals (v. 3), his precocious youthful courage in standing up to Goliath (v. 4), and his concern for the finest expressions of worship (v. 9). Thus David's physical attributes at the service of the people's security and his sense of worship as a priority illustrate his enduring concern for the common good. This is a model for all ages, especially for people of our own contemporary Western culture like ourselves so afflicted by self-centered radical individualism.

God as Source of Strength and Courage

Faced with daunting challenges embodied in the huge figure of Goliath, David simply called upon the Most High for precision of aim and strength of arm (v. 5). His humble recognition of God as the ultimate source of all gifts made him successful (v. 8). The same attitudes are required for any contemporary victory we may desire on behalf of our people. To arrogantly assume that any strength or talent is of our own making is a sure recipe for failure.

Antiphon (Year II)

Psalm 18:47b

Blessed be God, my salvation.

Twice-Told Songs

The fact that virtually the same song was recorded in both Psalm 18 and 2 Samuel 22 suggests that it was already known at the time of the composition of the Deuteronomic history (Deuteronomy through Joshua) in the sixth century BC, and may even have had its origins at the time of David himself. Some favorites never seem to lose their popularity! The title (v. 1), though not used by the Lectionary, suggests that it was placed on the lips of David whenever he was delivered from his enemies (v. 50). The generic reference also suggests that we can use it freely today as a song of praise at any moment we are rescued by God from serious opposition.

Divine Victory

The history of David has become so identified with God as to make all of David's victories into the victories of God himself (v. 50). The phrase "The Lord live!" (v. 47) is an ancient cry from Canaanite myths of conflict between Baal and his enemies. While we should be humbly cautious about too readily identifying our successes with God's as if God were always on our side, we certainly can celebrate the supreme power of our God and pray that we may be on God's side! It was Jeremiah who cautioned against such presumption when people in Jerusalem assumed that the presence of the temple would always and forever protect them from their enemies (7:3ff.).

Gospel

Mark 6:14-29

It is John whom I beheaded. He has been raised up.

Literary Link

A further example of misunderstanding during the Galilean ministry of Jesus is seen in the reaction of Herod to the growing reputation of Jesus (v. 14). Herod wondered if Jesus were the risen figure of John the Baptizer, whom Herod had killed. The reference became the occasion for telling the story of John's execution (vv. 17-29).

Guilt and Sorrow

The figure of Herod (v. 16), together with Judas who betrayed Jesus (Matt 27:5), remain two of the most classic New Testament representatives of people haunted by guilt. Usually, however, the sins and mistakes of life continue to live with and within us until, through the grace of God, they become the objects of repentance and atonement. We can only avoid being held hostage and trapped by prior sin when we realize that our human actions are never the last word in any situation. Rather it is God's final judgment, filled with his understanding and respect of our woeful limitations, that could conclude every human tale. Hope because of who God is, not despair because of who we are, marks the direction of our journey into God's future and ours.

Friday of the Fourth Week in Ordinary Time

Revenge and Human Respect

Two very dangerous emotions are illustrated in this exotic and dramatic tale of the death of John the Baptist: the revenge of Herodias (v. 19), which can also lead to violence if nursed and harbored for years, and the distressing human respect on the part of Herod (v. 26), which can lead the weak into tragic decisions. As evident from this tragedy, too narrow and blind a focus on ourselves can have terrible consequences for us and for the larger world. Once again, as is often the case, we are not punished for our sins as much as by our sins! Their consequences return to show their inherent evil.

Saturday of the Fourth Week in Ordinary Time

First Reading (Year I)

Hebrews 13:15-17, 20-21

May the God of peace, who brought up from the dead the great shepherd, furnish you with all that is good.

True Sacrifices

After the destruction of the temple by the Romans in AD 70, a variety of devotional practices came to be understood as "sacrifices." Praise of God with a personal sense of submission and homage was seen as sacrificial. This sentiment is familiar from Psalm 141, where prayer is compared to incense (v. 2). The letter also explicitly equates generosity and acts of goodness with sacrifice (v. 16). The piety of the Pharisaic tradition was ready to see daily family life and personal devotion as extensions and equivalents to temple worship. They considered domestic devotions as similar to temple ritual.

Community Leaders

It may seem self-serving to make a point of the deference to local leaders that this letter commands (v. 17). Nevertheless, it is commanded, and leaders are reminded of the account that they must give for their communities. The letter noted that respectful relationships within the community should be the occasion for mutual joy (v. 17). Such is not the case when conflict arises. It is interesting to note that contemporary Amish communities postpone their semiannual communion Sabbaths if there is discord or lack of harmony in their communities.

Grace at Work

The author of Hebrews concludes the letter with a quick summary of ethical admonitions regarding respect for leaders (v. 17), and then invokes a final blessing. This fits into the epistolary pattern so familiar from the letters of Paul. The letter's final blessing acknowledges that the God of Peace (v. 20) is the ultimate source of everything within us that is pleasing to God (v. 21). This sounds very much like the doctrine of grace, which we hold as a cherished portion of our Christian tradition, because it is only by grace that we can do what is pleasing to God.

Antiphon (Year I)

Psalm 23:1

The Lord is my shepherd; there is nothing I shall want.

Shepherd

The image of shepherd has been applied in many ways over the centuries. The original bucolic context from which it comes suggested personal self-sacrificing care for the flock, its nourishment, security, and well-being. In many ancient Near Eastern cultures it was also applied to royalty, who were expected to care for the people, especially the poor, as an important element in a king's responsibilities and duties. To speak of the Lord as a shepherd (v. 1) is to acknowledge God's personal interest in the lives of his people. Because the metaphor can seem remote for modern urban dwellers, countless modern alternatives have been suggested: legal guardian, security guard, personal primary physician, and even parole agent! What figure would we select for ourselves in order to describe the comfort and concern intended by the reference?

Table and Anointing

The flow of attributes and responsibilities suddenly veers to include a new context: table fellowship (v. 3) and the anointing of hospitality offered in the ancient world to honored guests (v. 4). By extension, over the centuries these verses have been applied to participation in the church's sacraments of initiation, including the Eucharist. Pastoral care today in the Catholic tradition regularly refers to these biblical passages and includes their historical and contemporary applications.

Saturday of the Fourth Week in Ordinary Time

First Reading (Year II)

1 Kings 3:4-13

Give your servant an understanding heart to judge your people.

An Understanding Heart

Later tradition, as found in the books of Chronicles, would omit any reference to the high place of Gibeon because it was an unauthorized sanctuary, but the Deuteronomic historians preferred to retain the event because of the famous prayer recounted in this passage. As noted, Solomon simply asked for *leb shomeʿa*, literally, "a listening heart" (see v. 9). Since there is no word in Hebrew for "obey," the more common expression for obey was "hear." Their presumption was that anyone who listened carefully and heard well, perhaps like a parent alert to a whimpering baby at night, would promptly respond by obedient compliance. Moreover, the heart was the symbol of personal planning and decision making. Whoever listens, acts accordingly. This prayer of Solomon should be the Morning Prayer for every human being.

Right from Wrong

While there were some basic creeds of belief in Israel's religious traditions that named God as the Lord of the covenant (Exod 24:8) or as a God ever gracious and merciful (Exod 34:6), the primary accent of Israel's faith was ethical. For this reason Solomon asked for the kind of "listening heart" that would distinguish "right from wrong" (see v. 9). Orthopraxis defined the devout Israelite, and this request made Solomon a worthy king in Israel.

Antiphon (Year II)

Psalm 119:12b

Lord, teach me your statutes.

Psalm 119: A Prayer for Instruction

Psalm 119 is a lengthy acrostic, namely, an extended prayer with 22 sections each composed of a subunit of 8 verses that began with one of the 22 letters of the Hebrew alphabet. Thus, somewhat artificially constrained to follow the format, the petitions are often repetitious and forced into a mold that doesn't fit easily. The verses of this response (vv. 9-14) each begin with the second letter of their alphabet, *beth*. Running throughout its 176 verses is a constant concern for the word and the law of God as central to every facet of daily life. The Lectionary imagines that such a prayer could have been used by Solomon.

God as Teacher

A pervasive image of God in this psalm that exhibits many characteristics of "Wisdom literature" is that of teacher who instructs and gives moral admonitions. The request of the antiphon stresses such a portrait of God (v. 12). Much of the instruction known to the ancient world was oral, and repetition was a primary mode of learning. The Talmud even forbade the establishment of a school in any area without the agreement of neighbors because of the noise that even the best disciplined place of learning entailed. The God who taught Israel had much knowledge, but also wisdom, that is, how to live successfully in a confusing and tempting world. That wisdom was considered a treasure beyond all riches (v. 14).

Gospel

Mark 6:30-34

They were like sheep without a shepherd.

Literary Link

Immediately after Herod learns about what people were saying about Jesus (v. 14) in yesterday's reading, the gospel proceeds to describe the return of the apostles and the report of their experience on mission (v. 30).

Accountability

Mark is careful to note that the apostles, who returned to Jesus after their initial "mission" earlier in the same chapter (v. 7), gave a report of their experiences (v. 30). Although they traveled with a mandate, they remained subject to the Lord's authority and accountable to him for the results of their work. One could easily imagine some form of group discussion and mutual critique as part of that "debriefing" in a relaxed and relatively "deserted" environment (v. 31). The Sabbath was not mentioned, but its reality in terms of "rest" was assumed in these sessions. The account is a reminder of the fact that every one of us remains accountable to God for graces and vocations received.

Desperate Yearning for Truth

No matter how often Jesus attempted to find the type of solitude needed for reflection and prayer with his disciples (v. 31), the crowds seemed to anticipate their moves (v. 33). Perhaps out of a desperate longing for understanding, the people continued to come from every direction, seeking knowledge about how their God was at work in their lives and in their moment of history. The fact that Jesus responded in this instance by teaching (v. 34) indicates the type of hunger experienced by those crowds as Mark described the scene. Curiously, when Matthew's gospel described that same compassion of Jesus, the response is healing (14:12)!

Monday of the Fifth Week in Ordinary Time

First Reading (Year I)

Genesis 1:1-19

God spoke and it was done.

The Book of Genesis

The Lectionary now begins two weeks of readings from the first eleven chapters of Genesis. Using profound theological motifs from a variety of "catechetical" traditions to describe the origins of material creation and the ancient peoples who inhabited that world, we are introduced to a tale of divine blessings and human disobedience. Gradual disintegration and violence is recounted to provide the background for the call of Abraham and God's plans for his chosen family. This is not history as we know it.

Pre-Scientific Tales

This excerpt from the first chapter of Genesis is a very familiar story based on an ancient worldview. The catechetical purpose of this first account of creation is to provide a basis for the command of God to observe the Sabbath. With the repetition that often characterizes children's literature in any age or culture, different successive steps in creation are assigned to the initial six days of the week, and indeed in a pattern that corresponds to basic human experience, such as the way in which the appearance of light precedes the rising of the sun (v. 3) and seems like a different reality. The poetry of these opening verses should never be made the criterion for evaluating modern scientific theories about the origin of our world. Primitive cosmology assumed a three-tiered universe without asserting that as a reality. It took centuries to understand that distinction between presumptions and affirmations.

The Word-Power of God

The effortless work of God in creation is the preliminary activity that culminates in the Sabbath rest. God speaks six times (vv. 3ff.) and the world comes into existence step by step. Behind the tale is the Semitic concept of "word/*dabar*," namely, a word-event that makes history subject to the divine command. This notion indicates the fact that a "word/act" is somehow at the core of everything that happens.

Primeval Benevolence

The first account of creation presents a God who is benevolent and concerned with good order, never arbitrary or capricious. Absolutely everything in existence depends on God. Creation itself, human beings included, is described as good (v. 12), not malevolent or hostile. There is not even a hint of the type of primeval conflict among competing powers as known from Canaanite creation myths. This is a portrait of a generous God, not one who is victorious in battle over primitive hostility.

Antiphon (Year I)

Psalm 104:31b

May the Lord be glad in his works.

Psalm 104: An Orderly Creation

Psalm 104 is often praised as the most beautiful of all the inspired poetic efforts to praise God for the beauties of creation. It is often seen as echoing in some fashion the hymn to the sun composed by Pharaoh Amenophis IV (1375–1358 BC). Filled with parallels and similarities to religious sentiments everywhere, the poem's beauty is unsurpassable, and is the perfect response of God's people to the first story of creation. Human beings are inserted into the wide scheme of creation without preeminence.

The Supremacy of God

Throughout the psalm's litany of praise, God remains the majestic source of order and the primary point of reference for every created being (v. 5). Abundant fertility marks all of creation. God is described as being thoroughly delighted with every aspect of creation. This is a wise God who is pleased with good order and the mutual relationships between all the elements of the material universe (v. 24). The psalm is the perfect response to the question of children, what makes God happy?

FIRST READING (YEAR II)

1 Kings 8:1-7, 9-13

They brought the ark of the covenant into the holy of holies, and a cloud filled the temple of the LORD.

The Ark as Enduring Divine Presence

This reading describes the final journey of the ark and other sacred objects associated with the meeting tent of the desert (v. 9) into the temple built by Solomon. It underscores the fact that God always desires to be with the chosen people, no matter what social or political form of organization they experienced (v. 13). God remained with them both in tribal association and in settled urban life. Part of our Christian sacramental tradition can be traced back to objects such as the ark of the covenant: items signaling a God who travels with his people. Never distant, disinterested, or disengaged, our God is a God with and for his people, always Immanuel! In a very real sense, God has always been taking flesh and dwelling among us!

Under the Wings of the Cherubim

The cherubim of the ancient world were extraordinary mythical creatures, incomparably different from the winged bare bottomed angels that populated ancient Roman art or now illustrate modern romantic imagery. They were figures composed of elements suggesting lions, bulls, and winged dragons with human faces; they were guardians of the invisible divine world, far beyond the limits of human experience. Cherubim also marked the boundaries of the world of Israel and protected humans from the burning presence of God (vv. 6-7). Their beautifully crafted figures were placed in the holy of holies to protect the ark. They warned of the power of God.

God Always Above and Beyond

No matter what sacred objects we may have and treasure, God always remains above and beyond them, ultimately and completely transcendent. The God of Israel also lives in a dark cloud of mystery (v. 12), almighty and beyond human control or manipulation. The very smoke of incense is also a symbol of divinity, visible, fragrant, and warning of invisible fire, immaterial as anyone knows when trying to capture a handful—but very real. Incense may be seen as a symbol of human prayers (Ps 141:2), but it is also always a symbol of God's elusive transcendence.

ANTIPHON (YEAR II)

Psalm 132:8a

Lord, go up to the place of your rest!

A Psalm of Renewed Dedication

The various elements of Psalm 132, including both temple and Davidic dynasty, may well have been part of the annual autumn covenant festival. A renewal of the dedication of the temple (v. 8) and a restated promise to the house of David (v. 10) were annual opportunities for Israel to refocus on the heart of the covenant and on the sacred places and relationships that embodied this bond. There was a moment in history when, after having traveled with Israel for forty years through the desert, God had finally entered into the temple built by Solomon, and in a sense, taken divine rest in that sacred place. The annual celebration of those holy moments were relived and renewed regularly. Daily Eucharist also renews that presence in the person of Christ, and under sacramental forms.

God's "Rest"

There is a "Sabbath" character to the divine presence. The temple is described as God's "resting place" (v. 8). Everyone entering the temple is invited to share in an anticipated final completeness of creation when everything will be fully reconciled, and when every element of creation will be in "right relationship" with everything else. Even when a person stood momentarily before God in humble prayer, he or she shared in God's eternal rest. That prayer provided a brief respite amid the activity of daily life. Similarly we believe that the church gathered at prayer participates in the heavenly liturgy with everything visible and invisible, as the Creed professes.

Gospel

Mark 6:53-56

As many as touched it were healed.

Monday of the Fifth Week in Ordinary Time

Literary Link

The Lectionary chooses to omit the accounts of the feeding of the five thousand (vv. 35-44) and the walking on water (vv. 45-52) in order to establish some liturgical continuity between Saturday's report on the compassion of Jesus and his teaching response (v. 34) and today's story of his healing ministry at Gennesaret (v. 56). Both teaching and healing were works of the kingdom.

Jesus the Healer

The appearance of Jesus in this portion of Mark's gospel immediately and almost automatically made people think of the sick and infirm (v. 55). That instinctive association between Jesus and concern for the sick, as Mark presents his portrait of Jesus, suggests that a contemporary image of Christ could be presented as wearing a white divine physician's coat and carrying a stethoscope. We might well make the same association with the work of Jesus today. Everyone is bruised by life's experiences, and everyone is in need of some type of healing, be it emotional, spiritual, or physical. Those who care for the sick are extensions of Mark's portrait of Jesus.

Touching the Tassels

Scholars remind us that touching the tassels of Jesus suggests more than mere contact with a readily available portion of his clothing. In the Pentateuch, the wearing of tassels were commanded of all Jews (Deut 22:12), and the Pharisees explained the practice as a constant reminder of the obligation to be faithful to God's will in every human activity, just as the loose tassels of a prayer shawl touched one's thigh at every step. This pious devotion was intended to teach that the commands of God accompany, measure, and judge our every human movement and daily activity. Reaching out to the tassels of Jesus was making contact with his supreme and constant obedience to the will of God that heals the world. Once again Mark acknowledges the Jewish customs of the day, perhaps without understanding them clearly.

Tuesday of the Fifth Week in Ordinary Time

First Reading (Year I)

Genesis 1:20–2:4a

Let us make man in our own image, after our likeness.

Image of God amid the World of Creation

This reading begins at a midpoint in the tale, namely, the fifth day's account of the creation of the sky and sea (v. 20). Then, surrounded by living things in motion, human beings are created on the sixth day and acknowledged as images of God (v. 26). Respectful stewardship for material creation and human recognition of the potential usefulness of every creature is one of the ways in which human beings are indeed made in the image and likeness of God. Although medieval scholastic theology often places the human likeness to God in the reality of human intellect and will, the Scriptures themselves see a different correlation, that is, the ability to put things in order and the duty to develop material creation from one level of being into higher forms and more able creatures. Those who abuse and misuse nature can never be honored as divine images. As our Scriptures would see it, a certain sense of eco-justice is therefore intrinsic to the identity of every human being.

Creation by Will and Word

Once again, God simply *speaks* a world into existence (v. 26). The act of speaking suggests God's ease of action and deliberate intentionality. Deeper reflection on this first account of creation reminds us that our own speech can also create worlds of hurt or happiness. What we say can also make a difference. Once spoken, a word cannot be taken back.

Caring for Creatures

There are many ways of exercising a personal concern for material creation around us. People who care for pets or maintain birdfeeders and aquariums are exercising one form of their care for creation. Because the stories of Scripture are always also about us, as a result of the proclamation of this reading we could find ourselves encouraged to pray for such creaturely neighbors in a special manner today! In the broader scheme of interdependent creation, animals also serve as instruments and helpers of God.

Divine Blessings

The words of God's blessing for all things at creation (v. 22) suggest prosperity and abundance. All words, but especially divine words, bring things into being. The Semitic notion of blessing usually implies fertility at some level. The blessings for believers at the end of each Eucharist, whatever their specific focus, are also a prayer that the number of believers be increased and multiplied. By its very nature, that daily blessing is both hope and promise of success for evangelization.

Nonviolence

Genesis imagines that the original world as God fashioned it was without violence between creatures, because each creature was nourished by plants (v. 30), not by preying upon one another. One could suggest, while acknowledging that such an attitude might be more of a religious afterthought than a specific divine command, that being a "vegan" was plan A for God's creation, at least as the Priestly tradition of Genesis saw its world. The freedom to eat meat was only given to Noah after the flood (9:3).

Antiphon (Year I)

Psalm 8:2ab

O Lord, our God, how wonderful your name in all the earth!

The Name

The name of God (v. 2) is celebrated in the refrain. This reference is a respectful manner of speaking about the Person of God! In our human society there are some family names that suggest social prominence, wealth, or heroic community service. Scripturally, the "name" encompasses the entire reality of a person, including everything the individual says, does, and is. In this sense the "name/person" of God is certainly wonderful in every way. That name in the special title YHWH has a universal character because by etymology it is literally translated as "he will make (all) things come into being." It is the name/being of the God who created the entire universe and who sustains it in existence every minute of every day. Such a being is indeed wonderful in all the earth, which can only exist because of God's ongoing creative love and mercy.

Tuesday of the Fifth Week in Ordinary Time

Material Creation

There is a deep logical relationship between the psalm's hymn of praise for creation and the personal name of the God who is praised and honored above all else. Although celebrating the exalted place of human beings in creation, the verses from Psalm 8 chosen by the Lectionary make a point of referring to the different types of animals: sheep and oxen as well as birds and fish (vv. 8-9). That inclusiveness makes Psalm 8 a very fitting response to the reading.

FIRST READING (YEAR II)

1 Kings 8:22-23, 27-30

You have said: My name shall be there, to hear the prayers of your people Israel.

The Prayer of Solomon

Solomon begins his prayer by acknowledging the absolute uniqueness of the God of Israel. He then specifies the precise nature of God's singular reality, namely, the divine desire to enter a "covenant of mercy" with those who are faithful to him with all their heart (v. 23). The type of "mercy" mentioned is, in fact, that of *hesed*, that is, a reciprocal concern for partners in a covenant. It is helpful to recall that the heart is the place in human anatomy where one's plans are formulated and decisions made. Israel is encouraged to be faithful in everything they think and do! Solomon stands in the newly dedicated temple as one committed to do just that!

Final Composition from Exile

Scholars tell us that the final draft of the literary work titled "the Deuteronomic history" (Deuteronomy through 2 Kings) was written after the destruction of the temple by the Babylonians and the total devastation of Jerusalem. For that reason the primary point of view and the final focus of Solomon's prayer is a sad look backwards. A plea for *pardon* and forgiveness is noted in verses after the section chosen for this day's liturgy (v. 30). All human needs and wants fade into insignificance before the reality of human sin and the necessity of divine absolution. Later verses in the full prayer even envision the scattering of Israel in exile and the prayers of those so geographically distant as to only be able to face the temple from afar and to beg God's forgiveness (vv. 47-50).

ANTIPHON (YEAR II)

Psalm 84:2

How lovely is your dwelling place, Lord, mighty God!

A Psalm of Pilgrimage

Psalm 84 is filled with references to the things that a pilgrim longs to see and experience when eventually entering the temple. In the last analysis, however, it isn't the architecture itself or the liturgical environment that truly makes God's dwelling place attractive, but rather the simple fact of God's presence above all else (v. 2). Even resting at the doorway (v. 11), like a beggar for alms at any famous shrine, is described as better than life in the palaces of the wicked. These sentiments make the psalm a fitting communal response to Solomon's prayer.

And Yet, Not Perfect!

Orthodox Jewish synagogues of Eastern Europe often left a patch of lathing exposed without plaster to signify that the building, however beautiful, was unfinished, and to remind worshipers that God was still at work among his people. The earthly building of the temple, like all places of human worship, was but a ragged imitation, according to the blueprints given to Moses by God (Exod 25:40) who dwells in a heavenly holy of holies completely exalted above any human imitation or construction.

Gospel

Mark 7:1-13

You disregard God's commandment but cling to human tradition.

Literary Link

Within the context of Mark's effort in this section of the Galilean ministry to show the incomprehension of the disciples, the gospel presents three acts of power (feeding the five thousand, 6:35-44; walking on water, vv. 45-52; and healing, vv. 53-56) followed by a controversy over purification (7:1-23). This will be followed by a similar series of three acts of power (healing of the Syrophoenician woman's daughter, vv. 24-30; healing of the deaf mute, vv. 31-37; and feeding the four thousand, 8:1-10) followed by another controversy over signs (8:11-21). There is a balanced structure to the stories.

Pharisaic "Fence" and Defense

The Pharisees were rightly concerned about obedience to the will of God. They counted out some 613 commandments woven into the Pentateuch and built a "fence" of mere human customs and practices around that divine will in order to be assured of full and complete human obedience to God. The inevitable problem is the human temptation to so focus on the fence as to forget the precious reality enclosed. Thus human customs, unfortunately, can take on an unwarranted and independent value of their own. That misplaced primacy is the target of the challenge of Jesus in this controversy over the washing of hands. Once there is a confusion between the commandment itself and its traditional "carrying case," it becomes very easy to think that "the way we've always done things" is at the heart of God's will for us forever. Cultures change and the customs of a prior age may no longer be helpful to protect the essential point of God's command. Human beings live, grow, and change, but the will of God does not. True religious devotion knows how to develop without losing the fundamental point of God's will for his people.

Pharisaic Hand Washing

For the Pharisees washing hands at meals wasn't primarily hygienic but rather their way of introducing spirituality into the home and family life. A main objective of Pharisaic spirituality was to imitate temple ritual in the home, and particularly at every family meal, even to the extent of following the temple rites of purification for sacred vessels. They saw this as a way of sanctifying their family meals at home. Contrary to the presumption of Mark, this was a custom enshrined in Pharisaic spirituality, not necessarily practiced by all Jewish people (v. 3). Home and family meals were accorded the special sanctity of respect for the work of God in daily human life. This is a worthy concern for Christians too.

Clean Hands

Even though the Semitic world reserved the left hand for bodily hygiene and the right hand for all social interactions, this reference to the washing of hands (v. 2) refers to those involved in the secular pursuits of life. Such persons were not automatically prepared for the fundamental holiness of meals with family and friends.

Love of God and Neighbor

To dedicate material gifts to God is a worthy practice. In refusing to give priority of such devotional offerings (known as *qorban*) over the care one owed to parents (v. 11), Jesus retains love of neighbor as somehow equal to love of God and insists that care for parents may not be lightly set aside out of convenience or piety. It may be helpful to remember that the commandments, even the obligation to honor parents (v. 10), were presumed to refer to adults over the age of twelve, when they underwent the bar mitzvah ritual of becoming a "son of the law."

Tuesday of the Fifth Week in Ordinary Time

Wednesday of the Fifth Week in Ordinary Time

First Reading (Year I)

Genesis 2:4b-9, 15-17

The Lord God planted a garden in Eden and placed there the man whom he had formed.

The Second Story of Creation

Having concluded the first "priestly" creation account, which was intended to provide background for observing the Sabbath, the Lectionary turns to viewing the world around us from a different perspective. There are several important teachings hidden in this second account of creation. The very fact, for example, that Adam is formed from *ʾadamah*/soil (see v. 7) is a powerful Hebrew way of insisting on the relationship between ourselves and the clay upon which we stand. We are linked together by the reality of material creation and the mystery of God's life-giving power. Whatever happens in and to the reality of creation happens to us human beings as well. Even the English word "human" carries the same connotation because it comes from the Latin *humus*/soil. We are, by history and by definition, creatures of mud! These images may even provide an anchor for contemporary scientific theories of evolution.

Living "Green"

Human beings were placed in the Garden of Eden (v. 8) and commanded by God to care for and cultivate the earth (v. 15). This command contains the beginning of a God-given ecological responsibility for the world within and upon which we live. Human beings are summoned to act as God's agents, instruments, and partners in God's own care for the cosmos.

Forbidden "Fruit"

Implicit in the curious command not to eat of the "tree of knowledge of good and evil" (v. 17), whatever that may have meant to those ancients who told the story to their children, there is also an ancient recognition of a moral distinction between the products of human enterprise and the morality of their use. Though material creation itself was judged by God as very good (1:31), there is the possibility of evil inherent in the manner in which human creativity is applied. Just because we can do something, should we? Why or why not? This is the fundamental question of believers in response to all the marvelous biological and scientific discoveries that have flourished in recent decades.

Antiphon (Year I)

Psalm 104:1a

O bless the Lord, my soul!

Praise for the God of Creation

Psalm 104 is an extended poetic meditation (v. 34) on the wonders of creation. This striking praise for the geological features of the planet and for the wondrous creatures that inhabit the earth is the basis for the psalm's litany of praise for God's power and ingenuity. The Lectionary is ingenious, therefore, in suggesting this psalm as the community's response to the double creation stories. The recitation of the psalm places the worshiping assembly in humble amazement at the Lord's loving power.

My Soul

One of the many insights derived from philological study of ancient Semitic languages has been the realization that the fundamental meaning of the Hebrew word used in this refrain, *nephesh*, is "throat" (see v. 1). Although often translated as "soul," because of the ancient equation of one's life principle as somehow identified with the experience of our human breath and voice, it still is helpful at times to revert to the primary meaning of the word in order to understand the meaning of this refrain. It is clearly one's voice that is commanded by the refrain to praise God always and forever!

Wednesday of the Fifth Week in Ordinary Time

First Reading (Year II)

1 Kings 10:1-10

The Queen of Sheba saw all the wisdom of Solomon.

Wisdom

In the ancient Near Eastern world, wisdom was initially understood as the practical ability to do something successfully and well. The quality was initially applied to the artists and architects as, for example, skilled craftsmen who were employed for the construction of the temple. Later the notion was expanded to include the ability to deal well with all of life's challenges as one matured and exercised responsibility. Solomon was remembered for possessing that ability to an extraordinary degree (1 Kgs 5:9). The queen came to experience Solomon's administration and marveled at his wisdom (v. 4). Contemporary society also marvels when things are done wisely and well. We often select mentors to share their ability with others.

The Queen of Sheba

The legendary territory of Sheba was located in the southwestern corner of the Arabian Peninsula, in the area now known as Yemen. In the eighth and seventh centuries BC (when the writing of the Deuteronomic history was finalized), Assyrian records refer to several famous queens from that area. They were known as traders of precious stones, gold, and spice. In this passage the Queen of Sheba became a personification of distant lands that heard of Solomon's reputation and were attracted to learn from his skill as well as to profit from trade with his kingdom. She was recognized as having her own wisdom in her ability to direct trade within her own nation wisely and well. This reading could be an occasion to pray for leading women in our contemporary American world of commerce.

Spice

The reference to the huge amounts of spice (v. 10) should not be casually overlooked. Spices were always viewed as a rare and precious commodity, as evidenced by the tales of sixteenth-century Western explorers from much later Dutch, English, and Portuguese nations who circled the earth in a desperate effort to find an easy route to the spice lands of the Far East. Even after so many centuries, the exotic spice markets of the modern Near East remain as evidence of the value of this gift from the queen.

Antiphon (Year II)

Psalm 37:30a

The mouth of the just murmurs wisdom.

A Psalm of Wisdom

Psalm 37 is a loose collection of proverbs that serve to exhort a person to live in humble trust and confidence before God, no matter what obstacles may arise in life. It could well have served as a "primer" of a teacher's reflections by way of help to a younger student facing a series of life's setbacks and heartaches. The royal schools of ancient Jerusalem prepared the children of the court for leadership; they probably used such poems as instructional materials. Wise sayings from heroes of the past are often presented to a new generation of young leaders to offer guidance in getting through the storms of life. This is the basic meaning of Israel's wisdom.

Trust

The psalm's collection of proverbs finds a thread of continuity in the fact that in three different verses the entire psalm encourages reliance on one's trust in God (v. 5). God strengthens, supports, and ultimately vindicates those who trust in his care (v. 40). In our own contemporary context, virtually any heartache experienced by those who gather for a daily Eucharist is addressed by the verses of this psalm. They reflect the first reading's praise for Solomon's wisdom.

Gospel

Mark 7:14-23

What comes out of the man, that is what defiles him.

Literary Link

The text articulates the general principle behind the controversy of Jesus (vv. 14ff.) and then gives further private instruction to his uncomprehending disciples on the question of inner purification (vv. 17-23). Notice that verse 16 has been omitted from the Lectionary passage because it is not found in the best Greek manuscripts, and was possibly borrowed from Mark 4:23.

Inner Purification

As people know from experience, there remains a daily need to wash hands after touching coffee grounds or undusted shelves or after polishing shoes. One of the consistent threads or themes in the teaching of Jesus is his focus on the importance of the inner intention of an individual's daily actions (v. 23). Both here in Mark's treatment of Pharisaic cleansing practices and in Matthew's Sermon on the Mount (5:21-28), we hear echoes of Jesus' stress on a person's mind, heart, and intention as the fundamental source of evil. Christianity, like many world religions, insists on the importance of doing the right thing for the right reason when performing good deeds. Similarly we also recognize the need for the more important inner cleansing of the heart demanded before one can truly hear the word of God or enter into the mystery of the Eucharist.

Spiritual Illnesses

The list of the diseases of the heart forms a handy examination of conscience (vv. 21-22) as well. These are the realities that define a person and separate him or her from God's kingdom and the community. The verses provide a useful measurement of personal spiritual health and suitability for eucharistic participation.

Thursday of the Fifth Week in Ordinary Time

First Reading (Year I)

Genesis 2:18-25

The Lord God brought her to Adam, and the two of them become one flesh.

Not Good to Be Alone

The comment of God (v. 18) speaks to the fundamental need of all human beings for relationships and community. By God's creative will, and therefore by definition, we are inherently bound to people we love and serve. Loneliness and alienation is not the will of God for anyone. We are each called into being by God, upon whom we depend completely. We are distinctively shaped by God. Moreover, we each possess unique strengths to be shared generously with others and personal weaknesses that require assistance from others. As Archbishop Tutu once observed, "The totally self-sufficient person is sub-human."

Naming the Animals

To know the name of someone is to understand and to possess some level of authority over him or her. Even the ability to call someone's name in a crowd is to cause that person to turn around in response. Similarly, naming the animals of creation (v. 19) is to know them well enough to intuit their deeper nature and to have an insight into how they may be used properly. Knowing the animals enabled Adam to recognize that they are not fully suitable partners in life (no matter how much we may care for a pet dog or cat). It would follow logically, then, that even knowing the name of God gives human beings some relationship and "authority" before God!

One Flesh

The ancient world struggled to understand the mysterious tug of human affection that results in the desire to share life together in physical intimacy. They explained the attraction in terms of the story of Eve made from Adam's rib (v. 21). They concluded that each individual, therefore, lives with a desire to return to that closeness of life (v. 24). Sexuality is a great mystery, embodying both great gift and perennial lifelong challenge for everyone.

Antiphon (Year I)

Psalm 128:1a

Blessed are those who fear the Lord.

A Psalm of Blessing

Scholars have suggested that the brief song of blessings in Psalm 128 was developed in further reflection upon the words of blessing in God's name (Num 6:22-26) by the priest of the sanctuary. Because in the Semitic mindset God's blessings implied prosperity and fertility, they inevitably suggested the gift of wife and children (v. 3). This psalm is therefore a fitting response to the day's reading from Genesis. The very same notion of "benediction" celebrated in this psalm also occurs again (v. 4) by way of emphasis, lest there be any doubt about the true source of blessings in life.

The Blessings That Follow from Reverence

Reverence and respect, not servile fear, for God is the source of the domestic blessings of spouse and children (v. 3) as well as the larger and more communal circles of prosperity for Jerusalem (v. 5) and salvation for the whole world. Obviously one's humble regard for God enables many blessings to ripple forth in every direction, for God is the ultimate source for everything. The same type of reverential respect that the head of a family has for God should mark the relationships within a family as well.

First Reading (Year II)

1 Kings 11:4-13

Since you have not kept my covenant, I will deprive you of the kingdom, but I will leave your son one tribe for the sake of my servant David.

David's Blessings

To have one's heart with God is to make God the center and source of every plan and decision of one's life since, according to the ancient Near Eastern sense of anatomy, the heart is the focal place for such human activity. That explained the negative judgment on Solomon's heart (v. 4). In retrospect, however, and by contrast, David, even in spite of his sins, was remembered for keeping his heart with the Lord, and thus making God the primary measurement for his actions. What would be the signs for someone having her or his heart with God today? How would one know for oneself or others that the human heart and the divine "heart" are properly aligned? Catholic devotion to the Sacred Heart of Jesus is rooted in this biblical concept.

The Punishment for Solomon's Idolatry

The multiplication of strange gods (v. 4) was the fundamental sin of Solomon because of the fact that his marriages of political expediency gave way to compromise in his religious allegiance (v. 8). Since the land had been a covenantal gift from God, the punishment for the human party's breaking of the covenant relationship was a partial retraction of the gift and a diminishment of land under Solomon's authority (v. 11). From a biblical perspective all punishment was somehow formed and shaped by the specific action committed by the human sinner. To place idols on the land was to lose the land upon which they were worshiped. God gave the land, and to worship another was to refuse to recognize the donor and to lose the gift itself.

ANTIPHON (YEAR II)

Psalm 106:4a

Remember us, O Lord, as you favor your people.

A Psalm of Grace and Sin

Like the Book of Judges and the entire Deuteronomic history, Psalm 106 offers a long litany of historic events throughout salvation history, all of which describe the successive gifts of God's grace and the repeated sin of rejection by Israel. Mingling with the nations and worshiping idols (v. 35), and even sacrificing their children (v. 37), are some of the major sins of Israel over the centuries. This human pattern has been constant from the beginning as far back as the time in the desert. This now even included Solomon, but the "favor"/goodwill (v. 4) of God will not be frustrated. Unfortunately, we today still stand in that same line of sin. Fortunately, God is gracious and "rich in mercy" (Exod 43:6).

National Idolatry

The sins described in Psalm 106 are more extensive and more serious than the worship of idols by weak individual persons. They represent the sins of the entire people as they imitated the worship of the neighboring pagan nations (vv. 35ff.). There are times in history when an entire nation is summoned to penance for violating the very commandments that should distinguish them and that could set them apart as unique members of God's chosen people. Israel was called to the love of the Lord alone, with all their heart, mind, and substance (Deut 6:4ff.). Are there national sins in our day that characterize us and define our culture? Is there an inevitable punishment that will flow from the very nature of the sins?

GOSPEL

Mark 7:24-30

The dogs under the table eat the children's scraps.

Literary Link

Mark now begins the repetition of an earlier literary pattern with the first of three acts of power, namely, the healing of the daughter of the Syrophoenician woman (vv. 24-30). He will conclude the series with the account of the controversy over signs (8:11-21).

The Uniqueness of Jesus

We have close friends whom we instinctively and immediately recognize in a crowd, even from a distance. A characteristic stride or toss of the head identifies them without a doubt! The report that Jesus could not escape notice (v. 24) inevitably leads us to wonder and speculate about precisely what it was that caught people's attention? Physical stature, a distinctive profile, or a characteristic gesture? Perhaps an extraordinary attentiveness to the people around him and their needs? A sense that he was so rooted and focused on his relationship with his heavenly Father as to radiate a share in divine goodness in his every action? Something made Jesus unique.

The Determined Woman of Tyre

The Syrophoenician woman was an outsider, not one of the lost sheep of Israel, and therefore initially beyond the borders of the mission of Jesus. Curiously, Jesus was also an outsider as he traveled through the seacoast district of Tyre (v. 24) in what is now modern Lebanon. The poor woman's maternal heart and desperate need (v. 26), as well as her humility and keen sense of reality in allowing herself to be compared to a family dog (v. 28), led Jesus to expand his mission and to heal the troubled daughter (v. 30). Did Jesus change his mind because of her determination and her perseverance or simply take advantage of her candid confidence to move to the next phase of his ministry? Jesus told his disciples to keep asking and knocking (Matt 7:7). Doing so reminds us of our dependence and our need.

Thursday of the Fifth Week in Ordinary Time

* "The Truth and Reconciliation Process—Restorative Justice" (Third Longford Lecture, Church House, Westminster, February 16, 2004).

Friday of the Fifth Week in Ordinary Time

First Reading (Year I)

Genesis 3:1-8

You will be like gods, knowing what is good and what is evil.

The Wily Serpent's Temptation

There is something perennially characteristic about all temptations, namely, the distortion of the command to make it seem impossibly burdensome or its disobedience very desirable. Eve astutely caught the exaggeration and quickly offered a correction (v. 3). She succumbed, however, to the suggestion that eating from the tree would make her know the reality of evil and its inherent difference from good (v. 5). She concluded that eating the fruit might make her understand her difference from God, the source of all goodness. That initially seemed like a good thing because the fruit would help her to gain wisdom (v. 6), that is, the ability to get through life wisely and well! The account of this first sin provides a template for understanding all human temptation and sin.

The Human Body

The human body is wonderfully made and an object of beauty in its own right. Nevertheless, the immediate effect of that forbidden picnic was described as the realization of their nakedness (v. 7) and the sense that this nakedness was potentially dangerous for their goodness. Both the temptations and the nature of the evil were very subtle. The culture of the Semitic ancient Near East was particularly sensitive to human nakedness, just as contemporary mores of that part of the world considers limited clothing of men or women a serious violation of modesty. Arab culture often finds casual Western styles of clothing offensive. Our modern culture could do well to retrieve some of that fundamental modesty.

Antiphon (Year I)

Psalm 32:1a

Blessed are those whose sins are forgiven.

A Psalm of Forgiveness

Psalm 32 is a brief penitential hymn that recognizes sin as sin (v. 5), and celebrates the blessing of forgiveness (vv. 1-2). Just as goodness is an occasion of blessing from God, so the honesty of labeling one's sins as such is the result of God's grace. Protection, deliverance, and freedom (v. 7) are among the gifts that can come to those who humbly acknowledge their sins. Even though the reading from Genesis does not yet describe God's forgiveness, the verses of the response anticipate that divine grace.

Subhuman Existence

The verses of Psalm 32 chosen for this response celebrate the blessings of God's forgiveness. Later portions of the psalm not used here by the Lectionary compare the stubborn sinner with senseless horses or mules (v. 9) in need of reprimand and training. That later portion of Psalm 32 implies that the lack of understanding regarding the reality of sin in one's life renders a human being less than human! Conversely, one is fully human only when one understands the reality of sin and its negative effect in one's life. That insight, especially when related to the passage from Genesis, would suggest that only when Adam and Eve become penitent will they rise to their full humanity again. This psalm is a very effective prayer for use as a personal preparation for the initial penitential rite of any morning's Eucharist.

First Reading (Year II)

1 Kings 11:29-32; 12:19

Israel went into rebellion against David's house to this day.

Punishment for Abusive Leadership

The prophetic judgment oracle of Ahijah (vv. 31ff.) is a punishment for Solomon's blatant idolatry (11:4-10) and for his arrogant, high-handed, and oppressive treatment of God's chosen people (9:16). We are told that because Solomon mistreated the people of the land and ruthlessly took their possessions for his court, God removed ten tribes from his rule and named Jeroboam king of northern Israel. This allowed a tragic return to the prior separated status of the northern kingdom. Acts of greed and injustice cast long shadows and eventually bring their own punishment. Perhaps God doesn't punish us for our sins, but allows us to be punished by them!

The Prophet Ahijah's Torn Cloak

Prophetic actions such as the ripping of Ahijah's new garment (v. 30) were commonly viewed as fearful and powerful because they actually began the punishment that they illustrated. The verses just prior to our reading explained that Jeroboam was a runaway foreman over gangs of workers who, in a strange twist of events, received God's blessing for his rebellion (vv. 26-28). There is a sort of "sacramental" aspect to prophetic actions in the sense that they accomplish what they signify. They also give insight into how God is at work in the situation. The northern kingdom thus began centuries of violence against leadership. The northern tribes experienced the instability of a series of newly risen charismatic leaders who were then rejected and killed by opponents.

Israel

The word "Israel" can mean many things: the clan tribe of Jacob the person who was renamed Israel (Gen 32:29; literally, "God will struggle"), or the northern kingdom after the rebellion as contrasted with Judah, or the entire people chosen by God. In this case, the entire people of God are divided after Solomon. Only a portion retained the ancient name of the patriarch (12:19), while the southern kingdom of Judea contributed the title that eventually became "Judaism." Listening to Scripture readings requires a sense of history because God is King of creation and Lord of history with all its circuitous twists and turns.

ANTIPHON (YEAR II)

Psalm 81:11a and 9a

I am the Lord, your God: hear my voice.

A Festive Psalm

From Israel's earliest days Psalm 81 has been associated with the ancient autumn festival of Tabernacles when the harvest is gathered, the renewal of the covenant celebrated, and the New Year begun. The blowing of the *shofar*/ram's horn (v. 3), not cited among the verses of this response, signaled holy time. The portion quoted as a response to the rejection of Solomon's heritage, however, acknowledges a history of disobedience and "hardness of heart" (see vv. 12-13) on the part of God's people. These verses do not seem very festive. Nevertheless, the verses are appropriate because the covenant always included curses for those who chose to disregard its stipulations.

The Uniqueness of the Lord

The refrain exalts the name of the Lord (v. 11) and demands appropriate hearing/obedience (v. 9). The reference to the "LORD . . . your God" (v. 11) forms the basis for the psalmist's expectation of a renewed positive response from God to Israel. The psalm's reference to past deeds of liberation (v. 7), again not cited in this response, provides an opportunity for God to offer a promise for its possible repetition. This is what gave a festive character to the entire psalm and explained its use in Israel's liturgy for Tabernacles. The negative effects of the sins of Solomon can still be reversed even for us.

GOSPEL

Mark 7:31-37

He makes the deaf hear and the mute speak.

Literary Link

This healing of the deaf man (vv. 31-37) is the second act of power by Jesus in this series leading up to the controversy over the signs (8:11-21). Note that both the healing of the Syrophoenician woman's daughter at Tyre (vv. 24-30) and this healing of the deaf man in the far northeastern area of the Decapolis were situated outside Galilee, where mounting negative reactions to the ministry of Jesus were recorded. Outer (more pagan) areas were more positive than Galilee!

The Basic Physical Impediment and Need

To be deaf with a speech impediment (v. 32) is not surprising. One naturally speaks thickly or poorly precisely because one hears poorly and simply repeats words as they are heard. Mark's gospel often contains precise concrete descriptions and details that reflect very real human situations and suggest an eyewitness character of the stories. The miracles of physical healing accomplished by Jesus were often also chosen because of their deeper spiritual significance. To hear in Hebrew meant to obey; to speak implied the ability to offer a vocal confession of faith in God. The absence of both abilities in this poor man suggested the need for physical as well as spiritual healing.

The Response of Touching and Healing

Although the crowd merely asked Jesus to lay his hands (v. 32) on the person so afflicted—which traditionally would signify welcoming and associating the man into the messianic healing power of Jesus (not power going out of Jesus)—Jesus preferred the more specific healing by physical contact with ears and tongue. This physical immediacy suggests that the passage provides one of the sources for our entire Catholic sacramental tradition. Human actions, especially of wonderworking prophets like Elisha, were used as both signs and instruments of divine power. Although our Western culture may feel a bit squeamish about the gesture of placing saliva on the tongue of another person (v. 33), that very gesture was once part of the Catholic baptism ritual. Both actions of touching ears and tongue are expressions of faith in a person who has been welcomed into the new creation, namely, hearing and speaking about God's mighty deeds.

Miraculously Renewed Hearing

The miraculous healing (v. 35) is also very symbolic for Christian discipleship because the results include both hearing the teaching of Jesus and speaking in witness to what has been done in our lives and our world. The great *Shema* prayer of Judaism, "Hear, O Israel! . . ." (Deut 6:4), stresses a type of attentive listening that spills over into human obedience. The specific miraculous healings repeatedly mentioned in the gospel are chosen for their reference to the spiritual realities of faith in action.

Saturday of the Fifth Week in Ordinary Time

First Reading (Year I)

Genesis 3:9-24

God banished him from the garden of Eden to till the ground.

The Blame Game

With remarkably perceptive insight the story reflects a classic human response to being found culpable for any evil action, namely, the uncanny impulse to blame someone else! Adam blames Eve (v. 12) and she blames the serpent (v. 13). More courageous and humble would be claiming one's own sins and attempting to make amends in some way. The Yahwist author of this creation story is a very astute student of human nature! The sacrament of reconciliation, which includes the opportunity to name our own sins, can be a moment of new truth and healing.

An Early Hint of Redemption

The divine pronouncement of enmity between the serpent and the woman, as well as between their respective seed/"offspring" (v. 15), has become a classic case of what scholars call *sensus plenior*, that is, a fuller meaning that may not have been understood by the original speaker but turned out to be true at a new and profound level. Perhaps the statement initially only referred to the instinctive antipathy between humans and snakes, with some erotic undertones, but the words eventually came to be understood as a hint of the way a woman's offspring would be victorious in definitive battle with the serpent.

Punishments Rooted in Reality

The serpent is cursed with the necessity of crawling legless on the earth (v. 14), the woman's childbearing becomes painful and yet related to the force of sexual desire (v. 16), and the man is condemned to difficult and physically demanding labor (vv. 17-19). Although somewhat conditioned by the cultural mores and gender roles of the ancient world, each punishment is related to the physical reality of life now made more burdensome by sinful rebellion. Daily experience has been theologically related to the bigger picture of sin.

Divine Compassion

When all is said and done, however, the response of God is one of compassion, not anger (v. 22). It is God who makes leather clothing for the couple (v. 21) and who acknowledges the spark of divinity they have in fact gained, namely, the ability to distinguish between good and evil (v. 22). The price is the loss of their immortality and their exclusion from the garden. God does not reject them outright but radically changes the context and character of their lives.

Antiphon (Year I)

Psalm 90:1

In every age, O Lord, you have been our refuge.

A Community Lament

The extended contrast between the eternal nature of God and the transitory character of humanity, which returns so easily back into dust (Gen 3:19) or dry rootless grass (v. 5), is a very appropriate response to the tasks of human beings since the sin of Eden and its punishment. Psalm 90 invites a serious review of human experience as a prelude and introduction to true wisdom (v. 12). Just as the story from Genesis in fact addresses perennial human experience, the psalm refrain attributes the same foolishness and its needed remedy to every generation (v. 1).

A Place of Refuge

The Hebrew word behind this antiphon is *ma'on* (v. 1), a dwelling (or den, in the case of animals) to which one can flee for safety. The psalmist recognizes that God alone is the ultimate place of security amid the changing realities and natural disasters of seasonal change (v. 6). The possibility of recourse is extended to every person in every generation. This even includes the people of today who gather for Morning Prayer. Amid all the challenges and anxieties of life, God alone provides the security and safety we need as well as the protection we desire from ultimate harm.

First Reading (Year II)

1 Kings 12:26-32; 13:33-34

Jeroboam made two golden calves.

Dividing the Nation

A certain deliberate political deviousness is ascribed to the new king of northern Israel (v. 27), specifically, the suggestion that the alternative shrines in Dan to the north and Bethel further south were established to entice people away from the temple sanctuary in Jerusalem (v. 29). The foundation of the shrines also undercut the temptation to any continuing loyalty to the king of Judah. Temple and throne were viewed as deeply connected. Furthermore, the northern king Jeroboam established a competitive feast in the eighth month (v. 32), close in time to the New Year festival in Judah, in order to lure people to a more convenient place. Deepening the division was the establishment of an alternative non-Levitical priestly dynasty—all aimed at establishing a separate and independent religious place of worship and social gathering. In retrospect these decisions were made exclusively to protect the king's new political power, without regard for the will of the Lord. How often political decisions in every age are self-serving.

Golden Calves

It was certainly not the animals themselves that were worshiped but the strength and fertility symbolized by the two new golden calves (v. 30). Those attributes, while exhibiting a certain pagan overlap with the fertility cults of Canaan, were also ascribed at times to the God of Israel. The images were very concrete and embodied forces necessary for survival. The calves were probably understood by the people as visible bases for the invisible throne of YHWH above. A subtle undercurrent to the story is its warning about the ease by which material objects associated with God in any age could quickly become superstitiously endowed with power in themselves! Even contemporary Catholic devotions merit the same warning. God, and God alone, is the true source of blessings, not some mechanical human action.

Antiphon (Year II)

Psalm 106:4a

Remember us, O Lord, as you favor your people.

Plea for Renewed Divine Favor

Although citing different verses, the Lectionary returns once more to Psalm 106 of Thursday's responsorial hymn for a liturgical reaction to the story of Israel's rebellion and division. The same refrain begs for the return of God's goodwill toward his people (v. 4). In a phrase that is similar to the words of the song of the angels at Bethlehem who praised God's goodwill to all people (Luke 2:14), God's favorable regard is once again sought.

Forgiveness before Favor

Coming after the account in First Kings of the primary sin of Israel's King Jeroboam in establishing the golden calves at Dan and Bethel (v. 30 above), Psalm 106 suddenly recalls the sin of the golden calf at Horeb (v. 19) while Moses remained with God on the mountain (Exod 32). Scholars see a relationship between the two events. Everything about the northern sanctuaries was roundly condemned. The actions of Jeroboam and his people needed radical forgiveness. All of Psalm 106 deals with the interplay of sin and grace, insisting that divine favor (v. 4) can only be received after the acknowledgment of the reality of human sin (v. 6). For those with open eyes, the psalm is a mirror for our lives as well.

GOSPEL

Mark 8:1-10

They ate and were satisfied.

Literary Link

The Lectionary proceeds, after reporting the cure of the Syrophoenician daughter (7:24-30) and the healing of the deaf man (vv. 31-37), to the third act of Christ's power in this series: the feeding of the four thousand (8:1-10). Thus this account forms a literary inclusion, because the first series of three acts of power and a subsequent controversy over hand washing began with the feeding of the five thousand (6:35-44). Note, however, that the Lectionary chose to omit Mark's earlier account of the feeding of the five thousand in order to focus on this feeding. Since the earlier multiplication left twelve baskets of leftovers, possibly referring to the tribes of Israel, and this multiplication left seven baskets, possibly referring to the seventy Gentile nations, Mark may have been quite deliberate in his duplication. Both have overtones of the final messianic banquet and the Last Supper as recounted in the gospels.

Saturday of the Fifth Week in Ordinary Time

Christ's Heart Moved with Pity

The physical hunger of the people was the cause for Christ's compassion (v. 1). The generic biblical term of "three days" (v. 2), like the number forty, indicated a short period of time preceding an extraordinary act of great favor and blessing. For a people often forced to stretch the fruits of the harvest from one year to another, and straining with very limited resources, hunger was a fact of life for everyone. The abundant fullness of the future heavenly banquet, signified and anticipated here by the unimaginable existence of leftovers (v. 8), remained an image of great blessing in the imagination and experience of the ancient world. One should not miss the fact that the amount of leftovers, seven baskets, corresponded to the number of initial loaves.

Disciples as Partners

It was the disciples themselves who acknowledged having a meager seven loaves (v. 5), presumably small and flat like pitas in form. They were also employed as distribution agents (v. 6). This is a perfect example of how the "disciples" were in fact apprentices as they learned how to care for the hungry and needy under the direction of Jesus. Imitation of that event falls upon modern shoulders as well because the hungry are ever present and always in need. Contemporary food pantries mark the presence of true disciples of Jesus. Moreover, generosity always leaves the donor herself greatly enriched by the act of giving.

Monday of the Sixth Week in Ordinary Time

First Reading (Year I)

Genesis 4:1-15, 25

Cain attacked his brother Abel and killed him.

Ranchers and Farmers

Apparently the argument between farmers/tillers of the soil and ranchers/keepers of the flock has some very ancient roots as the story from Genesis (v. 2) and the modern popular song from the musical *Oklahoma* attest. Reading the ancient tale carefully, it would seem that the keepers of the flock were viewed as the privileged group, and that there is some prejudice against the farmers in this account. Note that it is Cain the farmer who does violence and kills Abel the shepherd (v. 8). Care for all of God's creation, animal as well as vegetable, in both ancient and modern times, demands cooperation and mutual respect if the common good is to be served. Also note that God protects Cain the farmer from revenge/bloodshed (v. 15). Even today there are many competing interests that must be respected and balanced for the good of our society. Interclass conflict and hostility needs to be transformed wherever it exists.

Relationships

Human beings need social relations. This is confirmed from God's comment that man/*ʾAdam* should not be alone but needs a helpmate (Gen 2:18). That relationship, however, is also open to negative selfish and self-serving rivalry and even violence at times. Most adults experienced immature and strained relationships with siblings at some time in their growth. Burning unresolved resentments are dangerous. It is particularly tragic if that rivalry is somehow rooted in religious differences! Emotional and spiritual maturity is the growing recognition of mutual interdependence. Love of neighbor includes family too.

Appropriate Punishments

Why the Lord was described as not favoring the offerings of Cain the farmer remains a mystery. Perhaps the once nomadic tribes of Israel held on to this story as part of their historical experience when they were being chosen by their God. An irony of the story is that as a result of the murder of Abel, Cain is separated from the very *soil* to which he was attached, and forced to become a nomad (v. 12). God, however, punishes him through the added element of hard labor amid the very portion of creation that Cain was trying to protect (v. 11)! We are not only punished for our sins but also by our sins. Cain's determination to violently protect the preeminence of his way of life led to its loss. "For whoever wishes to save his life will lose it" (Mark 8:35).

A God of Second Chances

If we listen to the text carefully, we find that, curiously enough, the protective intervention of God, in preventing retaliation or even the murder of Cain, may be the first argument against capital punishment. The maxim of an "eye for [an] eye" (Exod 21:24) does not hold here. The "mark of Cain," however it may have been understood in the ancient world, is in fact presented as positive and protective. Cain is not forced by his serious sin to avoid the presence of God. Is the very wandering of Cain a means of providentially reincorporating him into the nomadic life of the deceased Abel and a way of reintegrating him into the very tradition of the brother he had hated? These ancient stories speak about us and our relationships too.

Antiphon (Year I)

Psalm 50:14a

Offer to God a sacrifice of praise.

Sacrifice of Praise

The first reading's account of the original rivalry between Cain and Abel focused on the two different sacrifices, from flock or field, that were offered. One was mysteriously accepted but the other not.

The praise of one's heart, not the material gift itself, is the issue here. The refrain (v. 14) suggests that any sacrifice that comes from an obedient heart, not "casting God's words behind" (see v. 17), is acceptable before God.

Fraternal Rivalry and Rumor

The psalm response is explicit in its condemnation of speaking evil against a brother or sister (v. 20). A person's contributions to family divisions by negative gossip or stewing resentment make that person's offerings to God unacceptable. The heart is the heart of the issue. This is another helpful example of the Lectionary's careful matching of themes in reading and response. In many subtle ways the love of God and neighbor are linked by these readings.

First Reading (Year II)

James 1:1-11

The testing of your faith produces perseverance so that you may be perfect and complete.

Monday of the Sixth Week in Ordinary Time

The Dispersion

James writes to the twelve tribes of Jewish Christians in the *Diaspora* (v. 1), that is, Jews scattered throughout Palestine or the larger world. He shares the best of Jewish religious wisdom with them. The fact of the explicit reference to those scattered abroad suggests that the addressees are surrounded by a culture other than their own, which often militates against the spiritual and moral values of their Judeo-Christianity. Maintaining fidelity and identity in a foreign land is not easy, especially if the different mores of neighbors have an allure and if the people desire to "fit in" for greater conformity and prosperity. Similarly, people of faith today can find themselves amid a very alien and radically secular world as well.

Trials as an Occasion for Joy

No one likes to be tested, neither the student before exams nor the adult before the temptations of life. To consider such trials and tribulations of life a "joy" (v. 2) takes a great deal of spiritual maturity. They are occasions, however, for the revelation of our deepest values and our real selves. Such an attitude of considering difficulties as "joys" demands that a person has absorbed the full meaning of the paschal mystery with the saving death of Christ as an essential part of his victory over sin. Often it is only in retrospect that we can eventually see hard times of one sort or another as times of grace and growth. Participation in daily Eucharist should help that process.

The Letter of Saint James

Like other New Testament letters, this Letter of James is called "catholic" because it is not directed to any single community. Its inspired character was not universally acknowledged until the fifth century. The letter is concerned with human moral conduct. Faithful to the Wisdom tradition of the writings of the first covenant, scholars still find some forty verses that show influences from the sayings of Jesus, especially from the Sermon on the Mount. The letter proposes the best of Judaism as expressed by the rabbi from Nazareth.

Perseverance

"Perseverance and endurance" or "hanging in there for the long haul" (see v. 4) is a sign of one's maturity before God. The more often we can reaffirm our moral convictions in different circumstances, the deeper they become ingrained into our personal moral habits and reflexes. There is a relationship between perseverance and wisdom (v. 5) because the latter is the ability to navigate through life wisely and well. A perennial habit of fidelity enables a person to choose wisely and to be successful in the long run. This perseverance also shows itself in a consistent attitude of prayer (v. 6) because it shows a personal recognition of our ultimate dependence on God, not ourselves. Conversely, people of wealth who depend upon themselves alone are like dried grass (v. 11).

ANTIPHON (YEAR II)

Psalm 119:77a

Be kind to me, Lord, and I will live.

Maternal Kindness

The "kindness" to which this psalm refrain (v. 77) refers is *rehem*, namely, that motherly womb-like regard, which cannot but care for one's closest family member. To attribute that attitude to God and to assume its existence indicates a remarkable relationship to God. The refrain's Hebrew word, however, is different from that found in the last verse of the psalm response itself (v. 76), which is *hesed*, that is, mutual covenantal care and concern for partners bound together. Of course, *rehem* is related to the gift of life. This very refrain, therefore, with its reference to God's maternal care has an implicit "pro-life" character to its approach to God. God's maternal kindness as described in the refrain would share the same quality as experienced by humans from the very first moment of existence in our mother's womb!

The God of Life

Many different considerations can be discovered in this short and simple refrain (v. 77). To predicate a quality of maternal compassion to the God of Israel is to acknowledge God as the source of all life. The use of the word *rehem* for God under his title of Lord/YHWH is also to gain insight into the feminine maternal nature of the Lord. This insight is further confirmed by the probable literal meaning of the Hebrew name for God, as scholars have suggested, that is, one who "makes creatures come into being."

GOSPEL

Mark 8:11-13

Why does this generation seek a sign?

Literary Link

After the double pattern of three acts of power, Mark's gospel concludes briefly with yet another controversy, the brief debate about "signs" (vv. 11-13).

Evidence and Freedom

Any generation that insists on the same type of compelling and incontrovertible evidence as found in science or mathematics will never be satisfied, because our response in faith must be free. It cannot be so forced by a type of logical proof as to be an inescapable conclusion. The very nature of faith in a God of First Causes lives in tension with a world of secondary causes. The latter are immediately felt, leaving a person free to speculate about the existence of yet another ultimate "Cause behind the cause." Even crossword puzzles often presume by their clues that the "true" or the "real" is equated with what is "verifiable." Some things are so profoundly true as to be beyond mere verification in human experience.

Signs

The question and argument over "signs" is puzzling (v. 11), especially given that the very passage of Mark's gospel immediately prior to these verses is the account of the second miraculous feeding of the four thousand with only seven loaves and a few fishes, leaving seven baskets of fragments and leftovers (vv. 1-10)! That should be a clear sign for anyone. The real issue for that group of Pharisees, therefore, must be about something else! So often we demand more and more compelling evidence because of our radical unwillingness to accept the consequences of the signs before us.

Divine Exasperation

The Jesus who "sighed from the depth" of his very being (v. 12) is a source of strength and courage for anyone who keeps trying in vain to explain something to stubborn or resistant children or colleagues. That reference is a phrase worth lingering over as a model for perseverance and patience. Jesus shared in everything human except sin; this passage is a consolation for anyone who has felt exasperation with a stubborn argument and has concluded to the need to walk away (v. 13) in the hope of better mutual understanding another day! Sometimes mere physical or temporal distance provides the needed remedy for disagreements.

Monday of the Sixth Week in Ordinary Time

Tuesday of the Sixth Week in Ordinary Time

First Reading (Year I)

Genesis 6:5-8; 7:1-5, 10

I will wipe out from the earth the men whom I have created.

Divine Second Thoughts

The exasperation experienced by Jesus amid those demanding signs, as described in yesterday's gospel passage, is continued and deepened in today's text from Genesis, a story of God's discouragement in the face of constant human inclination toward evil (v. 5). The larger picture seems to reveal that every human being, generation after generation, makes such terrible choices as to leave God regretting his decision to start the mess in the first place (v. 6). This "report" of God's tentative inclination to destroy everything (v. 7) reveals the underlying assumption in creation to begin with, namely, God's desire for partners in the work of creation. That initial intention, therefore, presumed that human beings would also live under the expectation of accountability for our stewardship. Thus judgment comes into our world for everyone.

Noah's Favor

We are not told what it was about Noah that found favor (v. 8) and thus opened up the possibility for a remnant of the human race and a hope of redemption and a fresh start. Was it the obedience he instinctively demonstrated in building the ark (7:5)? Was it the sacrifice and grateful praise of God (Gen 8:20), which Noah later expressed upon deliverance after the flood? In early patristic writings Noah became a Christ figure in saving the human race. He was also described as a metaphor of baptized Christians when he emerged alive and renewed from the waters of the flood. Because of his goodness, a representative group from every type of creature is preserved, and with them continuity with the prior world of creation (7:3). The Scriptures see material creation somehow inevitably linked to human moral behavior.

The "Yahwistic" Tradition

The use of YHWH, the personal name of God (6:5, 7; 7:1, 5), indicates that this portion of the flood story is not from the priestly source, even though the text speaks of the differentiation between clean/unclean animals, and the seven days (Sabbath?) of waiting for the waters (7:10). By the time the various strands of the story were interwoven, the seven-day weekly sequence was already deeply imbedded in the lives and religious practices of the sacred editors and their Jewish neighbors. They prepared for the Sabbath and renewed their labor by the energy obtained through its weekly celebration. It is helpful to see all Christian weekday assemblies in light of the prior and consequent Sunday gatherings. Just as in our own day, certain practices such as the Eucharist are too often simply taken for granted.

Antiphon (Year I)

Psalm 29:11b

The Lord will bless his people with peace.

Peace

The biblical concept of "peace/*shalom*," namely, the reintegration of all parts of creation into a single reality, ultimately comes from God, not human actions or political negotiations. The refrain's reference to peace is the consequence of God's blessing (v. 11), which alone can truly renew and reunite all of material creation. Israel is a people chosen by God for covenantal partnership, and as a consequence of that election, shalom is granted to God's people. It is both gift and challenge.

God's People

Psalm 29 celebrates the praise (v. 1) and glory (v. 2) given to God for all his mighty deeds. In particular, ancient Canaanite creation stories of God's primeval conflict with the great waters (v. 3) are invoked to describe the power of Israel's LORD. The antiphon (v. 11), though not recited in the responsorial hymn itself, offers a fitting conclusion because the verse celebrates the creation and blessing of God's people as the ultimate purpose for the creation of the world.

FIRST READING (YEAR II)

James 1:12-18

God himself tempts no one.

Perseverance

This passage encourages everyone to persevere in the face of any temptations to engage in action contrary to the gospel (v. 12). James' Christian admonition correctly identifies the source of the temptation, not in the object itself (for we are surrounded by objects and persons who pose no temptation) nor in God (v. 13), but in our own desires (v. 14). This comment poses an interesting similarity to the view of Buddhism, which finds human desire as the source of unhappiness. If we desire nothing, they say, except what is, we are happy. There is something of God's spirit of truth operating in all the major religious traditions of the world.

God as the Source of Good Gifts

In a marvelous counterpoint, James reminds his readers that God is the source of all *good giving*, that is, of the grace to be generous in doing the right thing for the right reason, and the source for every perfect gift (v. 17)—perhaps the gift without strings given only out of response to need and as respect for the dignity of the recipient. The divine ultimacy of goodness, within which alone all human kindness, generosity, and justice exist and from which human existence comes, is the point of this passage. The Father of Lights is complete and perfect goodness. The scholastic notion of first and secondary causes finds an echo in this teaching.

ANTIPHON (YEAR II)

Psalm 94:12a

Blessed the man you instruct, O Lord.

Unspoken Vengeance

The first eleven verses of this psalm, not cited in the Lectionary's responsorial song itself, contain a sustained passionate plea for God's punishment and retribution to evildoers. The sins of the wicked are described there together with a prayer for their fitting punishment. It is the second more positive portion of Psalm 94 that becomes the Lectionary's response to the teaching of James. These final verses praise the God who does not allow the feet of the good to slip under persecution or pressure (v. 18). Only with the echoes of the passion of the prior section can the thanksgiving and praise of the verses cited make full sense. Our own words of praise make fullest sense when the difficulties of the past, resolved by God's grace, are acknowledged.

Instruction

The specific word translated in this refrain as "instruct" (v. 12) is far more nuanced and reflects the prior half of this psalm. Often translated as "discipline, guide, or chasten," the word would seem to refer to the various corrections we receive in life. When we ourselves are admonished by experience or instructed by mentors "to do it again, and to do it right this time!" we learn a lesson, and our foot is prevented from slipping (v. 18). This action of God the Teacher is lifted up in the refrain as a correction for the "man" (v. 12), literally, a fighting military champion (*geber* in the Hebrew). Though translated simply as "man"/person (v. 12), the individual is in fact called a fighter, presumably on behalf of what's truly right and just. Everyone is asked by God to be enlisted in the fight for justice in our frail world!

GOSPEL

Mark 8:14-21

Watch out, guard against the leaven of the Pharisees and the leaven of Herod.

Literary Link

Mark retains a metaphor from the account of the miraculous feeding of the four thousand (vv. 1-10), namely, the yeast leaven needed for baking regular daily bread, and applies the notion of yeast to human attitudes.

The Correction from Jesus

The exasperation of Jesus surfaces again (v. 17) when confronted by the density of his disciples, whom Mark presents as continually misunderstanding the mission and message of Jesus. Jesus may have wanted to say, "Forget the loaves, for pity's sake, it's the leaven!" These dolts in the boat presume a literalness of loaves of bread while Jesus intends the word "leaven" (v. 15) to be symbolic for the inaccurate attitudes that permeate the teachings of those Pharisees as they continue to demand more signs. Perhaps in this very account Jesus himself is the source for giving us an implicit caution against presuming a literalness (and fundamentalism) in our contemporary methods of interpreting the gospel.

Leaven

The use of the word "leaven" (v. 15) signifies something that permeates and changes a reality from within, just as yeast permeates dough to create bread! It is the fundamental attitude of some of his opponents that elicits this warning from Jesus: stubborn request for signs in order to avoid the lifestyle changes it would require. Given the way in which Jesus so often identified with the Pharisaic tradition of spirituality in other gospel passages, we should be very careful not to project this attitude upon all Pharisees as such. This is also a warning to be conscious of our own fundamental attitudes that permeate our every word, action, and choice. Self-knowledge regarding our personal "default" values enables us to perceive our own "leaven" and perhaps to target specific conversion efforts in the precise direction of our errors.

Wednesday of the Sixth Week in Ordinary Time

First Reading (Year I)

Genesis 8:6-13, 20-22

Noah saw that the surface of the ground was drying up.

Learning from Our Material Environment

However the scientific (and political) debate about climate change may eventually sort itself out, we have much to learn from the state of material creation around us. Vast areas of our globe once fertile and productive have become Saharan deserts. Noah received signals for his next move from the messenger birds he released, from whether they returned or not (v. 7). He also learned from his personal observations of the state of his environment, namely, the fresh olive leaf (v. 11). Many of the parables of Jesus came from his close observations of nature. We should be no less attentive to material creation around us. Good prayer is always contextually aware of the world within which we live.

The Dove with the Olive Branch

Many familiar symbols have a biblical reference by way of origin. Consequently, the contemporary lack of biblical literacy limits modern appreciation for their full meaning! The appearance of the dove with the olive leaf (v. 11) is a good example, promising a new beginning after great destruction in some way caused by human evil. Fresh beginnings after the horrible devastations of the world wars of the last century made that symbol popular. For Christians who know the biblical use of the dove as a symbol of the Holy Spirit in the accounts of Christ's baptism (Mark 1:10), the symbol of the dove also suggests the multiple gifts of the Holy Spirit that are essential to the rebuilding of a truly new and fruitful human society. The image of the Holy Spirit is often painted on the ceiling of a church's sanctuary as a graphic reminder of the transforming power of that divine Spirit.

The Sacrifice of Noah

The very first action recorded after Noah's exit from the ark was his offering of a sacrifice (v. 20) to the Lord, who accepted his action with renewed divine pleasure. The Lord's response included a promise to retain and sustain the cycle of planting and harvest seasons forever (v. 22). Thus the good order of all of creation, not merely the benefit of individual human participants, is involved in every ritual sacrifice. Similarly, there is a cosmic aspect to every celebration of the Eucharist because the risen Christ is the Lord of all creation.

Antiphon (Year I)

Psalm 116:17a

To you, Lord, I will offer a sacrifice of praise.

Personal Praise

The immediate consequence after the devastation of the flood is a renewed personal relationship with God. In all religious rituals the relationship to God is personal. Moreover, God is acknowledged as the source of salvation from danger. The praise mentioned in this refrain is directed "[t]o you, Lord" (v. 17). Although the many forces of nature might seem merely the positive or negative convergence of climate factors, for believers there remains the personal presence of God at the center of everything. The verses of Psalm 116 chosen by the Lectionary refer to the fulfillment of vows in the midst of the people (v. 14). They offer fitting expression for the mindset of Noah described in the day's reading from Genesis.

The Cup of Salvation

The psalm's reference to the cup (v. 13) could recall the offering of the fruits of the harvest, thus creating a relationship between sacrifice and the promise of God that seasons of planting and reaping would again be sustained forever (Gen 8:20). This ritual is applied in yet another way when the cup drained by Jesus in his passion (Mark 10:38) is shared with his disciples at the Last Supper, or when the same psalm is recited at the Christian Eucharist.

First Reading (Year II)

James 1:19-27

Be doers of the word and not hearers only.

Quick to Hear

Two fundamental admonitions run through this portion of moral advice given by James. Both can serve as elements for a communal penitential rite. First, James focuses on the word to which believers should be eagerly attentive. That word is to be pondered thoroughly (v. 19). Jesus was a master teacher and his disciples are expected to remain avid listeners, hearing his actual words and exploring their implications. Careful listening is a spiritual practice, often emphasized in the gospel's stories of healing the deaf, who in fact represent each and all of us. We are often told that listening is a redemptive action that always changes the person who hears.

Slow to Speak

The second complimentary action regards human speech and the use of one's tongue (vv. 19 and 25). Native American cultures often insist upon the courtesy of a two-minute pause after each speaker at a meeting in order to demonstrate that the words are received respectfully and taken seriously before any oral response. Without a humble personal acceptance of a word, the reply can seem ungrounded and superficial. Such a pause makes sure that the response is not hurtful or harmful but rather truthful and helpful. Oral speech, like writing a potentially angry letter, is best served when first framed and then set aside for a bit rather than firing off the first thing that comes to mind.

True Religion

Again and again throughout the gospels, Jesus urges generous and just action, not merely talk! Jesus praises the one with a house founded on rock (Matt 7:24), namely, one who hears and does God's will. Christianity, like Judaism, is often described as orthopraxis, the doing of right actions. Care for widows and orphans (v. 27; cf. Deut 26:13), the traditional category for those most easily fallen through the cracks of society and who often have nowhere to turn in desperate need, demonstrates the intensely Jewish roots of the Christianity encouraged by James.

Antiphon (Year II)

Psalm 15:1b

Who shall live on your holy mountain, O Lord?

The Torah Psalm

As noted previously, Psalm 15 includes the type of priestly instruction offered by way of an examination of conscience for anyone desiring to enter and worship at a sanctuary. It is therefore labeled as a "Torah" or instructional psalm. Actions listed in the psalm, such as doing justice, speaking the truth (v. 2), avoiding slanderous speech (v. 3), and refusing usury (v. 5), pick up the themes from the day's reading from James. Calling people's attention to the original purpose and use of this psalm may even aid their prayer. We need to acknowledge our sinfulness each time we prepare for an encounter with God in individual prayer or communal worship.

Mountains and High Places

Within traditional religious imagination, places of geographical elevation have always been considered places for special communing with the divine. Somehow physically closer to the higher ranges of the trilevel of cosmology where God was imaged as dwelling, and affording a better view of the bigger picture as seen from God's point of view, mountains were regarded as different from the plains or valleys below and specially endowed with holiness. All this comes to mind in the refrain's reference to God's holy mountain (v. 1). Whether it be the ancient tale of the tower of Babel or more mundane sanctuary steps in parish churches, elevation is for more than mere visibility afforded for worshipers. Although God is always present in the midst of his people, reference to elevation offers its own unique religious symbolism.

Gospel

Mark 8:22-26

His sight was restored and he could see everything distinctly.

Literary Link

The reference to the arrival of Jesus and his disciples at Bethsaida (v. 22) signals a turning toward Jerusalem. This journey also offers a more focused opportunity for instruction to his disciples, a "crash course," if you will, regarding his mission and ministry. Between the accounts of two healings of the blind (8:22-26 and 10:46-52) there will be three passion predictions (8:31ff.; 9:30-32; 10:32-34). The solemn entrance into Jerusalem will occur immediately after the healing of Bartimaeus (11:1).

Wednesday of the Sixth Week in Ordinary Time

Double-Phased Healing

There would seem to be a deliberate parallelism between the healing of the first blind man (8:22-26) and Peter's confession (vv. 27-33). Moreover, in both instances a two-phased gesture seems to be present. The healing of the first blind man, for example, occurs by a laying on of hands twice repeated by Jesus (vv. 22-25); at first he only saw trees walking (v. 24). The later story of Peter's faith will be initially expressed in his solemn declaration of Jesus as "the Christ" (v. 29) but accompanied by a very limited appreciation of the full significance of that profession; Peter then receives a sharp rebuke from Jesus when he refuses to accept the possibility of Jesus' suffering and rejection (v. 32)! Thus there is also a similarity between physical and spiritual blindness. Both healing and revelation require a certain gradualism in reaching fullness of insight and maturity of faith. God is content to work in gradual steps accommodated to human limitations—and so should teachers, leaders, and parents.

The Messianic "Secret"

Repeatedly Jesus requests that those healed or helped by him not speak about the miracle, and in this instance, not even going back into the village (v. 26). This pattern, which marked the early ministry of Jesus, especially in Mark and in those portions of the other gospels dependent upon Mark, has been the object of much scholarly research and interpretation. Often it is stated that Jesus needed to reject the popular expectation of the Christ's glorious victory and easy restoration of Israel's independence, and to redefine his mission so as to include the essential element of suffering. A depoliticization and respiritualization was needed for their more accurate understanding. That would take time. Once again we see the gradual work of Jesus, always carefully adapted to the limited and often stumbling abilities of his disciples.

Thursday of the Sixth Week in Ordinary Time

FIRST READING (YEAR I)

Genesis 9:1-13

I set my bow in the clouds to serve as a sign of the covenant between me and the earth.

The Noahite Covenant

Jewish teaching has long recognized the difference between God's covenant with Noah (and implicitly with all humanity) and the covenant with Abraham. Judaism would insist that the specific commandments of the prior are binding for all peoples and all nations, namely, the obligation to be fruitful and multiply (v. 1), the possibility of using plants and animals as food (v. 3), the need to respect blood as singularly related to the source and bearer of life (v. 4), solemn obligation to avoid the taking of the life of another (v. 6), and the delegation of God's action in such cases to the human community ("by man shall his blood be shed," v. 6). These directives will be somewhat simplified and summarized much later by the early church at the Council of Jerusalem (Acts 15:20) when determining which commandments will be laid upon Gentile converts to the "Way," as the Jesus movement was first called.

Capital Punishment

Reading this text carefully, it would seem that human society under the Lord would be delegated by God for punishing anyone who takes the life of another: "by man shall his blood be shed" (v. 6). This passage, however, could well be an opportunity for a brief reflection on the contemporary neuralgic question of capital punishment. It is clear that the Catholic Church's teaching has demonstrated a strong desire (deepened by the writings of both John Paul II and Benedict XVI) to limit engaging in the violence of murder to punish the same action of one human against another. This is especially the case if other means of just punishment can be found without endangering the safety of society (see *The Catechism of the Catholic Church*, 2266, as amended in the 1998 revised edition). The instruction given to Noah continues to have great relevance, especially in our modern world of increasing violence.

The Rainbow

The end of this passage explains the rainbow as a sign of God's commitment to a renewed covenant and to peace vis-à-vis human beings and all of creation (vv. 12ff.). The choice of the rainbow resting on the horizon, God's laying down the most powerful weapon of that day, serves as a symbolic reminder of God's pledge of peace. It also remains an enduring promise and sign of hope for all ages. Note that the promise includes "every living creature" (v. 12) and the entire "earth" (v. 13). This expanded relationship that now includes the entire planet thus also offers a foundation for ecological stewardship and human responsibility for the entire world of creation. God is green!

ANTIPHON (YEAR I)

Psalm 102:20b

From heaven the Lord looks down on the earth.

Lament and Salvation

Psalm 102 is the fifth of the nine penitential psalms of the ancient church. After a sad litany of physical pain, social isolation, and persecution (vv. 1-11 not cited as the response), the Lectionary chooses the next portion of the psalm, namely, the verses celebrating the wonder of Zion and the veneration of pilgrims united in worship at the temple. The point is that God looks down in compassion on the prayer of the destitute (v. 18). God hears the groans of prisoners (v. 21). The use of these verses serves to suggest that God shows compassion and approval for worship such as that offered by Noah.

The Height of Heaven

God is utterly and completely supreme over all creation. The point of this refrain, however, is that exalted dwelling of God in heaven (v. 20) is not distant or isolated. Rather, the level of humble human habitation and God's transcendence is bridged by divine compassion and care. No matter how abject and wretched human beings may have become, God continues to offer salvation. Noah's new beginning was a new beginning for God too. That fresh start even includes us.

Thursday of the Sixth Week in Ordinary Time

First Reading (Year II)

James 2:1-9

Did not God choose those who are poor in the world? You, however, dishonored the person who is poor.

The Sin of Human Partiality

This reading contains the classic biting condemnation of human beings who exhibit economic and social partiality (v. 1). Preference for the wealthy and finely attired prominent members of society over the poor is roundly condemned. Anyone giving in to the temptation of according the wealthy special treatment is numbered among evil judges (v. 4) who are themselves worthy of punishment. Even one's inner inclination along such lines is a violation of God's justice. Although the passage concentrates on the sin of partiality toward the rich (v. 9), one might reflect further about the possibility of reverse partiality for the poor and any presumption that the wealthy are undeserving of care and consideration!

The Poor as Specially Chosen by God

The Letter of Saint James inherits the teachings of the great prophets of Israel and like them suggests that if there is any partiality in God's actions, it would be the reverse of customary human behavior, that is, to the poor rather than to the wealthy (v. 5). James viewed the poor as spiritually blessed rather than merely economically deprived. Echoing the Beatitudes of Luke (6:20), the poor are praised as inheritors of the kingdom.

Antiphon (Year II)

Psalm 34:7a

The Lord hears the cry of the poor.

The Cry of the Poor

Although there are times when the word "cry" is a technical term for a legal lawsuit (Exod 2:22), this refrain (v. 7) could also describe a liturgical prayer of lament uttered in worship. The psalm portion used by the Lectionary (vv. 2-7) is followed by the famous Christian Communion invitation, "Taste and see the goodness of the Lord" (see v. 9, though not cited in the response). Covenantal sacrifices were shared by the family; the poor and hungry were fed and nourished. Perhaps it would have been better to include the reference to nourishment for a fuller consideration of the challenge of poverty. Everyone present for a daily Eucharist should count himself or herself among God's poor.

Divine Hearing

If the fundamental concept inherent in human hearing includes obedience, the reverse can be said of God. When God truly hears (v. 7), God takes action and "obeys" the petition of people who are forced to live without personal resources, and who know only too well that they must be dependent upon others.

Gospel

Mark 8:27-33

You are the Christ. The Son of Man must suffer much.

Literary Link

As noted yesterday, this story of Peter's profession of faith in Jesus as Messiah (v. 29) is an intended parallel to the prior story of the man only partially cured of his blindness (vv. 22-26). The stories are meant to stand as two complimentary sides of the verbal icon.

A Very Imperfect Confession

Jesus insists that a Christ without suffering and rejection (v. 31) cannot be of God. As a matter of fact, we are all followers of Peter, for our individual confessions of Christ are very immature and imperfect (v. 32)! It takes a full lifetime for one's faith to mature properly. Perhaps the whole church, human and flawed, still has much to learn about the Lord we venerate. For an entire church to be humbled by its mistakes and sins, as has been the case in recent years, can be a moment of grace and growth. The "paschal imperative" may well exist for Christ's mystical Body as well as for his physical existence at the end of his earthly ministry.

Peter Rebuked

Ironically, the private rebuke of Jesus by his disciple Peter (v. 32) is reversed, and Peter himself is reprimanded in turn. To be called a "Satan"/enemy/stumbling block (v. 33) by Jesus must have been humiliating for Peter "the Rock," but the name illustrated very clearly how much Peter had yet to learn about the actual message and mission of his Christ! Unfortunately, every one of us also becomes, at some time or other, an obstacle to God's will for us and for our world.

Friday of the Sixth Week in Ordinary Time

First Reading (Year I)

Genesis 11:1-9

Let us go down and there confuse their language.

Human Arrogance

The tale of Babel has many levels of meaning. Behind the story, but close to its surface, may well have lurked a feeling of contempt for Israel's Babylonian oppressors and for those enemies who spoke a different language. They were despised as alien and morally inferior. The story itself deals with a sense of primeval unity (v. 1), arrogantly tempted to extraordinary self-aggrandizement by building their monument to the very heavens (v. 4). The existent ruins of the famous Babylonian ziggurat or temple tower exemplified that pitiful self-importance. The fact that the people exiled to Babylon after the destruction of the temple (587 BC) saw the ruins with their eyes (v. 8) convinced them that God had once humbled their now powerful enemies and oppressors. The ruins of the past gave confidence in the ultimate power of God for the future as well.

The Pain of Human Misspeaking

Among the many mysteries for the ancient world was the diversity of language and the need to explain its origin. Recognizing the reality of ethnic migrations (v. 2), the people of Israel saw how recent arrivals could often assume prominence and self-importance in their new environment. The story might even seem to be told from the standpoint of contempt for the speech of their Babylonian oppressors. The grandness of their architectural schemes almost anticipated quick destruction; they used perishable pitch and tar (v. 3) for cement. The punishment was the confusion of language (v. 7) and the scattering of the nations! In the eyes of later Christians, only Pentecost with the unifying gift of the Spirit of tongues could reunite such diversity! In the meantime, even when speaking the same language, we contemporary human beings misunderstand each other gravely and often, as any family can testify.

Antiphon (Year I)

Psalm 33:12

Blessed the people the Lord has chosen to be his own.

Response to Babel

The opening verse (v. 10) of Psalm 33's response is the assertion of ultimate condemnation for any national plans that are at variance with God's designs. The latter stands forever (v. 11), while the nations rise and fall with astonishing speed. This portion of the psalm raises the specter of failure for any nation that models itself after the arrogance of ancient Babylon and its gigantic building complexes. By contrast, the only nation truly blessed is the one that venerates the Lord (v. 12) and builds his temple.

The Divine Fashioner of Human Hearts

Because God knows the plans of his own heart (v. 11), God is able to know and judge human hearts. In this context, especially after the tale of the tower of Babel, it is very logical to refer to the human heart (v. 15) because for the ancient world the heart was the place of planning and deciding. This is the core element in any Christian devotion to the Heart of Christ whose plans are for the salvation of the world, not its condemnation (John 3:17).

First Reading (Year II)

James 2:14-24, 26

For just as a body without a spirit is dead, so also faith without works is dead.

Faith and Works

This is the classic text at the crux of many bitter sixteenth-century debates. James was not popular among the early Reformers. Only the Joint Declaration on the Doctrine of Justification (JDDJ), signed by representatives of the Vatican and the Lutheran World Federation on October 31, 1999, brought some resolution to that controversy. The document insisted that the precise point of justification of a sinner is by God's grace alone, and that no human efforts can achieve one's salvation. At the same time a person who truly accepts the gift of restored friendship with God will inevitably do good works as a sign of her transformation in Christ. James insists that faith without good works is dead (v. 17). Lutherans and Catholics alike need to be regularly reclaimed by this fundamental truth.

Abraham, the Model of Belief

Both here in this Letter of James (v. 24) and in Paul's Letter to the Romans (4:13ff.) Abraham is cited as one who heard God's promise of an heir and believed with all his being (Gen 15:6). For that reason Abraham's faith became the source of his righteousness before God. This righteousness is more than mere repayment of debts and balancing the human ledger; rather it established a person in right relationship with God and with all of God's creation.

ANTIPHON (YEAR II)

Psalm 112:1b

Blessed the man who greatly delights in the Lord's commands.

A Beatitude for God-Fearers

The Scriptures abound with the proclamation of blessings for those who are righteous and faithful. The New Testament continues that form, as evidenced by the famous Beatitudes of the Sermon on the Mount (Matt 5:1-11). The original word, *ʾasher* in Hebrew or *makarios* in Greek, includes two complimentary ideas: the reception of a gift from beyond one's ability and the human being's emotional delight upon its reception. Thus, to translate the word into English as "blessed" (as does the Lectionary in v. 1) only notes the giftedness; one of the alternatives, "happy," only connotes the positive human emotional response. More accurate, in fact, might be something like "fortunate" or "lucky." This refrain insists that those who have learned how to fear God have a gift and they are very lucky!

Delight in God's Commands

The immature feel that commands are burdens to be endured; the spiritually mature, however, understand that commands from a loving and beloved God are occasions for delight (v. 11) because they are fruits of friendship and they reflect the means to true human happiness. The refrain (v. 1) attempts to highlight a person's basic human pleasure in compliance with the wishes of a "significant Other." If such delight is an occasion for the pronouncement of a beatitude, it is itself a gift as well.

GOSPEL

Mark 8:34–9:1

Those who lose their lives for my sake and that of the Gospel, will save them.

Literary Link

Immediately after the first passion prediction (v. 31) and debate with Peter (vv. 32-33), Jesus proceeds to teach his disciples about the implications of his God-given messianic mission and their lives. To become his apprentice will cost something.

Accepting the Cross

The development of this foundational Christian maxim may well have been shaped in light of the "triumph" of Christ's crucifixion as a postresurrection teaching. True discipleship entails self-denial, accepting one's cross, and following Jesus down that same path (v. 34). The "cross" that we are commanded to take up refers to whatever specific dimension in our lives we would remove if we had the power to do so, but cannot! To come to accept that disappointment or heartache as a reality in our lives, and perhaps even to embrace it as a unique transforming gift, is another mark of spiritual maturity. Everyone has a cross; not all are wise enough to find it a blessing. We tend to make the cross of Jesus into jewelry but are unwilling to do so with our own.

Shame and Honor

Modern scholarship has offered some insightful comments on the ancient culture of the first century, highlighting the way in which familial honor and shame dominate thinking. Jesus warned of the consequences of being "ashamed of [him] and of [his] words" (v. 38). In this teaching one is "ashamed" of a word of Christ if we feel it very contrary to the values of our society and judge ourselves compelled to reject it and to explain it away for ourselves and our friends. Every word of Christ, our Teacher and Savior, must be interpreted in a way that sheds the outer clothing of his own first-century world, but may not be simply and arbitrarily eliminated as if it were a curious and quaint antique. The true word of Christ stands forever! He can never become the cause of embarrassment for a true disciple. Imagine the converse experience of ourselves becoming the cause of embarrassment to Jesus, Lord and Judge of the world!

Friday of the Sixth Week in Ordinary Time

Saturday of the Sixth Week in Ordinary Time

First Reading (Year I)

Hebrews 11:1-7

By faith we understand that the universe was ordered by the word of God.

Faith

This passage begins with the classic definition of faith: "the realization of what is hoped for and evidence of things not seen" (v. 1). The description thus presumes that a person of faith already possesses in some imperfect fashion what is hoped for, and already has basis for anticipating things not yet fully seen. Faith is the initial phase of the final full reality. We experience the future here and now; we already see signals of things that others do not. It is like the title for a car not yet fully paid for or the very real blueprint plans for a house not yet fully built or the acorn for a tree yet to grow. We see it and we have it, but not yet fully! We are, however, changed in the process.

Faith-Filled Figures

The passage offers three names of towering ancient biblical figures who lived with faith: Abel (v. 4), Enoch (v. 5), and Noah (v. 7). This list of examples indicates more concretely what the author of Hebrews means by "people of faith" who were pleasing to God. Popular Jewish piety developed teachings and legends about their lives. In some unique fashion these individuals wrapped their existence around a promise and already experienced some of the reality they anticipated and awaited! Turning to our own lives as people rooted in the graces of baptism, we see yet another example of that anticipated reality: participants in the life of God yet to blossom more fully, and heirs of a future kingdom who are already so transformed as to have a foot in each world.

Antiphon (Year I)

Psalm 145:1

I will praise your name for ever, Lord.

Praise

To praise, as the antiphon announces (v. 1), is to be conscious of the positive qualities or attributes that one then feels compelled to name and acclaim. To praise a child or an artisan for good work is to note the specifics that stand out and make the work remarkably notable and praiseworthy—and then to find the right words that can somehow describe the excellence of the work. Thus, awareness and articulation/verbal expression converge to make praise possible. Moreover, one can never be grateful unless one is first attentive.

The Name of God

We know that in the ancient Semitic world, name stands for person. To praise the "name" of God (v. 1) is to list the many marvelous deeds accomplished by God throughout history and in one's own life, and to lift them up for recognition and admiration. The psalms are filled with such poetic attributes, and those who pay attention to the work of the Lord are able to make their own litany. One cannot help but recall the existence of the famous ninety-nine names of Allah in the Islamic tradition.

First Reading (Year II)

James 3:1-10

No human being can tame the tongue.

Teachers under Judgment

The utter practicality of the spiritual wisdom offered by James is striking. The opening verse (v. 1) of this passage lifts up the importance of the role of teacher, and notes, therefore, the expectations they bear and the accountability under which they work. Those who teach, including parents, are models for what they say and responsible for passing on attitudes and values as well as fundamental facts. We probably all know teachers whose memories we cherish. We may even include those who are now revered even though demanding in their day, and those once popular but now are seen as ultimately wasteful of our time and attention. This is a day to pray for teachers, past, present, and future. The ministry of teaching is itself a gift from God among many special callings within the community of Christians who in turn build up the Body of Christ (Eph 4:11).

The Human Tongue

James cannot resist moving to a wise word of both praise and caution regarding the tongue of teachers and preachers (v. 4). In the third Servant Song the mysterious figure gives praise for the gift of a "well-trained tongue" (Isa 50:4) in order to encourage and instruct others well. James knows that restraint is often needed if a tongue is to guide one's life well, and that it is capable of great destruction in society, as demagogues and slanderous gossips know only too well (v. 6). It is the source for life-giving blessings and curses filled with deadly poison (v. 8). Turning for a moment to our contemporary eucharistic ritual, receiving Communion in the hand rightly blesses a person for the work of the kingdom, while those who receive on the tongue accept a summons to truth, justice, and charity.

Saturday of the Sixth Week in Ordinary Time

ANTIPHON (YEAR II)

Psalm 12:8a

You will protect us, Lord.

Deceitful Lips and Boastful Tongues

Behind the antiphon's refrain (v. 8) is a personal lament against the falsehood (v. 3) of so much speech that divides and destroys the community of the faithful. With a remarkable ability to continue the themes of the passage from James, Psalm 12 continues its diatribe against speech that falsifies or exaggerates the truth. The psalmist prays for punishment on smooth lips and insincere hearts (v. 3). It is rare to hear a homily on speaking/"living the truth in love" (Eph 4:15) or on the sin of lying.

Divine Protection

The protection of God, which is praised and sought in the context of Psalm 12, is not against military power or physical oppression but rather against all the harm caused by false speech. The very God who created the universe by a word (Gen 1:3) will shelter and protect his people from the type of human speech that destroys this world. How does God protect from deceit? Perhaps by exposing its error or by confronting the speaker with contrary truth or by destroying the fabric of tissue built by lies. The Hebrew word for truth, *ʾemet*, means at its root something sufficiently strong or stable as to bear leaning against and relying upon.

GOSPEL

Mark 9:2-13

Jesus was transfigured before them.

Literary Link

The Gospel of Mark follows the first passion prediction (8:31) and the teachings of Jesus about the consequences of that reality for the life of all disciples (vv. 34-36) with a promise of future glory. The account of the transfiguration (vv. 3-8) reminds readers of the glory hidden in the Person of Jesus throughout his entire earthly ministry. Perhaps inspired by the appearance of Elijah in conversation with the transfigured Jesus (v. 4), and recalling Jewish beliefs about the end-time return of Elijah (v. 11), the narrative easily connects the theme of resurrection with that great prophet.

The Mystery of Transfiguration

There is something of an anticipated postresurrectional glory in this event, which allowed the perennial personal radiance of Jesus (v. 3) to shine forth amid his three specially chosen disciples (v. 2). Three heavenly figures are contrasted with three earthly disciples. Positioned by Mark between the first two passion predictions (8:31 and 9:31), the account enables the listener to remember the inner radiance of this Son of Man whose mission included suffering as well as glory. Like all biblical events, the ultimate subject is not only an ancient personality but also ourselves, because we also bear the inner dignity of children of God while subject to the sufferings of our age. People at a weekday Eucharist are now numbered with the three amazed disciples.

The Heavenly Voice

It is curious that the voice at the baptism of Jesus in the Jordan said, "You are my beloved Son (1:11)," as a testimony directed personally to Jesus, affirming his special dignity. At the transfiguration, however, the addressee is subtly changed: "This is my beloved Son" (v. 7), with the added command to the disciple witnesses to "hear / obey" him. Suddenly noting the disappearance of Moses and Elijah (the Law and the Prophets), and the solitary presence of Jesus alone, the disciples are reminded that Jesus alone has become the voice of God and the source of truth for them. He summarizes for them everything from the past for the future.

Monday of the Seventh Week in Ordinary Time

First Reading (Year I)

Sirach 1:1-10

Before all things else wisdom was created.

The Book of Ben Sirach

Written in Hebrew in Palestine about 200 to 175 BC by a greatly revered sage named Sirach, and translated into Greek in Egypt by his grandson, Jesus ben-Eleazar ben Sirach, about 132 BC, the book attempts to preserve the best of ancient Israelite wisdom for an age under siege from contrary Hellenistic culture. Once called *Ecclesiasticus*, or the "Church book," it only existed in Greek until 1896 when portions of the original Hebrew were discovered. It is a priceless compendium of spirituality and good sense. Although the book was venerated as inspired by the early Greek-speaking churches, it was not included among the canonical Scriptures acclaimed by Saint Jerome and classical Protestant writers.

Wisdom

The word "wisdom/*Sophia*," used five times in this brief introduction to the book, is much more than the knowledge of facts and figures. Wisdom refers to God's ability to do all things wisely and well. Because such a capacity can only originate from God (v. 1) who created an entire world with its remarkable precision, wisdom was received as a gift "poured . . . forth upon all his works" (v. 8). This gift is granted to human beings who are able to navigate through the inevitable shoals and difficulties of life. Artisans, cooks, potters, parents, and court officials each also shared that capacity in special ways, enabling them to serve God's people successfully because of their skill. In every parish community there are very wise people.

Personification

Because Wisdom was shared and lavished upon human beings and material creation, the idea was quickly personified (v. 7) and lifted up as the first of all created reality. Before more sophisticated modern knowledge of physics, Wisdom was considered the "glue" that held the universe together. The magnificent things said about Wisdom easily enabled this quality to become identified with the Torah/Pentateuch among pious Jewish leaders, and subsequently identified by early Christian scholars with the Word/Logos (Second Person of the Trinity) or even the Holy Spirit. The smooth functioning of material creation was seen as the effect of God's wisdom.

Antiphon (Year I)

Psalm 93:1a

The Lord is king; he is robed in majesty.

Royal Psalms

Psalm 93 begins with an acclamation of divine kingship (v. 1). It formed part of a liturgical celebration, possibly associated with the covenant renewal each autumn. The psalm was chosen by the Lectionary as an echo of Sirach's reference to God upon his throne (v. 6). Even inspired poets can be literary "thieves," so the psalm may have been borrowed to some extent from Mesopotamian worship. The song acknowledges the exaltation of YHWH over all creation, even the deepest foundations of the world and the power of wisdom that holds it together. Over the centuries Israel had celebrated divine kingship. They also experienced human kingly agents whose ultimate success depended on their fidelity to the Divine King.

Clothing Imagery

The poetry of faith readily imagined God as clothed in many attributes of majesty, glory, and exalted royal power. This is repeatedly acclaimed in the antiphon (v. 1). The acclamation enabled Israel to recall the "mini gods" of their polytheistic neighbors, and to subordinate them to YHWH alone, converting them into personified apparel used and worn by God. Similarly the Letter to the Colossians speaks about human members of the churches as morally clothed in mercy, kindness, humility, meekness, and patience (Col 3:12). What one wears matters!

FIRST READING (YEAR II)

James 3:13-18

If you have bitter jealousy and selfish ambition in your hearts, do not boast.

Humility

True wisdom comes from God and remains humbly honest (v. 13) and truthful about the source of such a gift. In the wake of such modest wisdom come compassion, mercy, and peace (v. 17). True respect for other people, who are also gifted, creates in turn all the attitudes that unite and build up the community. These gifts do not travel alone but together as they find a home in the mind and heart of a truly wise person and in a wise community. The reading concludes with a marvelous reference to the type of justice and peace that is the foundation for a Christian's social ministry (v. 18).

False Wisdom

By contrast, any attitude that is filled with self-serving ambition will inevitably experience jealousy (v. 14) about the gifts of others. Bitter boastful rivalry (v. 16) will be the fruit of earthly wisdom and will lead not to truth but to falsehood. These also are gifts that travel in groups. By their fruits you will know them.

ANTIPHON (YEAR II)

Psalm 19:9a

The precepts of the Lord give joy to the heart.

Revelation

Psalm 19 is comprised of two very different parts, often judged by scholars to have had two separate human authors. The first seven verses (not used in this response) sing the praises of the firmament and celebrate the way the sun travels across the sky, revealing God's will. The second portion (vv. 8-15) is cited here as the response to the reading from James and treats of the many different commands and precepts of God that, like the sun, have a heavenly origin. They illuminate our lives (v. 9). Those with true wisdom can and will learn many lessons from the will of God and from surrounding creation.

Gladness of Heart

The various forms of divine instruction, like the beauty and wonder of material creation, cause delight. As the refrain proclaims, those with true wisdom experience a genuine gladness of heart (v. 9) in obedient response to the revelation of God's will. Sinners live with a shallow sadness because they are rooted in themselves. Saints are happy people. "Joy is the infallible sign of God's presence" (attributed to the French philosopher Léon Bloy).

GOSPEL

Mark 9:14-29

I do believe, help my unbelief!

Literary Link

After a slight distraction occasioned by the discussion of the mission of Elijah (vv. 9-13), Mark tells the story of the desperate father and his possessed son (vv. 14-29). The inability of the disciples to cure the lad may be linked to the statement at the end of the transfiguration story, namely, the necessity of depending on Jesus alone (v. 7) through prayer (v. 29).

True "Disciples"

Mark's gospel tells this story about the cure of the possessed child immediately after that of the transfiguration, showing the link between the inner glory of Jesus and service to the needy. This passage is perfect for explaining that the Greek word *mathetai*, usually translated as "disciples," might better be understood as "apprentices." The word disciple seems to include too much of the classroom or academic type of learning. The discipleship of the gospel, on the other hand, suggests a relationship with Jesus that includes training for service. Out of the radiant glory within the heart of Jesus come his power and his compassion. The disciples were helpless (v. 18). This secretly radiant Jesus, however, helps his followers learn how to deal with the sick, the hungry, the sinner, or other groups in human need. Only through dependence upon him can they become effective (v. 29). The famous painting of the transfiguration by Raphael shows both the dominant luminous figure of Jesus as well as the group of his helpless "apprentices" gathered in the lower right corner, puzzled over their inability to heal the boy. The painting is dramatically reproduced in mosaic form over a side altar in Saint Peter's Basilica in Rome.

Monday of the Seventh Week in Ordinary Time

The Desperate Father

Parents often say that they never stop worrying about their children; they just worry about different things as the years go by. This parent is clearly terribly concerned about his son who gives evidence of a malady similar to epilepsy (v. 20) and becomes a symbol for all parents who pray for their gravely ill children. Panicked by fear and worry but unable to provide any relief, comfort, or help for his son, he turns to the disciples of Jesus. His prayer of desperation (v. 24) can become the prayer of anyone caught in a tragic situation that seems beyond human help. In response to the calm reminder of Jesus, "Everything is possible to one who has faith" (v. 23), the father begs for the type of faith that can save his son (v. 24). The same prayer is ours today as well.

Belief and Unbelief

The honest plea of the father acknowledges his limited faith (v. 24), possibly compromised by worry and the inevitable challenges of daily life. Every disciple, if truly honest, should admit having a similar share of belief and nonbelief in the face of the truth of God's revelation and the human struggle to respond fully in generous self-dedication.

Prayer (and Fasting)

Older Catholics may recall that the verse familiar from their childhood included the need to cast out demons by "prayer and fasting." More recently, however, we have learned that the better ancient manuscripts only state "prayer" (v. 29). Prayer is not only petition but more essentially the act of assuming a stance of personal humility and dependence before God. If prayer is only asking, it might easily be presumed that lack of effect only means that the person hasn't begged enough or hasn't used the proper words. All the focus would be on the human effort. If prayer is a posture before God, however, then we are the ones who are changed by our prayer. Only then can God use us to be effective instruments of peace and emotional healing in the lives of others.

Tuesday of the Seventh Week in Ordinary Time

First Reading (Year I)

Sirach 2:1-11

Prepare yourself for trials.

Trials

As a result of much wisdom and experience Sirach reminds his student that true service to God inevitably entails many trials (v. 1) of sorrow, crushing misfortune (v. 4), and humiliation. Heartaches and headaches may come from the cost of our choices or the rejection of those around us. Early Christians understood that this was true of the ministry of Jesus and will also be verified in the lives of his disciples. Those found worthy of God's wisdom, however, will be treated like gold or silver, always purified by fire (v. 5).

Fear of the Lord

Four successive verses are each introduced by the address, "You who fear the Lord" (vv. 7ff.). Those who have learned to live in reverential "fear" before God are always also filled with trust (v. 6) and hope (v. 9). The end of the reading seems to invoke a level of trust difficult to sustain, for it asks if anyone who had hoped in God had ever been disappointed, forsaken, or rebuffed (v. 10). One cannot help but think of the struggles of Job and those saints like Therese of Lisieux or Teresa of Calcutta who apparently lived with long periods of desperate spiritual depression as a result of the purifying sense of divine absence. Perhaps in the last analysis, we are invited to borrow the prayer of the desperate father from yesterday's gospel, and to pray for the deeper trust that can and will carry us through the tough times. Professional spiritual counseling may also be helpful.

Antiphon (Year I)

Psalm 37:5

Commit your life to the Lord, and he will help you.

A Psalm of Confidence

Psalm 37 is not so much a hymn of trust as a string of individual proverbs on the same theme, arranged in such a manner that each alternating verse begins with a successive letter of the Hebrew alphabet. Picking up the motif of complete and total trust from the teachings of Sirach, these verses insist upon confidence in God (v. 3) and promise the rewards reserved for those who sustain that attitude. This is not easy for anyone, and therefore the prayer of the desperate father again comes to mind.

The Rewards of Trust

The verses of the psalm chosen to serve as a response list many of the rewards given by God to those who live in trusting confidence: security (v. 3), a lasting inheritance (v. 18), life without shame even in evil times (v. 19), abundance amid famine (v. 19), and ultimate salvation (v. 39). One might add the blessing that comes from communal support of those who share the same deep trust in the Lord, and the strength that comes from common prayer.

First Reading (Year II)

James 4:1-10

You ask but you do not receive,
because you ask wrongly.

The Dangers of Human Passion

Passion itself is not a bad reality, as in the case of one who has a passion for beauty or a passion for justice or a passion for learning. Only when one's passion is totally concentrated on one's self (v. 1) to the exclusion of others does it become problematic and possibly sinful. One can see a relationship between Buddhism and the warnings of this passage, because that religious tradition insists that human unhappiness comes from the passionate desire for things not possessed. Those driven by covetousness (v. 2) for what they do not have rather than supported by contentment for what they do have can never be happy. These teachings verify the wisdom of loving what one has rather than having what one loves.

Lamentation over Sin

The passage ends with a strange and unexpected suggestion, namely, to put aside laughter for mourning (v. 9). Humility before God is the acceptance of truth, and this includes openness to the bigger picture. The truth is that we live in a world that includes the existence of sin and the need for purification. Both are serious obstacles to trust and to contentment in the friendship with God who exalts those whom he humbles (v. 10).

ANTIPHON (YEAR II)

Psalm 55:23a

Throw your cares on the Lord,
and he will support you.

Temptations to Flight

Psalm 55 acknowledges that there are times when one would simply love to throw in the towel and run away from the tragic storms of life and its prowling dangers (v. 10). The troubles may be rural disasters (v. 9) or urban violence (v. 10). Unfortunately, however, the fears of our heart would travel with us no matter where we go. Therefore we would take our problems with us. For that reason the refrain summons us to cast our cares, whatever they may be, on the Lord (see v. 23).

Tuesday of the Seventh Week in Ordinary Time

Support from God

The most effective remedy for establishing stability of life is a renewed realization that ultimate peace comes, not from our limited human resources alone, but from God, as the refrain reminds us (v. 23). God has called each of us into being and desires to protect the creatures he loves. Human sin remains the obstacle to the peace and security desired by God.

GOSPEL

Mark 9:30-37

The Son of Man is to be handed over. Whoever wishes to be first, shall be last of all.

Literary Link

Just as Mark's first passion prediction (8:31-33) had been followed by a teaching regarding the consequences for disciples who must deny themselves and carry their crosses (vv. 34-38), so also the second passion prediction (9:30-32) is followed by a teaching on the consequences of caring for children and imitating them (vv. 33-37). In each case we find a prediction and then a teaching.

The Paschal Mystery

This second summary of the destiny of the Son of Man can be summarized by the notion of "the paschal mystery," namely, betrayal, death, and resurrection (v. 31). This triple convergence of human suffering and divine vindication remains at the heart of Christ's Gospel of salvation. It includes the final element that promises the vindication of the Christ. In a very real sense this is the nub of the Gospel, which is the proclamation of Christ's suffering and death with an added explanation of the context and causes for that death. From that sharply focused prediction/announcement, the entire Gospel of Mark was developed and filled out for catechetical purposes.

Definition of "Greatest"

The instruction of Jesus regarding the definition of the true notion of being "greatest" in the kingdom (v. 34) is immediately related to his teaching regarding his destiny in death and resurrection. There is logic to the way these ideas are linked together in the arrangement of ideas and stories. If rejection and humiliation is somehow at the heart of Christ's mission, then it is logical to train the disciples/apprentices for a lifestyle that values service (v. 35) rather than social or religious preeminence. In the kingdom, human values are turned upside down.

Child as Image and Model

Once Jesus lifted up a child as somehow identified with himself (v. 37), it becomes imperative to explore that reality and thus to understand the precise model of human existence in the kingdom embodied in a child: dependence, eagerness to help, openness to learning because of curiosity, and humble recognition of limitation. Jesus chooses to identify with all who have made those qualities their own. Whoever welcomes and values such a person, welcomes and values both Jesus and his heavenly Father (v. 37)!

Wednesday of the Seventh Week in Ordinary Time

First Reading (Year I)

Sirach 4:11-19

Those who love her the Lord loves.

Personification

The sequence of verses in this reading resists any easy logical divisions. The major link among the statements is that Wisdom as a divine attribute is personified and presented as (divine) mother (v. 11), friend, and teacher—each with a different task or function in a person's life. As such, Wisdom offers countless blessings to those who seek and treasure her presence. The reading insists that God's wisdom is present wherever we learn, wherever we find comfort, wherever we find true happiness.

Antiphon (Year I)

Psalm 119:165a

O Lord, great peace have they who love your law.

"Law"

In Hebrew the noun translated in the antiphon as "law" (v. 165) is really *torah*. This word is certainly far richer and less legalistic than the English version might seem to Western minds, because Torah more properly suggests instruction. Its basic literal sense is "something tossed out to be caught, received, and treasured." One might more properly think of students who really relish a particular subject or course, who eagerly await the class and who excel in mastering its contents. Such students seriously consider the subject as a possible lifetime occupation and companion.

Commands

The full psalm response itself (vv. 165-75), however, proceeds to use a variety of words that are specific imperatives of one kind or another: precepts, decrees, statutes, and ordinances. Each presumably expects a specific type of compliance; all are ways in which the general category of God's instruction is conveyed to the faithful member of God's chosen people.

Great Peace

This antiphon (v. 165) envisions that those who are completely open to God's wide-ranging "instruction" will achieve the integration of all the various elements of human existence into their mature life. Biblical "peace/*shalom*," as we know from other venues, is the possession of the big picture of life when all the elements coalesce into consistent unity, not merely into quiet tranquility. God's peace, like an eternal jigsaw puzzle, puts everything back together again.

First Reading (Year II)

James 4:13-17

You have no idea what your life will be like. Instead you should say: If the Lord wills it.

Fallacy of Human Planning

James insists that any human plans must be content to accept their fundamentally contingent character, because our plans are dependent on so many factors completely beyond our control (v. 14). The decisions of others, our shifting needs, and even the quality of the weather can so easily provide a different scenario at the dawn of a new day. This practical instruction from James echoes perfectly the customary qualifier familiar from Islam, namely, *Inshallah*/"If the Lord wills it" (v. 15). Each day requires a fresh review to determine the right and just response to its *kairos*.

Sin

There are many different descriptions for the reality of sin: deliberately missing the mark, violation of the love of neighbor, disregard for one's own nature, and so forth. Here James simply says that freely not doing what one knows is "right" (*kalos*) is a sin (v. 17). This Greek word usually signifies "noble, skillfully suitable, or proper." It is used for the "good" shepherd (John 10:11). This is different from the Greek word *agathos*, that is, something morally good. Even not doing the "noble thing" by way of omission is, according to James, sinful.

ANTIPHON (YEAR II)

Matthew 5:3

Blessed are the poor in spirit; the Kingdom of heaven is theirs!

Poor in Spirit

At first glance, the reading does not seem to refer to "poverty of spirit" and makes the refrain sound odd in context. Further reflection, however, reminds us that this type of poverty means seeing everything as gift, not personal achievement. If we learn of our inability to plan life, we approach the meaning of that attitude; then the refrain makes sense. This beatitude is expressed differently from its form in Luke's gospel, which is more physical, "you poor" (6:20). The refrain from Matthew's Sermon on the Mount would suggest the blessing is for those who are "poor in spirit," those who consider everything as gift and who therefore claim nothing as their own individual isolated achievement.

Blessed

The very nature of beatitude is a unique combination of two factors: the fact of a blessing or gift that comes from beyond our control, and the fact that it becomes the occasion for great personal delight. Both aspects converge to make one blessed.

Psalm 49: The Paradoxes of Life

Psalm 49 is a wisdom poem dealing with the riddles of life: dangers of trust in personal wealth (v. 7), priceless value of an individual life that, however, passes away (v. 10). These wise propositions are intended for rich and poor alike (v. 3) as something to be pondered when making plans and decisions. The psalm forms the perfect response to the teaching of James regarding the contingency of both human existence and personal wealth.

GOSPEL

Mark 9:38-40

Whoever is not against us is for us.

Literary Link

Perhaps Mark adds this vignette about the unauthorized exorcist (vv. 38-40) as yet another example of the paschal mystery. Living the second passion prediction means that the disciples must become like little children again (vv. 33-37), and that they cannot even control who will act in the name of Jesus (vv. 38-40).

Insiders and Outsiders

The disciples, and this would include men and women alike, seemed to presume that only those who live in complete agreement within the closer bond of friendship with Jesus and share a way of life together can confront evil and drive out demons in the name of Jesus (v. 38). In their minds, outsiders would be forbidden to use the name of Jesus as a basis for their actions. In a sense the basic question is an early form of the perennial question of "no salvation outside the church" because it presumes that all agree on the definition of "church" or live within the boundaries of the "community" of disciples. Apparently this was a topic of heated debate in the early church as well as in our own day, as evidenced by the fact that the very opposite (and more narrow) boundary is found elsewhere, namely, "Whoever is not with me is against me" (Matt 12:30).

Speaking Well of Jesus

Mark's community would seem to be satisfied with the fact that a person qualifies as a colleague and partner if he or she does not speak ill of Jesus, regardless of the nature of his community membership. Perhaps the deeper issue was the relationship of "God fearers" to the community. There were individuals on the edge of both Judaism and Christianity down through the ages who admired the morality or religious values of the community without accepting its full set of boundary marking practices. Jesus accepts and blesses their good deeds. Ultratraditional Catholics whose judgments are "more Catholic than the church" would seem to be people excluded by this saying of Jesus. Likewise the ultraliberal would be excluded if they act in their own name, not in the name of Jesus.

Wednesday of the Seventh Week in Ordinary Time

Thursday of the Seventh Week in Ordinary Time

First Reading (Year I)

Sirach 5:1-8

Delay not your conversion to the Lord.

Rationalizations

This passage from Sirach is masterful in listing the many ways in which human beings avoid the summons to conversion: trust in personal wealth or political power (vv. 1-2), the presumption of eventually getting (buying or bullying) one's way (v. 3), a long life of good fortune or even an unfounded presumption of God's mercy (v. 6). We each become masterful at avoidance and sidestepping the will of God at any given moment in life. The passage is a perfect penitential rite for a weekday morning Eucharist.

Conversion

Sirach strongly counsels conversion without delay (v. 8). Although we may not know the precise Hebrew word in the original text, we do know that their customary word for conversion is *teshuvah*, literally, a "return." The gospels often use *metanoia*, a fresh new way of thinking (about how God really works in our world). One might also suggest that the idea of conversion is to see things from God's point of view and to make sure that God is a partner in every conversation about human attitudes and behavior. No one can truly stand before the presence of God and then walk away unchanged!

Antiphon (Year I)

Psalm 40:5a

Blessed are they who hope in the Lord.

Hope

The refrain from Psalm 40 lifts up the importance of hope in God. The notion of confidence or trust has a slightly different flavor than "hope." To trust is to live with the personal conviction that things will work out well sooner or later, but to hope, as the verse translated in the Lectionary implies, adds the notion of justified expectation. With good reason based on the very nature of God, God's faithful people anticipate that God will save his people, somewhat perhaps like the child jumping into the arms of a parent simply assumes to be caught. Note, however, that the verses chosen for this response are from Psalm 1, which contrasts good and wicked individuals.

The Beatitude

To formulate this hope into a beatitude or "blessing" (v. 5) is to see such hope as a gift from beyond one's own native ability and a gift that makes the recipient delighted. The encyclical of Benedict XVI, *Spe Salvi*, speaks to these theological and spiritual realities of Christian hope with clarity and conviction. Those who delight in the law of the Lord (v. 2) will receive the spiritual gift of hope and the blessings that follow.

First Reading (Year II)

James 5:1-6

The workers from whom you withheld the wages, are crying aloud; their cries have reached the ears of the Lord of hosts.

Self-Centered Wealth

With a harshness very reminiscent of the condemnations of prophets like Isaiah (5:8-12) or Amos (2:6-8; 6:4-8), the wealthy are threatened with sorrow and punishment (v. 1) by James for their utter disregard for the needy around their homes. For the eighth-century prophets and for first-century urban advocates of justice, the bitter moral truth is that material prosperity had often been built upon the backs of the poor (v. 4). The very practical moral wisdom of James is clearly heir to the voices of the ancient prophets of Israel. Early church fathers taught that any superfluous wealth is not ours, but already belongs to the poor!

The Cries of the Workers

With poetic vigor James insists that the cries of the unjustly treated poor have risen to the very ears of God (v. 4). Wages withheld are almost personified in their pleas for justice. It is passages like this that give motivation for strong efforts for social justice in every age, particularly for factory and farm workers. Contemporary questions of immigration reform and compassion for families mired in poverty find root in teachings such as this passage from James.

Antiphon (Year II)

Matthew 5:3

Blessed are the poor in spirit; the Kingdom of heaven is theirs!

The Antiphon

This refrain borrowed from the first beatitude of Matthew's Sermon on the Mount (5:3) is an exact repetition of yesterday's response to similar strong moral teachings of James. Apparently the promise is too important to be the occasion for prayer and examination of conscience for only one day.

Thursday of the Seventh Week in Ordinary Time

Psalm 49: Social Teachings

Similarly Psalm 49 is also repeated from the prior day, but these verses are taken from a later portion of the psalm (vv. 14-20). The wisdom themes continue: the folly of total self-confidence (v. 14), the inevitability of death (v. 15), and punishment of the uncompassionate wealthy before the judgment of God (v. 20). These two days form a specially focused pair of readings on Catholic social teachings and a proper Christian response to the burning needs of God's poor.

Gospel

Mark 9:41-50

It is better for you to enter into life with one hand, than with two hands to go into Gehenna.

Literary Link

This teaching is probably included here as another example of action in the name of Jesus, similar to receiving children in his name (v. 37, sometimes translated as "for his sake") and expelling demons in his name (v. 38). Note that two possibly familiar references to the "undying worm and unquenchable fire" (see vv. 44 and 46) have been eliminated from the liturgical text because they are only found in less reliable manuscripts.

Motivation of Disciples

The promise of a reward for even such a small action as offering water to the thirsty is linked to the motivation of doing so as a result of the giver's relationship to Christ (v. 41). Such a gesture of compassion is proposed as an action of Christ himself, and underscores the enduring bond of identity between master and disciple/apprentice. This is another example of the concern of Jesus for a person's inner motivation as well as for the physical gesture itself. Another way of stating the teaching is to see it as a reminder of our obligation to do the right thing for the right reason!

Avoidance of Temptation

The historical experience of holy people over the centuries should remind us of the danger of taking these teachings of Jesus literally. The zealous and brilliant theologian Origen († ca. 255), who was named to head the catechetical school of Alexandria at the age of eighteen and who eagerly desired martyrdom, is said to have castrated himself as a means of avoiding temptation. The teaching regarding the removal of one's hand (v. 43), foot (v. 45), or eye (v. 47) is rather intended to illustrate a person's serious responsibility to eliminate every occasion of sin from one's daily life, even at considerable personal cost. The Semitic hyperbole does not negate common early Christian teaching regarding the sanctity of the body as a temple of the Holy Spirit, and the obligation to hold it in esteem (1 Cor 6:20).

Salt

The final verses (vv. 49-50) of the passage appear to be different in content from the rest of the passage. Three different meanings seem to be associated with salt in this brief summary: a practical burning purification for wounds (v. 49), a seasoning to make food more tasty (v. 50), and its symbolic use for wisdom (v. 50). One should not forget the use of salt in the prerenewed liturgy of baptism, nor the fact that the entire community is called the salt of the earth (Matt 5:13). Contemporary life includes salt for de-icing purposes as well.

Friday of the Seventh Week in Ordinary Time

First Reading (Year I)

Sirach 6:5-17

Faithful friends are beyond price.

Testing Friendship

With considerable wisdom and apparent wealth of experience, the author of this reading lists the types of superficial "fair weather" friendships that fail when no longer convenient or when under distress (vv. 8-10). Even though friendship is considered a precious gift from God and something to be cherished like "one in a thousand" (v. 6), it should also be tested for its sincerity and depth.

Faithful Friendship

A truly faithful friend is a source of protection like a "sturdy shelter" (v. 15) throughout life, remaining at one's side in adversity as a great treasure. Such a friend, in fact, could be listed among the blessings from God for which we should exercise a sense of stewardship. Enduring friendship should actually and actively be cultivated, because it remains a remedy in difficulties (v. 17) and even a constant source of health. Such men and women are irreplaceable!

Antiphon (Year I)

Psalm 119:35a

Guide me, Lord, in the way of your commands.

Statutes, Commands, Words, Laws, etc.

Throughout this portion of Psalm 119 we hear a litany of different terms for the expectations of God regarding human behavior. Each expresses God's will, and clearly suggests that God is the ultimate origin for the requirements. Thoughtful reflection on the commands and the need for discernment (v. 27) imply that human beings have a role in maturely understanding the value of the commands, without simply being compelled by force. The fact that this psalm responds to the reading on the beauty and blessing of friendship also teaches the value of a free and positive relationship between God and Israel (and us)!

Guidance

The various words, whatever their specific meaning, are the forms by which divine guidance is given to Israel. There is a respectful aspect to "guidance" that offers direction without imposition and invites compliance. The Hebrew verb form (v. 35) behind "guide" means literally to "cause someone to take steps," almost like a parent teaching an infant to walk.

First Reading (Year II)

James 5:9-12

The Judge is standing before the gates.

Complaint

Anyone who complains about neighbors bases their comments upon personal judgments. The letter's reminder of the invisible presence of the divine judge (v. 9) is a caution about the possibility of being subsequently judged according to the same criteria by God as well. To judge is to be judged.

Patient Perseverance

One of the values of hardship (v. 10) is the lesson learned by ancient prophets who were often opposed and even rejected by the people of their day, namely, the blessing of confident perseverance, no matter what the level of adversity. Without opposition there is no real perseverance. Certainly Job (v. 11) is a classic model of perseverance amid suffering and misunderstanding.

Antiphon (Year II)

Psalm 103:8a

The Lord is kind and merciful.

Mercy

This refrain echoes the final verse of the reading, the confession that the Lord is "kind and merciful" (v. 11). The sentiment is a comforting reminder of God's mercy toward those who remain patient in their suffering. The distinctive notion of the Hebrew word for "merciful" in this refrain (v. 8) is *rahum*, the maternal compassion of the womb from whence the very gift of life itself was nourished and protected.

Kindness

The meaning of "kindness" mentioned in the refrain and in the second portion of that same verse (v. 8b) is not easily sorted out. The refrain suggests "kindness" as graciousness that makes a person attractive, and the latter part of the verse (not mentioned in the refrain) is kindness as *hesed*, namely, the mutual care and concern of covenanted partners, one for the other. The combination is almost a creed for Israel's relationship to a God who is much more than judge.

Gospel

Mark 10:1-12

What God has joined together, no human being must separate.

Literary Link

A sad reality of marriage in any age is the potential existence of divorce. At the request of some Pharisees (v. 2), Jesus addressed the question of failed marriages.

Divorce

By their religious traditions Pharisees were committed to obedience to the stipulations of oral tradition as well as to the strict written text of the Torah. The priestly class of Sadducees upheld only the latter. Even though Jesus tended to live and teach from the Pharisaic tradition and viewpoint, he was inclined to hold a more literal interpretation of the unbreakable reality of the bond of marriage (v. 9). He was willing to set aside the permissiveness of even Moses (v. 5) in this matter as an ideal. In our contemporary culture divorce is often as painful as it is common. Jesus taught that the adultery is found in the remarriage, not the separation, and the Western Catholic Church tries to maintain respect for this teaching of Jesus by reviewing the marriage itself and making a judgment about the absence/presence of the bond from the beginning. Eastern Christianity holds that a first marriage remains forever, but due to the sinfulness of both partners, a human accommodation can be made for life in this age. This truth must be preached sensitively with an eye toward the people who may be present, and the perennial need for lifting up the ideal in our society.

Commitments

God does not will that anyone stay in situations that are truly harmful; we may even have an obligation to remove ourselves from such negative circumstances. At the same time, a sign of one's emotional and spiritual maturity is a personal willingness to keep one's promises. In an age and a culture that are radically individualistic, it can become easy to be so focused on our needs and wants as to simply do what we want, when we want and how we want it. This teaching of Jesus provides a caution against quick or easy solutions to genuine human heartaches.

Saturday of the Seventh Week in Ordinary Time

First Reading (Year I)

Sirach 17:1-15

In his own image the Lord made them.

An Image of God

The characteristics of being a true image of God are limited because of death (v. 3). They include, however, authority over the beasts of the earth (v. 4), wisdom and counsel in guiding creatures (v. 6), and the knowledge of good and evil. It is important for every person to have a clear sense of precisely what makes us images of the God we serve. There will be something common to all human beings, but also something specific to each individual!

Divine Knowledge

Even though God grants such knowledge (v. 9) and authority to human beings, he still holds us accountable for our actions, and knowing our "ways" (v. 13). The image of "walking a path" or "ways" is the biblical metaphor for human moral behavior that God sees thoroughly and judges clearly. There is a conceptual relationship between this moral metaphor and the gospel accounts of physically healing the lame (Matt 11:5), thus enabling them to walk and live well before God.

Antiphon (Year I)

Psalm 103:17

The Lord's kindness is everlasting to those who fear him.

Everlasting Kindness

The "kindness" celebrated in this refrain (v. 17) is *hesed*, namely, the mutual concern required of covenantal partners. The verse insists that such care, one for another, lasts forever, literally from age to age, or from one world as it unfolds endlessly to another similarly unfolding world. The psalm verses acknowledge the grass-like brevity of individual human existence (v. 15) but also celebrate the compassion of God's response to the covenant that he has granted to human beings (v. 18). God is just, that is, in right relationship, with all his creatures forever!

Fear of the Lord

The partners in a covenant do not live in servile fear, not even when one is God, but rather in respectful reverence (v. 17) for each other's inherent dignity. This is the type of "fear" that children and adults should exhibit to their parents. Even the children of children into the third generation are bound by this duty to offer respect and reverence.

First Reading (Year II)

James 5:13-20

The fervent prayer of a righteous person is very powerful.

Importance of Prayer

James insists on the obligation to pray, either in petition or in praise, no matter what the circumstances may be (v. 13). In suffering or sickness a prayer that acknowledges one's total dependence upon God is the beginning of reestablishing harmony and health in one's life. The same humble stance before God is the beginning of conversion (v. 19). The life-changing prayer described and encouraged by James is far deeper than the mere recitation of things humanly desired.

Anointing of the Sick

In this classic text, which the Catholic Church invokes on the occasion of celebrating the sacrament of the sick (vv. 14 and 15), we learn of the apostolic practice of prayer accompanied by anointing for the healing of the sick in mind and (when willed by God) body. The visible sacramental action is intended to signal the invisible action of God at the very center of a sick person's being by the use of oil that soothes, heals, and strengthens. The reading reminds us of the times when the disciples of Jesus themselves engaged in anointing the sick (Mark 6:13). This reading in the Lectionary may also be an occasion for instruction about the proper use of the sacrament as intended for the sick, not the dying! The former Catholic notion of "last rites" is clearly antithetical to the way this sacramental prayer is presented in the Letter of James.

ANTIPHON (YEAR II)

Psalm 141:2a

Let my prayer come like incense before you.

The Prayer of God's Faithful

Psalm 141 was often considered the perfect Evening Prayer of the early church, and the refrain's reference to prayer makes these words a fitting response to the comments of James regarding the importance of our personal relationship with God. The refrain enhances the notion of personal prayer by suggesting that even individual human verbal expression can take its place beside temple sacrifice as worship. In the absence of sacrifice, either because of distance from the temple or because of the inability to offer formal sacrifice after the temple's destruction by the Babylonians (586 BC), prayer itself takes the place of such physical sacrifice. This psalm was popular in Galilee, which was so geographically distant from the temple in Jerusalem.

Incense

We often understand prayer as a sort of incense because they both rise from the level of our human existence upwards toward the realm of God and both are judged as pleasing to God. Incense, however, not only symbolizes our own human actions but also was viewed by the ancient Israelites as the mysterious place where God dwelled. Immaterial and upward in motion, the incense signified the actual presence of God in the temple: fragrant and pleasing, immaterial yet real and associated with holiness. After the dedication of the tent (Exod 40:35), the "cloud" filled the sanctuary and no one was able to enter out of respectful "fear" of God. To understand our own prayer by analogy as a place where God dwells is a powerful and humbling insight.

GOSPEL

Mark 10:13-16

Whoever does not accept the Kingdom of God like a child will not enter it.

Literary Link

Perhaps the mention of divorce in the prior day's gospel passage (vv. 2-12) led to the logical reflection by Mark on the role and importance of children. One could say that the participation of a disciple in the passion prediction has consequences for one's attitude toward marriage and children.

Children

To suggest, as Jesus did in his teaching, that the kingdom of God belonged to children (v. 14) is to lift them up as models for anyone desiring to be part and partner in God's kingdom. The imagination of children is always open to things unseen. They are curious, helpful, inquisitive, and never afraid to be dependent on others. Such are the fundamental characteristics of kingdom people, eager to be instruments of God's sovereign action in the world, not obstacles.

Preventing the Children's Approach to Jesus

It may be helpful to recognize the three levels of history in the gospels as taught by the church: (1) the words and deeds of Jesus, (2) the preaching of the apostles about those words and deeds after the resurrection, and (3) the way in which each individual evangelist chose to paint the portrait of Jesus in a given gospel. I am sure that Jesus welcomed children during his earthly ministry, and fondly teased and taught them about God. While reporting that earlier reality, the passage may also be addressing an early controversy about whether children should be admitted to baptism and thus to a sacramental relationship with Jesus the Christ. The insistence of Jesus that they not be prevented from approaching him (v. 14) could have become the scriptural basis for infant baptism in an age when primarily adults entered the community. The entire household was welcome, children and adults, even if the former were not yet able to express a profession of personal faith.

Saturday of the Seventh Week in Ordinary Time

Monday of the Eighth Week in Ordinary Time

First Reading (Year I)

Sirach 17:20-24

Turn again to the Most High,
and learn the judgments of God.

Return

These five verses represent a strong and clear invitation to all who have gone astray, slipped into sin, or lost hope (v. 20). The customary Hebrew word for "conversion/penance" is *teshuvah*, namely, "return," the same word used in modern parlance for a return ticket on a train, bus, or airplane. The Greek word *metanoia*, by way of comparison, means "conversion/penance" in the sense of changing one's mind and thinking outside of customary categories. The passage speaks of divine compassion and encouragement and the strong dislike of God for sin (but not for the sinner). The passage would be perfect for a penitential rite!

Way Back: God's Work

Of special importance is the statement (v. 20) that God provides a way back for the penitent. This is God's work, not ours, in the sense that once a person experiences and expresses sorrow, God is the one to help the individual to reenter the community and to find his or her own place again. If a sinner feels overwhelmed by the prospect of dealing with the offended family members or neighbors, like the Prodigal Son (Luke 15), God's work is to help those losing hope and to bring them back again. This is very consoling. It is also found in the sentiments of Francis Thompson's *Hound of Heaven*.

Praise from the Living

It would seem from this passage that the author of the book did not have the strong or clear belief in the resurrection of the dead. The Pharisees of the first century, however, were committed to belief in the resurrection. Those who are deceased can offer no praise (vv. 22, 23), says the author. He stresses that the living stand among those whose prayers of praise rise to God. Because of the death and resurrection of Jesus, which made resurrection central to our faith, we have a different conviction.

Antiphon (Year I)

Psalm 32:11a

Let the just exult and rejoice in the Lord.

A Psalm of Repentance

Psalm 32, as noted earlier in this volume, is the second of the famous seven "penitential psalms" and a favorite of both Augustine and Luther. It offers a most fitting response to the initial portion of the reading from Sirach and continues his theme of our need to acknowledge our own sinfulness. The verses announce blessing to the forgiven, whose jubilant gratitude fills their hearts. The refrain (v. 11) makes that very clear.

The Just

The refrain (v. 11) describes the forgiven and now just (*tsadiq*) members of God's people. It is a favorite word in biblical tradition to describe, not merely one who pays all debts fully and promptly, but one who stands in right relationship to all things and all creatures. A different word is used elsewhere in this psalm response, namely, *hasid*, the completely faithful human partner to a covenanted God. Both terms, each with its own shade of meaning, can be used as adjectives expressing holiness. Those who are mutually responsible for each other—and who are properly related to their world—rejoice in the Lord.

Monday of the Eighth Week in Ordinary Time

First Reading (Year II)

1 Peter 1:3-9

Although you have not seen him, you love him; you rejoice with an indescribable and glorious joy.

The First Letter of Saint Peter

Although the Petrine authorship of this letter is controverted, it represents an address written in Rome (called Babylon, 5:13) to scattered Gentile communities. It may be helpful to understand the entire epistle as an extended baptismal homily with instructions for the practical day-to-day life of the baptized who live as aliens in a culture very different from their own. If written by Peter himself, the date could be close to his martyrdom under Nero (AD 64–67); otherwise it may be from a later time in the first century.

Baptismal Themes

This letter includes many references to baptism from the very first greeting, "a new birth to a living hope" (v. 3), with a further allusion to a heavenly and imperishable inheritance through the resurrection. If we begin by listing all the allusions to baptism in this expression of praise for God, we will have caught the spirit of the entire letter. The greeting (v. 2) includes references to the three Persons of the Trinity and subtly echoes the formula of baptism.

Real but Invisible

Love for someone as yet unseen (v. 8) by believers suggests that the supernatural gift of faith enables a person to make a full and personal commitment without the physical evidence normally required for human conclusions and promises. Without seeing, we can believe. The Nicene Creed acknowledges God as creator of "all things visible and invisible." Theologians sometimes suggest that the very structure of our minds is transformed by the grace of divine life at baptism.

Trials

The inevitable stress of trials (v. 6) is described as an opportunity for purification (v. 7). The baptized person will live amid people of very different values, and be asked from time to time to give witness to the teachings of Jesus the Christ. Christian witness may cost something because it is not always welcome. This reading invites both proclaimer and listener to see all the troubles of his or her own life in that same context, as occasions for purification. As such the trials and difficulties can become steps into a life of praise for the God who grants salvation (v. 9).

Antiphon (Year II)

Psalm 111:5

The Lord will remember his covenant for ever.

Remembering

In the language and thinking of the Scriptures, remembering is more than revisiting some cherished intellectual images stored in one's memory. To remember is to actually make those events once again present in the here and now. If the Lord remembers his covenant (v. 5), as stated in this refrain, he makes it present and recreates the covenantal relationship anew. All the effects of the covenant, as listed in the initial verses of Psalm 111, are renewed: sharing the company of the just (v. 1), food for the hungry (v. 5), a special inheritance (v. 6), and final deliverance from danger (v. 9). The psalm does not say that God eliminates the distress or anxiety, but simply promises that God will prevent long-term damage to those who love him.

Covenant

There is a temptation to consider the covenant mentioned in this refrain (v. 5) as a sort of agreement that God promises to uphold. In fact the essence of covenant is the relationship itself, not the things held in common upon which the agreement is based. Even if that relationship is weakened by human sin, God is committed to remember the covenant and to keep the relationship alive forever. At the same time, God respects our freedom and will not impose friendship upon us.

GOSPEL

Mark 10:17-27

Go, sell what you have and give to the poor.

Literary Link

The third consequence of the second passion prediction (9:30-31), after one's attitude to marriage (vv. 2-12) and to children (vv. 13-16), is a distinctive "kingdom approach" to the question of personal wealth (vv. 17-27).

Inheriting Eternal Life

By Mark's use of "inherit" (v. 17) the man's question is well phrased, for it indicates that the life of the next age is a gift that we cannot earn by our own actions. As one may recall, this was an issue at the very center of the bitter sixteenth-century discussions between Lutherans and Catholics. Obedience to the commandments (v. 19) is the result of God's grace, not the means of obtaining friendship with God! After careful modern dialogue, both groups recognized that they hold this truth in common: a sinner's initial reconciled friendship with God was not the result of any good works by the human being. Justification and reconciliation are only due to God's grace, which, once received, is able to produce the good works that signal a share in the new creation through Christ.

Selling Off Possessions for the Poor

The eventual sign of life in the kingdom is the generous gift of one's possessions to those in need (v. 21). It is not physical poverty that in itself pleases God, however, but an utter dependence upon God, not one's self. Such an attitude, when combined with care for the needy, even to the point of self-sacrifice, represents the way a person of the kingdom lives life. To say it differently, being a disciple means living in solidarity with others, especially the needy. Nothing we may call "mine" is really an exclusively personal possession. Only with such an attitude toward our possessions can we be perfected and brought into complete discipleship! "The totally self-sufficient person is sub-human" (Desmond Tutu).*

Children

When Jesus is described as having called his disciples "children" (v. 24), we are reminded that the word "child" has two levels of significance in New Testament communities. First, the word obviously refers to those who are young in a chronological sense, and viewed as minors in their families; in Judaism this status remains approximately up to the age of twelve, when Judaism celebrates the bar/bat mitzvah of a young person. Secondarily, however, the term can also signify those who, though technically adults in chronological age, are still immature in the faith. Jesus implies the latter when he addresses his disciples as "children." Similarly, an "elder" is someone mature in faith, no matter what his chronological age.

* "The Truth and Reconciliation Process—Restorative Justice" (Third Longford Lecture, Church House, Westminster, February 16, 2004).

Tuesday of the Eighth Week in Ordinary Time

FIRST READING (YEAR I)

Sirach 35:1-12

To keep the law is a great oblation.

Obedience as Oblation

Jewish piety often described personal spiritual devotions and attitudes in terms of sacrificial worship, as if prayer and praise were equated with the physical actions of altar sacrifice. In an extended, though very real, sense, obedience is a sacrificial oblation (v. 1). The development of that terminology was more pronounced in areas like Galilee, which were located some distance from the temple in Jerusalem, or during the time when the temple lay in ruins after its destruction by the Babylonians in 587 BC. It is interesting to note that observing the commandments (v. 1) is called a specific type of sacrifice, namely, a "peace offering/*shelamim*" (v. 2), which has social implications. This sacrifice is shared in a meal distributed to all participants (the offering family, temple priests, and even God). It is not a holocaust that is destroyed as it is offered.

Generosity

The command not to appear before God "empty-handed" (v. 4) is very ancient (Exod 23:15; Deut 16:16). The offering of sacrificial gifts presumed the active participation of the entire community, each bringing to the worship something from his or her own possessions for the needs of the poor (v. 2) and for the upkeep of the temple altar (v. 5). The intention of the person who offers such gifts is crucial, however, because Sirach notes that God is not open to "bribes" (v. 11). Acceptable prayer should never be a subtle form of trying to bribe God into doing what we want. That would be commerce, not prayer!

ANTIPHON (YEAR I)

Psalm 50:23b

To the upright I will show the saving power of God.

Divine Judgment

The reading from Sirach was a reflection on prayer as worship. Psalm 50 was chosen by the Lectionary as a fitting response to that passage because the psalm recognizes God as Judge (v. 6) and acknowledges the positive blessings of ritual sacrifices and burnt offerings (v. 8). The response concludes with a citation from God's point of view: offering praise as sacrifice (v. 14) glorifies God (v. 23). Fulfilling one's vows (v. 14) and keeping one's promises is also a form of praise. In this way God is acknowledged as supreme.

The Upright

The refrain describes those who experience salvation as the "upright" (v. 23), literally, those who "keep to the path." They are called "upright" because of their willingness to walk straight and tall in life, without deviations and with clear attention to God's will. Those who persevere in such an attitude will experience God's full and final saving intervention. Thoughtful preaching is never hesitant to pause over a commonly used term such as "upright" and to explore its deeper meaning.

FIRST READING (YEAR II)

1 Peter 1:10-16

They prophesied about the grace that was to be yours; therefore, live soberly and set your hopes completely on the grace to be brought to you.

Prophetic Searching

Early Christians spent much time and energy reviewing the Scriptures and seeking clues to explain the "sufferings destined for Christ" (v. 11). In so doing they recognized that the ancient prophets of Israel had also in turn searched out the events of their times (v. 10) in an effort to understand what

God was doing in their day. Strictly speaking, prophets do not predict the future (or they would be called "*pre*phets"). Prophets speak about what God is doing in a more hidden fashion in their own day; they speak for God and in God's name. Seeking the will of God demands personal discernment and cannot be satisfied with mere mechanical repetition of spiritual bromides or platitudes. Sometimes only in retrospect do we realize a deeper meaning in what the ancient prophets spoke. They ended up serving future generations unknowingly.

Long-Term Ministry

Because the words of true prophets often receive initial opposition from the human community they address, time may be needed to sort out the impact of their message and to appreciate the full truth of their statements. For that reason, a prophet can be understood as speaking to distant future generations, and even to those who would announce the Good News (v. 12). Every prophet is called to serve a larger span of history than just his own, even though he primarily speaks to his own contemporary neighbors. Although he proclaims rather than predicts, the truth of his insights has an enduring validity. It is the often repeated pattern of divine actions that the true prophet declares. Each generation of Christians depends on the past and also speaks to the future.

Antiphon (Year II)

Psalm 98:2a

The Lord has made known his salvation.

Ends of the Earth

Once again, the psalm chosen as a liturgical response to this portion from the First Letter of Peter echoes the theme of the far reaches of God's activities. Just as a prophet's words may have an impact on future generations not his own, God's salvation reaches far beyond the people immediately visible. The objects of God's care for Israel also include those living at the ends of the earth (v. 3). God's vision is always immensely larger than our own. The psalm reminds us of that truth.

Making Known Salvation

The saving power of God in the lives of individuals and communities is not intended to remain secret. As the refrain reminds us, God makes his salvation known (v. 2). Even though the Gospel of Mark reports Jesus as repeatedly requesting silence about his cures (usually disobeyed!), scholars conclude that the silence was requested in order to give Jesus the opportunity to adjust and expand the thinking of his contemporaries. They erroneously expected a fully glorious and militarily triumphant Christ without suffering! More normally God's great saving deeds are intended to be proclaimed. The deeper sense of contemporary Catholic evangelization is not handing out brochures door-to-door or street-corner preaching, but the willingness to speak candidly about what God has done for all of us during our lives (v. 4).

Gospel

Mark 10:28-31

You will receive a hundred times as much persecution in this age, and eternal life in the age to come.

Literary Link

The rich man (only called "young" in Matthew 19:20) had been told to give all his possessions to the poor and then to follow Jesus (v. 21). Although the disciples had done so, he could not. Today's gospel teaching follows that command. Peter observed that he and his colleagues had done precisely that, and wondered "what's in it for them" (see v. 28)? The editorial catchphrase is the idea of "giving up everything" and becoming "perfected." The answer of Jesus became the occasion for yet another passion prediction (vv. 33-34).

Returns and Rewards

Perhaps out of selfishness, the disciples implicitly inquire what they will get out of such self-sacrificing generosity (v. 28). Giving up one level of physical community in the form of a human family is promised the reward and the blessing of membership in a new and different type of community. Disciples exchange their natural families for the companionship of like-minded people of the kingdom who hear the Gospel (v. 29) and wrap their lives around it. This conversation with Peter reflects an earlier moment when Jesus ignored his own natural family in order to focus on those who do the will of God and become his family (3:35).

"With Persecutions"

The off-handed addition of the eventual experience of "persecutions" (v. 30) certainly doesn't seem to a casual listener like much of a blessing or reward. Moreover, the way in which the initial summary introduction to the Lectionary text is phrased, that is, receiving "persecutions a hundred fold," seems awkward at best and not even consistent with the text itself. The promise doesn't sound like a very good deal at all, and hardly a blessing or reward! The fact of the matter, however, is that many people go through tough times and finally in retrospect come to understand that the difficulties were truly moments of grace and growth. One's motivation can be purified by hardship. Dependence on others rather than self alone can become a source of encouragement. The new community of the kingdom is more than enhancement; it includes the purifying element of a completely different and new set of values. Experiences of hardship, as the saints remind us, can become means to spiritual maturity in ways that material security and unchallenged faith cannot. This is a profound truth.

Follow Me!

Mere self-denial is not enough, because the second part of the invitation includes following Jesus (v. 26, acknowledged by Peter in v. 28). Turning from something includes turning toward something else! To follow is to imitate. The person and mission of Jesus become the all-consuming value and goal in life. This is true apprenticeship. It inevitably entails a reversal of first and last, turning our natural world and its values upside down.

Tuesday of the Eighth Week in Ordinary Time

Wednesday of the Eighth Week in Ordinary Time

First Reading (Year I)

Sirach 36:1, 4-5a, 10-17

The nations will know that there is no God but you.

A Prayer for God's Intervention

Recalling that this is a prayer to the God of the universe (v. 1) for the people of Israel places the passage in context. This is a prayer for mercy (v. 1), restoration (v. 10), and reward for those who have lived in hope (v. 15). True to the biblical perspective, the community exists prior to the individual members who only find their identity in their belonging to the group. Our modern individualism finds it difficult to understand that perspective. The prayer envisions that the nations who see God's providential care for Israel will be impressed and brought to religious obedience themselves as well (v. 1). This is a prayer for use on the occasion of national holidays because it reminds us that God's choices are not ends in themselves, but are always intended for the larger world.

A Prayer in Hard Times

There is a certain "it used to be better" flavor to this prayer because it prays for a repetition of the "deeds of old" (v. 14) and expresses a hope that prophetic hopes and dreams from an earlier age might now be proven true (v. 15) and finally come to fruition. Mere repetition of the past, however, would not be enough. The prayer asks for "new signs" and "new wonders" (v. 5).

Antiphon (Year I)

Sirach 36:1b

Show us, O Lord, the light of your kindness.

Mercy/Kindness

The Lectionary reading differs from the text of the revised New American Bible because it adds the insertion, "Look upon us, show us the light of your mercies" (v. 1), which becomes the refrain. Without the Hebrew text, which was only recently discovered, we are not able to discuss the theological niceties of the word that is translated as "mercies" (v. 1) in the Lectionary passage itself. We do know that any mercy granted by God to a nation in the face of its enemies must by definition be manifestly evident and visible, both to Israel and to the nations. By seeing the results of God's mercy the nations will know that there is no other God (v. 1).

First Reading (Year II)

1 Peter 1:18-25

You were ransomed with the precious Blood of Christ, as of a spotless unblemished Lamb.

Community Background

One should never forget that the "you" of most statements in the New Testament is a plural, not a singular, even if English grammatical usage does not reveal that precision. Such is the case at the very beginning of this passage (v. 18). Therefore the address is primarily to the entire community "ransomed . . . with the precious Blood of Christ" (v. 19), and to the individual only to the extent of his or her membership in the group. The passage encourages us to see one's entire parish community addressed and described by the hymn of praise for God's grace and favor. The plural is used eight times in this brief section of the letter.

Ransom/Redemption

The reading begins with the announcement that the community had been "ransomed from . . . futile conduct" (v. 18). Behind this statement about the process by which a baptized person is incorporated into the community is the ancient Semitic practice of redemption. A redeemer (*go'el* in Hebrew) is a next of kin with an obligation to restore an indentured relative to freedom within his or her family of origin after being forced into servitude by economic hard times. In Israel's religious practice every firstborn son is offered to God, and then "bought back" by a substitute offering (Exod 13:13). In this instance the price paid is the blood of Jesus. His action restores a person to family friendship with God. Once again individuals now share that gift by being "born anew" (v. 23) through baptism.

Fraternal Charity

The effect of such reincorporation into the community of the baptized is *philadelphia* (v. 22), genuine concern and affection for brothers and sisters. The newly baptized and all who live within the community of the baptized have the obligation to express that fraternal/sororal love "from a pure heart," namely, for the right reason. Doing so for personal gain or for the community's admiration is unworthy of one who has passed through death and entered the risen life, even in this world.

Antiphon (Year II)

Psalm 147:12a

Praise the Lord, Jerusalem.

Jerusalem

Following from the plural address used throughout the reading is a refrain from Psalm 147 that speaks to the city of Jerusalem and her entire community of residents, inviting them to praise God as a chorus (v. 12).

Wednesday of the Eighth Week in Ordinary Time

"Urban" Blessings

The reasons for such praise are precisely the needs and desires of any residential town or city: security and protection (v. 13) as well as peace and prosperity due to abundant harvests (v. 14). These are the very blessings for which gratitude is often expressed at the time of national holidays. They are among the blessings for which nations pray in more difficult times.

Gospel

Mark 10:32-45

Behold, we are going up to Jerusalem and the Son of Man will be handed over.

Literary Link

With increasing intensity Mark's gospel peppers this portion of the gospel dedicated to the mission of Jesus with reminders of his inevitable rejection, death, and eventual triumph. As noted earlier, the teaching occurs three times (8:31; 9:31; 10:33-34). This prediction brings the series to completion, and prepares, as was the case in the prior two predictions, for a special new teaching on true discipleship. The second prediction had been followed by an instruction on servanthood (9:35) and on children as models (vv. 36-37). The teaching after this third prediction returns to leadership as service (v. 43).

A Third Passion Prediction

The number three is the Semitic manner of speaking in the superlative, as in the Isaian hymn of "holy, holy, holy" (Isa 6:3). The importance of this teaching, therefore, cannot be overemphasized. It is the entire gospel in nuclear form. The three constant elements in these predictions are rejection (v. 33), suffering unto death, and resurrection (v. 34). Each is theologically important for the full sense of the mystery of the mission of Jesus for his people and for the world. The "paschal imperative" governed the life of Jesus, the lives of each of his followers, and his entire Mystical Body the church.

A Petition for Honor

The request of James and John (elsewhere spoken by their mother in Matthew 20:20) for places of preeminence at the final victory banquet is met by the insistence of Jesus regarding the necessity of prior suffering, metaphorically symbolized by sharing the cup (v. 38). That very gesture can be associated with the contemporary restored Catholic practice of communion under both species. In the words of one of the refrains from the eucharistic prayer, "When we eat this Bread and drink this Cup, we proclaim your Death, O Lord, until you come again."

Apostolic Rivalry

One cannot miss the existence of rivalry between the disciples (v. 41). Even these specially chosen ones continue to forget that they were chosen to be apprentices in how to serve the community, not dominate over it. This is not merely an isolated event in the history of the earthly ministry of Jesus but a spiritual plague that has afflicted the entire history of Catholic Christian leadership—and the communities they serve. The gospels never speak only of the ancient past. They also speak about us! That same social plague was a major concern of Paul to the Philippians (2:3ff.). Whatever our gifts or callings, we are partners, not rivals.

Thursday of the Eighth Week in Ordinary Time

First Reading (Year I)

Sirach 42:15-25

The glory of the Lord fills all his works.

The Works of God

If the passage of yesterday was an extended prayer for the nation, this portion of Sirach is a hymn of praise for all the works of God in the world of nature: the ability to create with a mere word (v. 15), the orderly rising of the sun (v. 16), the depths of the sea, and God's knowledge of the human mind and heart (v. 17)! Even the fleeting sparks of a fire's blaze (v. 23) are the results of divine creation! The list of God's works in material creation and all its beauty are almost beyond count! The reading invites us to add our own favorite moments and places.

Without Counselor

The passage insists that all God's works are performed by his solitary, supreme, and almighty power alone, without assistance, advice, or counsel (v. 22). This powerful and poetic expression of monotheism bears no small resemblance to the praises of the One God as found in poetry of the prophet Isaiah, and even in the Qur'an, the other great monotheistic religion in the family of Abraham. The Scriptures may at times speak of personified Wisdom as an instrument of creation, but God reigns supreme in every way!

Antiphon (Year I)

Psalm 33:6a

By the word of the Lord the heavens were made.

Community Acclamation

Accompanied by music, as evidenced by the references to instruments such as harps and lyres (v. 2), Psalm 33 is a fitting response of the entire community to the proclamation of God's work in creation (vv. 6, 9). The refrain (v. 6) echoes the reading's praise for God's almighty word and adds a generic list of his mighty deeds. Scholars tell us that Psalm 33 may well have been traditionally used in the annual covenant renewal festival each autumn. This would emphasize the fact that all of creation remained within God's care and concern, as emphasized by the covenant with Noah (Gen 9:10). As a community response in our Lectionary, the ancient hymn has been reclaimed for Catholic liturgical usage as we celebrate the Word!

Justice

It should be noted that the litany of material creation also includes the works of human justice (v. 5) as a work of creation. We can't help but praise God, even for the things people do; after all, God gives the strength, wisdom, and opportunity. As noted elsewhere, biblical "justice" extends beyond the mere repayment of debts. It includes living in right relationship to all the creatures of creation. There is a moral component to creation and eco-justice must be included whenever we acclaim the wonders around us. That also is the work of God.

First Reading (Year II)

1 Peter 2:2-5, 9-12

You are a chosen race, a royal priesthood,
so that you may announce the praises of him
who called you.

Living Stones

It may be helpful to be reminded of the community focus of this portion of Peter's letter, the fact that all of the individuals are stones for the entire communal edifice, which in turn acts as a priestly agent in offering sacrifices of praise (v. 5). Perhaps they are living (v. 3) in the sense that they spontaneously conform themselves like coral reefs into the right fit with their neighbor's strengths and weaknesses. Each stone is not like the rigid field stones that never change except by erosion, and that must be cemented together with plaster in order to become strong walls of security and stability.

Metaphors

The fluid mixture of metaphors from human infancy (v. 2) to living stones (v. 3) to priestly action (v. 5) can remind us of the manner in which images are often heaped up in prophetic speech or spiritual exhortation, one on top of another, in an effort (ultimately inadequate and vain) to describe the transcendent nature of the community called into being by a fully transcendent God. A religious tradition that lives with the ancient Jewish caution about making of material images of God must find release in verbal efforts of imagination and poetry. God and God's community ultimately remain beyond human speech, no matter how hard we try to find useful images.

ANTIPHON (YEAR II)

Psalm 100:2c

Come with joy into the presence of the Lord.

Joy

We know the difference between joyful noise like that of children bursting energetically into play at recess time and mournful sound like that of a bagpipe at a funeral. We know the difference between liturgy celebrated flawlessly but mechanically and worship filled with a spirit of joy. Joy lifts up and unites people because it is contagious. It is said that the French spiritual writer Léon Bloy (among others) insisted that "joy is the infallible sign of God's presence." It is contagious and never superficial because it comes from a deep sense of gratitude for all the blessings of life, and possesses a spirit of love for those around us who conspire to make life itself a blessing. This type of profound spiritual joy as a gift of God's spirit can even coexist with human heartaches.

Presence

The Hebrew phrase that we translate as "presence" is literally "faces/*panim*" (v. 2). The term recognizes the various emotional realities that comprise a personality and that sum up that individual's shifting response to the many circumstances in daily life. They coalesce to comprise a person. This refrain invites people to gather in the invisible but very real presence of a God who lives in constant interaction with his chosen people. To enter into worship, as Psalm 100 invites, is to do so with gladness (v. 2), thanksgiving, and praise (v. 4). When we are joyful, God is pleased!

GOSPEL

Mark 10:46-52

Master, I want to see.

Literary Link

The arrival of Jesus and his disciples at Bethsaida (8:22) began their journey to Jerusalem, which they finally entered (11:1). During that entire time Jesus constantly attempted to provide instruction regarding his person and his mission, together with its implications for their lives and their work. The section began with the two-phased healing of a blind man (8:22-26) and now concludes with the story of blind Bartimaeus (10:46-52). The two "healing bookends," as it were, may also be a metaphor for the persistent lack of understanding on the part of the disciples.

Mercy

The Greek petition of blind Bartimaeus is the very familiar "have pity/*eleison*" (vv. 47-48), which was in turn the customary translation of the Hebrew *hesed*, namely, covenantal concern. As a result, the plea is more than an anguished call for pity because of desperate circumstances. Rather, the call is a reminder of a mutual obligation that one covenant partner must have toward another who had fallen into distress and need. In this case, and in our celebration of the Eucharist, it becomes a rather bold reminder to God of being somehow obligated by his own divine promise and fidelity to pay attention to this human person in need and to respond in the most helpful fashion.

A Crowd Transformed

The first effect of the summons of Jesus is upon the crowd who was traveling with Jesus on the way out of Jericho. From a group intent on silencing the blind beggar (v. 48), they changed into agents of encouragement (v. 49). From a group determined to maintain distance between Jesus and the blind beggar in need, they became people equally desirous to bring him into personal contact and conversation with the healing power of Jesus. The crowd listened to Jesus and changed, as must every congregation gathered for the daily celebration of the Eucharist. The congregation should be transformed into agents of care and reconciliation.

A Cloak Cast Aside

The cloak spread out before the seated beggar was the receptacle of alms and the means of the beggar's material sustenance. To cast it aside (v. 50) was to forgo his entire normal way of survival and suddenly to depend on Jesus. He abandoned one way of making a living to stand utterly and confidently before this popular rabbi from Nazareth. In his own way this beggar, who dismissed what little he had, became the antithesis of the rich man of Monday's gospel passage a few verses earlier who was unable to give away his many possessions in order to be a perfect follower of Jesus (10:22).

The Desire to See

In response to the question of Jesus, "What do you want me to do for you?" the beggar said, "I want to see" (v. 51). The Greek is more nuanced, because *anablepso* means to "look up." Anyone afflicted by poor eyesight is forced to look constantly and carefully at the ground in order to avoid tripping or falling. Bartimaeus asks for freedom from fear in order to be able to look up and around, and to see the bigger picture of life! All of us are limited to our own needs and concerns, and for that reason we should make the beggar's prayer our own every day, to seek the gift of "looking up," that is, of seeing everything around us in a new way.

Thursday of the Eighth Week in Ordinary Time

Friday of the Eighth Week in Ordinary Time

FIRST READING (YEAR I)

Sirach 44:1, 9-13

Our ancestors were merciful, and their name will live for generations.

Praise of Ancestors

These few verses introduce an extended ode of seven chapters of praise for the holy heroes from Israel's long history (v. 1) as God's chosen people. Many others were in fact forgotten by the passage of time. There were special figures, however, revered for their witness in their time and for the enduring example that they offered to subsequent generations. Every occasion when a parish congregation gathers for Eucharist, they should do so mindful of those figures of light and love who had gone before them! The men and women who occupied the very same pews are now among the cloud of heavenly witnesses. They are mindful of us as we are of them.

Merciful

Curiously enough, the word "merciful" is found in the introductory phrase for this reading, but not in the text itself! By the very fact that the final portion of our reading makes reference of the enduring covenant (v. 12), one could presume that the type of mercy exhibited by these heroes of faith was that of covenantal concern, namely, the mercy of *hesed*, for God and neighbor. Faithful and generous to the needs of others, they became remembered for all generations.

ANTIPHON (YEAR I)

Psalm 149:4a

The Lord takes delight in his people.

Liturgical Invitation

Psalm 149 is a joyous and lighthearted welcome to communal worship. The initial verse of the psalm encourages singing (v. 1) and praising with music; the final verses suggest that the same people should continue in the same spirit after they have returned home from pilgrimage and rest on their couches (v. 5). It could well be a Sabbath song celebrating the joy that endures throughout the "rest" of that special day.

The Lord's Delight

The refrain (v. 4) speaks of God rather than the people's spirit in worship, and makes a point of insisting that God himself is delighted by joyful worship. To acknowledge God as not merely pleased but "delighted" is to recognize the source of divine protection and blessings. The image of a delighted, laughing, joyous, and contented God is perhaps to imagine a beaming grandparent, proud and pleased with a family gathering! The poetry of the psalms is filled with the attribution of human emotions and experiences to the exalted God. They all fall short, however, of the utter transcendence of our God.

FIRST READING (YEAR II)

1 Peter 4:7-13

Be good stewards of God's varied grace.

Good Stewards

The Greek word for steward is *oikonomos*, someone in charge of "the law of the house," namely, the running of a household with responsibility for material possessions not one's own and with the duty to see that the welfare of all is served wisely and well. The diligent management of the family's resources, always with an eye to the health and happiness of family members, is paramount. That same dutiful attention is encouraged for spiritual gifts as well because each gift (v. 10) somehow belongs to the entire family. This letter reminds every leader and member of the Christian communities scattered throughout the known world of the day that they are accountable as "stewards" for the faith, hope, and charity of all! A steward is asked to make sure that every gift, be it of preaching (v. 11) or serving, is exercised properly for God's glory (v. 12). A steward is to be concerned with "quality control."

Trial by Fire

The image of fire (v. 12) may be exaggerated for the sake of making a point, but even the best managed community should presume the inevitable occurrence of difficulties and hardships. Whatever their source or nature, they are elevated in the reading to the big picture and described as a share in the sufferings of Christ (v. 13). Hardships purify the spiritual lives of the community members and remind the membership of their need to depend upon God and each other! Leadership and service each have their own burdens, blessings, and rewards.

ANTIPHON (YEAR II)

Psalm 96:13b

The Lord comes to judge the earth.

A Kingship Psalm

The response to Peter's admonition that community members are stewards of everything associated with the community's life and work is taken from Psalm 96, a song of praise for the Lord's work in creation and for God's supereminent exaltation over all creation (v. 11). The psalm provides the bigger picture into which every community is invited to exist. Any steward is an agent of the living God and ultimately remains in place by God's authority alone.

Friday
of the Eighth Week
in Ordinary Time

Judging the Earth

The entire earth is somehow related to the work of each community because the God of each community is the Lord of all creation (v. 11); consequently, there is a time of judgment (v. 13) and accountability as well! The biblical notion of judgment, however, includes the right to intervene. The judges of ancient Israel did more than issue decisions. They were powerful figures who rose up by God's invitation and power to change dangerous situations into times of safety, security, and prosperity. By acknowledging the Lord as "Judge" of the earth (v. 13), the psalm invites the entire people to be open to God's way of handling history and of directing the events that fill the days and years of our lives. This is an acknowledgment of God's action, not merely his words.

GOSPEL

Mark 11:11-26

My house will be called a house of prayer for all peoples. Have faith in God.

Literary Link

Curiously, the last verse (v. 26), though numbered in the citation, is not included in the reading because it is not found in the best ancient manuscripts: "But if you do not forgive, neither will your Father which is in heaven forgive your trespasses" (King James Version). Note that the very first action of Jesus upon entering Jerusalem is the purification of the temple (vv. 15-17).

Cleansing of the Temple

Jesus had entered the temple the evening before and viewed the situation (v. 11), and only after pondering and praying over what he saw did he return the following morning (v. 15) to confront the merchants and money changers. This was not an impulse but an intentional and deliberate action on his part—a prophetic action, if you will, that signaled the judgment of God, which would culminate in the temple's eventual destruction by the Romans in AD 70. The Synoptic Gospels, presumably written after that destruction, place this cleansing at the end of the public ministry of Jesus, almost as a final confrontation of Jesus with the religious authorities in Jerusalem. The judgment of Jesus, as Mark recorded it, was that the "house of prayer" had become a place of dishonesty and injustice by the actions of the merchants who are named "thieves" (v. 17). In John's gospel, however, the event is described at the beginning of the public ministry (2:13-17) and the complaint is not dishonesty so much as the commercial buying and selling of a bazaar, however honest.

Cursing of the Fig Tree

This is a troublesome passage because at first glance it seems to depict Jesus as impetuously piqued over no figs, even if out of season (v. 14). The poor fig tree is condemned for what was not naturally possible or even rightfully expected. Any fourth grader would say, "It's just not fair!" It is, however, the only miracle of Jesus in Jerusalem, and is presented as an action of divine power on his part, possibly a symbolic signal of the consequences of not providing the fruits of penance at the time of judgment. That day was a prophetic moment, signaling the imperative need for readiness at the time of divine visitation, no matter what our human schedule may be. It is a story of divine urgency, like the child who says, "Here I come, ready or not!" God will be God in God's time.

Mountain-Moving Faith

The danger of taking this account too literally is the possibility of thinking that everything depends on the level of our human faith alone (v. 24), and that astonishing miracles would happen if we had more faith. In other words, the fault is ours. God is the one, however, who is in charge of the natural order of the universe. Moving mountains (v. 23) is not within our normal human range of responsibility. Moreover, prayer is not only petition (v. 24) but also standing before the mystery of God, and being changed into God's view of the world, rather than changing God's mind about what we think we need and want! Offering forgiveness to others is one indication of our inner change (v. 26). Just because we ask never means that it will happen, no matter how insistent our request or demand. God remains in charge!

Saturday of the Eighth Week in Ordinary Time

FIRST READING (YEAR I)

Sirach 51:12cd-20

Give me wisdom and I will give you glory.

Wisdom the Teacher

In this, the final chapter of the book, Sirach returns to his hymn of praise for the way in which personified Wisdom became his beloved teacher (v. 16). After ardent and eager prayer for Wisdom, he visited her house and opened her gate (v. 19), almost like a young student going to school. The Hebrew text differs at times from the Greek, and includes an extended alphabetical hymn not reflected in this liturgical passage, inviting the reader to give thanks for such a gift. This Lectionary version is an example of the fruits of scholarly research since 1976, when the *imprimatur* was first given to the New American Bible.

Preparation for Wisdom

Although the liturgical text as found in the Lectionary only says "in cleanness I attained to her," the original NAB 1976 translation added, "I purified even the soles of my feet" (v. 20). Perhaps the point is a reference to an effort to be respectful when entering the home of Wisdom, almost like Moses taking off his shoes at the burning bush. Wisdom is holy and being in her presence requires physical and spiritual preparation and respect. Byzantine Catholic liturgy intones an admonition prior to the daily reading of the gospel: "Wisdom. Be attentive!"

ANTIPHON (YEAR I)

Psalm 19:9ab

The precepts of the Lord give joy to the heart.

Creation and Revelation

Psalm 19 is a combination of two very different poems. The first (vv. 1-6) speaks vividly of material creation's ability to speak of God's glory. The second (vv. 7-14), which has been chosen by the Lectionary, praises all the types of instruction and teaching that express God's will: law, decree, precepts, command, and ordinances. Each has its own nuance and original context, but all celebrate the importance of attending to God's will above all else. The psalm echoes the reading pointedly.

Source of Happiness

Many responses might be given to a question such as, what makes you happy? The psalm insists that among all the material gifts of food, friendship, comfort, and even social acclaim, one should acknowledge that obedience to the expressed will of God is paramount for the happiness of a spiritually mature person. This is the sense of the refrain (v. 9), which not only lists a special type of instruction but also lifts up the deep joyful response of those who are compliant with God's requests.

FIRST READING (YEAR II)

Jude 17, 20b-25

To the one who is able to keep you from stumbling and to present you unblemished and exultant in the presence of his glory.

The Letter of Saint Jude

This brief letter of a single chapter comprised of twenty-five verses is presumably not written by the apostle but by the relative cited in Mark 6:3 as locally known, and wondering about the origin of the wisdom and authority of Jesus. The letter warns strongly against proponents of false freedom and sexual licentiousness. It ends with the glorious doxology as expressed in this reading. This is the only time the Letter of Jude is included in the Lectionary.

Admonitions

The first portion of the letter, which is not included in the reading, warns against falling into the same behavior as those who live with unacceptable sexual freedom, and gives directions for confronting their behavior. The Lectionary's portion of the reading, however, is the classic teaching of avoidance of the occasion of sin, and the strategies for confronting those who have already been ensnared by such temptations: mercy for those who are wavering (v. 22) and efforts to reach out to the fallen (v. 23).

Doxology

This final hymn of praise (vv. 24-25) for God who is both Protector and Savior concludes with a litany of sublime attributes for the God whose grace assures full and final perseverance into the next age. Such praise is both the duty of followers of Jesus and the means of protecting oneself against the seduction of sin. Pausing often during the course of the day, whether at home or at work, with an expression of praise for God is fine habit to develop!

Antiphon (Year II)

Psalm 63:2b

My soul is thirsting for you, O Lord my God.

Soul

This refrain is the classic example of why it is helpful to remember that the Hebrew word *nephesh*, often translated as "soul" (v. 2), fundamentally refers to the throat, where thirst is most vividly experienced. This reference is not to the arid climate in which the person may be living but to the desperate spiritual yearning for God that a person may feel at certain times in life! For those who feel very distant from the presence of God, this refrain aptly describes the desperate longing that only the profoundly isolated individual can experience.

Communion Sacrifice

The psalm's references to food and drink (v. 6) seem to have in mind the "communion sacrifices" of temple worship, namely, *shelamim* (often translated as "peace offerings"), which described a familial offering from which human participants receive portions for a banquet. Rich food is offered and then shared as a reminder of a renewed bond between God and other members of the covenanted community. Much of this psalm reflects that type of worship. In the context of covenant, it is understandable that the reference to "kindness" (v. 4) is *hesed*, the mutual concern of partners for each other. The background makes the spiritual and physical thirst of individuals very obvious. From earliest centuries, Christians have applied this psalm to our hunger for the Eucharist.

Gospel

Mark 11:27-33

By what authority are you doing these things?

Literary Link

After the cleansing of the temple (vv. 15-17), Jesus was confronted by the religious authorities of the city with a loaded question. No matter how he answered, his reply could be twisted into something problematic and dangerous (v. 18). Jesus was clever enough to use a similar technique and posed a question of authority that they could not answer without creating equal problems for themselves! There are six controversies reported by Mark for the work of Christ's third day in Jerusalem. The first is this question of authority.

John and Jesus

Throughout the Gospel of Mark we find a parallelism between these two figures. Although each is different, both exhibit the general profile of a prophet whose deeds are inspired by God and whose actions are signs of God at work. One purified the people for God's presence (John); the other heralded the kingdom/sovereign action of God at work (Jesus). By definition a prophetic sign is charged with power, and people see it as the actual beginning of the divine action signified. The entire lives of both were prophetic actions. The mission of Jesus begins with that of John and builds upon it. The Gospel of Luke presents them as cousins; Mark simply shows the interrelatedness of their respective missions. In fact the works of all believers are also interrelated and bound together within the larger picture of God at work in our world!

Authority

The same people who were present for the first passion prediction of Jesus (8:31) now return in the temple precincts to question his authority for the prior day's cleansing actions. They intend to trap him into claiming some divine legitimacy, but he avoids the dilemma by a counterquestion regarding the actions of John and by astutely laying a trap of his own. If they are unable to acknowledge or deny the divine authority of John, they cannot charge Jesus' claim of divine authority as a religious blasphemy. Once again, by way of background, the three most common types of human authority are those based upon knowledge, experience, or deputation. All fall within the authority out of which Jesus lives and works. Asking which type of authority each of the morning worshipers might possess could be helpful for their further reflection during the day.

Saturday of the Eighth Week in Ordinary Time

Monday of the Ninth Week in Ordinary Time

FIRST READING (YEAR I)

Tobit 1:3; 2:1a-8

Tobit walked on the paths of truth and righteousness.

The Book of Tobit

Written in the second century BC, this religious novel describes the life of a wealthy Israelite deported to the city of Nineveh after the Assyrian conquest of the northern kingdom in 721 BC. Although literarily retrojecting the tale to seven centuries earlier, it is filled with teachings about true religious piety expected of Israelites living amid the Hellenistic paganism of nations conquered by Alexander the Great. Tobit's son Tobiah is sent to collect a debt, unknowingly guided by the disguised archangel Raphael the Healer. On the way he acquires a wife and obtains the means for healing his blinded elderly father. The Lectionary devotes six days to this popular story from the deuterocanonical books, original Aramaic and Hebrew portions of which were found in Qumran Cave IV.

The Family Name

The names of both Tobit and his son Tobiah are variations of the Hebrew word *tob*, "good." The term introduces us to a dynasty of genuine religious goodness. What a grace when such a characteristic can mark the intergenerational reality of any family! Because the activities of the family leaders are devout and praiseworthy in every way, the tale was undoubtedly catechetical in purpose. True goodness always includes a moral component. Do our names have any meaning? What do they ask of us?

Piety under Siege

The tale of Tobit is projected backwards in time from the Hellenists when the work was written to the earlier exile under the hated Assyrian domination (eighth century BC). Because of the similarity of life under persecution in both ages, the story's location is the capital city of Nineveh, in today's northern Iraq. The story, therefore, also provided motivation for fidelity to the law of charity (burying the dead) for people at the actual time of the story's composition in the second century BC. The latter was also a time of dreadful persecution under the Hellenistic royal Ptolemies who forbade possession of the Torah, observance of the Sabbath, and circumcision under the pain of death. How often the corporal works of mercy (like burying the dead, v. 4) can become sources for mockery or even persecution, rather than objects of admiration. Mockery can even come from coreligionists and family (v. 8).

Charity toward the Living and Dead

In this reading we have two of the corporal works of mercy, feeding the hungry (2:2) and burying the dead (v. 4). These actions, even under the threat of severe punishment, are presented as model behavior for the faithful Jew in exile. These two corporal works of mercy have been inherited from Judaism and are recommended for Christians as well. Often we relegate these ministries to others, for example, to the Saint Vincent de Paul Society for feeding the hungry or to the state for burying the unclaimed deceased poor, but it remains our Christian concern as well. Visitation of wakes for friends is a spiritual as well as a social duty. This is a providential introduction to the penitential rite for the day's Eucharist.

ANTIPHON (YEAR I)

Psalm 112:1b

Blessed the man who fears the Lord.

Psalm 112: A Faithful Person

Psalm 112's praise for the generosity (v. 3), mercy (v. 4), and justice (v. 5) of the faithful person is a fitting compliment to Psalm 111's praise for God that precedes it numerically and theologically. Both begin with successive letters of the Hebrew alphabet, and seem designed by the same composer as a pair. Although the utterly transcendent majesty of God remains infinitely supreme, there is the shadow of similarity between God and the lives of the blessed person (v. 1). The psalm promises that the just person will be remembered forever.

Practical "Fear"

Like the day's reading from the book of Tobit, to which these verses are a liturgical response, reverential fear of God is very practical, and includes mercy (v. 4) and lending to the needy (v. 5). Concern and care for those in need stand together with prayers and devotions as signs of true religious piety. The psalm's portrait of a just person is a reflection of the profile of Tobit in the reading.

FIRST READING (YEAR II)

2 Peter 1:2-7

God has bestowed on us the precious and very great promises, so that through them you might come to share in the divine nature.

Second Letter of Peter

Probably written by an unknown author at the beginning of the second century AD, this letter, literarily attributed to Peter for the sake of claiming authority, deals with false teachers, the misunderstanding of Pauline doctrine, and the pastoral challenge of the delay of the Lord's return (Parousia).

Knowledge

Monday of the Ninth Week in Ordinary Time

This reading insists on the importance of "knowledge of God and of Jesus our Lord" (v. 2) for growth in grace. At the time Christians were confronted by the beginnings of the heresy of Gnosticism, namely, salvation through secret knowledge revealed to the specially illuminated. Against that background the letter recommends instead the type of knowledge that results in humble awe before God's promises (v. 4), rather than the knowledge that is self-centered, arrogant, and proud.

Moral Guidance

The final portion of this passage (vv. 5-7) describes the practical effects of true knowledge in the lives of Christians: virtue (v. 5), self-control (v. 6), perseverance, devotion, mutual affection (v. 7) among community members, and the fullness of genuine love. The Hebrew sense of the verb "know" stretches beyond mere intellectual information to include care and concern. If we truly know someone or something, we cherish the object of our knowledge and submit ourselves to service rather than domination. We care about what we know.

ANTIPHON (YEAR II)

Psalm 91:2b

In you, my God, I place my trust.

Trust

The trust recommended in this psalm refrain (v. 2) is directed toward the person of God, not to our mere human strengths or abilities alone. The refrain is a very fitting response to the reading from Second Peter, which stresses humble knowledge before God. A constant theme throughout all of Scripture is the need to trust in God, not merely in our own skills or experience.

Dwelling in God's Shadow

The actual verses cited in the psalm response describe the experience of dwelling under God's shadow (v. 1) and shelter as the source of true trust and confidence. Those who acknowledge God's name (hear "person and power") are assured of a response to prayer (v. 15), deliverance, the gift of a long life, and ultimately salvation (v. 16).

GOSPEL

Mark 12:1-12

They seized the beloved son, killed him, and threw him out of the vineyard.

Literary Link

The third day of Holy Week contains six controversies, the second of which is the parable of the workers in the vineyard (12:1-12). It was directed to the chief priests, scribes, and elders (11:27). Mark presents the week as one of escalating confrontation with the authorities in Jerusalem.

Hard Work and Invested Energy

In the rocky land of Judea the establishment of a vineyard is very hard work, including the effort of protecting the grapes from wandering sheep or goats, terracing hillsides to protect precious soil from erosion, and chipping wine presses out of the native rock (v. 2)! This background for the parable prepared the hearers for the legitimate expectation of the owner to some share in the harvest from the tenants to whom he has leased the field. This symbol of God is no absentee landlord! The audience was certainly familiar with Isaiah's "song of the vineyard" (5:1-6), which spoke of God's hard work in preparing Israel as his "chosen vineyard"! The original song of Isaiah complained about a harvest of nothing except bitter grapes. In this parable Jesus changes the focus of the parable from the bad harvest to the bad workers.

Accountability

The original purpose of Mark's parable was to admonish the religious leadership in Jerusalem and to remind them of the inevitability of being called to account for their leadership (v. 2). The lack of faith among the people reflected their leaders' infidelity. Their leaders, therefore, stood under special divine judgment for their own misdeeds as well as for the sins of those they had been sent to serve and guide. Similarly in subsequent ages every single person in the world, not merely the leaders of ancient Israel, has been the recipient of some area of responsibility delegated by a God who expects accountability and results. We cannot hear this parable without asking ourselves, What do we "have"? What is expected of us by God? How will we be held accountable? The gospel is always also about us!

Stewardship

All the things that we claim as possessions are in fact on lease from a God (v. 1) who continues to claim radical divine ownership, no matter what our deeds on pieces of paper may indicate. This not only includes the material possessions in our attics, closets, basements, and garages but also physical health, intellectual abilities, friendships, and anything that others might admire about us. In the last analysis, it all belongs to God who will ask for an accounting.

The Beloved Son

The final purpose of this powerful parable as reflected in the gospels was to go beyond the question of accountability and to focus on the fate of the beloved son (v. 6) who was sent by God to obtain God's portion of the harvest. This parable, therefore, is christological and includes reference to the tragic murder of Jesus by the political/religious authorities of Jerusalem (v. 8). It lifts up again the theme of the three passion predictions (8:31; etc.) at the beginning of the disputes of the final week. Note that Mark's description of the son's fate, that is, being seized, killed, and thrown out of the vineyard (v. 8), is contrasted with the sequence as reported by Matthew 21:39 and Luke 20:15, who both transpose the actions into "thrown out and killed," thus making the final form of their parable more reflective of the actual events of the crucifixion when Jesus died outside the city walls. Mark's wording was original, and the others were modified to match history.

Tuesday of the Ninth Week in Ordinary Time

First Reading (Year I)

Tobit 2:9-14

I was deprived of eyesight.

Eyesight Woes

The slightly humorous explanation of the origin of Tobit's cataracts (v. 10) offers an opportunity to pray for people afflicted with eye diseases. The reference also provides an occasion to note the easy slippage from problems in the arena of the physical to the lack of moral insight embodied in the argument between Tobit and Anna. They were both blind, but in different ways. Moreover, a person's emotional stress often leads to family arguments, as illustrated in this story.

False Judgment and Anger

Tobit's presumption in his blindness led him to false judgment about his wife's actions and the very unfair accusation of her lack of honesty (v. 13). Anna's weaving work was the cottage industry of the day that enabled women to be viewed as economic agents and shrewd business leaders. She was rightfully offended by her husband, no matter how pious his reputation within the community. It's a rare passage because it offers a practical example and insight into a domestic squabble between Tobit and his wife Anna. There are endless examples in this "novel" for moral exhortation. The accusation of Tobit, occasioned by the bleating of the goat, illustrates the ease with which a devoutly religious person can move into a false sense of moral superiority and then to rash judgment and the presumption of wrongdoing in others (v. 14). The retort of Anna can illustrate the fact that anger often escalates and that truth can be spoken in anger. Rather than responding in kind, one might well pause to ponder the possibility that the other person in fact speaks the truth.

Family Charity

This passage also illustrates the need for charity to be exercised within the family as well as out in the community. Daily life within every family makes many demands for patience and mutual respect. One might recall the way in which the Synoptic Gospels command love of neighbor as contrasted with John's command to "love one another." Is it easier or more difficult to love people more proximate to our daily lives, since members of our families are regularly able to rub us the wrong way than more distant "neighbors"? Perhaps John, when faced with the challenges of loving neighbors, says, "Well, at least love your own community members."

Antiphon (Year I)

Psalm 112:7c

The heart of the just one is firm,
trusting in the Lord.

Heart

The ancient world's sense of anatomy included the fact that the "heart" was presumed to be not the location of romantic love but the place for a person's planning and deciding. The refrain, therefore, insists that precisely one's plans and choices should be oriented toward God in trust and confidence. Jesus is remembered as having said of himself that he was "meek and humble of heart" (Matt 11:29).

Firm

The word used by the psalm for a "firm" heart is the same word that describes the solid foundation of the world, understood in ancient cosmology as fixed on massive pillars that hold the earth's flat surface stable and strong. Similarly, the foundations of a house are securely solid, never simply placed on shifting sands or slippery mud. This is the type of firmness of trust that a truly just individual, namely, one in right relationship with the entire world, exhibits in decisions. She knows whom she trusts and her entire life achieves stability by that very fact.

First Reading (Year II)

2 Peter 3:12-15a, 17-18

We await new heavens and a new earth.

Patience

The exhortation to be patient in waiting for the "coming of the day of God" (v. 12) runs through this entire epistle, even suggesting that God's delay is an added opportunity for our response to God's call for conversion and true righteousness. Scholars suggest, as noted above, that this is one of the last of the New Testament's inspired letters, probably written by a later disciple of Peter at a time when early Christians were confused by the delayed return of Christ. Our human inclination is to dictate when and how we want God to act, even if God has other plans. God remains the chief architect of the new creation, not us!

Hastening the Day

Curiously, amid the invitation to wait in patience because the final power is in God's hands, we also discover the suggestion that we can somehow hasten that day (v. 12) and make it come more quickly. Our good deeds, therefore, might even prepare a world into which God will be welcomed more suitably and received. Living without personal moral blemish and in reconciled peace (v. 14) with others is at the very center of the new creation. Growth in the knowledge of the true God and his ways (v. 18) is also encouraged during this final age of human history. The doxology of praise ends the letter and provides an opportunity for the expression of our own gratitude.

Antiphon (Year II)

Psalm 90:1

In every age, O Lord, you have been our refuge.

Psalm 90: Divine Power and Human Frailty

If the prior passage from Second Peter is an encouragement during the time of delayed return, this psalm is a perfect response. It reminds us of God's eternal presence from the time before the creation of the great mountains (v. 2) through the ages of time during which each generation is reduced to the dust of its origin (v. 3) and natural destiny. This is summarized in the refrain's reference to "every age" (v. 1). Whether the fullness of our age be marked by seventy or even eighty years (v. 10), God remains a refuge. We pass quickly from the scene and others take our places.

Refuge

The Hebrew word for "refuge" is *maʿon*, a dwelling for security or even a place of safety like a cave. Amid all the changes that unfold over the centuries and across the lives of generations, God is recognized as a "place" of stability and security (v. 1). Although hardships come and go throughout our lives, God remains stable and those who live in his presence find a level of serenity beyond the vacillating times and circumstances of history. Every morning begins afresh as God offers his "kindness/*hesed*" (v. 14) and renews his covenant.

Gospel

Mark 12:13-17

Repay to Caesar what belongs to Caesar and to God what belongs to God.

Literary Link

The third day of the Lord's final "Holy Week" in Jerusalem is described as remarkably busy and filled with teachings. Today's gospel passage presents the third controversy, a discussion of taxes (vv. 13-17).

Pharisees and Herodians

The "Herodian" agents of the king were always concerned about potential rivals or covert political opponents. Apparently some of the Pharisees were politically aligned with them and offered religious counsel to the royal court. These are the very same groups mentioned earlier in Mark's gospel (3:6) as co-conspirators against Jesus. Since these were sent to entrap Jesus (v. 13), one wonders what/who might have been the original source and motive for the task given to these Pharisees and Herodians. Perhaps it was "the chief priests, the scribes, and the elders" who had questioned his authority (11:27) earlier and wanted to arrest Jesus (v. 12). Were these questioners used by others for less than noble purposes? It is part of "kingdom wisdom/astuteness" to be conscious of unlikely bedfellows and to confront them in the hope of their conversion, not condemnation. Disciples of Jesus are always on the lookout for others who might become instruments, not obstacles, of the work of God. In every generation God is at work for reconciliation with an eye toward the final transformation of the world. Among all the forces of our day, who could be invited to be partners?

Spokesperson for Truth

The initial words of the Pharisees and Herodians, though spoken out of deceitful flattery, are in fact a tribute to Jesus, an acknowledgment of his concern for the truth and lack of care to human respect (v. 14) or mere "political correctness." What a tribute that would be to anyone! Concern for the truth of things always marked the life and teaching of Jesus. Even though it may be a ruse for flattery in this case, it marks the qualities of speech expected of any true follower of Jesus. The quest for and permanence in personal integrity is a lifelong task, requiring careful attention each day as circumstances change and new pressures arise. Fudging the truth is not an apostolic quality. There may be reasons for not speaking the whole truth, but whatever we do say should be true.

Tuesday of the Ninth Week in Ordinary Time

The Coin

The coin requested by Jesus and presented to him (v. 15) was a *denarius*, the equivalent to the daily wage of an unskilled laborer. The very fact that such a coin was readily offered (v. 16) suggests that the coin was handy. Its very availability also implies the need for constant judgment and discernment because the will of God encompasses every part of life. As we know from archaeology, the tiny coin had the image of Caesar himself. Even our contemporary American coinage offers important evidence of our values because important personages, symbols, and mottoes are inscribed on them. What do the coins in our pockets actually say about us? As an aside, contemporary Orthodox Jews always protest the practice of using the name of God on our money. They do so, not because of disbelief or false separation between faith and politics, but because one never knows what unjust or ignoble purposes a coin may be used for.

Morality and Economics

Israel had a double set of currency, one allegedly "purer" that was used within the temple, and another, namely, the coinage of the idolatrous Roman occupiers used for the rest of life's transactions. For that reason the question was a valid moral one. It could be posed by people conscientiously desirous to obey God in every detail of their life. Nothing is merely economic. Christian morality has something to say about the values of our entire economy, as the 1986 pastoral letter of the American bishops, Economic Justice for All, insisted.

Hypocrisy

The Greek work "*hupokrisis*/hypocrisy" (v. 15) might mean "a dialogue with comments and responses, a dramatic role on stage (through a mask), a discussion covertly representing someone else, or a pretended conversation." Speaking for someone else does not necessarily have the negative connotation of our sense of "hypocrisy." Sometimes mistranslations or even transliterations have contributed to an unfair image of Pharisees among Christians. Jesus called it as he saw it; we must be cautious of unfairly or inaccurately imposing our own contemporary meaning on ancient language.

Wednesday of the Ninth Week in Ordinary Time

First Reading (Year I)

Tobit 3:1-11a, 16-17a

The prayer of these two petitioners was heard in the glorious presence of Almighty God.

Two Prayers

The book of Tobit contains six beautiful prayers. Today's reading offers two of the most powerful examples of personal prayer. The first is Tobit's prayer of sorrow for the moral and spiritual blindness that led him to say harsh judgmental things to his wife (vv. 2-6). It ends in a prayer to die rather than to keep living in such personal turmoil (v. 6). The second is the prayer of Sarah, fiancée to Tobiah, uttered in the far distant land of Ecbatana (Hamadan in modern Iran), who lived with the terrible heartache and subsequent social ignominy of having been widowed seven times (v. 11). Curiously, the passage chosen by the Lectionary omits the verses that claimed her innocence of fault (vv. 12-15). God's response was to send Raphael for all the levels of healing needed by each (v. 17). The prayer illustrates why the archangel Raphael (whose Hebrew name means "God healed or mended") has become the one invoked for healing and health in Jewish and Christian tradition.

Suicide

Sarah's desperation led her to consider taking her life (v. 10). This is an extremely rare topic for Scripture, though Saul seems to have taken his life after his final military defeat (1 Sam 31:4). Out of concern for the serious possible negative effects on her aged father, she reconsiders and simply asks for death and prays for God's mercy (v. 11). The passage could be an occasion for the congregation's prayers for the deeply discouraged wherever they may be, and for prayers for anyone within the community afflicted by a family heartache such as the suicide of a member. The pain of such families never really goes away because the conversation was stopped without any healing resolution.

Antiphon (Year I)

Psalm 25:1

To you, O Lord, I lift my soul.

Soul

As was noted above, the refrain (v. 1) translates *nephesh* as "soul," although the Hebrew word really means "throat, voice, and the place of personal living spirit." In trust and praise we use our throats to sing to the Lord as our response to the first reading. There is a clear physical and vocal aspect to the spirit we lift to God in confidence. No matter what troubles or burdens we may confront in our daily lives, we are invited to lift up our voices and spirits to God.

Shame

The first verses of the psalm response echo the shame (vv. 2, 3) that Sarah would have experienced if she had proceeded with her initial thought of suicide. Later in the psalm there is a repeated mention of covenantal kindness, *hesed* (vv. 6, 7), which God feels toward Sarah or any covenant partner overwhelmed by the sorrows of life. Those who are willing to wait (v. 3) for God's intervention according to God's timing can learn of God's love for them. Sometimes we want solutions too quickly. Sometimes our wants are not necessarily our needs!

First Reading (Year II)

2 Timothy 1:1-3, 6-12

Stir into flame the gift of God that you have through the laying on of my hands.

Apostleship

The vocation of apostle (v. 1), like most other authentic "vocations" in life, isn't simply chosen by the individual person, but rather the gift of God. A blending of interest, ability, and approval by the community of believers converges to make an authentic "vocation." There was a time when spiritual writers frequently spoke of the "apostolate" of the laity, namely, areas of special need in society to which men and women were sent by reason of their baptismal call and their personal abilities and interests. There are Apostles, and there are apostles. Paul was the former and we are often the latter.

The Second Letter of Saint Paul to Timothy
Although certainly the inspired word of God, the actual Pauline authorship of this letter has been seriously debated. Purportedly written from prison, Paul laments those who have left his team and strongly condemns false teaching. He encourages true holiness of life.

Imposition of Hands

Rooted in ancient Jewish practices, hands are imposed as a gesture of association with a reality larger then ourselves. An ancient example can be found in the case of rabbinic students upon whom hands were imposed to indicate their "ordination" or new association with the chain of teachers who had gone before them. We Catholics impose hands at baptism, confirmation, reconciliation, and ordination. In every Eucharist hands are imposed over the gifts and then (at least virtually) over the entire community. Paul's reference to hands imposed over Timothy (v. 6) presumed a ritual call to leadership. With that call came the grace of courage that equipped Timothy and gave him the ability to show "power and love and self-control" (v. 7). The earlier NAB translation stated beautifully that the spirit given by that action made us "strong, loving and wise." True gifts of God's grace also give whatever is needed to exercise them.

Wednesday of the Ninth Week in Ordinary Time

Hardships

Every single person has his or her own share in the hardships of life for the gospel (v. 8). Paul acknowledged the price he paid for his preaching over the years. Moreover, he knew well the burdens of ancient prison life. There is no cheap grace, but God also gives the strength needed to carry that hardship and benefit from it. Part of God's "grace/favor" is to have the blessing of a community of faith with whom to share the hardships.

ANTIPHON (YEAR II)

Psalm 123:1b

To you, O Lord, I lift up my eyes.

Prison

Perhaps this refrain was selected for the Lectionary as a response to Paul's letter from prison precisely because prisons were often underground dark and squalid places from which prisoners "lift up [their] eyes" (v. 1). In fact the Mamertine prison next to the Roman Forum, where Paul was allegedly confined, offered as its only entrance a hole in the ceiling of the cave/prison that allowed a minimum of air or light! He would certainly have lifted up his eyes.

Eyes on the Hands of God

In complete trust and utter dependence the handmaid carefully watches the hands of God (v. 2), awaiting some gesture of help or kindness. "Hands," as a material symbol of divine helping, holding, supporting, and feeding, are vivid images from the poetry of the psalm. Ours are lifted in supplication; God's are extended in assistance and blessing.

GOSPEL

Mark 12:18-27

He is not God of the dead but of the living.

Literary Link

This argument over the reality of resurrection (vv. 18-27) is the fourth controversy included in a very busy day dedicated to key final teachings of Jesus as Mark presents them. Each encounter contributes to the deepening confrontation between Jesus and the rulers of the city.

Resurrection

Sadducees did not believe in resurrection (v. 18) because they were committed to the literal text of the Scriptures, and they could not find any clear teaching about resurrection in the Torah/Pentateuch. The Pharisees, however, were strongly convinced of the resurrection and committed to that belief. In his general teaching Jesus seemed inclined toward the traditions of the Pharisees. In particular Jesus reflected the branch of that party inspired by the great Rabbi Hillel. As contrasted with his major rival, the literalist Rabbi Shammai, Hillel sought to understand the letter of the law as well as its intent. Pharisees taught a rising from the dead to a new way of life. Paul stirred up a similar argument when he proclaimed Christ's resurrection at Caesarea (Acts 23:6).

Argument from Marriage

Sadducees rejected resurrection but presumed that any life in the next age would be similar to life in this age, including marriage, and therefore resurrection was thought ridiculous! They chose an extreme argument to prove their case, the fictitious example of a woman required to marry seven brothers according to Deuteronomy 25:6. Jesus stepped aside of that passage and invoked a different and unexpected verse, Moses and the burning bush (Exod 3:6), for his side of the debate. Certainly we believe that relationships will endure in the next age, because they form our identity, but the way in which they will be expressed in that new creation remains mysterious and known to God alone.

Thursday of the Ninth Week in Ordinary Time

FIRST READING (YEAR I)

Tobit 6:10-11; 7:1bcde, 9-17; 8:4-9a

Call down your mercy on me and her and allow us to live together to a happy old age.

Ancient Marriage Formalities

In this reading we hear a very moving tale of a marriage proposal according to the customs of Israel (7:9): formal request and approval of parents, written agreement, banquet celebrations, and the beginning of a shared life. Because of the importance of marriage for the life of an individual as well as the entire community, every culture has its own marriage customs. Some elements such as formal agreement are always considered essential. Prior to our more modern times, all marriages were kept within family circles and were arranged by the families involved. Whatever the customs, a Christian congregation continues to pray for newly married couples. In our age Catholics are relatively adept at helping couples prepare for marriage but less accustomed to extend that pastoral concern to the first years of their adjustment.

Prayer

Given the tragic background in Sarah's previous relationships (7:11), it seemed essential to begin the marriage with a prayer (vv. 5ff.) from the lips of Tobiah, praising God, acknowledging the benefit of receiving a partner, and requesting God's mercy for a long and happy life together. It is easy to understand why this passage, or at least the prayer of Tobias, should be a frequent and favorite reading at marriage ceremonies. Presuming all the prior history and heartaches, the notion of happiness is finally introduced, but only at the end of the prayer (8:7). Because marriage is a sacrament, as sign of God's loving presence in the lives of people, the prayer of the couple, their families, and the entire community is always part of the picture!

ANTIPHON (YEAR I)

Psalm 128:1a

Blessed are those who fear the Lord.

Fear as Blessing

It may be helpful to pause for a moment and to acknowledge that fear/reverence for the Lord, as strange as it may seem initially, is indeed a blessing (v. 1). Such an attitude inclines one to recognize the source of all blessings and to seek those blessings that enable a person to be in right relationship with God and all creation. If truly a blessing, this reverence comes from outside our lives (because all blessings do) and is given beyond our control to be a source of goodness throughout all of life.

Wife and Children

This portion of Psalm 128 is the perfect response to the tale of Tobiah and Sarah because the psalm describes wife and children as fruitful vines and precious olive trees (v. 3) in the family home. Like a treasured family, vineyards and olive groves were the source of important nourishment, emotional pleasure, and security for the life of the ancient world. The image, though somewhat quaint to modern ears, is a charming and attractive allusion.

FIRST READING (YEAR II)

2 Timothy 2:8-15

The word of God is not chained. If we have died with Christ, we shall also live with him.

The Freed Word

In sharp contrast to the situation of Paul chained and fettered in prison (v. 9), the word of God is not held hostage to any single place. It moves freely through the world, echoing from one life and one person to another. When spoken and repeated with its promise of salvation through the death and resurrection of Jesus the Christ (v. 10), it tells the story of our redemption and promises glory to all who accept the Word and live accordingly.

Trustworthiness

God's words are eminently trustworthy because God is faithful to himself (v. 13). The letter seems to add something to the brief hymn about dying and living with Christ (vv. 11ff.) by noting that denying the truth of the paschal mystery under the pressure of persecution is a possibility due to frail human nature, but God remains faithful (v. 13) even when we are not. The enduring fidelity of God is a remarkable divine quality. God's fidelity will find reflection in our lives if we remain in friendship with God (v. 12).

ANTIPHON (YEAR II)

Psalm 25:4

Teach me your ways, O Lord.

God as Teacher

The best of human teachers influence us by their example, their encouragement, and their willingness to share knowledge in a patient fashion and even by discipline if needed. This refrain invites us to see those same qualities in God (v. 4) and in the manner in which God offers instruction and guidance to human beings. Reflecting back on our experience, we can find new ways of appreciating God's work with us as we mature and learn. Each title, like that of "teacher," applied to God offers its own insight into the ways in which God deals with us.

Psalm 25: Trusting Confidence

The acrostic alphabetical form of this psalm results in a repetitious and slightly strained tone to this poem, which uses the words "teach" and "instruct" repeatedly. Scholars tell us that this psalm may have been part of a lesson to be memorized by students in the royal court schools of Jerusalem. In any case the psalm forms a fitting congregational response to the reading from Second Timothy about the Word ever active in our world!

GOSPEL

Mark 12:28-34

There is no commandment greater than these.

Literary Link

This is the fifth conversation reported by Mark as having occurred during the third day of that final week in Jerusalem. Although not a controversy as such, it represented a discussion in which Jesus was asked his opinion about a serious and sometimes controverted topic. In Matthew's gospel the question was asked by one of the Pharisees to test Jesus (22:35).

Priorities

Among the 613 commandments deduced from different tales and portions of the Torah, it is logical and understandable that people should seek to know which were most important and which were most worthy of careful attention. After all, one would obviously be hard pressed to give equal energy to all, simply because of the human limitations under which we all live. The question of the first and greatest (v. 28) would be important. The response may have marked out differing schools of thought among the Pharisees.

Love

To best understand these two fundamental commandments (if one can ever command "love"), it is helpful to remember that romantic love, however wonderful in its own right, is but an early emotion that must mature. Rather than requiring sentimental affection on our part toward God (v. 30) and neighbor (v. 31), we are commanded to bring our personal concern for their welfare, well-being, and interests. Such an attitude can be commanded, and can also bring focus and cohesion to our lives and decisions. To insist on the commandment of love as the greatest is to place emphasis on relationships rather than mere obedient compliance. This makes Christianity with all its cherished Jewish roots a religion of friendship.

Friday of the Ninth Week in Ordinary Time

First Reading (Year I)

Tobit 11:5-17

God himself scourged me and behold,
I now see my son Tobiah!

Family Reunions

A return from college or military service or a reunion after years of separation can be a very happy moment for a family. The joyful tears of Anna over her son's return (v. 9) can reflect so many family joys. Moreover, when the reunion is accompanied by the recovery of health and well-being, as in this case of Tobit (v. 13), it is memorable indeed. Trusting that God is providing protection to all distant loved ones, whether in the form of guardians like Raphael or other forms of assistance and support, we pray for them all. It is God who brings people together in order to deepen the bond of mutual charity and to strengthen their mutual support. Human reunions are gifts from God. They are also faint foreshadows of our final reunion in heaven forever!

Restored Eyesight

Although the treatment for the cataracts of Tobit seems primitive in a world of lasers, and the popular use of anointing with fish gall (v. 12) is surprising if not downright dangerous, we are reminded of the symbolic importance of seeing clearly as a metaphor for faith. The tale of the symbolic cure of the blind man (John 9) and the medieval prayer of Saint Richard (to "see you more clearly") remind us of the long history of such interpretations. In the course of the story of Tobit and Tobiah, everyone's faith has been perfected. They begin to understand the larger picture of God's healing providence.

Daughter-in-Law Sarah

The warm welcome given by Anna and Tobit to their distant relative, now new daughter-in-law Sarah of Nineveh (v. 17), may be the occasion to speak of the graces present whenever a son- or daughter-in-law is newly welcomed into a family. They bring their own experiences, customs, and dreams. Although the initial adjustment may be challenging at times, they should be viewed as enhancing a family, not as providing an obstacle or new rival for attention or affection.

Antiphon (Year I)

Psalm 146:1b

Praise the Lord, my soul!

Psalm 146: Confidence at Dawn

Psalm 146 was often used as a Morning Prayer in late Judaism. As such it possesses the simple directness expected of prayer at the beginning of a new day. The eight verses selected by the Lectionary are filled with praise for God (v. 1) and grateful recognition of the wonder of God's perennial providential care for all in need. Each new day is an opportunity for God's generosity as well as for our gratitude.

Perennial Providence

With a certain classic ease this psalm describes the providence of God in every generation. Because the verbs are all in the present tense, they suggest that the actions of God are constant and perduring: securing justice for the oppressed (v. 6), giving food to the hungry, setting captives free (v. 7), restoring sight to the blind (v. 8), raising up those bowed down (v. 8), and protecting strangers (v. 9). All of these actions are listed as signs of ongoing divine care. These actions describe what God always does and who God is. Note that many of the same actions were listed as proof that Jesus was the "one who is to come" when he met with the inquiring disciples sent by John the Baptist (Luke 7:19, 22).

First Reading (Year II)

2 Timothy 3:10-17

All who want to live religiously in Christ Jesus will be persecuted.

Inevitable Persecutions

Paul reminds Timothy that everyone who attempts to live religiously will experience persecutions (v. 12). Resistance and persecutions can spring from many sources. Resistance could stem from the very inner nature of the personal changes required by conversion. Persecution could come from individuals who reject the messenger rather than accept the message because it would require unwanted change, make unwelcome demands, or sever existing friendships. Not only do the gospel's triple passion predictions describe with vivid power the experience of Jesus but they also form a universal template for all Christians. The necessity of the "paschal imperative," namely, suffering and vindication encompassed Jesus, the church over the centuries, and every individual disciple. Not without reason does Paul state that only through "many hardships [does one] enter the kingdom of God" (Acts 14:22).

The Nature of Scripture

The letter pauses to make a point of the true purpose for the inspired word of God in Scripture. The Scriptures are not for scientific accuracy or historical precision but rather for catechetical instruction and the salvation of those who proclaim and those who hear alike (v. 13). The Scriptures are intended by God for teaching, refuting, correcting, and training (v. 16). Those who attempt to find scientific truth in biblical literature are expecting what the Scripture cannot and should not provide. The books of the Bible are perennial sources of great wisdom that enable people to be well equipped for good work (v. 17).

Antiphon (Year II)

Psalm 119:165a

O Lord, great peace have they who love your law.

Peace

The "peace/*shalom*" described in the refrain (v. 165) is the reintegration of scattered elements back into their original or intended unity. It is not the serene tranquility of a house without noise after the children have gone to bed but rather the restored interrelationships of a jigsaw puzzle put together again. The refrain insists that those who love God's teaching find that very type of renewed unity with family, friends, and neighbors because of a commonly shared big picture into which each individual fits smoothly. Humble docility before God enables a person to find his or her proper configuration into the overarching plans of God.

Loving the Law

The biblical sense of "love" (v. 165) is respect and concern, not romantic or sentimental affection. The refrain recommends that we strive to come to love God's instructions. The clarity of divine teaching may in fact actually delight those who have achieved maturity in holiness. The same saints, however, may also experience periods of spiritual dryness at times. The great saints have acknowledged such times because God wishes us to depend upon him, not upon any good feeling that good deeds may evoke in our hearts.

Gospel

Mark 12:35-37

How do the scribes claim that the Christ is the son of David?

Literary Link

The sixth and final controversy in this series addresses the title of "son of David" and "Lord" for the Messiah. Each successive discussion focuses on some aspect of the person and mission of

Jesus to sharpen the image and to prepare for Mark's account of the inevitable passion and resurrection of Jesus, who will be called "Son of God" by the Roman centurion at the foot of the cross (15:39).

Rabbinic Debates

Sometimes very heated and even seemingly harsh in tone, the debates of the Mediterranean world provided entertainment as well as enlightenment for those who sought truth. The discussions were occasions for bringing together differing texts, each with its own nuance. The arguments were a form of entertainment (v. 37) for those who wished to learn more and to become immersed in the sacred texts. Like heated courtroom debates among modern lawyers, the argument could be proposed and parried, and then be followed by sharing a drink in fellowship. One should, therefore, know the culture of the time before presuming serious antagonism between Jesus and his Pharisee opponents.

Biblical Titles for Jesus

Throughout Mark's gospel we are regularly confronted by titles for Jesus and by the effort of the gospel to explain the implications of those titles: Son of Man/Son of God or Christ. Second-generation Christians debated the use of LORD for Jesus, especially because that was a translation for the sacred name of God alone. In the final writing and editing of the gospels later debates between followers of Jesus and Jewish scholars were sometimes written back into earlier arguments when Jesus engaged in the debates of his day, even though the full flashpoint of the issue only became apparent at a later date. It is important to keep the different chronological periods separate in our minds when explaining the controversies noted in the gospels.

Psalm 110

Psalm 110 is a classic example of the sources used by early Christians as they attempted to explain the person and mission of Jesus. The Messiah was to be the "son of David" (v. 35), yet also acknowledged as the "Lord" in the psalm (v. 1). This is an example of the confusing mix of titles that early Christians utilized to prove their belief in the divinity of Jesus. Precisely who is the "Lord/*kyrios*" mentioned in the psalm and what did the title mean to those who entered the debate? Throughout the centuries these types of arguments have helped Christians to sharpen and clarify their beliefs about sonship and lordship. Even when heated, however, debates should always be respectful and eager for God's truth in the matter, not mere polemical vindication.

Friday of the Ninth Week in Ordinary Time

Saturday of the Ninth Week in Ordinary Time

First Reading (Year I)

Tobit 12:1, 5-15, 20

So now praise God. Behold, I am about to ascend to him who sent me.

The Rest of the Story

Raphael calls Tobit and Tobiah together after the wedding to reveal his real identity as one of the seven spirits before God. He was the one whom God sent to care for the troubles of his faithful servants, the Tobiad family (v. 15). This helps to explain the big picture of human events as a framework of God's involvement in the affairs of the family and in all human events. God uses others, human as well as heavenly, as partners and agents of divine healing for human hurts. As we travel through life, we never know who might be the actual instrument of God and a messenger of healing.

Praise

As Raphael makes perfectly clear, the expected human response to the entire story is praise for God (v. 6). This chapter is a fine example of true evangelization, namely, the proclaiming of God's wondrous deeds by those who were the beneficiaries of such kindness (v. 7). Twice Raphael contrasts the expected sense of confidentiality for royal secrets (vv. 7, 11) with the public proclamation demanded in response to the deeds of God that should elicit praise. By way of example the final thirteenth chapter of the book is an extended hymn of Tobit's praise for God, the supreme source of goodness, justice, and compassion. This is the same sentiment written into the very institution narrative of the Eucharist.

Almsgiving

One should not leave this reading without an acknowledgment of the importance attributed by Raphael to almsgiving. Righteous (i.e., not merely for human adulation) almsgiving is stated as more important than prayer and fasting (v. 8). Raphael notes that almsgiving "saves one from death and expiates every sin" (v. 9). Looking back over the story of Tobit it becomes clear that feeding the hungry and burying the dead, though not an actual exchange of money, are also examples of the almsgiving that atones for sin.

Antiphon (Year I)

Tobit 13:1b

Blessed be God, who lives for ever.

The Canticle of Tobit

It is precisely the final hymn of Tobit that is used by the Lectionary as the response to the denouement of the story as explained by Raphael. The angel/messenger commands "praise" (v. 20) and Tobit promptly obeys, as this entire thirteenth chapter makes very clear. The refrain (v. 1) is repeated six times to emphasize the human duty of praise and blessing. Anyone who receives blessings without offering thanks and praise in return is shortsighted and narrow-minded.

Land of Exile

The story of Tobit and Tobiah is recited as taking place in Nineveh in the land of the Assyrians, a place of exile (v. 6). It is precisely in that social context of an alien land that they are commanded to speak of the mighty deeds of the Lord. It is, one might say, a command to "evangelize" and to do so amid pagans and people in need of learning about the God of Israel. Although there is some debate regarding the degree to which Israel was "missionary" in nature, the earlier experience of "proto-Jews" was more outgoing than subsequent Judaism (possibly in reaction to the strong missionary impetus of early Christianity) in the first centuries of the Common Era. Both the Judaism and the Christianity of the Diaspora, namely, religious existence in distant foreign lands, provide endless opportunities for witness to the marvels of God.

FIRST READING (YEAR II)

2 Timothy 4:1-8

I am already being poured out and the crown of righteousness awaits me which the Lord will award me.

The Urgency of the Word

"In season and out of season" (as the earlier NAB used to phrase it), or "whether it is convenient or inconvenient" (v. 2), Paul insists on fidelity to the task of proclaiming God's word with patience and urgency. He notes that the Word is useful for convincing, reprimanding, and encouraging (v. 2) those often subjected to false teaching (v. 4). A maxim often repeated in catechesis or adult formation is the conviction that good teaching is the most effective antidote to bad teaching!

Athletic Imagery

Whether the letter was written by Paul himself or by a later disciple, the use of athletic metaphors is characteristic of Paul's style. The reference to competing well, finishing the race, keeping the faith, and winning the crown represents a fine example of the various Olympic festivals celebrated in the Greece of the first century. In particular it may be interesting to note that the word "faith/*pistis*" (v. 7), while now a traditional word for one's religious response under grace to grace, also had a specific application in the ancient athletic world. "Faith" was the technical word for the deposit that a runner laid down at registration by way of concrete pledge that he or she would keep the rules of the competition. Upon so doing, the athlete received the money back. Paul knew the language of Hellenism around him and used it well in service to the Word.

Saturday of the Ninth Week in Ordinary Time

ANTIPHON (YEAR II)

Psalm 71:15ab

I will sing of your salvation.

Sung Psalms

It may be helpful to remember that the psalms were, for the most part, used as song in the temple worship and in early synagogues scattered throughout the areas more distant from Jerusalem. It was natural to speak of "singing" (v. 15) as a response to the salvation offered by God. In that sense, a "spoken" psalm, though common, is less traditional. This psalm speaks of a "mouth . . . filled with your praise" (v. 8). One should be encouraged to use psalms as religious music. Missionaries to Africa often speak of the marvelous manner in which every sermon was reduced to a refrain that could be repeatedly sung throughout the instruction, and thus memorized as a mantra for the week!

Salvation

When the people of God assemble, they sing of the deeds of God who delivers and saves his people (v. 15) from all the tight spots of history. One of the pastoral problems of an affluent culture is the lack of anything people feel a desire to be freed from! Those who have all possible material comforts may not hunger for salvation. At the same time there is a price for affluence because it often comes without a desire to care for others or to find inner growth. Is there anything from which our society wishes/needs to be saved?

GOSPEL

Mark 12:38-44

This poor widow has given more than all others.

Literary Link

Two widow stories—a warning against charlatan religious who prey on widows (v. 40) and a commendation of a widow's lavish generosity (vv. 42-44)—are presented as complementary teachings. They are presented here because the teachings took place in the temple area. This selection is the final passage chosen by the Lectionary from Mark's gospel. Next week we will begin to hear Matthew's portrait of Jesus.

Widows

Throughout the history of Israel widows and orphans were the prime examples of people who easily fell through the safety net of family support. Once a woman's connection to a family (into which she had moved at the time of her marriage) was disrupted by the death of her husband, she could be at the mercy of others who would have been her sole material support for food and lodging. She was often desperately vulnerable to exploitation by unscrupulous religious figures (v. 40). This is an appropriate day to pray for widows and to praise them. It is also a day to recall the Order of Widows in the early church (1 Tim 5:3-16).

Generosity

The praise of Jesus for the extraordinary generosity of the poor widow who gave her entire livelihood to those poorer than herself (v. 44) illustrates the fundamental relativity of that virtue. The dime from a youngster may mean much more than a casual gift of millions from a very wealthy adult. By way of side observation, the "poor boxes" at the back of our parish churches are often labeled "for the poor," but the metal boxes along the entrance to the Western Wall of the temple site in Jerusalem are labeled "*tzedeqah*/justice." The latter word in Jewish religious practice indicated right relationships between all creatures. Gifts, large and small alike, are intended to restore that universal balance among all of God's creatures. Human generosity is a tiny echo of the lavish generosity of God, who simply cannot stop scattering dandelions everywhere!

Monday of the Tenth Week in Ordinary Time

First Reading (Year I)

2 Corinthians 1:1-7

God encourages us that we ourselves may be able to encourage those who are in any affliction.

The Second Letter of Paul to the Corinthians

Because of the discontinuity of the various sections and themes addressed in this letter, many scholars have concluded that the document under this title is in fact a collection of several briefer communications from Paul. One can divide the contents roughly into three portions: a crisis in the relationship between Paul and factions of local leadership (1:12–7:16), the collection for the poor in Jerusalem (8:1–9:16), and a defense of Paul's style and method of leadership (10:1–13:10). His personal passion and emotional engagement are very evident in the way he addresses issues within the Corinthian community.

Teamwork

Paul is associated (v. 1) with Timothy in writing this letter, which is yet another example of teamwork in the ministry of the early church. According to the customs of the ancient world, a scribe would have been used to record Paul's oral messages. Moreover, even the initial oral proclamation was accomplished by the trio of Paul, Silvanus, and Timothy (v. 19). Different gifts are always needed to mutually support and complement each other's work in missionary efforts or community development.

Encouragement

The word "encouragement/*paraklesis*" is found ten times in these few verses (NABRE). The term serves to set the stage for the entire passage, even though other parts of this letter may seem harsher in tone and purpose. Sometimes encouragement includes a critique and a word of "tough love" as well as the expression of gentler sentiments. One could ask what role "encouragement" plays in child education or faith formation. Paul is a wise, perhaps even shrewd, psychologist in his approach. On occasion it is helpful to ponder all the possible subelements included in any action of encouragement: respect for another person, appreciation for each and all of his or her gifts, efforts to assist in developing and honing those same gifts as well as partnership in searching out areas of ministry or social action for justice in which those gifts might be used well. Imagine the implications of invoking the "God of all encouragement" (v. 3), or the example of a "coaching God" who insists on repeating, "Come on, you can do it!"

Communal Mutuality

We can think of God's love and mercy as divine qualities extended to us on the condition that we are to extend the same considerations to those around us (v. 4). That was also true of "forgiveness," as the Our Father reminds us so pointedly (Matt 6:12). This introduction from Paul and Timothy's letter suggests that the very same should be said of encouragement. We are encouraged so that we can in turn encourage others. No spiritual gift is only given for ourselves!

Antiphon (Year I)

Psalm 34:9a

Taste and see the goodness of the Lord.

Psalm 34: Praise and Thanks

Because Psalm 34 is an alphabetic acrostic, namely, with each verse beginning with a successive letter of the Hebrew alphabet, the ideas are loosely connected and the contents generic. Many verses sound like proverbs or generic invitations to praise God's kindness to the lowly (v. 3). That same sentiment reflects the gentle tone of the day's initial reading from Second Corinthians.

Tasting and Seeing

"Tasting" implies a meal of sorts (v. 9). It seems, however, as if we could search in vain for further indications of the use of this psalm with "communion sacrifices," namely, those that include sharing the offering among all the participants in the worship. The rest of the psalm is very generic and devoid of clear sacrificial references. Because of this one verse, the ancient church used the psalm for the celebration of Holy Communion. The refrain's sudden reference to tasting (v. 9) does, however, provide a concrete poetic image for our delight and good pleasure when experiencing God in any form. God's goodness is so good that you can almost taste it!

First Reading (Year II)

1 Kings 17:1-6

Elijah stands before the Lord God of Israel.

The First Book of Kings

In the light of the Lectionary's practice of alternating readings from the first (Old Testament) and second (New Testament) covenant readings, we suddenly follow Second Timothy with a portion from First Kings, beginning with the majestic figure of the great prophet Elijah. All these "historical" books are in fact intensely catechetical. They judge the rulers of the north and south kingdoms according to the principles of the theology of Deuteronomy. Those who obey the prophetic messengers from God and who uphold the laws of sacrifice to the Lord alone are praised, the others condemned, often harshly and severely.

The Mighty Elijah

The inspired Scriptures of Israel revere Moses as the "Founder" of Israelite covenantal piety, and Elijah as the Reformer and Renewer of Israel's fidelity to its Lord. Elijah suddenly appears on the scene (v. 1) with the threat of a terrible drought by divine authority. Elijah then rushes off under divine command to the wilderness east of the Jordan (v. 2), where he is fed by ravens (v. 4) during the years of the terrible dry period. Crops withered in punishment for lack of faithfulness to the God of Israel, the true source of wine, grain, and prosperity. This text is an invitation to review the truly prophetic figures of every age and to single out those who best speak the word of God in times of crisis.

Ahab

The tale of Elijah seems precipitated by confrontations with King Ahab of Samaria and his wife Jezebel. Those figures had been introduced into the story in the prior chapter (1 Kings 16:29-33). In Israel's sacred memory, prophets rose and served as challenging opponents to the kings who strayed into idolatry (v. 32). The prophets were the strong consciences of the nation, and when kingship disappeared during the Babylonian exile, prophets seem to have virtually disappeared from the scene as well. They may even have morphed into the temple choirs (1 Chr 25:1). It is to the person of Ahab that Elijah announces the drought with all its dreadful consequences for the people (v. 1). This is an example of corporate communal punishment.

Antiphon (Year II)

Psalm 121:2

Our help is from the Lord, who made heaven and earth.

Times of Need

Psalm 121 acknowledges the Lord as the source of assistance and aid (v. 2) in times of trouble. Many different human predicaments are then listed in this response as examples of situations of need for help: physical or moral slipping (v. 3), safety from danger during slumber (v. 4), protection from sun and natural calamities (v. 5). Members of a congregation could add their own contributions to the litany, which could in turn become the rough material for the day's general intercessions at the morning Eucharist.

Creator of Heaven and Earth

By invoking the God of creation as the ultimate source of assistance and protection, the refrain (v. 2) dismisses personal wealth, political power, or social prestige as legitimate resources for human confidence in times of difficulty. They are all "vanity," as Qoheleth/Ecclesiastes insists, perhaps visible but inevitably as insubstantial as smoke or mist (1:2)!

Gospel

Matthew 5:1-12

Blessed are the poor in spirit.

The Gospel according to Matthew

The beginning of the tenth week in the Lectionary also marks the change from Mark to Matthew, who will remain our guide through the Twenty-First Week in Ordinary Time. Following the introductory suggestions from the NAB, the gospel is divided into the infancy story (1:1–2:23); the proclamation of the kingdom (3:1–7:29); the Galilean ministry and mission (8:1–11:1); opposition from portions of Israel (11:2–13:53); teachings on Jesus, the kingdom, and the church (13:54–18:35); Judean and Jerusalem ministry (19:1–25:46); and the passion/resurrection account (26:1–28:20). Arranged within that structure there are five discourses, possibly alluding to the first five books of the Pentateuch: Sermon on the Mount (5:3–7:27), missionary discourse (10:5-42), parable discourse (13:3-52), church order (18:3-35), and eschatological discourse (24:4–25:46).

Jesus is presented by Matthew as the royal Davidic Messiah and the new Moses. For the mixed Matthean community of Jews and Gentiles, the Jewishness of Jesus is clearly presented with respect and conviction.

Literary Link

Monday of the Tenth Week in Ordinary Time

The Beatitudes (vv. 3-12) introduce the Sermon on the Mount and the teachings of Jesus regarding the kingdom of God. Jesus is presented as a new Moses, teaching from the mountaintop. Obviously, each of these blessings could be a launching pad for a brief weekday homily. The first two are selected for brief comment. The eight Beatitudes of Matthew for the disciples are contrasted with the Ten Commandments of Sinai. They also form a bookend for the requirements demanded of the nations in the great judgment parable (25:31-46).

Jesus the Teacher

Sitting down (v. 1) was always the ancient form for teaching. The posture suggested authority and signaled that respect was proper toward an elder, at least in wisdom if not in age. The liturgical postures in both synagogue and early Christian churches embodied that same practice. To be a teacher implies having some experience and knowledge to share as well as a community of learners.

Poor in Spirit

Although the first beatitude as phrased in the Gospel of Luke seems to emphasize the physical dimension of poverty (6:20), Matthew qualifies the concept with the addition of "in spirit" (v. 3). The renowned British preacher Simon Tugwell, OP, suggested that "poor in spirit" includes the ability to consider absolutely everything in life as pure gift. We possess nothing as our own. For the spiritually mature, therefore, that would even include those things that seem initially troublesome and painful, and only in retrospect are seen as filled with grace and growth. Even the cross is a gift!

Those Who Mourn

The second beatitude should not imply God is especially pleased with sad sacks. In fact we are told by the French spiritual writer Léon Bloy that "joy is the infallible sign of God's presence." Granted, no one passes through life without bruises, but what is lauded here (v. 4) is the ability to live with life's sorrows and disappointments without anger, bitterness, or thoughts of revenge. Such individuals have much to teach the community, and might even merit chairs of their own for teaching.

Tuesday of the Tenth Week in Ordinary Time

First Reading (Year I)

2 Corinthians 1:18-22

Jesus was not "yes" and "no," but "yes" has always been in him.

Jesus as "Yes"

Sometimes Paul was accused of waffling in his responses to situations, perhaps because he had thought about the matter further and developed his mind (a sign of wisdom or a gift of the Spirit), or because the circumstances were new and different. Here Paul invokes the memory of Jesus who embodied the total and complete "yes" to God's will and his own mission. In imitation of Jesus, it is imperative to give a consistent "yes" to God in everything we do. It is always helpful to know that God is the precise object of our fundamental fidelity (v. 18) as we move through life. In Christ we find the pivotal point of unified consensus between the divine "yes" of God's promises to us and the human "yes" of grateful response and commitment to the Father. Jesus is the great "amen" in both directions (v. 20). The great doxology of the Eucharist embodies that response.

God's Constancy

God is faithful (v. 18). All of God's promises find expression and embodiment in Christ: the offer of forgiveness, love for creation, the enduring covenant, and divine fidelity toward God's people. Although God respects our human free will and its choices, God's fidelity is found in the offer of second chances. For us who waffle so often between our frail "yeses" and our "noes," the image of God as constant in his promises remains a source of hope and confidence. The gospel begins with an invitation to repentance/*metanoia* (Matt 4:17). Sometimes a change of mind enables us to become faithful again.

Antiphon (Year I)

Psalm 119:135a

Lord, let your face shine on me.

Shining Disc

One of the common images for the Semitic God of justice was the burning winged solar disc. Assyrian bas-reliefs often picture the king associated with that image of an all-seeing and illuminating God. As the refrain states, the God of Israel shines (v. 135) and sees everything without shadow or obscurity. Moreover, divine revelation "sheds light" (v. 130). The notion is also included as a special benediction in the blessing of Aaron (Num 6:25), which later became familiar in the "Blessing of Saint Francis."

Psalm 119: Blessings of Obedience

For a full 176 verses this alphabetic psalm sings of the glory and wonders of the will of God. The psalm endlessly recounts the blessings that compliant obedience brings to the faithful who embrace God's illuminating commands. The teachings of the God of Israel even bring light to all nations.

First Reading (Year II)

1 Kings 17:7-16

The jar of flour shall not go empty, as the Lord had foretold through Elijah.

A Widow's Hospitality

The story of the kindness of the desperately poor widow of Zarephath presumes the image of a widow as among the most vulnerable among the people of Israel, utterly dependent and without resources. Of all people, it is to a widow without personal resources that the prophet is sent (v. 8), thus making it very clear that salvation comes from God alone. Famine made her plight even more desperate. Her generosity (v. 15) therefore acknowledged God as the ultimate source for her meager sustenance, which she freely shared with Elijah. When we share what we have, no matter how modest, God's reward is abundant.

Multiplication of Resources

One cannot help but see the similarity between the widow's ready generosity (v. 15) and the multiplication of the loaves and fishes as recounted by the evangelists (Matt 14:14-21). Only when we acknowledge that we have virtually nothing, and allow our poverty to be revealed, does God step in to make clear that God alone is the true source of any successful endeavor! The jar did not go empty or the jug run dry (v. 16). Later in the same chapter (vv. 17-24) Elijah even raised the widow's son as further evidence of God's power. This miracle was often used by the early church writers to illustrate the life-giving power of the miraculous Eucharist.

ANTIPHON (YEAR II)

Psalm 4:7a

Lord, let your face shine on us.

Psalm 4: A Plea for Help

This brief psalm was considered an Evening Prayer in the early church because it expressed great confidence, even amid distress (v. 2), at the end of the day (v. 9). The psalmist rebukes his contemporaries who are so dull of heart as to be unable to see God's enduring fidelity (v. 3).

(Curiously, this is the same antiphonal refrain, though cited from Psalm 4 rather than from Psalm 119, as used for the response to the first reading from 2 Corinthians in Year I's cycle on this same day of the Tenth Week in Ordinary Time.)

GOSPEL

Matthew 5:13-15

You are the light of the world.

Tuesday of the Tenth Week in Ordinary Time

Literary Link

After eight beatitudes in the third person, a final blessing was given to "you who are persecuted" (see v. 11). This direct address is now continued with images of salt and light. The effect of that change is to make the teaching personal and perennial for every generation of disciples.

Salt

The image of salt is very engaging: seasoning for bland foods, warming chemical for melting ice, and preservative. In the ancient world it was also a symbol for wisdom, hence the church's older baptismal ritual included the act of placing some salt on the tongue of the (often infant) candidate. Salt was a very valuable commodity in the ancient world, and is still regulated and taxed by governments in the modern world (i.e., Italy, where it is sold in special stores with tobacco). One should not overlook the fact that salt was only obtained by difficult and extended labor, either by underground mining (as indicated by the phrase "back to the salt mines") or by the lengthy process of distillation. The metaphor presumes intensive personal labor if the quality of being salt (v. 13) and light is to be achieved.

Light

In an ancient world whose nights were only illuminated by small oil lamps at best, the suggestion that the disciples should be the light of the world (v. 14) seems more than a bit hyperbolic. The phrase suggests that they have value, importance, and usefulness for others. Torches were rare and signs of affluence. The obligation to allow the light to be seen and used makes it clear that the light is not for us alone. Light, like every other creature, exists to serve neighbors and to give glory to God.

The Community's Witness

In the Greek text the "you" who are the salt and light is plural, suggesting that only when our varied gifts are joined together in a mutually interdependent way can our church community be salt or light. It is the entire community that is summoned to be seasoning and illumination for others. Contemporary ecclesiology often points out that the church's activities should be viewed as models for the way the rest of the world's citizens undertake social ministries and offer help to those in need.

Wednesday of the Tenth Week in Ordinary Time

First Reading (Year I)

2 Corinthians 3:4-11

He has qualified us as ministers of a new covenant, not of the letter but of spirit.

Human Qualifications

Job descriptions customarily list the qualifications and background expected for acceptable performance of the tasks. If Paul is qualified for his own vocational calling (v. 5) only by the grace and gift of God, we might also consider every "qualification" we possess when volunteering for an activity or filling out a job application as sheer gift from God. That fact alone gives true confidence (v. 4) when we are faced with a difficult job to be done. Moreover, if all qualifications come from God, they are ultimately directed to God's glory, not to our own prestige. Any achievement on our part comes from our cooperation, not initiative.

Ministry of the Spirit

Being involved in sharing and transmitting God's Spirit is what gives true and lasting glory to our life and work. Paul insists that the Spirit gives life (v. 6). The transforming Spirit of God is the source, medium, and ultimate destiny of everything we do for ourselves and for the larger community. The life-giving Spirit of God is the glue that holds the universe together. Paul contrasts the passing radiance of the physical face of Moses (v. 7) with the enduring radiance of the ministry of the Holy Spirit (v. 8). Paul imagines that even the works of charity, peace, and justice done by the baptized are luminous before God.

Antiphon (Year I)

Psalm 99:9c

Holy is the Lord our God.

Holy

It is always helpful to remember that the fundamental meaning of the Hebrew word "*qadosh*/holy" is "different." The truly "holy" is radically different from the normal human emotional reactions (such as anger, envy, lust, etc.) to things and people. In some manner "holy" is different from the entire created order. Divine transcendence is at the heart of this refrain (v. 9), which is repeated at the beginning (v. 5) and the end (v. 9) of the verses chosen by the Lectionary from Psalm 99 as a response to the reading. Note the things listed as part and parcel of this specific "holiness" of God: holy heroes of faith (v. 6), the pillar of cloud from Exodus (v. 7), and forgiveness (v. 8).

Lord our God

The personal title of the God of Israel is "YHWH/Lord," often, though not with utter certainty, vocalized as *Yahweh*, which means "He makes come into being." The sacredness of the name is indicated by the use of the word "Lord" when it occurs. The personal God of Israel is acclaimed in this refrain (v. 9), therefore, as One who remains the eternal source and origin for all things and peoples. There is a sense of confidence, dependence, and relationship that is conveyed by this title. Catholics have recently been cautioned by the Holy See to avoid the use of "Yahweh" in liturgical songs out of respect for Jewish sensitivities. That personal divine name is considered so revered and sacred to Orthodox Jews as to be unspeakable by human tongues.

First Reading (Year II)

1 Kings 18:20-39

Let it be known this day that you, LORD, are God.

The Call for Decision

The prophet Elijah, confronted by the multitudes who worshiped Baal, the Canaanite god of fertility, called people to end their vacillation (v. 21) between the Lord/YHWH and Baal. The cult of Baal had grown in the northern kingdom under the influence of Queen Jezebel and her husband, King Ahab. This story is masterful in its literary drama, pastoral urgency, and theological acumen. Summoning an assembly on Mount Carmel after a long hard drought, Elijah demanded that the people make a definitive choice (v. 21). Generation after generation the same religious demand confronts us as well: decision for God and lifelong perseverance in that choice.

The Two Sacrifices

Elijah insists that the priests of Baal offer their sacrifice and gives them every opportunity to demonstrate the reality and power of Baal, but to no avail (v. 29). Then Elijah dramatically made every effort to dampen the altar and gifts, and thus to make it more difficult for the Lord to consume them with fire from heaven, but the blaze was ignited (v. 38) and the authority of the Lord asserted and established in the sight of all. The final verse concludes with an act of faith in the Lord God of Israel (v. 39) who is also the God of Jesus and his followers. As Pope Benedict XVI often insists when offering encouragement to members of the Catholic-Jewish dialogue, "We worship the same God."

ANTIPHON (YEAR II)

Psalm 16:1b

Keep me safe, O God; you are my hope.

Psalm 16: A Prayer of New Converts

Psalm 16 has been seen by scholars as a sort of RCIA ritual by which converts to the faith of Israel rejected other/former gods and reaffirmed their faith in YHWH alone (v. 2). Recognizing the sorrows of those who worship other gods (v. 4), and rejecting their sacrifices, the worshiper of Israel's God accepts everything as an inheritance from the Lord (v. 5) and pledges fidelity to the Lord (v. 8).

Wednesday of the Tenth Week in Ordinary Time

Safety

The refrain (v. 1) highlights the fact that fidelity to the Lord brings security and provides the only sure source of hope for the future. No matter what may lie ahead, those who pledge their lives to the Lord are able to live in the hope that no difficulty or disaster can hold final victory. Crossing guards may offer temporary safety to children after school, as do warning signs to motorists approaching faulty bridges, but confidence in God alone provides lasting security.

GOSPEL

Matthew 5:17-19

I have come not to abolish the law, but to fulfill it.

Literary Link

After addressing the enduring light (v. 16) of the faithful community, the gospel presents Jesus now turning to speak about the Torah/law by which and from which the faithful community finds its light for others. To Matthew's mixed community of Jews and Gentiles the enduring validity of the "*torah*/*nomos*/law" is proclaimed (v. 17). The sermon will then proceed to offer six new interpretations of that "law."

Enduring Validity of the Torah

The community, from which the Gospel of Matthew came and to which it was spoken, was one comprised of both Gentiles and Torah-observant Jewish Christians who obeyed all the prescriptions, even the maintenance of a kosher kitchen (strictly separating meat from dairy products). Even with all the differences, they were united in their deep fidelity to Jesus the Teacher, their fierce passion to seek and do God's will, and their mutual respect for each other. That mutual respect remained in place even when they acknowledged different notions of what God's will might respectively demand of each. After considerable struggle, it was finally concluded (Acts 15) that Gentile followers of Jesus were not required to become Jewish in order to become Christian. Nevertheless, the Torah was the guide for all (v. 18).

Fulfill, Not Abolish

Jesus does not simply obey or comply with the law but embodies it perfectly (v. 17). The apostle Paul insisted that God's covenant with Israel remained eternally valid and irrevocable (Rom 11:29). All the different prescriptions of divine teaching and daily practice converge in his being and his witness to God's sovereign action in our world. Prophets, rather than merely predicting or promising some future blessing, primarily gave witness to God's actions in the currents of history or the events of their day. Jesus embodies that witness definitively and for all time. Precisely how to hold in tension the Christian convictions about the eternal validity of Israel's covenant and the universal redemptive mission of Jesus is the challenge of our day in interreligious dialogue.

Teaching the Little Ones

There is a perennial obligation to hand on the faith to children and also to all newcomers (v. 18) to the Christian faith community. Sometimes it may seem that catechists are tempted to teach their personal prejudices rather than the fullness of the faith as handed down through the generations of faithful and holy people under the guidance of their pastors. This gospel is an occasion to pray for all the wise and well-informed adults who pass on the faith to successive generations. This catechetical ministry has been acclaimed as the most important lay ministry in the church. It is the work of the entire church, even though some individuals may exercise it in the name of others.

Thursday of the Tenth Week in Ordinary Time

FIRST READING (YEAR I)

2 Corinthians 3:15–4:1, 3-6

God has shown in our hearts to bring to light the knowledge of the glory of God.

Veiled Hearts

Paul struggles with the fact that people, Jews and Gentiles alike, to whom he preached, did not always accept the person and mission of Jesus. By way of explanation he recalls how with unveiled face Moses spoke with God face-to-face (Exod 34:34). By contrast, human beings do not understand Jesus because, using a metaphor of impaired sight/belief, their minds and hearts are veiled before the truth (v. 15) as a result of their human ignorance or fear or selfishness. Resistance to faith is a perennial challenge. Ancient Jewish leaders as well as modern Christians live with the same problem. Moreover, contemporary atheism is a special challenge in our world of empirical science. If we are honest, we must admit that atheists exist to some degree because they see no compelling light in our lives.

An Easter Implication

The traditional Pharisaic reasoning of Paul in these sections of the letter may seem convoluted at times and difficult to follow for contemporary Christians. Paul's reference to "gazing with unveiled face on the glory of the Lord" (v. 16) could be an encouragement to see Christ as he is without our "blinders" of sin and ignorance. The concept may also offer a clue to the puzzling significance of the head wrappings left separately from the shroud in the empty tomb after the resurrection (John 20:7). Just as Moses put aside his veil when speaking face-to-face with the Lord (Exod 34:34), so Jesus in his glory now sees his Father face-to-face without the veil of the humanity that he had accepted during this earthly life. He left the veil in the empty tomb.

ANTIPHON (YEAR I)

Psalm 85:10b

The glory of the Lord will dwell in our land.

God's Glory

The refrain (v. 10) picks up the explanations of Paul by recalling the shining brilliance of God's presence. The Hebrew word for glory is *kabod*, something weighty, valuable, and somehow eye-catching because of its luminous nature, perhaps like gold. Human beings, however, because of our utter distance from the transcendence of God, cannot behold that splendor directly. Ancient Israelites were even convinced that no one could see the face of God and live. Are there any places or situations where we see some reflection of God's glory?

Temple Presence

When the tent of the meeting was finished and the sacrifices offered by Aaron, the dwelling of God was filled with incense and with the solemn presence of God (Exod 40:34). That same divine presence was believed to fill the holy of holies in the temple of Solomon (1 Kings 8:11). The psalm reminds us that the Lord chose to dwell mysteriously in the land of Israel amidst God's own people (v. 10). The prologue to John's gospel proclaims the same truth regarding the incarnation of the Word (John 1:14). Catholics continue that conviction by the practice of the reservation of the Eucharist in our churches and chapels.

FIRST READING (YEAR II)

1 Kings 18:41-46

Elijah prayed and the sky gave rain (James 5:18).

Prophetic Prayer for Rain

Omitting reference to the killing of all of Jezebel's four hundred prophets of Baal (v. 40), the tale of Elijah on Mount Carmel picks up the story of the end of the terrible three-year drought. As if to demonstrate that the water poured on the sacrifices to the Lord was more significant than merely making the fire more difficult, Elijah had also prayed for rain (v. 42). Prophetic signs not only imitated but also initiated the reality they proclaimed. Recognizing that the Lord alone is the source of fertility and agricultural prosperity, Elijah continues to pray for rain. He repeatedly sends his servant to look for its initial sign in the clouds to the west (v. 44). The books of Kings are always eager to describe prophets as the representatives of God whose words are powerful and effective.

The Fields of Our Time

The story of Elijah on Mount Carmel is a perfect time to pray for the fruitfulness of our farming fields at the approach of spring and for the meteorologists who attempt to read the signs of weather in our skies (v. 44). The story of God's mysterious use of rain and Elijah's search for signs in the heavens is also a good occasion to pray for all contemporary analysts who try to explain what God is about in all the historical currents and movements of our time.

ANTIPHON (YEAR II)

Psalm 65:2a

It is right to praise you in Zion, O God.

Psalm 65: A Farmer's Prayer

Psalm 65's poetic praise for the blessings of fertility and especially for the gift of rain (v. 10) that enables the production of a fruitful harvest (v. 12) is the perfect response to the end of the terrible drought at the time of Elijah. Each aspect of agricultural need and human labor is celebrated as fruitful because of God's blessings. There are always portions of our earth in desperate need of water and areas where pollution of those resources indicate a terrible violation of stewardship. For them we pray as well.

Praise in Zion

The fact that the refrain places the praise at the site of the temple on Zion (v. 2) suggests that this is to be sung at a liturgical service of thanksgiving. Such services at the various agricultural seasons of the year are reminders of our dependence on nature and on the work of others. This is a good time to warn against petty complaints when spring rains come at what we selfishly judge to be inopportune or inconvenient times. Regular prayers for planting and reaping are always timely.

GOSPEL

Matthew 5:20-26

Whoever is angry with his brother will be liable to judgment.

Literary Link

The text moves from a general admonition to teachers regarding faithfulness (v. 19) to the first of the five reinterpretations of the commandments, namely, regarding killing (vv. 20-26). Jesus is a teacher ever faithful to the letter as well as the spirit of the law.

Anger and Killing

Although Jesus teaches the same values as those of the Pharisees, he brings certain new emphases of his own. The immediate reference to "righteousness/Hebrew *tzedeqah*/Greek *dikaiosune*" (v. 20) places his instruction within Jewish tradition, but puts a new focus for that teaching on the inner anger that precedes any act of killing. When Jesus refers to "righteousness," he presumes the biblical notion of right relationships to all creatures, not merely justice in the sense of paying bills and resolving debts. In his focus on anger, Jesus insists on the importance of a person's interior sentiments as well as one's external actions. This is dramatically illustrated by listing angry words with the prohibition of killing (v. 21). Once again the teaching is directed toward doing the right thing for the right reason.

Gifts at the Altar

A somewhat shocking aspect of this passage

is that we are called to be somehow responsible for the inner sentiments of others as well as ourselves, hence the command of Jesus to deal with the hurt and resentment of others (v. 23) before presenting our gifts at the altar. The teaching of Jesus about the entire context of offering gifts referred to the temple ritual in Jerusalem. It also includes our experience of offering the Eucharist in our assemblies of faith and charity. If someone harbors sentiments against us, we are commanded to attend to that reality as part of our reconciliation and communal worship.

Thursday of the Tenth Week in Ordinary Time

Friday of the Tenth Week in Ordinary Time

First Reading (Year I)

2 Corinthians 4:7-15

He who raised the Lord Jesus will raise us also with Jesus.

Earthen Vessels

The ministry of mercy, the shining presence of God in our hearts, and the knowledge of God's glory are all contained in our individual, personal, and very frail human existence. This magnificent image brings to mind the common earthenware flower pots (v. 7) that are found on porches as well as in backyard gardens and sheds. They are useful, inexpensive, and contrast wonderfully with the invaluable beauty of the flowers they contain. Paul's self-depreciating humility has given us a remarkable and perennial metaphor, drawn from everyday life in the ancient world as well as our own, for ourselves and for the entire material world in which we live. Everything human is fragile, but God's surpassing power shines forth amid all our weaknesses (v. 11).

Ultimate Success

Paul's list of the hardships that marked his own apostolic ministry and journeys included affliction, persecution, and even puzzlement at times (vv. 8ff.), none of which was able to deaden his conviction or terminate his sense of calling (v. 11). Paul's conviction remained strongly rooted, not in himself, but ultimately and necessarily in the one who raised Jesus from the dead. That same victorious God is also our source of personal confidence (v. 13).

Antiphon (Year I)

Psalm 116:17a

To you, Lord, I will offer a sacrifice of praise.

"To You"

The beauty and the blessing of using the psalms as inspired responses to a text, such as Paul's laments about the hardship of his call, is the personal focus they provide. The community at prayer is invited to address God personally in, above, and beyond the human experience described in that reading (v. 17). It is in God, and in God alone, that we find the big picture of our lives. It is to him that we direct our thanks and praise.

Sacrifice of Praise

The only suitable response to the hardships that seem inevitably connected with attempting to do the right thing, even under duress, is praise for the God who makes all things possible. This is the entire community's reaction to the heartaches of life and to the difficulties entailed at times in submission to God's will for the transformation and salvation of our world. Praise is itself a sacrifice (v. 17) because it pays attention to God alone without self-serving motivation.

First Reading (Year II)

1 Kings 19:9a, 11-16

Stand on the mountain before the Lord.

Tiny Whispering Sound

Part of the uniqueness of the God of Israel as contrasted with the Canaanite fertility cults of neighboring people was Israel's refusal to identify God with any natural phenomena around them. Wind, earthquake, and fire might be instruments of the true God, but never true symbols of God. The Lord/Yhwh was "One who would be what he would be" (see Exod 3:14). The tiny whispering sound (v. 12) remained a pointer to the utter mystery of the divine. We may have favorite devotional practices and "reminders" of the utterly divine presence, but they are not God!

Prophetic Dejection

Self-pity is a very human reaction to a task with major obligations, but God is not willing to allow that emotional state to hold a permanent place in an authentic prophetic spirit (v. 14). Elijah, like Isaiah (Second Servant Song, Isa 49:4) or Jeremiah (15:18) before him, may have had moments of weariness over the seeming futility of his task. That sentiment, however, was merely allowed by God as a refining and purifying test to teach his prophet that ultimately any results must be ascribed to God alone. God's response is simply to send Elijah out again into the currents of political and military history (v. 16) in order to designate new Israelite leadership more acceptable to God.

ANTIPHON (YEAR II)

Psalm 27:8b

I long to see your face, O Lord.

The Face(s) of God

A frequent description for God's "presence" is the Hebrew word for "faces" (v. 8). Admittedly anthropomorphic, the poetic image suggested the various divine responses to human beings as if concretized in a divine "face" of benevolence, compassion, benign indulgence, anger, or scowling rejection. The combination of such "faces" became equated to God's presence. The Hebrew behind this refrain is precisely the plural for whom we seek. Later Christian writers have detected early hidden clues to the Trinity in that phrase.

Elijah's Desire

This refrain captures well Elijah's deepest yearning, namely, the consolation of God's presence (v. 8) even in his state of depression and dejection in the face of such hostile human opposition. That very human desire for vocational perseverance, no matter what the current and transitory emotion might be, is itself a gift from God and a grace. Perhaps when we are really down, God is in fact most present to us because we are forced to depend on God, not ourselves!

Friday of the Tenth Week in Ordinary Time

GOSPEL

Matthew 5:27-32

Everyone who looks at a woman with lust has already committed adultery with her in his heart.

Literary Link

The second reinterpretation of the Torah/law of God offered by Jesus in his Sermon on the Mount deals with adultery and divorce (vv. 27-32). Not only does Jesus stress the inner motivation of our actions but he also highlights the effect that our decisions may have on others if a divorce forces someone to marry out of desperation for physical and material survival (v. 32).

Internal Sin

A constant and consistent teaching in the gospels is the fact that true sin is found in the intention before any external action can take place to carry the evil decision into external practice. In this case, it is adultery of the eye or of the mind (v. 28) where sin is to be found. A very wise district attorney once stated that the longer he worked in the public sector, the more convinced he became that the sisters who had taught in his parish school years earlier were right when they insisted, "Don't entertain bad thoughts, because if you think about anything long enough, you'll do it."

Eliminating the Occasions of Sin

One should be very careful to avoid presuming literalness to these two examples of eye or hand (vv. 29-30) because they are meant figuratively. The physical body given us by God and pronounced "good" at creation and even further sanctified by baptism is a temple of God that should be respected. A subtle dimension of the teaching is found in the fact that, although the left hand is customarily reserved for hygiene, the right hand is used for social relations, and therefore to lose its use is to separate oneself completely from the community. The commandment of Jesus is to resist all evil, not to amputate or disfigure. Catholic exegesis always seeks to ascertain the type of literature in question before determining the proper response sought by God.

Saturday of the Tenth Week in Ordinary Time

FIRST READING (YEAR I)

2 Corinthians 5:14-21

For our sake, he made him to be sin who did not know sin.

Christ's Love as Motive

Paul's famous phrase "The love of Christ impels us" (v. 14) suggests that the very fact of Christ's love for us, and the extent by which that love was expressed in his total gift of self for everyone, should become a motive for extending our love toward all others in need. To say it differently, Christ's love for us is both model and driving force for our own actions toward others. That transforming love is one of the special marks of the new creation (v. 17). It is not that we love God but that God loved us first (1 John 4:10).

Ministry of Reconciliation

The word "reconciliation" occurs five times within a few verses (vv. 18-20). The notion and the reality imply putting parts back together again, and restoring relationships broken by sin, misunderstanding, or distance. Every family has some heartache, often related to the rupture of the bonds between parents and children, siblings, or spouses, which human efforts alone do not seem able to heal or rectify. Paul sees Christ's redemptive work as healing the breach between God and human beings (v. 19). We bring those wounds to every Eucharist and ask for the insight, humility, and courage to address them in God's name. Every Christian is called to be an "ambassador" of "reconciliation" (v. 20). God's righteousness includes a passion for reconciliation (v. 21). The admonition makes more sense than ever in our terribly divided world.

ANTIPHON (YEAR I)

Psalm 103:8a

The Lord is kind and merciful.

"Kind and Merciful"

The two adjectives in this early creedal confession regarding the true character of the God of Israel are not quite what they may seem. The first Hebrew word in this refrain (v. 8), translated as "kind," is *rhm*, the quality of mercy that is best characterized by a maternal womb-like compassion that loves no matter what. Likewise, the second Hebrew word is *hnn*, conveying grace, favor, and attractiveness to its object. If God is gracious in that sense, God is the source of everything that makes us attractive and loveable. God's compassion loves us into being attractive!

The God of Israel

Every so often it is pastorally helpful to pause and to remind ourselves and our people of the utter fallacy of the assumption that the God of the first covenant is a God of anger and judgment. The two characteristics expressed in the refrain (v. 8) represent a forceful argument against any such (occasionally anti-Semitic) misrepresentation of the God of Israel. To the contrary, the words celebrate God's mercy to Israel and to all who have become members of God's family through the extended gift of covenantal membership.

FIRST READING (YEAR II)

1 Kings 19:19-21

Then Elisha left and followed Elijah.

Elisha, a Prophetic Colleague and Successor

By definition there is something solitary to a prophet's vocation: called by God to speak clearly to a present moment, explaining precisely what God is doing even if the rest of his contemporary world can't see it yet. At the same time such a message requires testing by the community, because not everyone who comes running over the hill, claiming to speak in God's name, is to be accepted blindly. Elisha was chosen to be a disciple to Elijah (v. 19), helping to sift his word and supporting his work. God's will always includes a community because we are social creatures by definition and God does not want any of us, even prophets, to be alone.

Elijah's Choice

The text doesn't indicate why Elisha was chosen (v. 19). Perhaps Elijah's cloak was thrown over his shoulders because he was busy at work and clearly not lazy or indolent; after all, working with a dozen teams of yoked oxen is no small task! Elisha's willingness to leave everything in order to be embraced by the prophetic call suggests that it was a good choice, however it was made (v. 21). Elisha's request to offer farewell to his parents was affirmed, not denied, by Elijah as long as that gesture was a sign of "closure" to one way of life and an opening to another. Although we are not always able to choose successors, we can select colleagues and partners. The major criterion in partners in the work of the Lord should be those who make us strong and effective, not merely those who make us look good.

ANTIPHON (YEAR II)

Psalm 16:5a

You are my inheritance, O Lord.

Allotted Portion and Cup

The actual wording of the verse chosen by the church to serve as a response to this reading is specific: "my inheritance"/"portion and my cup" (v. 5). As a member of a family, one would receive daily food rations from the common granary and family provisions. The psalm puts family aside to be replaced by God alone from whom daily sustenance now comes. The liturgy describes that portion and cup for what it is, namely, the inheritance given to us by God whose family we now join. In this liturgical response Elisha, having said farewell to his parents, is now given words by which he can profess his dependence upon God and upon the great prophet Elijah for his sustenance.

Saturday of the Tenth Week in Ordinary Time

Communal Relationship

In claiming God as an inheritance (v. 5) the entire praying community accepts its relationship with God as the defining characteristic for its entire existence. People gathered for eucharistic prayer are related to each other first and foremost because they are related to God as the source and cause of their unity. No longer strangers and aliens, we have become fellow citizens with the holy ones and members of God's household (Eph 2:19). This communal summons to membership in God's family is an important antidote to the radical individualism of our culture.

GOSPEL

Matthew 5:33-37

I say to you, do not swear at all.

Literary Link

The third reinterpretation of the Torah offered by Jesus concerns the taking of oaths (vv. 33-37), something done all too casually even in our modern Western society.

The Power of an Oath

Contemporary society has fallen into a great casualness about the taking of God's name (v. 34). This use of the divine name has become an interjection of surprise, joy, or almost any other human emotion. Strictly speaking, to swear is to utter the name of God in testimony to the truth of one's statement. To swear is to invoke God's presence as witness to our firm intention to do something. This passage offers an opportunity to teach the difference between vulgarity, which is often incorrectly labeled "swearing," and the misuse of God's name. If we are sensitive to the pejorative use of the names of family members or those we love, how much more attentive should we be to the misuse of God's name?

Disciples as People of Truth

This portion of the Sermon on the Mount insists that true disciples of Jesus should be so clearly and forthrightly people of recognized truth that the invocation of God's name as further testimony should never be necessary (v. 34). We do what we say we will do, and we speak the truth without embellishment because of who we are and what we stand for.

Monday of the Eleventh Week in Ordinary Time

First Reading (Year I)

2 Corinthians 6:1-10

In everything we commend ourselves as ministers of God.

Acceptable Time

Immediately prior to this passage, Paul had called everyone to be reconciled with each other and to see him and themselves as servants of that ministry of reconciliation (5:18-20). Now he begins with the principle of not rejecting God's grace (v. 1). Presuming discernment, the apostle insists that such reconciliation should not be postponed or delayed for any reason. The Greek word, translated as "acceptable time," is *kairos* (v. 2), the proper time for a decision because all relevant factors converge to demand a particular response. Every inspiration of grace should be taken seriously and can become a *kairos*, the right moment for decision. We know what it is to miss an opportunity for doing good. Spiritual writers tell us that time is the one thing that cannot be redeemed; it rarely, if ever, returns to offer a second chance.

Hardships beyond Measure

Paul proceeds to list all the difficulties that have attended his apostolic ministry to the Gentiles (vv. 4ff.). In announcing the resurrection and the new creation, which had been introduced into human history by that decisive event, Paul's life has not been one of ease and comfort. He has not personally profited in terms of material comfort or social advantage. All these obstacles are invoked as authentication of his mission. Precisely because Paul depends so totally upon God and God alone, he remains victorious and unwaveringly optimistic in his conviction that ultimate success will be God's. Although human beings and even nature itself at times may seem to stand as impassible obstacles, God will not be thwarted, nor will Paul in his unfeigned love for the truth (v. 6) and for the people whom God wishes to claim his own. That love is the model for Christian pastoral leadership and for the entire community summoned to be instruments in the transformation of the larger world in every age. And we think we have it tough?

Antiphon (Year I)

Psalm 98:2a

The Lord has made known his salvation.

Salvation

Literally, the Hebrew word for "salvation" (v. 2) means freedom from "tight spots" over which the individual or the entire people have no control. Precisely when we recognize that we are unable to make any decisive moves by our own power, God fulfills the promises of old and achieves that purpose.

Make Known

It is God who not only accomplishes that liberation but also makes it known (v. 2). The community in prayer, responding to the reading about Paul's apostolic ministry in spite of all obstacles and hardships, must acknowledge that God is the source of his apostolic courage and determination. Even though God may choose to use many human instruments and events as occasions for interventions, the Lord alone remains the ultimate cause that the community at prayer announces and praises.

First Reading (Year II)

1 Kings 21:1-16

Naboth has been stoned to death.

The Terrible Injustice to Naboth

The passage tells the story of Ahab, a greedy and self-centered king who does not hesitate to violate the rights of a neighbor in order to obtain a nice view from his palace window. Israel lived with an ancient respect for the way in which land was passed from one generation to another within the same family. All property was considered held in an extended "lease" from God and allotted to specific families of covenanted members. The rights of Naboth were unjustly and ruthlessly violated (v. 16). Respect for the property of others is a deeply held value in our Judeo-Christian tradition and may never be violated for personal whim or unjust gain. Naboth was killed for a garden view. The entire community was somehow complicit in the injustice.

Community Corruption

The willingness of the elders and nobles of the city (v. 8) to be compliant instruments of the ruthless designs of Jezebel is a terrible example of cooperation in evil injustice. It was a grievous violation of the responsibility for the common good, which should be exercised by all who share community leadership. This is reprehensible in any society, but especially wicked within the community of the covenant where members are called by God to care for each other's welfare and well-being. Community members today continue to be summoned by God to serve as agents for justice against all those who would exploit the poor and vulnerable for their own selfish benefit.

ANTIPHON (YEAR II)

Psalm 5:2b

Lord, listen to my groaning.

Groaning

The Hebrew word translated here as "groaning" (v. 2) refers to an inner thought so powerful as to be audible to those nearby. Deeply felt emotions of loss, pain, or injustice escape from our lips and easily find external expression. In this liturgical context, the prayer of Naboth, who was so unjustly accused and finally even executed for the whim of the king, becomes such a prayer. Unfortunately communities rich and poor, ancient and modern, have always been filled with such sounds.

Divine Attention

It is the conviction of Israel that God hears the prayers of the poor against evildoers (v. 7). God also responds through the reaction of covenant members whose ability to hear the groans of injustice is enhanced by God's grace in order to become an instrument of God's concern for justice. This is an occasion for the entire eucharistic community to renew advocacy efforts against all who would exploit the vulnerable and illegally, as well as unjustly, take over their possessions. Members of a parish social justice committee could easily be called "Friends of Naboth."

GOSPEL

Matthew 5:38-42

But I say to you, offer no resistance to one who is evil.

Literary Link

Always reflecting the concern of Jesus regarding inner motivation, the Sermon on the Mount considers a fourth area of reinterpreting the demands of the Torah, namely, retaliation for injury and offenses (vv. 38-42).

"An Eye for an Eye"

The command cited from Leviticus 24:20 was intended to moderate human retaliation for offenses. It aimed at limiting the reciprocal punishment one might invoke in response to harm done to one of a family's members. Especially in a culture of honor and shame such vindication could escalate dangerously. The principle of "an eye for an eye" (v. 38) did not demand such reaction but tried to restrain it. Christian response to injustice should promote justice, not merely express anger. The teaching of Jesus recognizes that violence inevitably begets more violence; for that reason those who choose to refrain completely from retaliation are powerful instruments for the transformation of our world. Our contemporary

Monday of the Eleventh Week in Ordinary Time

initiatives for "restorative justice" reflect that concern.

No Resistance to Evil

This is a very difficult teaching, and should not be taken in an isolated fashion without reference to other biblical admonitions and instructions. Care for the poor, the innocent, and the vulnerable is also a biblical injunction to be respected. There are times when compliance with unreasonable demands can disarm an adversary and even effect a conversion from a violent way of life. There are also times when resistance is a form of protecting the poor and innocent. The criterion for any legitimate response should be "What does the person who makes such demands really need?" It is charity that should be the ultimate measure of our reaction, together with discernment by the entire community. We are at our best when we are thoughtful and moderate together.

Tuesday of the Eleventh Week in Ordinary Time

FIRST READING (YEAR I)

2 Corinthians 8:1-9

Christ became poor for your sake.

The Great Collection

Saint Paul decided to work at healing the divide between Jewish and Gentile followers of Jesus by taking up a collection from the Gentiles for the famine-struck Jewish believers in Judea. The idea of contributions as means of establishing unity was a novel one, and one that may still be of use for any fundraising efforts in modern times. The effort was a risk, however, in the sense that even hungry people could reject the gift out of pride or bitter convictions regarding the Gentile/Jewish divisions of the early church. Perhaps all divisions can only be healed by respectful generosity (v. 4) and humble gratitude.

Example of Macedonia

Rivalry and competition may not be the noblest motives for contribution to a good cause, such as the needs of the faithful in Judea, but such sentiments can be useful at times. Paul mentions the Christians of Macedonia (northern Greece) rather as an example of generosity (not rivalry), even suggesting (v. 4) that they begged to be part of the effort. Communities as well as individuals can serve as powerful examples and inspirations for doing good. Good works together with noble intentions are at the very heart of every authentic Christian community. In reference to charity, generosity is the test of authenticity. Their charity was a "gracious act" (v. 6).

The Poverty of Christ

Paul provided the bigger picture by invoking the example of Christ himself (v. 9). Jesus became poor so that we in turn might become spiritually wealthy. The image and reference to Christ is a remarkable example of the manner in which Paul was creative in the development of his early Christian theology for the sake of pastoral exhortation. As a result the incarnation and the passion of Jesus (Phil 2:7) become models for fund and friend raising everywhere.

ANTIPHON (YEAR I)

Psalm 146:1b

Praise the Lord, my soul!

Praise

The psalm's refrain (v. 1) is perfect for the portion of Paul's letter selected by the Lectionary for the liturgy of the day. In response to the exemplary actions of fellow Christians over the centuries, we are invited to praise God whose grace is the ultimate cause for such goodness. These human individuals themselves are only instruments and agents of God at work in our communities.

Soul

The praise that is encouraged and commanded is more than an inner attitude. The Hebrew word *nephesh*, often translated as "soul" (v. 1), is literally the "throat." The refrain therefore presumes that the instrument for a person's praise for God would be words and song (v. 2). Part of Jewish spirituality is the conviction that the entire body and all its faculties should be actively involved in a person's prayer and praise. Prayer without song is therefore only halfhearted.

FIRST READING (YEAR II)

1 Kings 21:17-29

You have provoked me by leading Israel into sin.

Prophets and Kings

It is a curious fact of Israelite history that prophets rose to preeminence during the same years as the kings of Judah and Israel were in existence. One of their major prophetic tasks was to confront royal authority and to keep its actions in conformity with the requirements of the

Tuesday of the Eleventh Week in Ordinary Time

covenant. In the Deuteronomic theology, the prophets were the primary servants of God and voices for God's will. They confronted the ancient equivalent of the government. Such individuals are needed in every age lest the rights and dignity of the voiceless poor be exploited by the more powerful. Authentic faith always finds a voice. The prophets may suffer for their mission (and many did), but truth and justice will ultimately prevail. We believe in a God of justice, not caprice.

Oracles of Judgment

The mystery of God's justice is that the punishment announced by the prophets for any sin is invariably correlative to the sin itself. Because Naboth's blood was shed, that of King Ahab (v. 19) and Jezebel (v. 23) would also be shed. People are punished for what they do wrong as well as by what they do wrong. Moreover, the Bible's ancient sense of the social nature of sin often included punishment for subsequent generations as well as for the offenders themselves. For this reason Elijah included Ahab's son in the punishment for violating justice and leading Israel into sin (v. 29).

ANTIPHON (YEAR II)

Psalm 51:3a

Be merciful, O Lord, for we have sinned.

Repentance

Because the account of Ahab's sin concluded with the king's dawning realization of the horror that had been committed in his name, and because of some level of humble acknowledgment of his sin (v. 27), the story concluded with a mitigation of the punishment. Thus the refrain from the great penitential psalm, the *Miserere*, serves as a fitting liturgical response (v. 3) to the account. True repentance is more than merely being sorry for past actions. Like all experiences of *metanoia*, it involves suddenly seeing everything from a different perspective, namely, God's point of view.

Be Merciful

The actual Hebrew refrain (v. 3) is a petition for renewed favor and grace. Rather than the various Hebrew words for "mercy," the psalm begins with the word *hanan*, which is a plea for the gift that will make God look upon us with favor once more. "Grace" is the biblical quality that makes someone attractive and worthy of a second glance. It is this subtlety that is the focal point of the psalm's petition in the refrain.

GOSPEL

Matthew 5:43-48

Love your enemies.

Literary Link

The prior teaching regarding the obligation to do what we promise without oaths (vv. 23-27) easily leads to the need expressed in today's passage, that is, to love others in action, not merely in word. This teaching represents the fifth reinterpretation (vv. 43-48) provided by Jesus for the Torah in this portion of the Sermon on the Mount.

Semitic Contrasts

Often Semitic expressions advocate one attitude and stress its importance by commanding "hatred" for its opposite. Although one should never hate one's parents, that is precisely and literally commanded by Jesus in contrast to the importance of becoming his disciple (Luke 14:26). Disciples are forbidden to call anyone "father" or "teacher" (Matt 23:8-9). It is an error to follow such admonitions literally without attending to its contrast as the more important factor in the equation. As a matter of fact, there was no written command in the Torah to hate one's enemies. The command was to love one's neighbor (Lev 19:18) and tradition may have deduced that hate for an enemy was tolerated. Knowledge of a language's particular idioms and its culture is always important for properly understanding the Scriptures. That is the reason for the church's requirement that explanatory notes accompany any Scripture translations made available to the faithful (canon 825).

Love for Enemies

"Love" or concern, even for those who may wish us harm, is the command of Jesus in this portion of the Sermon on the Mount (v. 44). It might be helpful to substitute the word "unlovable" for enemy in order to help us understand the full import of this teaching. To love the unlovable (from our limited personal perspective) is to recognize that they may in fact possess unseen value, or may even need love more than others. It is also to imitate the attitude of God who embraces all people by his love in the hope that they will be transformed in the process. Even we, sinners as we are, don't have to be good for God to love us because he will love us into goodness if we but let him. God respects our free decisions but always hopes that we will find a way back to him. The members of the praying community are invited to be divine instruments and to provide encouragement in that journey. Note that rain was considered a blessing; therefore the intent of the teaching is that God even allows rain on the unjust (v. 45).

Wednesday of the Eleventh Week in Ordinary Time

FIRST READING (YEAR I)

2 Corinthians 9:6-11

God loves a cheerful giver.

Generosity Begets Generosity

The first motive of encouragement for contributing to Paul's great collection is the reminder taken from agricultural life that generous sowing of seed (v. 6) is a requirement for a bountiful harvest. One could extend the same metaphor into many areas of human life, for sparseness in use of ingredients makes bland cooking, and cutting corners in most endeavors produces the likelihood of minimal results. God is lavish by nature, and generosity gets results.

The Burden of Reluctance

A second motive is offered by Paul: the necessity of avoiding any sense of acting grudgingly when making a contribution (v. 7). Anyone who gives reluctantly loses the deep satisfaction of generosity and in fact never really gives from the heart. In effect anyone who gives resentfully still holds onto the penny in spirit and forfeits the blessing of cheerfulness in extending a hand to others in need. Paul is masterful in such fund and friend raising, especially in his uncanny ability to understand the human psyche. It is God himself who is invoked as the model and patron of beneficence (v. 8).

ANTIPHON (YEAR I)

Psalm 112:1b

Blessed the man who fears the Lord.

Fear and Blessing

The refrain is a profound statement because it is reverence for God (not fear in the servile sense) that makes a person truly blessed (v. 1) and such an attitude helps one to know that absolutely everything is gift. The things we have should never be viewed as the result of entitlement. They have been generously received from God to be used for others, not merely or exclusively for ourselves (v. 4). This is the attitude that enables a person to feel deeply blessed and contented throughout life, even in more difficult days.

Care for the Poor

Psalm 112 concludes with the reminder that such an attitude of gratitude enables people to be lavish in their concern and response to others less fortunate (v. 9). The psalm celebrates the interrelationship between gratitude and generosity.

FIRST READING (YEAR II)

2 Kings 2:1, 6-14

A flaming chariot came between them, and Elijah went up to heaven.

The Second Book of Kings

This division into a First and Second Book of Kings was an artificial break for the sake of convenience in the length of the scroll. The same theological concerns of First Kings continue through this work, highlighting the role of prophets and explaining the final downfall of the northern kingdom of Israel and the Babylonian destruction of the temple. Those who ignore the demands of God's covenant inevitably suffer the loss of the blessings promised to the faithful. They incur the curses pronounced against the unfaithful ones.

Prophetic Mentoring

Sensing something ominous or at least very significant in the air, Elisha refused to abandon his teacher, even when asked to do so (v. 6). Sometimes immediate obedience is not really what is needed. Elijah's command that Elisha remain behind was an opportunity for Elisha to pause and consider the implications and consequences of moving forward. The life of a prophet can cost a great deal in terms of opposition and distress. Elisha chose to continue because of his earlier experience of the transforming power of his friendship with the great Elijah. Imagine what it might be like to have a zealous prophet like Elijah as a personal mentor and trainer. The intensity of Elijah's devotion to the will of God must have impressed Elisha, as it did everyone else in his day, and made him feel very humble. This account could be an opportunity to recall those who have been the most important influences in our lives and to be grateful for them.

The Fiery Chariot

Rationalistic explanations of the event abound, some requiring more credulity than a miracle. There was no tradition regarding any grave of the great Elijah, refounder of Israel. He seems to have had the nickname of "warhorse of Israel" because of his zeal and powerful personality (v. 12). Perhaps the dust devils of the hot southern sirocco winds were the starting point for the tradition of Elijah's ascent to the final presence of God. Fire was a powerful symbol for God, illuminating, comforting, destructive, and immaterial. Elijah's prophetic vocation was from God and his destiny completed that cycle. Sometimes it is best to allow the metaphor to remain a metaphor without any definitive explanation other than wonder at the power of God.

Spirit and Mantle

Elisha's request for a double portion was not greed or self-aggrandizement, but rather a reflection of the customary practice of an elder son receiving a double portion of any inheritance (v. 9; Deut 21:17). The double portion was given because the firstborn had special obligations to care for other members of the family. Elisha simply asks to be recognized as an older child and heir. He also receives Elijah's abandoned cloak, which apparently had its own power by association (v. 14). Each person throughout history receives his or her unique vocation in life, and is asked by God to respond wisely and well to whatever circumstances arise.

Antiphon (Year II)

Psalm 31:25

Let your hearts take comfort, all who hope in the Lord.

Psalm 31: God's Goodness

The verses chosen from Psalm 31 as a response to the story of Elijah and his chariot enumerate the ways in which God cares for his faithful ones in good times and more difficult ones, providing refuge (v. 20) and protection (v. 21) as needed for those faithful to him.

Comfort and Hope

The refrain itself (v. 25) would be the perfect prayer for both Elijah and Elisha. It expresses utter confidence in God's ultimate care, no matter what royal opposition might devise as punishment or retaliation. The refrain's invitation to have hope and take comfort is also offered to anyone in the daily eucharistic assembly who may be experiencing hardship, heartache, or difficulty on any level.

Gospel

Matthew 6:1-6, 16-18

And your Father who sees what is hidden will repay you.

Literary Link

The three traditional "righteous deeds" of almsgiving, prayer, and fasting are familiar from the readings selected for Ash Wednesday each year. Note that the Lectionary here extracts the fuller teaching on prayer (vv. 7-15) for proclamation the following day.

Modeling versus Preening

One of the special challenges of Christ's teachings in these verses is finding the right balance in the contrast between giving good example, namely, doing things so that others may be encouraged to imitation, without wanting the attention to focus exclusively on ourselves. Love for

Wednesday of the Eleventh Week in Ordinary Time

others wants them to act wisely and well, so the ultimate intent is on the welfare of others. Once again, the point of Christ's instruction is the intention behind the action. Performing these religious deeds merely so "people may see them" (v. 1) is a form of idolatry. The gospel's warning is to make sure that the public action is not short-circuited into mere attention for ourselves. Spiritual maturity demands attention to motive as well as to the external action (v. 1). As the years go by we grow in our ability to acknowledge that in fact we have often done the right thing for the wrong reasons, and sometimes conversely, the wrong thing for the right reasons. The Lord reminds us that intention is even more important than outward action because our thoughts are the source of all external behavior. The reality of sin depends on the state of our knowledge and consent as well as on the inherent nature of the action itself. Those items remain the church's three traditional measurements for assessing the gravity of sin.

Almsgiving

Giving assistance to those in need is an obligation well rooted in ancient Jewish piety (v. 3). The tradition was often to single out widows and orphans and resident aliens, namely, outsiders and immigrants residing in the midst of the covenanted people of God, but without the social network of tribal support. They were examples of the most vulnerable members of any given society. The attendant obligation is to respond to those in need without judging their "worthiness" since in a real sense none of us are ever "worthy" of any of God's generous gifts! Our charity is measured by need, not merit.

Thursday of the Eleventh Week in Ordinary Time

First Reading (Year I)

2 Corinthians 11:1-11

I preached the Gospel of God to you without charge.

Hidden Rivalry and Polemics

The theme of money seems to run through this letter (or, as many scholars suspect, the portions from several letters editorially joined into a single unit). There were factions among the early Christian communities, and very different, sometimes conflicting, approaches to the way in which missionaries worked. It would seem that some criticized Paul for his lack of attractive personality traits or speaking abilities, but also for the fact that he did not accept material support from those to whom he spoke. He was demeaned and dismissed for his insistence on supporting himself by tent making. Efforts to understand a person's motivation are always key elements in assessing the effectiveness of the action; perhaps Paul simply wanted the freedom to preach the Gospel without social constraints. Among Christians, differences in method or strategy always exist and can be mutually complementary. Criticizing others to enhance ourselves, however, as the "superapostles" (v. 5) seem to have done, is never acceptable before God who desires that our unity remain an important part of our witness.

Jealousy

It may be surprising, but one of the early creeds of Israel acknowledged that the Lord is a "jealous God" (Exod 20:5; Deut 5:9), who brooks no rival in his care and love for his people. Protectiveness without becoming unduly controlling or disrespectfully possessive can be a sign of genuine love for others. Since God can be jealous, Paul unabashedly admits the same quality in his care for the Corinthians and their welfare. Could anyone of our parish membership ever be called "jealous" in the biblical sense about the parish community, its leadership and its mission?

Antiphon (Year I)

Psalm 111:7a

Your works, O Lord, are justice and peace.

Justice and Peace

Both these realities are profoundly relational, but perhaps not exactly as we might expect. Biblical "justice" as mentioned before means being in right relationship with all creatures. Biblical "peace" means working hard to make sure that every single element in creation is restored to its proper place within the constellation of reality.

God's Work

There are countless different metaphors that are useful for describing the diversity and span of God's work in our world. God constantly creates, sustains, supports, transforms, and perfects the world and all its parts. Our refrain (v. 7) chooses to describe those divine activities in terms of making sure that everything is related properly to everything else. This is God at work, and we are called to be instruments, not obstacles. It may be helpful to recall that Psalm 111 addresses the work of God and its companion Psalm 112 speaks to the human counterpoint in the partnership. The Lectionary uses these psalms frequently.

First Reading (Year II)

Sirach 48:1-14

Elijah was enveloped in a whirlwind, and Elisha was filled with the twofold portion of his spirit.

Flash-Forward to Sirach

The sequence of readings from 2 Kings is interrupted to add some reflections on Elijah from a book written over six hundred years later. The community of Israel continued to ponder the prophet's person and message, and to be ever more deeply en-

Thursday of the Eleventh Week in Ordinary Time

riched by his life and indebted to his witness. Elijah possessed a fiery personality (v. 1), filled with passion and zeal. He was so beloved by God as to be the instrument of initiating a terrible drought by way of punishment for Israel's infidelity, and the means of calling it off. Israel remembered him as a person unmarred by anything and totally marked by his fidelity. His wondrous signs of raising people from the dead (v. 5) made him a historical template for describing the future public ministry of Jesus. The prophet Malachi lifted up Elijah's memory as a final sign of the Day of the Lord, reconciling parents and children (Mal 3:24).

Political Action

The witness of Elijah embraced both liturgical reform and political renewal. Neither area of life was considered alien to the prophet's keen eye. He insisted on pure covenantal worship untainted by any hint of the popular fertility cults of his age. He also confronted kings and worked for "regime change" when the royal human agendas were contrary to the covenant of Sinai (vv. 6 and 8). As such he was a member of the covenant community, not merely a lone ranger. Faith as nonviolent witness matters and always has a place in the public forum.

ANTIPHON (YEAR II)

Psalm 97:12a

Rejoice in the Lord, you just!

Justice and Ecology

Although faithful covenant people are presumed to pay their legitimate debts, the type of person described here as "just" is more comprehensive. Those who can truly rejoice in the Lord are those who live in right relationship with all of creation, including wind, rain, soil, and water. The Lord is surrounded by clouds and darkness (v. 2) as well as fire and lightning (vv. 3, 4), all of which are described as servants of God. Rarely does one think of the ecological implications for being "just people," but relationship to the material reality in fact presumes and demands it.

Covenantal Witnesses

In the literary form prescribed for entering covenants, witnesses were always required. Even the heavens and the earth were invoked by Moses as witnesses against those who broke the covenant relationship and worshiped idols (Deut 4:26). Clouds, darkness (v. 2), and fire (v. 3) were servants at the throne of God and witnesses against his foes.

GOSPEL

Matthew 6:7-15

This is how you are to pray.

Literary Link

This prayer (vv. 9-13) is taken from its context in order to serve as a concrete illustration of Christ's admonition regarding how his disciples should pray, that is, in community, comprehensively for all human needs, and without calling attention to oneself ("our"). The Lectionary presumes that this teaching is too important to have been left in the liturgical context of yesterday's gospel passage, and provides a day of its own.

Effective Prayer

The prayer recommended by Jesus is one that does not needlessly multiply words (v. 7) and does not bargain with God, namely, promising to do something if God does something else. Prayer is not a *do ut des* negotiation. Acceptable prayer is fundamentally about one's relationship with God. To say it differently, authentic Christian prayer is about the reciprocal presence of God. The one praying should not be presumed to be only preoccupied with petition. What friend would only ask for things? God knows what we need before we say it, but the saying of our need serves as a reminder of our dependence on God and each other.

The Perfect Prayer

The "Our Father" (v. 9) has often been called the "perfect" prayer because it contains all the elements that should mark our prayer: relationship, community, reverential awe, respect for the unfolding kingdom in history, obedience, dependence, contrition, and the recognition of the power of evil that remains ever subordinate to the almighty power of God. It is always possible to select only one of the petitions and make that verse an entire weekday homily of instruction on how to pray humbly and well.

Friday of the Eleventh Week in Ordinary Time

First Reading (Year I)

2 Corinthians 11:18, 21-30

Apart from these things, there is the daily pressure upon me of my anxiety for all the churches.

Self-Defense

Following from yesterday's passage, Paul continues to feel the need to defend the legitimacy of his apostolic ministry (v. 18), distinctive though it may have been, against the dismissive charges of other visitors to the church in Corinth. There are times when speaking the simple truth about our own belief and practice is a matter of humility, not pride, especially when we present the truth without attempting to elevate ourselves in the eyes of others. Humility is truth and the truth has its own right to be told, even about ourselves. In the last analysis, what we might boast of (v. 18) are gifts from God, not simply personal accomplishments. Our witness should therefore also include the hardships and dangers (v. 26) without trying to inflate our image in the eyes of others!

Anxiety for the Churches

Paul was legitimately concerned for the spiritual health and well-being of the communities that he had founded (v. 28). He wrote his letters to show his ongoing concern for their spiritual and moral development. The entire First Letter to the Thessalonians, for example, seems inspired by that same concern. There are many implications from this admission. Following that model, for example, it would be important for a parish to keep in touch with those whom we have accompanied into the Catholic tradition over the years. Converts need encouragement when the novelty is over and the drudgery of daily belief becomes old hat. Moreover, Paul's attitude is also the basis for our active participation in missionary work as well as in the church's ecumenical movement. In that light we pray for neighboring congregations of all traditions. Such universal concern is often proposed as something every bishop, pastor, and lay leader must keep in mind.

Antiphon (Year I)

Psalm 34:18b

From all their distress God rescues the just.

Distress

The actual Hebrew word translated as "distress" in this refrain means a "tight place/*tzarah*" (v. 18, reflecting v. 7 in the response) without space to move and beyond our ability to extricate ourselves. Everyone has some heartache that he or she is unable to resolve and therefore can only trust in God's rescue when and how God chooses to act. The poor are particularly prone to such hardships (v. 7) because they have few resources and little social prestige. This is a perfect prayer for Paul, especially when faced, as the reading so vividly describes, with so many hardships, calumnies, and untruthful complaints.

The Just Who Suffer

God never promised that his faithful people would be freed from distress and heartache, but only that he would stay close and accompany the just person through it all until final vindication (v. 7), whenever and however that would occur. Even the just have distress, and perhaps especially the just, since God wishes to purify and perfect them (v. 5).

First Reading (Year II)

2 Kings 11:1-4, 9-18, 20

They anointed him and shouted: "Long live the king!"

Rivalry

With the excessive brutality that has often marked the actions of those who feared the loss of power, Queen Athaliah proceeded to systematically kill off all possible related rivals for her throne (v. 1).

The example may be extreme, but it is a reminder of how easy it seems to ruthlessly remove anyone who threatens our more modest claim on power or authority in the community. Talented people are colleagues and partners, not adversaries. Even when they express criticism, their abilities can complement ours and serve the community well if truly heard and respected. Focus on the needs of the entire community rather than on ourselves can avoid rivalry. Paul's Letter to the Philippians (2:3-5) makes the same point.

Nurturing Young Leadership

The brutal story contains an important element, especially in the protection that Jehosheba, a relative of the royal family, courageously extended to the lone remaining prince (v. 2). Scripture thus upholds the positive witness of one woman who negates the evil of another. The legitimate successor was hidden away and secretly trained until the time when she could present him to the people as a young leader. This is yet another example of the brave actions of women in service to their community's welfare. Every one of us has the obligation to be conscious of all the talents of our young and to provide care for their development into the leadership needed by the next generation of faithful.

ANTIPHON (YEAR II)

Psalm 132:13

The Lord has chosen Zion for his dwelling.

Divine Election

Some of the early Gnostic heresies described God as producing creation in a sort of automatic mental fashion without the participation of the divine will. In contrast, however, the Scriptures consistently declare that God has freely chosen to create, redeem, and perfect the entire world and all its inhabitants. God chose Israel, and Mount Zion, as the refrain reminds us (v. 13), freely and with full purpose. Psalm 132 speaks to the choice of David (v. 11) and God's covenant with David's family (v. 12). So many years later, we also are the result of God's choice. That enhances the personal value of every individual, and also raises a further question of "purpose." Precisely for what has Zion been chosen? Every choice implies "from what?" and "for what?" Remaining mindful of that larger context keeps us focused in life.

Dwelling

The refrain speaks of God's dwelling (v. 13) and reminds us of King Solomon's prayer on the occasion of the dedication of the temple. At that time he admitted that even the heavens cannot contain the full majesty of God (1 Kgs 8:27). He suggested, consequently, that the temple can only be a place for God's name to dwell. Nevertheless, Solomon insisted that the temple should be a place toward which people, even from a great distance, can turn in times of repentance or need. It is worthy of our personal prayer to ponder and explore how such a material building can be understood as "God's address" on earth. How can God be said to "dwell" in the community and in each member? Does this also apply to a parish church? What would that mean for the neighborhood?

GOSPEL

Matthew 6:19-23

For where your treasure is, there also will your heart be.

Literary Link

Matthew adds six short instructions of Jesus to his disciples. Two are united in today's reading: care of true treasure (vv. 19-21) and maintaining keen spiritual vision (vv. 22-23). It may be helpful to remind ourselves that the parable of judgment regarding care for the needy with whom Christ identifies himself (Matt 26:31-40) is addressed to the nations, while the Sermon

Friday of the Eleventh Week in Ordinary Time

on the Mount speaks of the duties of disciples. These admonitions in the sermon should not be easily dismissed as less important than care for the needy.

Treasure

The Greek word for treasure is *thesaurus* (v. 19) and suggests something stored up because of its value. The precise nature of the value could be monetary or sentimental, as we learn from seeing what people instinctively and quickly take from their possessions in a moment of home fire or natural disaster. While it might be deeds, insurance documents, or money, it might also be precious photographs or items attached to a loved one. The gospel is an invitation to recognize the truly valuable realities in our life, and to make sure that the list includes more than merely material objects. Actions of generosity and justice should also be on our list. Some things are beyond moth and decay (v. 20). Spiritual apathy could also be resisted as destructive at another level!

Eyes

Sight is itself a great treasure and one never to be taken for granted (v. 22). In the ancient world where most people suffered from various diseases of the eyes, this was a well-known reality. In their ignorance of physiology and optometry, they easily concluded that the eye allowed light to enter a person's being. Experience teaches that in fact blindness can induce inner darkness and that such darkness may be spiritual as well as physical. Miracles of healing for the blind (Matt 9:27-31) were important portions of the gospels. This gospel passage, obscure as it may be for us today, could become an occasion for prayers of gratitude for the gift of sight, and for those whose medical profession or gifts of spiritual direction includes care for the vision of so many people.

Saturday of the Eleventh Week in Ordinary Time

First Reading (Year I)

2 Corinthians 12:1-10

I will rather boast most gladly of my weaknesses.

Boasting

To boast (v. 1), namely, to speak honestly about some personal accomplishment or attribute, is wrong only if it is inspired by a sense that everything is completely and totally one's own doing (v. 5). On the other hand, it can be an act of humility if inspired and accompanied by a strong conviction that everything we have and do is the result of God's grace and, as such, remains a gift from God. Paul boasts about his spiritual experiences (v. 2), clearly and ultimately attributable to God alone.

A Thorn in the Flesh

The guesses regarding the precise nature of this humbling "thorn" (v. 7) have been countless over the years, ranging from some physical disability to a moral limitation. Some conjecture that the thorn may be Paul's irascibility or temptations of a sexual nature. No one knows, and the guesses might reveal more about the writer than about Paul himself. In any case, including that element of personal experience served to balance out the picture and to keep Paul humble even though he was apparently blessed by extraordinary spiritual graces (v. 1) during his life. For the spiritually mature, such "thorns" can even be the occasion for gratitude to God because they remind us of our frailty and ultimate utter dependence on God alone (v. 9).

Antiphon (Year I)

Psalm 34:9a

Taste and see the goodness of the Lord.

Psalm 34: Thanksgiving

This psalm was used by the ancient church as a song that accompanied Holy Communion because it is permeated by a sense of gratitude for divine care and sustenance (v. 10). The verses chosen for the response pay tribute to the poor and humble before God who are fed, while those who are "great" (v. 11) in their own eyes (literally, "young lions") and who boast of their strength and prowess are left diminished and needy.

Taste

Complete dependence on God easily accepts the metaphor of hunger (v. 9), and all of God's gifts can somehow be combined into the notion of physical food and nourishment. We say that someone "wants something so badly that he or she can taste it" as an image of profound need and personal desire. That God's gifts taste good in general, and are somehow symbolically combined into the Eucharist, is part of the reason why the psalm was chosen for Communion. We know that the eucharistic gifts of bread and wine symbolize all the gifts of the earth. In response to Paul's words to the Corinthians the phrase may be used for everything that nourished the weakness of which Paul speaks at the end of this first reading (vv. 9ff.).

First Reading (Year II)

2 Chronicles 24:17-25

They murdered Zechariah between the sanctuary and the altar (Matthew 23:35).

The Second Book of Chronicles

This scroll, together with its first volume, treats of the same history of royal figures as recounted in the books of Kings, but from a different perspective. Rather than seeing everything through the Deuteronomic lenses of covenant and prophets, Chronicles tells the story from the viewpoint of temple worship and liturgy. The following small portion is used in the Lectionary as a further commentary on the dramatic events narrated the day before in its selection from 2 Kings.

Saturday of the Eleventh Week in Ordinary Time

Ingratitude and Punishment

King Joash, who had been carefully protected by Princess Jehosheba and the priest Jehoiada in his youth (as narrated in yesterday's passage from 2 Kings), was sadly convinced by his noble counselors (v. 17) to abandon the exclusivity of the temple and to allow fertility cults on high places (v. 18). Zechariah, son of the priest Jehoiada, rose up in condemnation of the new practices (v. 20) and was killed for his courageous loyalty to God's covenant (v. 21). The utter ingratitude of King Joash for the protection he had received from Zechariah's father and his compliance with the murder of the priest Zechariah in the temple were punished in turn by the king's own murder and burial outside the royal cemetery (v. 25). The tale is of soap opera quality and is taught to uphold the sacredness of holy places and the obligation to be grateful to those who have been kind to us. Second Chronicles is included in this one day's Lectionary cycle at the end of the week to complement and conclude yesterday's story.

The Spirit of God

The passage attributes Zechariah's courageous denunciation to the gift of God's Spirit (v. 20). This is the same reality found in Acts of the Apostles, where the first disciples of Jesus spoke with candor and forthright courage after the gift of the Spirit at Pentecost. *Parresia,* boldness and courageous candor, is one of the many gifts of the Holy Spirit. The gift, which marks prophets and apostles, was recognized as present in the priest's son as well. In the Christian context we see that same gift given to young adults in confirmation as they are sent into the larger world for witness and action.

Antiphon (Year II)

Psalm 89:29a

For ever I will maintain my love for my servant.

Psalm 89: God's Promises

Psalm 89 contains an extended tribute to God's care for David (v. 4), and God's fidelity to his oath to sustain David's throne forever (v. 5). Perhaps in response to the tragic murder of the priest Zechariah, the psalm's original focus on the Davidic king is implicitly extended by this liturgical citation to the memory of the faithful priest Zechariah (v. 30).

Love

The psalm refrain itself, though not completely faithful to the precise citation (v. 29), uses the word *hesed* for God's promised support. Covenantal loyalty and mutual concern, or "steadfast kindness" as it is often called, for each other's well-being is God's pledge to his servant, whether it be the king or the high priest or any person baptized into Christ in the new dispensation.

Gospel

Matthew 6:24-34

Do not worry about tomorrow.

Literary Link

After the teachings of Jesus regarding treasure and vision, today's liturgical text contains two more instructions added to the teachings of Jesus for his disciples, that is, the teachings about God and mammon (v. 24) and those regarding trust in divine providence (vv. 25-34).

Two Masters

The introduction to the gospel's teaching about providence is important, namely, the admonition against two masters (v. 24). Once having established the importance of submission to God alone, rather than to material possessions, as the prime value in life, the teaching of Jesus can continue. *Mammon* is a Semitic word for money or wealth; it has been interpreted at times as a name for one of the ancient gods. It is only logical and realistic for a healthy integration of one's life to accept the fact that there can only be one supreme value. This is a fundamental principle in Islam as well, and a conviction that we Christians have in common with that great world religion.

Providence

Life itself (v. 25) is important in God's eyes and ours. The gospel teaching therefore continues to acknowledge that the importance of clothing (v. 28) and protection, as well as food and nourishment, must remain relative and subordinate to the supreme value of our faith in God. Ultimate dependence upon God is an attitude expected of all who are poor in spirit, as the first of the Beatitudes commends (5:3). At the same time God expects us to act as prudent householders, using his gifts wisely and extending generosity to those in need around us. No one verse can serve as a complete basis for our spirituality or life. Earlier in the Gospel of Matthew the tempting invitation to throw oneself off the temple pinnacle (4:5) is rejected by Christ, because God will not protect his son from human foolishness. Being a son or daughter of God does not give us the license to place ourselves at physical risk in the expectation of a miraculous salvation. Both prudence and providence are servants to our confidence in God's care. Neither past nor future is ours. For that reason the passage concludes with the reminder that "[s]ufficient for a day is its own evil" (v. 34).

Monday of the Twelfth Week in Ordinary Time

First Reading (Year I)

Genesis 12:1-9

Abraham went as the Lord directed him.

The Book of Genesis

Woven together from strands of several different literary and theological traditions, Genesis is a story of new beginnings. The book begins with the fact of creation and then its demise into sin, followed by a fresh beginning with Noah and his family amid a renewed material creation. The book finally provides the story of a new beginning for humanity through Abraham and Sarah, together with their children. The catechetical history of the great patriarchal figures will be described for the next three weeks.

Trusting Confidence

Without introduction, Abram is abruptly summoned to leave his familiar land and beloved family for a completely new location yet to be described (v. 1). It is difficult for us in our individualistic culture to understand the full abruptness of this radical change for a world in which family is the principal point of identity and means of social security. It was a summons to total trust in a future beyond his control. As a matter of fact, this is also true for every individual of all time and age, because none of us knows our future from one moment to another. The call to leave extended family and familiar turf is one that God extends not simply to Abram but to every single human being as we leave childhood and move into adulthood. It is a summons that can be challenging, frightening, and adventuresome.

Abram as Source of Blessing

Inherent in Abram's call is the promise that his faithful response will be a source of blessing for himself (v. 2) and for everyone associated with him. God looks at Abram and sees through him to countless generations whose faithful obedience will open doors and windows to endless divine blessings (v. 3). Perhaps we might say that every blessing, no matter how individually granted, always has a social dimension because others are invariably affected. A blessing of health or prosperity enables others to be assisted; every gift from God is also in some fashion destined for others as well.

Places for Praise and Thanks

When Abram came to Shechem (v. 6) in the land of Canaan, he experienced another vision from the Lord, who promised that the land where he stood would be his. No matter which new land Abraham visited as he journeyed with his family and flocks, he paused to acknowledge the God who had brought him there (v. 8). Building an altar and offering sacrifice enabled Abram to acknowledge his total dependence on the Lord in every new situation. Wherever we may be, it is always appropriate to express gratitude to God. This is a daily duty as we enter any new time or new situation because everything in life remains under the Lord's direction and guidance.

Antiphon (Year I)

Psalm 33:12

Blessed the people the Lord has chosen to be his own.

The People

The fact that the refrain speaks about a people (v. 12) rather than merely an individual by the name of Abram serves as a reminder that Abram is a corporate personality from the very beginning. Biblical categories of thought presume the priority of the community, and assume that any individual is first and foremost the member of his or her family or tribe. Our contemporary Western radical individualism stands in sharp contrast to that revealed biblical truth.

The Mystery of Election

No creature can exist without God's summons into being, and therefore every creature belongs to God in a unique fashion. We are chosen, however, not only from something, but also for something! This unique destiny of Abram's family, to provide a special pattern for understanding God's dealings with humanity, is the reason for becoming "his [God's] own" (v. 12).

First Reading (Year II)

2 Kings 17:5-8, 13-15a, 18

In his great anger against Israel, the Lord put them away out of his sight. Only the tribe of Judah was left.

A Sad and Sorry Fact of History

The account of the Assyrian destruction of the northern kingdom of Israel and its capitol, Samaria, is very sober and almost matter-of-fact (v. 6). It happened. Its consequences were enormous. This passage introduces a week of first readings, each of which recalls a time of terrible devastation for God's people. They show that God is a God of history, and that our God is in the midst of the sufferings of his chosen people, even the suffering brought down on their heads by their own wrongdoings (v. 7). These readings provide historic templates for the more contemporary tragedies of our lives and reminders that terrible things continue to happen in our world.

The Price of Ignoring God's Prophets

The final explanation of the ultimate cause for the destruction of Samaria, namely, the refusal of the people to heed the warnings of the prophets (v. 14) and the rejection of the covenant (v. 15), is an illustration of the importance of the prophets in the Deuteronomic history, which we call the books of Samuel and the books of Kings. Not everyone who comes over a hill, claiming to speak in the name of God, deserves the title of true prophet, but they are vindicated when history confirms the truth of their judgments. This account of the end of the northern kingdom of Israel also, therefore, makes the point that all our actions have consequences, often even for a wider circle than merely our own lives!

Antiphon (Year II)

Psalm 60:7b

Help us with your right hand, O Lord, and answer us.

Psalm 60: Human Sorrow

Psalm 60 is a hymn of deep sorrow and lament, probably after a terrible and heartbreaking defeat. The liturgical text chosen by the Lectionary deliberately omits the temple oracle of verses 8-10 in order to allow the cry of the psalm full range of feeling and sentiment. This is offered as an appropriate response to the stunning defeat by the Assyrians as described in the reading.

Help and Answer

The refrain (v. 7) is a desperate plea, born out of utter helplessness (v. 13). The refrain provides words for anyone caught in terrible tragedy, sorrow, or loss. All Scripture is useful for human needs (2 Tim 3:16) and provides words for our prayerful response to the events of our lives.

Gospel

Matthew 7:1-5

Remove the wooden beam from your eye first.

Literary Link

After the warning to avoid preoccupation with material necessities and to rely on God's righteousness (6:33) comes this caution about judging the righteousness of others and their inner motivation.

Human Freedom

One of the remarkable aspects of the teaching of Jesus is that God respects our human freedom so profoundly as even to allow us to establish the criteria for our own final judgment. Our judgments of others in the course of our daily lives become the very criteria (v. 2) by which we ourselves will be judged. God in fact allows us in some fashion to set our own bar. Splinters and logs are perfect examples. Almost as if to preclude the human tendency to be easy on ourselves but hard on others, God makes the very demands we place on others to rest on our own heads as well.

The Danger of Judging

Not every act of judgment is automatically forbidden by this teaching because, as a matter of fact, we are called to make judgments every day. Making a judgment is simply one step in decision making no matter what the issue may be. It is judging others that can be problematic. Some actions are wrong and we must say so clearly and humbly. The fact is that we also bring our own biases to our judgments, and they can impede our vision. Any judgment about the motives of others, therefore, must be tentative, provisional, and open to God's view of things, not merely our own. Only God, who is all-knowing, can make a final judgment about us. Ignatius of Loyola recommends that at all times we give the best possible interpretation to the actions of others, rather than presuming the worst.

Hypocrite?

The original Greek word *hupokritai* (v. 5) refers to someone who speaks from underneath a mask, such as an actor in theater productions and drama. It could mean someone who pretends to have knowledge not really possessed or someone who assumes a stance unwarranted by the facts. Perhaps a case can even be made for translating the Greek word as "hypercritics," not simply "hypocrites." Demanding more of others than of one's self would be condemned by this teaching. This explanation would fit neatly in the context of the Lord's warning against judging others unfairly.

Tuesday of the Twelfth Week in Ordinary Time

First Reading (Year I)

Genesis 13:2, 5-18

Let there be no strife between you and me, for we are brothers.

Family Rivalries

Material wealth and abundance (v. 2) can sometimes lead to arguments and bitter disagreements, especially within a family or neighborhood. It is a sure recipe for conflict if our primary concern is to protect our own possessions without any respect for others or their needs. Abram and Lot saw the problem (v. 8) and decided to create some distance between themselves (v. 9). This story demonstrates the importance of early discussion to resolve potential conflicts or disagreements before they come to a head or leave permanent scars.

Ecological Tensions

Curiously, the fundamental issue for the flocks and families of Lot and Abram was one of water rights for their flocks (v. 7), a very contemporary question in modern times. Lot saw the well-watered plains of the Jordan and chose that area (v. 10). Experts sometimes surmise that the next world war will be precipitated by the urgent need/desire for water. Sometimes the land simply cannot sustain the lifestyle we have adopted, and therefore respect for the earth and its resources requires changes and modifications in the way we live and the places we choose to dwell. Agricultural irrigation, urban sprawl, or central city density may be moral problems as well as demographic challenges. Even in his more arid land in the Negev, Abraham built an altar in gratitude (v. 18).

Second Choices

The story reports that, given the choice, Lot quickly opted for the fertile Jordan valley and the edges of the not-yet Dead Sea for his flocks, leaving the more arid areas for Abram's flocks (v. 10). At first glance it would seem that Abram certainly got the lesser benefit of the deal. Later the very lush territory chosen by Lot came under the destructive anger of the Lord (v. 13) and was reduced with its key cities of Sodom and Gomorrah to utter ruin and desolation. God always remains with those left to second choices and shows himself ever generous and unexpectedly provident. The very dust became "the stuff" of God's promises (v. 16). Things ultimately remain under God's control, not our own.

Antiphon (Year I)

Psalm 15:1b

He who does justice will live in the presence of the Lord.

Psalm 15: Prayer at the Church Door

Psalm 15 is often called a "torah liturgy," an instruction given by a priest guardian of a temple regarding who might be found worthy to enter the holy place. Although the full psalm response omits the initial question regarding who may dwell on the holy hill (v. 1), the refrain seems incorrectly attributed by the Lectionary to verse 1. In reality it is part of verse 2's response to the invisible question. The subsequent verses list the moral qualities expected in anyone judged acceptable to God: justice, truth, respect, and rejection of interest or bribes. It can be used as a fine examination of conscience in any time and any age.

Justice

The Hebrew word to which the refrain refers, "*tzedek*/justice," refers to more than mere human debts, even though the litany does refer to the ancient biblical prohibition against usury (v. 5). Only a person in right relationship with all of creation is truly "just" in the biblical sense and worthy of living in God's presence. This is an attitude that needs to be reestablished each day of our lives as new realities arise and demand fresh human responses. This type of justice is very dynamic and very contemporary for each of us.

FIRST READING (YEAR II)

Tuesday of the Twelfth Week in Ordinary Time

2 Kings 19:9b-11, 14-21, 31-35a, 36

I will shield and save this city for my own sake and for the sake of my servant David.

Military Threats and Power

With human hubris and arrogance the great Sennacherib is described as proudly invoking his military victories and powerful forces (v. 10) in a threat to Hezekiah, who was remembered as a holy and faithful servant of the Lord. Earlier Hezekiah had taken advantage of Assyrian distractions and weakness to reestablish the worship of the Lord in Jerusalem, and to eliminate the type of pagan worship demanded by Assyria from all its subordinate nations. This tale of the victory of faith over military power is a reminder of who is ultimately in control of the forces of the world, not human kings but God alone. The book of Revelation at the climactic end of the New Testament is God's final response to the pride of the Roman Empire and all similar human claims.

Trust and Confidence

Hezekiah's beautiful prayer (vv. 15-19) provides a pattern for any human expression of trust in God's sovereign power over mere human governments. This invitation to trust is precisely the attitude recommended by the prophet Isaiah (30:15) in response to the threats of hostile Assyrian human power. It is a divine response to a particular historical human situation, but not necessarily the only response of God because a hundred years later the same God would speak through Jeremiah and would refuse to protect Jerusalem when a similar danger was posed by Babylonian forces. At the later time, people were asked to trust in the wisdom and spiritual remedy of defeat. In each case, it is the word of the prophet that provides the key insight into God's will and plan for that specific situation.

ANTIPHON (YEAR II)

Psalm 48:9d

God upholds his city for ever.

Psalm 48: God's Own City

This is a hymn to the glory of God whose references to Zion (v. 3) make it an appropriate response to the reading. God chose to preserve and safeguard the city (v. 4) at the time of Hezekiah, as described in the day's reading from 2 Kings. It is God whose will and power alone dominates the scene and declares the way things will play out in history.

"For Ever"

As demonstrated by the contrast between the times of Isaiah and those of Jeremiah, "for ever" is not necessarily forever. At least, one must acknowledge that the manner in which God chooses to uphold the city (v. 9) can change. Physical protection in one age might turn into a need for spiritual correction and punishment in another. God is faithful, as the refrain indicates, but divine fidelity takes different forms and differing faces, as any thoughtful parent or teacher knows all too well.

GOSPEL

Matthew 7:6, 12-14

Do unto others whatever you would have them do to you.

Literary Link

The opening verse's caution about giving holy things to dogs (v. 6) stands as a note of further correction and caution about judging, as noted in yesterday's gospel reading. One is required to discern the appropriateness of decisions. Judging takes many forms and not all judgments are forbidden; some are even required. Three separate teachings on aspects of judging are included in this passage. For some reason the Lectionary's liturgical text omits a teaching on the way God answers prayer (vv. 7-11). Perhaps the editors wished to offer these three simple teachings as a single unit.

Respect for Value

Respect for wisdom or for any of God's creation demands that we treat them with the care they deserve. Holy things, as well as dogs, pearls, and swine, each deserve the care and concern proper to it (v. 6). Careless tossing of valuables to people incapable of appreciating them may be a sin against creation too. The value of soil is different from that of pearls or precious gems. The latter may be more beautiful to the eye, but the former is more essential for life!

The Narrow Gate

The image of the "narrow gate" (v. 13) represents anything and everything that requires a change in us as we move forward into the future. In our time it might be equivalent to an attempt to squeeze through a small window in an emergency. Life and its faithful journey toward the fullness of God's will requires at times that we dispose of some prized possessions, or turn sideways to fit into more straitened circumstances. Not everything can fit through narrow gates! The fullness of life requires some discipline on our part (v. 14). Those unwilling to make any accommodation, or to shed any luggage, can't get through the gate.

Wednesday of the Twelfth Week in Ordinary Time

First Reading (Year I)

Genesis 15:1-12, 17-18

Abraham believed God, and it was credited to him as righteousness (Romans 4:3b), and the Lord made a covenant with him.

Heir by Trusting Faith

In the ancient world where any sense of life after death was often restricted to living on in one's children, Abram's concern for an heir was significant. No matter how deep the affection and personal bond may have been between Abraham and his servant, the choice of a steward of possessions and general manager like Eliezer was not sufficient (v. 2). God promised a son (v. 4), and Abram put his trust in God's word (v. 6). The action was credited to him as an "act of righteousness," something Saint Paul used centuries later as an explanation for Abraham as the father of all believers (Gal 3:6). This phrase also became crucial in the sixteenth-century Reformation debates.

Mystical Experiences

Spiritual experiences such as the one that accompanied Abram's covenant are very difficult to describe or comprehend. Sacrifice, terrifying darkness (v. 12), and the appearance of a flaming torch are mysterious symbolic elements that signaled God's presence and God's promise of the gifts of descendants and land. Contemporary experts in spirituality tell us that virtually everyone has some powerful spiritual experience over the course of a lifetime. God will be God, utterly transcendent and always beyond our human limits. That same God is determined, however, to remain in our midst forever!

Antiphon (Year I)

Psalm 105:8a

The Lord remembers his covenant for ever.

Covenant

Although "covenant" is often described as an agreement of sorts, such an explanation is inadequate. An agreement is always between persons about something else, a third object, so to speak. The deeper meaning of covenant, however, is the actual relationship between the persons that binds them together in peace and mutual concern. In the refrain (v. 8) God promises to keep that relationship alive forever.

Remembering

The biblical notion of "remember" is more than abstract mental recollection. To remember is to make the person or event remembered present again in all its fullness. The antiphon (v. 8) is a very fitting response to the first reading's account of God's eternal covenantal relationship with Abram, which the entire eucharistic assembly now makes its own.

First Reading (Year II)

2 Kings 22:8-13; 23:1-3

The king had the book that had been found in the Temple read out to them, and he made a covenant before the Lord.

The Pivotal Importance of This Scroll

Scholars tell us that this simple event of the accidental discovery of an ancient forgotten scroll amid the debris of a temple under renovation marked the turning point of Israel into a people of the book. The scroll was probably the original nucleus for the book of Deuteronomy. The formal acceptance of that written document by Josiah (v. 3) as a basis for Israel's national existence was a major event in salvation history. Subsequent kings were expected to carry a copy (Deut 17:18) and to make decisions in light of its commands. The symbolic relationship of this event to the way in which contemporary Christians are expected to refer to the gospels as a norm for our lives should not be missed. At the same time, our Christian loyalty is to the person of Christ the Word, not to a book.

The Invisible Hulda

The verses omitted in the story, perhaps to provide clarity and continuity in the narrative, introduce the prophetess Hulda (v. 14), whose insight made her the key figure in that development. It seems unfortunate, nevertheless, that the reading proceeds without reference to her prophetic judgment that the scroll was indeed the word of God and obligatory for all faithful Israelites. This woman deserves much more attention than is here given by our Lectionary to her role in the history of salvation. The liturgical selection could be an occasion, therefore, for a comment on all the important but often invisible women in the biblical witness to the history of salvation. We preach about what is said, and what is not said!

Antiphon (Year II)

Psalm 119:33a

Teach me the way of your decrees, O Lord.

Psalm 119: A Plea for Instruction

All the 176 verses of Psalm 119 represent an extended mediation on the word of God and all its forms, demanding reverential obedience from anyone who claims to be a faithful member of God's covenant with his people. Arranged alphabetically with eight verses dedicated to each Hebrew letter, the psalm may seem repetitious and tedious, but it represents an extended mediation of the way God speaks to his people.

Teach

The best of teachers is able to combine knowledge of a subject about which he or she feels a certain passion with care for the student being introduced into a new appreciation for the value and importance of the subject. That is precisely what the psalm response attempts to do by way of response to the discovery of the scroll. Our readings insist that people's lives depend upon their relationship to the scroll and to the God whose word and will are revealed within it!

Gospel

Matthew 7:15-20

By their fruits you will know them.

Literary Link

Immediately after the teaching of Jesus regarding the need for inner discipline in order to enter the narrow gate (vv. 13-14), and prior to his teaching about the inadequacy of merely saying "Lord, Lord" for entrance into the kingdom (vv. 21-23), we hear in today's teaching something about the need for "good fruit," not only words (vv. 15-20)! Results are the proof of goodness.

Prophets

A prophet is one who speaks for God. This gospel passage is a perfect follow-up to the reading from 2 Kings (Year II) because it addresses the faith community's obligation to test the person and the message. Not everyone who comes running over a hill claiming to carry God's message is necessarily authentic (v. 15). Consistency and conformity with the rest of revelation is one criterion of truth, as well as the patience to see if the message plays out in history and leads to the true God. Even recent years have witnessed some tragic situations where people foolishly followed a leader to their own destruction and death. Community discernment is the needed complement to prophecy. The fruits (v. 16) are important.

Orthopraxis

Deeply rooted in the Judaeo-Christian tradition is the inclination to value correct action (orthopraxis) over precisely stated belief (orthodoxy). Although the latter is important, God and the work of God remain a mystery. Doing the will of God after humble discernment is possible for all people of goodwill. The exasperated exclamation of an impatient elderly nun always rings true: "Don't just talk about it; do it!"

Thursday of the Twelfth Week in Ordinary Time

First Reading (Year I)

Genesis 16:1-12, 15-16

Hagar bore Abram a son and he called him Ishmael.

Sarah's Dark Shadow

It was Sarai (earlier form of her name) herself who first suggested that Abram have a child by Sarai's maid, Hagar (v. 2). The subsequent relationship between the two women, however, became one of bitter rivalry and physical abuse (v. 6). Though not described at length in the actual text, the situation seems hidden, often like similar situations in modern family life where abuse is never spoken of and too often painfully endured. In this case Hagar finally runs away. Though no one should be forced to endure mistreatment, she returns (v. 9), possibly for the protection of her son until the fullness of God's plan unfolds. For Hagar to have remained alone in her flight could have been dangerous to her and her son. This is almost a "text of terror" for situations of contemporary domestic abuse, and should be very carefully but honestly treated, even if a full and satisfactory biblical explanation does not seem within reach. No one should remain in a harmful situation of physical abuse or dangerous mistreatment.

Ishmael's Promise

Biblical tradition assigns Ishmael as the father of all the non-Jewish Semitic peoples. Abraham through Ishmael is venerated as the patriarch of all the Islamic nations. A recent book by John Kalter titled *Ishmael Instructs Jacob* was written to show the relationship between the major biblical figures in the Bible and the way in which those same individuals are presented in the Qur'an. In the latter they are all pictured as people who were totally submissive to the will of God, even in complicated and difficult human situations. The Scriptures of Israel remember Ishmael as "a wild ass of a man" (v. 12), feisty, apparently easily at odds with his neighbors but having an important role in God's providence for the world. The fact that Abraham himself gave the name to Ishmael is understood as the act by which Abraham claimed Ishmael as his own son (just as Joseph is instructed by the angel to named the baby Jesus; Matt 1:21).

Antiphon (Year I)

Psalm 106:1b

Give thanks to the Lord, for he is good.

Psalm 106: Praise before Confession

The first few verses of Psalm 106 are used as a liturgical response to God's care for Ishmael (no matter what Sarai may think). They are a song of praise for God's goodness and for those members of the people who remain faithful (v. 3). The rest of the same long psalm (not used in the response), however, describes a litany of significant situations when the people were sinfully disobedient and disregarded God's will. In its entirety the psalm becomes a confession of sin and a call to repentance for the mistakes of history.

God's Goodness

A prevailing and enduring conviction in the Scriptures is the fact that God's goodness ultimately will prevail (v. 4), no matter how misguided the actions of Israel may be over the years. That goodness remains forever (v. 1), and should be celebrated with humility and confidence rather than arrogance and self-centered pride. The psalm is about God, not about us!

First Reading (Year II)

2 Kings 24:8-17

The king of Babylon also led captive to Babylon Jehoiachin and the chief men of the land.

The First Babylonian Exile (597 BC)

By way of punishment for their rebellion, all the leadership of Judea as well as the artisans were forced into Babylonian exile (v. 14). This was a great tragedy for the poor community left at home without skilled and trained people to serve their common good. The reading can become an occasion for a community at eucharistic prayer today to be grateful for the wide range of professions and service industries present in any contemporary community. A weekday homily might even name them, category by category, in a prayer of thanksgiving.

The Appointment of Zedekiah

Zedekiah was a twenty-one-year-old puppet king, appointed by Babylonian authorities to ensure enduring compliant cooperation with the occupying powers (v. 17). He turned out to be remarkably vacillating in his response to Jeremiah's prophetic message and ministry. Though not explicitly mentioned in this particular passage, the appointment and its consequences for the history of Judah became a tragic example of authority so beholden to other powers (military, economic, and political) as to cause serious harm to the nation. Leadership in times of crisis demands integrity and courage. This is true for any time in history.

ANTIPHON (YEAR II)

Psalm 79:9

For the glory of your name, O Lord, deliver us.

Psalm 79: The Tragedy of Sacrilege

Psalm 79 was a lament over the destruction and profanation of the temple and its sacred vessels. The examples and description of violence reflect the more grievous results of the Babylonian devastation, providing a complement to 2 King's more sober account. War and its effects are always terrible, no matter what the cause or motivation. In later Judaism the psalm became part of the community's prayer on the occasion of the anniversaries of the temple's destruction by Babylon (587 BC) and then six centuries later by the Romans (AD 70). The psalm is also a plea for compassion (v. 8) and deliverance (v. 9). Every nation has its own historical tragedies. This would be a fitting prayer for any of our own.

Glory of God's Name

In this prayer for redemption and deliverance, the refrain (v. 9) chooses to acknowledge the damage done to God's name by sin. Any consideration for the comfort or vindication of the people is set aside for the moment. Our natural instinct is to pray out of self-pity in times of tragedy, but this antiphon places the focus upon God's reputation and power in seeking restored justice and renewed human fidelity to the covenant.

GOSPEL

Matthew 7:21-29

The house built on rock and the house built on sand.

Literary Link

This passage is the conclusion and final summary of the Sermon on the Mount. It emphasizes orthopraxis as an important value in Judaism. Only those who listen and act can provide true stability for community life. The final verse (v. 29) is repeated at the end of each of Matthew's great sections of teaching. One should not miss this expression of praise for the authority of Jesus as an initial anticipation of the great judgment (Matt 25:31-46).

Actions over Words

One of the consistent teachings of the New Testament, especially in Matthew's gospel with its roots in a community comprised of Torah observant Jews as well as Gentiles, is the importance of obedience and action (v. 21), not merely words alone. Keeping one's word and fulfilling one's promises are obligations that cast a long and large shadow over one's entire life. The examples of prophecy, expulsion of demons, and mighty deeds are all actions that seem extraordinary in evoking public acclaim (v. 22). However, even if such deeds are done in the name of Jesus himself, Jesus prefers a lifetime filled with obedience in all aspects of daily life in community. Occasional showy actions are not enough! Accepting one's cross and entering the new family of those who hear and do God's will are the true and important elements of being a disciple. Mere verbal devotion or actions glorifying oneself alone are not sufficient. Moreover, those actions cannot sustain a person throughout life.

Thursday of the Twelfth Week in Ordinary Time

Solid Foundations

Recent natural disasters, be they hurricanes, tornadoes, or tsunamis, provide countless examples of the importance of solid foundations for homes and buildings. The gospel, however, is not really speaking of basements or solid concrete slabs (v. 24) but of entire lifetime habits of obedience to the teachings of Jesus. Only faithful discipleship can provide comfort and stability in times of disaster. Those habitually faithful are able to stand firm when threatened by forces of evil or self-centered temptations. Sand washes away immediately, but rock remains. It may be time to list the qualities of the spiritual rocks that can do the job: regular prayer, community service and solidarity, acceptance of one's cross, and so forth.

Friday of the Twelfth Week in Ordinary Time

First Reading (Year I)

Genesis 17:1, 9-10, 15-21

Every male among you shall be circumcised: thus is my covenant with you. Sarah shall bear you a son.

Circumcision

To speak of this ritual, especially in a mixed community, can be awkward (v. 10). This is true even when the surgery has been secularized in people's minds and understood as simply hygienic. The primary intent of this external sign of Israel's covenant, however, is the insistence that the transmission of life from one generation to another is the work of God, not merely human beings, and that God is concerned about the future (v. 16), not merely the past or present. Ancient peoples with an undeveloped notion of the afterlife stressed living on in one's children. Human life is a precious gift to be welcomed and cherished.

Respecting the Elders

The promise of children to this couple at such an advanced age (v. 17) inevitably brings a smile of wonderment to any generation. Such a promise also invokes the immediate human acknowledgment of the difficulty of coping with children at that advanced time in life. Grandparents love children but are content to send them home at the end of the day. We say that "all things are possible with God," but we also recognize that the wisdom and experience of the elderly should be respected. Our elders continue to give life on many levels to their families and their larger communities. This can be an occasion to pray for the elderly who offer wisdom and even take up family burdens generously after tragedies.

Antiphon (Year I)

Psalm 128:4

See how the Lord blesses those who fear him.

Blessings

There is an undercurrent of biblical meaning that links the notion of blessing with that of fertility. For that reason this refrain's promise of blessing (v. 4) is an apt response to the story of God's promise of children to Sarah and Abraham. The list of blessings can be many and very diverse. There are often surprises in life, and only in retrospect are they viewed as "blessings." These readings can become an occasion to become newly conscious of such events in people's lives that were subsequently seen as sources of grace, spiritual growth, satisfaction, and gratitude.

Fear of the Lord

Sincere reverence for God (v. 4), not servile fear, is the beginning of understanding. So many experiences in life are seen as blessings only when placed in the larger picture of God at work making all things contribute to the good of those who love the Lord (Rom 8:28). We believe that God deals with our needs, not our wants. We recognize that it may take time for us to fully appreciate the ultimate value and the salutary importance of major events in our lives. That development can only begin with reverent faith.

First Reading (Year II)

2 Kings 25:1-12

Thus was Judah exiled from her land.

Zedekiah's Punishment

When he did rebel some ten years later, unleashing the fury of the king of Babylon and the destruction of Jerusalem (v. 9), Zedekiah was forced to watch the murder of his sons, and then blinded (v. 7) so that the horror would be the last thing he saw. He was then taken off in chains to exile in Babylon. This was a terrible punishment for a parent. The Deuteronomic historian wanted to document the bitter consequences of ignoring God's prophetic servants and of violating the covenant. The shadow of sin is large and long.

Friday of the Twelfth Week in Ordinary Time

Temple Destruction

The utter spiritual desolation of these events can hardly be appreciated by those of us so removed from the temple by theology, time, and distance. Loss of the temple (v. 9), the land, and the dynasty of David seemed to be the end of everything God had promised to give and protect. It provoked a terrible crisis of faith far beyond a mere building, no matter how sacred! It was the end of the "first temple era." In retrospect, however, even such a tragedy enabled God to initiate a new and different relation with his humbled people. Jewish communities continue to mourn that destruction by a day of fasting on *Tisha b'Av* (the ninth day of the month of Av), which falls in the Gregorian calendar each autumn. For them it is a day for prayers of repentant sorrow and for prayerful petitions for renewal of faith.

ANTIPHON (YEAR II)

Psalm 137:6ab

Let my tongue be silenced, if I ever forget you!

Psalm 137: An Exile's Prayer

This is a bitter and melancholic song for exiles who live far from the beauty and graces of God's presence in an earlier time and in a distant land. It is a psalm for those experiencing great personal loss and grief. The destruction of the temple with everything it signified and promised became the symbol for all the great sorrows of life. Even for us Gentiles grafted into the olive tree of Judaism (Rom 11:17) the memory should become a moment for personal contrition, not merely reproach of others.

Silenced Tongue

The spirit of this refrain (v. 6) is similar to a self-administered curse of punishment if forgetfulness ever takes over one's life to the point that the sorrow is relegated to the oblivion of history by a future generation of God's people. Some things are simply too important to forget! Our age could well add the horror of the *Shoah* (Holocaust of Nazism) to that category of tragedies that embody a profound lesson for subsequent centuries. Anyone who has ever visited the concentration camps knows the utter silence of those terrifying places.

GOSPEL

Matthew 8:1-4

If you wish, you can make me clean.

Literary Link

Having finished the body of teachings gathered into the Sermon on the Mount, Matthew turns to a series of three cures: the leper (vv. 1-4), the centurion's servant (vv. 5-13), and Peter's mother-in-law (vv. 14-15).

Cure of the Leper

This account is much simplified from Mark's version (1:29-34), where Jesus himself takes on the ritual uncleanness of contact with leprosy and is therefore prevented from entering any town. In Matthew's account we simply hear a straightforward story of healing offered to an outcast of society. It might be well, however, to remind people of the consequences of this action by the mere touching of a leper in the ancient world (v. 3). Because of the great popular fear of the disease, the unknown factors regarding how contagion is spread and the ritual uncleanness resulting from any touch, physical contact with a leper was forbidden (Lev 13:45ff.). This passage is an opportunity to pray for all who are ostracized from a community. By complying with the law and sending the healed man to the priests (Lev 13:2), Jesus restored him to the worshiping community once more.

Healing by a Word and Touch

The cure is accomplished by the combination of precisely the same elements as the sacraments of the church (v. 3): an action whose intent and purpose is clarified by a verbal statement/command of Jesus. Action and word (matter and form) comprise the sacraments of our faith. In declaring, "I will do it," Jesus makes it very clear that the cure is accomplished by his desire and intent. He has come to heal the world on all levels. The Son was sent not to condemn but to save the world (John 3:17).

Saturday of the Twelfth Week in Ordinary Time

First Reading (Year I)

Genesis 18:1-15

Is anything too marvelous for the Lord to do? I will surely return to you and Sarah will then have a son.

Hospitality

One of the primary virtues of the people of the first covenant was that of hospitality. Life in the desert could depend on the kindness of others, especially for travelers or families experiencing famine. Abraham considered it a "favor" to serve (v. 3). The reference to the baking of "rolls" may sound odd in context; at issue are small cakes or pita breads for soaking up gravy. Abraham's lavish generosity is richly blessed by God's promise of a descendant (v. 10). From this story one could go further (depending on the issues of the local parish community) to speak of our duty to welcome immigrants and to provide meal programs for the needy.

Three Visitors

This event of the three visitors (v. 2) has been used by saints, artists, and spiritual writers of Eastern Orthodoxy to symbolize the Trinity, source of life and guiding spiritual power in the history of God's people. It is the most common and favorite iconic representation of the triune God, often seated at table as guests of Abraham. They also viewed the bread on the table (v. 6) as evocative of the Eucharist. This biblical interpretation might be termed typological inasmuch as the original text provides a pattern that is reinterpreted in a deeper sense by a later generation. Similarly, the flood of Noah and the crossing of the Red Sea at the exodus have become "types" of Christian baptism.

Laughter of Sarah

One can't help but smile at the utter humanity of the tale as it pictures Sarah listening from within the tent and laughing at the utter impossibility of the entire promise (v. 12), and then quickly denying her reaction when confronted by the guests (v. 15). So many actions of God seem completely beyond imagination when considered from the standpoint of mere human rationality, but nothing is impossible with God, as we are often told by biblical witnesses over the centuries, including the archangel Gabriel at the time of the annunciation (Luke 1:37)!

Antiphon (Year I)

Luke 1:54b

The Lord has remembered his mercy.

The *Magnificat*

The Lectionary suggests Mary's *Magnificat* as an appropriate response to the announcement of a future son for Sarah and Abraham. In most other circumstances her hymn is associated with the canticle of Hannah, mother of Samuel (1 Sam 2:1-10). In this case, however, the Lectionary contrasts the disbelief of Sarah with the total obedience of Mary. Most people would probably sense a mixture of the two responses when confronted by either a promise or an actual gift of such normally impossible proportion.

Remembering Mercy

In this refrain (v. 54) the Greek of the New Testament does not demonstrate the subtle nuances and differences in the various Hebrew notions of mercy. The "memory" of God is another manner of speech to state that God extends his goodness to successive situations again and again. Divine mercy moves from generation to generation (v. 48) through history because of God's fidelity to his people. That even includes those of our generation who gather for a weekday parish Eucharist.

FIRST READING (YEAR II)

Lamentations 2:2, 10-14, 18-19

Cry out to the Lord over the fortresses of daughter Zion.

The Book of Lamentations

Five laments were written shortly after the tragic fall of Jerusalem in 587 BC, the first four of which were composed as acrostics, namely, with each stanza beginning with a successive letter of the Hebrew alphabet. The grief of that time is immortalized, and now placed immediately after the book of Jeremiah's prophecy in the established canon of the first covenant to emphasize its connection to that event.

Destruction of the Temple and City

In reading the book's second lament, one can almost hear the shrill cries of the Near East when grief-stricken women wail their sorrow and grief over the death of a beloved child (v. 11) or the starvation of children (v. 12). Similar grief is shown on contemporary television at the murder of an innocent person caught amid the spiraling violence or political turmoil of those lands. The selection of this lament is the perfect conclusion to the biblical reports of the final devastation of the Holy City, as described in the Second Book of Kings.

The Human Horrors of War

The text describes the dreadful effects of famine (v. 12) and all the suffering of innocent children and families caused by the destruction of cities in any war-torn zone. The physical sufferings themselves add to the spiritual sorrow over the ruin of the holy place. They demonstrate the impact of war on the lives of families. This can be an occasion to pray for all the victims of war throughout the contemporary world! One of the church's traditional criteria for judging a war "just" is the avoidance of harm to innocent people. That standard is virtually never met today. The more impersonal the weapons, the greater the tragedy and devastation.

ANTIPHON (YEAR II)

Psalm 74:19b

Lord, forget not the souls of your poor ones.

Psalm 74: The Sadness of Desecration

Similar to the tone of Psalm 79, Psalm 74 is a lament over the destruction of the temple. Whether the psalm commemorates the physical ruin of the temple in sad response to the Babylonian destruction of 587 BC (v. 6) or describes in hyperbolized account the desecration by Antiochus Epiphanes IV in 168 BC (v. 7), the sorrow of the people is still almost audible and tangible even after all this time! Sadness has not fled or been consoled. Some sorrows are so deep that they simply never go away.

Remembrance of God

If people cannot forget such a sorrow, neither can God. The refrain (v. 19) begs God not to forget his people, especially the poor, vulnerable, and utterly dependent. The prayer begs God to care for them in their need, even if the sorrow is caused by their own sin and misconduct. God never abandons those who turn back to him in true repentance (v. 20).

GOSPEL

Matthew 8:5-17

Many will come from east and west and will recline with Abraham, Isaac, and Jacob.

Literary Link

These accounts of healing describe the second and third of the cures that demonstrate the mighty deeds that accompany the teachings of Jesus. In an ever narrowing circle, the mercy of Jesus moves from ostracized leper (vv. 1-4) to a Roman soldier's servant (vv. 5-13) and then to Peter's mother-in-law (vv. 14ff.). Mark's reference to the Sabbath has been eliminated, but the account concludes with a brief generic description of the actions of Jesus as the fulfillment of the ancient prophecies (vv. 16-17), a favorite literary technique of Matthew.

Saturday of the Twelfth Week in Ordinary Time

The Centurion's Servant

As a leper remained an outcast because of his sins, this Gentile centurion, member of the hated Roman occupying army, was considered an enemy and often thought beyond God's mercy, especially by the Torah observant members of Matthew's community. To hear Christ's praise for his faith (v. 10) would have been unsettling and even shocking. In every age God's grace goes out to the most unlikely of persons, especially those judged unworthy by the more pious and faithful members of the community. Our liturgy even borrows his expression of faith (v. 8) for use as we approach the eucharistic table.

Peter's Mother-in-Law

Physical fevers were common in the ancient world, especially when food had remained unconsumed in a world without refrigeration or when infections were easily transmitted from person to person in daily circumstances without hygiene. Her cure is prompt by the touch of Jesus (v. 15), and her service to the needy nearby immediate. In merciful solidarity a divine hand touches on human hand. All gifts, even physical ones, are for others in some way. Nothing, not even a kind touch by God, is ours alone.

Monday of the Thirteenth Week in Ordinary Time

First Reading (Year I)

Genesis 18:16-33

Will you sweep away the innocent with the guilty?

God and the Visitors

The passage begins with a reference to the three visitors to whom Abraham showed great hospitality (v. 2), even offering the courtesy of walking with them for a bit on their way (v. 16). God was in their midst mysteriously. This is yet another reason why the Eastern Byzantine tradition sees the three as somehow foreshadowing the Trinity.

God as Examiner and Judge

Out of friendship for Abraham and transparency, God decides to share his decision to examine closely the cries of the poor and to determine the sinfulness of the inhabitants of Sodom and Gomorrah. Our God must know the facts (v. 21) and must himself act justly if he expects us humans to be just (v. 19). There can be no judgment, human or divine, unless it is based upon the truth. In a delightful extension of the conversation Abraham probes the amount of wickedness required for God to move into judgment and punishment (v. 23). The first discussion in this account takes place within the heart and mind of God and deals with God's debate over whether to share the divine decision to destroy the cities with his friend Abraham (v. 17). The cry of the poor and oppressed is deafening and so God finally decides to share his decision. Note that the word "cry" (v. 20) is a technical term for a legal lawsuit in Israel, which therefore out of justice elicits God's actions.

Abraham's Famous Bargain

The second portion of the reading (vv. 22-33) considers a more external argument, over the least number of innocent beings that would still force the punishing hand of God against a city. Like a shrewd business merchant, Abraham is successful, haggling and arguing the number down to ten (v. 32). This account is the origin of the Jewish custom that a group gathered for prayer must number at least ten (named a *minyan*) for the prayer to be recognized as fulfilling the law and being capable to be heard by God. That symbolic number becomes a faithful community and could save a community. A lesser number remains merely a group of individuals.

Antiphon (Year I)

Psalm 103:8a

The Lord is kind and merciful.

Kind

The refrain almost sounds like a confession of faith. The Hebrew word translated here as "kind" (v. 8) is in fact *raham*, the quality of being merciful and compassionate like the maternal womb. The word is associated with the love of a mother who can never forget or abandon a child. To apply this feminine quality to God is a significant, though hidden, poetic metaphor. No matter what our limited human language, God remains beyond human gender.

Merciful

By contrast the refrain's second Hebrew word is *hanan*, the quality of being favorable and making other things/persons gracious or attractive. This is the fundamental word for "grace" in the first covenant. God is the source of all beauty. The refrain (v. 8) is much richer than might first appear!

First Reading (Year II)

Amos 2:6-10, 13-16

They trample the heads of the weak into the dust of the earth.

Demeaning Poor Neighbors

The ironic willingness of the affluent to trade the life of a poor person for a bit of silver or a pair of nice new sandals (v. 7) demonstrates their utter lack of respect for human beings. The poor, possibly because they were forced by debts to become indentured servants, were almost considered mere chattel possessions. The actual comprehensive crimes as listed (vv. 7-10) combine lack of respect for both parties of the covenant, namely, God and neighbor, especially the poorest! It was partially against this dreadful economic inequality that Deuteronomy expanded the laws of freedom after seven years to include women (15:12) and any debts (15:1). Freed slaves were never to be sent away empty-handed (15:14)!

Monday of the Thirteenth Week in Ordinary Time

The Book of Amos

The prophet Amos rose in the early half of the eighth century BC to condemn the wealthy who had built their newfound prosperity on the backs of the exploited poor and oppressed. Such actions were grave violations of the covenant. The words of the prophet are harsh, insisting on greater continuity between liturgy and life. With astonishing accuracy the prophet's judgments seem very contemporary in mid-America some twenty-eight centuries later!

Prophetic Arithmetic

Even the numbers ascribed to the crimes are significant, and they contribute to the seriousness of the charges leveled against the northern kingdom by Amos (v. 6). The number "three," for example, signifies the superlative (cf. "holy, holy, holy") or intensity. The number "four" refers to the four directions and suggests universality and completeness. These symbolic numbers, therefore, identify the severity of these crimes and sins in the eyes of God. Similarly, we might use "dozen" or "million" to exaggerate the number of things to be done in a day! Such numbers mean more than the numbers.

Antiphon (Year II)

Psalm 50:22a

Remember this, you who never think of God.

Psalm 50: A Condemnation of Sin

Psalm 50 is a powerful critique of faulty dispositions brought to worship: words without commitment (v. 17), ongoing complicity with evildoers (v. 18), harmful speech against family and covenantal members (v. 20), as well as a variety of offenses against authentic worship not included in the verses actually chosen by the Lectionary as a response to the judgments of Amos. The psalm could easily be a penance rite for parish liturgy or social action committees.

Those Never Thinking of God

A perennial complaint against routine mechanical liturgical participation is the charge that it is divorced from life. Words, music, and action are performed without any sign that the God of worship is also the God of everyday life during the other six days of the week. The refrain (v. 22) is a strong word of judgment that could easily have been included in the words of Amos.

Gospel

Matthew 8:18-22

Follow me.

Literary Link

After the three healing stories, Matthew's gospel proceeds to consider two potential disciples who are impressed by the actions of Jesus and who offer themselves to be his disciples/apprentices in the healing of the world. The individuals set conditions for their willingness or ability to follow Jesus.

Crossing to the Other Shore

The manner in which Jesus moved away from the crowds (v. 18) seems at variance from his usual welcome and outreach to those seeking his help and attention. This may be a reminder that Jesus also left the crowds to spend time in prayer. The reliance on personal prayer underscored the source of his love and the origin of his concern for those in need around him. Something greater is at work here than human sympathy. The gospel describes Jesus as regularly withdrawing as a reminder to disciples of their need for spiritual centering and renewal. Only when we are truly rooted in the presence and power of God are we able to be instruments of his kingdom.

The Offer of the Scribe

Usually it is Jesus who invites others to discipleship. Here we have an example of self-selection and a scribe's desire to follow Jesus to that other side (v. 19). This clearly reminds us that not all scribes were hostile to Jesus. It also shows that Jesus himself had to deepen and intensify the understanding of those who sought to follow him. True discipleship is a lifelong process. The reference to lack of nest or den or home (v. 20) teaches us that following Jesus is not a matter of geographical journey from one place to another, but rather a matter of internal imitation. The "follow me" is closer to the general command of mentoring for a young cook, carpenter, or apprentice.

Burying Parents

Although the dismissal of the potential disciple's concern to bury one's father (v. 22) could seem callous, it reflects the admonition uttered elsewhere in the gospels by Jesus: "If any one comes to me without hating his father and mother . . . , he cannot be my disciple" (Luke 14:26). The expression is a Semitic manner of stating priorities. Parental respect is one of the Ten Commandments, and indeed a commandment for adults, not merely for children! Imitation of Jesus, however, is presented as even more important.

Tuesday of the Thirteenth Week in Ordinary Time

First Reading (Year I)

Genesis 19:15-29

The Lord God rained down sulphurous fire upon Sodom and Gomorrah.

The Unity of All Creation

All of creation is bound together, providing blessings for the good and punishment for the evildoers. The natural catastrophe is described as happening because of the sinfulness of the inhabitants. Those who sin will be punished by the very material creation within which they live! This never occurs in a mechanical fashion, however, because God remains mysteriously involved in everything and on occasion even allows tragedy by his permissive will. In the short run, sometimes bad things happen to good people, but good will triumph and justice will prevail. One should be very careful about presuming that any natural disaster is a punishment for specific sins. At the same time, as the apostle Paul insisted (Rom 8:19-22), all of material creation is somehow bound together with human goodness and human sin. It can be said that we are punished by our sins, not for them. Unstated in the account, but implicit in its unfolding, is the sadness that God could not even find ten good people in the city, so it was destroyed!

The Refuge of Zoar

Because of age and physical limitations, Lot could not travel in haste very far; for that reason God's plan made accommodation for his human infirmities (v. 21). Perhaps this distance was the stuff of Lot's haggling with God, just as Abraham had used numbers! God never expects more than we can handle, though God does give us the assistance to handle what we must. God wanted Lot's safety even more than Lot did himself! God pulled and urged him to get at least as far as Zoar (literally, "a trifle"). It was still large enough to save him.

Pillar of Salt

The story of the pillar of salt (v. 26) may simply be a folktale to explain a curious rock formation shaped like a woman looking back at the valley of desolation. The fact is, however, that looking back, though necessary at times, can also be dangerous. We are called to understand the past in retrospect, and to see it from God's point of view, but we can not remain so bound to that past as to be unable to become rooted in God's present or open to God's future. To be frozen in the past or by it is lethal.

Antiphon (Year I)

Psalm 26:3a

O Lord, your mercy is before my eyes.

Psalm 26: A Plea of Innocence

This psalm is a solemn protestation of personal innocence in the face of accusations from evil people. The worshiper begs to be tested (v. 2) in order to be vindicated, and insists that he or she has avoided association with those who indulge in violence (v. 9) or bribery (v. 10). The verses would easily fit on the lips of Lot as he left the cities of evildoers with his integrity intact. There are times in life when this psalm should become our prayer as well, especially if we feel compelled to disassociate ourselves from evil colleagues! There may be a price to be paid, but it cannot even compare to the value of integrity (v. 11).

Mercy

The mercy placed before the eyes of this innocent person, as the refrain states (v. 3), is *hesed*, the steadfast covenantal kindness exhibited by God to those who live faithfully bound to him. Precisely because of God's fidelity, this individual finds courage and confidence to remain faithful in turn, no matter what pressures may suggest otherwise!

First Reading (Year II)

Amos 3:1-8; 4:11-12

The Lord God speaks—who will not prophesy!

The People of the Exodus

The simple reference to the "family that I brought up from the land of Egypt" (v. 1) is a reminder of the covenant, since the Ten Commandments (Exod 20:1) begin with that same self-identification by God. Thus the crimes listed by Amos as the basis for judgment and condemnation are proposed as violations of that covenant relationship. Any person or group specially favored by God has corresponding duties (v. 2). To whom more is given, more is expected (Luke 12:48).

Cause and Effect

The list of experiences linked by cause and effect, such as, for example, those who walk together out of agreement (v. 3), the roaring of a lion because of its prey (v. 4), or the fall of a bird because of its trap (v. 5), prepares for the prophet's explanation of God's revelation and the prophet's response. When God speaks, a person cannot help but prophesy (v. 8). From the event or effect one can go back to the cause. True prophecy never appears out of nowhere. Punishment follows crime (v. 11). Our world and our lives are filled with examples of cause and effect. This is not automatic or mechanical because bad things do happen to good people. Even then, God remains in ultimate control.

Prepare to Meet Your God

This final invitation (v. 12) is a call to judgment. Scholars often surmise that it is a phrase of invitation from Israel's worship that now is invoked as a preparation for condemnation. This statement could be proclaimed at any number of different times in formal worship. The phrase could also become a prayer before every single human activity, since God is present at the center of everything.

ANTIPHON (YEAR II)

Psalm 5:9a

Lead me in your justice, Lord.

Psalm 5: A Humble Worshiper

This psalm seems most suited to accompany the morning sacrifice (v. 4) and contains the elements expected in humble prayer. The psalm acknowledges that God rejects evil (v. 5), arrogance (v. 6), falsehood, and violence (v. 7). Because of the mutual concern of covenant members for each other, namely, "*hesed*/abundant mercy" (v. 8), the psalmist (and the Christian morning worshiper) enters the assembly with trusting confidence (v. 9).

Justice Leading

This refrain (v. 9) comes from the verse immediately following the portion chosen by the Lectionary for this response, and singles out God's justice as leading people by example and transforming power. Perhaps justice is poetically personified as a servant or minor "deity," and perhaps God himself is proposed as the model of justice. Biblical justice means being in right relationship with all of creation. It also can serve as the virtue that prepares people to enter worship each morning.

GOSPEL

Matthew 8:23-27

Jesus rebuked the winds and the sea,
and there was great calm.

Literary Link

After the Sermon on the Mount, Matthew's Jesus engaged in a series of three healings to make different groups of people whole again. Now he commands the natural elements. Yesterday's passage began with the command of Jesus to cross the lake (v. 18), and in so doing they encountered the storm described today. Tomorrow the liturgy's gospel will present Jesus as even forgiving sins (9:1-8).

The Power of the Sea

The sea with its raging waves and powerful storms (v. 24) was frightening to people who lived in the desert. Even those who lived by fishing from the fruits of the sea respected its power. They celebrated the shorelines, which indicated the edges of its power. People of any age who live close to large bodies of water know to respect its force, especially in storms. In such circumstances its apparently hostile nature easily became an ancient symbol of evil. The storm described in this passage is physical, but we know that emotional and financial storms can also overwhelm people. Humble trust is essential for anyone caught amid any disaster.

Tuesday of the Thirteenth Week in Ordinary Time

The Plea of the Disciples

Sensing their great danger, the disciples ask to be saved (v. 25). This petition is contrasted with the account in Mark's gospel, where the disciples never seem able to comprehend the whole picture and are often pictured as misunderstanding self-centered individuals; there they simply confronted Jesus with an accusation, "do you not care that we are perishing?" (Mark 4:38). Jesus offers salvation even to those who ask poorly. Matthew's disciples are more straightforward and focused.

Power over Creation

Jesus exercised power over the winds and the sea (v. 27). In this account Jesus is presented as the God of creation. It is a "pantocratic" moment in the narrative, namely, a point after cures over individuals with various illnesses, when Jesus is revealed as Lord of all creation. The amazement of the disciples is a sentiment that should be evoked by all of the natural and astonishing wonders accomplished in our world. At the same time contemporary Christians should remember that God has chosen to share responsibility for the world; therefore we should sense a shared obligation to be active in concern for the ecological protection of the world in which we live. We are called to be partners as well as mere spectators or consumers.

Wednesday of the Thirteenth Week in Ordinary Time

FIRST READING (YEAR I)

Genesis 21:5, 8-20a

No son of that slave is going to share the inheritance with my son Isaac!

Family Disagreements and Divisions

Virtually every family has some sort of tension and heartache, so there can be a bit of comfort in overhearing the all too human squabbles between Sarah and her maid. In Sarah's desire to protect her son and his inheritance, she attacks Hagar and Ishmael (v. 10). She even drives them out of the settlement (v. 14). Life lived in close quarters can generate friction. Faith doesn't take away misunderstandings but offers respectful ways to confront, minimize, and resolve them.

The Danger of Anger

How often anger demeans, depersonalizes, and even demonizes those with whom we disagree or fear. Years of service are suddenly forgotten. The fact that Sarah doesn't even use Hagar's personal name but only refers to her as "that slave and her son" illustrates the point perfectly (v. 10). Putting a face on an opponent and using a personal name is the first step toward renewed understanding and reconciliation. Recognizing the absolute uniqueness of every person is also important in family and neighborhood life. Things once said can never be taken back and often leave a permanent scar on relationships. Sarah's lack of charity and compassion tarnished her own reputation in history and left an impression of basic mean-spiritedness.

An Infant's Cry

God heard the child's "voice/*qol*" (see v. 17) in the desert and responded to the need of infant and mother Hagar. Although the "cry/*tzaʿaq*" of the people in Egypt so many years later (Exod 3:7) used a different Hebrew word, that is, the technical term for a lawsuit, God responded with care to both situations. God's care for this child in desperate need of assistance is an inspiration to make our contemporary children a special personal cause in our communities too. Children need the advocacy of adults; this is important for any community that sees itself as "pro-life." Jesus followed the same tradition when he encouraged the little children to come to himself (Matt 19:14), even though the New Testament issue in that case may have been the question of infant baptism in the early church.

ANTIPHON (YEAR I)

Psalm 34:7a

The Lord hears the cry of the poor.

The Poor

The Hebrew word used in this refrain (v. 7) is *ʾanawim*, those who are afflicted and oppressed by the circumstances of life or by more powerful members of a community. The term gradually came to imply, as the prophet Zephaniah insisted (3:12), that these individuals were utterly dependent on God and therefore honest and holy in their humbleness. Attitude is more important than bank accounts, but meagerness of resources is the point. It could be helpful to devise a list of the people who fit into this category in each community.

Heard by God

Because of their total dependence upon God, not their own human resources, these poor people are much beloved and heard by God (v. 7). The refrain offers an unspoken contrast with the proud and arrogant whom God casts down from their thrones, as the *Magnificat* points out (Luke 1:51ff.).

FIRST READING (YEAR II)

Amos 5:14-15, 21-24

Away with your noisy songs! Let justice surge like an unfailing stream.

True Worship

Both Isaiah (1:11-15) and Amos (v. 21) have some harsh things to say about worship because they witnessed prosperous people of their day being generous in support of the sanctuary but unjust toward their poorer neighbors. Some sixteenth-century Reformers erroneously concluded that worship itself was condemned by the prophets. The prophets' more precise judgment, however, was against any experience of worship that does not spill over into justice for others (v. 24). These prophetic voices claimed that such isolated and unfruitful liturgy was simply unacceptable to God. The language is strong, even suggesting that their hymns gave God a headache and their sacrifices made God sick. If Amos came to morning Mass at the parish, could he find any signs of greater care for the needy because of the worship?

Wednesday of the Thirteenth Week in Ordinary Time

Justice

Once again the notion of "justice" (v. 24) in the religious language of Israel includes much more than paying one's bills or resolving debts. Biblical justice includes personal effort to place ourselves together with all of creation in right relationship with God and each other. It is the entire covenanted people who gather for worship, and for that reason care for the more marginal and needy must be a concern for all who claim to be God's chosen ones. Paul VI lamented at times the isolation of liturgy from life as one of the great crises of our day!

ANTIPHON (YEAR II)

Psalm 50:23b

To the upright I will show the saving power of God.

Psalm 50: God's Call for Inner Integrity

Psalm 50 is a strong criticism of faulty attitudes found in those who worship with a concern for public impression rather than genuine piety before God. The verses are, therefore, most fitting as a response to the judgments of Amos. The response insists that God has no need of sacrifices because all animals, beasts, and birds already belong to him by reason of creation (v. 10). Any benefit is for the human participants! Moreover, the psalm condemns those who participate in the ritual, but ignore the statutes (v. 16) of the covenant in the rest of their lives. They are condemned by the psalmist because they reject discipline and quickly throw God's words away (v. 17).

Upright

The Hebrew is obscure (v. 23), but its sense is that those who walk God's path with integrity, honesty, and compassion can stand tall. It is emotional and spiritual "uprightness" that is praised, not simply good physical posture. To them God promises to reveal his salvation and to save them from harm. God "shows" his saving power by making sure that people actually experience and participate in the salvation they see.

GOSPEL

Matthew 8:28-34

Have you come here to torment us before the appointed time?

Literary Link

Some characteristics of genuine discipleship (vv. 18-22) were chosen by the Lectionary for Monday's gospel reading, followed by the story of the stormy journey by sea on Tuesday (vv. 23-27). Now, in the pagan Gadarene territory, Jesus brings his authority over the sea to the two demoniacs who lived among the tombs. The same power was exercised over both evil forces. This illustrates the logical flow to the biblical narrative.

The Gadarenes: A People Living without God's Torah/Instruction

The land of the Gadarenes was Gentile, east of the Sea of Galilee and beyond the area normally embraced by Israel. Matthew greatly abbreviates the story as told by Mark (5:1-20) and simply presents the area as troubled by two savagely disturbed people who were ritually unclean because of their contact with the dead (v. 28). The presence of forbidden swine underscores the distance of that population from God's will as revealed to Israel (and to devout Muslims even to this day). Even though Matthew elsewhere described Jesus as "sent only to the lost sheep of the house of Israel" (15:24), his compassion brought peace and healing to the two troubled individuals. By his actions Jesus was teaching his disciples to reach out to all in need, no matter whether they fit within "the rules" or not. This was part of the "apprenticeship" that he provided for his chosen disciples. The account could inspire a brief survey of the needs of similar "outsiders" in any community.

Dismissal

The reading's last sentence is one of the saddest in the New Testament, namely, the conclusion and final response of the townspeople to the liberating and saving presence of Jesus: Just go away! (see v. 34). The love and power of Jesus upset their Gadarene customs and social equilibrium, and left them with two cured demoniacs. The loss of the pigs was perhaps more important than the healing of neighbors. It was too much to absorb, so they told Jesus to go away and leave them alone. Things can never be the same after healing and conversion. The whole town must change. Not everyone is willing to do so—sometimes not even ourselves.

Thursday of the Thirteenth Week in Ordinary Time

First Reading (Year I)

Genesis 22:1b-19

The sacrifice of Abraham, our father in faith.

The Demand of God

The thought of killing one's own child and doing so under obedience to God is a terrible and chilling situation. Whether it was an explicit divine command (v. 2) or merely the personal conclusion (as some interpreters suggest) of Abraham who saw pagan neighbors sacrificing their firstborn and decided that his God was just as worthy, the terror of the situation remains. How could God ask such a thing, even as a test (v. 1)? The very fact that Abraham and Sarah had yearned so desperately for an heir and had received Isaac as a quasi miraculous birth in old age only made it worse. There are times in life when we must stand mute before dreadful circumstances. Careful discernment is demanded lest we project our thoughts upon God or create a god in our own image and likeness. We can only trust that God is always involved for our welfare!

The Chilling Trust of Abraham

This story is masterfully told, with short staccato sentences almost echoing a compliant wooden journey burdened by sorrow. In his dark night Abraham can only trust the God who had promised to make him a blessing and give him an heir (19:10). There are terrible moments in life when nothing makes sense and we have not a clue as to how to proceed—and yet we trust. Perhaps real trust in God can only be present when our human reaction is so bereft of understanding as to conclude that it is God, not we, at work.

God Will Provide

At the very last moment, already under the shadow of the raised knife, a substitution replacement is provided in the shape of an animal whose horns were caught in the thicket (v. 13). Some will say that this story offered the foundational justification of animal sacrifice. The initial innocent question of Isaac evokes Abraham's grieving response (v. 8). Later the name of the place reflected that the invocation of Divine Providence had deeper meaning than Abraham had realized (v. 14). Countless heroic saints have found in this story the basis for their unwavering trust in the providence of God for his people. The name became "God [who] will provide" (v. 8; literally, "will see to it").

Antiphon (Year I)

Psalms 115–16

I will walk in the presence of the Lord, in the land of the living.

Psalm 115—Rejection of Idols

The psalm response to the story of Isaac's sacrifice as recounted in Genesis is a confession of the utter transcendence of Israel's God, especially as a contrast with the lifeless idols of their neighboring nations. Perhaps Psalm 115 was a hymn frequently used on the occasion of the great annual festival of covenant renewal in Jerusalem. Israel's allegiance is to the Lord alone who remains their covenantal help and their shield of protection, even in hard times of trouble and trial.

Psalm 116:9—Refrain

The single-verse refrain, though not so indicated in the Lectionary, is actually found in Psalm 116. Its reference to walking "in the land of the living" finds easy application to the lips of Isaac who was fortuitously released by divine providence from the threat of being sacrificed by the trembling hand of his father Abraham. The very same refrain could easily become the prayer of anyone preserved from serious misfortune or harm. "Walking" is the most common biblical metaphor for an upright life of ethical morality. It embraces all the lifelong actions of one who is faithful to the will of God in all things.

First Reading (Year II)

Amos 7:10-17

Go prophesy to my people Israel.

A Priest/Prophet Confrontation

Amos went to the northern royal sanctuary of Bethel (v. 10) to deliver his condemnation of King Jeroboam. The priest sent word to the king of the treason of Amos and attempted to send the prophet away (v. 12), but Amos would not comply. Sometimes religious functionaries clash, collide, and contradict. It is the larger community's task to discern which, if any, truly speaks in the name of God. Sometimes both are correct, but about different things! The response of Amos was a harsh promise of family tragedy, exile, and death for the king (v. 17). The final judgment can only come after waiting to see whom God upholds in the unfolding of history.

Dresser of Sycamores

Amos can only defend his actions by claiming a personal divine call without any prior training or experience as a "professional" prophet associated with a sanctuary or guild (v. 14). Sycamores produced an inferior type of fig, but provided valuable wood for coffins; Amos may have worked in a sanctuary orchard. Personal charisms originating from powerful religious experiences of the living God are given to individuals at times. Such spiritual gifts, however, must be further tested by the community of the faithful. Do the things described come to pass (Deut 18:22)? Do they lead toward or away from the true God (Deut 13:3)? It is helpful to remember that a prophet is one who speaks in the name of God, not one who predicts the future. God will choose whom God will choose.

Antiphon (Year II)

Psalm 19:10cd

The judgments of the Lord are true,
and all of them are just.

Psalm 19: God's Spoken Word

Although some commentators would completely separate the first seven verses of this psalm from the rest of the poem by reason of disparity of content, there is a logical inner cohesion and relationship. The first section addresses the way material creation reveals the glory of God. The second portion, chosen by the Lectionary for this response, describes the way that the revealed word of God also discloses God's glory under words such as law, decree, precepts, command, and ordinances. Amos stood under God's command. The judgments of the prophet reflected his faithful obedience to his living God. In reciting these verses we dare to claim a share of that same obedience for our lives today.

Judgments

A "judgment/*mishpat*" (v. 10) is a decision made by a leader that gradually becomes sufficiently repeated as to become a custom and a standard of behavior. They were originally associated with the ancient judges of Israel, namely, military leaders who intervened in Israel's history and brought peace and prosperity. This refrain insists that God makes similar pronouncements. They are "true" in the Semitic sense of being reliable enough to lean against. They are "just" in that they promote the proper interrelationship of all creatures. This refrain is a response to the oracles of condemnation spoken by Amos against Amaziah, the king's sanctuary guardian. By God's judgment the priest, who attempted to send Amos away, will himself die in exile (v. 17). The refrain suggests that this is only fair.

Gospel

Matthew 9:1-8

They glorified God who had given such authority to men.

Literary Link

After curing the cemetery demoniacs on one side of the lake (8:28-34), Jesus comes back to his own shores to heal a paralytic (9:1-8). To each he brings new inner serenity and peace. His people at Capernaum glorify God (v. 8) in stark contrast to the Gadarenes who had simply sent him away (8:34).

Thursday of the Thirteenth Week in Ordinary Time

The Faith of the Carriers

Although the account as told by Mark is much more dramatic, with the stretcher bearers tearing up the roof and lowering their colleague (2:1-12), in both cases it is the faith of the carriers that caught the attention of Jesus (v. 2) and inaugurated the cure. The community's faith and efforts for the sick man would seem to be a key element in the healing. In contrast to contemporary individualism, it is profoundly biblical to stress the community as prior to any member. This conviction offers a scriptural basis for recognizing the influence of the community's faith in the lives of its members. We celebrate God's willingness to reward individual members because of the larger community. This is one of the biblical roots for the Catholic sense of church as a mediating community.

Authority to Forgive Sins

One should not move too quickly over the scandal of human beings capable of forgiving sins. The surprise of the scribes makes a valid point (v. 3). Not only does the text see and celebrate that authority possessed by the person of Jesus (v. 6) but it also implicitly acknowledges that the early Christian community claimed the same authority on earth. By the time that the Gospel of Matthew was written, Jewish leadership encountered those very claims made by the Jewish Christian members of Matthew's community. Traditional Judaism would insist that only the person offended could forgive. Catholicism believes that the church mediates God's truth and forgiveness. This gospel story about the power of Jesus to forgive sins is also a story about his community's power and authority to do the same in his name.

Friday of the Thirteenth Week in Ordinary Time

First Reading (Year I)

Genesis 23:1-4, 19; 24:1-8, 62-67

In his love for Rebekah, Isaac found solace after the death of his mother Sarah.

The Burial of Sarah

The account of the death of the great mother of our faith is important for the larger story of salvation history, particularly since she died in the land of promise, where she was buried. Abraham's purchase of the field in Hebron gave his family a legal right to a portion of the land (v. 19). The reading ends with an acknowledgment of the enduring grief of Isaac until his marriage (v. 67). Our contemporary society is so mobile that it often ignores or at least becomes insensitive to being "rooted" in a particular place through the loss and sorrow of the death of parents and the place of their burial. A community of faith shares each other's grief and sorrows. Surveying the burial locations of the parents of a weekday congregation can bring people together in sharing their losses and their faith.

Wooing Rights and Customs

According to Semitic custom, Abraham was determined that his beloved son should be married to someone from their same extended family. Therefore, he sent a servant under oath (24:2-4) to seek the willing compliance of someone back in Haran who might serve as wife to Isaac. Omitted in the Lectionary's selection is the long detailed account of their meeting at the well and the subsequent negotiations. We are simply told of this arranged marriage that blossomed into love (v. 67). God is always at work in human cultural customs, even our own. Everything works together for the good of those who love the Lord (Rom 8:28). Human relationships, perhaps modeling the Persons of the Blessed Trinity themselves, seem to be the preferred location for God's transforming grace.

Antiphon (Year I)

Psalm 106:1b

Give thanks to the Lord, for he is good.

Psalm 106: Humility before Acknowledging Sin

For almost fifty verses this psalm rehearses a litany of all the sins and rebellions of Israel in the wilderness after the exodus, insisting at the beginning (v. 1) and at the end (v. 47) that God's goodness even overlooks so many multiple examples of faithlessness. The goodness of God's fidelity to his promise of enduring mercy/*hesed* is a fitting response to the story of Isaac and Rebekah. The rest of the psalm would not be quite so appropriate for the reading. The Lectionary chose wisely.

Thanks

The refrain's invitation to give thanks (v. 1) may evoke an awareness of the many blessings that fill our present lives. Seldom, however, do we look backwards into our heritage or family roots for further examples of God's goodness. The tale of Isaac and Rebekah encourages us to include the past regularly in our litany of blessings.

First Reading (Year II)

Amos 8:4-6, 9-12

I will send famine upon the land:
not a famine of bread or thirst for water,
but for hearing the word of the Lord.

The Prophetic Condemnation of Amos

The fundamental moral insight of Amos was that the prosperity of his day was built upon the backs of the poor and needy (v. 4). In the eighth century BC Amos witnessed an unprecedented surge in prosperity around him but also saw that it was accompanied by a great disparity between the wealthy and the impoverished. He concluded that the lowly and the poor were traded off for trivial items like shoes (v. 6). That is an unsettling fact of contemporary life as well. This is verified especially if we think about the fact that supermarket tomatoes in February depend on the labor of underpaid workers in places like the Dominican Republic, or that clean executive offices and restrooms are frequently provided by desperate single mothers doing night shifts, often without health insurance.

Friday of the Thirteenth Week in Ordinary Time

Greed and Dishonesty

Slightly modifying measures and weights in the days of Amos stemmed from greed and dishonesty, cheating the poor in the markets (v. 5) and considering them worth nothing more than a pair of sandals (v. 6). Such injustice in the ancient world is cut from the same bolt as any dishonesty in current grocery markets, public service, or customer relations. Seldom do we hear sermons about the dishonesty woven into so much of our capitalist economy because of the greed of the human heart at all levels. Amos's condemnation of his contemporaries for trading the lives of the poor and their fundamental needs for greater profit is not so far stretched from our twenty-first century. So often unacceptable methods of biomedical research are justified and promoted with the sole rationale of providing jobs and promoting economic benefit for a society. The voiceless of society could even include the embryonic poor and needy.

Crimes and Punishments

Prophetic condemnations were always somehow proportionate and conceptually related to the sins and crimes that merited the punishment doled out by God. Thus unjustly obtained money for banquets would become funeral dinners of mourning (v. 8), and high living would be punished by famine (v. 11). Amos's condemnation of common disregard for the prophetic word is then extended to a famine for such nourishment of the spirit. Amos envisions a situation in which people will experience terrible famine for divine presence and direction. Mother Nature will not be tampered with. Imagine the corresponding punishment for the sins of our own day.

Antiphon (Year II)

Matthew 4:4

One does not live by bread alone, but by every word that comes from the mouth of God.

Not by Bread Alone

The refrain is taken from Christ's desert temptation as told by Matthew. That verse in turn is a citation from Deuteronomy 8:3, which stated that God allowed the Israelites to experience hunger during their years of wandering in the wilderness to teach that spiritual hunger and obedience is more important than mere physical hunger. In this way the liturgy links the voices of Jesus, Moses, and Amos. Likewise our worship is always surrounded by a cloud of historic witnesses.

Psalm 119: Obedience to the Word

The response itself is formed from six verses selected almost randomly from the great extended alphabetical meditation on the many different teachings of God. These instructions nourish the minds and spirits of all generations including our own.

Gospel

Matthew 9:9-13

Those who are well do not need a physician;
I desire mercy, not sacrifice.

Literary Link

The call of Matthew follows the account of the healing of the paralytic. The authority of Jesus to forgive sins (9:1-8) also included his power to seek partners like Matthew. The same Jesus who forgave the sins of the paralytic also sought out sinners such as those who surrounded Matthew and his tax collector friends (vv. 9-13). He extended grace to all, group by group.

Professional Reform

The call to Matthew did not require his total abandonment of the colleagues associated with the work of tax collection (v. 10), even though they were enmeshed in the very corrupt and unjust tax system of his day. Rather, Matthew apparently remained in conversation with former coworkers in order to help them to make their daily work more just and generous. The call to discipleship is not a divine summons to flee the political or economic world but to transform it. Everyone is encouraged by this story to imagine Jesus with his or her contemporary coworkers for similar conversations.

Meals as Invitations to Conversion

The experience of eating in the ancient world was not fast food nourishment on the run but extended time for conversation and conversion. The Pharisees practiced fellowship meals among themselves, as did Jesus with his disciples. Jesus knew that meals with tax collectors (v. 10) could also become similar opportunities for change of heart (v. 11). Almost invariably the accounts of meals with Jesus were opportunities for conversion either accepted or rejected. Every eucharistic meal is intended for conversion. Authentic Pharisee spirituality would presume that family tables should accomplish the same effect. While washing dishes after a meal, it might be good to ponder whether any ideas were changed in the process.

Mercy

The quotation about "mercy, not sacrifice" (v. 13) comes from Hosea 6:6; it is a richer comment than it may first appear. The Hebrew word translated as "mercy" is really *hesed,* covenantal kindness and concern for the well-being of one's neighbors. There is a level of presumed mutuality in the mindset of Jesus, and a care for tax collectors as part of God's people. Jesus the great reformer of Israel invites these tax collectors back into the Jewish community within which they were to show care and concern for their poorer fellow covenant members. If one must choose between community and self-denial, the prior wins out.

Saturday of the Thirteenth Week in Ordinary Time

First Reading (Year I)

Genesis 27:1-5, 15-29

Jacob displaced his brother and usurped his blessing (Genesis 27:36).

Special Blessing

In Israel the firstborn son had the right of primogeniture, namely, special recognition. Deuteronomy required that a double portion be given to him (21:17) even if his mother was not favored. This consideration was given by law because the firstborn also bore certain obligations of sustenance toward the rest of the family. Isaac was aware of his duty toward his firstborn and began preparations for that blessing by asking for a special festive meal with Esau (v. 4). At all times throughout history God distributes gifts differently. God always expects that any such gifts granted will be used for the welfare of others, not merely for oneself.

Rebekah's Deviousness

Unfortunately, rivalries and favoritism within a family have been a perennial challenge to mutual harmony in every age. Rebekah, mother of both Esau and Jacob, takes advantage of her husband Isaac's infirmity. She intervenes to deflect the blessing with a deceitful sleight of hand, thus assuring that the double portion would go to her favorite son rather than to its rightful recipient by law (v. 15). Her action was unjust and wrong, but God used that wrongful deed to assure Jacob's place in the history of human salvation. Once again the unexpected becomes the crooked line for God's plan. God brings good out of evil in mysterious ways. The blessing obtained by deceit is still a blessing that cannot be taken back or reversed. The words of blessing and curse (v. 29) echo the blessings once given to Abraham when first called by God (12:3).

A Blessing of Fertile Fields

Encouraged by the musky fragrance of Esau's borrowed clothing, Isaac's blind blessing for Jacob invokes the dew of the fields and the fertility of the earth as symbols of economic wealth and social prominence (vv. 27ff.). These same words could well be used even today for a springtime blessing of fields in rural areas. They could also become a springboard of prayer for abundant harvests among people who live in more urban environments and who depend on the work of others who live and work those distant acres.

Antiphon (Year I)

Psalm 135:3a

Praise the Lord for the Lord is good!

Choice of Jacob

The initial portion of Psalm 135 offers praise for the selection of Jacob (v. 4). When all is said and done, and in spite of the human deviousness and manipulation involved in that choice, God is praised for arranging matters in accord with the larger divine plan. Even the less than noble characteristic of duplicity, which was associated with Jacob throughout his entire life, was used by the Lord of history. Our God does not condone human wrongdoing but finds a way to use it ultimately for good. Even our faults become a means of salvation.

God Is Good

In so many human situations, the spiritually mature are able to proclaim the goodness of God by the regular use of this refrain (v. 3). God's goodness surpasses ours in every way. Even disappointments and heartaches can become moments of grace and eventually can inspire a sense of gratitude before the God who shapes and purifies his chosen ones. One is also mindful of the apostles who "rejoic[ed] that they had been found worthy to suffer dishonor for the sake of the name" (Acts 5:41).

First Reading (Year II)

Amos 9:11-15

I will bring about the restoration of my people Israel; I will plant them upon their own ground.

Final Salvation

In spite of the multiple visions and proclamations of judgment and destruction by Amos throughout his prophetic career, the final editors of the book arranged the work so that it would conclude with this promise of God's renewed beneficence toward his people. The fallen hut of David would be raised up and the breached walls repaired (v. 11). Though sinful and punished by the consequences of their bad choices, Israel remained God's people in good times and more difficult ones. Sin is never the last word in God's vocabulary, and the possibility of conversion was always an implicit part of a prophet's worldview for those who heard and complied with the prophet's admonitions.

Final Abundance

The poetic images used to depict that final salvation remain attractive and heartwarming: rebuilding of the city walls (v. 11), even after Assyrian and Babylonian destruction (possibly due to the hand of later editors who had a longer range view of past tragedies), and harvests so abundant that the next year's plowing came before the reapers had finished gathering the harvest of the prior year (v. 13). The final blessing of the book concludes with a promise of enjoying the wine and fruit of their gardens, never to be removed from their given land again (v. 15). Whenever left to himself, God is always lavish in goodness. Only sinful human freedom can limit that generosity.

Antiphon (Year II)

Psalm 85:9b

The Lord speaks of peace to his people.

God's Peace

Once again it may be useful to remember that biblical peace/*shalom* (v. 9) entails the restoration of all things to their original interrelated unity. All the parts are fitted together again by God's grace. As in the story of creation from Genesis, whatever God proclaims by an effective divine word comes into being. Likewise, if God speaks of such peace, it will happen.

Litany of Virtues on Parade

The virtues cited in the various portions of Psalm 85 selected as a response represent a magnificent list of every blessing for a good society: kindness (*hesed*), truth (v. 11), justice, peace (*shalom*), and truth (v. 12). They are God's doing, not our achievements. These metaphors for a perfectly operating community represent a most fitting description for the type of blessed nation that concludes and climaxes the hope of Amos. Any congregation and village would be blessed to have such virtues and strengths flourishing in their midst. The words could even serve as an examination of conscience for contemporary leaders and members alike. Would anyone see our parish in that description?

Gospel

Matthew 9:14-17

Can the wedding guests mourn as long as the bridegroom is with them?

Literary Link

Perhaps the dinner described as an opportunity for Jesus to meet tax collectors in the prior call of Matthew (v. 10) was the link to the question of fasting for the final editors of Matthew's gospel. For the Torah observant Pharisees in Matthew's community there was a need to explain the nonfasting practices of Jesus and his Gentile disciples.

Fasting

Pious Jews fasted at times of family mourning. They also fasted as a community on the anniversaries of the two destructions of the temple (Babylonian and Roman). Early on, the more pious Jews fasted on Mondays and Thursdays while Christians fasted on Wednesdays and Fridays (*Didache* 8:1). The wording of this passage acknowledges a change in practice from the days of Jesus (v. 14) to later generations (v. 15). The ultimate question is one of meaning rather than the mere physical fact of abstaining from food. For Christians it was sorrow over the historical mistreatment of Jesus, personal discipline in preparation for prayer, solidarity with those less fortunate, and a new sense of dependence on God.

New Cloth and Wineskins

The similarity of the teachings of Jesus with many of his contemporary rabbinical leaders suggests that complete discontinuity and total novelty was not the point of these two sayings. New patches were only suitable for new cloth (v. 16). Similar practices might differ greatly because of motive or meaning. The question seems, therefore, to be suitability, not novelty. We choose suitable practices appropriate for our needs so that the values we have embraced will be protected and transmitted wisely and well. The rabbis spoke about some practices that were likened to a fence around the Torah, that is, the means of making sure that the instructions of God were respected and observed. An example might be their regulations against lighting fires on the Sabbath, not because fires were wrong, but because they could come dangerously close to the daily work that was proscribed on that day. The fence was appropriate for preserving the value.

Monday of the Fourteenth Week in Ordinary Time

First Reading (Year I)

Genesis 28:10-22a

Jacob had a dream: a stairway rested on the ground and God's messengers were going up and down on it and the Lord was speaking.

A Dream on the Journey

One should not forget that this famous dream of Jacob at Bethel was part of his journey back to the land of his family origin to find a suitable bride. It was fitting in that context, therefore, to reaffirm for him the Lord's promise of land and descendants as abundant as the dust of that earth (v. 14). Thus the third generation of those especially blessed, namely, Jacob as well as Abraham and Isaac (v. 13), would be added and folded into the recipients of that promise. Jacob returned to his homeland in order to reaffirm his future back in Canaan. In the dream the messengers of God linked Jacob to God (v. 12) and to his ancestors, for Abraham had previously worshiped in that very place as well (12:8 and 13:4). It is the repeated grace and renewed calling of God that creates the intergenerational blessing. This is not the work of mere human beings alone. Even today, the same God who worked in the lives of those who went before us continues to be active in our times and indeed with the same goals and purposes.

Ancient Shrines

Places become holy by the experiences of "the Holy" in the lives of people. In the Bible's account of the lives of the great patriarchs and matriarchs of Israel, ancient shrines celebrated by the Canaanites long before the arrival of Abraham took on new meaning because of the faith of those cherished ancestral figures in Israel's history. Holiness is not static but rather dynamic and ever expanding to include the generosity and justice of the lives of visitors. In the last analysis, even in our day, buildings are not truly consecrated by ritual words alone but by the lives of those who enter (v. 16)!

Antiphon (Year I)

Psalm 91:2b

In you, my God, I place my trust.

A Liturgical Chorus

From as early as the Targums of second century AD, these psalm translations of the Hebrew into the spoken Aramaic of the people suggested that the different verses be allocated to distinct groups of people for a sort of antiphonal recitation. Thus verses 1 and 2 (the refrain), as well as verses 3 and 4, could be spoken by a priest or sanctuary guardian to visitors and worshipers, while verses 14 and 15 could be understood as the voice of God from within the shrine. Psalms are communal or personal; they may even have been designed for community liturgies. The psalm response fits the shrine dream.

Trust and Confidence

The verses express a profound sense of personal trust in the Lord's protection (v. 2), especially in travel or in times of distress. Because members of the covenant are pledged to care for each other, any individual person could have an enduring sense of confidence wherever he or she may be. God will always and everywhere eventually provide whatever is needed for security and salvation.

First Reading (Year II)

Hosea 2:16, 17c-18, 21-22

I will espouse you to me forever.

A Second Honeymoon

Even after the tragedy of Israel's infidelity (described in almost definitive terms in the first chapter), which Hosea sees as spiritual adultery, the prophet envisions a fresh start. Hosea speaks of an opportunity to go back to the desert (v. 16) where the first love of God for Israel had been experienced and celebrated. Imagine the utter largesse of a God who would be so forgiving! This is the notion of God that Hosea proclaims to us today as well.

The Book of the Prophet Hosea

In the early years of the eighth century BC when the northern kingdom was on the verge of being carried away into exile by the Assyrians, Hosea arose to speak strongly against the nation's disregard for the God of the covenant. His own painfully broken marriage became a metaphor for the nation's infidelity. Hosea is capable of great tenderness as well, recalling God's kindness like a parent teaching a child to walk and refusing to cast the child (Ephraim) away.

The Qualities of a First Love

Monday of the Fourteenth Week in Ordinary Time

There is something very attractive about the love of a young newly married couple. Older and more experienced people are touched by that example and sometimes painfully conscious of the work it may take to preserve and deepen those same qualities: justice, love, mercy (v. 21), and fidelity. They are gifts of grace that require human cooperation in order to flourish for a lifetime. These same qualities of marriage are also desperately needed in our contemporary world. More mature spouses understand the value of such long-term fidelity and the cost it may require to sustain it over a lifetime. These verses should be brought to the attention of all those who would erroneously claim that the Old Testament only shows a God of anger. Hosea almost seems eager to expand the Deuteronomic notion of faithful love of God and neighbor to include even sentimental and romantic affection of one person to another. God has embraced everything fully human (v. 22). All things human reflect the wonder of God.

ANTIPHON (YEAR II)

Psalm 145:8a

The Lord is gracious and merciful.

"Gracious and Merciful"

Once again the divine qualities exalted in the refrain (v. 8) are those that show God as tender and loving. God reaches out to his creatures with the gifts of grace (*hanan*), which in turn make them attractive, namely, gracious, for that is precisely what "grace" means. God also demonstrates the loving maternal mercy (*raham*) that makes him so protective of his people.

Slow to Anger

The second half of that same verse from which the refrain is taken (v. 8) includes one of the creedal formulas of the first covenant (Exod 34:6), which the psalm translates as "slow to anger and of great kindness [*hesed*]." This tender summary of God's regard for his people, even amid human infidelity, remains consoling. The sentiment beautifully reflects the prophetic poems of Hosea. It also anticipates the love of the prodigal father for his erring son (Luke 15:20).

GOSPEL

Matthew 9:18-26

My daughter has just died,
but come and she will live.

Literary Link

After having concluded the series of stories about banquets (vv. 10-13) and fasting (vv. 14-15), Matthew turns to a series of three healing stories, each building upon the prior event, followed by a summary statement of the great compassion of Jesus.

The Dying Young Daughter

The loss of a child is a terrible tragedy for any parent. This first healing story combines the healing of an older woman with the healing of a young girl, the child of a local official at Capernaum (described additionally in Mark and Luke as a prominent official in the local synagogue). Presumably a person of personal faith, the official approached Jesus (v. 18) in the hope that, possibly like Elijah and Elisha of old, he might raise her up again. After the interruption posed by desperate need of the older woman along the way (vv. 20-22), Jesus entered the official's home, took the girl's hand, and she rose back to life. The life-giving touch of Jesus triumphs over the disbelief of the mourners (v. 24). This account is an opportunity to pray for grieving parents and for all who have lost children amid the terrors of warfare or the grief of disease around the world.

The Woman with the Hemorrhage

In each of the Synoptic Gospels, the story of the woman with the hemorrhage (vv. 20-22) is woven into the account of the prepubescent young girl's restoration to life. The combination of healing for both younger and older woman must have been the way the story was told from the beginning. Both generations were members of early Christian communities; both are objects of the special compassion of Jesus. The public ministry of Jesus as well as that of the church (and every parish) is intergenerational. It is probable that the younger girl's age and the duration of the older woman's suffering are about the same, namely, twelve years. In touching the tassel on the cloak of Jesus (v. 20), the woman makes contact with a bit of clothing worn by the Pharisees as a sign of their desire to be completely faithful in their obedience to God, because the tassel touches every step taken. The faith of the woman reaches out to the religious symbol of the faith of Jesus.

Tuesday of the Fourteenth Week in Ordinary Time

FIRST READING (YEAR I)

Genesis 32:23-31

You shall be spoken of as Israel, because you have contended with God and have prevailed.

Wrestling with God

In the irony of history the devious Jacob had been punished in turn by the deceit of Laban (29:23) and had married both Leah and his beloved Rachel. Now after fourteen years of service, Jacob travels homeward again. Chastened by his life experiences, Jacob was forced to confront the very estranged brother from whom he had wrongfully wrested their father's blessing. The story of Jacob's wrestling with the messenger (v. 25) is a very strange tale, ending in the odd reference to the sciatic muscle (v. 33). Perhaps Jacob needed to wrestle with his conscience before God in order to discover what and how to seek forgiveness from God before meeting his brother, against whom he had also sinned. A limping Jacob, he remained forever physically affected by his struggles (v. 32). This wrestling with God's angel has often been used as a metaphor for the struggles of every human being who attempts courageously to do the right thing amid so many conflicting emotions. The story is an opportunity to prayer for all who struggle in conscience, and for all suffering ailments of the hip.

Seeing God Face-to-Face

Only at the end of the struggle does Jacob, now called Israel ("He will contend"), conclude that it was indeed God himself with whom he had struggled throughout the night (see v. 31). God takes many forms in calling us to conversion and integrity with justice. Little children, mysterious figures of our imagination, rivals, and family friends can assume the voice and call of God for us. If we remember Jacob, we can be reminded that God wants what is the best for us, even in all the struggles we may experience in our effort to attain a peaceful conscience and family reconciliation. Perhaps this story is one of the many reasons why the Hebrew word for God's "presence" is *panim*, "faces."

ANTIPHON (YEAR I)

Psalm 17:15a

In justice, I shall behold your face, O Lord.

Psalm 17: A Cry from the Innocent

Psalm 17 is difficult, and several of the verses are open to different translations. The portion chosen for this response comes from the beginning of the psalm. It is a claim of innocence before God (v. 1) and a repeated plea for hearing and help (v. 6). It was chosen by the Lectionary as a prayer placed on the lips of Jacob in his struggle with God. It is fitting for anyone caught in a moment of desperation and need.

Seeing God

The verb translated as "see" (v. 15, NAB) often refers to the visions of a prophet. The refrain is taken from the last verse of the psalm. It concludes with an expression of faith in the fact that the person's desire to flee to God and to be kept safe under God's protection will be finally rewarded. God's response is not only the grace of security but also a vivid personal vision of God's care and concern. This is achieved, says the refrain, by living one's entire life out of biblical justice, that is, maintaining a right relationship with all creatures. Only then does one "see" God and begin to understand how God operates in our world.

FIRST READING (YEAR II)

Hosea 8:4-7, 11-13

When they sow the wind, they shall reap the whirlwind.

Choosing Leaders

There was a long-standing difference between the manner of choosing leaders in the northern kingdom of Israel and that used by Judah in the south. While the latter relied upon the dynasty of David and his successors, the north was more likely to change rulers by violent rebellions and assassinations, thus producing a series of short-lived ruling families. Hosea's complaint that rulers were chosen without the Lord's approval (v. 4) states that they were selected for mere political or economic motives, without consideration for the traditional religious values required by the Lord's covenant. All methods of leadership selection, ancient or modern, should be based upon God's justice, care for the needy, security for the people, and concern for the common good.

Idolatry

Gods of one's own making (v. 4) and sanctuaries crafted in disobedient rebellion against God are doomed (v. 7). Hosea insists that we are called to be images of God rather than to be busy about making gods in our own image and likeness (v. 6). Handmade gods of silver and gold bring destruction (v. 4), not salvation. Gods who bless our wants (as contrasted with our true needs) are unable to lift us up into becoming better people. They are like the wind that returns to destroy us and like wheat that produces no ears for harvest or sustenance (v. 7).

ANTIPHON (YEAR II)

Psalm 115:9a

The house of Israel trusts in the Lord.

The Impotence of Idols

The entire response continues to mock the helpless statues worshiped by Israel's neighbors with crafted mouths, eyes, ears, noses, hands, and feet incapable of functioning or moving (vv. 7-10). The psalm simply extends Hosea's diatribe and summons us to consider our own idols more carefully. Whatever is the primary motive for our actions and decisions is an idol if different from or contrary to the God of the covenant. Our idols, whatever they may be, are no less helpless than those described in the psalm. (Note that the same verses from Psalm 115 were used in Year I's response on Thursday of the Thirteenth Week.)

God of Action

Contrasting with such idols, Israel's God calls nations into being. He freely decides to create, redeem, punish, and bless. Whatever this God wills, he does (v. 3)! He remains the King of the universe and the Lord of history. The God of Israel is a living God, and therefore the refrain repeats the invitation to trust in him always.

GOSPEL

Matthew 9:32-38

The harvest is abundant but the laborers are few.

Tuesday of the Fourteenth Week in Ordinary Time

Literary Link

Matthew describes the healing of the two women (vv. 18-26), the healing of two blind men (vv. 27-31, omitted in the Lectionary), and the healing of the mute (vv. 32-34), followed by a summary conclusion (vv. 35ff.) to this healing phase in the public ministry of Jesus. He is repeatedly presented as one who is filled with compassion, deeply conscious of the enormous needs of people for healing and help. The final verses of the gospel's chapter speak of the great harvest (vv. 37-38). They form a bridge to his decision to choose partners in the work of the kingdom (10:1), which forms the substance of the next day's Lectionary reading.

The Speaking Mute

After the cure of the young girl and the mature woman, the gospel proceeds to help the mute man speak. Modern Western culture might suspect that all three were deprived of voice in their ancient world. When the crowds express their amazement (v. 33), it is almost as if the newly articulate fellow is himself one of that chorus of praise! We are all called to speak God's praise for all the mighty deeds done in our lives and for us. Once again, perhaps without our initially recognizing the fact, the story is about us and our newfound ability through faith to offer praise and witness.

God's Need for Partners

Sheep without shepherds and harvests without reapers form the final observation of Jesus at the end of this series of cures and healings (v. 38). A God powerful enough to seek and to empower partners is part of the gospel's image of the heavenly Father of Jesus. The same invitation is also addressed to all those who gather for weekday Eucharist. The gospel is a divinely inspired social movement as well as Good News!

Tuesday of the Fourteenth Week in Ordinary Time

Wednesday of the Fourteenth Week in Ordinary Time

First Reading (Year I)

Genesis 41:55-57; 42:5-7a, 17-24a

Alas, we are being punished because of our brother.

Joseph the Provider

The Lectionary cannot complete the story of the patriarchs without including something about Joseph, beloved son of Jacob, sold into slavery by his jealous brothers, only to rise to become the instrument of their deliverance from starvation. That intervening history is presumed by the editors of the Lectionary, but is important for the irony of its conclusion. God's mysterious, perhaps even devious, providence had provided the very gifts in the person of Joseph that would eventually be recognized by the Pharaoh and rewarded by high responsibilities. Ever the dreamer, Joseph became the organizer of possible strategies for feeding the world's hungry (42:6). Popular Catholic piety has appropriated the pharaoh's command ("go to Joseph," 41:55) in our devotion to Saint Joseph, protector of families and patron of the universal church. What talents do the members of today's worshiping community possess that could become useful in time of future need?

The Sorrow of the Brothers

Only when caught in the painful situation of the demands of this foreign royal bureaucrat do the brothers begin to understand the consequences of their sin so many years earlier (42:21). To force their hand, Joseph demands that their/his youngest brother (Benjamin) be held as hostage in Egypt. On one level the ploy will intensify the punishment for their sin, but at a deeper level it will reunite the family of Jacob. True sorrow for sin repairs the breach and rectifies the harm done. This is God's purpose, and we are often unknowing partners and accomplices in the designs of God. Every family has some heartache, and the shadows of that hardship can stretch out for decades.

Antiphon (Year I)

Psalm 33:22

Lord, let your mercy be on us,
as we place our trust in you.

Psalm 33: The God of History

The portions of the psalm selected by the Lectionary are perfect for the account just read. The verses move from praises for God to a confession of belief in a God able to control the plans of nations according to his will. The response concludes with a final expression of praise for the God who knows the humble reverence of faithful people (v. 18) and preserves them from famine (v. 19). The final phrase is precisely the point of this portion of the Joseph story.

Mercy and Trust

The "mercy" to which the refrain (v. 22) refers is *hesed*, the mutual concern that characterizes true covenant membership. All who pledge themselves to care for the needs of each other are bonded together in mutual trust. Because the brothers of Joseph violated that bond so grievously, they are now confronted with the pain of possibly losing yet another family member. They are punished by their sin rather than for it. The refrain is proposed as a possible prayer said by the brothers and by all in need of help.

First Reading (Year II)

Hosea 10:1-3, 7-8, 12

It is time to seek the Lord.

The Bitter Price of Israel's Fertility Cults

Israel had been seduced into thinking that the origin of its rich harvests was due to the Canaanite fertility cults of their neighbors and had imitated them, building altars and sanctuaries everywhere. The Lord was determined to destroy them all by famines and dearth of harvests and to make them pay for their guilt (v. 2). In the imagination of Hosea the vineyards were replaced with thorns and thistles on the altars (v. 8). In typical prophetic thinking crime and punishment are interrelated. The irony of the prophet's poetry is magnificent. The hills and mountains, once the foundation for the high places of false worship, are begged to become part of the people's punishment and ruin (v. 8). Only the Lord of the covenant is the true source of grain, wine, and oil.

Repentance

The image for repentance is to substitute new plants for the lush vineyards of their fields, namely, fields of "justice"/*tzedeqah* and "piety"/*hesed* (v. 12). Only by returning to a true relationship with the Lord/YHWH in mutual covenantal care and relationship with all of creation can the fields become truly fertile again and the people be fed.

Wednesday of the Fourteenth Week in Ordinary Time

ANTIPHON (YEAR II)

Psalm 105:4b

Seek always the face of the Lord.

Singing Praise

The psalm response begins with an invitation to sing (v. 2). Praise and lyrical celebration of God's power is this psalm's first communal response to the possibility of new beginnings. Even though we may usually make the psalm responses into recited vocal statements, we should remember that they were written to be sung.

Seeking God's Face

The refrain (v. 4) is an invitation to "seek," that is, to enter the sanctuaries of Israel's God, in order to experience the "face/*panim*" of God. The Hebrew word translated as "face" is literally in the plural. The word refers, as noted elsewhere, to the many different personal responses of God to the human worshiper who brings foibles and selfishness into the temple. The psalmist understood that the presence of God was uniquely experienced by those who participated in worship. They may not physically see God's face, but they are gathered in his presence and seek divine blessings. The repeated refrain stresses the heart of liturgical prayer, namely, the community that looks for signs of God's presence in our world.

GOSPEL

Matthew 10:1-7

Go rather to the lost sheep of the house of Israel.

Literary Link

The immediate consequence of the observation of Jesus regarding the immensity of the harvest (vv. 37ff.) is the account of the selection of the Twelve (10:1-7). They will be told of their specific commission in tomorrow's gospel.

Disease and Illness

The ancient world knew, as do we, that the mind and body are inherently interconnected and that sometimes destructive forces from within a personality could cause great harm. Jesus gave power to his specially chosen disciples and apprentices (v. 1) over such demons and unclean spirits. The seven capital sins are certainly among the compulsions from which people need freedom. Jesus sent the Twelve to confront such harmful realities and to summon people into healthy relationships with God in community. Doing so is the work of the kingdom (v. 7).

The Names of the Twelve

There is some debate among scholars over whether the title "Apostles" (v. 2) came from the public ministry of Jesus or from a later time after the resurrection under the impulse of the Holy Spirit. The "Twelve" individuals were certainly specially chosen by Jesus and sent in his name. Twelve very different people, with distinctive personal names, were selected to represent a renewed Israel of twelve tribes. They were diverse in their political loyalties and professions, as evidenced by the presence of Matthew, the tax collector representing Roman authority, as well as Simon, the zealot firebrand opposed to that authority. Through the personal presence of Jesus they become united in service to the kingdom of God that they were sent to announce (v. 7). In one sense we could add the individual names of every single subsequent baptized disciple of Jesus. All are called to be partners in healing human society and proclaiming God's sovereign work in our world.

Thursday of the Fourteenth Week in Ordinary Time

FIRST READING (YEAR I)

Genesis 44:18-21, 23b-29; 45:1-5

It was really for the sake of saving lives that God sent me here ahead of you.

Lifelong Sorrows

The figure of Joseph in Genesis is a perfect example of a person of wisdom, living a life of singular integrity (as demonstrated by his reaction to the seductions of Potiphar's wife; cf. 39:6-20). He possessed many outstanding qualities such as his clever organizational abilities in preparing for famine, his loyal service to the pharaoh, his care for family values, and his studious avoidance of bitterness against those who had done him harm as a young man. At the same time Joseph lived for years with quiet awareness of the sorrows that resulted from his family's treachery and the violence of his brothers (45:4). Countless people have similar pains and sorrows that they carry quietly through life, and for which healing may be needed, even after many years. The beatitude for those who mourn (Matt 5:4) does not imply that God is pleased with suffering but rather that God is pleased with those who live with sorrow while avoiding anger, bitterness, or revenge in their lives. These folks are objects for our prayer and our imitation.

Divine Providence

There remains a marvelous and mysterious sense of providence in the conclusion of this family saga (v. 5). The very brother who was once rejected out of jealousy had become their savior in later times of drastic need. Joseph had been sold off to Egypt by mysteriously complicated routes, all under the hand of God, in order to serve God's ultimate purposes in unexpected ways. One can never praise God's almighty ways sufficiently. All our lives we can only see the ragged backside of the tapestry of history; only at the end does the true pattern become evident in each of our lives and in the entire history of the church. We can understand the fullness of truth when we look backwards.

ANTIPHON (YEAR I)

Psalm 105:5a

Remember the marvels the Lord has done.

Psalm 105: God's Care for Joseph

Psalm 105 is a recitation of all the ways in which God had guided and saved Israel in times of turmoil and trouble. The litany reflects one of the important portions of every covenant treaty text, namely, the recitation of the history of the deeds of a great king toward his covenanted partner. The fact that the story of Joseph is included in that list (vv. 16-21) makes this psalm a fitting communal liturgical response to the reading from Genesis. Other interventions mentioned in the psalm, but not selected by the Lectionary, include the signs of Moses, the actual exodus, the wandering in the wilderness, and the gift of the Promised Land.

Marvels

Today's refrain speaks of the marvels of the Lord (v. 5). The deeds of God for his chosen people over the centuries, however, need not always be extraordinary or astonishing in themselves. The God whose providence uses what philosophers call "secondary causes" can make ordinary things fall wondrously into place for those whom he loves. Contemporary calls of the church for greater evangelization don't necessarily expect contemporary people to knock on neighbor's doors or pass out pamphlets. What we are asked, however, is to speak freely about the blessings we have received from God throughout life and to give that type of witness whenever appropriate.

FIRST READING (YEAR II)

Hosea 11:1-4, 8e-9

My heart is overwhelmed.

A Tender God

This text is almost explicitly designed to counter the popular but very erroneous modern Christian assumption that the God of the Old Testament is one of anger, wrath, and punishment. By way of correction to that error, Hosea depicts the Lord God of Israel as lovingly teaching an infant to walk, uncertain step by step (v. 3), and holding his people close to his cheek in affectionate care (v. 4). Even when irritated by Israel's foolish behavior (and what parent doesn't have that exasperated feeling at times!), this God refuses to destroy his beloved child. He remains God; he will never react like a mere human being (v. 9).

The Passion of God

Hosea is willing to imagine a God internally conflicted by feelings. Perhaps this may seem excessively anthropomorphic in ascribing human feelings to the utterly transcendent God, but the Scriptures of Israel do so often. This is a God with a broken heart over his people (v. 8), weeping over their hurts and determined to seek a fresh start whenever and wherever possible (2:16ff.). Abraham Heschel, the great Jewish spiritual writer, speaks of this divine passion with remarkable brilliance in his two-volume work on *The Prophets*.

ANTIPHON (YEAR II)

Psalm 80:4b

Let us see your face, Lord, and we shall be saved.

Psalm 80: A Plea for Divine Protection

The Lectionary chooses two brief stanzas from Psalm 80 as a response to the tender words of Hosea, and simply asks in confidence for God's protective care (vv. 15ff.). Addressing God as shepherd and farmer, the psalm seeks the enduring concern of God in all times of new spring planting and fresh starts. A favorite prophetic symbol for Israel was a cherished vine, transplanted from Egypt to the rich soil of Canaan (Ezek 17:6-8).

Seeing God's Face

The refrain itself is taken from elsewhere in the psalm. In fact the same prayer is repeated three times (vv. 4, 8, and 20) in the context of a community lament. Amid so many sorrows in the history of Israel, the refrain begs for a new glimpse of God at work. The refrain is a perfect prayer for people in moments of hardship that seem to have no easy human solution. Note that the refrain of yesterday's response to the reading from Hosea also refers to the face of God.

GOSPEL

Matthew 10:7-15

Without cost you have received;
without cost you are to give.

Literary Link

This instruction of Jesus follows the selection of the Twelve. Jesus gives them further directives regarding how to go about the mission they have received. The portion of the instruction dealing with the hardships of their mission, however, is reserved for tomorrow's reading (vv. 16-23).

Missionary Mindset

The Twelve are sent out to herald the kingdom (v. 7), namely, to announce publicly something about the way in which the sovereign action of God is at work in the world. They are sent to be active instruments of that great commission, not merely people who point it out. As missionaries, they are expected to live and work with an acute sense of the "from" and the "for" of their lives. The sick, deceased, diseased, and troubled (v. 8) are the objects of their concern. They are commanded to travel without any extra human resources (v. 10) in order to show their total dependence on God, not themselves. One could even stay at home and be permeated by that zeal.

Worthy Recipients

If the Twelve (and by inference all members of the Christian community) are to be so totally dependent on others, they are commanded to seek appropriate hosts

(v. 11) as sponsors for their evangelical work. Note that Matthew's charge, unlike other gospel accounts, does not contain any reference to "eating what they place before you," possibly because that historical reference envisioned the challenge of kosher dietary restrictions. Matthew's community was comprised of both Torah observant Jews and Gentiles who were not obliged to follow such rules. Perhaps Matthew simply thought it wiser to omit any reference to that neuralgic issue in early Christian community life. In any case, hospitality remains an important virtue in every age. The support offered by others, whether immediate or distant, is essential for missionary work.

Thursday of the Fourteenth Week in Ordinary Time

Friday of the Fourteenth Week in Ordinary Time

First Reading (Year I)

Genesis 46:1-7, 28-30

At last I can die, now that I have seen for myself that Joseph is alive.

Jacob's Vision

This portion of the story begins with a vision (v. 2) given by God to Jacob, who had suffered as a result of the apparent loss of his beloved son. It was ironic that Jacob himself had in a different fashion deprived his own father Isaac of a beloved Esau by the ruse of stealing the blessing destined for the heir. Jacob was reminded that the Divine Speaker was "the God of [his] father" (v. 3). The land of Canaan had been promised to Abraham and Isaac, and now Jacob was leaving it for a different foreign territory (v. 5). Things can change in our lifetime, and God can ask new and unexpected things of us as part of our journey. Perhaps Jacob needed assurance that this change was not a self-serving convenience but still within the will of God for him and his family.

Security in Elder Age

Jacob's move to a new situation in Egypt (v. 3), not originally his own, can be compared to the mature years of so many elderly who give up their independence and feel forced to move to homes for assisted living or special care. Time for grieving may be necessary and more time for an adjustment to the unexpected demands of God's will for them. Did Jacob's sons have to talk him into this? How do we help our parish members faced with this same challenge? Our culture and the complication of modern medicine no longer allow families to care for the elderly and infirm as we once did.

Family Reunions

If ever there was a fractured family, it had to be this extended group of brothers who had sold one of their own into slavery out of jealousy. In spite of the remarkable providence of God in this case, the brothers had much to be sorry for and many amends to make. At the heart of the reunion was that of Joseph with his long-lost father, and Jacob with his long-lost son (v. 29). We can imagine the emotions of the sheepish brothers who witnessed the reunion. Virtually every family has some heartache in need of healing, and some divisions in need of new understanding. How can a parish community assist that healing?

Antiphon (Year I)

Psalm 37:39a

The salvation of the just comes from the Lord.

Plenty in Times of Famine

Perhaps Psalm 37 was chosen as a response because of its explicit mention of food for those struggling under famine (v. 19). The desire and the need for security, however, can take many forms (v. 3). The psalm encourages trust in all difficult situations. Struggling families and anxious elderly all need assistance in tough economic times.

Salvation from the Lord

The refrain (v. 39) promises salvation. Because our lives are filled with so many apparently serendipitous events that end up saving us from harm or pain, it is helpful to remember that our God works with "secondary causes." Things converge to introduce us to different individuals at one time in life who become sources of assistance at other times. Circumstances occur that distract us momentarily only to save us from accidents. Even though bad things continue to happen to good people, and not everyone is so preserved, we believe that it is still God who is behind all the various "salvations" we receive over the years.

First Reading (Year II)

Hosea 14:2-10

We shall say no more "Our god" to the work of our hands.

Words of Repentance

Hosea's final chapter includes a suggested formula for expressing sorrow for sin (vv. 3 and 4). Israel's humble acknowledgment of the fact that military strength and political allegiances can never save a people is an important part of any true repentance; the concepts are as contemporary as anything we could ever imagine. A perennial "firm purpose of amendment" always includes the rejection of idolatry in all its forms (see 1 John 5:21). Creating a god in our own image and likeness is a sure recipe for disaster. Hosea understood that the rejection of idolatry needed to be stated clearly for any true renewal of life and forgiveness.

Friday of the Fourteenth Week in Ordinary Time

Divine Response

The answer of God to his own suggested prayer is filled with poetic imagery of fresh beginnings: life-giving dew at morning time, deep roots, fragrance of cedar, and rich harvests (vv. 6-8). The God of prior humbling also promises prosperity to those wise enough (v. 10) to see the dire consequences of their sinful actions. Nations and individuals suffer from the effects of misguided alliances with their great neighboring powers.

Antiphon (Year II)

Psalm 51:17b

My mouth shall declare your praise.

Psalm 51: A Plea for New Beginnings

The Lectionary fittingly chooses selected verses from the great penitential Psalm 51 as an echoed response to Hosea's prophetic effort at reconciliation. Just as Hosea offers a suggested formula for the expression of true sorrow, these verses (especially vv. 3-14) spell out the various sentiments associated with the human quest for forgiveness.

Inner Sorrow

Among the verses cited from Psalm 51 we hear the classic request for a clean heart (v. 12). Not satisfied with mere external reunion with the people of God at prayer, the psalmist asks that his heart, the place of human planning and decision making, be purified for the future. One senses a similarity between this petition and the portions of the Sermon on the Mount that command inner freedom from thoughts of anger or adultery (Matt 5:21-30). Once that inner purification has been achieved by grace, we can proceed to offer the praise promised by the refrain (v. 17).

Gospel

Matthew 10:16-23

For it will not be you who speak, but the Spirit of your Father speaking through you.

Literary Link

Yesterday's gospel commanded all "missionaries" to live in complete dependence on God and their generous human hosts. Here the gospel adds, possibly in the light of experiences around the time of its publication, that the initial entrance into a new town or community may even involve resistance and hostile anger.

Arrest and Court Action

Early Christians were accused of the crime of atheism because of their refusal to participate in pagan sacrifices, and of cannibalism because of garbled rumors about the nature of the Eucharist. Their belief was viewed as seditious, and this popular charge was probably enhanced by the fact that knowledge of certain ritual practices and prayers were reserved to the baptized. The missionaries were handed over to civil and religious authorities (vv. 17ff.). Even the apostle Paul's journeys are filled with disruptions, court appearances, and imprisonment. Like the apostles in Jerusalem who rejoiced at "dishonor for the sake of the name" (Acts 5:41), these early followers of the risen One are to regard their suffering for doing the right thing as a badge of honor.

Gift of Words

Jesus promises a sense of confidence to those brought before tribunals because of their witness. They are assured that responses will be provided on the spot by the Holy Spirit (vv. 19-20). The publication of Matthew's gospel came decades after Pentecost. The early Christians already had felt the consequences of the Spirit's gift of tongues and bold speech. Even if their professions of personal faith should divide families (v. 21), God's Spirit was promised as the divine source for the right words. Unfortunately, families have long been divided over religion. Not only the Spirit's word at the moment of persecution but also the further development of apologetics (the reasoned defense of the faith and its practices) are gifts of the Holy Spirit. When all is said and done, however, the best witness is that of one's entire life, not merely a few well-crafted persuasive words in court.

Saturday of the Fourteenth Week in Ordinary Time

First Reading (Year I)

Genesis 49:29-32; 50:15-26a

God will surely take care of you and lead you out of this land.

The Death of Jacob

In order for the story to come full circle and find a suitable conclusion, the body of Jacob, at his request (v. 29), was returned for final burial at the cave of Machpelah (currently called Hebron). It was the site that Abraham had purchased for the tomb of Sarah (23:16). In this manner the land promised by God to Abraham became the place of their life and death. The text says simply that he "breathed his last, and was taken to his kindred" (49:33; not in the Lectionary). To understand death as a reunion with one's ancestors, known and unknown, is yet another biblical testimony to the family bonds that hold us together forever.

The Devious Brothers

Taking advantage of the silence of their deceased father, the brothers approached Joseph for full amnesty and pardon for their crimes against him so many years before (50:15). Even though they put words in the mouth of their father, and perhaps even though Joseph wisely read the true situation, he granted their request fully and freely (v. 19). A truly wise person knows the human heart as well as the value of forgiveness and reconciliation. Perhaps the brothers, knowing full well their own prior wickedness, feared the same sentiments in the heart of Joseph and betrayed their guilt by this action. They are who they are.

The Death of Joseph

Joseph, like his father Jacob, asked to have his bones returned to the land of promise (v. 24), from which he had been driven by the jealousy of his brothers. It may have taken centuries, but the bones of Joseph were finally taken with his people when Moses led them out of Egypt (Exod 13:19). The complete patriarchal account of the origins of Israel is now complete. The story of Genesis is over. The tale of the three primal generations tells the history of the entire family. Moreover, in life and in death, home is home. How often contemporary elderly who have migrated to warmer climates request final burial "back home" with their families. Thoughtful families honor those wishes out of respect and love.

Antiphon (Year I)

Psalm 69:33

Be glad you lowly ones; may your hearts be glad!

Psalm 105: God with His People

Very uncharacteristically, the Lectionary has selected a different psalm for the response than for its refrain. Psalm 105 appropriately celebrates the praise given God for his actions among the nations, and addresses Abraham and his chosen sons of Jacob (v. 6). The choice reflects the situation of Jacob's death in the foreign land of Egypt. The verses praise God's constant protection of that people during their many journeys.

The Joy of the Lowly

Amid the chosen people of God, it is precisely the lowly/*ʾanawim* who are invited to rejoice by the refrain (v. 33). In so doing, the entire family of Jacob is recognized as "lowly," not necessarily socially and economically, but spiritually. They depended totally on God's goodness and generosity. In this liturgical context the Lectionary presents God's entire people as humble and holy. Centuries earlier poverty had been understood as a punishment for infidelity; now it was the mark of God's special favor.

First Reading (Year II)

Isaiah 6:1-8

I am a man of unclean lips; yet my eyes have seen the King, the Lord of hosts!

The Book of the Prophet Isaiah

For the next week the Lectionary offers readings chosen from First Isaiah, namely, the initial forty chapters of that prophetic work. Isaiah calls for trusting confidence and repentance before the ominous threats of the Assyrian power.

The Call of a Prophet

Isaiah's call is described as a profound liturgical experience in the temple, with swirling clouds of incense imagined as a royal robe filling the temple (v. 1). In response to Isaiah's sense of total unworthiness, God purifies his lips with a burning coal (v. 7). This experience forms the background for the prayer placed on the lips of someone preparing to proclaim the gospel at Mass, and on the lips of the congregation's response after the preface to the eucharistic prayer. This great call story of Isaiah is rehearsed at every Eucharist as a reminder that everyone is unworthy of speech before the transcendent mystery of God.

"Send Me"

With purification comes the prophet's willingness to be used howsoever God may choose (v. 8). Once a person understands that worthiness is completely dependent upon God alone, a new generosity and confidence arises in the human spirit. This same spirit animated the life of the apostle Paul, former persecutor, and then later a specially summoned herald of the Gospel.

Antiphon (Year II)

Psalm 93:1a

The Lord is king; he is robed in majesty.

Virtues as Clothing

The refrain picks up a theme from Isaiah's call and announces God as robed in majesty (v. 1). Often liturgical imagery in the psalms speaks of spiritual values as so ingrained in daily life as to be considered virtual clothing that we put on at the beginning of every day. Similarly, the Letter to the Colossians speaks of the qualities that a follower of Christ should wear like clothing (3:12). In this spiritual sense, we wear what we are.

The Lord as King

In describing and venerating their God, Israel did not hesitate to borrow words and ideas from their Canaanite neighbors. Initially God alone was the king without human counterpart. Later in the time of the prophet Samuel, some of the people began to ask for a human king to serve as a focal point for defense and security (1 Sam 10:19). Traces of both sides of that argument can still be found in the First Book of Samuel. The opposing arguments were vivid reflections of the actual historical abuses that followed. God alone should be their king, and this was celebrated in the temple's liturgy.

Gospel

Matthew 10:24-33

Do not be afraid of those who kill the body.

Literary Link

The third and final section of the mission chapter of Matthew concluded with an invitation to confidence in God's providential presence and care in spite of rejection and persecution.

Calumny and Mockery

Jesus reminds his disciples that they will be treated just as he was (vv. 24-26). This, however, may not have been much consolation. The early Christians considered it an honor to share the experience of being called "Beelzebul" (v. 25), as was their Master (Matt 12:24). Rejection by mockery and by ascribing false motivation has been a perennial manner of avoiding serious conversation and possible conversion.

Divine Providence

Beside the tiny sparrows and the hairs of one's head (vv. 29-31), the world is filled with countless seemingly insignificant things that remain under God's providential protection and care. Not everything is protected materially, however, because predators prowl and people suffer violence. God remains with his world, even in their suffering. Divine Providence presumes human discernment and partnership.

Saturday of the Fourteenth Week in Ordinary Time

Monday of the Fifteenth Week in Ordinary Time

First Reading (Year I)

Exodus 1:8-14, 22

Come, let us deal shrewdly with them to stop their increase.

The Book of Exodus

This second scroll of the Torah/Pentateuch recounts Israel's growing oppression in Egypt and their wondrous departure by divine protection under the leadership of Moses and Aaron. The work includes the story of the great gift of the covenant on Mount Sinai. Several classical sources, each with its own theological perspective, have been woven together to describe the origins of God's chosen people and their first travels toward the Promised Land.

Increase as Threat

The Lectionary's introduction to the people of Israel begins with recognition of the effectiveness of God's promised fertility and the threat of that fact as perceived by Egyptian authorities (v. 10). Rather than acknowledging the giftedness of this population and seeking ways to utilize those gifts and to live/work together, the Egyptians decided to enslave them with very hard work (v. 14). The text emphasizes that dreadful condition by repeating verbal and nominal variations of the same Hebrew word, "to work/*ʿabad*," four times in rapid succession. Given the fact that the Israelites were alien residents in Egypt, this could be a suitable time to speak briefly about immigration reform and the need to treat newcomers and their families with dignity and respect.

The Crime of Infanticide

The pharaoh's ruthless command (v. 22) stands as a perennial warning against any effort to resolve even the most difficult of human problems by simply eliminating the weakest and most vulnerable persons in the area. God can never be pleased by such responses. In acknowledging such realities, one should also understand the dreadful social pressures that can force individuals, such as young single unwed mothers, into actions they find morally untenable and the lifelong guilt that follows. Though not mentioned in this passage, one should note the determined disobedient resistance of the midwives (v. 17).

Antiphon (Year I)

Psalm 124:8a

Our help is in the name of the Lord.

Psalm 124: God's Protection

Psalm 124 is an emotional expression of communal thanksgiving for deliverance from danger. It is particularly fitting as a response to the story of Egyptian oppression because of its description of human hostility (v. 3) and the mortal danger of drowning waters (v. 4). This is a prayer of thanksgiving for children saved from drowning.

The Name of the Lord

Because the "name" represents the entire person in Semitic anthropology, the practice of referring to the "name of God" quickly became a way of expressing reverence for God without explicitly mentioning the personal name itself. In this case, it is precisely the Hebrew name of "YHWH/LORD" that is invoked (v. 8) because it means "he who makes to be." The very God who calls creatures into existence is here called upon to sustain and protect his chosen people.

First Reading (Year II)

Isaiah 1:10-17

Wash yourselves clean! Put away your misdeeds from before my eyes.

Separation of Liturgy from Life

Immediately after introducing Isaiah's call last Saturday, the Lectionary quickly reverts to an introductory summary of his prophetic message. Isaiah's bitter charge against the people of Jerusalem and Judah is their inability or unwillingness to see that temple worship demands the exercise of justice (v. 17) toward the most vulnerable in their society, widows and orphans (v. 16). This bold prophetic expression of divine abhorrence is not an out-and-out rejection of liturgy, negative and forceful though its wording might be. Rather, the text offers a condemnation of any worship that does not produce a more just society. Isaiah demanded that ritual ablutions (v. 16) reflect their deeper inner moral purpose as well.

Sodom and Gomorrah

To be named with imputed citizenship in these two immoral and cursed cities (Gen 19:4) was a dreadful insult to people and leaders alike (v. 10). To use such an expression in his denunciation and negative judgment did not gain Isaiah many friends. Generally any name-calling is wrong because it demeans and creates stereotypes among people, but in this case the names make associations with earlier historical events in order to provoke repentance and change of behavior. Though often remembered for sins against sexuality, the more serious crime of Sodom in ancient Semitic culture would have been their contemptible violation of hospitality toward travelers who were passing through the area.

Antiphon (Year II)

Psalm 50:23b

To the upright I will show the saving power of God.

Upright

The original Hebrew is a bit more complicated than this word "upright" (v. 23) might suggest, as evidenced in various translations: "to those who go the right way" (NRSV), "to him who follows my way" (REB), "to the obedient" (NAB), and "to the upright" (NJB). The presumption behind the metaphor is that those who walk on God's prescribed paths are able to walk strong and straight, not burdened or bent over toward themselves. One classic definition of sin is being "turned into oneself."

Saving Power

The Hebrew refrain (v. 23) simply says "salvation/*yashaᶜ*," namely, the action by which the Lord extricates people from tight spots over which they have neither control nor any ability to extricate themselves. It may be of interest to note that this is the same root word for the Hebrew name of Jesus whom we acknowledge as the Savior of the world.

Gospel

Matthew 10:34–11:1

I have come to bring not peace, but the sword.

Literary Link

After last Saturday's reminder of the full embrace of Divine Providence over everything, even the most minute of creatures, Matthew proceeds to acknowledge the possibility of division as a consequence of discipleship, followed by some final comments on its costs and rewards. This concludes Matthew's extended instructions regarding the commission given by Jesus to the Twelve (10:1). The final summary (11:1) echoes that given at the beginning of this section (7:28).

Family Division

The sad reality, undoubtedly already experienced by the time of the gospel's writing, is that the good news of the kingdom of God at work can and does sometimes divide families (v. 35). A desire to care for the nearby needy or the duty of forgiveness may not be embraced by everyone. Differing strategies for achieving a goal may put individuals at odds with each other, as evidenced in the often bitter contemporary partisan debates. The social teaching of the gospel can divide. The remedies include clarity of communication, concern for truth, and mutual respect. This passage reminds us of the priority of Christ's teaching even over the bonds of affection normally associated with family life (v. 37).

Rewards

Among the earliest and most central of early Christian teachings is the unity and shared identity of Jesus and his followers. Paul was confronted by this truth when the risen Lord insisted that Paul's persecution of early Christians was a persecution of Jesus himself (Acts 9:4). Some scholars have suggested that the earliest division among the members of Matthew's community was that of prophets and the righteous (v. 41). Each has its gift to contribute to the faith community, and each will receive its own proper reward. The basic unity of the Christian community, primitive or modern, does not rule out diversity of functions for its spiritual health and the success of its mission.

Tuesday of the Fifteenth Week in Ordinary Time

First Reading (Year I)

Exodus 2:1-15a

She called him Moses for she said, "I drew him out of the water." After Moses had grown up, he visited his people.

The Biblical Heritage of Moses

This charming human story takes pains to assure the legitimacy of Moses within the traditional tribal structure of the chosen people. The Levites, from whom both his mother and father stemmed (v. 1), were set aside for sanctuary worship and were presumed to have knowledge of how God could best be served. Moreover, in Semitic lore the nationality of a person was transmitted not through conception and birth but through a mother's milk (v. 7). Early readers would have enjoyed the artifice of the tale and the fact that Moses was nursed by a woman of Israel (v. 9). That fact alone was crucial. We each receive physical, spiritual, and cultural DNA from our parents, however the transmission is explained.

Royal Protection

Almost as if deliberately negating the pharaoh's edict to destroy the male children (1:22), the pharaoh's daughter purposely saves young Moses and defiantly raises him within the pharaoh's own household. This is a pro-life tale that includes concern for rearing children as well as intervention at the beginning of their existence. The princess is aligned with the midwives in protecting life. It takes an entire community to raise a child.

Early Action for Justice

The first act narrated about the young Moses' coming of age was the intervention of Moses to save his Israelite kin from violence and injustice (v. 12). His own overreaction, however, contributed to the spiral of violence and required further mature reflection on how to serve his people wisely. The flight of Moses into the desert (v. 15) gave him the opportunity to think things through again. The biblical mentality understands the present by learning about its beginning.

Antiphon (Year I)

Psalm 69:33

Turn to the Lord in your need, and you will live.

Psalm 69: A Desperate Prayer

Psalm 69 is a lament expressed because of the desperate and dangerous situation in which God's people found themselves. Echoing the sentiments of deep anxiety felt by the mother of Moses, and the precarious situation of the baby among the reeds, the psalm speaks of hazardous swamps and floods (v. 3). The response also acknowledges that God does not ignore those in bondage (v. 34).

Hearing the Cry of the Poor

In the later periods of biblical thought, the poor (in spirit) are those who are totally dependent upon God, for they understand that all is gift. Because of their reverence and trust, God hears them and does not dismiss their needs. This verse is a summons for everyone in the contemporary eucharistic community to acknowledge that their dependence gives them a hearing before God. The refrain (v. 33) encourages us to turn to the Lord for help. The psalm presumes that we will hear others in turn once God hears us.

First Reading (Year II)

Isaiah 7:1-9

Unless your faith is firm, you shall not be firm!

Ahaz and Plans for War

Even though Isaiah had constantly proclaimed God's protection of Jerusalem in the face of the hostility of neighboring nations, King Ahaz lacked trust in God and in the prophet who spoke in God's name. For that reason the king was busily preparing the city's pools and cisterns for possible siege and famine (v. 3). Those who prepare for war will find it. Isaiah begged him to trust in God's protection and assured him that such would be given if requested. Being providential on our part is not contradictory to a fundamental trust in God. Of the latter, the king had none. Good leadership needs a balanced combination of both. At stake is the true source of one's security.

Ahaz and Isaiah

There is supreme irony hidden between the lines of this account. With deep concerns about having an heir to his throne, Ahaz was busy in the upper portion of the city preparing for war when he was met by Isaiah. The prophet held the hand of his own son (v. 3), and asked that Ahaz trust God for an heir and protection. Unmentioned is the fact that Ahaz had sacrificed his son at the foundation of a city gate (2 Kgs 16:3), and subsequently worried about succession. When Ahaz refused to trust God on the grounds of false piety, Isaiah promised a better son than Ahaz could ever have imagined. We are always invited to ask for what we need (as contrasted with what we want) and to trust in God's goodness. From the standoff between prophet and king came the great promise of the future birth of Hezekiah/*Immanuel* (v. 14).

Source of Personal Firmness

The recurring message of Isaiah was his invitation to trust in God alone rather than in military prowess or political alliances. Firmness of faith is the only enduring source of strength (v. 9). Isaiah often comes across as being a strong antiwar figure in his day (31:1) because he insists that neither horses nor chariots can save the nation of Israel.

ANTIPHON (YEAR II)

Psalm 48:9d

God upholds his city for ever.

Psalm 48: Divine Protection for Zion

Psalm 48 is primarily a hymn to the glory of God. Only tangentially does the psalm note that the praise is offered in the city of God (v. 2) and in the fortresses of Zion (v. 3) where God dwells. For that reason, the Holy City and its temple give perennial honor to God as well. Isaiah was committed in his day to the God who had promised to protect Jerusalem forever. Because that promise was conditionally related to the fidelity of God's people residing in that city, the people could not hear Jeremiah's very different message a hundred years later, namely, that Jerusalem would be destroyed by the Babylonians (Jer 7). In every age we need to pray for our towns and cities, and to work at making them citadels of justice for all inhabitants.

True Security

Once again security comes, not from ramparts, moats, and fortified gates, but from the protection of the living God (30:15). Similarly in our day, security comes not from accumulated savings, strong physical health, or political position because all that could change in an instant. God, however, does not change. Would God endorse the prayers we utter for our cities?

GOSPEL

Matthew 11:20-24

It will be more tolerable for Tyre and Sidon and for the land of Sodom on the day of judgment than for you.

Literary Link

Perhaps to provide a tighter logical link with yesterday's teachings on reward, the Lectionary omits the story of John the Baptist (11:2-19) in order to excoriate the towns that refused or dismissed the announcement of the kingdom (vv. 20-24). Jesus wished to remind his listeners (and us) of the possibility of punishment lurking in the background of everyone who refuses to listen, and therefore assures his or her own ruin.

Tyre and Sidon

In speaking of recalcitrant communities, Jesus gives an example of punishment in his references to Tyre and Sidon (v. 22), famous port cities off the coast of present Lebanon. Those cities were historically infamous for their arrogance but were destroyed by the Assyrians. Any people that prides itself in being totally self-sufficient is doomed. The cities of Chorazin (now only large chunks of basalt scattered in the fields a few miles northwest of the Sea of Galilee) and Capernaum (once a center for taxes and commerce) are warned of such a destiny unless they accept the call to repentance. More contemporary names might be Silicon Valley, Fort Knox, and Wall Street.

Mighty Deeds for Change of Heart

It is important to remember that God's mighty deeds (vv. 20, 21, 23) of healing are not for mere entertainment, but rather they are aimed at changing the way we think about God and God's work in our world. The very first word of Jesus in announcing the kingdom was "repent" (4:17). Those who choose to ignore the invitation are left out of the kingdom.

Tuesday of the Fifteenth Week in Ordinary Time

Wednesday of the Fifteenth Week in Ordinary Time

First Reading (Year I)

Exodus 3:1-6, 9-12

The angel of the Lord appeared to Moses in the burning bush.

The Burning Bush

Several sacred symbols converge to signal the presence of God in a special manner: mountain/high place (v. 1), bush/tree as a sign of hidden life giving water, fire (v. 2) as a sign of God's visible but immaterial presence, consuming or consoling as the situation may demand. The sacredness of the spot is also indicated by the presence of an angel/messenger/guardian of the sacred place. All these elements find cohesion in the burning bush (v. 3). This is much more than a mere natural curiosity. One could also look around the parish church to see the signs that indicate holiness of location for us.

Curiosity: A Holy Place

Not only is the location shown as holy by the convergence of the symbols described above, but also by the fact that Moses is possessed by a spirit of holy curiosity before the mystery of God. Moses admits a desire to look more closely (v. 3). Curiosity can be inspired by the Holy Spirit who impels us to seek the Lord and learn about him. The questions of people preparing for full communion with the church or for confirmation are signs of the Holy Spirit at work. The very location of inquiring questions is holy too; one perhaps should remove one's shoes in places of serious searching inquiry.

A Sign from the Future

Although Jesus may complain at times about the people of his generation always asking for signs, the practice began with the spontaneous offering of signs by God (v. 12). It was God who offered signs in the desert by a promise that they would return to the same holy mountain and recall the divine assurance. There were also the many signs performed by Moses before the pharaoh. The search for signs can be an indication of serious discernment, or a device to avoid commitment. The difference lies in our motivation.

Antiphon (Year I)

Psalm 103:8a

The Lord is kind and merciful.

"Kind and Merciful"

Once again we can unpack the deeper meaning of these two words by noting that the first Hebrew word translated as "kind" is *raham*, a maternal womblike compassion that a mother would have for a child. The refrain's (v. 8) second word in Hebrew is *hanan*, the quality that creates in people something attractive, graceful, and eliciting divine favor.

"O My Soul"

Twice (vv. 1, 2) within the portion selected as a response by the Lectionary, the psalmist says with exultation, "Bless the Lord, O my soul." The Hebrew word for soul is *nephesh*, and means "throat/life principle (often experienced as breath in one's throat)/voice." The more literal meaning is often highlighted, for example, when a psalm says "my soul thirsts for God" (see Ps 42:2-3). It is the voice that is lifted up and that blesses God. The psalmist is encouraging worshipers to sing joyfully as they praise.

First Reading (Year II)

Isaiah 10:5-7, 13b-16

Will the axe boast against the one who hews with it?

Mere Instruments

Isaiah is willing to recognize the military power of Assyria but insists that such human power is only an instrument in the hands of God. By describing the mighty

Assyria as only "a rod" in God's hand (v. 5), the prophet insists that all of creation, even the mighty empires that attack Judah, are only instruments created by God to be used as God sees fit. Any arrogant assumption that human mighty deeds are done by human strength alone is destined to be rendered useless and brought low. To God alone is the glory, either now or later. Mere instruments can never be self-satisfied or self-sufficient. Does the broom or the stove or the wrench or the power tool boast?

Punishing Political Powers

If God uses foreign nations as punishment for Israel, those nations still remain nothing but instruments (v. 5). They will themselves be punished for arrogance. This is even true about us contemporary Americans, because if we act arrogantly when God uses us, God will eventually punish us in turn. Would it ever be instructive to read the international headlines as if the nations were simply God's chess pieces?

Wednesday of the Fifteenth Week in Ordinary Time

ANTIPHON (YEAR II)

Psalm 94:14a

The Lord will not abandon his people.

Psalm 94: God's Justice

Psalm 94 is sometimes called a "psalm of vengeance" because of its conviction that God will punish those who unjustly afflict his people (v. 10). The fact is that God's sense of justice, though not always immediate, will triumph. Those who suffer innocently have not heard the last word (v. 6). The just ones simply wait patiently for their vindication. Note that it was the decision of Paul VI to remove ancient cursing psalms from our liturgy (e.g., Psalm 137:9)—perhaps lest we be tempted to have specific individuals in mind. The psalm portions used in this response are petitions for help, not prayers of revenge.

Abandonment

As noted in the reading, Isaiah proclaimed eventual and ultimately inevitable divine punishment on those who act arrogantly against his people. The refrain (v. 14), therefore, is a heartfelt conviction about God's fidelity even in hard times. Even if one feels all alone and isolated, utterly defenseless and without resources, God will never abandon his people. Great saints of history have experienced periods of terrible spiritual aridity, however, as God weans them from the comforting feelings of divine presence to the reality of that enduring presence.

GOSPEL

Matthew 11:25-27

Although you have hidden these things from the wise and the learned you have revealed them to the childlike.

Literary Link

The eleventh chapter concludes with a contrast between proud and arrogant cities that refuse the invitation to repentance (vv. 20-24) and the childlike (v. 25) to whom God gladly reveals his mysteries. This contrast will in turn prepare for the following day's passage, the prayer of Jesus (vv. 28-30) and his invitation to the weary and burdened.

These Things

It is a remarkable gift to eavesdrop on Christ at prayer! It is difficult to avoid some puzzlement regarding the precise reference of "these things" (v. 25) that Jesus reveals so readily to the childlike. Given the preceding verses scholars might suggest that the phrase echoes the value of repentance and the blessings that come to those who change their minds. Children do that much more readily than adults; they are willing to learn when their elders are not. A perennial theme in the gospels is the summons to be childlike in devotion, namely, to live without pretense, with curiosity to know, and with a willingness to help.

The Father

Gospel references to the Trinity are mostly indirect and as yet undeveloped. Only after centuries of careful debate would the mystery find its proper language. Matthew's gospel seems more explicit than most because of verses such as this one (v. 27) and the final great commission (28:19) at the end of the gospel after the resurrection.

Thursday of the Fifteenth Week in Ordinary Time

First Reading (Year I)

Exodus 3:13-20

I AM WHO AM. I AM has sent me to you.

The Name of God

The Lord's mysterious answer to Moses from the burning bush has continued to engage the minds of scholars and saints through all subsequent centuries. The Hebrew grammar is puzzling and inconsistent (which reveals a history of varying usages). The familiar form "Jehovah" is based on a misunderstanding because later ages combined the consonants of God's verbal name with the vowels of "Lord/*ʾadonai*" to remind Hebrew readers to say *ʾAdonai* out of respect for the unspeakable name of God. To have "I will be what I will be" (see v. 14), which seems to be the most likely interpretation, as one's personal name is extraordinary. God's name is a verb. God's name is a promise to be whatever the chosen people may need at any given time. God's name is an eternal commitment.

Moses on Mission

Armed with the knowledge of God's name, Moses is sent to announce and promise divine intervention, deliverance from slavery, and freedom (v. 16). An inadequate instrument to be sure, Moses will face countless obstacles from the pharaoh and his servants. Nevertheless ultimate success will be theirs and Israel will eventually leave Egypt because their God will be with them and will lead them into freedom (v. 17). Human instruments are only instruments. Throughout the ages, every person has his or her own mission as part of the overarching plan of God: the spiritual deepening of God's people and the transformation of the larger world.

Antiphon (Year I)

Psalm 105:8a

The Lord remembers his covenant for ever.

Signs of the Times

By choosing portions of Psalm 105, the Lectionary wishes to connect God's covenant with Abraham (v. 9) to the mission of Moses and Aaron (v. 26). There is a large divine plan for the salvation of the world, and every age plays its own part, including our own. Determining what might be appropriate for our modern age seems dependent on reading the "signs of the times." Prior to the formal sessions of the Second Vatican Council, John XXIII established a commission to ponder the "signs of the times." Would a parish benefit from having such a standing committee?

Remembering

In biblical parlance, to remember is more than mere nostalgic treasuring of the past. Rather, to remember (v. 8) is to make present anew, and to render the power and the promise of a prior event fully activated in the present. One remembers a gift when one puts it to use (like driving the car given at graduation or wearing a wedding ring). Everything the gift symbolizes comes alive again.

First Reading (Year II)

Isaiah 26:7-9, 12, 16-19

Awake and sing, you who lie in the dust.

Isaiah 24–27

Often labeled the "Apocalypse of Isaiah" (Fourth Isaiah?), this section of the collected words attributed to Isaiah and his disciples seems more recent in focus and purpose. Placing the sufferings of Israel under post-Babylonian empires, these chapters deal with final victory, vindication, and prosperity by divine intervention and protection. Israel was home again but still under foreign domination. They confidently assume a final judgment (v. 9) and enduring peace (v. 12). These verses have the feel of a more cosmic resolution to human problems than the more narrowly focused national issues of Isaiah's own historical time.

Resurrection

Verses 18 and 19 are grammatically obscure and have endured various corrections by scribes and commentators to render them clearer and more intelligible. In their location amid end-time promises, and in the form chosen by the Lectionary, they seem to promise resurrection to those who have died (v. 19). They even suggest a possible manner in which that resurrection might be effected by God, namely, by a special life-giving dew (v. 19). In reality it is natural dew that increases in Israel during the rainless months of summer and provides the irrigation needed for growth and harvest. Jewish speculation regarding the possibility of resurrection increased and deepened over the centuries. It is "Catholic" to want to know the histories of our beliefs because we are committed to the reality of doctrinal development.

ANTIPHON (YEAR II)

Psalm 102:20b

From heaven the Lord looks down on the earth.

Psalm 102: Invoking God's Protection

Psalm 102 is a "prayer of one afflicted" (v. 1) and was listed as the fifth penitential psalm by the early church. Omitting descriptions of personal suffering in the verses used as the Lectionary's liturgical response, however, the day's portion turns to consider the restoration of the entire people. The individual in the psalm serves as a sort of "corporate personality" for the nation. Love for the very stones of the city (v. 15) inspires the worshiper to pray for a new beginning for everyone. In the radical individualism of our contemporary American culture we often forget to link our sorrows with the larger world around us, and neglect to pray for the entire community's similar needs beyond our own.

A Time for Pity

In a truly remarkable reminder to God, the psalm suggests that it is the proper *ʿet* (Hebrew)/*kairos* (Greek)/"time" for mercy and grace (v. 14). How does one know that this is the case? Daring to tell God what to do, the prayer is deeply rooted in the reality of the covenant by which both God and Israel promised to care for each other's needs and welfare. The refrain (v. 20) establishes God's posture throughout history and presumes that God is alert and eager to do what is both needed and wanted by his people.

GOSPEL

Matthew 11:28-30

I am meek and humble of heart.

Literary Link

After the brief prayer of Jesus in which he indicates his desire to reveal the truth to the childlike (v. 25), this portion moves to an invitation addressed to God's poor.

The Community of Matthew

The Christian community out of whom and for whom this gospel was written included both Torah observant Jewish members and Gentiles. Jewish believers brought a sense of the "Sabbath rest" to their fellow Gentile believers who in turn found that tradition from Genesis helpful for their daily lives. Every Christian community should respect the diverse spiritualities of individual members and benefits from them. It is in the person of the risen Jesus that all the various spiritualities find unity (v. 28). Rest and relief for the poor and oppressed is everyone's concern, because it is the Lord's concern, no matter which tradition of spirituality the community members may have embraced.

The Nature of Work

Some types of labor are eagerly accepted and happily pursued because they promise positive results and benefits to those engaged in them. Other kinds of labor seem mere drudgery because they are either necessary or imposed by others and seem devoid of personal reward. Jesus invites all workers everywhere (v. 28) to himself. Faith can provide the bigger picture of how all human effort fits into the original activity of God as described in Genesis, that is, putting order into the world and transforming material creation into forms that are beneficial to people. The fact is that human beings need work to find completeness and meaning in their lives.

True "Rest"

The notion of "rest" in this saying of Jesus (v. 28) is more than mere cessation of effort or the end of hard work. Human beings need rest as well as work. This is the true Sabbath, the God-given opportunity to pause and re-create a sense of right relationship to all of creation, especially family members, neighbors, and distant people. The gift of *Shabbat* is associated with the teachings of Jesus whose doctrinal "yoke" makes life easier, clearer, and truly productive. Without the larger picture and deeper root, human labor could be very oppressive.

Meekness

To be "meek" is not to be a pushover or wishy-washy. Moses was once called the "meekest man on the face of the earth" (Num 12:3), and he stood toe-to-toe with the pharaoh during his mission of bringing freedom to Israel. Jesus is strongly self-confident, inviting rather than imposing his will. The beatitude for the meek (Matt 5:5) is aimed at those who exercise authority wisely and responsibly within the community. Jesus promised that they will inherit the earth.

Thursday of the Fifteenth Week in Ordinary Time

Friday of the Fifteenth Week in Ordinary Time

FIRST READING (YEAR I)

Exodus 11:10–12:14

It shall be slaughtered during the evening twilight.
Seeing the blood, I will pass over you.

Making the Pharaoh Obstinate

The Exodus account of Israel's struggle for freedom deals with the mystery of grace and free will in its own manner. The Pharaoh freely refuses freedom to the Israelites, but God is ultimately involved in every human decision, so it might be said that God was the one in some fashion who hardened the Pharaoh's heart (11:10) against the request. Isaiah states that God creates good and evil (45:7). God will be God, and his plan for the salvation of the world will unfold in its own way, occasionally using human beings as instruments, but also on occasion dealing with them as obstacles so that his will remains ultimately the sole power at play.

The Passover of the Lord

In this text we are treated to the fundamental rubrics of Israel's celebration of the Passover set into the original context of their historic departure from Egypt under divine protection and guidance. An unblemished (v. 5) lamb, which may be a sheep or a goat, is to be shared by family and neighbors as needed after being publicly sacrificed (v. 6). Its blood is to be smeared on the outer doorframe of every Israelite's home by way of protection (v. 7). Symbolic foods comprise the meal for those dressed and poised as if to flee for freedom. It is Israel's festival of freedom from political oppression so that they might become God's people to the core. Every celebration of the Eucharist invokes the same fundamental grace and calls Christians to freedom from sin for the work of God.

ANTIPHON (YEAR I)

Psalm 116:13

I will take the cup of salvation, and call
on the name of the Lord.

Psalm 116: A Prayer at Sacrifice

This psalm of thanksgiving serves as the Lectionary's most fitting response to the institution of the Passover. Reference to the cup of salvation echoes the Passover meal theme (v. 13) in the presence of all God's people (v. 18), as does the allusion to having been freed from bonds (v. 16).

The Cup of Salvation

This image of a cup unites two important themes in Israel's experience. There is its reference to communion sacrifices and meals at which the participants experience a sharing with God and each other, always in gratitude for reconciled relationships and for the blessings of the covenant. There is also the cup's imagery for whatever may be poured out by God as punishments to be accepted or as the sovereign will of God for salvation. Israel was forced to drink of God's anger before being relieved of that punishment (Isa 51:17, 22). In his garden prayer at Gethsemane Jesus hesitates and then accepts the pain of his role in salvation (Mark 14:36). For a community celebrating the Christian Eucharist, the refrain can evoke both memories.

FIRST READING (YEAR II)

Isaiah 38:1-6, 21-22, 7-8

I have heard your prayer and seen your tears.

Note

The Lectionary has curiously chosen to transpose the order of events in this passage, making the sign of the changed shadow of the sun as a conclusion to the story (vv. 7-8), rather than as a sign of God's determination to heal and extend Hezekiah's reign. In the original Hebrew text the "pause/rewind" button was an immediate response to the king's prayer rather than a finale to the entire event. This brings the prophetic narrative of Isaiah into conformity with the story's sequence as found in 2 Kings 20. The liturgical Lectionary has reconciled different biblical traditions.

Hezekiah's Almost-Mortal Illness

With mysterious logic, probably based on a desire to find some correspondence between the themes of the first reading and that of the gospel, the Lectionary turns from yesterday's promise of final vindication and resurrection to the illness of King Hezekiah. After Jerusalem was miraculously liberated from the threats of Assyrian King Sennacherib whose armies were camping outside the city walls (Isa 37), Hezekiah falls terminally ill, weeping bitterly and rehearsing his fidelity to God throughout his reign (v. 3). In response to the king's prayers, Isaiah is sent to promise recuperation in three days and an added fifteen years of life (v. 5). Serious illness, with or without physical healing, is often the occasion for much spiritual grace and growth. Family wounds can be healed, hurts resolved, and relationships deepened.

Time in Reverse

Friday of the Fifteenth Week in Ordinary Time

After the curious but effective prescription of mashed figs packed atop a boil, Hezekiah is cured (v. 21). This tale of the reversal of daily time (v. 8) and its accompanying shadow on the steps may have had a separate history, and was only introduced into the story by the editors. In any case, what seemed physically impossible and therefore miraculous became the confirming sign of Hezekiah's cure and extended reign. All biblical stories are ultimately about both God and us. In this case God is the Lord of history for them and for us.

Antiphon (Year II)

Isaiah 38:17b

You saved my life, O Lord; I shall not die.

Hezekiah's Hymn of Thanksgiving

Rather than using a psalm as the liturgical response to this reading, the Lectionary chooses to take advantage of the beautiful hymn attributed to the newly cured king (38:10-20). The gift of health and life (v. 16) changes the bitterness of the seriously ill king (v. 15). The response reflects the very real emotional states of anyone seriously ill, and perhaps even reflects the stages of personal adjustment to such situations at life's end. As the refrain (v. 17) suggests, Hezekiah moves through the classical stages of acceptance to discover, not death, but new life.

Radical Recoveries

The refrain is adapted from the hymn's verse 17, and is liturgically placed on the lips of Hezekiah. The words can also become the personal prayer of anyone cured from serious illness. Celebrating the sacrament of anointing of the sick with them unites their experience to the Lord's saving death and resurrection. That ritual is the church's primary contribution to pastoral care. As we know, however, not everyone is cured. In any case, assisting the seriously ill by speaking thoughtfully about their impending "journey to the stars" is important. Many go to Lourdes, for example, and even the ability to deal with sickness for another year can be itself the "miracle" of grace and spiritual healing needed.

Gospel

Matthew 12:1-8

The Son of Man is Lord of the sabbath.

Literary Link

The notion of "mercy" links the invitation of Jesus to the oppressed and overburdened (v. 28) in yesterday's reading to the teaching of Jesus about the priority of mercy (v. 7) over sacrifice in today's text. Today's reading is one of the controversy stories that illustrate the rejection of Jesus in several different contexts.

Feeding the Hungry

The combination of Torah observant Jews and Gentiles in Mathew's community may well have occasioned regular discussions of diet and food preparation, including the question of harvesting fresh produce for the hungry (v. 2). What was forbidden "work" and what was community service? The story of Jesus defending his disciples (v. 3) served as a reminder of the priority of charity over mechanical obedience to the rules of Sabbath rest. In fact, this priority was already part of the Pharisaic tradition of Jewish spirituality. This was not a new teaching of Jesus setting one practice aside for a higher one. Pharisees themselves debated such issues with passion because at issue for all of them was the will of God, a supreme value.

The Sabbath

Maintaining the proper interrelationship of humanity and Sabbath rest is a perennial pastoral task for the rhythms of daily life. Sabbath rest is certainly a major religious value (v. 2). The practice was in fact an identity tag for Jewish life in the centuries when they lived under Hellenistic persecution and under threatened punishment for their uniqueness (1 Macc 1:45). As Jesus pointed out (v. 8) the practice is not primarily for God's sake, as if God needed people to settle down and live in greater dependence upon his Father's providence, but rather for the sake of human beings. The citation from Hosea (6:6) insisted that covenantal love for each other's needs and concerns (*hesed*) always remained more important than ritual sacrifices. Mercy never dismisses the spiritual importance of ritual but keeps it in perspective when encountering unusual circumstances and pressing needs. Retrieving a proper sense of the Sabbath, however, is crucial for our busy modern world too.

Saturday of the Fifteenth Week in Ordinary Time

First Reading (Year I)

Exodus 12:37-42

This was a night of vigil for the Lord as he led them out of the land of Egypt.

The Numbers Game

To imagine 600,000 men marching on foot out of a country (v. 37) sounds rather impressive. It could hardly have escaped the notice of their contemporary record keepers or historians. Then there would be women and children added to that number. An alternative interpretation is to point out that the Hebrew word *aleph* can either be translated as "thousand" or "a basic unit of fighting men." Six hundred smaller warrior units of soldiers is a more credible number. The reference could also be an opportunity to point out the existence of phrases in every language and culture that serve to suggest generic numbers rather than factual historical documentary. To speak of "a million things to do" or "three hundred problems" in a challenging biblical text might be examples of exaggerations to make a point. God uses ordinary human expression to communicate his salvation, even colloquial exaggerations.

Unleavened Bread

The rushed departure precluded the time needed for yeast to rise before baking. Unleavened cracker-like bread (v. 39) became one of the distinguishing marks of all subsequent annual Passover celebrations. Western Latin Catholics have kept the practice of unleavened bread as a faithful reminder of the Passover roots of the Eucharist, while Eastern Byzantine Catholics seem to have used leavened bread from the beginning. The Second Vatican Council stressed the important historical tradition of the use of unleavened bread, but asked that effort be made so that the hosts used at Mass seem more like our forms of bread while still unleavened. Bread is formed by grinding and baking in a self-sacrificing form for the nourishment of others. It remains a remarkable sacramental sign of Christ's love for all people.

Antiphon (Year I)

Psalm 136:1

His mercy endures forever.

Psalm 136: History Clothed in Mercy

Psalm 136 is an instructive rehearsal of the manner in which God's saving presence has endured and been repeated in so many countless difficult historical situations. In example after example over the centuries, God has been at work for his chosen people. Note that the Lectionary cites the generic praise of verses 23-24 before reciting the references to the Exodus (vv. 10-12, about which Egyptians may have a different perspective!) and the passing through the Red Sea (vv. 13-15) in their proper historical sequence. These verses serve to remind our contemporary assemblies of the rest of the story still to come.

Mercy

Once again our understanding of the spiritual significance of this refrain (v. 1 and repeatedly throughout the entire response) will be enhanced by the recognition that the Hebrew word is *hesed*, mutual covenantal concern between God and human beings. The constant repetition of this fundamental belief of Israel represents one of Christianity's deepest gifts from historical Judaism. It is even the literary background for our use of the Greek petition *Kyrie, eleison*!

First Reading (Year II)

Micah 2:1-5

They covet fields, and seize them; houses, and they take them.

Evil Plans

Micah condemns the continuity between nighttime plotting of violence and theft by evil people and their daytime actions to accomplish the aims of their greed (vv. 1-2).

So often one's internal thoughts and desires, when frequently contemplated, become reality. If one thinks about something long and often enough, good or bad, one will do it. The warning against evil thoughts, whether of anger (Matt 5:21-22) or lust (Matt 5:28), was one of the primary teachings of Jesus as found in his Sermon on the Mount.

The Book of the Prophet Micah

A contemporary of Isaiah, the prophet Micah saw the same exploitation of the poor and vulnerable by the rich, especially violating the age-old sense of hereditary tribal lands for the sake of greed. Like Isaiah, Micah was a critic of worship that was not linked to justice, insisting rather on justice, mutual covenantal concern, and humility (6:8).

Prophetic Judgment

Once again with ironic precision the crime of unlawful seizure of the property of another (v. 2) will be punished by the subsequent seizure of their own lands by occupying armies (v. 4). In the prophet's judgment the greedy land grabbers are punished by becoming the victims of what they themselves had done to others. The multiplicity of contemporary heartbreaking foreclosures in our own time may not be far from this ancient state of affairs. The moral issue is greed in all its forms (Luke 12:15).

Antiphon (Year II)

Psalm 10:12b

Do not forget the poor, O Lord!

Psalms 9 and 10

These two were originally a single unit. In fact they are presented as such in the early Greek translation (Septuagint) of the Psalter. They both lament the sufferings of a faithful person in the context of an experience of a God who seems indifferent and aloof (v. 1) to the misery of his people (v. 14).

Unjust and Evil Rich

Because the crimes of the greedy rich are pictured in remarkably similar terms in the psalm (v. 3) as in the reading itself, they provide a fitting response to Micah's words of prophetic condemnation. The poor depend utterly and totally on God alone (v. 14). The refrain (v. 12) repeats the plea of the psalmist for divine attention and intervention. Just as God is implored not to forget the poor, so also is the same plea directed to human covenant members who gather for weekday Eucharist in their parish churches.

Gospel

Matthew 12:14-21

He warned them not to make him known to fulfill what had been spoken.

Literary Link

For some reason the Lectionary omits the story of the Sabbath curing of the man with the withered hand (vv. 9-13). Perhaps this was done because it was thematically similar to the preceding story of the Sabbath picking of grain and because the editors wished to report the plot of some of the Pharisees against Jesus (v. 14). The principle opponent of Torah observant Jews within Matthew's Christian community were Pharisees. That would explain this gospel's generalization, even though elsewhere Pharisees were reported as among the disciples of Jesus (Nicodemus in John 3:1; Acts 15:5).

First Servant Song

The subsequent departure of Jesus from the area (v. 15) provided Matthew with an opportunity to summarize the multiple healings performed by Jesus. Matthew also takes the occasion to introduce a citation of Isaiah 42:1-4. From the very beginning (4:15; 13:35; 15:8; etc.) Matthew uses citations from the prophets to explain the life and mission of Jesus. Jesus embodies the entire history of Israel, and his genealogy (1:2-16) provides the perfect link between the Old Testament and Matthew, the first of the gospels of the New Testament.

Justice and Gentleness

The first Servant Song makes a point of stressing the quiet justice and gentleness of Isaiah's mysterious servant. Not even a smoldering wick will be quenched by his nonviolent preaching of justice (v. 2). In keeping with the Messianic secret of Mark, Jesus does not want publicity for his cures (v. 16). In everyone's life there are areas of preferred confidentiality and family information that is not appropriate for public discussion. This attitude also reflects the teaching in the Sermon on the Mount to give alms in such a fashion that the left hand does not even know the actions of the right (6:3).

Saturday of the Fifteenth Week in Ordinary Time

Monday of the Sixteenth Week in Ordinary Time

First Reading (Year I)

Exodus 14:5-18

They will know that I am the Lord when I receive glory through Pharaoh.

Consequences and Costs

Almost immediately after the pharaoh's decision to let Israel go, he had regrets (v. 5). There are always consequences to any decision we may make, be it for good or evil. Releasing the Israelite slave force either left work undone or necessitated that others take up the burden at considerable cost to themselves. If we decide to do something good, there will also be implications. We speak of the cost of discipleship in reference to accepting the invitation of Christ to gospel living: generosity to the needy, simplicity of life, offering forgiveness, accepting one's cross, and living in hope. Saying "yes" to some things necessitates saying "no" to others.

Temptation to Blame Others

As soon as Israel saw the Egyptian armies bearing down upon them, they complained in horror and fear, blaming Moses for their predicament (vv. 11-12). Totally forgetting how willing they had been to cast off their slavery, they could only see Moses as the source of their problem, not the occasion for their freedom. Refusal to take responsibility for our own decisions and their consequences seems deeply rooted in the sinful human heart, as evidenced from the Garden of Eden where Adam and Eve were all too ready to blame each other and the serpent for their situation (Gen 3:12-13). The lament of children, namely, "He started it!" never seems to go away.

Antiphon (Year I)

Exodus 15:1b

Let us sing to the Lord; he has covered himself in glory.

Miriam's Refrain

Although the text introduces this jubilant hymn by attributing it to Moses (v. 1a), scholars are fairly agreed that the truer historical source would be Miriam, as indicated in the same words found in the ancient chorus at the end of the account (v. 21). Attributions and stories tend to gravitate to more prominent personages over the centuries as a means of emphasizing the individual's importance and the antiquity of the tale. Miriam's role in celebrating Yahweh's victory over Egypt, however, should not be easily dismissed, and her partnership in the decisive event of Israel's foundation should be remembered with respect and honor.

Destruction of the Enemy

The first section (vv. 2-12, not all of which is cited in the response) of this hymn of praise and thanksgiving focuses upon the total devastation suffered by the Egyptian armies (v. 4). In poetic terms that have echoes of ancient Canaanite myths, the Lord is proclaimed as triumphant over the watery forces of evil (v. 5), no matter what specific concrete form that evil may take over the course of centuries. Even the liturgical blessing of that baptismal water at the Holy Saturday Vigil retains some of this ancient imagery and proclaims victory over sin and death forever. The paradox of water is that it can both kill and give new life. Israel was born from the Red Sea.

First Reading (Year II)

Micah 6:1-4, 6-8

You have been told, O man, what the Lord requires of you.

A Perfect Penitential Rite

This text is easily broken into three sections: the threat of God to begin a lawsuit against Israel for breach of promise (vv. 1-4), a human question regarding possible satisfaction (vv. 6-7), and a prophetic response in the name of God indicating the fundamental requirements for pardon and a renewed upright life before God (v. 8).

It is almost as if this text contains an accusation, satisfaction, and firm purpose of amendment.

Good Friday Lament

Micah's conviction was that the breakdown of basic covenantal concern between the poor and the wealthy was equivalent to a rejection of the exodus itself. All had been equally led forth into freedom, no matter what their economic status. God's legal lawsuit as spoken by Micah (vv. 3-4) is used in the Good Friday liturgy. In that latter liturgical context the accusation serves to illustrate the divine complaint against all of humanity. When the church commemorates the death of Jesus as redemption for the sins of the world, it is all humanity who bears the guilt, certainly not the Jewish people. Once again, rich and poor alike, humanity stands guilty under the cross.

Threefold Requirement for a Good Life before God

Monday of the Sixteenth Week in Ordinary Time

The profile offered in the final verse (v. 8) is a magnificent summary of God's expectations for any just and faithful person. Relativizing all liturgical rubrics and more marginal commands, three non-negotiables are presented for Israel's fresh start before God: (1) doing justice (*tzedeqah*), namely, being in right relationship with all people and all creation; (2) mutual covenantal kindness (*hesed*) between each and every human partner in God's covenant; and finally, (3) living in personal humility before God. This is a magnificent summary of first and second covenant morality.

Antiphon (Year II)

Psalm 50:23b

To the upright I will show the saving power of God.

Psalm 50: God's Complaint

The verses selected for the communal response to the condemnations announced by Micah take up the same theme of God's accusations against his errant people. Sacrifice itself is not the point of complaint (v. 8) but the fact that the ritual is without impact on daily life (v. 17). Mere verbal commitment without action constitutes the essence of God's accusation. The justice, kindness, and humility of Micah's teaching are left in the sanctuary.

Saving Power

The refrain is taken from the very last verse of the response (v. 23). It highlights the fact that only those who acknowledge the need for salvation from God, and demonstrate that need in the daily rhythm of their lives, will receive the gift. Contrary to the accusations expressed by both the prophet and the psalmist, liturgy spilling into life and words into action are the requirements for experiencing God's saving power.

Gospel

Matthew 12:38-42

At the judgment the queen of the south will arise with this generation and condemn it.

Literary Link

After a reference to good fruit as a sign of a healthy tree (12:33), Matthew turns to the request of some Pharisees for signs of the healthy authenticity of the ministry of Jesus himself. Note, however, that the Lectionary has chosen to omit the controversy over Jesus casting out demons by Beelzebul (vv. 22-32) and his teaching about healthy trees and good fruit (vv. 33-37). The result is the Lectionary's pointed association of Jesus, first with the Servant of Isaiah (last Saturday), and then with Jonah (today).

The Request for Signs

Sometimes it is helpful to remember that God was the One who first offered signs to the Israelites in Egypt, giving proofs of the authority of Moses in order to impress the Pharaoh's court (Exod 3:12; 4:2-9). Signs are useful in one's discernment process. Our faith must be reasonable. Only when signs are demanded (v. 38), however, as a ruse for evading and dismissing the invitation do they become problematic.

Resurrection

One of the ways in which the tale of Jonah was suggested as an anticipated "sign" of the mission of the Son of Man was found in the three days and nights (Jonah 2:1) spent by the prophet in the belly of the great fish (v. 40). In that story God used material creation to stop the prophet's flight from obedience and to bring him back to the true purpose of his life. Although in itself a familiar biblical symbol for a short time, the phrase "three days and nights" quickly became an early Christian reference to the passion of Jesus and his final vindication by his glorified resurrection. Our own earthly lives are also filled with moments of anticipation pointing to the fullness of final life with God. Sometimes losses and disappointments teach us how to die to ourselves; at other times gestures of human compassion and kindness can prefigure the life of total social harmony in the next age when all will be welcomed into the messianic banquet forever. Sometimes life is lived in segments of "three days" at a time.

Fruitful Proclamation

Another primary way in which Jonah is lifted up as a sign can be found in the fact that his word was so positively heard and embraced by the Ninevites, the most unlikely of penitents. Cruel and ruthless by reputation, disliked and judged unworthy of grace by Jonah, the Ninevites stopped in mid-step, listened carefully, and wrapped their lives in repentance (v. 41). They became the prototype of the prostitutes and tax collectors who listened to Jesus when many of the more official religious figures of his day would not.

The Person of the Herald

Perhaps what made the legendary figure of Jonah so effective was the fact that his very person incorporated the message he proclaimed. Reduced to grudging compliance after resisting and even fleeing God's command, his second effort embodied obedience to the God who offered salvation to those who needed that grace desperately. Only teachers who have conformed themselves to God can be credible and effective heralds. Basic integrity of life is demanded of anyone who would preach or teach others. Life gives greater witness than words. When Jesus said, "Repent, for the kingdom of heaven is at hand," (Matt 4:17), he referred to the model of himself as well as to the circumstances around him.

Tuesday of the Sixteenth Week in Ordinary Time

First Reading (Year I)

Exodus 14:21–15:1

The children of Israel marched into the midst of the sea on dry land.

Historical Hints and Poetry

Scholars often point to the casual reference to the strong east wind (v. 21) as a possible hint to a natural occurrence of the searing African winds that dried the shallow waters of the Red Sea and enabled people to pass on foot (v. 22). The heavier bronze chariots of the pharaoh's army, however, sunk in the mire (v. 25). Other verses seem more poetic in describing the waters as congealed walls on either side of the marching peoples (vv. 22, 29). Ever since the teachings of Pope Pius XII (*Divino Afflante Spiritu*, 1943), Catholic scholars and preachers have been called to note the different literary types found in our Scriptures. Exegetes are instructed to beware of presuming that everything biblical was the equivalent of a historical documentary. These accounts are catechetical in purpose; they are written to teach and deepen faith.

"Holy War"

One of the ancient traditions of Israel was a conviction that God was the primary force in every battle fought by the chosen people. That motif, found even in ancient Canaanite religious tales, celebrated the fact that even a glance from God was a mighty military weapon (v. 24). They believed that it was the power of God, not human warriors, that threw the Egyptians into the sea and destroyed them (v. 27). The only requirement from the human instruments was faith and the avoidance of greed in taking the spoils of such wars, which then belonged to God alone. Solid moral teaching will differentiate this ancient belief from seeing the horrors of modern warfare in any similar light. Human violence in the name of religion is never acceptable. In Lent of 2000 John Paul II asked for public pardon for the sins of the Catholic Church in this regard.

Respect for Contemporaries

Christians ought to be very cautious about projecting the actions and motives of earlier generations or nationalities upon their contemporary descendants. That includes the obligation not to hold Jewish peoples responsible for the deeds of a few leaders in Jerusalem at the time of the crucifixion, and the duty to avoid presuming that Egyptians are eternal enemies of God (v. 25) or that they have always hated Jewish people because of the actions of a pharaoh over three thousand years ago. To say "they've always been that way" about anyone is to fall victim to false and unjust stereotypes.

Antiphon (Year I)

Exodus 15:1b

Let us sing to the Lord; he has covered himself in glory.

Miriam's Chorus

As noted in yesterday's commentary on the antiphon, the refrain (v. 1) is probably attributable to the jubilant faith of Miriam, not Moses, even though the actual text says differently. Unfortunately, the Lectionary's reading doesn't include verse 21 where the song is explicitly associated with Miriam and her chorus. The entire community celebrated the victory and the liberation of God's people from slavery in Egypt. While the liturgy is not the place for community debate, it is appropriate to acknowledge the many heroes and heroines who go unmentioned. They are the ones celebrated by the church on All Saints' Day.

Poetry

The poetic references in the hymn of Exodus, which fittingly serves as a response to the reading, illustrate the fact that this is not pure documented history. Waters are piled up (v. 8), water congeals, and people sink like lead (v. 10). The song, however, keeps one foot in history by referring to the wind (v. 10). It is Catholic to recognize the difference between history and poetic hyperbole.

First Reading (Year II)

Micah 7:14-15, 18-20

He will cast into the depths of the sea all our sins.

Israel as Inheritance

To refer to the people of Israel as God's "inheritance" (vv. 14, 18) is to suggest that the entire nation was a precious treasure, received as gift, but now completely possessed as one's own. The image must be understood in light of Israel's conviction that inheritances were precious and were to be kept through all generations forever. By analogy one can look at any weekday congregation and see them as God's precious possession, redeemed by God from sin and darkness and now received into the divine family forever. They do not even belong to themselves.

God Most Merciful

The God of Israel can be described in many ways, but the prophet Micah prefers in this luminous passage to highlight mercy, compassion, and forgiveness (v. 18). Human guilt and sin are trampled into the dust of the earth and thrown into the sea (v. 19) to be forgotten forever. One could easily extend the metaphor by listing all the concrete ways in which moderns discard and eliminate anything we no longer value or care about. That is precisely how God acts toward sins now forgiven. These words could be well used in a communal reconciliation service. Often the liturgy's first reading is an extension of the Eucharist's penitential rite.

Antiphon (Year II)

Psalm 85:8a

Lord, show us your mercy and love.

Showing the Bigger Picture

The Hebrew text of the antiphon suggests more than merely "show." The verb is causative, namely, "make us see" that mercy (see v. 8). God's grace not only puts the signs of his love in plain sight but almost forces us to pay attention to that reality by enabling us to see those experiences over the centuries for what they really are, that is, gestures of true kindness. The antiphon is found at the very end of the response, which gives examples of God's actions of restoration and forgiveness over the years, especially return from exile (v. 2).

Mercy

Once again the actual word for mercy in the antiphon is *hesed* (v. 8), the reciprocal kindness and care that members of a covenant are obliged to demonstrate toward each other. To think of God as somehow self-obligated toward us and to understand the refrain as a bold reminder to God of his promised duty is a remarkable prayer for a weekday congregation. Precisely because covenantal mercy is such a crucial notion in Scripture, this commentary continues to point out its presence in our liturgical texts.

Gospel

Matthew 12:46-50

Stretching out his hands toward his disciples, he said, "Here are my mother and my brothers."

Literary Link

This passage returns to an earlier theme: Jesus as a cause for family divisions (10:35) and his prohibition against loving parents more than himself (10:37). Now after a series of stories regarding Sabbath violations and controversies, the gospel returns to highlight the members of the true family of Jesus.

Outsiders

The mother of Jesus and his relatives are "outside," not simply on the edge of the crowd but pictured as standing outside the walls of the house (v. 46). Ordinary homes in ancient Israel were U-shaped structures built around an enclosed courtyard or open space where daily work could be done and family gatherings could occur. The rooms of the house itself were small and often windowless. The focus of Jesus was on the people directly before him. By extension, there are many "outsiders" unseen and distant from every eucharistic gathering, of whom we are called to be conscious, and for whom we pray.

My "Family"

The utter clarity of the metaphor is almost stunning. Everyone who actually "does the will of [the] heavenly Father" (v. 50) becomes part of the new family and the definitive "tribe" of Jesus. More than merely the objects of momentary affection, these new family members are bound to Jesus and to each other in a permanent fashion, both in easy as well as more difficult times. They have a common language of communication and shared values. Those who choose to enter must become assimilated into a new gospel culture and a different way of kingdom life. Obedience, not blood kinship, becomes the defining mark of this eschatological family. It is for this reason that the letters of the New Testament speak of "brothers and sisters." It is, curiously enough, a value shared with Islam, which by definition means "obedience/submission."

Tuesday of the Sixteenth Week in Ordinary Time

Wednesday of the Sixteenth Week in Ordinary Time

First Reading (Year I)

Exodus 16:1-5, 9-15

I will rain down bread from heaven for you.

The Price of Freedom

The journey from slavery to the freedom of the desert brought unanticipated challenges and difficulties. Things taken for granted are suddenly no longer available. There is always a price to be paid for freedom, and independence brings new responsibilities. Food available in the rich delta of the Nile (v. 3) is not found in the deserts of Arabia. Young adults, suddenly on their own for the first time, know this experience very well.

Grumbling and Murmuring

The rhythm of life in the arid wilderness is very different from that along the banks of the Nile with its annual floods to renew the soil and produce abundance of food (v. 3) each season. The people simply could not resist the refrain of "it used to be better." It is a perennial human temptation to compare what we don't like about the present with what we did like about the past. The very different limitations of a new leader are contrasted with the gifts of a predecessor. It's "apples and oranges" again and again. Moreover, human memory is inevitably selective in what we choose to remember.

Nourishment

Whatever the original historical context may have been for the daily collection of "bread/*lehem*" (v. 4) in the morning and "quail" (v. 13) in the evening, the Scriptures remember that the people were fed and sustained in the wilderness. Whether by some natural resource that becomes miraculous in the telling, or by some other means, Israel was nourished and sustained for many years. Somehow utter dependence upon God does result in sufficient food, as the lives of so many saints indicate. Those who trust in Divine Providence are provided for in some way.

Manna

Though named after the puzzled question, "What is it?/*man-hu*," the account presumes some nourishing white substance that appeared regularly and provided for the needs of the people. Subsequent generations may have exaggerated its nature, frequency, and abundance, but the biblical tradition remembers the reality with gratitude and respect. Manna became a symbol for the Eucharist because of its heavenly origin, nourishing nature, and gift-like character.

Antiphon (Year I)

Psalm 78:24b

The Lord gave them bread from heaven.

Psalm 78: Nourishment in the Desert

The portion of Psalm 78 selected as a response to the tale of manna and quail focuses on the "riddles" of history and the repeated demands, sometimes unreasonable, of God's people in the wilderness (v. 18). They ask the question, "Can God?" and God does! This hymn celebrates God's providence and also provides several poetic images for the idyllic life of Israel in the wilderness. The behavior was repeated so often in history as to become almost characteristic of people who acted like pouting children as a "default" response to everything and anything.

The Refrain

"[H]eavenly bread" (v. 24) was the reversal of normal nourishment from the fields of the earth. The people of old are remembered as having collected manna amid the dew each morning. Dependence on Divine Providence is a necessity for a healthy life. It is easy to see how this food could become a type for the Eucharist, and how the references to "bread from heaven" could become such a powerful Christian prayer.

FIRST READING (YEAR II)

Jeremiah 1:1, 4-10

A prophet to the nations I appointed you.

The Book of the Prophet Jeremiah

Spanning a lifetime of prophetic ministry from the late seventh into the early sixth century BC, the prophet Jeremiah bore the terrible burden of announcing the destruction of the temple to a people who could not imagine such a catastrophe and refused to listen. In an age of consummate tragedy, he stayed with his people through the bitter end. Jeremiah will be our liturgical companion for two weeks.

Wednesday of the Sixteenth Week in Ordinary Time

Original Destiny

Jeremiah lived with a strong sense of having been created, called, prepared, and summoned by God for his life task from the very first moment of his existence (v. 5). A prophet is able to perceive God's work at a deeper level before anyone else. That ability would have been his throughout his entire life. Every human being has a similar existential summons, not necessarily to the task of prophecy, but to some task of our own because each of us is absolutely unique. We are called into existence by our Creator for some purpose singularly our own. Our talents and interests converge with the special needs of others to create a "vocation."

Human Inadequacy

Jeremiah's hesitations because of young age and inexperience (v. 6), like those of Moses in Exodus (4:10), only serve to highlight the fact that all God's human instruments are unlikely and limited. This inadequacy either leads people to reject them out of hand as inappropriate, or enables people to see that the work is really God's. Improbable servants like Moses, David, Jeremiah, and Mary of Nazareth indicate God's pattern in our world.

Two-Sided Call

Jeremiah's mission was "[t]o root up and to tear down" (v. 10), namely, to announce the destruction of the temple by the Babylonians but also to speak of the people's eventual return, restoration, and renewal. He was also summoned "to build and to plant," that is, to prepare for a renewed place of worship and a recovenanted people as well (31:4, 31-34). God's work of tearing down is always for an eventual positive purpose, to establish the new creation. This is the same God who sent Jesus, not to condemn the world but to save it (John 3:17).

ANTIPHON (YEAR II)

Psalm 71:15ab

I will sing of your salvation.

Youth in Retrospect

Psalm 71's perspective would be that of old age (v. 18) looking back to the confidence of youth (vv. 5, 17) in spite of troubles over the years. In this response one hears repeated expressions of enduring confidence and trust (v. 5) over a lifetime. This is a most fitting response to the story of Jeremiah.

Salvation

The refrain (v. 15) sings of God's salvation and deliverance, not merely speaks of it. Though not cited in the Lectionary, a second account of Jeremiah's call (vv. 11-19) makes reference to opposition and resistance from his audience (v. 17), and offers divine assurance of final deliverance (1:19). Thus the psalm's refrain echoes God's promise to Jeremiah and to all who struggle to do God's will in the face of hostility.

GOSPEL

Matthew 13:1-9

The seed produced grain a hundredfold.

Literary Link

After the reference to those who do God's will as true family members (12:50),

Matthew proceeds to a collection of parables describing how God is at work in the world. The true family members of Jesus would share that perspective with him. The first parable in the series is that of the sower and the seed (vv. 3-9).

Nature of a Parable

Parables of the kingdom by definition are almost always about God, not us. Even though it may be easy to slip into simply moralizing about the different types of human recipients of the Word (which is exactly what a later interpretation supplied, as seen in vv. 18-23), such an interpretation bypasses what the parable teaches first and foremost about God's work in our world. Typical questions to any parable might be the following: What situation provoked this teaching? How is the vignette an insight into how God works? Where is the same divine action taking place in our day?

Confident Hope for Eventual Success

The primary point of this parable of the sower and the seed is that God's purpose may be initially foiled by human limitations or resistance, as symbolized in the obstacles of birds (v. 4), stones (v. 5), or thorns (v. 6), but that purpose will not be rendered null and void! In the end God will inevitably produce his desired and intended extraordinary harvest (v. 8)! Human instruments are frail and counterforces may be many and often powerful, but God will prevail. This first parable was originally intended as a parable of hope, possibly addressed to the disciples at a moment of deep human inadequacy.

Thursday of the Sixteenth Week in Ordinary Time

FIRST READING (YEAR I)

Exodus 19:1-2, 9-11, 16-20b

The LORD descended on Mount Sinai before the eyes of all the people.

Journey to Sinai: Preparation

After only three months into the wilderness (v. 1), the Israelites arrived at Sinai, almost as if encounter with God were the first and foremost objective in their minds. They prepared themselves ritually for that meeting by external cleansing of themselves and their clothing (v. 10). One can never approach the living God except through a sense of profound unworthiness. Daily worshipers and pastoral staff members should remember that familiarity can breed lack of respect and reverence, even toward God. All the way to church should be church. How can we prepare wisely and well? The heart, of course, is the main issue, but externals make a difference too.

Ritualized Encounter

The story of Sinai is told in a form that reflected the manner in which it was subsequently celebrated over the centuries. Ritual purification (v. 10), prayer amid loud thunder-like trumpets (vv. 16, 19), and the presence of fire (v. 18) and smoke all signaled aspects of temple worship. The original account may have been associated with a volcanic eruption but was told with the wrappings of its later liturgical reenactment. The memory of that past is now clothed in the celebration of what is. In a similar fashion the first Christian Eucharist at the Last Supper is described with the actions used in the celebrations of the early Christian communities (Matt 26:26-30). Attention to our rituals, the meaning of every gesture and the significance of the words, is part of our prayer. This is similar to the Zen Buddhist sense of "mindfulness."

ANTIPHON (YEAR I)

Daniel 3:52b

Glory and praise for ever!

Psalm Response

The entire response is taken, not from the Psalter, but from the hymn of the three young men in the fiery furnace, unharmed amid the flames and praising God (Dan 3:52-56). Six blessings, almost like beatitudes of praise chosen from the hymn, are offered to the Christian congregation by the Lectionary as words of praise for the transcendent God of Sinai. The liturgical alignment of the fire of Sinai with the flames of Daniel shows the unity of all God's people in every time and place.

The Refrain

The simple refrain (v. 52), repeated six times, provides an expression of the congregation's grateful response for the overwhelming experience of God in their midst. The hymn itself offers praise for God in the temple (v. 53), on the throne (v. 54), and amid cherubim (v. 55) in the highest heavens (v. 56). In every situation, whether liturgical or mundane, God is to be praised!

FIRST READING (YEAR II)

Jeremiah 2:1-3, 7-8, 12-13

They have forsaken me, the source of living waters; they have dug themselves broken cisterns.

Divine Nostalgia for First Love

In words clearly reminiscent of Hosea's fond memories of early love, Jeremiah describes Israel's first love of God in the wilderness (vv. 2, 3). We know from human affection that an idealism and romanticism can characterize initial human infatuation before the full reality of a beloved's limitations settles into daily life. That initial fondness is remembered in retrospect as flawless. Jeremiah brings the same fondness to his idealized description of Israel's life in the desert. There is a blessing in only remembering the good things. The special group of Rechabites who focused their perennial spirituality in the ancient simplicity of the desert was a powerful and attractive example for Jeremiah (35:1-19).

The Failure of Priests and Prophets

Even after entering the Promised Land, priests did not bother to serve by pointing out the way God was at work in their midst; prophets spoke in the name of worthless Canaanite gods (v. 8). What would it mean for us to ask, "Where is the LORD?" (v. 8) in suffering, in dull daily routine, or in disappointment? Here, as often throughout the book, Jeremiah condemns religious leaders who do not fulfill their duties to God's people. The word of God challenges every generation.

Broken Cisterns

The vivid poetic imagination of Jeremiah concludes with the observation that the people were deliberately digging useless broken cisterns, dry and empty in times of need (v. 13) but not seeking the living, moving waters of God. Thirsty people were looking in the wrong places! This is the same prophet who would later accuse God of being a deceptively dry wadi in times of his own greatest need (15:18). The poetic imagery used by a prophet like Jeremiah invites readers and listeners to explore the metaphors and to spend time in developing a contemplative response to this word of God.

ANTIPHON (YEAR II)

Psalm 36:10a

With you is the fountain of life, O Lord.

Psalm 36: Praise for God's Mercy

The first four verses of Psalm 36 speak of an individual completely under the sway of evil. Although that would have echoed the condemnation of Jeremiah, the Lectionary, however, omits that portion of the psalm in order to focus on praises for God's merciful generosity (v. 6) and goodness. Feasts and banquets are described for those who are faithful to the Living God, with streams of fresh water available to all (v. 9).

Fountain of Life

The refrain (v. 10) describes God as a fountain. That reference may well be the primary reason for the Lectionary's use of this psalm as a response to Jeremiah's condemnation. This provides a sharp contrast to broken cisterns! In times of sorrow, disappointment, or loss, one's trust in God can be refreshing. In times of joy and gladness, confidence in God as the true source of whatever makes us happy can be renewing and energizing. We are not our own refreshment!

GOSPEL

Matthew 13:10-17

Because knowledge of the mysteries of the Kingdom of heaven has been granted to you, but to them it has not been granted.

Literary Link

Wedged between the first parable (vv. 3-9) and its later interpretation (vv. 18-23) is a mysterious explanation of the use of parables by Jesus, almost as if he chose the stories to prevent their being heard and understood. The passage is borrowed from Mark (4:10-20) but softened by the reference to "healing."

The Mystery of Rejection

Matthew makes a clear distinction between the inner circle of disciples (v. 11) and the larger crowd of listeners who reject the teachings of Jesus about the kingdom. Jesus quotes Isaiah (6:9ff.), including the final promise of healing (v. 15), to acknowledge the mystery of grace and free will. The God who gives freedom is, in a remote sense of ultimate causality, somehow responsible for the misuse of that freedom by those who reject the Gospel. It is false, however, to interpret this text in some form of hard or soft "predestination," as if God created some for reward and others for punishment. All are called and offered grace but respected for their free will. Missionaries of all generations have sought reasons for the rejection of their message, often blaming the recipients. The way the message was expressed, however, may have been the deeper problem.

Prophets and Righteous

Some scholars conclude from the two titles of those who longed to see what the disciples had witnessed (v. 17) a reference to the major groups in Matthew's community. There were the "prophets" who spoke the word of God to the assembly. Others were the "righteous" who comprised the larger numbers, living each day in faithful response to God's will, either as Torah-observing Jews or God-fearing Gentiles. Modern parish communities are often divided into professional staff and parishioners, or into clergy and lay. Matthew's categories offer another set of lenses for viewing the life and mission of every community. Have we lost something of value by no longer seeing ourselves in this differentiated but mutually supportive way?

Thursday of the Sixteenth Week in Ordinary Time

Friday of the Sixteenth Week in Ordinary Time

FIRST READING (YEAR I)

Exodus 20:1-17

The law was given through Moses.

The Decalogue

The biblical context for the famous "Ten Commandments" is completely covenantal. A new relationship has been granted by God to his people Israel. The text follows the traditional ancient pattern for expressing such relationships: the name of the "grantor" followed by a brief recitation of prior historical actions demonstrating the grantor's goodwill and concern (v. 2). The Decalogue itself (vv. 3-17) represents a series of requirements expected from the recipient of the relationship. They serve as good-faith evidence of having accepted the friendship offered and having taken it seriously. Blessings and curses were often added as further motive for compliance. Some ritual sacrifice cemented the relationship and made it real. An annual renewal ceremony brought each new generation into the friendship, including ourselves as we hear the ancient words of God, now also addressed to us.

Historical Basis

To be complete the same historical introduction should be repeated at the beginning of each of the commandments. In other words, "I, the LORD, am your God, who brought you out of the land of Egypt, that place of slavery" (v. 2) should serve as an introduction to each of the individual "words/commandments" (as they are called in the Hebrew). This is the manner in which God once acted on behalf of the chosen people; it is the enduring rationale for compliance. Each commandment indicates an area of life in which God cares for his people. Our relationships today are still rooted in the history of God's love for us. They point to the God who entered human history and who continues to unite us into a single people, generation after generation!

ANTIPHON (YEAR I)

John 6:68c

Lord, you have the words of everlasting life.

Psalm 19: Life-Giving Commands

After celebrating the wonders of natural creation (vv. 2-7), the second portion of Psalm 19 praises God's revelation in decrees, precepts, commands, and ordinances (vv. 8-11). Each section is an insight into the different ways we learn about our God. It is the latter verses that serve as the liturgical response to the reading from Exodus. By being attentive to what people ask of us, we learn something about them, their needs and wants. Similarly, attention to God's commandments reveals much about God. While our God is utterly beyond all human limitations, the commands still give us the opportunity to know our God and to understand what is most important in our relationship with him.

The Refrain

With striking creativity this refrain of the Lectionary's response to the Decalogue is taken from a later and very different context, namely, the conversation between Jesus and the Twelve after his extended discourse on the Bread of Life (John 6). Many walked away from Jesus after his insistence that eternal life comes from eating his body and drinking his blood (6:66). Jesus sadly turned to the Twelve and asked if they also wished to leave. Peter's reply brought together the first and second covenants, saying, "Master, to whom shall we go? You have the words of eternal life" (see v. 68). This in turn echoes the teaching of Moses, cited by Jesus at the time of his temptations in the desert: "One does not live by bread alone, but by every word that comes forth from the mouth of God" (Matt 4:4; Deut 8:3). God's word feeds all our hungers.

FIRST READING (YEAR II)

Jeremiah 3:14-17

I will appoint over you shepherds after my own heart; all nations will be gathered together at Jerusalem.

Lord and Master

By a very curious, even startling, turn of phrase God invites Israel to return to himself and now claims to be their true *Baal* (v. 14), that is, their Lord, master, and husband. God is even willing to accept their existing (pagan) titles for God in order to repair the ruptured relationship and give that title a new meaning. The God of Israel is the Lord of their history as well as the source of their fertility of field and flock (v. 16). This use of the word "lord/master" for husband may not be readily understood by contemporary Americans, especially given our properly refined sense of radical equality between spouses and friends. For ancient Israel, however, God's acceptance of the title demonstrated the distance to which God would go in order to reclaim his people!

Friday of the Sixteenth Week in Ordinary Time

Shepherds after God's Heart

The passage dreams of a renewed and restored Israel. A word of clarification might help to appreciate the full import of God's promise regarding a renewed leadership in Israel. For the ancient Semitic world, "*leb*/heart" is not a place of romantic affection but rather the place for human planning and decision making. A shepherd "after God's heart" (see v. 15), then, is one whose leadership implements God's will and follows God's wishes. The larger picture of the world's salvation and final transformation should be the sole aim for all human decisions. An effective leader always keeps that in mind in making decisions with and for his or her people. God's will is the gathering and uniting of everyone at Zion, the place of God's first love. Parish councils, trustees, and catechists should all be "after God's heart"!

ANTIPHON (YEAR II)

Jeremiah 31:10d

The Lord will guard us as a shepherd guards his flock.

Homecoming

The Lectionary invites us to use the words of Jeremiah himself (31:10-13) as a response to Jeremiah. The poem of Jeremiah is a jubilant promise of return from exile and reunion, accompanied with all the music and dancing of a homecoming celebration (v. 12). Exile was a historical event but also a lifelong process. The fact is that God wants everyone, like the Israel of old, to be able to return to a renewed home as if for the first time and to start all over again together. Each decade and each generation must determine what needs to be reunited and how they "after the heart of God" might again be human partners with God in that endeavor.

God as Shepherd

Israel did return from exile in Assyria and in Babylon. The fundamental force and power behind that movement of nations, however, was the shepherding power of God himself, as the refrain (v. 10) reminds us. Humans may be the partners, but God is the divine CEO. We all want to "go home" again even if we may not be sure of where home is! In this response to the word of Jeremiah, God as shepherd promises to guide us there. Our contemporary urban cultures have little contact with the reality of shepherding. The closest we come to that reality may be an elementary teacher guiding a gaggle of little children on a walk through the neighborhood.

GOSPEL

Matthew 13:18-23

The one who hears the word and understands it will bear much fruit.

Literary Link

After a brief distraction, addressing the mystery of why some people do or do not respond (vv. 10-17), Jesus now offers a moralized explanation of the same parable taught earlier in the chapter (vv. 3-9).

Words about the Kingdom

This collection of parables is explicitly linked to the kingdom of heaven (v. 19). There was apparently some mystery and confusion about the kingdom preached by Jesus. The people of his day were convinced that God would restore full political and military power to their nation. Jesus offered an alternative new vision. This was even more important for a later age after the destruction of the temple and the city of Jerusalem by the Romans. Jesus used parables to explain how God works in our world. God's "kingdom/sovereign action in the world" is one of respecting the decisions of human freedom and weaving human decisions together in such a way that the world rises to new levels of generosity, justice, and mutual respect. God will make it happen! We are again invited to be partners, not obstacles, in that work.

The Seed

In the explanation found in Mark (4:14), the seed is "the Word," namely, the message and invitation uttered by God and addressed to each person. It is of God, from God, and related to God. In Matthew's explanation, however, the seed is rather identified with the recipient (v. 19), the one who hears the word, and so forth. To consider ourselves as the seeds sown by God into all the human situations in which we live and work is a powerful image for our identity and purpose. If John could say, "I'm the voice crying in the wilderness" (see 3:3), we can say, "I'm a seed." What a remarkable garden that would be if all of us were busy about our mission! The obstacles are now presented as different groups of people.

Friday of the Sixteenth Week in Ordinary Time

Saturday of the Sixteenth Week in Ordinary Time

First Reading (Year I)

Exodus 24:3-8

This is the blood of the covenant that the Lord has made with you.

Peace Offerings

This particular type of sacrifice, distinguished from holocausts in which the entire victim is burnt in expiation, is often called a "communion sacrifice/*shelamim*" (see v. 5). This was a sacrifice in which the family who gave the offering and the temple guardians (representing God) shared the meal and were reunited and reconciled. The Hebrew notion of *shalom* was reconciled unity, not tranquility. The sacrifices celebrated on Sinai made that possible.

Covenant of Adoption

The explicit ritual of this primeval covenant is a powerful gift. Because blood was viewed in the ancient world as the location of life, it was a vital force. Anyone who had ever witnessed a fatal injury and seen the person's life ebb away as the blood ran out into the ground understood that identification between life and blood. For God to take the blood of the sacrifice and to splash some on the altar (v. 6) and some on the people signified that God and the people were of one blood, one life, and one family! This was a powerful ritual of being adopted into God's own family. In this new context the Decalogue becomes a series of expectations for all who would live as members of God's own family. Like parents of all ages, God says, "This is my house and as long as you live here, this is the way you will treat me and each other" (see v. 8). The Eucharist renews that family bond, as we are reminded each time we hear the words of consecration over the bread and wine.

Antiphon (Year I)

Psalm 50:14a

Offer to God a sacrifice of praise.

Psalm 50: An Inviting God

Psalm 50 as a whole is a powerful description of God's sovereign action, summoning his people to an assembly of judgment because of their false worship. The verses chosen for the response, however, simply single out the section of God's public invitation (v. 5), the proclamation of justice by the heavens (v. 6), and the promise of a positive divine response to those who worship properly, with attention to the words and care to make the words a daily reality (v. 14)! This seems a very fitting liturgical response to the first reading's description of the great primordial event on Sinai.

Praise

The refrain repeats the psalm's invitation to praise of God (v. 14). True praise cannot be feigned before a God who knows the human heart and who judges the external deeds that follow from one's intentions. Praise must be sincere and inspired by admiration for God; it must be accompanied by a willingness to do what is promised, even if the worshiper has to pay a price in daily life to do so. Word and action are both essential components of praise.

First Reading (Year II)

Jeremiah 7:1-11

Has this house which bears my name become in your eyes a den of thieves?

First Temple Speech: The Messenger

The terrible prophetic burden of Jeremiah was his duty to announce the destruction of the temple. It was a message he dreaded and a task he abhorred. As a matter of fact, he was severely punished for his words and forbidden to enter the temple again (36:5). A prophet invariably pays a price for his words and actions, but he cannot "not speak" when the word burns in his bones (20:9). Jeremiah's personal experience provided a pattern for Jesus, who knew that he would be rejected by the temple authorities of his own day. The disciples of Jesus also often suffer, sometimes from their own colleagues in the faith, for speaking words of truth and justice.

The Message

Jeremiah was compelled to attack and condemn the mechanical dependence of his contemporaries upon the physical presence of the temple in their midst. In spite of the fact that Isaiah had insisted on the perduring presence of the temple in the face of Assyrian aggression a century earlier, Jeremiah's mission was to remind Israel of the essentially conditional character of God's salvific love. Jeremiah's mission began with the conditional warning expressed in this passage. Without justice (v. 5), compassion for the vulnerable (v. 6), respect for the physical well-being of others, and avoidance of idolatry, God would not remain in their midst with protection and prosperity. God respects human freedom; he can be forced to step away from the covenant if the actions of the people show little regard for their part in it. At this early moment in Jeremiah's mission, he offered a chance to his people. God's presence in our midst shares the same conditions!

ANTIPHON (YEAR II)

Psalm 84:2

How lovely is your dwelling place, Lord, mighty God!

Psalm 84: Joyous Temple Residence

By contrast to Jeremiah's condemnation, Psalm 84 sings of the spiritual joy experienced by truly faithful people when entering the temple precincts and joining the worshiping community there. Those who love the Lord yearn eagerly for the opportunity to enter the temple's beautifully decorated courts (v. 3) and to stand in the presence of the God who dwells there (v. 4). Jeremiah's negative assessment of the temple is contrasted with the idealized image of the psalmist.

Pilgrimage Songs

Given the lyrical nature of this song of praise, and the manner in which its physical and spiritual character is described, scholars have suggested that it was a favorite hymn for groups of pilgrims as they traveled by foot up the Judean hills to Jerusalem. This same song would well be prayed today by anyone setting out for a weekday Mass at the parish church because it is filled with such an appreciation for the spiritual beauty of the people and the church building within which they (except for the sparrows!) gather.

GOSPEL

Matthew 13:24-30

Let them grow together until harvest.

Literary Link

This is the second of four parables of the kingdom gathered together in this chapter by Matthew. After insisting on the eventual fruitful harvest (vv. 3-9), no matter what the obstacles (as I suggested for the original intent of the parable of the sower and the seed), we now turn to a parable about the initial mixed results of the planting. This parable acknowledges the presence of weeds too.

The Problem of Weeds

How does one know which plants are truly weeds when they first appear? How does one know that what we judge to be a weed today may not turn out to be the source of some marvelous cure in future generations? Even dandelion leaves make great spring salads! There was once a rectory cook in Milwaukee, an immigrant from Eastern Europe, who walked to work each day through the alleys because she found so many "weeds" that made great soups.

The Compassion of God

The fundamental point of this parable seems to be the patience of God who is willing to let things grow at their own pace (v. 29), always in the hope of achieving their conversion. God takes things as they are and tries to make them better and more useful. To say it differently, we do not have to be good for God to love us because God is willing to love us into goodness if we let him. At the same time, God's compassion includes truth, and knows the reality of accountability and judgment too. Without truth, there is no compassion. Without compassion, there is no truth.

Saturday of the Sixteenth Week in Ordinary Time

Monday of the Seventeenth Week in Ordinary Time

FIRST READING (YEAR I)

Exodus 32:15-24, 30-34

This people has indeed committed a grave sin, in making a god of gold for themselves.

Ancient Idolatry

Images of calves (v. 19) and bulls were common idols in the ancient Near East. These figures were chosen because they were images for divine strength, fertility, nourishment, and new beginnings. It may well be that each age and each person has his or her own inner "idols," things so symbolically important to us that we might be willing to push aside the actual will of God in order to honor a different priority. It might be public fame, financial prosperity, or personal pleasure. Does everyone have his or her own privileged area of life sometimes judged more important than commitments to God? The passage reminds us of the fact that things of beauty and even precious ideas can becomes idols for us, supreme values that displace the real God and make us idolaters in subtle ways. Gold, for example, is very beautiful, and the fact that it has always been such a treasure only confirms that fact. Whatever may attract our attention and claim our desire could become a golden idol.

Divine Punishment

The story includes the fact that Moses ground the idol into powder that he mixed with water and made the Israelites drink (v. 2). The popular belief was that the ritual was a curse because the guilty would become very ill, while the innocent would be preserved from sickness. The wisdom of the ancients, affirmed by revelation, insists that God does punish wrongdoing, but perhaps in unexpected ways. We can be punished by our sins rather than because of them. Bad choices are wrong because they cause us harm sooner or later.

ANTIPHON (YEAR I)

Psalm 106:1a

Give thanks to the Lord, for he is good.

Psalm 106: Ancient Sins Rehearsed

Scholars suggest that Psalm 106 may have been used each autumn as part of a covenantal renewal ceremony associated with the feast of Tabernacles/Booths. Major events of salvation history are rehearsed, even those that had been followed by negative human response to God's goodness in ancient times. Because of the psalm's litany of sins, it easily became a frequent element in services of penance. We have our own history of such failures. Fortunately, our history also includes forgiveness as well as God's gracious gifts.

Sins of Horeb

The Lectionary has selected these specific verses that deal with the golden calf (v. 19) as the response to the tale of its construction. Horeb is the site of the burning bush, and seems to have been another name for Sinai. Scholars have noted that the name of Sinai occurs in the Yahwist and Priestly traditions of the Pentateuch, while Horeb is found in the Elohist and Deuteronomic materials. Different people often have special preferred names for their sacred experiences and places. If we were asked to list the "holy places" for our encounters with God, where would they be?

FIRST READING (YEAR II)

Jeremiah 13:1-11

This people shall be like a loincloth which is good for nothing.

People as Rags

The graphic image of undergarments worn close to one's person (v. 1) and then discarded after use and buried is used by the prophet to indicate the utterly useless and disgusting reality (v. 7) that Israel has become because of its sins. By sin, Israel had become like a soiled rag. Like dirty torn rags or diapers thrown away into an abandoned lot Israel is described, once beloved and chosen, and then rejected by God as utterly useless because of its prior sins. To consider one's entire society in such terms inevitably produces a sense of guilt and shame, which is precisely what Jeremiah wished to achieve. His is a prophetic judgment.

Election and Mission

Anyone or anything chosen by God is always intended for a purpose. People are called "from" and called "for." Those who refuse to see the larger picture become useless in graphic ways. In a real sense, therefore, people had chosen to become what they were. Jeremiah's prophetic oracle of judgment, however, was not the last word. God would eventually invite them back, but would not force conversion upon them. There is something sad about the final verses of this reading, treating as it does, God's genuine love for Israel, and their refusal to listen (v. 11).

Antiphon (Year II)

Deuteronomy 32:18a

Monday of the Seventeenth Week in Ordinary Time

You have forgotten God who gave you birth.

The Anger of God

The Lectionary has selected an excerpt from the song of Moses (Deut 32) as the formal response to the tale of the golden calf. We hear the strong rebuke of Moses for that sin of "no-god" (v. 20), taking up once more God's words of judgment and condemnation. The repetition of Jeremiah's judgment and the hymn's echo is almost a liturgical double dose of prophetic disappointment and anger.

Absence of God

The prophets and psalms speak of God's anger at times as being so profound as to cause God to turn away and hide his face (v. 20). Like a furious human parent who needs to go away in order to control personal feelings before returning to carry out discipline, God's face is hidden. God takes away the signs of his presence in the world within which Israel lives. They are left without spiritual consolation, satisfaction, or any sense of accomplishment. They have only the emptiness of a "no-god" amid a "no-people." In fact, however, God can never be completely absent, at least as philosophy teaches us, because that would cause the world to disappear!

Gospel

Matthew 13:31-35

The mustard seed becomes a large bush and the birds of the sky come and dwell in its branches.

Literary Link

Matthew completes this collection of his parables of the kingdom by adding two final teachings: the mustard seed (vv. 31-32) and the yeast (v. 33). The chapter is finally concluded with a statement about the way parables are used by Matthew's Jesus (vv. 34-35).

Mustard Seed

Mustard seed (v. 32), as we know from spice shelves, is very small (v. 32), but so are many others, such as carrot, poppy, common grass, and herbs of many kinds. Matthew's purpose, however, is not the fact of small size alone, but the further truth that this particular plant grows to be of service, even to the birds of the air. The unanticipated growth so beyond expectation, therefore, is the teaching of the Lord in this parable, as well as the fact that it even becomes a place of refuge for other creatures. Sometimes human beings truly surprise friends and family members by their eventual stature and public reputation. Teachers might never have guessed the final development intellectually or financially of some students. If that stature is combined with remarkable service, the parable comes true again. Perhaps in the story of the magnificent harvest the first disciples were overwhelmed by their own insignificance and limitations, thus becoming the occasion for the Lord's reminder that God can and does make great things from the insignificant. This clearly shows the power to be God's alone! Jesus offers assurance to those who think themselves worthless.

Yeast

The final parable is that of yeast (v. 33), which permeates and transforms dough into material for delicious nourishment. The world in which God works is not separate or parallel from our world and its society. Rather, God completely permeates and changes everything in our world. Similarly, an attitude of compassion can permeate everything we do; so can a spirit of self-sacrificing love. These sentiments can become like yeasts that change what we think and do; they can make us useful. God works subtly in everything, hidden yet capable of producing transformation. This parable may have been told to those who expected to see public showy signs of God at work like miracles or astonishing natural phenomena! The final verses about Christ's purpose in using parables avoid any hint of intended confusion from God's part as was suggested in the earlier omitted verses (vv. 10-15). The Lectionary keeps the message positive.

Tuesday of the Seventeenth Week in Ordinary Time

First Reading (Year I)

Exodus 33:7-11; 34:5b-9, 28

The Lord spoke to Moses face to face.

The Tent of Meeting

Though somewhat distant from the main camp of the Israelites (v. 7), that sacred place where Moses met God face-to-face was the point toward which the entire camp was oriented. When Moses entered, the people faced the tent and attended that encounter from a respectful distance. This was one way of insisting that every life is in fact oriented toward meeting God as individuals and toward the community's corporate worship of God. No daily life or human activity was isolated from the divine presence in the midst of God's people. Moreover, all turned toward Moses because the prayer of every individual belongs in some way to the entire community.

The Cloud

Among the more popular and familiar signs of God's presence was the cloud (v. 9): visible yet intangible, unable to be controlled by human effort yet permeating all our lives, possibly bringing life-giving moisture to the earth. The origin of this symbol may have been associated with incense. Although we Westerners have tended to equate the smoke of incense with our prayers rising, the more ancient use of the symbol would have been associated with God, not us. Such a divine presence might even leave a trace of fragrance on our person, clothing, and possessions.

The Name of the Lord

The Lectionary text gives the impression that the encounter begins with the action of Moses, calling out the name of God (v. 5), but a closer reading of the original wording would indicate that it is God alone who first reveals his name to Moses and thus establishes the friendship inherent in such an exchange of personal names. To know someone's name grants a certain social power over that individual. To call out the personal name of God, namely, Lord, is to stand in the very presence of God. God is present wherever God is addressed! The descriptive summary of the Lord's nature, "merciful and gracious . . . slow to anger and rich in kindness and fidelity" (vv. 6-7), is placed on God's lips as a revelation. The statement may well have been an early creed that was recited regularly by Israelites who gathered for worship. Christians could do well by making that same description a summary of our own faith today, just as it was for the Jewish disciples of Jesus in the earliest days of the church. Imagine reciting that creed when we gather for communal prayer! If Moses stayed with God for forty days without eating (v. 28), one might wonder if fasting enhances a person's sense of the divine. Did God's presence in itself provide nourishment?

Antiphon (Year I)

Psalm 103:8a

The Lord is kind and merciful.

The Refrain

Because the English translation isn't always consistent, it may be helpful to pause for a moment over the statement of the refrain (v. 8). As noted before, the Hebrew word translated here as "kind" is *raham,* that is, maternal, womb-like mercy such as a mother might have for a child. The Hebrew word translated as "merciful" is *hanan,* namely, very gracious and attractive in himself but also giving grace to someone else and thereby making that person gracious and attractive as well.

Psalm 103: God's Forgiveness

The sections of Psalm 103 chosen by the Lectionary serve to unpack and explain more concretely the elements in that early creed as expressed in the refrain (v. 8). They explain the nature of the God who has entered into covenant with his chosen people. The Lord obtains justice for the oppressed (v. 6), instruction for Israel (v. 7), and does not constrain himself only to anger over our sins (v. 10). His covenantal kindness is as high as the heavens (v. 11) and he has placed our sins as far away as possible (v. 12). The compassion affirmed in the refrain is like that of a parent for his children (v. 13).

First Reading (Year II)

Jeremiah 14:17-22

Remember, Lord, your covenant with us and break it not.

True Prophecy

In the verses immediately preceding this text, God rejects the false prophets who insist that God will give lasting peace without sword or famine (v. 13). The truth of the matter, however, as Jeremiah points out with tears (v. 17), is quite the opposite. Jeremiah acknowledges the sins of Israel (v. 20) and wonders if the covenant has been cast off forever (v. 21). A true prophet speaks the mind of God, not simply what people may wish to hear. This demands careful discernment in every instance lest our words reflect the desire of the speaker alone, not God. That would be false prophecy! Children put on extra clothes because their mother is cold. The congregation is scolded because the preacher is piqued. Such self-centered speaking would be human speech, not prophecy.

Disasters

The reading begins with the acknowledgment of disasters such as violence and hunger (v. 18). One must always ask if violence and tragedy automatically indicate God's anger and the end of the covenant (v. 19) or if they signal a time of grace for possible repentance and renewal. The simpler *quid pro quo* morality of early Deuteronomy would suggest that prosperity comes from obedience and suffering from disobedience, yet we do know that bad things happen to good people! Once again discernment and patient endurance is the recipe for the day.

Antiphon (Year II)

Psalm 79:9

For the glory of your name, O Lord, deliver us.

Pleas and Petitions

The lament of Psalm 79 was used in later Judaism on the anniversaries of the destruction of the temple by the Babylonians (587 BC) and the Romans (AD 69). It was the prophets who explained the disasters in terms of divine anger. Though true in those cases, is it always the correct explanation? Conceding the legitimacy of God's anger, the verses beg for forgiveness, compassion (v. 8), and deliverance (v. 9). The Lectionary omits the prayer for revenge (v. 12).

Ultimate Motive

Humbly acknowledging that human conduct itself cannot be sufficient reason for forgiveness (v. 9), the psalm invokes God's own nature, and dares to express the hope that God will wish to demonstrate the nobility of his own name and nature by such forgiveness. One recalls the scene from the film *Schindler's List*, where the compassionate industrialist tries to convince the brutal Nazi camp officer that mercy is a sign of self-control, and therefore of greater strength than violent killing.

Gospel

Matthew 13:36-43

Just as the weeds are collected now and burned up with fire, so will it be at the end of the age.

Literary Link

After the parables of the mustard seed and the yeast in yesterday's gospel, plus a reminder of why Jesus used parables (vv. 31-35), Jesus is now pictured as turning toward the small group of his disciples for a further explanation of the weeds (vv. 36-43). Jesus dismissed the crowds (v. 36) to signal a shift in his attention.

Deeper Understanding

The request of the disciples for further explanation (v. 36) suggests that every person who is truly a disciple will want to go ever deeper into the mysteries of God's revelation and the teachings of Christ. Similar to the manner in which the parable of the sower and the seed had been explained allegorically (vv. 13-23), Jesus now applies the same technique of explanation to the weeds and wheat (vv. 37-43). Scholars and preachers note the danger of moralizing too quickly in order to explain each element. Although the refocus may make the parable very clear and easily applicable to the lives of the audience, they point out, it could also risk obscuring the original point of the Lord's parable, namely, divine tolerance for coexistence until the right time. The further explanation of the good seed as good people (v. 38), however, can be spiritually and pastorally useful. Focusing on us rather than on God enables each of us to imagine ourselves as seeds cast and sowed into the larger world. Our missionary task is emphasized. We understand that we have been called by God to bring forth a harvest of justice and charity.

A Prophet of the Last Age

Jesus is rightly called a Prophet of the Eschaton, that is, the last age, for all his teaching acknowledges the dynamic flow of human history to our ultimate destiny. He reminds us that all our human actions as well as our entire lives remain under the judgment of God. Although the Sermon on the Mount teaches us how to live life well, a major focus of Jesus is the final age and the consummation of the universe (v. 39). Final accountability as well as partnership is part of God's work in our world. Evildoers burn (v. 42), but the righteous shine (v. 43).

Tuesday of the Seventeenth Week in Ordinary Time

Wednesday of the Seventeenth Week in Ordinary Time

First Reading (Year I)

Exodus 34:29-35

Seeing the face of Moses, they were afraid to come near him.

The Radiance of Moses

This text pays special attention to the radiance of the face of Moses (v. 29). When we enter into the presence of God and engage in genuine prayer, we are the ones who are changed. True prayer includes praise and thanksgiving and repentance, not only petition. Even then, God isn't changed by our prayer, but we are, as we come to know the serenity and peace that can be the result of the great grace and gift of prayer, especially in times of uncertainty and anxiety. This text may also be one of the sources for the account of the transfiguration. Jesus, Moses, and Elijah all became radiant as a result of their conversation together (Matt 17:1-8).

Veil Put Aside

When Moses spoke with the people, he covered his face with a veil to allay their fears (v. 30). When Moses spoke directly with God, however, he removed the veil from his face (v. 34). Scholars suggest that this is the proper biblical reference for a detail in the resurrection story of John's gospel. There we are told that, when Peter and John entered the empty tomb after the resurrection (John 20:7), they noticed the cloth that covered the face of Jesus was not with the rest of the burial clothing; it was rolled up in a separate place. Just as Moses had removed the veil over his face when speaking with God face-to-face (v. 34), so did Jesus when speaking directly with his Father after the resurrection. Furthermore, the First Letter of John promised that when the full mystery is revealed, "we shall be like [God], for we shall see him as he is" (3:2).

Antiphon (Year I)

Psalm 99:9c

Holy is the Lord our God.

Holiness

The refrain (v. 9) proclaims the holiness of God. A defining characteristic of biblical holiness is the fact that it renders someone radically different from others around him or her. Thus there is a fundamental countercultural dimension to holiness that enables those so blessed by God to see things differently. They are able to view things from God's point of view rather than from a merely human perspective. Isaiah often calls God "the Holy One." The response to the eucharistic prefaces proclaims that quality in a threefold (superlative) manner.

Psalm 99: Praise for God

The response to the memory of the radiance of Moses serves as a reminder of the fact that Moses and Aaron served God as priests, and that Samuel was one of God's prophets (v. 6). The heroes of old were holy because they heard God speaking (v. 7), paid serious attention, and were transformed. We might receive a similar blessing!

First Reading (Year II)

Jeremiah 15:10, 16-21

Why is my pain continuous?—If you repent, you shall stand in my presence.

Jeremiah's Laments

One of the more poignant "charms" of Jeremiah is his willingness to invite us into the turmoil of his spirit and to overhear his bitter complaints to God. He bares his heart so fully as to give his personal name to this type of literary cry that is labeled a "Jeremiad." As a moral analyst of his society, Jeremiah saw all too clearly the tragic bad choices being made around him, and the disasters that would follow for the entire city. He was truly indignant (v. 17). Those who follow God's laws scrutinize the whole of society as well as other individuals and their own lives. They speak candidly as did Jeremiah. They also suffer greatly because of what they are forced to behold around them and to say (v. 10). In his bitterness, Jeremiah dares to call God a "treacherous brook" (v. 18), namely, one that offers the hope of water, but upon closer inspection is revealed utterly dry. The burden of speaking the truth from God's point of view entails paying a price as did Jeremiah. Left in anger (v. 17), isolation, and sorrow, he watched the tragedy unfold around him as the Babylonian powers began to move against the city of Jerusalem.

Divine Sternness

When Jeremiah felt sorry for himself, however, and was filled with anger (v. 10), God's surprising response was to take the prophet to task and chastise him (v. 19). God warned him to make sure that his prophetic speeches remain precious and valuable, unmixed with personal venom or vile ranting (v. 19). Only then did God promise to protect and defend him, making the prophet strong as a brass wall (v. 20). Jeremiah was the one who had to change, not God! Jeremiah's experience of divine "comeuppance" in the face of his human anger toward God might also be given to us if our own anger is too self-centered at times.

Wednesday of the Seventeenth Week in Ordinary Time

ANTIPHON (YEAR II)

Psalm 59:17d

God is my refuge on the day of distress.

Psalm 59: The Cry of the Innocent

This psalm is the prayer of one who feels innocently persecuted by powerful adversaries (vv. 2ff.), and left without protection. Three times God is invoked as a stronghold (vv. 10, 17, 18). The psalm concludes with an expression of total confidence in God's ultimate ability to deliver and save his faithful servant (v. 11).

Refuge

The refrain uses a specific Hebrew word for refuge, *manos* (v. 17), literally, a place to which one flees quickly in times of danger, like a storm cellar in a tornado or high ground in a flash flood. God's constant immediate presence to our hopes and fears makes God a perfect "refuge"! Studies of the Psalms note the relationship between life's "path" and its destination of "refuge."

GOSPEL

Matthew 13:44-46

He sells all he has and buys that field.

Literary Link

After the allegorical explanation of the weeds and the wheat to the disciples (vv. 37-43), the gospel adds two more brief parables that would seem specifically directed to the personal effort and search expected of an individual disciple. Both a buried treasure (v. 44) and the pearl (vv. 45-46) demand action on our part.

Buried Treasure

Even in our own day, the news periodically reports the discovery of valuables long buried in attics, vacant lots, or backyards, possibly back from the Depression of the 1930s when people did not trust banks or financial institutions. The elements of the parable (v. 44) include diligent effort, sudden discovery of something not of our doing, joy, and the need to make a decision in order to make sure that the treasure is legitimately one's own. Normally, parables of the kingdom are about God, not human beings. Perhaps the implicit point about God is the manner in which God hides treasures amid familiar surroundings for us to discover and make our own. God works below the surface of everything we do and invites us to find the fingerprints of his secret efforts.

Pearl of Great Price

The Greek word for pearl is *margarites* (v. 45), and refers to a rare and precious stone unknown in Israel prior to the conquests of Alexander the Great in the later fourth century BC. Imported from the Red Sea and similar distant areas of salt water, pearls represented luxurious wealth and exceptional beauty, which is why the book of Revelation described the whore of Babylon decked in such excessive and rare jewels (18:16). For a merchant to find such a treasure in the bazaar (v. 45) is rare; his willingness to risk all for one single gem is the point. This parable praises the merchant as a disciple with refined values and good taste! If parables are about God at work, this parable insists that God has priorities and God expects us to make his priorities our own as well. Some things are more valuable than others. A true disciple knows the difference.

Thursday of the Seventeenth Week in Ordinary Time

First Reading (Year I)

Exodus 40:16-21, 34-38

The cloud covered the meeting tent and the glory of the Lord filled the Dwelling.

Perfect Obedience

The very fact that Moses did everything precisely as the Lord had commanded (v. 16), underscores the fact that the covenant and God's new relationship with Israel is purely by divine initiative, not the result of any mere human effort. The reference to the obedience is repeated twice (vv. 16, 21) as if to underscore that truth. Everything is grace and gift! It can only be God alone who determines how he will be present in our world and where he will dwell. Eight times within this brief passage we hear the same word, "dwelling/*mishkan*," as if to emphasize God's intent and purpose. It is a place where one settles down, builds a home, and rests regularly. God asked Moses the "home builder" to prepare the place, and Moses obeyed.

A Complex Reality

This reading is about place, presence, purpose, and people. The intricacies of building the temple with all its pedestals, boards, and bars (v. 18) almost remind one of the incomprehensible instructions for something purchased "to be assembled." The final "tent" product still remains difficult to imagine, and that underscores the mystery of God's presence in our midst. This type of sacred architecture provides a designated space for the symbol of divine presence, namely, the commandments, and also provides shared space for the human encounter of Moses with God. The mystery of God's presence includes both a relationship and a shared self-revelation.

Cloud and Fire

The cloud in itself is a symbol of divine presence (v. 34). When illuminated by fire from within (v. 38), the cloud clearly teaches that the mysterious power and presence of God, immaterial and intangible, visible yet beyond human control, is the center of Israel's existence and the source of guidance for them on their pilgrim journey—which endures throughout all of history. There seems to be some liturgical background to this symbol, perhaps a charcoal fire that was carefully tended as an "eternal flame." Under the ashes and in the incense remained the burning fire of God's presence.

Antiphon (Year I)

Psalm 84:2

How lovely is your dwelling place, O Lord, mighty God!

Psalm 84

As noted elsewhere, Psalm 84 was a song of pilgrims en route to the Holy City for a major annual festival. As they eagerly anticipated their arrival (v. 3), they sang the praises of the temple and celebrated the wonder of God's presence therein throughout history. They praised those fortunate enough to live in close proximity to the temple throughout the entire year (v. 5). Hmong refugees immigrating to the United States tend to instinctively look for new residence near a church just as they had sought to live near temples in their native land.

Mighty God

The Hebrew behind the refrain's title "mighty" is *Sabaoth*, literally, the Lord "of armies" (v. 2). The implied poetic reference is to the armies of stars that move across the heavens each night in formation under the divine command. In the ancient Semitic mind, anything that moved was alive. To celebrate such a divine cosmic presence as somehow dwelling in the temple was to be humbled by the presence of the enormous power of Israel's God. God's armies are those of the cosmos, peaceful, orderly, and under divine command. In a modern world constantly seeking to understand the universe, we stare at the galaxies of heaven, and stand humbled before our God.

First Reading (Year II)

Jeremiah 18:1-6

Like the clay in the hand of the potter, so are you in my hand, house of Israel.

Prophetic Poetry

Jeremiah was one of Israel's finest poets. As such, he was constantly alert to situations from daily life that could illustrate God's actions in regard to Israel. A simple potter, throwing lumps of clay onto his wheel and starting all over from the beginning when things did not turn out as desired (v. 4), provided a perfect illustration of God's judgment and determination to make a fresh start if needed. The image may well have been inspired by the second creation tradition where God is described as shaping a human being out of the clay of the earth (Gen 2:7). With poetic insight Jeremiah knew that each of us comes fresh and unique from the hand of God. He also knew of God's willingness to reshape us by the experiences of our lives.

Insight and Metaphor

In the midst of an experience the prophet suddenly saw a metaphor at work, and realized that the common action of the potter was like God at work! Where does such an insight come from? Jeremiah ascribed it to God speaking to the very core of his understanding. The prophet called it a "word" from God (v. 5). The notion of divine inspiration makes God the author of the idea but allows the human partner to provide the verbal expressions needed to clothe the idea. This would seem a far better explanation of the doctrine of inspiration than simple divine dictation. Do we ever see our ideas and insights as coming from God?

Antiphon (Year II)

Psalm 146:5a

Blessed is he whose help is the God of Jacob.

The True Source of Help

Psalm 146 is a simple but profound invitation to see in God alone the sufficient strength and stability to be a help in times of need. Trusting in mere human "princes" is chancy at best. Because God alone provides the help we need, God becomes a dependable partner in life, as contrasted with the fickleness of human beings (v. 3) whose life is limited and whose days are numbered (v. 4).

God of Jacob

The people of Israel took the name of their ancestor Jacob/Israel. The intergenerational character of Israel's faith makes those who have gone before us models of fidelity and trusting hope in the Lord (v. 5). Often teenagers choose a sponsor for confirmation from among their grandparents, whose unwavering faith has been tested by experience and found solid. That elders can become such models should be a reminder of their obligation to provide the stable examples needed by the next generation when they invite and inspire without nagging.

Gospel

Matthew 13:47-53

They put what is good into buckets, what is bad they throw away.

Literary Link

The chapter's collection concludes with a final (seventh) parable about how God is at work in the world, the parable of the net cast into the sea (vv. 47-50). The mysterious sovereign action of God has a final purpose, and judgment is part of the big picture.

The Divine Agent as Judge

Parables are always about God, and about God's action in the world; for that reason the actions of throwing and hauling and sorting (v. 48) are primary points of the story. Not every fish story is about the big ones that got away. Some of the catch, as illustrated in this parable, are simply found unworthy and tossed away by a discriminating God. Any experienced fisherman instinctively knows what isn't worth cleaning and taking home. Our God, wise, loving, and compassionate, is also a God of accountability and judgment!

Further Depth of Meaning

Although the disciples quickly responded that they understood (v. 51), the fact is that each parable takes a lifetime of thought and experience to unpack. In a church that acknowledges the fact of "doctrinal development," we all are called to ponder Christ's teaching and find new depths of meaning for our lives and work. The parable isn't really about fish at all, but rather about the wisdom of a human being who is finally able to determine what is of lasting value in life. A scribe of the kingdom is more than a warehouse employee because he or she brings forth the new as well as the old (v. 52)!

Thursday of the Seventeenth Week in Ordinary Time

Friday of the Seventeenth Week in Ordinary Time

First Reading (Year I)

Leviticus 23:1, 4-11, 15-16, 27, 34b-37

These are the festivals of the Lord on which you shall proclaim a sacred assembly.

The Book of Leviticus

The book is called Leviticus because it is primarily composed of instructions for sacrifice and ritual as performed by the temple Levites. The Lectionary has chosen to conclude the account of God's instructions regarding the building of the tent/temple with a summary of the major festivals scattered throughout the year when the people of Israel came together on pilgrimage to that holy place.

Passover

At the beginning of Israel's ancient year came the feast of Passover (vv. 4-11), which remembered the exodus out of Egypt and their flight into freedom. This is the foundational festival for Israel, and the feast that coincides with Christian Easter. It provides the fundamental meaning for Christ's death to the slavery of sin and resurrection to the freedom of a new life. At a later time, Israel's calendar was changed so that the New Year (as celebrated today) began in autumn. Passover, however, remained in the spring.

Pentecost

The first spring harvest (vv. 15-16) occurred about seven weeks into the ancient year. Called "*Shevu'ot*/Weeks," the festival provided an opportunity for gratitude to the God of abundance who cared for his people and provided fresh grain precisely when the supplies so carefully hoarded from the previous year were finished. Israel gradually associated this feast with the springtime gift of the law on Sinai. Christians celebrated the gift of the Spirit and the renewed law of God's love for his people.

Atonement

Here the Lectionary offers only a single verse (v. 27) for the annual feast of "Atonement/*Yom Kippur*" when sins are acknowledged and forgiven. This annual autumn feast seems to have been influenced by Babylonian ritual and grew in importance after the exile. Its significance for Christians was merged into Christ's redemptive Passover from death to life.

Booths/Tabernacles

Originally the final fall harvest festival of the year (vv. 34-37), the feast of Tabernacles was celebrated by building temporary shelters in the fields where workers could stay close to the harvest and engage in the joys of that season. Even today urban Orthodox Jews build shelters on balconies or in backyards to celebrate the renewal of the covenant in gratitude.

Antiphon (Year I)

Psalm 81:2a

Sing with joy to God our help.

Song and Dance

The festivals of Israel, like their prayer, were always celebrated with song (v. 2), so that the entire physical body could participate in the event and render suitable thanks to God for the blessings of that particular memorial. The psalm mentions timbrel, harp, and lyre (v. 3) as well as trumpet (v. 4) among the sacred instruments of temple worship. All sounds have their respective place in the worship of the Lord. We might add organ, piano, and guitar.

One Lord Alone

The psalm insists as part of its invitation to praise that the focus of that worship should be the Lord alone (v. 10). Moreover the enduring motive for that praise remains God's interventions on behalf of his people throughout history. This is the same rationale that introduced the Ten Commandments

(Exod 20:2). God's historical journey with us is no less a motive for our praise and obedience today.

First Reading (Year II)

Jeremiah 26:1-9

All the people gathered about Jeremiah in the house of the Lord.

Announcing Destruction

Jeremiah was commanded to stand in the temple and to proclaim its destruction like that of the shrine of Shiloh centuries earlier (v. 6). Although little Samuel had lived there (1 Sam 3), curiously no account of Shiloh's destruction has been preserved in Scripture. Jeremiah's prediction was directly contrary to the oracles of Isaiah, who a century earlier assured the people of Jerusalem that God would save them and their city if they only trusted in him. Jeremiah was caught in a moment not of his choosing and with a task not to his liking, but he had to find God in that moment because it was the only one he had! Determining precisely what is the right thing to do demands discernment; doing so can demand a great price. Prophets have no choice because of their commitment to the living God. An excellent examination of conscience: when is the last time we did what was right even though it wasn't popular?

Friday of the Seventeenth Week in Ordinary Time

Popular Reaction

Sometimes negative popular reaction to prophetic comments comes from fear or anger or some other less noble motive. Morality cannot be based upon majority votes or popular opinion because self-interest often clouds moral thinking. The cry for the death penalty (v. 8) for Jeremiah was a travesty of justice. Mob rule never reflects true moral reasoning. After the news reports of public opinion must come the more thoughtful moral reasoning of the Judeo-Christian community. Their moral resources gleaned from centuries of life and faith amid conflicting values must be brought to bear on the neuralgic questions of the day.

Antiphon (Year II)

Psalm 69:14c

Lord, in your great love, answer me.

Psalm 69

This psalm, after Psalm 22, is the second most cited psalm in the New Testament because it describes so vividly the distress of someone unjustly insulted and persecuted (v. 5), something easily attributed to Jesus in his final sufferings. The psalm speaks of shame, insult, and family rejection (vv. 8-10). Through it all, the psalmist trusts in God's fidelity (v. 14), as must we all when life becomes overwhelming. Spiritual writers say that such a moment of utter helplessness comes into every human life at some point in God's effort to bring us to ultimate dependence upon God alone, not ourselves!

Love

So often the translation offered by the Lectionary fails to do full justice to the original. Once again, as in this case, the English word "love" in the refrain (v. 14) in fact translates the Hebrew *hesed*. As noted often, this is covenantal concern by which God is obliged to come to the aid of a human partner who, in this case, is suffering persecution for doing the right thing. This response, picking up the desperate situation of Jeremiah in the temple, begs God to exercise his covenantal duty of protection for the prophet so unjustly condemned.

Gospel

Matthew 13:54-58

Is he not the carpenter's son? Where did this man get such wisdom and mighty deeds?

Literary Link

Matthew's great collection of parables ends with the brief and sad description of rejection by the people of Nazareth. The end of the prior chapter (12:46-50) described the true members of the family of Jesus, those who do the will of his heavenly Father. This account reveals that the former neighbors and family "friends" at Nazareth, especially after having heard the parables, are definitely not in that category!

Rejection

In Luke's gospel the rejection is described in terms of the unwillingness of Jesus to grant former neighbors preferential treatment (Luke 4:23). Here it simply says that they "took offense" (v. 57) at him. There is a perennial perversity of the human heart that would keep others at lower levels lest they outshine us in some way! The fact of his rejection, however, remains puzzling and filled with sadness. Perhaps it was simple jealousy or envy at his gifts and increasing fame that led to that negative dismissal, or their reaction may have been a way of avoiding the claims made by his teaching on their lives and attitudes! Even the simple fact that Jesus spoke in new and unfamiliar ways may have become the occasion for his rejection; they may have refused to allow him to grow beyond their early memories of the lad at play in the neighborhood. Rejection has many motives.

Brothers

It might be helpful to remember that the Hebrew language, unlike Greek or most modern languages, has no specific word for cousins. Hebrews rather used the phrase "brother" (v. 55) or "sister" (v. 56) for any of the various degrees of family relationship. This is one of the challenges of translation from one language and culture into another. The question must be asked: To what degree does one retain the flavor of the original without conveying something erroneous in the new language? Too literal a translation can cause theological misunderstandings.

Saturday of the Seventeenth Week in Ordinary Time

First Reading (Year I)

Leviticus 25:1, 8-17

In the year of the jubilee you shall return, every one of you, to your own property.

Social and Economic Realignment

One of the great insights of the Torah was its divinely inspired effort to engage in periodic adjustment of economic inequities. First slaves were released after six years of servitude (Exod 21:2), then debts were added to the list of things forgiven after six years (Deut 15:2), and finally, wherever possible, property was returned to its original owners (Lev 25:10). Whether this system was ever truly implemented in practice is unknown, but the ideal remains remarkable. The same sense of justice and the common good must lead contemporary Christians to seek new ways for regularly eliminating poverty from our communities and alleviating economic oppression.

Jubilee

Every fiftieth year all property was to revert to its original owners (v. 13). Any social or economic inequity that may have developed over the five decades would thus be erased. Social justice was a prime value of Israel and was enshrined in the stipulations or commandments associated with the covenant. Each culture or nation may have its own system for the social realignment of citizens, but concern for economic stability and the compassionate elimination of poverty remains an obligation and duty for all people in all ages! The original rules for jubilee may have developed as families returned from exile in Babylon and sought to reclaim their ancestral lands that had been overtaken by squatters during their absence from Jerusalem. The Catholic Church has embodied this ancient jubilee custom in the practice of spiritual jubilees of justice and peace every fifty years.

Antiphon (Year I)

Psalm 67:4

O God, let all the nations praise you!

Harvest Joy

Psalm 67 has been described as a song for the celebration of a fruitful harvest, as indicated in verse 7 where the blessings of God are gratefully acknowledged. The fact that verse 2 refers to God's face shining upon his people has been seen as a reference to the blessing of Aaron (Num 6:24ff.), which may have either preceded or followed this song in worship. This special blessing at the time of harvest serves to remind everyone that the ultimate source of any abundance is God alone.

Nations

Like all good and acceptable prayers, the harvest song is not self-centered or limited to the needs and wants of Israel alone. It maintains a broader frame of reference and includes all the nations of the world (vv. 3-6). Although scholars may debate the pace and extent of Israel's growth toward universalism in the first covenant, there are many signs of Israel's concern for the salvation of a larger world than merely its own. Abraham's call included blessings for all nations (Gen 12:3). National isolationism is never a viable path for true Catholic Christians. We can do no less, especially in light of Christ's command to make disciples of all nations (Matt 28:19).

First Reading (Year II)

Jeremiah 26:11-16, 24

For in truth it was the Lord who sent me to you, to speak all these things for you to hear.

Rejection

This reading describes the negative response of the priests and prophets (v. 11) of Jerusalem to the message of Jeremiah. They of all people should have been most attentive to the message of God, but they were too immersed in protecting their own domains and could not see the truth of Jeremiah's pleas. By the very fact of his submission to such rejection, Jeremiah became a model for the event some six centuries later when Jesus stood before the rulers of Jerusalem and experienced their rejection of his message of repentance (Matt 26:65-68).

Jeremiah's Confidence

Even in the face of such formal and official rejection, however, Jeremiah remained confident in God's commission. Twice (vv. 12, 15) the prophet insists that he had been sent by God himself who became his rock of stability amid all the controversy and rejection. We need a similar source of strength whenever we are rejected for doing the right thing because it is not popular. Confidence in God is never foolish.

ANTIPHON (YEAR II)

Psalm 69:14c

Lord, in your great love, answer me.

Great Love

The original Hebrew for "great love" speaks of an abundance of *hesed*/covenantal mercy (v. 14) as the source for God's favorable response to the psalmist's prayer. Because covenantal mercy is invoked, it follows that the people expect God to respond, and to do so with care for his people. The covenantal obligation to love is reciprocal. It goes both ways!

Watery Depths

The initial verses of the response allude to mire and watery depths (v. 15) and flood waters (v. 30). This provides a perfect prayer for the lips of Jeremiah, who was punished by being thrown into a cistern that could have been dangerous in any sudden rainfall (38:6). Even in that desperate situation Jeremiah retained his sense of trust. Like Paul who sang hymns from his Philippi prison (Acts 16:25) the psalmist sings praise to God's name (v. 31).

GOSPEL

Matthew 14:1-12

Herod had John beheaded; John's disciples came and told Jesus.

Literary Link

After the gospel's summary of the teaching regarding the kingdom and the subsequent rejection at Nazareth, the fourth book (13:54–18:35) deals with the establishment of the kingdom and the type of authority embodied in the community that is called to serve that kingdom. Speaking the truth, training his disciple apprentices, contrasting their call with the other authorities in Jerusalem prepares for his final teachings regarding intracommunity relations (18:1-35).

The Cost of Truth

One can often pay a price for speaking the truth to individuals who are not willing to hear it. Prophets who suggest God's point of view about moral or political issues are regularly rejected and punished, as was John for his challenge (v. 4) to the illicit relationship between Herod and his brother's wife, Herodias. Being countercultural in our contemporary world can result in similar dismissal or mockery. At the same time the truth must be spoken, and spoken with love (Eph 4:15), so that the listener is disposed to hear the message. Arrogant self-righteousness or dismissive contempt on the part of the messenger never accomplishes that purpose. One must love those addressed.

Human Respect

One of the great sadnesses of this story is the fact that Herod realized the terrible mistake of his boastful promise to young Salome (unnamed in Matthew), but could not bear to take it back in the presence of his courtiers and guests (v. 9). Violating one's integrity and one's deeper sense of justice for the sake of public appearances is what

Herod chose as the "lesser evil." Choices of this sort can reveal the hidden weaknesses and idolatries of our hearts. They can demonstrate the prime values to which, when push comes to shove, we are willing to sacrifice everything else. How often we prefer to do what we know is wrong in order to avoid the momentary mockery of friends and colleagues at the office watercooler or corner tavern.

Saturday of the Seventeenth Week in Ordinary Time

Monday of the Eighteenth Week in Ordinary Time

First Reading (Year I)

Numbers 11:4b-15

I cannot carry all this people by myself.

The Book of Numbers

This third scroll of the Pentateuch receives its name because of the census described at the beginning and end of the book (chapters 1 and 26). Between these head counts, the work contains a collection of stories about the temptations and purifications entailed in the people's forty years of life in the wilderness prior to their entrance into the Promised Land.

Revisionist History

Any reader can't help but note the way in which the past, difficult and oppressive as their Egyptian slavery had been, suddenly became such an idyllic existence! Brick making without straw was a terrible life of punishment, but suddenly they only remember the produce of fields fertilized by the annual Nile flooding. Their prior menu (v. 5) became a haunting fantasy amid the arid wilderness of their existence after the exodus into freedom. In one sense, it is a blessing to be able to forget the bad and only remember the good. In another sense, forgetting the difficulties of the past may also include forgetting what we should have learned in the process. Our own murmurings about how "it used to be better" are so often only rooted in imagination rather than in reality. All we have at any moment in life is "now," and our obligation is to find life and grace in this time—in which God remains active and generous in God's own way.

Lament of Moses

This passage contains the prayerful lament of Moses who feels overwhelmed by the constant whining of his people (v. 11). Anyone with a demanding task can move into a self-pity mode, presuming that the entire burden of leadership falls upon one's own shoulders alone. The popular cry for meat, or for any other nourishment than the manna that had become wretchedly familiar, wore Moses down and he complained in turn to God. Complaint in itself can be a recognition of dependence on someone else. It must also become an occasion for doing our part to become part of the solution.

Antiphon (Year I)

Psalm 81:2a

Sing with joy to God our help.

Psalm 81: Israel's Deafness

By ironic contrast, this psalm's exultant rejoicing in God's goodness has often been associated with Israel's festivities of the harvest at the time of Tabernacles and the New Year. It certainly does not echo the complaints of Israel in the wilderness. The psalm's response serves as a reminder of the gift of covenant at Sinai, and the quickness with which that blessing was forgotten (v. 13). The psalm appeals for renewed obedience in order to experience the covenant's blessings again (v. 14).

Singing for Joy

A prophetic word was assumed to have been fulfilled by its very utterance. For that reason, people sing for joy, as the refrain commands (v. 2), because God has already mandated a response to their need (v. 17), even if the fruits of that response are not as yet felt by the people. When African Americans were burdened by slavery, they sang even in hardship because of their confidence. We sing hymns to the God who supplies our need, though not always our immediate want.

First Reading (Year II)

Jeremiah 28:1-17

The Lord has not sent you, and you have raised false confidence in this people.

Hananiah the False Prophet

The fact that Hananiah came from Gibeon (v. 1) was already a signal. The

Gibeonites were infamous at the time of Israel's first entrance into the Promised Land for deceitfully pretending to be distant travelers in order to protect themselves and their interests (Josh 9:3ff.). Not everyone who comes running over the hill with a message from God is a true prophet. Jeremiah suggests caution if the prophet proclaims the words we want to hear (v. 9). Restoring the way it all used to be may not be God's plan. Those announcing woe, war, and pestilence may be the ones really sent by God (v. 8). Community discernment by believers is essential for true obedience.

The Yoke of Domination

Mechanized farming has removed yoked oxen or horses from our modern experience. The prophetic image chosen for Babylonian occupation was the yoke (v. 10), a sign of forced labor, domination, and oppression. Hananiah chose wood to signal its temporary nature, but after prayer and thought, Jeremiah returned insisting on a yoke of unbreakable iron (v. 13). There are circumstances in life that seem to restrain and remove freedom. They may be the result of our own bad choices and ingrained selfish habits, but they may also be sent from God to purify us and to remind us of our dependency on God and each other. Once again community discernment by believers is essential! The yoke offered by Jesus to his faithful followers, however, was one of partnership in the work of the Gospel (Matt 11:29-30).

Monday of the Eighteenth Week in Ordinary Time

ANTIPHON (YEAR II)

Psalm 119:68b

Lord, teach me your statutes.

Psalm 119: An Obedient Community

As often noted, Psalm 119 is an extended meditation of 176 verses on the various forms in which God's law is expressed in our world: ordinances, decrees, and statutes. The category seems primarily legal, but the reality is something interpersonal by which God embraces an entire well-ordered community, not merely individuals. A radically individualistic society like our own tends to reject anything that feels like a constraint on freedom. Good rules, however, bring order to society and prevent harm to its members. The psalm attempts to evoke gratitude from God's people.

Divine Teaching

The true source of God's statutes can only be God, who may, however, use a variety of human instruments and events to convey the truth and justice that is rooted in God's will. God teaches us in many ways, as the refrain points out (v. 68), using our successes and failures, our experiences and our convictions to communicate God's truth and "best practices" for a successful life. Everything we might use to teach children or to train new employees can be the means chosen by God to teach us as well!

GOSPEL

Matthew 14:13-21

Looking up to heaven, he said the blessing and gave the loaves to the disciples, who in turn gave them to the crowds.

Literary Link

The cowardice of Herod at the festive banquet that tragically led to the martyrdom of John (14:3-12) is contrasted with the compassion of Jesus (vv. 13-14) and the multiplication of loaves to feed the five thousand in the wilderness (vv. 15-21).

The Limited Compassion of the Disciples

As Matthew recounts the story, it is the disciples who come forward to point out the needs of the crowd for nourishment. They seem, however, to presume that the crowd should take care of themselves (v. 15). Perhaps the recognition of the meager resources of the men and women traveling with Jesus was the reason for their expressing the need to send them away. The text doesn't seem to include any attempt on the part of the disciples to survey available help before suggesting the crowd's dismissal. Their compassion was not linked to any sense of self-sacrifice or sharing. They are kind enough to see the problem, but without the imagination to seek a different solution.

The Partnership of the Disciples

With clearly eucharistic overtones, especially in the "rubrics" of the prayer of Jesus prior to the distribution of the five loaves and two fish (v. 19), Jesus insists that the disciples act as the distributors of the food. The disciples both distribute the pita breads and gather the leftovers (v. 20). Behind the wording of the early church's memory of this event was their regular practice of gathering for Eucharist and feeding the hungry members of that community as well as outsiders in need. The participants in any contemporary celebration of Eucharist bear the same shared responsibility for the hungers of our world as well. Only a Eucharist without walls is Eucharist in the full sense!

Tuesday of the Eighteenth Week in Ordinary Time

First Reading (Year I)

Numbers 12:1-13

Not so with my servant Moses! Why, then, did you not fear to speak against him?

Jealousy among Leaders

The marriage of Moses to an Ethiopian woman (v. 1), presumably different from a daughter of Jethro (Exod 2:21), is indicated as the occasion for the jealousy of Aaron and Miriam. They felt further marginalized from central leadership by that development. They seem to have presumed that their own call to leadership implied total equality and complete identity in function with Moses (v. 2). Their self-centeredness ignored the diversity of contributions made by various community members and leaders. The fact is that priests and prophets made different contributions to the spiritual well-being of God's people! A small side note might be pastorally helpful, namely, that the biblical witness of the Scriptures never gives any indication of racial discrimination or superiority. An Ethiopian, or Cushite as they were once called, would have come from an African background. Diversity of skin color, however, seems not to have even been noticed in Israel or their surrounding neighbors.

The Uniqueness of Moses

The special friendship between God and Moses, also expressed in Exodus 33:11, is a recurring theme in the Pentateuch. This was a special gift from God that surpassed that of prophecy (v. 7). The face-to-face communication and relationship extended by God, however, did not make Moses arrogant or give him a sense of superiority (as contrasted with Miriam and Aaron). The wonder of that gift rendered Moses meek (v. 3) before the utter grace of God. True meekness is self-imposed gentleness in exercising leadership. Meekness merits a beatitude of its own (Matt 5:4). True charity, as the apostle Paul pointed out, is not jealous, nor does it seek its own interests (1 Cor 13:4-5). Moses even prayed for Miriam to be forgiven and cured of her leprous punishment (v. 13).

Antiphon (Year I)

Psalm 51:3a

Be merciful, O Lord, for we have sinned.

Psalm 51: A Prayer for the Envious

In this liturgical context the church's great penitential psalm is offered to Aaron and Miriam, providing words for their sorrow and repentance, as the refrain indicates (v. 3). They were asked to change their minds about their relationship to Moses and his relationship with God. The refrain could also serve as a prayer for anyone in the modern eucharistic assembly troubled with thoughts of jealousy against some other person in the community of believers. God chooses whom God chooses.

Divine Mercy

The conflated character of the refrain (v. 3) leaves the precise reference from the original somewhat in doubt. That mercy is probably rooted in the Hebrew *hanan*, the gift that makes people attractive and once again objects of God's favor. The refrain offers the entire assembly an opportunity to accept the sin of Aaron and Miriam as its own. The eucharistic congregation thus begs forgiveness for every form of jealousy and for all other sinful attitudes toward others.

First Reading (Year II)

Jeremiah 30:1-2, 12-15, 18-22

Because of your numerous sins, I have done this to you. See, I will restore the tents of Jacob.

The Diagnosis

This passage is clearly divided into two distinct sections in our Lectionary, eliminating any references that might distract hearers. First there is God's command to write down the message of judgment

(vv. 1-2) and then the clear recognition of the wounds and running sores (vv. 12-13) of the people of Jerusalem and Judea. A physician's diagnosis may be shattering. God's judgment is based upon truth. Truth is sometimes very painful (v. 15), and not always easy to hear.

The Promise

As dreadful as Jeremiah's message was to proclaim, and as burdensome as it made his life, judgment and condemnation was not God's last word. Again here, and in sharp contrast to the prophet's negative words, God also envisions a future age of restoration and prosperity (v. 18) with political leaders of their own (v. 21), not merely those who had been imposed by Babylonian occupying armies. The unmerited renewal of the covenant, as articulated in the mutual relationship of God and people (v. 22), is also Jeremiah's proclamation!

ANTIPHON (YEAR II)

Psalm 102:17

The Lord will build up Zion again, and appear in all his glory.

Psalm 102: A God of Second Chances

Ignoring for the moment the character of the penitential lament expressed in the first portion of this psalm (vv. 1-11), the Lectionary chooses instead the latter section, that is, praise for God's willingness to redeem the people and restore the buildings of Zion (v. 17). The refrain celebrates that divine intent. This in turn echoes the promise of Jeremiah's second portion of the reading, and provides words of praise for God's goodness and compassion (v. 22). Every good prayer, as Origen once reminded his second-century contemporaries, begins with praise.

God's Glory

In the faith of Israel, God's actions are focused on the reality of our concrete physical world. The plans of God for the salvation of his people are never isolated or separated from physical realities such as the beauty of Jerusalem and the buildings of the temple in Zion (v. 17). The God of Israel "will be what he will be" (see Exod 3:14), and that reality is intimately associated with the physical history and needs of God's people in this world!

GOSPEL

Matthew 14:22-36

Command me to come to you on the water.

Literary Link

Having established the creative power and authority of Jesus in yesterday's feeding of the multitude (vv. 15-21), Matthew now continues by illustrating that same power over other elements of creation, including the waters of the sea (vv. 25-33), which had a perennially ominous character in the minds of the ancient Israelite nomads.

Divine Authority

Jesus is presented as walking on the crashing waves of a terrible storm at sea (v. 25). Although the English translation somewhat hides the reference, the self-identification of Jesus, namely, "it is I" (v. 27) is in fact the citation from the divine title "I AM/*ego eimi*" in Exodus 3:14. Jesus thus reveals himself to those in desperate need of salvation and protection. Within the literary context of this portion of Matthew's gospel, Jesus demonstrates that he does indeed possess God-given power and authority, which he can delegate to his disciples and their successors throughout subsequent future generations. The church's response should be humble service, never arrogant authoritarianism.

Matthew's Peter

This gospel insists on presenting a figure of Peter as impulsively good, fearfully weak, and very vulnerable. There is no arrogance in Peter's servant leadership. Peter is described as identified with the weak and needy of whom he is a prime example. As an ultimate test of the authenticity of Jesus, Peter suggests the command to join him in walking on the waves (v. 28). It's almost as if Peter knew that Jesus habitually invited partnership in the impossible, at least from a natural standpoint. Typically Peter then wavered and began to sink (v. 30), especially when he realized the perilous situation into which he had thoughtlessly stepped out of his lack of full foresight. Humble and total confidence in God who makes all things possible remains an essential characteristic of anyone who would accept the role of leadership in the Christian community. "Take courage" is Christ's command (v. 27), both before and after the invitation to join him.

Tuesday of the Eighteenth Week in Ordinary Time

Wednesday of the Eighteenth Week in Ordinary Time

First Reading (Year I)

Numbers 13:1-2, 25–14:1, 26a-29a, 34-35

They despised the desirable land (Psalm 106:24).

The Grace of Reconnoitering

It was by divine request that representatives were sent forth to check out the proposed gift of a new land (v. 1). God seeks partners, not servants, and desires free acceptance from those to whom gifts are given. God asks us to test out the graces given so that we may understand them and make them our own. The forty days spent checking out the land (v. 25) is symbolic, since that biblical number regularly represents a period of time for special preparation prior to a great gift from God: days of Moses on Mount Sinai, years in the wilderness before entering the land, time of Elijah on Horeb before the renewal of Israel, days of temptation in the desert before Christ's public ministry, days after the resurrection. In contemporary American culture a fortieth birthday is sometimes celebrated with playful black crepe, but nothing could be further from the truth from a biblical perspective!

Original Sin?

Curiously, each of the major theological traditions woven into the Torah makes a point of describing some initial event in which Israel seriously questions or rejects the grace of God. Here the land is reported as indeed rich and bountiful (13:27), but is rejected by the people out of fear due to the reported size and might of its inhabitants. The people forgot that God had provided the power for their escape from Egypt. They did not believe that God would continue to work for the welfare of his people in an exercise of his divine covenantal fidelity. Could one not label this initial rejection as an "original sin," preparing for a history of habitual rejection? The forty years of preparation became punishment and purification.

Antiphon (Year I)

Psalm 106:4a

Remember us, O Lord, as you favor your people.

Psalm 106: Sin upon Sin

Psalm 106 describes the history of Israel's salvation, but with a sharp focus on their repeated acts of rejection and sinful rebellion (vv. 13-14). This is an appropriate response to the first reading, as the psalmist accuses his people of their ancient sin but also recalls the way in which Moses interceded for them (v. 23).

Ironic Refrain

The refrain (v. 4) is almost sarcastic here, ironically presuming that everything is fine between Israel and their God. As the chosen verses of the responsorial psalm indicate, however, God is angry and doesn't favor his people at all. Nevertheless, God is faithful even when we are not. The refrain reminds us of that truth.

First Reading (Year II)

Jeremiah 31:1-7

With age-old love I have loved you.

The Book of Consolation

After Jeremiah's harsh judgment against Israel and Judah, and especially immediately after his letter to the exiles (chap. 29) in which he commands them to settle into their alien land of residence for the long haul, this promise of loving restoration is a surprising and very welcome message (v. 3). Scholars debate the history and literary unity of these chapters and wonder to what degree Deuteronomy's theology of covenant influenced the renewed bond between God and his people (v. 1). God chose Israel, not because of their merit, but because of his love. The God of Israel always ends communication on a high note of hope, no matter what the background or prior history of sin may have been. Our God is a God who is determined to save (v. 4)!

"Age-Old Love"

The love that God describes as his own for his people is "*ʿolam*/age-old" (v. 3) or "everlasting," literally, "of the unfolding world." As history develops over the centuries, certain patterns of God's actions are regularly repeated often enough to be viewed as characteristic of God. No matter what happens, somehow God can figure out a way to be forgiving and faithful. Even in light of all the harsh prophetic judgments and condemnations, such as those announced by Jeremiah, God remains the faithful God of "mercy/*hesed*" (v. 3) and is ever eager to work around the sins of his people.

ANTIPHON (YEAR II)

Jeremiah 31:10d

The Lord will guard us as a shepherd guards his flock.

The Response

The response, taken from the verses immediately following the first reading, originally promised that God would bring home the northern tribes that had gone into Assyrian exile some hundred years earlier. But the text now includes God's care for the Babylonian exiles of Jeremiah's time, as well as those of us living far from the home of our heart's desire.

A Personal Memory

Wednesday of the Eighteenth Week in Ordinary Time

Some years ago I spent an afternoon amid the ruins of Jeremiah's home town of Anatot, where I noticed a shepherd guiding his flock over a hill and then stopping at a major highway to wait for traffic. I watched in horror as a small lamb dashed across the highway directly in front of an oncoming truck, only to be rescued at the last second by the vigilant shepherd who, with the crook of his staff, snagged the lamb's rear leg and yanked her to safety. With a new respect for the practicality of the shape of the staff I thought of all the situations from which God's providence saves us each day.

GOSPEL

Matthew 15:21-28

O woman, great is your faith!

Literary Link

Within this gospel's fourth book about the establishment of the kingdom and its church, Jesus cures outsiders to the northwest (Gennesaret, 14:34-36) and the Canaanite woman to the northeast (15:21-28). Moreover, between these accounts the gospel deals with the cleansing traditions of the Pharisees and the need for internal and intentional discipleship, not merely external compliance and cleaning (vv. 1-20)!

Targeted Audience of Jesus

As Jesus noted, his primary concern has been the "lost sheep of the house of Israel" (v. 24). Toward that end he was presented as a prophet of renewal and reformation within Israel. Suddenly the pleas of the Canaanite woman seem to change his mind! Jesus sparred with her but then reached out to her needs. Given the fact that Matthew's gospel was somehow rooted within his community of Torah-observant and Gentile Christians and embraced both segments of believers at that time, this new concern for Canaanites makes sense. Did Jesus change his mind, or was this simply the right time, the *kairos*, for a second phase in his ministry?

Dyspeptic Disciples

Although Mark's is the gospel most inclined to dismiss the disciples as misunderstanding and misguided, we have several instances of narrow-minded followers of Jesus in Matthew as well. They attempt to send the hungry ones home (14:15) and the little ones away (18:6), either because they couldn't be bothered or didn't have the means to respond. Their attempt to get rid of this pesky woman (v. 23) fits that pattern. The temptation to dismiss the aggressively persistent is all too great. But keep knocking, said Jesus, "and the door will be opened" (7:7).

Thursday of the Eighteenth Week in Ordinary Time

First Reading (Year I)

Numbers 20:1-13

Water gushed out in abundance.

A Desperate Thirst for Water!

The contrast between their situation in the wilderness and the former abundant waters along the Nile River in Egypt and the succulent produce harvested there remained a temptation for Israel. It was so easy to think back to the past with yearning for its blessings (v. 5). Their time in the wilderness was intended to bring them to a new sense of utter dependence upon God, but their first response as a people was grumbling. Nostalgic memories only heightened the contrast and increased their thirst. We easily become impatient over what we do not have at the moment. The very element through which they fled in terrified fear during their escape from Egypt now became their deepest need. God has a sense of humor about us. Stories like this became part of the pattern used by Christians to describe baptism (1 Cor 10:4) and the entrance into the new creation it heralds!

The Sin of Moses and Aaron

The reprimand and punishment given by God to Moses and Aaron for their infidelity (v. 12) seems to come out of nowhere and remains puzzling for readers of all generations. A common explanation, though one that seems to require imagination and exegetical effort, is the fact that they struck the rock twice (v. 11), possibly out of doubt, rather than once out of obedience. That proposal can only be a conjecture because the text seems deficient. That such needed water should come out of the improbable rock (v. 11), however, suggests again that God can and will do the impossible when needed!

Antiphon (Year I)

Psalm 95:8

If today you hear his voice, harden not your hearts.

Psalm 95: Prayer before the Rock

The ancient Jewish tradition of the Mishnah associates this psalm of praise with the New Year festival, and thus with gratitude for the autumn harvests. The verses chosen by the Lectionary begin with a very appropriate reference to the Lord as a "rock" of salvation (v. 1), thus alluding to the rock from which the water came at the command of Moses.

Hard Hearts

The refrain's reference to their hard hearts (like rock?) at Meribah and Massah in the desert (v. 8) clearly refers back to the very episode described in the reading, and rebukes the people for their facile forgetfulness of God's prior beneficence over the years. The mighty works of God are themselves also a pattern (v. 9), as is the forgetfulness of Israel a sin against trusting confidence in God. Do we experience some of that same forgetful hard-heartedness in our own time? The irony is that the very hard-heartedness once ascribed to the pharaoh in Egypt now becomes the sin of the people in the wilderness!

First Reading (Year II)

Jeremiah 31:31-34

The days are coming when I will make a new covenant with the house of Israel and I will remember their sin no more.

Renewed Covenant

In this classic oracle of Jeremiah, the prophet presumes that the same teaching/*torah* (not a new teaching!) will be placed in renewed hearts (v. 33). This nuance is important for understanding the essential relationship and bond between Judaism and Christianity, at least as Christians have come to understand the text. Interiority, forgiveness, and a new direct relationship with God will characterize this renewed covenantal union with the Lord. Jesus appropriated this text as having special significance and implications for the meaning of the Eucharist since the words over the wine (Luke 22:20) contain explicit references to this oracle. "Renewed," not "new," is the point of the promise. Judaism has not been rejected in favor of Christianity.

Need for Teachers

Early Christianity saw themselves in this oracle from Jeremiah, but that did not lead them to an immediate dismissal of teachers from their midst, even though the prophet had promised no further need for them (v. 34). Jesus recognized the teaching authority of the scribes and Pharisees who sat on the seat of Moses (Matt 23:2). Among the gifts given by the Spirit one repeatedly finds that of teaching (Eph 4:11). True teachers not only provide explanation and instruction but they also give witness by the quality of their lives to the effect of God's presence in their world. Paul considered himself called to be "preacher and apostle and teacher" (2 Tim 1:11). In our contemporary parish communities, qualified dedicated teachers and catechists can rightfully be recognized as engaged in the most important lay ministry of the church!

ANTIPHON (YEAR II)

Psalm 51:12a

Create a clean heart in me, O God.

Thursday of the Eighteenth Week in Ordinary Time

Psalm 51: The Grateful Prayer of the Forgiven

Psalm 51 has become the preeminent prayer of the church for forgiveness and new beginnings. As such, its reference to a fresh start makes it the Lectionary's perfect response to Jeremiah's oracle (v. 12). The fact that Jeremiah envisions the insertion of God's instruction into the depths of the human heart also makes this prayer most appropriate as a preparation for that gift. Jeremiah's oracle had promised the forgiveness of sin (v. 34), and this psalm celebrated that gift.

Clean Heart

The refrain's prayer for a purified heart (v. 12) serves as a reminder of the fact that the heart was considered the place where human planning and decision making occurred. The gift of God's cleansing grace produces a new sense of purpose and the ability to make decisions according to God's priorities.

GOSPEL

Matthew 16:13-23

You are Peter, I will give you the keys to the Kingdom of heaven.

Literary Link

The Lectionary has chosen to omit several events: a summary report of the healing ministry of Jesus (15:29-31), the feeding of the four thousand (vv. 32-39), the request of the Pharisees for a sign (16:1-4), and the warning of Jesus against the leaven of the Pharisees (vv. 5-12). Therefore, a preacher may miss the gospel's contrast between the "leaven/teaching" of the Pharisees and Sadducees (v. 6) to be avoided and the "teaching/confession" of Peter regarding the person and mission of Jesus (vv. 13-20) to be accepted.

Peter's Profession of Christ

In response to the question of Jesus, Peter speaks in the name of the Twelve and confesses Jesus as "Christ" and "the Son of the living God" (v. 16). An earlier version of the New American Bible chose to separate those two phrases by a "he said" in order to distinguish the actual historical confession of Peter from what may have been a slightly later articulation of the church's faith regarding the nature and mission of Jesus. The singular and preeminent sonship of Jesus as a profession of trinitarian belief took some time to reach its full expression. Peter is reprimanded because his confession of Jesus as the Christ is still inadequate. Peter refuses to recognize the role of suffering as the only acceptable path to final glory (v. 22)!

Christ's Confession of Peter

Peter's faith, impulsive though it may have been, has become the cornerstone of our Catholic sense of the church (v. 16). At the same time, the centuries of post-Reformation polemic have made these verses about Peter as the rock foundation of the church (v. 18) and the keeper of the keys (v. 19) into a sort of "canon within the canon." The verses should, however, also be nuanced and balanced by other texts such as Peter's need to be strengthened (Luke 22:31-32) and forgiven for his denial (John 21:15). Nevertheless, this passage reveals a profound truth: one's vocation is ultimately articulated from within the community of belief, never in an individual and isolated fashion. Jesus asks Peter about his own mission and responds by defining Peter's vocation in turn.

Friday of the Eighteenth Week in Ordinary Time

First Reading (Year I)

Deuteronomy 4:32-40

For love of your fathers the Lord chose their descendants.

The Book of Deuteronomy

After a few selections from the book of Numbers, the Lectionary now turns to this final book of the Pentateuch/Torah, which includes the final summary of the teaching of Moses as Israel pauses before entering the Promised Land. The mighty acts of God are recounted a second time (hence the book's name, which means a "second law"). In fact, this summary, as finally edited, looks back at Israel's history through the later experience of exile. In that light Deuteronomy introduces the six books of Deuteronomic history, namely, Joshua through Second Kings, and recounts the tragic consequences of Israel's historic disobedience to God's covenant.

The Singular Actions of God for Israel

Moses is remembered as inviting Israel to look backwards in order to appreciate the unique actions of God on their behalf: the communication on Sinai (vv. 33 and 36), the election of Israel as his own people, as well as the signs and wonders of the exodus (v. 34). We live life forward, but understand it backwards! In the midst of daily life we rarely see the pattern, but in retrospect things fall into place for us. The regular pattern of our contemporary prayer should always include a look backwards and a familiar litany of gratitude for what God has done for each of us as individuals and as communities. If the actions are unique, so is the God who performs them. There is no other (vv. 35 and 39).

God's Motive: Love

Purely and simply out of his love for Abraham and Sarah, God chose their descendants (v. 37) as his own people. In the Semitic mentality at least three generations are always included in blessings and curses. Here the contemporaries in the sixth through eighth centuries BC are addressed as still chosen because of that initial divine love. Biblical "love" is not romantic in our modern sense but practical and focused on concern for the object's well-being. One can easily see how false is the assumed dichotomy between the God of anger in the first covenant and the God of love in the second (New Testament). True love includes truth, and does not shrink from recognizing the faults and failings of the beloved. Scholars point out that Deuteronomy's use of the word "love" is borrowed from ancient political treaties in which the partners promised to love each other. For that reason, sentimentalism is excluded, and care for the common good is always included.

Antiphon (Year I)

Psalm 77:12a

I remember the deeds of the Lord.

Psalm 77: God's Deeds of Old

After some words of lament (v. 3), Psalm 77 turns in verse 12 to recall all the wonders done by God through history. The purpose is not to wallow in a sort of pity under the theme of "it used to be better," but rather to provide a foundation for expecting that God might renew the pattern of historical goodness in a new age of wonders (v. 14).

Remembering

The Semitic concept of remember (v. 12) does not allow the things recalled to remain in the past as objects of awe but makes them present again. It is this same anamnesis that explains the perennial presence of the paschal mystery in the daily celebrations of the Eucharist. They are not repeated (as if the death of Christ were not sufficient) but are renewed and "stretched into the present moment" for the benefit of present generations of believers and disciples!

First Reading (Year II)

Nahum 2:1, 3; 3:1-3, 6-7

Woe to the city of blood!

The Book of the Prophet Nahum
After eight days of readings from Jeremiah, the Lectionary moves to the pronouncements of one of Jeremiah's contemporaries, Nahum, a prophet of the seventh century BC who detested the Assyrians because of their legendary cruelty and exulted over the destruction of their capitol, Nineveh, in 612 BC.

Consummate Joy Over the Destruction of Evil

Like popular jubilation at the end of any war, especially if achieved by victory, Nahum cannot contain his rejoicing (v. 7). Older parishioners can recall the celebration at the end of World War II and the popular rejection of the horrors perpetrated by the Nazis. They should bring that memory to their hearing of this prophecy. The sounds of ancient warfare are duplicated and echoed through this poetic text of wheels, horses, and chariots (v. 2). As children of a later age, we hear this reading and we are invited to share the exhilaration of that historic moment. The prophetic issue for Nahum is triumph over evil, not the pain of people out for revenge.

Restoration

The passage speaks of the renewed peace and prosperity of Judah (2:3) before describing the brutality of war (3:1-3). It might seem more logical to transpose the two interrelated realities, but the current order of the text highlights the contrast and shows God at work. Peace is described in terms of bucolic imagery, that is, tender vines growing again in a new springtime (v. 3) after the jubilation of the news of Nineveh's destruction. That detested city of Nineveh is the same site that evoked so much disgust from Jonah and impelled him to run the other way when called by God to give the people of that city a second chance. God's restoration is larger than the human heart and includes nations we would not choose. God sent his son to save, not to condemn (John 3:17).

Antiphon (Year II)

Deuteronomy 32:39c

It is I who deal death and give life.

Deuteronomy 32

As the book of Deuteronomy comes to a conclusion in its account of the death of Moses, it offers a summary of God's gracious and mighty actions for Israel (vv. 1-14), Israel's ungrateful idolatry (vv. 15-29), and the eventual destruction of Israel's enemies (vv. 30-43). It is a few verses from that latter portion that the Lectionary utilizes for its response to the announcement of the fall of Nineveh. The response describes God as the God of justice (v. 36) and vindication (v. 41).

Death and Life

A common motif in prophetic writings of that age was the recognition that death and life, hurt and healing (v. 39), evil and good all somehow come from the hand of a single transcendent God. If there is only one Supreme God, then everything, directly or permissively, comes from that one source. Second Isaiah says the same thing repeatedly as well (45:7). To put it differently, God has everything to do with everything! Even hardships and sorrows in retrospect can be viewed as times of grace and growth because they come from a God who wishes the salvation of his people.

Gospel

Matthew 16:24-28

What can one give in exchange for one's life?

Literary Link

Immediately after Peter's confession (v. 16) and the correction of Jesus regarding the necessity of suffering as part of his mission (v. 21), Matthew added the first passion prediction of Jesus (vv. 21-23) as heard in yesterday's gospel reading. Now Matthew follows up with the teachings of the cost of discipleship.

The Cross

Undoubtedly influenced by the later actual circumstances of the tragic execution of Jesus, all major difficulties of life are presented in the words of Jesus as symbolized by a cross (v. 24). We each have our own. It is easy to turn someone else's sufferings into a piece of artistic jewelry, but its reality remains severely painful and traumatic. Whatever difficulty in our own lives that we would change in an instant if we could, but remains beyond our control, is what we are invited to describe as our "cross." By embracing that hardship with trusting confidence, we are saved by God's grace. Eventually spiritual maturity may even bring us to say a word of thanks for our crosses!

Personal Death and Final Coming of Christ

Time is very relative, as any child knows who impatiently waits, seemingly forever, for Christmas or birthdays! Jesus was perceived by his followers, both before and after his resurrection, as an eschatological prophet, someone announcing the end of the age and the inception of a new creation. One of the early church's primary challenges was the delayed return of the Master (v. 28). They gradually came to understand that his Second Coming was to be an experience first for the individual through personal death and only latter after an extended time for the entire world's population. The prediction of a second coming prior to the physical death of people in the historical audiences of Jesus reflects that initial Christian conviction, and proves that these teachings are somehow rooted in the words of Jesus himself. "[T]aste death" (v. 28) is used here negatively in contrast with things desired so greatly that we say we can almost "taste" them!

Friday of the Eighteenth Week in Ordinary Time

Saturday of the Eighteenth Week in Ordinary Time

First Reading (Year I)

Deuteronomy 6:4-13

You shall love the Lord your God with all your heart.

The *Shema*

This reading begins with the great prayer of Judaism (vv. 4-5), which extols exclusive loving devotion due to Yhwh, the Lord of Israel's covenant. By Jewish custom this prayer is repeated several times a day, and the devout Jew hopes to die with the words of this prayer on his lips. A small copy of this creed is inserted into the *mezuzah* (literally, "doorpost"), an ornamental metal container attached to the doorposts of every devout Jewish home. It is displayed for personal veneration when entering or leaving home. Jesus, echoing the great rabbis of his day, taught that the *Shema* embodied the first of the great commandments, namely, love of God. Like many of the rabbis, he also added love of neighbor (Lev 19:18) as the second great command (Matt 22:34-40). This prayer insists on the fundamentals of faith to which we must return regularly. The entire person is swept into this response, heart (where thinking and planning occur), soul (where vitality flourishes), and strength (literally, one's possessions).

Everything Is Gift

The reading continues with a list of all the blessings that will be experienced upon entering the land, none of which were the work of their hands and all of which were received as gifts: cities (v. 10) together with homes, cisterns, vineyards, and olive groves (v. 11). Seeing everything as gift is precisely the attitude commended by the first beatitude of the Sermon on the Mount, that is, being "poor in spirit" (Matt 5:3).

Antiphon (Year I)

Psalm 18:2

I love you, Lord, my strength.

Psalm 18: David's Faith

This psalm is a royal thanksgiving attributed to David and repeated in 2 Samuel 22. It affirms David's abiding love for God (vv. 2-3) and commemorates God's gift of deliverance and victory over enemies (v. 51). Ingeniously the Lectionary thus suggests that David's legendary devotion is but an echo of the great Mosaic teaching and witness, even with the colossal moral failures of David so well documented in the Bible's writings. These verses of response represent David's human attempt to live out the *Shema* prayer in response to God's goodness.

The Refrain

By selecting this verse as a repeated refrain (v. 2) for congregational use, the liturgical response to the *Shema* echoes the theme of love for God and connects a title for God, namely, "Strength," with the human quality that should measure the generous extent of our response to God, "with all your strength" (Deut 6:5). God is the source of any strength we might use in measuring our own response to his love for us!

First Reading (Year II)

Habakkuk 1:12–2:4

The just, because of their faith, shall live.

The Complaint

Habakkuk gave voice to the just person's perennial complaint about the wickedness of evil people and their prosperity (v. 13). This prophet's lament is suitable for every age, and for every generation that must in turn supply the specifics to fill in the blanks. There are those who arrogantly treat others, especially the poor and vulnerable, like fish to be caught (v. 14) and exploited (v. 15), then stupidly and idolatrously worshiping the net (v. 16). Habakkuk insists that such people are objects of contempt. Habakkuk sees it all so very clearly, and wonders why God can't do likewise (v. 1)!

The Book of the Prophet Habakkuk

This prophecy was written by the prophet Habakkuk, a contemporary of Jeremiah who dared to question the way God governs the world, and to challenge God's apparent willingness to tolerate injustice and violence without intervention. Habakkuk's solution is simply, hold on to the vision (2:2).

Living by Faith

God's response as cited by the Lectionary in this passage is twofold. First Habakkuk is reminded kindly but firmly that the vision should be held firmly because it will have its own day and time (vv. 2-3). The act of holding on to the vision in tough times is perennially good advice and wisdom. Then the prophet is told that a truly just person lives by faith (v. 4), namely, with trusting confidence. Because of that faith, a person who is truly just will live to eventually experience victory. This verse became a major truth in the apostle Paul's debate about salvation by faith rather than good works (Rom 1:17) in mere obedience to the law.

Saturday of the Eighteenth Week in Ordinary Time

ANTIPHON (YEAR II)

Psalm 9:11b

You forsake not those who seek you, O Lord.

Psalm 9: Praise for a Kingly God

This psalm with its partner, Psalm 10, is a song of praise for the divine king and his victory over enemies and opponents. It celebrates his royal enthronement. In singling out God's care for the oppressed members of the covenant (v. 10) and his willingness to hear the cry of the poor (v. 13), the psalm serves as a divine response to the complaint of Habakkuk, and a rebuke to human leaders who do otherwise.

Seeking God

The refrain acknowledges the people who seek God (v. 11) from the midst of their doubt, ignorance, persecution, and sorrow. In the world of first-century Judaism and in the New Testament, "God seekers" are those who have great respect for the high morality and strict monotheism of Judaism, yet are not quite able to embrace all its practical precepts such as the kosher diet or circumcision. That God would not forsake these slightly marginal folks who have not as yet become actual practicing members of the covenant was a blessing. The same term could rightly be applied to all believers still on their journey through life in this world, living with their own personal mixture of belief and unbelief.

GOSPEL

Matthew 17:14-20

If you have faith, nothing will be impossible for you.

Literary Link

The complaint of Jesus about faithless and perverse generations (v. 17) could be a logical follow-up after the story of the transfiguration (17:1-8) and the subsequent discussion of Elijah (vv. 8-13), who struggled with similar generations in his day. Both are omitted by the Lectionary, which moves from the conditions of discipleship (16:24-28) to the healing of the boy (17:14-20). Similarly, the complaint of Jesus about the little faith of his disciples (v. 20) is a preparation for Matthew's second passion prediction (vv. 22-23). Note that the best manuscripts omit the verse referring to driving such demons out by "prayer and fasting" (v. 21) as a later borrowing from Mark 9:29.

A Parent's Care for a Child

One cannot help but be moved by a parent's desperate concern for his son (v. 14). The Greek calls the poor boy a "lunatic," namely, someone afflicted by the moon (v. 15). The anger of Jesus seems uncharacteristically harsh, somewhat similar to his equally puzzling response to the Canaanite mother two chapters earlier (15:21-28) whose faith he had praised. Matthew's account changes the focus from the poor distraught father (Mark 9:14-29) to the disciples whose lack of faith is excoriated, not the father. Most parents worry, pray, and sacrifice for their children; they never stop worrying but simply worry about different things as the children grow older. This father turns to the believing community for help, and it is the members of that community who should offer more help than they do.

Faith the Size of a Mustard Seed

As Jesus sees it in this healing story, even a minimum of faith can be part of "moving mountains" (see v. 20). From the rebuke given to Peter (16:23), this gospel continues to note the lack of faith among the disciples of Jesus. The pastoral challenge of this story is the need to avoid giving the impression that any miracle could happen if the petitioners had sufficient faith. It is God who cures and possibly moves mountains, not the disciples. Our task is to trust in God who can do what seems impossible if that is truly for our benefit. God responds to human needs, not necessarily to our wants. Desperate parents do not need another layer of guilt over things not under their control!

Monday of the Nineteenth Week in Ordinary Time

FIRST READING (YEAR I)

Deuteronomy 10:12-22

Circumcise your hearts. Befriend the alien, for you were once aliens yourselves.

Fundamental Human Behavior

With consistent teaching Deuteronomy returns often to four interrelated fundamental norms for our human response to our God: reverential fear or awe, loving concern, service to the divine will (v. 12), and obedience to specific commandments (v. 13). This list is similar to the way in which the prophet Micah answered the same question in his day: What does God ask of you? (6:8; love justice, do kindness, be humble). Both the response of Micah and that of Deuteronomy could well serve as a daily examination of conscience. What other human response is conceivable in the face of the fact that the God of the highest heavens has chosen Israel (v. 15) as his own?

The Neediest of Neighbors

After addressing our relationship to God, the text then turns to our human neighbors, and offers the three classic examples of the most vulnerable and needy members of society: widows, orphans, and aliens (v. 18). Each case represents someone bereft of the normal family support systems that would provide care. Israel is commanded to provide that care to such members of the covenant. Each group mentioned in the reading offers an opportunity for homiletic recommendations to support our contemporary efforts to protect children, support the elderly, and treat immigrant aliens justly. Aliens are singled out for special care by Deuteronomy, with the additional motive of remembering that such was once their own situation in Egypt (v. 19). Caring for immigrants makes one an image of God.

ANTIPHON (YEAR I)

Psalm 147:12a

Praise the Lord, Jerusalem.

The Blessings of God

The verses chosen for this response list the major gifts of God to his chosen people: urban security (v. 13), peace and abundant harvests (v. 14), as well as the gift of his commandments (v. 19). These are the blessings granted to those who obey the will of God as described in today's reading from Deuteronomy.

Jerusalem

The mindset of ancient Israel was fundamentally communal, as contrasted with the radically individual culture in which we contemporary Americans live. Thus it is the entire city that is invited to praise God (v. 12) in grateful response for being the focus of God's love, generation after generation. The words of Moses are addressed to contemporary generations, whichever they might be in succeeding ages. All successive generations are invited to consider themselves citizens of Jerusalem. These are the ones invited to sing communal songs of praise to God who chooses Israel forever! Our community is larger than those we might see at morning Mass because it includes past, present, and future.

FIRST READING (YEAR II)

Ezekiel 1:2-5, 24-28c

Such was the vision of the likeness of the glory of the LORD.

The Inaugural Vision

Although Isaiah and Jeremiah might regularly describe the immense military power of Assyria or Babylon as generic "enemies from the north," Ezekiel chooses to identify that same ominous threat with the movement of God who rides hostile chariots and makes them instruments of his punishment! God appears surrounded by storm winds, flashing fire, and strong metallic gleam (v. 4). The normal din of armies (v. 24) is projected upon heavenly beings that always accompany God's presence described in human form, clothed and surrounded by the fiery splendor of the rainbow (v. 28). The vision again illustrates the utter impossibility of adequately describing the glory of God in human language. Every attempt stutters and falls woefully short. Spiritual writers tell us that every single human being at some time or other experiences a profound sense of God's presence. Idols were forbidden, so Israel used words to describe the indescribable.

The Book of the Prophet Ezekiel

Ezekiel was a contemporary of Jeremiah. They both witnessed the tragic destruction of Jerusalem and its temple by the Babylonians. Moreover the priest Ezekiel was forced into exile together with his colleagues in 597 BC. Influenced by the figure of Elijah, Ezekiel was overwhelmed by the transcendence of God and the horror of idolatry on any level.

Human Response

What happens when a human being encounters the living God? The ancients claimed that no one could live after such an experience, as noted in the story of Samson (Judg 13:22). Certainly something of one's prior convictions or assumptions must die! Pre- and postvision "Ezekiels" were different personalities. A new burning conviction filled his spirit once the "hand of the LORD" (v. 3) came upon him in such a manner. The community must test such visionaries and seek the positive moral qualities that inevitably mark the effects of such experiences. By their fruits you will know them.

ANTIPHON (YEAR II)

Psalm 148:12 + Isaiah 6:3

Heaven and earth are filled with your glory.

Refrain

Contrary to its customary practice, here the Lectionary does not use a verse from the psalm response as its refrain, but rather composes a new acclamation comprised from a reference to divine majesty above heaven and earth (Ps 148:12) and the cry of the seraphim from Isaiah's inaugural vision (Isa 6:3).

The Psalm Response

The verses chosen from Psalm 148 to respond to Ezekiel's vision describe different groups of people that comprise all of Israel: princes and leaders (v. 11), young and old (v. 12). All are now summoned to join their voices in a chorus of praise. One could add an extended litany of other contemporary groups from within our own society also being invited to join that same heavenly choir with us.

GOSPEL

Matthew 17:22-27

They will kill him and he will be raised.
The subjects are exempt from the tax.

Literary Link

Perhaps it is the prior reference to the dangerous demons and mysterious inner forces harming the boy (v. 15) that led the editors of Matthew's gospel to add the second passion prediction (vv. 22-23) at this point in the text. Similar demonic forces in society converged to oppose Jesus and to attempt to kill him. The story of the temple tax may have been added to show the unwillingness of Jesus to antagonize temple authorities over the wrong issue.

Second Passion Prediction

Jesus lived with the conviction that the authorities in Jerusalem would eventually find his ministry too dangerous for the status quo, and would attempt to still his voice and remove his presence. There is value in comparing this brief prediction with the more extended elements found in its predecessor (16:21-23). There we read references to the city of Jerusalem, to suffering at the hands of Israel's elders, chief priests, and scribes. Here more succinctly Jesus sees himself handed over to human beings (v. 22) and killed before being raised (v. 23). Jesus saw this rejection as necessary on some level. The finest of the church's spiritual writers always note that no one enters heaven without scars. In contrast to Mark's disciples who didn't understand (9:32), these disciples experience grief (v. 23).

Taxes

Faithful Jews were expected to pay a special tax for the temple upkeep beyond the required taxes to imperial Roman authorities. It was a mark of Jewish identity, and therefore the early disciples voluntarily paid that tax as a sign of respect for their religious and ethnic heritage. The custom was even recognized by the emperor as legitimate. Behind the question of the collectors (v. 24) is the issue of whether Jesus considered the temple administration legitimate. Several groups such as the Essenes did not. Many even fled to the desert in protest against the political corruption of the day. The gospel points the question of obligation to Simon Peter (v. 25), perhaps in an effort to help Peter understand the specific nature of the one whom Peter had just confessed as the Christ and "the Son of the living God" (16:16). Putting aside for a moment the extraordinary fishing venture (v. 27), Jesus indicates that he has so totally assumed human nature as to even take on the burden of taxes! Those who refuse to do so in our times can come across as less than full disciples of Jesus. The incarnation embraces everything human except sin (Heb 4:15).

Monday of the Nineteenth Week in Ordinary Time

Tuesday of the Nineteenth Week in Ordinary Time

First Reading (Year I)

Deuteronomy 31:1-8

Be brave and steadfast, for you must bring this people into the land.

Succession of Joshua

Perhaps Moses simply died outside the Promised Land, and that death was later interpreted as the result of God's decision that Moses could not enjoy that blessing because of his prior association with the people punished by forty years in the wilderness. In any case, his right-hand colleague Joshua became the man of that hour (v. 3) and God promised to work in tandem with him. This was evidenced by the fact that Israel is told that both God and Joshua will "cross before you" (v. 3). Leadership is chosen by the force of history within which God works invisibly and often indirectly. What happens is willed by God, either permissively or directly. Each generation has its own task to do, and each task requires its own skills and strengths.

Being "Brave and Steadfast"

The same admonition is addressed both to the entire people (v. 6) and to Joshua as an individual leader (v. 7). Similarly both are reminded that in fact it is God who marches before them and will never abandon them (vv. 6 and 8). Ultimately it is God alone who leads his people, no matter which human figure may stand in that role. Human leadership shares the same strengths and weaknesses as the people who are led. The very same command will be given to Joshua again (Josh 1:7). These words of Moses also provide an opportunity to speak of the characteristics required for true leadership in any age: knowledge, competence, the ability to inspire and motivate, a sense of vision for the future, and a compassionate bond with the people being led.

Antiphon (Year I)

Deuteronomy 32:9a

The portion of the Lord is his people.

Psalm Response

The Lectionary has chosen the song of Moses as its response to the speech of Moses, thus highlighting the greatness of God (v. 3), especially as expressed in the stories handed down from prior generations (v. 7). The God of Israel and of Christianity is a God of history (v. 8), as our Creed illustrates so well, ever active in marching with his pilgrim people and shaping their experiences along the way.

God's "Portion"

The refrain (v. 9) insists that the entire people of Israel represent the hereditary portion that became God's "special possession" (Exod 19:5). Separated from the rest of the nations, Israel belongs to God in a unique manner, almost like an inheritance, to be accepted and cared for throughout all generations. It is almost as if God gives himself that gift. Anyone who has ever received a bequest from a relative or friend should again ponder that experience and find insight into the metaphor of "inheritance" selected by the Lectionary for this refrain.

First Reading (Year II)

Ezekiel 2:8–3:4

He fed me with this scroll, and it was as sweet as honey in my mouth.

The Word as Nourishment

Part of Ezekiel's inaugural vision as a legitimately authorized prophet was to receive a message written on a scroll and to be commanded to eat the scroll (v. 1). Chewing on papyrus or parchment seems neither enjoyable nor nourishing. Nevertheless, because it was the message of God, it initially tasted sweet (v. 3). Because God's word gives courage, stamina, purpose, energy, and direction, it does strengthen and nourish those who receive it on many levels. In John's gospel, the bread of heaven refers both to revelation and to the Eucharist (John 6).

Mission

The Lectionary passage concludes with God's command to go to the house of Israel and to speak the given message (3:4). Even though the communication initially seemed sweet, one should not forget that the words written on both sides of the scroll were bitter "[l]amentation and wailing and woe!" (v. 10). This task would in fact be neither easy nor sweet for Ezekiel and for the people so stubbornly hard-hearted and unwilling to see the gathering storm around them.

Antiphon (Year II)

Psalm 119:103a

How sweet to my taste is your promise!

Psalm 119: Praise for God's Commands

Once again this entire and lengthy psalm is an extended meditation, sometimes tediously repetitious, on the laws and teachings of God. This impression is to a large extent the result of the fact that Psalm 119 is structured alphabetically with eight verses devoted to each letter of the Hebrew alphabet. Even an inspired writer has difficulty dedicating 176 verses to the topic. Each verse taken separately may be worthy of meditation, but the entire work is somewhat overwhelming.

Tuesday of the Nineteenth Week in Ordinary Time

Sweet Promises

Promises can be sweet if they are positive and offer something deeply desired. False promises can, however, be very attractive for that same reason. The promise of punishment is not so welcome. The Lectionary has chosen this verse as the refrain (v. 3) in order to reflect the command given to Ezekiel and the sweetness of its initial flavor.

Gospel

Matthew 18:1-5, 10, 12-14

See that you do not despise one of these little ones.

Literary Link

The fourth book of Matthew's gospel (13:54–18:35) deals with Christian authority from different aspects and concludes with this fourth discourse on concern for aspects of community life (18:1-35). The liturgical passage omits the obligation to remove hands or feet that lead to sin (vv. 6-9), and prepares for dealing with community members involved in sin. This keeps the focus of the reading on children and on the wandering weak.

Children as Models

Because Jesus repeatedly recommended children as models for the type of person who qualifies for entrance into the kingdom of heaven (Mathew's respectful way of avoiding the use of the name of God), it is always valuable to pause for an exploration of the characteristics so praised: dependence, curiosity and openness to learning, desire to assist, lack of self-importance, and absence of false pretense. Children are models (v. 3) with whom Jesus himself identifies (v. 5), and therefore should never be despised (v. 10) or lost (v. 14). This illustrates the unspeakable tragedy of sexual abuse of minors in the church and in society. Note that these "little ones" (v. 6) refer not only to the chronologically young but also to recent converts and innocent newcomers into the community of faith.

Lost Sheep

From the beginning Jesus considered the lost sheep of Israel to be the special object of his ministry (15:24). Here in parable form Jesus suggests that a special focus for the exercise of authority in the Christian community should be those who no longer live their lives in accordance with the primary norms of discipleship (vv. 12-14). By application those who do not live "kingdom lives" should be sought out and encouraged, and that same concern is extended to the "little ones" (v. 14) who enter the community but then wander off for any number of reasons. Without being judgmental, a parish community at Eucharist should be mindful of those no longer present for whatever reason.

Wednesday of the Nineteenth Week in Ordinary Time

First Reading (Year I)

Deuteronomy 34:1-12

There Moses died as the Lord had said, and since then no prophet has arisen in Israel like him.

Vision but No Entrance

With generosity and as a sign of special friendship, God showed Moses the entire land that would be given to Israel (v. 1). We are reminded that there was no other prophet in all Israel's history like Moses, whom God knew face-to-face (v. 10), and that Moses had no equal in signs and wonders (v. 11). God's friends always have some sense of the future, whether they actually see and share it in their own lives or not. They live with a deep future orientation. Then Moses died in full vigor at the age of 120 (v. 7) and was buried in an unmarked grave of a ravine in the land of Moab (v. 6). Thus both Moses and Elijah shared mysterious, though differing, fates. As human beings we long for the future, hoping that our children and our projects will continue as we desire, but the future is never in our hands or under our control.

Joshua the Successor

Again we are reminded that Joshua was the chosen successor of Moses, and we are told that he was filled with wisdom (v. 9), namely, the practical ability to do things well. The imposition of hands has been a ritual for the call to leadership from ancient biblical times. It may be helpful to remember that this gesture is not one of delegation or of authority given outwards to others, but rather of drawing the recipient into the authority of the one who extends hands. Hands are laid on a sacrificial animal to associate the victim with the person seeking renewed relationship with God. The hand of God is upon prophets (Ezek 1:3) to signal their new association with God. A similar dynamic is expressed in any Christian ritual of imposition of hands, be it the gift of the Spirit at confirmation and ordination or the gift of forgiveness.

Antiphon (Year I)

Psalm 66:20a and 10b

Blessed be God who filled my soul with fire!

Psalm 66: Testimony to God's Goodness

This psalm is a combination of community praise for God's majestic glory (v. 1) and the praise of an individual helped by God in distress (v. 16). As such, its verses are a fitting response to the report of God's dealings with Moses. The words could also serve as individual hymns of praise from Moses and Joshua for what God has done for them (v. 16). Anyone could easily and rightfully make these words one's own.

The Refrain

The combined phrases used for this refrain are interesting, especially since they are taken from verses not used in the Lectionary. The initial beatitude from verse 20 is directed to God who has neither rejected prayer nor removed grace. The rest comes from verse 10, which, however, has no reference to fire in the Hebrew text except implicitly as the presumed manner of purifying silver. The New Vulgate has made it explicit by adding the word "*igne*/by fire." What we have in this refrain, therefore, is a concrete testimony to the way in which generations, cultures, and languages over the millennia have shaped the prayers we use.

First Reading (Year II)

Ezekiel 9:1-7; 10:18-22

Mark a "Thau" on the foreheads of those who moan and groan over all the abominations in Jerusalem.

The Mark of the "Thau"

In preparation for the destruction of Jerusalem, God summoned an individual scribe or professional letter writer to carry his portable equipment through the city and mark the forehead (v. 4) of everyone who opposed and lamented the idolatry practiced in that place. The thau/cross, therefore, became the sign of everyone to be saved from destruction and death (v. 6). It is easy to see how this letter of the alphabet became associated with the cross of Jesus, and then with salvation from final damnation. The same ritual gesture has been incorporated into the church's ritual for the sacraments of baptism and confirmation. It is regularly renewed by each person who prepares to hear the gospel in the Western Latin liturgy. To bless ourselves in this fashion is to remind us of the salvation promised by God to his faithful. Ezekiel's witness has touched us all!

The Departure of God's Glory

The day's reading concludes with a brief description of the glory of God enthroned above majestic cherubim rising to depart from the temple (vv. 18-19). Originally the cherubim were mythical temple or palace guardians imaginatively composed of the head of lion or man, the body and legs of lion or bull, and the wings of dragon or eagle. They were fearful creatures. Their departure represented the reverse of the earlier action when God had filled that same temple with his glory at the time of its consecration (Exod 40:34). It was a moment of tragic sorrow. Although God is eternally present to everything that exists by the very fact that it exists, God is only uniquely present as he wills, and can always choose to be somehow distant if deeply offended by sin. We may never take that special presence of God for granted as if it were our due. Entitlement is wrong, no matter where it may be found. God will be God.

Antiphon (Year II)

Psalm 113:4b

The glory of the Lord is higher than the skies.

Psalm 113: Invitation to Praise

Again we hear exuberant praises for the majesty of God from east to west (v. 3) and from below to above (v. 4). The psalm strikes a note of universality in its attempt to trace the origins of the world's praise and to document the fact that such praise is right and just. One could easily add other spans of measurement such as from each continent, each nation, each historical generation, and so forth. The point is the psalm's desired inclusiveness of everyone in the chorus of praise for God!

Heavenly Glory

In placing praise for God's glory in the highest of the heavens, the refrain (v. 4) invokes spatial categories to express divine supremacy. The "highest of heavens" is beyond our reach and our intelligence except in most generic terms. The poetry of religious experience uses spatial and temporal categories to express divine immensity and transcendence. The point is praise, not cosmology. The measurements of science belong to a very different realm of human thought.

Gospel

Matthew 18:15-20

If your brother listens to you,
you have won him over.

Literary Link

Immediately after the parable of the lost sheep for whom the community has responsibility (vv. 10-14), Matthew proceeds to describe the sequence of interventions to be followed when initially confronting a "lost sheep," namely, an errant member of the community (vv. 15-20). This in turn will prepare for tomorrow's parable of the unforgiving servant who receives forgiveness but is adamant in refusing to extend that same forgiveness to others (vv. 21-35).

The Proper Sequence in Addressing Unacceptable Behavior

The offended Christian is directed to first speak to the offender privately and directly (v. 15), and then, if that proves ineffective or fruitless, to bring witnesses in a private fashion (v. 16). Only in the last resort should the entire community be brought into the discussion. So much community hurt and turmoil could be avoided if this sequence were always followed. Confidential letters of complaint to superiors without speaking with the alleged offender often seriously violate this evangelical process. In that first step the facts of the matter need to be clarified, and then only after determining what actually happened should one proceed to explore the intention or purpose of the accused individual's action. Respecting the sequence prevents so much heartache and community division!

In the Midst of Two or Three

Popular piety often applies this mention of the Lord's presence in the midst of two or three disciples (v. 20) to the practice of prayer, and that is certainly correct. Upon closer study, however, the intent of this particular verse in its context would seem rather to be that of making community judgments about the misconduct of a member. Christ is present in the midst of those who confront the sinner. God is at the heart of our human, and therefore necessarily tentative, judgments regarding the negative behavior of others. It is God who provides the love that should be the motivation for our action.

Wednesday of the Nineteenth Week in Ordinary Time

Thursday of the Nineteenth Week in Ordinary Time

FIRST READING (YEAR I)

Joshua 3:7-10a, 11, 13-17

The ark of the covenant of the LORD will precede you into the Jordan.

The Book of Joshua

This biblical work was shaped by the same Deuteronomic theology as that of the book of Deuteronomy and the books of Samuel and Kings. Against the background of God's fidelity to his people, the initial campaigns of military action are described as victorious. They are used to justify later claims of political jurisdiction by the Davidic dynasty.

Miraculous Crossing of the Jordan

Any student of the Scriptures cannot help but see the similarity between the way this crossing of the Jordan is described and the accounts of the earlier crossing of the Red Sea with waters stopped like massive walls (v. 13; Exod 14:22). Scholars suggest that the parallelism was developed to show the continuity of God's saving presence, but also to incorporate other newer groups that had joined Israel during their forty years in the wilderness. Israel was a combination of several diverse tribal groups, each with its own religious history and its own experience of the Lord/YHWH! At issue is the welcome of newcomers into Israel's salvation history.

John the Baptist

Over a thousand years later John the Baptist summoned the people of Judah and their leaders back to the Jordan for a baptism of repentance (Matt 3:5). So many compromises had been made and so many national sins of apostasy had been committed since that first moment of God's gift of the land. John summoned them back to the very point of their initial and purer response to God's gift. His hope as reformer was that Israel could be restored to new innocence and thus begin all over again as God's chosen people! Jesus himself shared John's baptism and thus also the history of his people.

ANTIPHON (YEAR I)

(Multiple References)

Alleluia!

Psalm 114: Creation Astonished

This short song of praise celebrates the exultant joy of creation (v. 4) at the time of Israel's exodus from Egypt. The psalm thus provides a very fitting response to the crossing of the waters of the Jordan, including a playful interrogation of the waters (vv. 5-6) to determine why they had run away from God's intervention. Desert nomads lived with fear of the sea and considered it somehow associated with evil. It was banished from the new creation (Rev 21:1).

The Refrain

Although not appearing at all in this particular psalm, the refrain's joyful shout of *HalleluYAH* is most appropriate—literally, "Praise [you all] Yah" (a shortened form of God's personal name), the expression is found at the end of the next psalm (115:1) and frequently throughout the entire Psalter. For Christians, the words mark the entire paschal season. Communal praise, reflected in the plural form of this verb, is one of the most important forms of prayer.

FIRST READING (YEAR II)

Ezekiel 12:1-12

You shall bring out your baggage like an exile in the daytime while they are looking on.

Prophetic Signs

Prophets not only spoke their messages verbally but they also sometimes acted them out in symbolic gesture or movement. Ezekiel is commanded to pretend publicly and in bright daylight that he was desperately gathering a few precious possessions and secretly digging his way out of the clay walls of his own home (v. 5) to escape the approaching Babylonian armies. Ezekiel is further ordered to say that he was himself "a sign for [them]" (v. 11). Elsewhere, in a curious tale about his burning beard, Ezekiel was commanded to say, "This is Jerusalem" (5:5). People were angered because they were convinced that any such symbolic action by a prophet actually initiated the eventual action itself and made it inevitable. One can see in gestures like this the biblical antecedents for the prophetic action of Jesus at the Last Supper when he broke the bread, saying, "this is my body" (Matt 26:26). The "sacramental" sign creates the reality. God uses human actions to instruct, warn, and promise.

Israel the Rebellious House

Ezekiel's prophecies often simply characterize Israel as a family of rebellious people (vv. 2, 9), refusing to cooperate or obey well-known commands of God. To receive such a pejorative label from God is itself a condemnation and a punishment. Most individual members comprise a more complicated texture of response, but in general, the prophet describes them as he sees them, and the single word is not complimentary! Are there any single words that could be used for the worshiping eucharistic community at your parish? How would others, perhaps neighboring families or congregations, describe the parish and its members?

Antiphon (Year II)

Psalm 78:7b

Do not forget the works of the Lord!

Thursday of the Nineteenth Week in Ordinary Time

Psalm 78: The Price of Rebellion

The verses selected for the response continue listing the sins of God's people that Ezekiel condemned in the reading: rebellion and disobedience (v. 56), infidelity (v. 57), and idolatry (v. 58). As a response to God's gift of the land (v. 55), it was a shameful expression of ingratitude.

The Refrain

In contrast to the historical behavior of Israel, the refrain (v. 7) sounds like a desperate plea to remember God's mighty deeds, and to respond in gratitude and fidelity. A recitation of past beneficence was always an initial section of any covenant text. The Ten Commandments began with a reference to Israel's redemption from Egyptian slavery (Exod 20:2). Thus the request to keep history in mind is also an invitation to return to Israel's covenant partnership with God. Our own salvation history should make us equally grateful and faithful today.

Gospel

Matthew 18:21–19:1

I say to you, not seven times
but seventy-seven times.

Literary Link

As in his confession of the nature of Jesus (16:16) and the inquiry about paying tax (17:24), Peter continues to act as a spokesperson for the group (18:21). The question of the obligation to confront an erring fellow community member (18:15) leads logically to the question of recidivism. How often should one confront and forgive? Peter wants to explore the limits of patience and charity. This in turn prepares for the parable of the unforgiving servant (18:23-35).

The Number Game

Of itself the number seven implies a certain universality: three being the superlative in Hebrew as in "holy, holy, holy," and four expressing universality as in the four directions. As a matter of fact, the Greek phrase (v. 22) can be correctly translated as either "seventy-seven" (NAB, NRSV) or "seventy times seven" (KJV, RSV), hence the differences among contemporary English translations. The subtle biblical background for the cipher is found in the number of times Cain forgave (seven) as compared with Lamech (seventy-seven), who was remembered as a mighty avenger (Gen 4:24). Whether it be 77 or 490, the point is that there can be no limit to human forgiveness. The parable (vv. 23-35) highlights the fact that our forgiveness should mirror that of God!

The Measure of Love

At the same time, forgiveness should be extended out of genuine love for the sinner/offender. There can be a point when repeated forgiveness becomes enabling and reduces the possibility of true conversion or change in behavior. The "tough love" response to alcoholism or domestic abuse may at times be the best form of Christian love. Determining what is truly in the best interest of the offender can be difficult.

Friday of the Nineteenth Week in Ordinary Time

First Reading (Year I)

Joshua 24:1-13

I brought your father Abraham from the region beyond the River; I led you out of Egypt, I brought you to your land.

Historical Review

After Joshua's farewell speech (23:2-16), he summoned all the tribes of Israel to the great sanctuary at Shechem (v. 1) for the first great covenant renewal ceremony in the land that the Lord had promised and given to his people. As an initial section of the covenant renewal, Joshua again recites the major elements of the history of their salvation. We read them carefully because they are compositions by the author who reveals his theological perspectives woven throughout the entire book. In any age the same history told by different people will reveal their individual values and concerns. Joshua as Israel's leader uses the traditional prophetic messenger formula of "Thus says the Lord" (v. 2), and speaks in God's name. The word "I" (the Lord) appears fifteen times within this short summary—an effort to state as clearly as possible that God is personally active in all of Israel's history. The same God continues to be dynamically present in ours as well.

"Holy" War

Repeatedly during these summaries, the biblical text refers to the way in which God accompanied the Israelite people and fought for them (v. 8). God demanded faithful and devout soldiers who obeyed the Torah. God gave the victory to such an extent that all the spoils of warfare belonged to God. All living inhabitants, as, for example, at Jericho (Josh 6:21), were to be killed: men, women, and children alike. They had to be destroyed lest they subsequently enter in profane human use. The practice rightfully sounds brutal and repulsive to the modern conscience. Scholars call this entire concept "the holy war." Modern Catholic theories of "just war" have been developed to limit warfare and to impose severe restrictions before any war could be morally acceptable. In the ancient world victorious military warfare was seen as a metaphor for supreme divine power. Moderns have seen the savagery of war too universally and closely; we prefer other metaphors for divine power.

Antiphon (Year I)

Psalm 136

His mercy endures forever.

The Refrain

Psalm 136 repeats this same phrase (v. 1) in each of its twenty-six verses, thus indicating that gratitude is a duty before each of the constant saving interventions of the Lord throughout history. Killing enemy kings and hostile opponents over the centuries has been seen as expressions of divine presence and protection for his people. Generations after generations of God's chosen people encountered opposition that God removed by his grace, mercy, and power. Refrains are intended to emphasize an idea and to help interiorize a value.

Mercy

The precise quality acknowledged so repeatedly in this response is *hesed*, the mutual concern that flows from the covenant. In that relationship God promised to care for his people, and recommended that they similarly care for each other. That same concern has been exercised again and again throughout history unto this very present age.

First Reading (Year II)

Ezekiel 16:1-15, 60, 63

You are perfect because of my splendor which I bestowed on you; you became a harlot.

Sexual Infidelity

With a harshness that is even crude at times, Ezekiel has chosen to describe in very graphic terms Jerusalem's physical growth (v. 7) and eventual turn toward idolatry/prostitution. In similar expressions as found in Ezekiel 23, the prophet described Judah's covenantal disobedience as harlotry, and condemned that infidelity as if it were a violation of marital bonds. Accurate translation is challenging because of the crudity of the language at times. Perhaps the recurring popularity of fertility cults provided the occasion for the metaphor, but it is strong and unavoidable in its message. Because of the perennial prophetic relationship between religious infidelity and prostitution, some scholars have suggested that the challenge of Jesus to the Samaritan woman (John 4) was idolatrous rather than sexual in nature.

Reconciliation

In spite of the strongly worded rejection, the possibility of a renewed relationship remained possible in the view of Ezekiel just as in the judgments of his prior prophetic colleagues. The Lectionary retrieves two verses (vv. 60 and 63) from the end of the chapter to signal available forgiveness and a renewed everlasting covenant again. Like the renewed courtship suggested by Hosea (2:16-25), Ezekiel will not exclude marital reconciliation and renewed love. Somehow, the end is not the end as far as God is concerned! Note that the shorter reading offered by the Lectionary omits the graphic descriptions and concentrates on the new beginning in love (only vv. 59-63).

Antiphon (Year II)

Isaiah 12:1c

You have turned from your anger.

Isaiah's Song of Thanksgiving

Precisely in response to the reading's final promise of possible rediscovered love (vv. 60 and 63), the response borrows the song of thanksgiving from the book of Isaiah (12:1-6). The original context of that song was God's promise to dry up the River Euphrates and the Red Sea so that Israel could return from exile. Isaiah's song of thanksgiving was offered as a hymn for the journey. The Lord is acclaimed as Savior (v. 2) and, in typical Isaian terms, revered as the "Holy One . . . in your midst" (v. 6). Isaiah's God is "holy," namely, different, precisely because he does not act as human beings would naturally and instinctively act in similar circumstances.

The Refrain

That God could turn from his anger (v. 1, not cited in the response itself), even in such a traumatic event as the faithless prostitution condemned by Ezekiel, is judged by the Lectionary as worthy of celebration! Anger can be justified at times because of the gravity of the offense, but forgiveness demonstrates God's even greater strength and mercy.

Gospel

Matthew 19:3-12

Because of the hardness of your hearts Moses allowed you to divorce your wives, but from the beginning it was not so.

Literary Link

After the discussion of authority and forgiveness, the parable of the unforgiving servant (18:21-35) concludes the fourth discourse of the gospel. Matthew then begins the fifth section with a consideration of the question of divorce and its implicit assumption of the need at times for mutual forgiveness in marriage as well.

Motives for Divorce

The Pharisees began the discussion with a question about the possibility of acceptable reasons for divorce (v. 3). It was a much debated issue between the rabbinic schools of Shammai and Hillel. Jesus turns the issue into a discussion of divorce itself, and acknowledges only one reason, that is, *porneia*/unlawful marriage (v. 9). The question was uniquely debated in the community of Matthew because of its combination of Gentile converts who assumed the Roman practice and Torah observant Jews who may have affiliated themselves with a variety of Jewish schools in the matter. The school of Hillel was more liberal in recognizing divorce than Shammai. The Essenes of Qumran seem to have been opposed in principle. In these verses, as well as in the teaching in the Sermon on the Mount (5:31-32), Jesus seems to uphold the indissolubility of every legitimate marriage for Matthew's community. Jesus entered the biblical controversy (vv. 4-5) by upholding the teaching of Genesis 1:27 and 2:24. At the same time, Jesus always welcomed sinners, ate with them, and invited the entire world to enter the society of people engaged in the deep repentance/*metanoia* (4:17) needed by all, whether they are single, married, or divorced!

Reception of the Teaching

The Lectionary passage seems to conclude with the recognition that there are teachings that not everyone is able to receive (v. 12). Perhaps this acknowledgment accepts the difference between the abstract principle and its concrete application (called *ekonomia* in the Byzantine Catholic tradition) to very diverse human situations and lives. All are sinners, and each person has his or her own area of personal need for spiritual growth and reform. We are asked to uphold the ideal and to be compassionate with those who struggle in these areas, just as they are asked to be compassionate with our struggles.

Friday of the Nineteenth Week in Ordinary Time

Saturday of the Nineteenth Week in Ordinary Time

First Reading (Year I)

Joshua 24:14-29

Decide today whom you will serve.

A Covenant with the Lord Alone

Upon entrance into the new land of promise, Joshua felt the need to insist on the unique religious identity of Israel, especially in the midst of people who affirmed different gods in relation to different territories. There was a constant temptation to assume that the fertility of the new land was the result of the blessing of its god, and to follow suit in order to obtain abundant harvests in new territories. Joshua demands fidelity to the God of Abraham, Isaac, and Jacob alone, not to the gods of the land or even to those of their most ancient ancestors (v. 15). The shared voiced response of the people linked themselves irrevocably with the God of the exodus from Egypt (v. 17). As the story unfolds they repeated that allegiance (vv. 18, 21, 24). Joshua died at the age of 110 (v. 29), 10 years younger than Moses (Deut 34:7), to show his beloved but lesser status.

The Stone of the Covenant

A covenant is a relationship, not an agreement. The latter is about some third element that all parties acknowledge, but the relationship is a bond of mutual concern between the parties themselves. The statutes and ordinances (v. 25) written by Joshua were merely the ways in which this new relationship would be respected and lived. A large stone, probably covered by the blood of the sacrifices associated with the covenant ceremony (Exod 24:6), was erected as an enduring witness to the relationship and its obligations (v. 26). In the tradition of Catholic eucharistic liturgy, the altar stone with relics of the saints recalls that ancient covenantal practice of representing Christ, the source of our unity with God through the blood of the cross, and the larger community of holy ones who have been members of the covenanted community over the centuries by reason of that same redemption.

Antiphon (Year I)

Psalm 16:5a

You are my inheritance, O Lord.

Psalm 16: A Convert's Prayer

Although the text is at times corrupt and controverted, this psalm would seem to be a profession of faith in YHWH (v. 1). Thus it serves as a very fitting response to the account of Israel's historic entrance into relationship with the Lord alone. Only from the Lord do the blessings of life (v. 11), sustenance, and security come. Each individual and each successive generation must renew that allegiance and make it its own anew.

Inheritance

The land was apportioned to each tribal group as a gift from the Lord to be held and worked as long as they were faithful to that God. The refrain (v. 5) makes God alone the actual inheritance, received from prior ancestors, and "leased" to each generation in turn for its benefit. To consider the relationship itself as a bequeathed gift is a unique idea. How many people, when making a list of personal valuables for insurance or wills, would list first and foremost their relationship with God?

First Reading (Year II)

Ezekiel 18:1-10, 13b, 30-32

I will judge you according to your ways.

Personal Responsibility

The ancient Semitic world considered tribal membership a primary value. They viewed the value of each individual in the light of that affiliation. Upon birth children were identified as "son" or "daughter" of such and such a person and retained the title throughout life. They saw life as lived under the responsibility of whatever prior generations had done; they even formulated a proverb about sour grapes (v. 2) to express that conviction. Ezekiel chose to counter that easy blame on prior generations by insisting on the personal responsibility of each person for acts of virtue (v. 5) or sin (v. 13). To maintain the sharpness of the point, the Lectionary omits the further example of conversion (vv. 14-22). Ezekiel demands personal accountability for one's life and actions; blessings and punishments come from God to the individuals involved, but the actions have consequences for subsequent generations.

Examination of Conscience

Ezekiel provides a brief listing of sins (vv. 6-9) that a truly just and virtuous individual will avoid: idolatry, adultery together with violations against justice, honesty, compassion, and the duty to lend without usury. These are the things that comprised virtuous living amid Israel's covenant members. If each person drew up his or her personal list, favorite failings could easily be minimized or overlooked. Ezekiel takes no chances and provides a more comprehensive listing. It is worth noting that although Ezekiel was of priestly lineage, he does not mention ritual violations here but restricts his concern to ethical and moral behavior as primary in one's relationship with God and neighbor.

ANTIPHON (YEAR II)

Psalm 51:12a

Create a clean heart in me, O God.

Saturday of the Nineteenth Week in Ordinary Time

Psalm 51: A Plea for Purification

Most fittingly the Lectionary returns to the great penitential psalm for a response to this teaching of Ezekiel. The psalm's acknowledgment of personal sin (v. 5) reflects the fact that everyone stands guilty in Ezekiel's judgment. All live in need of personal penance. No one is allowed to quickly take a position among those fully righteous before God, even though the reading from Ezekiel acknowledges the possibility.

Clean Heart

The verses chosen by the Lectionary for this response seem to focus on new beginnings rather than former sins. This attitude finds expression in the refrain (v. 12). It may be helpful to remember that in Semitic anatomy the "heart" (v. 12) is the place where a person does planning and makes decisions. The "heart" is the place where the Holy Spirit is active (v. 13) to produce humble contrition (v. 19). This inner source of one's motivation for one's actions is precisely what the psalm asks to be purified and renewed.

GOSPEL

Matthew 19:13-15

Let the children come to me, and do not prevent them; for the Kingdom of heaven belongs to such as these.

Literary Link

It is with understandable practical logic that the gospel moves from the question of divorce (vv. 3-12) to concern for children. This also reprises the teachings of Jesus about children as models (18:1-5) and his concern about giving "scandal/a stumbling stone" to little ones (see v. 6). This in turn prepares for the story of the rich young man whose spiritual maturity is tested and found wanting because of his numerous possessions (vv. 16-30).

Children

At the beginning of the discourse marking the conclusion of the fourth section of the gospel, Jesus had proposed children as models of the qualities needed for entrance into the kingdom (18:1-3). The gospel now encourages that those same youngsters become disciples (v. 14), even at an early age, so that the instinctive characteristics associated with their youth might be strengthened and intensified for the benefit of the entire community. It may be helpful to recall that the term "children/*paidia*" could refer to newcomers and converts to "the Way" as well as to the chronologically young. Both groups deserve the blessing of personal contact with Jesus and the encouragement of the rest of the community.

Eligibility for Baptism?

Invoking the benefits of the historical-critical method, it is always useful to seek the issues of the community behind the words of Jesus, which were in turn remembered because they continued to provide illumination and instruction for community questions. Thus it could well be that the issue of whether children of adult converts to Christianity should also be baptized with the entire household was a matter of pastoral discussion. Invoking this saying of Jesus helped to resolve the question in any early community of disciples.

Monday of the Twentieth Week in Ordinary Time

First Reading (Year I)

Judges 2:11-19

When the Lord raised up judges,
they did not listen.

The Book of Judges
In this book twelve heroes are memorialized from the history of early Israel for their military prowess and ability to save Israel in a time of oppression. They "judge" in the biblical sense of intervening to make things better, not merely offering opinions about culpability.

The Nature of God

In abandoning the God who led them out of Egypt (v. 12) for other gods, the children of Israel turned away from the God of history who had accompanied them on their long journey and through their evolution in faith. Instead they choose to worship the Baals and their consorts the Ashtaroth (v. 13), Canaanite gods of fertility and protectors of the annual cycles of harvest and planting. These two alternative options are very different, as are the people who worship them. The God of history has a chosen plan and a purpose, freely selecting partners and instruments toward that goal. The god of fertility is held captive by the annual life cycle of growth and death, unable to move out of what always was and will be. In continuity with Israel, the God of Christians seeks the ultimate transformation of the world in Christ, and us with it.

Consequences

Choosing values of pleasure and agricultural profit in the fertility cults of Canaan, the Israelites lost the protection of the God of the covenant (v. 13). The covenant always included curses and blessings for the human partners depending on their respective disobedience or fidelity. The people of Israel ended up being exploited by surrounding nations (v. 14) who took advantage of their weakness and plundered them of their wealth (v. 15). Choices always have consequences.

Judges

The sign of God's protecting presence was the existence of a series of heroic tribal leaders called judges (v. 16). Twelve such judges were remembered, perhaps to mirror the twelve tribes. They were not judicial figures like our modern courtroom figures but rather skilled military leaders summoned by God in times of special need. In saving the people from the result of their sins (v. 18), these judges were laying a remote foundation and pattern for the incarnation of the Savior. The repeated sequence of sin and salvation formed a tragic pattern of life (v. 19), and demonstrated the people's inherent proclivity to evil. It was a pattern that only God could break from.

Antiphon (Year I)

Psalm 106:4a

Remember us, O Lord, as you favor your people.

Psalm 106: The Sins of the Past

This psalm rehearses the history of Israel's infidelity throughout generations before and after their entrance into the Promised Land. Portions of its recited litany of sins and rebellion have been used elsewhere in the Lectionary. Here we are reminded of idolatry (v. 36) and child sacrifice (v. 37). In a larger sense the particular verses used in this response focus on Israel's reluctance to maintain their own unique religious identity as well as the way they mimicked the nations around them (v. 35), much to their eventual dismay and destruction.

The Refrain

In contrast with the psalm's sad story of disobedience, the refrain (v. 4) takes a phrase from the beginning of the psalm and repeats its reference to God's repeated efforts to begin anew as noted in the last verse of the response (v. 44). The repetition of the refrain echoes the repeated willingness of God to offer freedom and salvation from oppression, even if it was self-caused. Our God is a God who opens up graves, even the ones we dig for ourselves (Ezek 37:12-13).

First Reading (Year II)

Ezekiel 24:15-23

Ezekiel shall be a sign for you: all that he did you shall do when it happens.

Death without Mourning

Ezekiel was commanded to endure a terrible suffering, to forgo any sign of mourning when his beloved wife died (v. 15). The world of ancient Israel expressed sorrow by going bareheaded and barefooted, fasting, and wailing in grief, but this was to be forbidden to Israel (v. 17) when their misfortune would come. The description highlights Ezekiel's affection for his wife and his terrible loss at her death. The point of prophetic instruction was that God would not even mourn at the destruction of the temple, which had been so beloved and treated as the "delight of [his] eyes" (v. 21). It was inconceivable that God should not mourn in such a tragedy; yet God's punishment demanded the destruction of the temple, which God allowed and even commanded.

Prophetic Sign

Prophetic signs were events that anticipated and actually initiated the blessing or punishment announced by God through his spokesperson. The very person of Ezekiel himself (v. 14) became the expression of God's intentions, motives, and purposes. It was a very tough price to pay for being a sign to the people. As a matter of fact, God uses every single one of us, each in our own way, for the instruction of those around us. The texture of our lives should be both personal witness and sources of wisdom for others.

Antiphon (Year II)

Deuteronomy 32:18a

You have forgotten God who gave you birth.

Song of Moses

The responsorial psalm chosen by the Lectionary for the nonmourning of Ezekiel is a portion from the song of Moses, who laments the anger of God over the rebellion and idolatry of Israel (v. 21). God even threatens to hide his face from them (v. 20), to see what a mess they will make of things when left to themselves!

Prophetic Punishment

With typical irony a prophetic judgment usually announces a punishment that reflects and echoes the crime. In this case, the people become a "no-people" for turning their worship to a "no-god" (v. 21). The refrain repeats the charge, namely, forgetting the God who brought them into being (v. 18) and gave them life! Unfortunately, sin and punishment is part of the present as well as a legacy from the past. A cursory contemporary review of our idolatries might remind us of our own guilt.

Gospel

Matthew 19:16-22

If you wish to be perfect, go sell what you have and you will have treasure in heaven.

Literary Link

Perhaps Matthew saw a logical development between the reference to children as immature disciples (v. 14) and the young man who, though an adult, was physically unable to make a full decision for Christ (v. 22). The subsequent parable of the grumbling vinedressers of tomorrow's gospel will describe those who are not able to understand God's goodness (20:1-15). Neither the young man nor the vinedressers can measure up to God's invitation and generosity.

The Problem of "Good Works"

A fundamental problem inherent in the young man's question (v. 16), whether from a genuine spiritual interest or from the mindset of a self-satisfied braggart, was the presumption that anyone could in fact "gain" eternal life by human actions. We do not know the actual motive of the young man; therefore we must be cautious of any presumption in that regard. Eternal life is a gift from God for which one can only prepare and wait in trusting confidence. Often such events and stories point to the issue that became so neuralgic during the sixteenth-century Reformation, namely, whether one's good works gain salvation or whether salvation is pure gift from God alone (Eph 2:9). The good works in a person's life are never the cause for our justification, but rather they are evidence that one has accepted the grace of God!

Obeying the Commandments

It is curious that the commandments cited by Jesus in this story are only those that deal with human relationships (vv. 18-19). The list provided by Jesus deals with murder, adultery, theft, false witness, honoring parents, and love of neighbor. Perhaps the further final admonition of selling all for the poor (v. 21) is intended to open the young man's life to the entire spectrum of human need, and thus to the mystery of God as a fundamental prime value in life! So many of the expectations of life in covenant deal with mutual concern (*hesed*) for other human beings. Once again, we obey, not to win God's favor, but to demonstrate that we have received that favor and live accordingly.

Monday of the Twentieth Week in Ordinary Time

Tuesday of the Twentieth Week in Ordinary Time

First Reading (Year I)

Judges 6:11-24a

Go and save Israel; it is I who send you.

Divine Nicknames

The name "O champion" given to Gideon (v. 12) seems to suggest a secret "nickname" from God, revealing Gideon's deepest personal identity before God and his individual destiny within the plan of God for the salvation of the world. This is something like the name "highly favored one" given to Mary by Gabriel at the time of the annunciation (Luke 1:28). Even Gideon's initial sense of personal unworthiness by way of response (v. 15) seems to suggest an echo of resonance between the two accounts. The fact of the special names for Gideon and Mary leaves us wondering if each of us has a similar name known to God alone.

Gideon

Although Gideon may be the most insignificant of the lowliest of families (v. 15), it is God who provides the strength for his task and the victory for his efforts. God seems to prefer the most unlikely and improbable of human instruments for the achievement of his purposes in order to make clear the true source of success (v. 16). This fits nicely into the perennial pattern of God choosing the unlikely, as in the case of David or Mary, to illustrate the ultimate cause for the victory. See Gideon, but think "God at work!" This also might apply to each of us.

Antiphon (Year I)

Psalm 85:9b

The Lord speaks of peace to his people.

Psalm 85: Divine Blessings

Psalm 85 seems to be a good example of materials composed and used in public worship with the first section (vv. 1-8) addressed to God by priest or congregation, and the second portion expressed in a single voice by way of response (vv. 9-14). Although the specific details can be argued, it seems clear that the psalms were part of Israel's liturgical chants. We even know that after the return from exile, the temple chorus was composed by people called liturgical "prophets" (1 Chr 25:1). The use of antiphons in the renewed liturgy of the church seems to hearken back to the practices of ancient Israel.

Divine Works

The verses selected by the Lectionary for a response to the account of Gideon's call indicate the ultimate purposes that God has in mind: peace (v. 9), kindness, truth, justice and peace (v. 11), agricultural prosperity (v. 13), and salvation (v. 14). Since one understands people by their works, these divine works suggest a very loving and beneficent God in our midst. Perhaps because Israel was under attack from marauding enemies at the time of Gideon, the repeated references to peace (vv. 9, 11) respond to the precise needs of his time.

First Reading (Year II)

Ezekiel 28:1-10

You are a mortal and not God, however you may think yourself like a god.

Condemning the Idolatry of Tyre

The city of Tyre was located about fifty miles south of Beirut. In its prime the city was a major source of commerce, culture, and sea power. Its artisans had made major contributions to Solomon's temple (1 Kgs 5:15ff.). At the time of Ezekiel its prince was resisting the fourteen-year siege of Nebuchadnezzar with a great deal of confident arrogance, hence the prediction of his eventual humiliation and violent death (vv. 7-10). Ancient Solomonic friends became the later target of prophets after the time of Jezebel because she reintroduced the Canaanite gods of Phoenicia to the northern kingdom (1 Kgs 16:31). The sin of Tyre remained its idolatry (v. 9), which became more and more objectionable in the eyes of the prophets.

Human Hubris

Throughout all of human history material wealth and political power have contributed to a false sense of invulnerable supremacy in the human heart. Ezekiel's condemnation of Tyre's leadership was sarcastic (v. 3), alleging for themselves a false sense of wisdom and commercial shrewdness (v. 4). Whenever human beings attribute such false importance to themselves, God brings them down. These oracles are not only directed to the past but also have us in mind, should we exhibit similar arrogance and blindness. Mary's *Magnificat* reminds us that God throws down the mighty and lifts up the lowly (Luke 1:52).

ANTIPHON (YEAR II)

Deuteronomy 32:39c

It is I who deal death and give life.

Song of Moses

Once again the Lectionary chooses the song of Moses for its response to the condemnation of Tyre, particularly those verses that describe God's negative response to self-inflating human arrogance (v. 27). Such pride can only reap disaster and doom (v. 35).

Life and Death

Like the confession of Second Isaiah (45:7) attributing weal and woe to God alone, Deuteronomy acknowledges that both life and death (v. 39) come from God alone. Ultimately they are neither accidents of history nor the results of mindless evolution. This reality of limited human life confronts the rich and powerful. The verse readily becomes a refrain against people like the prince of Tyre or any modern political leader who views his work as self-serving domination rather than service.

Tuesday of the Twentieth Week in Ordinary Time

GOSPEL

Matthew 19:23-30

It is easier for a camel to pass through the eye of a needle than for one who is rich to enter the Kingdom of God.

Literary Link

The Lectionary chooses to separate the private explanation given by Jesus to his disciples regarding riches (vv. 23-30) from the preceding story of the young man (vv. 16-22). This may serve to underscore the fact that the rich man's story is everyman's in its universal applicability to human beings of all time.

The Camel Problem

Although the image of a camel (v. 24) moving through the eye of a needle is very graphic and improbable, it clearly points out again the fact that final salvation is the gift of God alone. Our efforts only prepare the ground of our lives to receive that gift from God. Some scholars have attempted to clarify the image and make it more reasonable by suggesting that the original text was "*kalos*/rope" rather than "*kamilos*/camel," but there is little textual justification for such a reading. The principle of presumption for the more difficult reading should govern the interpretation of this text. The "camel reading" makes the observation of the disciples about impossibility (v. 25) more logical.

Peter's Question

Although Peter's question, What's in it for us? (see v. 27), may seem human enough, it indicates a mindset, however, that remains fundamentally selfish and self-centered, rather than an enduring attitude of love and concern for others. Peter's humanity remains ever present! Because the gospel overturns natural human instincts and values, the kingdom of heaven proceeds along a different path. Like the distance of heavens above earth, God's ways are not ours (Isa 55:9). The exchange of discipleship for thrones of glory (v. 28) is a typical example of the reversal of all things, namely, the rich brought down and the lowly lifted up, as the *Magnificat* heralds (Luke 1:52).

Wednesday of the Twentieth Week in Ordinary Time

First Reading (Year I)

Judges 9:6-15

It is said: The king will reign over us, when the Lord God reigns among you (1 Samuel 12:12).

The Parable of the Trees

This odd parable of the various trees is a sarcastic tale told by Jotham, a rival opponent to Abimelek, who had just been anointed king of Shechem. The tale concerned a series of plants (olive, fig, and grapevine), each asked in turn to become king. Each was clearly limited, and the parable is pointed in underscoring the weakness of the successive candidates and indeed the entire system. Each of the proposed rulers is asked to renounce its own central identity. That automatically disqualifies them for true leadership. None was willing to "wave over the trees" (vv. 9, 11, 13), probably a reference to the pompous ceremonial and arguably useless activity of such kings. A true leader considers the good of others as primary, and one's own benefit as secondary.

Buckthorn

Finally chosen and anointed is the useless buckthorn (v. 15), pretentiously assuming that it had shade to offer and that fire from its scraggly self could consume even the mighty cedars of Lebanon. Scripture is filled with alternative pro- and antimonarchical sentiments that lift up the potential of such leadership but also document the bitter experience of that leadership in practice over the centuries. Deeply conscious of all human limitations, we are invited to beg for the strength and wisdom that only God can and does provide.

Antiphon (Year I)

Psalm 21:2a

Lord, in your strength the king is glad.

Royal Psalm

Although commentators vary in their interpretations, this psalm is probably a generic hymn used repeatedly on the occasion of the anointing and coronation of a new king. Its positive descriptions of royalty, especially in those verses selected by the Lectionary, serve as a counterpoint to the parable of the trees in Judges. References to strength (v. 2), long life (v. 5), and majesty (v. 6) as blessings from God serve to stress God's support for the institution and its ideal practice. In so doing Psalm 21 contributes to the traditions of Israel that found ultimate convergence in the biblical witness to an anointed king/Messiah whom Christians would later acclaim as Jesus of Nazareth.

The Refrain

The refrain (v. 2) simply acknowledges that it is the strength of God alone that confers the blessings of majesty and splendor on any human royal figure. To the degree that every Christian shares Christ's royal character through the anointing at baptism, all can anticipate God's enduring strength in their lives.

First Reading (Year II)

Ezekiel 34:1-11

I will save my sheep, that they may no longer be food for their mouths.

Condemnation of Judah's Kings

Conscious of all the bitter failings and failures of the kings of Judah, with only David, Josiah, and Hezekiah as notable exceptions, Ezekiel condemns them roundly (v. 2). Under the common image of a "shepherd," as kings were called across the entire Near Eastern Levant from ancient times, Ezekiel excoriates them for their many self-serving practices at the expense of the very people they were summoned to protect and nourish. They used milk, wool, and meat (v. 3) from the sheep without feeding, healing, or tending them as was their duty. These royal shepherds are judged by God through the words of Ezekiel, therefore, as irreparably wanting (v. 10). The institution of prophet in Israel exercised a unique voice of criticism and existed as the primary anti-monarchical foil for centuries. For that reason, when the monarchy finally went out of existence after the exile, prophecy vanished from the scene as well. All leadership is blessing and burden; it awaits judgment from a just God.

God's Takeover

In view of the utter failure of Israel's royal shepherds, at least as viewed by Ezekiel, God vows to take over the role directly and personally (v. 11). Perhaps in the light of the exile when the people lived in Babylon without active royal figures, that direct divine governance and guidance was understood as a consolation. God promises to claim his sheep as his own (v. 10), to save them and to pasture them properly. In every age human religious and political leadership is judged by God and punished if found wanting. At the same time, the Letter to the Hebrews encourages prayer and respect for those called to the office of servant leadership (13:7, 17).

ANTIPHON (YEAR II)

Psalm 23:1

The Lord is my shepherd; there is nothing I shall want.

Psalm 23: The Shepherding God

It should be no surprise that the Lectionary would select the famous "Good Shepherd psalm" as the response to the equally famous judgment and promise of Ezekiel. The classical imagery of verdant pastures (v. 1) and restful waters (v. 2) have become literary masterpieces. These references echo what God promised to do for his people in the reading from Ezekiel.

Care for Humans

Wednesday of the Twentieth Week in Ordinary Time

The psalm moves quickly to clarify that it is the individual who is first and foremost addressed as a recipient of God's care. The verses shift to the abundant table and the anointing of hospitality as well as the overflowing cup of prosperity, all indications of divine "kindness/*hesed*" (v. 5). God has obligated himself through the covenant to provide the best of care to those who are faithful to him! One can easily understand why the early church in turn used this psalm as an instruction for the sacraments of initiation. The figure of the Good Shepherd was the favorite artistic image for Christ as found in the catacombs.

GOSPEL

Matthew 20:1-16

Are you envious because I am generous?

Literary Link

Matthew moves from the promise of twelve thrones to those who follow Jesus faithfully (19:28) and the reminder that the first will be last (v. 30) to an illustrative parable that recognizes diversity of human work and the generosity of God. Not all who leave everything to follow Jesus receive the same responsibilities, even if they receive a similar reward.

Divine Justice

Although it might seem unjust from a merely human standpoint that the hired help were paid equally for vastly different amounts of work (v. 14), the equal treatment underscores the fundamental teaching of Jesus that the kingdom is a gift (v. 15), not something we earn by our efforts alone. Grace is given diversely, but that fact does not eliminate the truth that it is given, not merited. Once again we find hints of the true doctrine of salvation through faith and not good works!

Divine Generosity

The utter generosity of God (v. 14) simply will not be outdone, and should never provoke sentiments of comparative rivalry or envy. The fact that some were not hired during the entire day leads to a logical speculation about their physical ability for work. Were they left behind because they were physically weak or limited? Was the equal pay also a recognition of special need? The lavishness of creation in spreading seeds and flowers and fruits points to a God who simply will not be outdone. Parables are primarily about God, not ourselves; for that reason any exegetical effort to allocate the different classes of hired hands or moralizing about their sins risks missing the point of it all.

Thursday of the Twentieth Week in Ordinary Time

First Reading (Year I)

Judges 11:29-39a

I shall offer whoever comes out of the doors of my house as a burnt offering.

Text of Terror

Recent feminist scholars have labeled this story a "text of terror" because of the manner in which the daughter is seemingly disvalued and disposed of by her father (v. 35). It becomes a passage that may be "preached against" rather than proposed as a model or standard for others. The Scriptures witness to a God at work amid the total range of human sin and grace, including the blind spots of any culture. Those blind spots must be confronted in order to serve the fullness of God's truth and justice. Countercultural criticism is an obligation in every age. At stake in this story is the inherent dignity of every individual, the importance of concern for life, the equality of women, and the ultimate nature of God who is not open to bargaining as a way of getting one's human will. The end, namely, reverential obedience to God, does not justify the means. One cannot help pondering the relationship of this story with the account of Abraham's readiness to sacrifice his son Isaac (Gen 22) or Isaac's willingness to distance himself from Rebekah as only his "sister" (Gen 26:7). Promises are serious, but not every promise is morally good. What kind of God would hold a person to a morally bad promise?

Human Oaths and Promises

Is this act of compliance with a thoughtless promise truly pleasing to God and should Jephthah be held bound to it (v. 31)? In dealing with the promise of marriage or any other human moral action, knowledge and freedom are key considerations in determining the validity and binding nature of the action. This tale underscores the seriousness of all oaths and the way in which we should be very conscious of the implications of the promises we make and the prayers we utter. A new situation demanded a reconsideration of the promise. God may be served generously, but badly.

Antiphon (Year I)

Psalm 40:8a and 9a

Here I am, Lord; I come to do your will.

Psalm 40: The Person Who Trusts

Interpreters have noted that this psalm concludes with a desperate cry for help (vv. 13-17). It is the first section of the psalm, however, with its words of praise and thanksgiving that was chosen by the Lectionary as the response to Jephthah's dilemma. Although the refrain (vv. 8-9) stresses the utter importance of giving priority to God's will over our own, it seems ironic that this refrain should follow such a terrible situation, making it look as if Jephthah's decision was automatically equated with that divine will.

Obedience over Sacrifice

It is interesting that a psalm, presumably originating in the public worship of Israel, should relegate sacrifice to second-place status in favor of obedience. When defending his willingness to eat with tax collectors, Jesus cited the prophet Hosea in upholding the importance of covenantal "kindness/*hesed*" over sacrifice (Hos 6:6; Matt 9:13). Elsewhere the Letter to the Hebrews cites this psalm when contrasting the obedience of Jesus with the sacrifices of the temple (10:7). Inner submission is the fundamental human stance before the mystery of God. In this matter Christianity and Islam find common ground.

First Reading (Year II)

Ezekiel 36:23-28

I will give you a new heart and place a new spirit within you.

Proving the Holiness of God

Ezekiel echoes the anguished resolve of God as described by Hosea when God proclaims himself radically different from the common human instinct to punish opponents (11:9). In this passage God's holiness is demonstrated (v. 23) by a divine resolve to give a fresh start to the people in exile. That includes bringing people home (v. 24), cleansing their impurities (v. 25), and giving them an inner new beginning (v. 26). God promises this rather than following a darker human inclination to punish and destroy them. We are called to be images of God's holiness in our reaction to those around us. Destruction can only be a last resort because God promised to respect our decisions and our free will.

New Heart

The promise of a new heart (v. 26) highlights the full import of God's gift. As noted elsewhere, the ancient world considered the heart as the place for human planning and decision making, not romantic sentimentality. A divinely given new heart will assure that all plans will be completely consistent with God's will. The gift of a "new spirit" (v. 27) will enable Israel to abide with ("live with," not merely resignedly "tolerate") God's will. This text from Ezekiel is often used by the church for the liturgical celebration of the sacrament of confirmation. Decisions made by candidates on the edge of adult maturity, since that is how Western Latin Christianity celebrates confirmation, are blessed by the gift of a new heart and spirit. Those who gather for weekday Eucharist today could be invited to renew their respective confirmation commitments to be open to all the gifts of God's Spirit!

ANTIPHON (YEAR II)

Ezekiel 36:25

I will pour clean water on you and wash away all your sins.

Psalm 51: A Fresh Start

The response echoes the theme of cleansing from Ezekiel (v. 25) and uses that verse as the refrain. The congregation is invited to use verses from the great penitential Psalm 51 that celebrate a renewed "clean heart" and "steadfast spirit" (v. 12) as well as the importance of humble contrition over sacrifice (v. 19). This renewal and fresh start as intended by God, however, will not occur without the free agreement of human beings; that's how much God respects our freedom! God offers the help of grace but does not force compliance.

National Renewal

Although our contemporary culture, ecclesial and national, may understand this promise in terms of individual actions, Ezekiel (and the entire biblical witness) prefers to think communally and socially. It is the whole nation that will be purified as part of the return from exile in Babylon. The refrain's "you" (v. 25) is inherently plural, signifying all of Israel, and not merely an aggregate of individuals. What would a national spiritual renewal look like in our culture? How can the worshipers at a morning Eucharist be occasions and instruments of such a new Pentecost?

GOSPEL

Matthew 22:1-14

Invite to the wedding feast whomever you find.

Literary Link

The Gospel of Matthew immediately follows Wednesday's parable of workers hired at different times of the day (20:1-16), with a third prediction of the passion (vv. 17-19). Curiously, however, the Lectionary omits that prediction, as well as the request of James and John for special places (20:20-28) and several parables. Perhaps the solemn entrance into Jerusalem (21:1-11), the cleansing of the temple (vv. 12-17), and the parable of the tenants who treated the Master's servants so brutally and shamefully (21:23-42) were judged more appropriate for later Lenten proclamation. Therefore the Lectionary has chosen to follow the parable of the grumbling hired help (Wednesday) with today's parable of the wedding guests who were unworthy of their invitation (22:1-14). Grumbling help and ungrateful guests have much in common with our resistance to God's grace.

Religious Leaders or General Populace?

Jesus' parable of the wedding feast was addressed to the chief priests and elders of his day (v. 1). It was a logical development from the debates of prior sections (21:45). A wedding in any community would have made sure to invite its prominent leadership. Passages from the gospel often begin with Jesus speaking "in reply" (v. 1) and lead the hearer/reader to be curious about the question that might have produced such a parable. The teaching of Jesus in this parable becomes universal by reason of Matthew's final general concern for all nations (28:19). All are invited by God into family friendship and into the final celebration of the victory of the Son of Man!

Fifty Ways to Say "No"

Ignoring the invitation (v. 5), demeaning the credibility of the messenger, or simply mistreating them (v. 6) may be typical human responses to God's invitation. The human heart is perennially skilled in finding ways to avoid demands that might force a change in personal comfort or lifestyle. Fortunately God loves us even more than we love ourselves and seeks ways to turn the "no" into a "yes."

The Problem of the Wedding Garment

The additional teaching about proper attire (vv. 11-14) adds a different question to the mix. This portion of the parable always seems unfair because it calls people off the streets and from the midst of their daily occupations, but then condemns the same "come as you are" folks for not being properly dressed. Rather than allegorizing the tale and finding meaning in each of its details, it might be best to simply recognize the fundamental teaching of God's gift and human cooperation with that gift as essential to the way God has chosen to work with us.

Thursday of the Twentieth Week in Ordinary Time

Friday of the Twentieth Week in Ordinary Time

First Reading (Year I)

Ruth 1:1, 3-6, 14b-16, 22

Naomi returned with the Moabite daughter-in-law, Ruth, to Bethlehem.

The Book of Ruth

The Lectionary contains two readings from this book, which locates its history in the time of the Judges, exemplifies family loyalty, prepares for the Davidic dynasty, and reflects a positive attitude toward outsiders. That latter teaching contrasts with the more closed notions of Ezra, for example, who counseled separation from non-Israelite spouses after the exile.

A Time of Famine

It was the experience of famine (v. 1) that drove Naomi and her family from Bethlehem, and the subsequent abundance of harvest in the same land that then brought them home again (v. 6). God can bring many blessings from hardship and times of want. Relearning dependence upon God and each other is one of the positive lessons from simplicity of life, even if forced by circumstances beyond our control. Every year there are enormous areas of famine in our world. We are asked to feed the starving as if we were feeding Christ himself (Matt 25:35). By extension the physical hunger of Naomi's family might be similar to the hunger for word and sacrament that draws people to the daily Eucharist.

Family Loyalty

Ruth's choice to remain with her mother-in-law Naomi, even to the point of abandoning her own Moabite family, illustrates her fidelity and enduring love. This is the true family sense of "piety," not sentimental affection. No wonder the statement of Ruth in accepting Naomi's people and their God (v. 16) is used so frequently at weddings to express the new and exclusive bond between husband and wife.

Open yet Faithful Religious Identity

The example of Ruth in accepting Naomi's religious convictions contrasts with the more rigid exclusivity of Jewish identity as found in Ezra (9:1ff.). There are times in history when one's religious identity needs to be sharpened against the challenges of culture, but there are other times when religious narrowness must be broadened. In God's larger vision the covenant with Israel is also for others, not merely for themselves. The people of Israel are chosen from the nations in order to be a blessing for the nations (Gen 12:3). The fact that Ruth, the Moabite outsider, becomes an ancestor of David (4:22) and ultimately of Jesus illustrates that bigger picture.

Antiphon (Year I)

Psalm 146:1b

Praise the Lord, my soul!

Psalm 146: A Saving God

The actual literal verbs of this psalm are present participles. That suggests that care for the poor and oppressed (v. 6), the hungry and imprisoned (v. 7), the blind and bowed down (v. 8) are perennial activities of God in every age. These activities are characteristic of Yhwh, the God of Israel. The story of Ruth illustrates that truth in the concrete circumstances of her time in history.

Refrain

The refrain (v. 1) invites the soul to praise God. Since the word "*nephesh*/soul" literally means "throat," it is logical that praise for God would be vocal. Jewish notions of prayer presume that every physical sense and every human ability would be involved. The refrain, brief as it is, carries a subtle encouragement to full active participation in the actions of ritual and in the religious singing in worship. Silent prayer is not what this refrain is really all about.

First Reading (Year II)

Ezekiel 37:1-14

Dry bones, hear the word of the Lord. I will bring you back from your graves, O my people Israel.

Dry Bones

In a time of utter despair over the loss of everything that assured their distinctive religious identity, namely, land, temple, and Davidic dynasty, Israel considered itself dead and without hope (v. 11). Although the familiar Negro spiritual may exhibit a bit of playful vitality in its rhythm, the fact is that the historical situation as described in the Scriptures was humorless, devastating, and hopeless for everyone. It is precisely the desperation of dry bones (v. 4) that Ezekiel addressed in the name of God, promising a new spirit and a new life (v. 5) to the entire nation, not merely individuals.

Opening Graves

In Ezekiel's words God repeatedly identifies himself as one who opens graves (v. 13). This is even the case with those graves we dig for ourselves by our sins and stupidity. The prophets often warned that all God's gifts would be taken away because of so many grievous violations of the covenant, but God would not be content to allow his great experiment of election to end that way. The primary focus of the prophecy was Israel at the time of exile (587 BC), but its distant shadow had unexpected fulfillment in the tragedy of Calvary. Ezekiel was not speaking of the resurrection, but the words took on a fuller meaning (*sensus plenior*) in the light of that later experience.

Antiphon (Year II)

Psalm 107:1

Give thanks to the Lord; his love is everlasting.

Friday of the Twentieth Week in Ordinary Time

Psalm 107: Water in the Wilderness

This psalm fittingly begins with a powerful description of the parching thirst (v. 5) experienced by those who were lost in the wilderness, desperate for water lest they perish. Such references provide additional background for the dry bones. Images from the devastating pressures of life in the terrible arid regions of our California Death Valley or those of northern Africa or Asia could provide the backdrop for our use of the psalm. God satisfied the longings of the "soul"/ throat (v. 9).

The Refrain

Gratitude for God's everlasting covenantal concern/*hesed*/mercy/"love" (v. 1) is the point of the refrain. Even in that desperate situation of dire thirst, the Lord cannot and will not refrain from exercising his covenantal kindness (*hesed*) toward us. The refrain as translated speaks of "everlasting love" (see vv. 1, 9). God is faithful in ways we cannot even imagine, even if we are not. For this we can only express our gratitude.

Gospel

Matthew 22:34-40

You shall love the Lord, your God, with all your heart and your neighbor as yourself.

Literary Link

The allusion to the silencing of the Sadducees (v. 34) refers to the prior passage that described the debate of Jesus with them over the doctrine of resurrection, which they did not hold (vv. 23-33). Once again, perhaps to avoid premature liturgical consideration of themes reserved for Lent and Passiontide, those sections that were important in the development of Matthew's theological trajectory were omitted by the Lectionary. Our readings, therefore, move from yesterday's parable of the wedding feast (22:1-14) to today's teaching about the greatest commandment (vv. 34-40).

Testing

One cannot resist pausing for a consideration of what it might mean to test anyone as the Pharisee did with Jesus (v. 35). Does one "test" to determine qualification for acceptance into a school or promotion to the next grade? Then the Pharisees, who believed in resurrection, would have tested Jesus to see if he was acceptable as a true colleague. Abraham was tested to see if he loved his son more than his God (Gen 22). The people of Israel were tested in the wilderness for the purification of their motivation and the determination of their suitability for entrance into the land of promise. Jesus was tested early in his life after the baptism (Matt 4:1-11) to demonstrate what being a "Son of God" truly implied and demanded. One can even test things we are proud of, such as physical stamina, endurance, or memory. The response of Jesus mirrored and echoed that of the prominent Pharisees of his day. Testing is not necessarily negative.

Torah as Instruction, Not Law

This passage demonstrates the limitations of translating *torah* as "law" (v. 36), since love cannot really be commanded. A better term would be "instruction" or "teaching," which presents a value and then encourages people to figure out how such a concern for God and God's values might be integrated into one's daily life. Instruction suggests cooperation and personal participation in exploring the meaning and implications of a truth, rather than forced compliance. The Hebrew word *torah* literally refers to something "tossed out" or "thrown" to be caught by another. This is not the way we understand "law."

Saturday of the Twentieth Week in Ordinary Time

First Reading (Year I)

Ruth 2:1-3, 8-11; 4:13-17

The Lord has not failed to provide you today with an heir. He was the father of Jesse, the father of David.

Gleaning after the Harvesters

One of the specific laws of Israel was the stipulation that harvesters not be so greedy as to gather every grain. Rather they were obligated to leave the fringes and corners of the fields for the poor and hungry (Lev 19:9-10). Whether out of religious piety or out of attraction for the young widow, Boaz even instructed his workers to leave extra for Ruth's gleaning (2:16). One obeyed the command by being "forgetful." Ruth's activities clearly position her among God's *ʾanawim* and thus allow her vulnerable dependence to become a moment of grace and blessing for her. Even Naomi was not above a bit of scheming and matchmaking in this charming tale. In the Near East arranged marriages were the norm. This reading is about care for the needy, and about Divine Providence.

Davidic Genealogy

The ways in which people find their places in the humanly contorted genealogy of David (and Jesus) are very mysterious and often improbable. Ruth's son Obed, which means a worker or a worshiper (i.e., religious worker), was the grandfather of David, as Matthew's genealogy notes (1:5-6). Thus a foreign refugee and immigrant whose need for food and whose loyal piety toward her mother-in-law motivated her move to Israel became part of the Davidic dynasty. All human circumstances were used by God in shaping the family influences upon David and ultimately upon Jesus, who became like us in all things but sin (Heb 4:15). We in turn need to be mindful and grateful for the quirks in our own family lineage.

Antiphon (Year I)

Psalm 128:4

See how the Lord blesses those who fear him.

Blessings for Fidelity

The first verses selected by the Lectionary to serve as a response to the story of Ruth fittingly promise food (v. 2), favor, and fertility (v. 3) to those who live in reverential awe of Israel's Lord. While not reverting to a naïve or mechanical promise of blessings for covenantal obedience (because bad things do happen to good people), the psalm promises ultimate prosperity for those who remain faithful, even in adversity (v. 4). The psalm is one of those included in the "songs of ascents" (v. 1), namely, psalms for the use of pilgrims on journey to Jerusalem.

Family Life

The image of children as "olive plants / around your table" (v. 3) may evoke a smile or a nostalgic memory of Norman Rockwell's paintings, but the total impact of the poetry suggests an idyllic portrait of family life in simple happiness, ever conscious of their blessings before God. Olive trees, however, are not within the life experience of many people today. If we were to create our own images for happy family life, possibly out of our memories or out of the way we wish our earlier lives had been, what descriptions would we use?

First Reading (Year II)

Ezekiel 43:1-7ab

The glory of God entered the temple.

Future Restoration and Glory

Ezekiel's first vision of God was amid a "stormwind . . . from the North" (1:4), and his earlier terrifying sense of God's departure from the temple and abandonment of his people (10:18) is now to be reversed amid a sound like roaring waters (v. 2). Reminiscent of the way in which God's glory filled the tent at the time of Moses (Exod 40:34) and the temple at the time of Solomon (1 Kgs 8:11), Ezekiel promises a return after the people's exile and purification in Babylon. The pattern of God's enduring presence, even amid a sinful people, had been set and would not be revoked. The God who opened graves also would rebuild his temple in one way or another forever. The book of Revelation concludes the pattern forever when the luminous presence of God became the temple (21:23).

Glory

One of the more elusive notions in Scripture is that of "glory/*kabod*." With subtle and mysterious implications of heavy value, brilliance, and attractive beauty, this concept becomes the aura for the divine presence as he reenters the temple (v. 4). For all its blinding splendor one cannot turn one's gaze away because of God's utter attractive nature that fills space and leaves no place for anything other than God (v. 5). This same overwhelming presence in the temple became the fullness of divinity that in a later age would fill the person of the glorified Jesus as well (John 17:5). A share of that same gift of God's glory is also given to every person at baptism.

Antiphon (Year II)

Psalm 85:10b

The glory of the Lord will dwell in our land.

Psalm 85: A Benevolent God

After acknowledging the reality of God's anger (vv. 1-6), the Lectionary prefers to cite the second section of Psalm 85, which describes the positive effects of God's presence: covenantal kindness, truth, justice, and peace (v. 11). These qualities have a cosmic effect with truth from the earth and justice from the heavens (v. 12). God's blessings will even provide abundant harvests (v. 13).

The Refrain

The refrain (v. 10) celebrates God's return to the temple after the desolation of its destruction by the Babylonians. The worshiping community, whether in the temple of ancient Jerusalem or at a morning Eucharist millennia later, recognizes that all these blessings flow from the presence of God who chooses to remain amid his people. Can anyone see those same blessings in the parish's eucharistic community?

Gospel

Matthew 23:1-12

They preach but they do not practice.

Literary Link

Matthew's gospel groups together several accounts of discussions and debates between Jesus and the Pharisees. After their agreement on the great commandment (22:34-40) and their disagreement on the title of the son of David (vv. 41-45; not selected for use in the Lectionary), Matthew concludes the section with a series of teachings about religious authority (23:1-23) before the eschatological discourse (24:1–25:46) at the end of his fifth book.

Authority of the Pharisees

It seems clear that Matthew continued to recognize the basic religious authority of the scribes and Pharisees who occupied the teaching chair of Moses (v. 1). This was one of the curious challenges inherent in the fact that Matthew's community was comprised of both Torah observant Jews and Gentiles. The debates described in the gospel may well have reflected the deepening hostility between disciples of Jesus and Jewish leadership in the first decades after the resurrection. Issues such as the divinity of Jesus and dietary laws gradually separated neighboring religious communities. The gospel presumes that Jewish Christians would continue to re-spect the teachings of the Pharisaic leadership still operating in the larger community. Instructions from the Holy See regarding contemporary

Jewish/Catholic relations suggest that Catholic preachers use stories from rabbinic sources whenever appropriate.

Religious Leadership

Reading through this list of the complaints of Jesus against the Pharisees makes it very clear that the issue is religious leadership itself, not merely an "us" versus "those Jews." Among the possible faults of Jewish or Christian leadership would be errors such as imposing burdens without compassion (v. 4), engaging in devotional practices merely to be seen and admired (v. 5), and seeking signs of social prestige and preferential treatment at public gatherings (vv. 6-7). The literal translation of this section of the teaching dismisses and even forbids human titles as unimportant (vv. 8-10), but the real intent is probably closer to the Semitic practice of affirming one thing, in this case service, by rejecting alternatives. A similar example could be the way true disciples are asked to hate their parents (Luke 14:26), which surely was not intended to countermand the fourth commandment.

Saturday of the Twentieth Week in Ordinary Time

Monday of the Twenty-First Week in Ordinary Time

First Reading (Year I)

1 Thessalonians 1:1-5, 8b-10

You turned to God from idols to await his Son, whom he raised from the dead.

The First Letter to the Thessalonians

This, the first of Paul's apostolic letters, was written about AD 51 to the members of the second community that he had founded (after Philippi) upon leaving Asia and entering Europe. His comments and encouragement are typical of a wise pastor's concern for the spiritual growth and perseverance of recent converts.

Team Ministry

Although the letter is traditionally ascribed to Paul, note that Silvanus and Timothy are also listed as members of the team (v. 1), supporting each other's respective strengths and supplementing each other's weaknesses. Paul's sharper edges, when insisting on the principle of things, for example, may well have benefited from the assistance of these others who were willing to work with given human reality as the starting point. We are by definition and creation social beings that need each other for success as God would define the term.

Thanksgiving

The letter begins with gratitude to God for the community, and for the abundance of their faith, charity, and hope (v. 3). Note that this seems to be the earliest mention in the New Testament of that fundamental trinity of theological virtues and their grace. Paul's gratitude includes the entire manner of the team's apostolic approach, that is, through powerful words and actions (v. 5). Paul's gratitude is primarily to God, rather than to the human community itself. That sense of appreciation includes the two basic facets of their new Christian faith, the rejection of idols (v. 9) and faith in the resurrection (v. 10). Those are the effects of grace for which Paul is grateful.

Antiphon (Year I)

Psalm 149:4a

The Lord takes delight in his people.

Psalm 149: Jubilant Rejoicing

The praise of the entire Psalter begins to reach its climax in the exuberant praise of this psalm, whether expressed in liturgical assembly (v. 1) or at home (v. 5). Origen, one of the truly brilliant early Christian writers (†255), wrote a commentary *On Prayer* and spoke of its basic components: praise, gratitude, penance, petition, and a final return to praise. Among the litany of divine qualities that Psalm 149 invites us to celebrate with song (v. 1), dance, and music (v. 3) are God's almighty power, knowledge, and compassion. There is always much to praise, and the object is God, not ourselves, except from the vantage point of our relationship to God whose images we are.

Thessalonians

The Lectionary does not hesitate to take a poetic verse from the psalms that originally celebrated a renewed Israel and now to apply it fittingly to the Christian community at Thessalonica. Paul's letter noted that they were admired by other Christian communities in the area (1 Thess 1:8). We believe that God truly takes delight in every Christian and Jewish community that responds to grace and lives with generosity, integrity, and joy.

First Reading (Year II)

2 Thessalonians 1:1-5, 11-12

May the name of our Lord Jesus be glorified in you and you in him.

Team Ministry

Once again the mention of Silvanus and Timothy as "sources/authors" of this letter, as well as Paul himself (v. 1), is a reminder of the inherently communal

Monday of the Twenty-First Week in Ordinary Time

nature of all Christian ministries. We may never know their specific individual contributions, but the fact that Paul sends Timothy back for further encouragement (1 Thess 3:6) gives us some insight. There should be no "lone rangers" among us. Paul may receive the full credit although others share the work with him. "The totally self-sufficient person is sub-human" (Archbishop Desmond Tutu).*

The Second Letter to the Thessalonians

Although many of the expressions in this letter are also found word for word in its predecessor, there is a different sort of distance in its tone, leading some scholars to conclude that it was written by a disciple of Paul rather than by the apostle himself. In either case, this is shorter and sharply focused on two challenges faced by the community at Thessalonica: the presence of Jewish Christian missionaries who seemed to undermine Paul's earlier work with different teachings, and the worry of the Thessalonian converts over the delayed second coming of Christ.

Visible Community Growth

The fact that the deepening faith and the mutual charity of the church is visible to others and praised by other early Pauline Christian communities is stressed by the apostle who remained justly proud of the reputation of this local church (v. 4). How does one measure the example of our own contemporary congregations within their larger neighborhoods? What judgment should be made if no one sees any growth or development in us from year to year? Would anyone in the larger community miss our parish if we stopped existing? This reading ends with a prayer for their continued growth (v. 11). We should echo the prayer for our parishes today!

ANTIPHON (YEAR II)

Psalm 96:3

Proclaim God's marvelous deeds to all the nations.

Psalm 96: Endless Praise for God

Although the word "king" is not found in this response, Psalm 96 was probably used for any enthronement festival that celebrated God's kingship. Its praise for the supremacy of God echoes Paul's initial praise and prayer of thanksgiving. We celebrate what we value and admire.

The Refrain

The refrain (v. 3) chosen by the Lectionary reflects and echoes the way other Christian communities near Thessalonica viewed and admired the witness given by the Thessalonians. It was to all the nations that the example of the Thessalonian Christians gave witness. Every Christian community is chosen to give that sort of example to others.

GOSPEL

Matthew 23:13-22

Woe to you, blind guides.

Literary Link

After Saturday's more generic teachings of Jesus regarding the temptations and sins of religious leadership (vv. 2-12), the gospel now adds a collection of seven "woes" related to specific charges, each introduced by the same Greek expression of astonishment, abhorrence, pain, and anger ("woe/*ouai*"). Only the first three are proclaimed today, while two are reserved for tomorrow (vv. 23-26) and the final three for Wednesday (vv. 27-32). The culture of the ancient Near East (somewhat like contemporary Mediterranean cultures today) was inclined to expressions of heated emotion in arguments that sound harsher to our Western ears than they would have to the people of that world. Note that the Lectionary (and NAB) omits the "woe" of condemnation for those who devour the houses of widows (v. 14) because it is a word-for-word repetition of Mark 12:40 and may have been inserted into Matthew later for completeness.

Hypocrites

Technically the word "hypocrite" (vv. 13, 15) refers to an actor who speaks through a mask, and therefore hides his or her true feelings. The words spoken are therefore not the individual's true ideas. The same word could also be stretched to describe a hypercritic who dramatically pays more attention to tiny details rather than to the substance of the matter. That could change depending on the precise point of the accusation.

Oaths

After the gospel's denunciation of leaders who seek converts (v. 15) but do not themselves enter the kingdom (v. 13), the denunciation adds a lengthy statement about foolish distinctions among different oaths (vv. 16-22). Pharisees and modern Orthodox Jews avoid speaking the name of God out of reverence. Thus, rather than invoking the name of God to attest the truth of one's statement, they tended to use temple or altar as a substitute and to transfer the focus to the gold or the gift as if that were closer to God and therefore binding. The gospel would have none of those subtleties, and insists that all oaths are very serious matters. This is a pastoral opportunity to address the importance of avoiding all inappropriate uses of the divine name.

* "The Truth and Reconciliation Process—Restorative Justice" (Third Longford Lecture, Church House, Westminster, February 16, 2004).

Tuesday of the Twenty-First Week in Ordinary Time

FIRST READING (YEAR I)

1 Thessalonians 2:1-8

We were determined to share with you not only the Gospel of God, but our very selves as well.

Paul's Apostolic Methods

Paul was an inveterate salesman, and he was a Pharisee who wanted desperately to comply with the will of God—in his case to share the Gospel of God's offer of salvation. As a salesman concerned with morality/God's will, Paul would neither fudge the truth about the product (v. 3) nor engage in mere flattery (v. 5) to make a sale. Both of these temptations are explicitly rejected by Paul as he describes his relationship to the people of Thessalonica whom he treated with affection, not spiritual domination (v. 8). Every Christian is invited to be an evangelist, and to follow Paul's example of method.

A Credible Life

Apostolic witness is more than mere words proclaimed, but includes the entire life and being of the one who gives testimony (v. 7). Once again, the medium is the message! Paul, like anyone who preaches the Good News, must place his verbal testimony as well as his very life on the line to be judged by those who listen (v. 8). Like the witness of a "before/after" advertisement, the personality and conviction of this apostle is what ultimately counts before human beings and God as well.

ANTIPHON (YEAR I)

Psalm 139:1

You have searched me and you know me, Lord.

Psalm 139: An Open Life before God

This remarkable poem is a sort of "verbatim" conversation between the author and his/her God. The realities of God's presence, power, and perspective are acknowledged, not in abstract principles or concepts, but in the realities of the psalmist's inner personal experience (vv. 1, 4) and genuine relationship to God. This is a real God of majesty at work in the emotional life of a devoted servant (v. 4).

Divine Knowledge

In several different ways, even within the few verses chosen by the Lectionary for this response, God's knowledge is celebrated: knowledge of human actions (v. 1) even from afar and of human speech even before it is spoken (v. 4). The Hebrew notion of knowledge, however, also includes an emotional element of care and affective concern for the object known at a deeply personal level. To know is to experience genuine concern for the object of that knowledge.

FIRST READING (YEAR II)

2 Thessalonians 2:1-3a, 14-17

Hold fast to the traditions that you were taught.

The Return of the Lord

Even in our own day, the media provides an occasional report of some evangelist predicting the precise date of the end of the world and of Christ's return in the immediate future. Seemingly rational people sell their possessions and gather at some predetermined place in vain. Whether the phenomenon stems from excessive incredulity or a deep desire to escape the heartaches and hardships of life, it does demonstrate the perennial nature of what Paul confronted. He instructs and even begs them to pay no attention to such rumors or promises (v. 3). That Christ will return in victorious glory is a fact of faith. The timing, however, is known to God alone. The passage ends with a prayer of encouragement (vv. 16-17).

Criterion for Credibility

In Paul's reference to the rest of what they had been taught, he invokes what we have come to call "the rule of faith," namely, the way in which apostolic teaching should be the measure of credibility for all subsequent teachings (v. 15). Our Christian faith has its own logic and intellectual constancy. What is not consistent with "the traditions that you were taught" should be ignored. This Pauline teaching may also be the beginning of the distinction between public revelation (expressed in the Scriptures and the apostolic preaching, which is binding on all) and private revelation (stemming from private prayer or mystical experience, which is only binding on the person who receives it).

ANTIPHON (YEAR II)

Psalm 96:13b

The Lord comes to judge the earth.

Divine Kingship

When the realm of human royal ideology was applied to God, its functions were easily transferred. Marshaling armies, demanding (temple) taxes, caring for the poor, and sitting in judgment over injustices were among the actions expected of a good king, and therefore attributed to God. Prophets announced God's judgment in individual cases such as King Ahab's power grab of poor Naboth's vineyard (1 Kgs 21), but also gradually spoke with increasing conviction of a final judgment of the world by the Lord to establish justice (v. 13) once and for all. Psalm 96 was easily conceived as an element in the annual celebration of God's daily individual and final universal judgment.

The Refrain

The Lectionary chose this refrain (v. 13) as a response to the reading that described Paul's teaching regarding the Second Coming. In this manner the Lectionary is able to insist on the truth of Paul's teaching, no matter how it might be twisted or misapplied by others. The early church knew with certainty that Christ would return but had to deal with its fading sense of imminence. Paul taught that truth and twenty centuries later we still expect it, but in God's time.

GOSPEL

Matthew 23:23-26

But these you should have done without neglecting the others.

Literary Link

After a brief distraction regarding oaths (vv. 16-22), the gospel returns to the litany of condemnations of the sins and mistakes of religious leaders. Today's passage adds two more errors or mistaken emphases to the list.

Preoccupation with Details

The positive aspect of the attitude of the Pharisaic leadership that is lifted up here for critique is not their burning concern for the will of God (a good thing!) but their relentless devotion to minutiae like tithes on herbs while overlooking the big picture (mistaken preoccupation). Small details may be important, but not nearly as important as the God they served. In an earlier age Catholics could fall into the same mistake by carefully weighing ounces of food during the Lenten fast, but forgetting what the fast itself was all about. Pharisees remain guides, mentors, and teachers, but are expected above all to keep the big picture in mind.

External Cleansing

A similar preoccupation about less significant matters is illustrated by the accusation of being so concerned with external washing of utensils (v. 25) as to forget to cleanse the inside of the person using them. Both hands and hearts are important. Our behavior needs to look good, but also *be* good! Human actions must look just, but also be just. Inner motivation is even more important (v. 26) than the external action itself. The fact that we are called to give good public example can lead to forgetting the insides of things.

Wednesday of the Twenty-First Week in Ordinary Time

First Reading (Year I)

1 Thessalonians 2:9-13

Working night and day we proclaimed to you the Gospel of God.

Ministerial Entitlement?

Paul's life made it very clear that he rejected any type of special "entitlement" in his work to support himself while proclaiming the Gospel. He freely chose not to be any financial burden to his new friends in Christ at Thessalonica during his stay there (v. 9). Although he may have had a right to receive support for his ministry, he chose to forgo that practice in order to make his motivation as clear as possible. The purpose of such support from a community is to enable the minister to have the freedom required for response to pastoral needs as they arise. All support, however, is really intended for the work of the Gospel, not the comfort of the minister.

The Word at Work in Believers

Paul insists that the word of God, once heard, continues to percolate, as it were, and to work in a transforming fashion in the minds and spirits of believers (v. 13). Almost like a marinade that gradually gives intense flavor to meat, or medication that gradually transforms and heals the recipient, the Word continues to work in the lives of those who hear and embrace it. The Catholic tradition believes strongly in "doctrinal development," namely, the possibility of holding a truth firmly while unpacking its fuller meaning and implication for the life of the church. Sometimes a new age can present new questions to be addressed by God's eternal Word.

Antiphon (Year I)

Psalm 139:1

You have searched me and you know me, Lord.

Psalm 139: A Life Still Open to God

Contrary to general practice, the Lectionary has chosen to continue the use of Psalm 139 as an antiphon from yesterday. Perhaps Paul's personal relationship to the Thessalonians as gifted teacher and encouraging mentor contributed to that decision. The end result is that the psalm again maintains the tone of an "I/Thou" friendship that inspires and unites both partners.

Distance Overcome

The verses used in this antiphon celebrate the fact that God surpasses and transcends the greatest of distance or diversity to remain closely involved in personal care for his faithful servant. Distance (v. 9) and even darkness (v. 11) mean nothing to God who is all light and life. Divine omnipotence and omnipresence are not abstractions but simply the personal affect that God brings to the lives of his friends. God knows us far better than we know ourselves!

First Reading (Year II)

2 Thessalonians 3:6-10, 16-18

If anyone is unwilling to work, neither should that one eat.

"Disorderly" Community Members

Because all the gifts of the Spirit are for the common good (1 Cor 12:7), every authentic Christian community should give evidence of its members working together in an orderly fashion. Paul condemns those who do not do their part in whatever work needs to be done. "Disorderly" would seem to refer to those who enjoy the food without helping to obtain it by work or preparation (v. 10). Anyone who takes advantage of the work and talents of others without making their own contribution to community life is out of order and should be shunned (v. 6).

Modeling by Leaders

Paul was not embarrassed to offer himself as a model of that behavior while living in their community. He recommended that all leaders do something similar in order to give a good example (v. 16). This is not contrary to the Lord's teachings against doing something to be seen (Matt 6:1) because the intention is not to seek praise for oneself but to give good example to others. Once again, the intention is the key! The true witness of our lives is found in our example as well as in our words.

ANTIPHON (YEAR II)

Psalm 128:1

Blessed are those who fear the Lord.

Psalm 128: Family Blessings

The first verses of Psalm 128 were chosen because they echo Paul's teaching regarding the basic motive for giving good example, namely, fear of the Lord (v. 1). Maintaining an attitude of basic awe and reverential respect for God in everything we do is presumed in Paul's admonitions to the Thessalonians. Continuity of thought, therefore, between the reading and the responsorial psalm develops the idea and explores its meaning for life.

Walking God's Paths

Those blessed for their reverential attitude toward God are described as engaged in daily walking the paths laid out for us by God's will (v. 1), and eating the fruit of their labors. The psalm, therefore, links conduct and cuisine. To be able to do so, especially amid the poverty of ancient urban life, was seen as itself a sign of God's favor (v. 2). Without being simplistic, Paul sees a link between morality and meals. In times of contemporary economic pressure, many of our own community members know all too well the need for employment sufficient for putting food on the table. Mutual concern helps bridge the gaps.

GOSPEL

Matthew 23:27-32

You are the children of those who murdered the prophets.

Literary Link

The litany continues the critique of religious leadership in the renewed Israel to which Jesus felt himself sent (15:24). In today's gospel passage Jesus offers two more areas of admonition, especially in terms of his rejection of their excessive concern for mere externals (v. 27).

Whitewashed Tombs

Preoccupation with externals is a common human affliction. "Keeping up appearances/with the Joneses" can be a terrible disease of the spirit; it is certainly not restricted to any group from the ancient world! One should remember the ritual uncleanness contracted by contact with the dead (Lev 21:11) in order to appreciate fully the imagery of this condemnation. To give the name of a "tomb" (v. 27) to a devout Pharisee was a special insult. The charge of preoccupation with external comeliness vs. internal corruption could be a temptation for anyone.

Respect for History

One of the major problems of contemporary "postmodern" American culture is that we have no sense of history. For that reason we can arrogantly claim that we would have never made the mistakes of the past (v. 30)—and yet we are prone as a people to make the same mistakes generation after generation. These Pharisees are charged with washing their hands of all past guilt (v. 29) but establishing a bond with prior evildoers by building the tombs of the present, and so sharing their guilt. One should be very cautious about claiming to be more insightful and more moral that those who have gone before us! In so many contemporary debates, we need to be careful about reading current standards into the mindsets of the past. Jesus insists that those who build the tomb, even so many years later, are somehow complicit in the deaths! Only those who respect the prophets of their own day can claim innocence regarding the fate of the prophets of the past.

Thursday of the Twenty-First Week in Ordinary Time

First Reading (Year I)

1 Thessalonians 3:7-13

May the Lord make you increase and abound in love for one another and for all.

Firmness of Faith

Like any parent undergoing hardships, Paul is encouraged by the reports of the steadfastness of his convert community at Thessalonica. As an indication of the importance of the Thessalonians for Paul, the apostle acknowledges that his very life and vitality (v. 8) are determined by the firmness of the faith of his early converts to Christ Jesus. The success of those whom one has mentored is a source of gratification to any teacher or coach. Their daily lives amid Thessalonian society provided evidence that they had shared Paul's own firmness in the faith that he had received prior to his arrival in their city.

Deepening Love

Paul encouraged the Thessalonians to keep up and deepen their love for one another (v. 12). True charity is never static; it either grows and deepens or it diminishes. Paul's constant and enduring desire to offer a remedy for the deficiencies of the faith of his early converts (v. 10) illustrates his ongoing concern for their spiritual maturing and for lifelong faith development. Paul becomes an example for our need to invest energy in the spiritual development of all our recent contemporary converts and for the deepening faith of every parish community. These issues could well become a portion of an annual audit of the spiritual life of the parish community. What would be the criteria for concluding that a community's love had deepened? How would we know?

Parousia

In the first years after the resurrection, the early Christians were preoccupied with awaiting the imminent return of Christ; Paul was no exception (v. 13). This reality that was described as Christ's Parousia (coming/appearing) remains the final measurement for all our human activity. He will return as Judge and Reaper. Even after so many centuries when the delay becomes something taken for granted and increasingly remote, the sustained urgency of Christ's return is a vital element in the spirituality of a disciple and in one's desire to be found blameless (v. 13). Alertness to all the signs of God's approach should not be restricted to the season of Advent alone!

Antiphon (Year I)

Psalm 90:14

Fill us with your love, O Lord, and we will sing for joy!

Psalm 90: Humble Dependence

The overriding theme of this psalm is the contrast between the utter majesty of God and the weak limited nature of human beings who return to their dust (v. 3) at God's command. For that reason human beings should rise each morning in gratitude for their enduring existence. We humbly ask the Lord to prosper the work of our hands (v. 17), because success cannot come from our effort alone!

The Refrain

The word translated as "love" (v. 14), as one might guess from the context, is *hesed*, mutual covenantal concern. This mutual attentiveness is a gift to be renewed every morning. The petition for its presence could easily become an important element in a person's first prayer each day, followed by the petition that human work be prospered (v. 15) by God's interest and grace. Just as human marriage and friendships are realities in need of constant attention, so the covenant with God needs daily care. The translation as "love" may have been chosen to reflect more directly Paul's admonition to "abound in love for one another" (1 Thess 3:12).

FIRST READING (YEAR II)

1 Corinthians 1:1-9

In him you were enriched in every way.

The First Letter of Paul to the Corinthians
To a small but vibrant community troubled by divisions on many levels, Paul writes his first letter of admonition and advice. The community was established in about AD 51 while Paul was on his second missionary journey, and he never ceased caring for its spiritual growth. The apostle's teachings and method are perennially valuable and remarkably contemporary, especially for a world so fraught with partisan division and rivalry.

Social Character of Christian Holiness

The fact that the letter comes from both Paul and Sosthenes (v. 1), and is addressed to the entire community at Corinth, once again underscores the social nature of our Christian calling. Moreover, the "you" (v. 2), who are sanctified and called to be holy, concerns the entire community because it is in the plural. How is this community, or any community, "holy"? "Holiness" in its radical sense means to be different. To what extent is the holiness of a contemporary parish community different from the larger cultural community? If its membership is indistinguishable in their responses to any survey regarding values or attitudes, how are they "holy"? Spiritual writers often suggest that the signs of holiness are honesty, generosity, and humility before God.

The Gift of Grace

"Grace/*charis*" is one of the elements in Paul's greeting (v. 3). It is also a motive for his prayer of thanksgiving. It signifies something that makes a person as well as a community attractive and appealing. Paul insists that it was a gift from God (v. 4), which enriches everyone. Deeper than mere physical comeliness or beauty, this "favor" is expressed in the spiritual gifts of eloquence and knowledge (v. 5), relating the individual and the entire community to the person and mission of Christ himself. By insertion into the redemptive action of Christ, each person finds his or her ultimate attractiveness and authentic contribution to the community and the larger world. A community gathered for prayer or scattered for service is very attractive.

ANTIPHON (YEAR II)

Psalm 145:1

I will praise your name for ever, Lord.

Psalm 145: Praise for a Generous God

Because of the psalm's reference to giving food in due season (v. 15, which is not included among the verses chosen by the Lectionary for this response), this psalm was often used in the early church as a midday meal prayer. The response focuses on praise for God and for the way in which that praise is handed on from one generation to another. The psalm is also fitting for a meal prayer because of the reference to more than one generation (v. 4) gathered around a table of praise.

The Refrain

As an echo of Paul's praise and thanksgiving, this refrain (v. 1) highlights Paul's perennial pride in the Corinthian community that he loved dearly, even in spite of his serious concerns about their unity and behavior. One loves most those in most need of that love. Their eloquence and knowledge as well as the presence of so many spiritual gifts inevitably led Paul to give praise to God for their existence.

GOSPEL

Matthew 24:42-51

Stay awake!

Literary Link

The Lectionary moves from the final criticisms of religious leaders mentioned

Thursday of the Twenty-First Week in Ordinary Time

in yesterday's gospel to the conclusion of the discourse at the end of Matthew's fifth book (v. 42). Much of the eschatological discourse of Jesus, therefore, was omitted because it is presented more fully at the end of the liturgical year. Thus in Lectionary logic, today's admonition seems directed to religious leaders, even though its original focus was upon the entire community and all its members.

Vigilance and Watchfulness

The Greek word for "stay awake" is *gregoreite*, "be vigilant, alert" (see v. 42); it is the origin for the Christian name "Gregory." Because of its position at the end of the Lord's eschatological discourse, immediately after the teaching on the suddenness of the Lord's coming and the lack of knowledge regarding its precise timing (v. 36), the original focus of that vigilance was the signs of God at work in the world. What a wonderful sense of meaning for a personal name, and what a fine motto for lifelong adult Christian spirituality!

Thief in the Night

Scholars remind us that the image of an unexpected visit from a thief or robber (v. 43) is a very improbable illustration for the coming of Christ. They conclude that it would never have been developed by a later generation of early Christians who would surely have exhibited more respect and reverence for their Lord and Master. Like any of the biblical images and parables, therefore, it merits our further reflection for the implications of such an audacious metaphor. God surpasses all our preparations and moves at a level of time beyond our own limited and mundane sense of life's rhythm. Christ is no thief, but he does come very quietly at times and unexpectedly. Christ also recognizes what is of genuine value in our lives, and knows where to find it!

Food Distribution

The Lord's praise for one who gives out food in a timely fashion (v. 45) envisions more than simply the person in charge of serving three meals a day. The saying is meant, therefore, for more than school cafeteria cooks, restaurant employees, or family household managers of the kitchen. Every single person has received gifts from God to be shared with the larger community. Each gift can "nourish" other members of the community in some way. The obligation, then, is to distribute the benefits of our talents to others properly: respectfully, in a timely fashion, and when they need them. Like Jesus who gives himself away under the appearance of bread, all our lives, talents, and resources are expected to nourish the lives and needs of others.

Friday of the Twenty-First Week in Ordinary Time

First Reading (Year I)

1 Thessalonians 4:1-8

This is the will of God, your holiness.

Daily Conduct

Paul's admonition that the Thessalonians conduct themselves well (v. 1) underscores the fact that genuine belief always overflows into daily actions and personal behavior. One's relationship to others flows from what one believes about oneself and about others. Biblical images for the larger reality of God's work include the Body of Christ, people of God, and temple of the Spirit. Each image has its own implications for the importance of each member's function and inherent value. Actions and attitudes matter!

Holiness

The meaning of these verses is somewhat obscure and scholars debate whether the entire text is devoted to sexuality (NAB) or to sexuality and business practices. Presuming for a moment the former, since that is the interpretation preferred by our Lectionary, the Thessalonians are directed to honor their spouses (v. 4) without selfish exploitation (v. 5). Paul therefore stresses that Christian holiness includes proper physical relationships. Given the reality of the incarnation and the opposition of the biblical witness to any form of dualism, these verses are very important for family life and love. To disregard our relationships is to disregard God (v. 8). One shorthand description of Christian holiness toward others might include honesty, generosity, and humility.

Antiphon (Year I)

Psalm 97:12a

Rejoice in the Lord, you just!

Psalm 97: A God Majestically Enthroned

Long considered a hymn for an annual enthronement festival, Psalm 97 celebrates divine kingship (v. 1) and describes the rejoicing of the entire world before the supreme throne of God (v. 6). In selecting this psalm as a response to Paul's teachings about Christian sexuality, the Lectionary places human sexuality and holiness within the larger context of God's justice (v. 2) and promises divine protection for the lives of his faithful ones (v. 10).

The Refrain

The assembly of praise is described in the refrain as comprised of people called "just" (v. 12). "Justice" is invoked as a foundation for God's throne (v. 2). Justice remains a reality proclaimed by the very heavens (v. 6). More than merely the payment of one's bills fully and in a timely fashion, the biblical notion of justice presumes being in right relationship with all of creation. Only such individuals are truly able to rejoice (v. 12) before God and be judged worthy of divine protection.

First Reading (Year II)

1 Corinthians 1:17-25

We proclaim Christ crucified, foolishness to Gentiles, but to those who are called, the wisdom of God.

Christ Crucified

Paul felt that his philosophical address to the Athenians (Acts 17) had been a failure, especially after he was casually dismissed for his reference to the resurrection (vv. 31-32). For that reason he felt the need to review his kerygmatic style and to change his missionary methodology. Thereafter, as this passage clearly states, Paul decided to speak only of "Christ crucified" (v. 23). Profoundly countercultural to human ideals of prosperity, acclaim, and social status, Paul's message focuses on self-sacrificing love for the well-being of others. For Paul, this is the only means to human happiness. To many of our modern contemporaries that message will quickly be dismissed as foolishness.

Friday of the Twenty-First Week in Ordinary Time

Wisdom

Behind the scenes and between the lines, Paul continues to do battle with the prominent philosophers of his first-century Greek world (v. 20). In the ancient biblical world "wisdom" was the ability to do things well like a good cook or carpenter. Only later within the developing biblical witness was the idea of wisdom extended to apply to one's ability to make one's way through life. The sense of self-sacrificing love, exemplified in the way Jesus gave himself away under the appearance of bread, was the supreme illustration of that wisdom, something the teachers of Greece could not understand. Paul concluded that they were the real fools of the world (v. 23). God's good news in Christ completely surpasses human values (v. 25)! To place ourselves at the service of those we love is to become fully human and holy.

ANTIPHON (YEAR II)

Psalm 33:5

The earth is full of the goodness of the Lord.

Psalm 33: God beyond All Human Plans

The psalm combines generic praise of God accompanied by music (v. 2) with a sweeping dismissal of the nations who foolishly plot against the God of Israel (v. 10). The Lectionary may have selected this psalm precisely as a further confirmation of Paul's comments because of his rejection of the designs and plans of Jews and Greeks alike (read respected pagan philosophers).

The Refrain

When all is said and done, the psalmist simply returns to the way in which the entire earth is filled with God's goodness (v. 5). Goodness in reference to the earth can at times mean good weather, sufficient rainfall and fruitful climate. However this "goodness" is described, it is more important than human reasoning and philosophic theories. In no way is this sentiment to be thought anti-intellectual; rather, in typical Semitic fashion, the response dismisses foolish human plans (v. 10) in order to emphasize better use of time for praising God.

GOSPEL

Matthew 25:1-13

Behold, the bridegroom! Come out to meet him!

Literary Link

Immediately following the teaching regarding punishment for unfaithful servants (24:51), Matthew's gospel launches into three major end-time parables: the ten virgins in the wedding party (25:1-13), the distribution of talents and the ensuing accountability expected from the recipients (vv. 14-30), and the judgment of the nations (vv. 31-46). Punishment from God can take many forms in response to human sin: personal unpreparedness, cowardly unwillingness to take risks, and lack of generosity toward the needy. The gospel provides a teaching parable for each category.

Parables

A New Testament *parable* is usually an instruction about how God works in our world, with its primary focus on God. Although the temptation might be to move quickly and exclusively into a consideration of the two types of young women in the bridal party, the reader/listener should first and foremost consider how God is described in the parable of the kingdom (v. 1). Our God is one who arrives on the scene at unexpected moments. Our God depends on partnership with human beings, and expects that people be prepared for the sudden arrival of his grace in our world and in our lives. Because of human positive or negative reactions, our God is also a God of "plan B" who is willing to accept "what is" as he welcomes the smaller number of attendants properly prepared.

Weddings

The example of the young women in an ancient Near Eastern wedding procession

(v. 1) offers the perfect illustration of a combination of delay, waiting, sudden arrival, and the need to be prepared! One might include for consideration a few more contemporary examples of such a convergence of human activity and idle expectation: the family gathering at an airport to await the arrival of a relative returning from foreign military service or the last-minute hushed gathering of friends for a surprise birthday party of a colleague. Careful preparedness for any contingency and eager anticipation mark the events in which God often acts. What other examples might we suggest?

Saturday of the Twenty-First Week in Ordinary Time

First Reading (Year I)

1 Thessalonians 4:9-11

You have been taught by God to love one another.

Thessalonian Charity

The real teacher of charity is not Paul but rather God (v. 9), who provides the grace and enables the Thessalonians to become an object of admiration among the neighboring Christian communities in Macedonia (v. 10). They were taught by God (v. 9), who remains the best model for their charity toward each other. As the First Letter of John insists (4:6ff.), God is love, and where God abides, loving concern for others flourishes.

Signs of True Love

Paul, the ever practical teacher who was deeply immersed in the orthopraxis of his Jewish tradition, offers three indications or effects of the presence of authentic love (v. 11): tranquil life in community without inner agitation or turmoil, minding one's own business rather than everyone else's, and working with one's own hands to earn a living rather than depending on the generosity of others. That was his instruction to his new converts at Thessalonica. It remains a fitting instruction for our contemporary communities as well. Mindless gossip about others and idleness are never signs of a truly Christian community.

Antiphon (Year I)

Psalm 98:9

The Lord comes to rule the earth with justice.

Psalm 98: Welcoming Voices of Creation

This enthronement psalm may have been chosen for its initial invitation to sing a "new song" (v. 1) because of the new activity of God in raising up the newly converted community at Thessalonica. Even the sea and mountains (vv. 7-8) of material creation found at the edges of that Greek city are invited to join the chorus of praise.

The Refrain

The response to the arrival of God (v. 9) is jubilation, not fear. The entire created world shares that joyful welcome. Part of the reason for the positive response is Israel's conviction that God's judgment (v. 9) will be fair and evenhanded, not arbitrary or capricious in any way, even though his judgments are so vastly distant from ours (Isa 55:9).

First Reading (Year II)

1 Corinthians 1:26-31

God chose the weak of the world.

God's Improbable Choices

There is a long-standing pattern in the biblical witness to the effect that God seems to prefer choosing weak and improbable instruments, at least according to the criteria of the secular world around us (v. 26). Young David chosen as king, still betrothed Mary chosen as mother, and persecutor Paul chosen as prime apostle are examples that eminently verify that truth. Here again the Corinthian community gives yet another example of God's values because they are not generally known as wise, powerful, or noble in the eyes of their world (v. 26). Those perceived as foolish, weak, and lowly (vv. 27-28), or perhaps more to the point, *especially* those folks, are the ones chosen by God for his purposes.

No Boasting

Paul suggests that the ultimate purpose of such choices is to preclude any human being from boasting about personal merits or qualifications (v. 29). Everything is grace and gift! Learning how much we depend on God and each other is a humbling process through which every single person must go. The weaker the instrument, the more clearly God is revealed as the real source of any subsequent success (v. 31).

ANTIPHON (YEAR II)

Psalm 33:12

Blessed the people the Lord has chosen to be his own.

Psalm 33: Human Eagerness

In a surprising fashion the Lectionary chooses the same Psalm 33 two days in a row, although using different verses, in order to respond to the varied messages of the days' respective readings from 1 Corinthians. Yesterday it was the initial portion of the psalm that focused on the praise of all creation, but today's response stresses the hopeful anticipation of the human recipients and beneficiaries of God's goodness (v. 18). They all wait for the Lord (v. 20).

God's Free Choice

The refrain (v. 12) stresses the fact that God deliberately and freely chose his people, even though they were less eminent than others of the same generation. The utter freedom of God in his choices is exercised repeatedly: at creation, redemption, and salvation. Especially when the people chosen seem so limited in normal human qualifications, it seems necessary to take note of the fact that it is all God's doing! Thus God becomes king, shield (*magen*, v. 20; also vocalized differently in Hebrew by some scholars as *mogen* to mean "emperor"), and protector for those who are weak and in need of help.

GOSPEL

Matthew 25:14-30

Since you have been faithful in small matters, come, share your master's joy.

Literary Link

The second parable of the kingdom in this collection of Matthew's gospel is that of the diverse distribution of talents (vv. 14-30), "each according to his ability" (v. 15). Matthew had collected several parables of the kingdom at the end of the third book (chap. 13), and now concludes the teaching ministry of Jesus with another "end-time collection" of three parables at the end of the fifth book. The new Moses, suggested by the gospel's five "books" in imitation of the five scrolls of the Pentateuch, has something to say by way of farewell. With this reading the Lectionary concludes its annual review of Matthew's gospel.

Diverse Talents

Initially a talent was a large piece of precious metal, almost the size of a garbage can lid, and obviously too heavy and too valuable for easy portability. The parable gives a hint of the reasons for the different size of the investments, namely, ability (v. 15), as well as perhaps prior experience or former responsibilities. The parable, by the fact that it is ultimately God-centered, recognizes that God knows all creatures intimately and profoundly. Once again the parable presents a God who knows people, seeks partners from among them, shares gifts, and expects accountability.

Risk Taking

Running throughout the New Testament one finds the theme of a God who is willing to bet on his people and who rewards those who are willing to take risks in doing the work of the kingdom. The first people cast out of the heavenly Jerusalem are the cowards (Rev 21:8). The so-called "unjust steward" (Luke 16:8) is commended, not for dishonesty (which is never proven), but for his creative and enterprising decisions to make friends for himself in this age and the next. The parable's one servant too fearful of a mistake is called "wicked and lazy" at the final accounting (v. 26). God shares in partnership but also expects results according to our abilities.

Monday of the Twenty-Second Week in Ordinary Time

FIRST READING (YEAR I)

1 Thessalonians 4:13-18

God, through Jesus, will bring with him those who have fallen asleep.

Resurrection

The first Christians at Thessalonica lived with a strong belief in the resurrection and a vivid anticipation of the Lord's second coming (v. 15). Their pressing worry, which had been communicated back to Paul, however, was the concern that fellow believers who died before the second coming of Christ might be left behind, as if only the living would be taken into God's eternal embrace. We never know the practical questions that could arise in people's minds as a result of their beliefs. Paul writes to give further information and assurance on the matter (v. 13). To fill out the picture he uses familiar images such as divine commands, angelic voices, and trumpets (v. 16) from the apocalyptic literature that was so familiar and popular in his day. What type of assurance do our contemporary believers need at this time in their lives?

Living in Hope

The basic question of the Thessalonians about the resurrection of family and friends serves to underscore the importance of living with a strong and hopeful sense of our final destiny in Christ as baptized believers. Baptized into the Lord's paschal mystery, we are expected to live in the hope (v. 13) that our redemption will be complete at the end of our lives on earth. Like faith, hope is both a desire for things not yet possessed (Heb 11:1) and a confidence that the promise and the gift will be experienced sometime in the future. Anticipation and confidence are the two essential marks of genuine Christian hope.

ANTIPHON (YEAR I)

Psalm 96:13b

The Lord comes to judge the earth.

Joyful Praise

The anticipation of the coming of God to judge the world is neither negative nor fearful for God's faithful people. That future event is anticipated with joy and enthusiastic welcome (v. 4). Its positive nature is illustrated by the poetic imagery as if even the seas and plains (v. 11) are laughing and the trees (v. 12) singing at the prospect!

Judgment

In the biblical tradition the primary meaning of "judgment" is a decisive intervention to make something happen. One can recall the book of Judges and the twelve heroic leaders described there for a fuller biblical sense of salvific intervention. This is much more than judicial action in a court of law. In the Scriptures the verb "judge" implies the action of appearing on the scene, and secondarily affirms that God's appearance makes a difference because he is able to separate the good from evildoers and to reward them accordingly.

FIRST READING (YEAR II)

1 Corinthians 2:1-5

I came to you proclaiming Jesus Christ, and him crucified.

Message over Method

Paul felt the need to remind the Corinthians that his approach had been one of truth, not preoccupation with persuasive or flattering speech (v. 1). He is not ashamed of his weakness (v. 3) or the uncertainty of his public speaking style (if we are to accept at face value the comments about his speech in 2 Corinthians 10:10). Paul's primary concern was the truth of the paschal mystery, and its implications for daily Christian living. Since God was the force behind his words, Paul felt no need to pretend more talents than he actually possessed! The same humble honesty should characterize all our efforts. Similar to AA spirituality, none of us needs to pretend to be better than we are.

Christ Crucified

With the clarity of good rhetoric, Paul prefers to focus exclusively on Christ crucified (v. 2) in his preaching, not even the resurrection. With self-sacrificing self-abnegation Jesus handed his life over and accepted the fact that his public ministry had frightened the religious leadership in Jerusalem. The fact that Jesus loved the unlovable and wanted to make them whole seemed to challenge the status quo so profoundly that they had to still his voice and remove his example from daily sight. The death of Jesus and his divine motivation, however, transformed the world. Paul wanted everyone to know about it. The true power of God was made evident in the death of Jesus.

ANTIPHON (YEAR II)

Psalm 119:97

Lord, I love your commands.

Psalm 119: Love for God's Law

With some frequency the Lectionary chooses to use verses from Psalm 119 as a response to a biblical reading. Again and again the list of various terms for God's will, namely, law, commands, decrees, and precepts, is presented and described as occasions for the loving and eager response of God's people to the goodness and love expressed by their God.

Joyful Opportunities

Divine commands are not burdens but opportunities for human beings to demonstrate their love for God as requested by the great *Shema* (Deut 6:5; Matt 22:37). The refrain (v. 97) is presented as an example of loving God with all our being.

GOSPEL

Luke 4:16-30

He has sent me to bring glad tidings to the poor.
No prophet is accepted in his own native place.

Literary Link

Today the Lectionary turns to the Gospel of Luke. After the "infancy narratives" (1:1–2:52), Luke described the preaching of John the Baptist, including the baptism of Jesus himself and the descent of the Spirit (3:1-22). This event was followed by an extended genealogy (vv. 23-38). Then Luke presented the temptations in the desert (4:1-13) as the event that clarified the role of a true "son of God" and prepared him for his first return to Nazareth (vv. 16-30).

The Gospel of Luke

This is the first volume of Luke's two-part work, first dealing with the public ministry of Jesus of Nazareth in the gospel, then with the life of the early church in Acts. The work's purpose is to give assurance to educated readers and to present a portrait of Jesus as a new Elijah, filled with the Spirit, loving the poor, recognizing the role of women, confronting self-righteous arrogance. The work of Luke-Acts was also eager to avoid seeming to blame Pilate for the tragic death of Jesus in Jerusalem.

Anointed for Action

The core of the inaugural hometown speech of Jesus in the context of a Sabbath (v. 16) synagogue service is a series of citations from the prophet Isaiah (61:1; 58:6; 61:2). Fresh from his experience in the desert, and in the presence of family and friends, Jesus declared his mission and purpose in life, saying, "This is who I am and what I am doing!" The initial verb (v. 18) cited in the passage from Isaiah, that is, Hebrew *mashah*/Greek *chrisein*/"anoint," includes many related ancient ideas: being chosen, selected, prepared, and empowered for a specific purpose. The ancient ritual included the use of aromatic oil. That oil was absorbed into the person's physical being for healing, transformation, leadership, and service. Its full meaning should not be lost on those anointed in the Christian sacraments of initiation today.

Monday of the Twenty-Second Week in Ordinary Time

Reaction of Nazareth

The major problem with this group of folks from Nazareth, as Luke described it, was their strong sense of entitlement! Because they were former neighbors and perhaps even relatives of Jesus, they presumed some sort of special treatment. They didn't seem to have heard the reference of the citation to the poor, the blind, and the incarcerated (v. 18). The references of Jesus to the works of Elijah and Elisha outside of Israel confronted the presumed entitlements of his former neighbors. This is the very opposite of the point of the first beatitude, the blessing for the "poor" (6:20) who are praised because they live in utter dependence upon God's gifts alone. His departure from their midst marked a moment of sadness and their loss (v. 30).

Tuesday of the Twenty-Second Week in Ordinary Time

First Reading (Year I)

1 Thessalonians 5:1-6, 9-11

Jesus Christ died for us so that we may live together with him.

Children of the Light

People who are "children of the light" (v. 5) have lives of faith, hope, and charity marked by transparency, integrity, and justice. With nothing covert or hidden, they shine forth in giving good example. They have no fear of the "day of the Lord" (v. 4) since it will only intensify the visibility of their normal daily lives as grace and gift from God, fully received with a spirit of humble cooperation. There will be revealed a luminous consistency about their activity and motivation. An ancient Near Eastern symbol of divine presence, power, and justice is a burning sun disk of light. The Day of the Lord will reveal that presence as eternally active in our world and ultimately judging everything we are and do.

Christian Destiny

Living in God's light is not static or immobile, but dynamic! To recognize that we are destined for salvation is to acknowledge an internal dynamism and purpose in our existence that moves toward the fullness of life, not death. As food is to be eaten, clothing to be worn, cars to be driven, our entire individual beings have been created and sustained by God for the final perfecting (v. 6) of everything we are. To stay "alert and sober" is to live with a sharp focus on the will of God and on our role in that mission. Almost like a seed catalogue we always exist in God's mind in the full-blown image of the beauty we might become if we cooperate with the gifts and graces we receive each day. Each of us is brought to our unique individual perfection. God will do it if we cooperate.

Antiphon (Year I)

Psalm 27:13

I believe that I shall see the good things of the Lord in the land of the living.

The Refrain

The hope of Christian life as Paul described it to the Thessalonians included an assurance of life beyond death as partners in Christ's resurrection (v. 13). Without any fear of darkness (v. 4), neither from evil powers in this world nor from death in the next, the Thessalonians are encouraged to live in light and to look forward to sharing Christ's victory over darkness.

Dwelling in the Temple

One way to sustain that sense of life and light, suggests the psalm, is to spend time in the temple of God's presence (v. 4). Frequent awareness of God's presence and power keeps hope alive. It also keeps God in mind and heart. Those blessed with the spirit of contemplation (v. 4) can find peace even amid much tragedy and heartache. Perhaps programs of adult formation on the methods of prayer are needed now more than ever!

First Reading (Year II)

1 Corinthians 2:10b-16

Natural persons do not accept what pertains to the Spirit of God: spiritual persons, however, can judge everything.

The Work of the Spirit

The ancient world experienced, as do we today, the ability to discover the depth of our own thoughts, and sometimes even to intuit what someone else is thinking. There are many occasions when we seem to know things beyond the material and physical world. There is, nevertheless, much about ourselves that we do not know (v. 11). We can at times sort out in retrospect our motives, mysterious as they may be, even to ourselves. The ancients labeled that action the work of "the Spirit." As Paul reminded the Corinthians (and ourselves as well), all the more is that Spirit needed to understand God (v. 12)!

Tuesday of the Twenty-Second Week in Ordinary Time

Natural/Spiritual Persons

When Paul speaks about the merely "natural/*psychikos*" person (v. 14), he means someone restricted to the material world of objects and feelings. Such an individual is not able to understand the larger world from God's point of view and requires the gift of the Holy Spirit to do so. The "spiritual/*pneumatikos*" person (v. 15), however, is more discerning because she has received the ability to see things from God's standpoint. That includes the possibility of forgiveness and reconciliation as well as the need for justice and loving respect. All these abilities are among the gifts of the Holy Spirit!

ANTIPHON (YEAR II)

Psalm 145:17

The Lord is just in all his ways.

Just and Fair

To confess that God is just (v. 17, which is not among those verses selected for this response by the Lectionary) can mean that eventually all God's actions reflect the justice of God. That includes the fact that God treats people fairly and gives each one's due, even if tragedies often do afflict good people as Job insists. The gospels speak of the great final reversal when all things will be made right, and when the mighty will be taken from their thrones and the lowly lifted up (Luke 1:52 in the *Magnificat*). We may struggle with the problem of evil in our world, but we confess that our God is just.

God Is Justly Related to Everything

The biblical notion of justice goes beyond merely repaying debts and balancing out the ledger of personal relationships. In this sense to speak of God as "just/*tzadik*" (v. 17) is to acknowledge that God remains in right relationship with every creature and every material object of creation in the entire galaxy. Personal and material objects in turn are called just when they are what they should be. A path, for example, is just if it leads to where the path should lead.

GOSPEL

Luke 4:31-37

I know who you are—the Holy One of God!

Literary Link

After leaving the synagogue at Nazareth, Jesus went to the synagogue of Capernaum (v. 33), where he immediately put into practice the mission he had just proclaimed for himself. He healed the man held captive and troubled by an unclean spirit.

Respect for a Synagogue

Jesus regularly visited the local synagogues and participated in the weekly Sabbath services. Recalling that pattern in his earthly ministry, we might well renew our respect for those same services in the synagogues of our own day. When we hear that Jesus spoke in the synagogue, we might wonder if he suddenly rose to make a comment and offer a teaching, or if he was invited as a newcomer or guest to offer a few reflections on the reading of the day. They were astonished by the authority of his teaching (v. 32). Virtually everyone has something spiritual to say or some personal question of faith to raise for the common good. Looking at any congregation we might wonder in genuine awe about the wisdom gathered each time the community comes together for worship. This may not be possible within formal liturgy with a substantial number of participants, but that reality illustrates the value of faith-sharing groups in other settings for the growth of the church and its membership.

Demons

The Greek word *daimon* (v. 33), which we sometimes translate as demon, originally meant an uncontrollable urge or impulse to some type of activity. Without denying the possibility of invisible supernatural forces, such "demons" might also be powerful psychological or emotional drives that seem to control our lives, even propelling us into dangerously harmful areas. Such were named "unclean" in the ancient world if they involved ritually forbidden contact with the origins or final ends of life and death or led to the consumption of forbidden foods. Jesus showed power and authority even over such runaway human inclinations and addictions. Encountering Jesus is to find new integrity and peace.

Wednesday of the Twenty-Second Week in Ordinary Time

FIRST READING (YEAR I)

Colossians 1:1-8

The Gospel has come to you just as in the whole world.

The Letter to the Colossians

This letter was written from a unique perspective, emphasizing as it does Christ's cosmic redemption and his relationship to angels and spiritual powers, as well as to unique ascetical practices. There is considerable similarity to the ideas found in the Letter to the Ephesians, raising questions among scholars about the actual author of this inspired work, whether it be Paul himself or someone else, possibly a disciple, writing in his name.

A Community Effort

From the very beginning there was a social and communitarian aspect to Christianity. The team of Paul and Timothy addresses the entire community at Colossae. Although possibly numbering as few as two dozen individuals, that Colossian community was praised for their example of spiritual growth (v. 6). Moreover, one should be conscious of the fact that the phrases when the epistle mentions "you" are inevitably in the plural, not singular. Our English words often do not differentiate between the persons. This constant communitarian mentality remains a remedy for the radical individualism of our American culture. It also provides a biblical basis for our Catholic sense of church as a mediating instrument of divine revelation and forgiveness.

The Theological Virtues

Once again we hear a very early reference to the three theological virtues of faith, hope, and charity (v. 5). These are not abstractions but concrete characteristics of the community's relationship to God and to each other. Faith is the acceptance of God's salvation in Christ, with the confident hope of future participation, and it is love that unites them all together. This combination under the inspiration of the Holy Spirit is a novel Christian contribution to the spirituality of our human existence. The writer of this letter knows of the community's fine reputation from the reports of others, including Epaphras of nearby Ephesus (v. 7) who may have founded the community. What would neighbors say about our parish?

ANTIPHON (YEAR I)

Psalm 52:10

I trust in the mercy of God for ever.

Trust

A green olive tree (v. 10) is suggested in this brief portion of Psalm 52 as a symbol for trust: green and fruit-bearing, sturdy and long-lived, deep-rooted and able to endure, even in challenging climates. American culture might prefer the imagery of an oak or an ancient sequoia. The refrain (v. 10) nicely expresses Paul's sentiments as a result of the positive report he heard of the stability of the Christian community at Colossae. His trust was always in God, not in himself or in them. Once again, the mercy in which we trust is *hesed*, the mutual and reciprocal concern of the covenant.

FIRST READING (YEAR II)

1 Corinthians 3:1-9

We are God's co-workers; you are God's field, God's building.

Divisions

One of Paul's biggest headaches at Corinth was the jealous rivalries and factions that divided that community (v. 3). Instead of viewing differences as ultimately complimentary and mutually helpful, the Corinthians held on to them firmly as if the variations were mutually contrary and perhaps even contradictory. Leaders of each faction seem to have insisted on a loyalty that was exclusive. Both Apollos and Paul were gifted teachers who inspired loyalty (v. 4). Paul insisted on unity in God, however, which integrates all merely human differences (v. 9). One reality by way of remedy for healing Corinthian debates was the existence of God's truth, which is always larger than any human mind, and the other issue was the need to constantly seek the common good.

Images for the Community

To speak of the entire community as a field (v. 6) is to discover considerable insight into the nature of any local church community: acknowledgment of a community's origin in a seed from outside, the need for water (baptism), different species of plants each needing diverse nourishment and care, an expectation of future harvest, and the recognition of an inevitable succession of seasons and generations. The brief reference to a building (v. 9) as an image offers different insights: the value of an initial blueprint, the cooperation of many hands and skills in its construction, an openness and an ability to welcome others and provide shelter as well as the presumption that entire families would live therein, not merely individuals. Every image provides its own insight and contribution to our understanding of the church.

ANTIPHON (YEAR II)

Psalm 33:12

Blessed the people the Lord has chosen to be his own.

Psalm 33

The first portion of Psalm 33 served as the response last Friday. By using different verses from the same psalm today, the Lectionary is able to refocus on larger social groupings: nation and people (v. 12), mankind (v. 13) and earth dwellers (v. 14). This enables the day's liturgy to maintain a sense of concern for the unity and harmony of the entire community.

His Own Inheritance

Reading the refrain (v. 12), one would not realize that the point is God's choice of the Colossians, a once pagan people (*goy*), as his very own inheritance. The word "inheritance" is not mentioned in the liturgical text. The unusual aspect in this unspoken phrase of the refrain is that one does not normally choose one's own inheritance by explicit request. One normally receives an inheritance as gift rather than selects it. God, however, has decided to treat Israel as absolutely unique and to bind the people to himself for all ages! Doing so also creates a bond across the generations with both past and future. In this fashion God remains active throughout all of their history.

GOSPEL

Luke 4:38-44

To the other towns also I must proclaim the Good News of the Kingdom of God, because for this purpose I have been sent.

Literary Link

The healing of the man during the synagogue service (v. 33) and the healing of Simon's mother-in-law immediately afterwards (v. 38) illustrates Luke's concern to balance men and women among the recipients of the Lord's cures. In spite of the reference to preaching in Judea (v. 44), the entire section seems devoted to a Galilean ministry (4:14–9:50).

Cures and Healings

The gospel curiously described Jesus as talking to fevers and other maladies (v. 41), almost as if they were personified realities, somewhat like the way we might speak in exasperation to a computer, automobile, or oven! The people came after sunset

(v. 40) because the Sabbath had formally concluded at that time and they were free to engage in the "work" of bringing the sick and infirm to the healing presence of Jesus. Implicit, therefore, in the "postsunset" passage is a respect for the obligations of the Sabbath rest. Equally implicit is an invitation to follow the example of Jesus and to embrace the gift of the Sabbath in our own modern lives as a time to acknowledge the Christ (v. 41) and to rejoice in the wonders of creation.

Wednesday of the Twenty-Second Week in Ordinary Time

Movement to Other Towns

The healing offered by Jesus is marked by an evangelical universalism. Jesus will not be held hostage to the needs of any single community. He is sent to other places as well (v. 43); a true disciple/apprentice lives with that same perspective of divine generosity. In the insistence of Jesus that he announce the Gospel to entire communities, not merely to individuals, we hear an echo of the message of Gabriel who (if we read the text closely) was sent at the time of the annunciation to an entire town in Galilee (1:26). By God's definition and through his grace we are always and forever interdependent social creatures with a care for the larger common good.

Thursday of the Twenty-Second Week in Ordinary Time

First Reading (Year I)

Colossians 1:9-14

God delivered us from the power of darkness and transferred us to the Kingdom of his beloved Son.

Communion of Communions

By the very fact that Paul acknowledges that his first contact with the Colossians was secondhand, namely, having "heard about [them]" (v. 9), he admits that he was not the founder of that Christian community. Care and prayers for communities founded by others should be a mark of the larger "Catholic" point of view. A distinctly Catholic approach to the church is to believe that all communities are united together into the Body of Christ through the bishop who is obligated to preserve their bond with others. As Catholics we are not merely "congregational" in our approach to the world in which we live as if every individual community could make its own laws and live in virtual spiritual independence.

Knowledge

Two elements consistently mark the Christian life: intellectual knowledge of God's will (v. 9) and the capacity to walk/live ever worthy of our calling (v. 10) to comply with that will. This means that we are expected to act and behave in a manner consistent with our knowledge of God's will. Paul notes the capacity of our knowledge to provide power and patience in our daily life (v. 11), fidelity under adversity, and confidence through more difficult times in life. When we know something with certainty, we can manage many difficulties and burdens wisely and well. That knowledge enables us to understand that we have passed from darkness (v. 13) by God's help, casting off ignorance, fear, sin, and eventually death itself. Certain knowledge provides light for the journey.

Antiphon (Year I)

Psalm 98:2

The Lord has made known his salvation.

No Secrets

The way in which God has revealed the salvation offered to Israel has never been secret. The Lectionary's choice of this refrain serves to reject any hint of the "secret knowledge" such as was found in the Gnostic heresies of early Christianity. God's sense of justice is visible to all nations (v. 2), even to the ends of the earth (v. 3). It is a mark of true "evangelization" to feel the freedom and even the need to speak of all the blessings that God has given to Israel and to ourselves over the years. Only in this way can we be examples of faith and life for others. God uses us to make his salvation known!

First Reading (Year II)

1 Corinthians 3:18-23

All belong to you, and you to Christ, and Christ to God.

Biblical Wisdom

The Semitic concept of "wisdom"/Hebrew *hochmah*/Greek *sophia* suggests the ability to do something well. Thus a truly good cook, seamstress, carpenter, or artist is called biblically wise. From there the idea was extended to include a person who has learned how to navigate life well with all its challenges, heartaches, and joys. The contents of the books of Wisdom, Qoheleth, Proverbs, and Ben Sirach all fit into this category of biblical "Wisdom literature" and are well worth leisurely reading for spiritual profit and growth.

Wisdom of This Age

There is a certain ability of individuals to excel in areas of life in society. Among these we could readily list a celebrated rock star, a popular model, an astute investor in the stock market, or a brilliant scientist who becomes wealthy by patenting genetic discoveries. This type of "wisdom" describes individuals who have mastered an area of existence or a realm of nature for their own advantage (v. 18). Paul would see all this as ultimately merely foolish (v. 19) because it remains essentially self-centered and restricted to the merely material set of values and goals. He asked the Corinthians to become foolish again, as the world might see it, namely, living simply and generously in order to possess eternal wisdom.

Thursday of the Twenty-Second Week in Ordinary Time

Wisdom in the Kingdom

Paul insists that a higher wisdom only comes when each set of individual gifts and personal talents is placed in the larger picture of interdependence and of final subordination to the needs of others, the victory of Christ's resurrection, and the final glory of God (v. 23).

ANTIPHON (YEAR II)

Psalm 24:1

To the Lord belongs the earth and all that fills it.

Torah Psalms

Scholars call Psalm 24 a "Torah liturgy," a psalm that could be sung as a sort of "instruction" at the entrance to a sanctuary. After a profession of faith in the Lord's majestic power (v. 1), one asks about the moral requirements for standing before such a divinity and offering worship (v. 3). The response, presumably by a temple guardian or priest (v. 4), then leads to a moral examination of conscience including avoidance of violence or dishonesty, refusal to desire forbidden or immoral actions, or any other basic values unacceptable to the God of Israel's covenant. Only if the visitor can indicate compliance with these moral criteria would he or she be admitted to the sanctuary.

Divine Majesty

The psalm's initial refrain (v. 1) is a recognition that all of creation and everything in the entire world belongs to God. This acknowledgment is the beginning of holiness and happiness. The refrain also gives basis for considering care of the earth and the environment as an important aspect of faith. Our God is green! The basic faith as expressed presumes that human beings will act as divine agents in the care for the earth.

GOSPEL

Luke 5:1-11

They left everything and followed Jesus.

Literary Link

After Jesus had announced his mission was to all the towns (4:43) came the miraculous catch (v. 6) with the call of Peter to be a partner in that mission (v. 10). Then after two healings, Levi the tax collector will also be called to be a partner (v. 27). The cures and calls are interwoven because they illustrate the fact that care for the sick and infirm was part of the mission.

God in the Details and in the Happenstances

At first blush the meeting of Jesus and the fisherman seemed so casual and spontaneous. They happened to be working at their nets (v. 2), and Jesus happened to see the value of using this nearby boat (v. 3) to create a little distance from the pushing crowds—but Divine Providence was at work from the beginning. How often do we just happen to meet people who change our lives? The great catch (v. 6), in spite of prior long and hard fruitless human activity, is a fine reminder of the fact that God is the true source of any success we may have in life.

Out into the Deep

The phrase has been used in recent years to describe the unknown and often dangerous areas that may cause uncertainty and trepidation on our part. To launch out into the deep (v. 4), however, is not merely an encouragement to have confidence and trust in God but also a command to travel where the fish can be found! It is the first step in embarking on a missionary career. In the metaphors of the gospel, shepherding often referred to residential life in a settled Christian community (John 21:15, where fishing and shepherding are presented side by side), while fishing had a clearly missionary aspect, bringing others into the group. The invitation of Jesus to Peter remains a reminder that we are summoned to a type of missionary witness to the larger world, not merely local work with familiar faces. One cannot be a missionary unless one is willing to travel to the places where potential new members live. Paul invariably went to the crowded cities of the ancient world! Mother Teresa went to Calcutta.

Friday of the Twenty-Second Week in Ordinary Time

First Reading (Year I)

Colossians 1:15-20

In him were created all things.

A Hymn to Christ

This reading is in fact a hymn (vv. 15-20) sung by the early believers at Colossae to honor the all-encompassing mystery of Christ. Many translations, therefore, actually print this text in verse format. Scholars conjecture that the Christian community at Colossae may have only numbered about two dozen persons as they gathered to celebrate the Eucharist weekly and to proclaim their faith in God. Therefore, the passage is also a reminder of the importance of song and the value of vital small communities of conviction and faith throughout the history of the church.

A Christological Creed

If one were to list the various elements contained in this hymn, one would note their comprehensiveness: image of the invisible God, firstborn of creation (v. 15), the instrument used by God for all creation (v. 16), the "glue" that holds the universe together (v. 17), the head of the church, the firstborn from the dead into resurrection (v. 18), and reconciler/restorer of all creation to unity through the cross of Jesus (v. 20). The hymn is about Christ. Note that the hymn's references to thrones, dominions, principalities, and powers (v. 16) are all in fact names for various classes of angels, and may well reflect an ancient preoccupation of the Colossians with angelology. In a later section this letter will warn against excessive preoccupation with angelology (2:15, 18). The city of Colossae was famous in the fifth century AD for a large basilica dedicated to Saint Michael the Archangel.

Antiphon (Year I)

Psalm 100:2b

Come with joy into the presence of the Lord.

Psalm 100: Prayer at the Doorway

This brief psalm, virtually all of which is reproduced by the Lectionary as the response to the reading, is an entrance hymn. This is evident from the double invitation (vv. 2, 4), each of which is followed by a statement of praise for the God honored by the worshiping assembly.

Presence

The Hebrew word, here translated as "presence," is literally "*panim*/faces" (of God), a recognition of the many moods and facets of God's relationship to us and to our world. Although the word suggests a very anthropomorphic approach to God, as if he were a human with shifting emotions, it does recognize the various divine responses to human activity: compassion, condemnation, forgiveness, or cooperative support. The use of this psalm as a response to the christological hymn of Colossians recognizes that God's revealing grace is also present in the very hymn that joyously celebrates divine greatness and expresses our faith!

First Reading (Year II)

1 Corinthians 4:1-5

The Lord will manifest the motives of our hearts.

Servants and Stewards

Paul labels himself both a servant who devotes his entire life to the needs (not necessarily the wants) of those to whom he was sent by Christ and a steward ultimately responsible for giving an account of the gifts, graces, and duties he had received (v. 1). Although both titles demand trustworthiness (v. 2), each title looks in a different direction and has a separate focus. Paul lived out of his original experience of the risen Lord's identity with the disciples, a lesson learned on the way to Damascus (Acts 9:5). Because of that insight, his faithful communities became the primary reference points of his life; they were the presence of Christ for him. The gifts he received were never his own. We also could bear the same titles in terms of our own responsibilities and abilities, namely, servants and stewards.

Human Judgment

Although tentative judgments on the morality or effectiveness of actions, our own or those of others, are often required for community discernment and planning (v. 3), our judgments are always only tentative and can never reach to the inner motives of those around us (v. 5). The Lord alone remains the ultimate judge of everything (v. 4). All else is provisional at best.

ANTIPHON (YEAR II)

Psalm 37:39a

The salvation of the just comes from the Lord.

Salvation

The Hebrew word for "salvation/*teshuʿah*" suggests the result of being freed from a tight spot, physically, morally, or financially. Only God can be the ultimate source of such freedom and salvation. Although the title given to God in this refrain (v. 39) is "Lord/YHWH," one can easily recall a resonance with the name of "Jesus/*Yeshuʿa*" who was promised as Savior to Joseph when he was commanded to take the mother and child as his own and name the baby "Jesus" because he will save his people from their sins (Matt 1:21).

Just One

We need to be reminded often that the use of the word "just/*tsadiq*" in the psalms, and in this refrain in particular (v. 39), refers to one who lives in right relationship to everyone and everything. It is only such a person who becomes just by God's grace, and who is therefore saved by God. To think merely of paying debts and balancing the ledger of life is too narrow a notion of justice. One's entire personal integrity is the point of the phrase.

GOSPEL

Luke 5:33-39

When the bridegroom is taken away from them, then they will fast.

Literary Link

The calls of Simon Peter (v. 10) and of Levi (v. 27) lead to the question of how Jesus is training his disciples, and why they are not taught to fast as are other disciples at the time. The parables address the discontinuity between the teachings of Jesus and those of John or the Pharisees. Later differences may have been read backwards into the earlier public ministry of Jesus.

Fasting

The gospel contains a collection of the teachings of Jesus gathered by Luke and often held together by common words and ideas, even though they may have been given at differing times and places. This text unfolds from a consideration of an external action, that is, fasting (v. 33), to a consideration of one's motivation and rationale. Each different group—the disciples of John, the Pharisees, and the disciples of Jesus—has its own respective reasons. Thus it would seem that all Pharisees fasted annually to commemorate the destruction of the temple, and some extended that practice to twice a week. John's disciples may have borrowed the custom from Qumran, and replicated life in the wilderness as a renewed preparation for the renewed gift of the land. The example of the bridegroom (v. 34) suggests that the early Christians, who eventually fasted, did so in solidarity with the poor who shared food in common, and in preparation for the great messianic banquet at the Second Coming of their Master. Later their fasting bound them to the sufferings of Jesus and provided an opportunity to exercise self-discipline.

The New and the Old

In the end the real question is not fasting itself but the need for inner consistency and logic in what we do and why. New wine and new skins (v. 27) need to age together; older clothing fits poorly with newer cloth. The very fact that Jesus promised to come again resulted in the devotional practices of his disciples who looked forward to the future and fasted accordingly. Those of John and the Pharisees turned their attention backwards. Every Christian assembly should gather in that same light, anticipating the great dawn of the full and final redemption. The old wine is good (v. 39), but so is the new!

Friday of the Twenty-Second Week in Ordinary Time

Saturday of the Twenty-Second Week in Ordinary Time

First Reading (Year I)

Colossians 1:21-23

Christ has now reconciled you to present you holy and unblemished before him.

Alienation and Reconciliation

The letter presumes that evil deeds have a definite and direct effect upon the human agent, rendering him or her separated from God and hostile to God. Actions matter. The first effect of any action or thought is upon ourselves, making it easier to repeat that reality for good or for evil. If evil, such deeds both isolate and harden (v. 21) a person in opposition to the plan of God from us and for our world. Evil actions separate and alienate. God's gift of reconciliation through Christ (v. 22) goes to the heart of the matter and changes the inner reality of a person's being into reuniting existence and holiness.

Perseverance

Personal holiness is achieved by grace and demands continuity and enduring perseverance in goodness (v. 23). Repetition is necessary for an isolated individual action to become a stable habit in life. The letter insists that habits come into being when rooted properly, in the hope of the Gospel (v. 23). Daily prayers, devotions, and outreach to the needy become the exercises needed to maintain spiritual health and true holiness.

Antiphon (Year I)

Psalm 54:6

God himself is my help.

Psalm 54: A Plea for Help

This brief psalm follows the general pattern of a lament: an initial plea for assistance in a difficult situation, followed by a confession of trust and confidence, and then a final ritual of thanksgiving. It is a "one-size-fits-all" type of petition that can be used in virtually any human predicament. God is called upon as savior and defender (v. 3) as well as helper and sustainer (v. 4). God is acknowledged as being and having everything needed by the person in distress. The liturgy brings this psalm together with the statement of Colossians regarding a person's alienation because of sin.

God the Helping One

The Hebrew word rendered as "help" (v. 6) is *ʿozer*, which in fact is a present participle and thus speaks of God as one who by definition regularly and instinctively offers help as needed. Ezra is the personal name formulated from that verb. Occasionally a person is playfully mocked for acting in a type of arrogance that considers God "a mere helper," but the fact is that God is the unseen help in every life. This refrain celebrates that truth!

First Reading (Year II)

1 Corinthians 4:6b-15

We go hungry and thirsty and we are poorly clad.

Admonition Clothed in Sarcasm

Paul indulges in sarcasm when he calls the Corinthians rich as kings, strong and wise (v. 8)—the very opposite of the way he had described the community at the very beginning of this epistle (1:26). The lifestyle, attitudes, and general disposition of both Paul and Apollos give good example in this matter (v. 6), not boasting because all is grace and nothing done is accomplished by their own unaided effort. In contrast to their self-ascribed "wealth" Paul notes his own poverty (v. 11) and his apostolic life often marked by deprivation in service to the people of Corinth. Modern religious leaders and parish members alike would do well to imitate Paul in these matters today, just as he asked the Corinthians to do in the first century (v. 14). This is profoundly countercultural in a world, suburban or central city alike, that inordinately prizes wealth, power, and pleasure.

Saturday of the Twenty-Second Week in Ordinary Time

Father in Christ

Contentious as the Corinthians were and often troubled with rivalries, Paul still saw himself as the one who had generated their faith in Christ, and therefore viewed himself as their father in faith (v. 15). Like any family, the relationship was tested at times, and even required some strong corrections and discipline in order to assist the Corinthians toward full and responsible spiritual Christian maturity. A parent provides nourishment and example for living as well as giving the initial gift of life. One never stops worrying about one's children, and constantly works to love them into mature goodness.

ANTIPHON (YEAR II)

Psalm 145:18

The Lord is near to all who call upon him.

The Nearness of God

The God of Israel is never distant from his people or disinterested in their lives. The verses of the response list the divine qualities of justice and holiness (v. 17), proximity and attentiveness to the needs of his people (v. 18). That special proximity is not primarily spatial because God by definition is close to all creatures, good and bad. Any distance is created by us human beings who choose to distance ourselves emotionally from God's loving mercy. The very formula for establishing the covenant was "I will be your God and you will be my people" (see Exod 6:7). Moreover, the title given by Isaiah to a future king is *Immanuel*, "God with us" (Isa 7:14), a title invoked by Matthew's gospel in the infancy narrative (1:23).

Calling on God

To call upon God (v. 18), as the refrain recommends, is to invoke his name in prayer and worship. The knowledge and use of God's name presumes a relationship and the right to seek assistance and aid. Because of the sacredness of the action and the holiness of the name of God, one should be reverential in its use, and very careful not to casually invoke the name as witness to any human promise made or truth told. The name of God has become far too carelessly stated in contemporary speech!

GOSPEL

Luke 6:1-5

Why are you doing what is unlawful on the sabbath?

Literary Link

Luke's gospel logically moves from the question of fasting (5:33-39; not automatically required of his disciples by Jesus) to the account of casually gathering a handful of grain (v. 1), which was seen as a violation of the Sabbath. The issue of "eating" serves as the link between the two sections.

Sabbath Work

After the destruction of the temple by the Babylonians (587 BC), certain religious practices grew in importance as distinctive markers of Jewish identity: Sabbath, circumcision, respect for the written Torah, and dietary rules. Particularly in terms of the observance of the Sabbath, "hedges," so to speak, were grown around that command to protect it from any casual or creeping violation. Thus anything that could seem like the work of the week, as in the case of harvesting, was forbidden. Plucking a handful of grain was hardly reaping but came close enough to fall under the ban as described by some groups of Pharisees. Lighting the oven for baking seemed to come close enough to blacksmithing as to fall under the ban. The purpose was noble and wise, but an excessive preoccupation with the external could always lead to forgetting the true intent of the practice. The great Rabbi Hillel was famous for noting both the literal law and the intention behind that law. He developed a tradition of flexibility, and Jesus often spoke along the same vein. This is true for Christianity as well.

Lord of the Sabbath

Chapter 5 of Luke's gospel had proclaimed Jesus as source of health by his cures and as Lord of created matter by calming the storm. In this event Jesus is now proclaimed "lord of the sabbath" (v. 5). Thus we now have health, creation, and time. By that title Jesus is recognized as a reformer who teaches the true meaning of the Sabbath observance. In a fuller sense, as faith in his divinity deepened, he was also acknowledged as one with the Father who was uniquely worshiped on that day each week (Gen 2:2). This human Sabbath in our own experience was a faint echo of the rest taken by God at the end of the first week's work of creation. Jesus became associated with the work of creation and with the Sabbath that followed. Contemporary Christians need to reclaim the Sabbath in our culture too. It is in our benefit to do so. The Sabbath is for people. God does not need it, we do!

Monday of the Twenty-Third Week in Ordinary Time

First Reading (Year I)

Colossians 1:24–2:3

I am a minister of the Church to bring to completion the mystery hidden from ages past.

Rejoicing in Suffering

The only way in which one's suffering can be a cause for rejoicing (v. 24) is if the purpose and result itself gives hope and comfort. Paul understands that the hardships of his life are profoundly united with the afflictions of Christ's passion for the salvation of his Body the church. Baptized into Christ, Paul's entire apostolic life has been inserted into the growth of the Body of Christ. The same can be said for each and all of us these many years later. Christ is sufficient, but we make up whatever might be lacking in each successive generation by becoming part of his person and mission in our day. By grace we are the Body of Christ, and our sufferings as well as our joys belong to him and to the work of transforming the world.

The Mystery of the Gentiles

That all Gentiles, or "the nations" as the ancient prophets had named them, are called to become part of the Body of Christ is now revealed (v. 26) and proclaimed by Paul's ministry (v. 27). Everyone can come to his or her own respective perfection in Christ (v. 28). Christ's death, resurrection, and glorification represent the big picture to which everyone is called and by which all lives find their ultimate meaning. The presence of so many "Gentiles" at morning Mass is the proof of Paul's mission and the sign of his success.

Antiphon (Year I)

Psalm 62:8

In God is my safety and my glory.

The Refrain

Curiously, the response's refrain (v. 8) comes from the verse that the Lectionary omits from the portion of Psalm 62 chosen for this response. It forms a summary of what is sung in this answer to Paul's comments, for the psalm claims God to be hope and rock, salvation and stronghold (v. 7), even amid challenges and difficulties. If God is the supreme and ultimately the only dependable refuge, the hardships of life can be sustained and endured.

Trusting Confidence

The responsorial psalm concludes with an invitation to trust in God (v. 9). To trust is to acknowledge a need beyond our abilities at the moment, and to experience an assurance that what is needed will be provided in God's way and in God's time. God as "rock," "salvation," and "stronghold" (v. 7) is the source of our confidence.

First Reading (Year II)

1 Corinthians 5:1-8

Clean out the old yeast; for our Paschal Lamb, Christ, has been sacrificed.

A Community's Challenge

In some way Paul learned of the scandal present in the Corinthian community, that is, a man living with his father's wife (v. 1). He reacted strongly to that blatant immorality. Whatever the reason for the community's reticence to confront this morally unacceptable behavior (possibly alleging the new freedom of the Gospel), Paul was more forthright (v. 3). Paul requested that the guilty party be temporarily removed from their midst by way of remedial punishment (v. 5). Apparently Paul's apostolic boldness empowered him to confront moral aberrations in the community as well as to proclaim his countercultural convictions about Christ's death and resurrection. Contemporary Christianity can do no less. Without judging the inner motivation for unacceptable moral behavior, we are called to deal with the actions themselves and to call a spade a spade! This demands love for the welfare of all concerned and no little discernment. We depend on each other's example on every level.

Old Yeast

Paul supplies an image for what must be done, the cleansing of a home at the time of the feast of Unleavened Bread/Passover as required by the domestic ritual for Passover (Exod 12:15). Every year Orthodox Jewish homes scrupulously remove every crumb of leavened bread in preparation for the *mazzot* of Passover. Precisely this type of housecleaning (v. 7) is recommended to the Corinthians in regard to unacceptable moral behavior by their members. Even stale yeast ferments and, if unchecked, can spoil the whole batch with mold.

ANTIPHON (YEAR II)

Psalm 5:9

Lead me in your justice, Lord.

Psalm 5: Prayer Offered by Blameless Hands

Psalm 5 is often associated with the morning sacrifice of the temple (v. 4). It has been chosen by the Lectionary as a response to the first reading precisely because of its praise for God who does not tolerate any form of human sinfulness: falsehood, bloodthirsty behavior, or deceit (v. 7). Human arrogance is condemned and rejected (v. 6) by God. By the use of this refrain (v. 9) God is remembered as giving an example of what real justice/holiness looks like.

Divine Protection

God's protection (v. 12) for the just includes concern lest the bad example of others cause harm to the rest of the community. In other words, harm can come from within a community as well as from external sources. This is precisely the danger of scandal, putting a stumbling stone in the path of others. We believe that God respects human freedom, but still works to protect the innocent from undue permanent harm.

GOSPEL

Luke 6:6-11

The scribes and the Pharisees watched him closely to see if he would cure on the sabbath.

Literary Link

Immediately after proclaiming himself as the Lord of the Sabbath in response to the casual gathering of grain by his hungry disciples (v. 5), the gospel presents another Sabbath question in the form of a man with a withered hand (v. 6). This cure of a withered hand (vv. 6-11), like those of the leper and the paralytic in the prior chapter, illustrates what the work of the kingdom entails.

The Withered Right Hand

Contemporary Western society may not understand the problem posed by a right hand that was withered and useless. In many parts of the Near East the right hand is used for eating and social relations, while the left hand is reserved exclusively for personal hygiene. Extending the left hand or touching someone with it can be very offensive in those circles. Consequently, this was a man excluded from society and forced to a life isolated from meals with family, friends, or colleagues. To cure his right hand (v. 6) was to restore him to society and to enable him to join the Sabbath celebrations. If the genuine purpose of the Sabbath is to honor God by rejoicing in the produce of the fields among family, Jesus fulfilled that goal (v. 10) rather than violated it.

Reframing the Question

One of the great gifts of Jesus the rabbi/teacher was his ability to reframe a question so that it might be approached from a different perspective. In this case, Jesus neatly sidesteps the issue of work and introduces the questions of "do[ing] good" (v. 9) and participation in the community. He does so in order to instruct his observers and critics. Often good pastoral leadership is exercised in precisely that same manner.

Tuesday of the Twenty-Third Week in Ordinary Time

First Reading (Year I)

Colossians 2:6-15

God brought you to life along with Christ having forgiven us all our transgressions.

The Fullness of God

In an extraordinary application of teaching, the fullness of God (*plērōma*), which was applied to Christ himself in the great christological hymn (1:19), is now extended to all baptized Christians (v. 10). This was originally a term used by the early Gnostic heretics to describe the entire totality of heavenly powers and spiritual emanations. Perhaps they were the false teachers condemned by Paul (v. 8), but the concept is now applied by Paul to the Colossians because of their association with Christ through baptism (v. 12). Paul insists that Christ is the point of connection with God's "fullness." The entire cosmos is somehow united and energized by Christ and his disciples.

Revived and Glorified

Paul considered the prebaptized life of the Colossians as carnal and uncircumcised (v. 13). Although an awkward reference for a mixed community, the image is helpful because of its ability to demonstrate the shedding of a way of life for a new existence that is still bodily but incorporated into a new risen (v. 12) people of grace and truth. This new life demands new behavior (v. 6), described as "walking" in Christ. Elsewhere the letter also uses the metaphors of being rooted and built to describe the relationship of the newly baptized with Christ. Because of our baptism, what might be new or different about the way we live, at least in comparison with the world around us?

Antiphon (Year I)

Psalm 145:9

The Lord is compassionate toward all his works.

Psalm 145: Praising the God of Goodness

Prescinding from its use in the early church as a midday meal prayer (v. 15), the psalm's repeated references to blessing (v. 1) and praising (v. 2) God provide a fitting response to the reading's insistence that we share in God's own fullness. One can only be filled with awe and gratitude at such divine magnificence that surpasses all the individual gifts we have received. The ancient creed, which celebrates God's grace and mercy as well as his slowness to anger (v. 8), is also included in this response.

The Refrain

The refrain (v. 9) uses the English word "compassion." That choice hides, however, the psalmist's Hebrew reference to God's maternal mercy (*rehem*). That particular type of compassion is extended toward all God's works. It implies an enduring fondness for every creature and each event as history unfolds. Our God is never remotely distant but rather personally invested in the welfare of all creation.

First Reading (Year II)

1 Corinthians 6:1-11

A believer goes to court against a believer and that before unbelievers.

Faith and Judgment

The report that Corinthians were taking their disputes to local civil courts for resolution (vv. 1, 6) was something that stunned Paul. The repeated use of the word "judge/judgment" amply demonstrates the impact of that news upon Paul's sense of right order. He was convinced that the "holy ones" (v. 2), namely, the baptized, brought additional wisdom to the resolution of human disputes because of the insights given by their faith. The mutual unity effected by the bond of baptism in Christ and the Gospel's call to generosity, especially toward the needy, were considerations not normally prominent in the minds of outsiders. Paul even suggests that Christians learn to live with injustice (v. 7) for the sake of harmony and good example to outsiders.

This text could also provide an occasion for an instruction regarding the existence of diocesan church courts and their ministry.

Excluded from the Kingdom

Paul's list of the actions that render some persons excluded from the kingdom (vv. 9-10) is very explicit and even graphic. Without the necessity of explaining each category, it suffices to note that the list reflects typical morality of the first-century Greco-Roman world, and indicates the manner in which early Christian community, like the Jewish communities of the Diaspora, stood as a countercultural witness to paganism. Since aspects of this same list occur elsewhere (Rom 1:26-27; 1 Tim 1:10), it is clearly a litany of moral expectations throughout that world, not merely a teaching aimed exclusively at Corinthians. Non-Christians of the ancient world, however, found the monotheism and morality of Judaism and Christianity very attractive. Our contemporary secular world of excessive individual rights and freedoms may need a similar set of moral standards. The kingdom has specific moral expectations, and the witness of the community speaks louder than words.

Antiphon (Year II)

Psalm 149:4

The Lord takes delight in his people.

Psalm 149: Praise for the God Who Chose Israel

The description of joy (v. 2) among God's people celebrates the fact that they are "faithful/*hasidim*" (vv. 1, 5). The Hebrew word is related to *hesed*, namely, covenantal kindness, and therefore literally signifies those who live in mutual covenantal concern for God's will. A community comprised of such people represents the moral standard that Paul is holding up for the Corinthians in the day's reading about lawsuits. The word also indicates the type of community in which God takes great delight because they are truly his people!

Songs of Praise

In four different verses and ways this psalm response makes allusion to the song of God's joyful people. Praise should find sung form for its exuberant gratitude, not mere verbal recitation. Too often our weekday celebrations are content with the latter, and our praise is diminished accordingly.

Gospel

Luke 6:12-19

He spent the night in prayer. He chose Twelve, whom he also named Apostles.

Literary Link

One of Luke's special perspectives is the fact that Jesus spent time in prayer at major turning points in his ministry: in the desert at its beginning (4:1), at the selection of the Twelve (6:12), and at Gethsemane (22:41-42). After the two Sabbath incidents, Jesus is presented as selecting the Twelve to be human agents for a renewed Israel. That the names are immediately followed by a generic list of the activities of the kingdom (vv. 18-19) delineates the activities they now share.

The Twelve

One should not miss the significance of the number twelve (v. 13), and its relationship to the twelve tribes of Israel. Like Elijah with his disciples, Jesus is pictured as a great religious reformer and renewer of Israel. Many scholars suspect that the actual word "apostle" came later, perhaps after the resurrection, when it became necessary to send representatives from one Christian community to another. The actual number of such "apostles" would seem to be more than twelve (Acts 14:4, 14). The Byzantine traditions of Eastern Christianity celebrate many names of saints endowed with the title of "apostle." The actual names listed by Luke are distinct individuals with specific personalities, as the inclusion, for example, of both Matthew the tax collector and Simon the zealot (bitterly opposed to Roman occupiers) demonstrates (v. 15)! A presider might be tempted to continue the list with the names of those present at a morning Mass, each of whom are now called to be partners in the spread of the kingdom.

Tuesday of the Twenty-Third Week in Ordinary Time

The Listening and Healed Crowd

The presence of the great crowd comprised of Judeans and Gentiles from the coast shows the universalism of the teaching of Jesus and the diversity of the crowds that came to listen (v. 17). Everyone responded positively and was therefore healed (v. 19). This presents a different picture than that of Matthew where Jesus feels himself sent primarily to the lost sheep of Israel (Matt 15:24; that story, by the way, is not found in Luke, who has more universalism in mind from the beginning). This summary provided the introduction of the work to the Twelve. A similar generic description should be offered at the final rite of dismissal for the works to be performed by the weekday Mass crowd each day.

Wednesday of the Twenty-Third Week in Ordinary Time

First Reading (Year I)

Colossians 3:1-11

You have died with Christ; put to death, then, the parts of you that are earthly.

Seeking What Is Above

The first verses of this passage (vv. 1-4) are also offered as an alternative second reading for Easter Sunday each year. To seek what is above (v. 1) is to live according to the life of one who is baptized into the new creation. To live a risen life already here and now is to put aside the various types of immorality listed in the letter's litany of vices (vv. 5, 8), the first list more characterized by sexual impropriety and the second by inner anger and hostility. Both are rejected as contrary to the attitudes of anyone living in God's kingdom. By contrasting the "above" with the "earthly" (v. 5), the letter introduces the image of a spatial dichotomy, but that is only one manner of illustrating the different perspective inherent in the new creation. The "new self" recommended by this text (v. 10) leads us to wonder precisely what a "new and improved" version of our own individual selves might look like.

Neither Jew nor Greek

Entering the new creation erases many of the distinctions (v. 11) that have marked the ancient world as well as our own. By baptism there is a new fundamental equality before God among all the social and economic groups within any given society. In fidelity to the New Testament's teachings, however, one should be cautious about presuming that this equality translates into availability for all the different ministries or tasks within the assembly. There still remains the reality of a functionally differentiated community from the beginning (1 Cor 12:1-11; Eph 4:11). Each baptized person is equipped for whatever God calls that person to do.

Antiphon (Year I)

Psalm 145:9

The Lord is compassionate toward all his works.

Psalm 145: Still Praising God

Curiously, and in fact contrary to the usual practice of the Lectionary, the same psalm (with slightly different verses and the omission of the ancient creed in v. 8) and the same refrain are provided two days in a row. Perhaps it is the praise and blessing of the community elevated to participation in the new creation as described in the reading that elicits such repeated and everlasting gratitude (v. 13).

Unsearchable Greatness

We use many words to describe the goodness and greatness of God. Most descriptions are taken from different aspects of our daily experience. We are reminded, however, that in the last analysis all our words fall short because God's goodness is ultimately unsearchable (v. 3). We sometimes speak of "apophatic" theology, namely, the recognition that our praise fails so profoundly as to almost demand that we deny God's goodness, wisdom, and so forth. God so surpasses our experience as to almost quickly add by way of correction, "God is not good" (as we limited human beings understand "goodness")!

First Reading (Year II)

1 Corinthians 7:25-31

Are you bound to a wife? Do not seek a separation. Are you free of a wife? Then, do not look for a wife.

The Shadow of the Parousia

Because all the early Christians assumed that the second coming of Jesus our Lord and Christ was imminent, all stable human institutions were under judgment and were to be approached with caution. Paul, together with all his early Christian colleagues, was convinced that the world in its present form was passing away quickly (v. 31). The point of this passage is that the shadow of the Second Coming fell upon every aspect of life and all human institutions. It colored all their emotions. This is a perspective that we need to reactivate and renew periodically.

Marriage

Obviously, the enduring relationship of marriage easily became a set of obligations that some ancient teachers rejected as obstacles to the kingdom. Confronted with such pastoral questions, Paul's basic response is "stay as you are" (see v. 26), even though the choice to change one's marital status would certainly not be sinful. As a faithful Jew, conscious of all the obligations of the Torah to increase and multiply (Gen 1:28), scholars suggest that Paul may himself have been married once, and simply was following his own advice since there is no hint in any letter of a wife in his life.

Wednesday
of the Twenty-Third Week
in Ordinary Time

ANTIPHON (YEAR II)

Psalm 45:11

Listen to me, daughter; see and bend your ear.

Psalm 45: A Wedding Song

Psalm 45 is generally considered to be a royal wedding hymn, describing the life and duties of a young king and his consort. Any efforts to pinpoint the precise occasion for its composition seem fruitless. It is easy to understand why the editors of the Lectionary chose this psalm as a response to Paul's thoughts about marriage. The psalm's positive attitude toward marriage was helpful in the early church because the final messianic banquet was often described as the wedding feast of the Lamb (Rev 21:2, 9).

Advice to the Bride

Curiously, the advice to the groom in the first portion of Psalm 45 has been ignored, and the entire response is directed to the bride as a symbol of the entire Christian community. She is told to henceforth forget her family (v. 11), share her beauty with her new husband (v. 12), wear glorious clothing (v. 14), and care for her children (v. 17). This portrait of an ideal wealthy royal wife is offered as a response to Paul's advice to "stay as you are."

GOSPEL

Luke 6:20-26

Blessed are you who are poor. Woe to you who are rich.

Literary Link

After being confronted by a large crowd when Jesus came down to the plain (v. 17) subsequent to his appointment of the Twelve, Luke presents Jesus as teaching his equivalent to the Sermon on the Mount. The summary gathers material from different contexts in a thematic rather than geographical context.

Lukan Beatitudes

If one compares Luke's beatitudes with those more familiar from Matthew's Sermon on the Mount, we find only four (vv. 20-22). We note that these are shorter, and more directly personal because of the repeated use of the "you" and "now." In contrast to Matthew's list (5:3ff.), Luke also supplements his blessings with corresponding woes (vv. 24-26) to sharpen their point. Note that Luke does not include peacemakers, the meek, the merciful, or the single-hearted in his list. The Lukan list therefore invokes Christ's blessings in a manner that is more focused on the physical needs of the poor.

The Lukan Community

Some commentators read between the lines of these beatitudes and conclude that Luke's community was more affluent, and therefore more in need of regular encouragement toward generosity to those who were physically needy. Luke was also more attentive to moral behavior that could be overly influenced by public respect and peer pressure. This may explain the final warning regarding a woe to those who are spoken well of within the community (v. 26). Human praise is fleeting; God's alone endures!

Thursday of the Twenty-Third Week in Ordinary Time

First Reading (Year I)

Colossians 3:12-17

Put on love, that is, the bond of perfection.

Getting Dressed

In the early church the newly welcomed Christians wore their white baptismal robe for a week after Easter. That may well have been the inspiration for the image that introduces this reading, the command to "put on" various new virtues and attitudes (v. 12). Daily apparel was much simpler in the ancient world, especially for workers and servants, than for us moderns, but at least a moment for dressing each morning was always required for most folks. That remains all the more true for us today. Imagine the extra daily effort, not simply to think about color coordination or climate, but to put on the virtues needed for the work of a given day. The letter names them for our convenience (v. 13). All the "clothing" listed in this spiritual wardrobe seem to refer to relationships with others, including forgiveness.

Gratitude

After suggesting that love is the belt that holds the rest together and in place (v. 14), the letter stresses the fundamental attitude of gratitude, even mentioning that disposition three times (vv. 15, 16, 17). Whether the day promises joy or threatens sorrow, we are always asked to approach life with truly grateful hearts. Everything we have is gift, even the more difficult aspects of life. The truly mature disciple can even say "thanks" for them!

Antiphon (Year I)

Psalm 150:6

Let everything that breathes praise the Lord!

Psalm 150: The Last Hurrah

The response chosen for this reading, perhaps inspired by the encouragement of the letter to songs and canticles (v. 16), is the Psalter's entire final concluding hymn of praise. Perhaps eight or nine different musical instruments are listed in the temple orchestra (v. 1). No wonder the final verse also invites everything that breathes to join the effort because plenty of wind would be necessary for all the music! This response is an opportunity to encourage congregational singing because God deserves it (v. 6).

Mighty Deeds

The praise is encouraged because of God's actions throughout history (v. 2). By one's deeds one is known, and that also applies to God whom we cannot see with our physical eyes. Praise is offered to "who God is" because of what God does. The congregation is always encouraged to update the list with more recent events as further grist for praise.

First Reading (Year II)

1 Corinthians 8:1b-7, 11-13

When you sin against your brothers,
weak as they are, you are sinning against Christ.

Knowledge

At a time of the year when back-to-school issues are paramount for modern young people in families and parishes, it's helpful to think about the reality of human knowledge as a moral question. The ancient Corinthians were confronted by the early Gnostic heresy that claimed to possess certain secret knowledge. The Gnostics explained how to use that knowledge to gain access to heaven. In Paul's emphasis on the paschal mystery, he resisted their approach mightily. For the Corinthian community he suggested that the ultimate test of all knowledge is not what one knows, but how one uses what one knows! If someone's knowledge produces merely a self-centered pride and arrogance (v. 1) or disdain for the less "educated" colleagues, without either awe or a concern for the common good, it is a waste of time. It may even be dangerous to one's salvation because it places the accent upon us, not God. The desire to know is in itself the gift of God and the fruit of the Holy Spirit, but only when expressed with humble generosity.

Care for the Weaker in Any Community

Weakness can be religious and moral as well as emotional and physical. A genuinely Christian community at prayer is always marked by concern for its weaker members (v. 11), whoever they may be. Paul uses the issue of eating meat that had been sacrificed to idols at the local butcher shop as an illustration of that concern (v. 4). Even though a spiritually mature Christian might eat such meat without qualms because idols are in fact nothing, one is cautioned not to partake if the action would create spiritual harm to the weaker members of the community (v. 12). The presider's role at daily Eucharist is to keep everyone mindful of the larger and often invisible community around them.

Thursday of the Twenty-Third Week in Ordinary Time

ANTIPHON (YEAR II)

Psalm 139:24b

Guide me, Lord, along the everlasting way.

Psalm 139: God the All-Knowing

Influenced by the Wisdom tradition of Israel, Psalm 139 celebrates the universal knowledge and presence of God in very personal language. Acknowledging the fact that God knows one's inner thoughts (v. 1) and every action of the day (v. 2), the psalm is an apt response to Paul's teaching in the day's reading from Colossians about the inner worries of the weak and the mature spirituality of the strong. In both instances, compassionate discernment is needed; hence the refrain's request for guidance (v. 24).

Knowledge

The responsorial psalm refers to "knowing" four times. The Hebrew concept of knowledge includes personal concern and care as well as objective understanding. Like the medical technician reading the X-rays of a family member or dear friend, one experiences affectionate concern as well as offers expert diagnosis. God knows and cares a great deal about each person.

GOSPEL

Luke 6:27-38

Be merciful, just as your Father is merciful.

Literary Link

Luke's beatitudes present blessings and contrasting woes (vv. 20-26). They then logically flow into the biblical commandment of love for one's enemies (vv. 27-35), which begins to turn everything upside down. Luke's sermon on the plain (vv. 20-49) uses some of the same material as Matthew in a much abbreviated form, beginning, as did Matthew, with beatitudes and ending with the parable of building a house on rock or sand (vv. 46-49).

The Great Reversal

One of the main themes of Christ's eschatological teachings is the promise of the final judgment when the mighty will be cast down from their thrones and the lowly lifted up. That sweeping current of God's grace in human history begins within the mind and heart of the individual Christian who counters hate with love (v. 27), violence with respect, and greed with generosity (v. 29). The constant concern of Jesus for a person's inner attitude beyond the external act is evident in this series of teachings. It is precisely the inner Christian attitude that is often so contrary to human reasoning.

True Love for Enemies

To set the record straight, these gospel verses do not require that devoted followers of Jesus simply accede without discernment to the demands of those around them (v. 30); rather the command is to love such individuals wisely and well. The mercy of God toward everyone is the criterion for our mercy toward others (v. 36). That type of loving concern for the welfare of others may even mean loving someone enough to say "no" and to do so for the right reason! Once again there is a danger when one makes any single verse the sum and substance of an entire theology or spirituality because every verse is somehow nuanced by another teaching elsewhere in the Scriptures. One may even be required to make a tentative judgment about others (v. 37), always respectfully and out of genuine love. God alone, however, has the final say.

Friday of the Twenty-Third Week in Ordinary Time

First Reading (Year I)

1 Timothy 1:1-2, 12-14

I was once a blasphemer, but I have been mercifully treated.

The First Letter to Timothy
Similar to Second Timothy and Titus, this letter is written to an individual religious leader out of concerns for proper doctrine and organizational structures. The false teachers are philosophers rather than Judaizers. For that reason these are often judged later letters, possibly even written by a colleague other than Paul himself. Their pastoral challenges resonate well with our age's concerns. Timothy was Paul's companion on the second and third missionary voyages, and was assigned by later tradition as the bishop of Ephesus.

Candid Sharing

The Lectionary chooses to omit the initial portion of this letter that deals with false teachers (vv. 3-11) in order to highlight the personal nature of Paul's opening greeting. He writes candidly as if to a familiar friend and rehearses his conversion from persecutor (v. 13) to become God's trustworthy minister and partner. By his example we are also encouraged to unburden our hearts and to share our joys with those whose lives have been similarly claimed by the Gospel of Christ. Faith-sharing groups can be moments of great grace. Faith instinctively leads to community.

Child in Faith

Every so often Paul will adopt some paternal language in addressing a community because of the relationship he had to the manner in which faith had been generated in their lives. Similarly here, Paul calls Timothy his "true child in faith" (v. 2), intimating that it was Paul who initially instructed—and possibly even baptized and welcomed—him into the Christian faith. This close relationship is consistent with the teaching of Jesus that a new family is created by baptism in Christ! His sisters and brothers are those who do God's will.

Antiphon (Year I)

Psalm 16:5

You are my inheritance, O Lord.

The Refrain

There is a certain logic in the Lectionary's choice of the word "inheritance" (v. 5) because of the close quasi family/filial relationship that Paul had with Timothy. Families share possessions (spiritual as well as material) and receive them one from another by way of bequest and inheritance. They also share like-minded attitudes that are passed from one generation to another. In the new creation all such inheritances come ultimately, however, from God alone. They are to be shared wisely and generously with other believers. What "inheritance" have we received through baptism or parish membership?

Allotted Portion

Psalm 16 has been interpreted as a hymn that described the event by which a person embraced the God of Israel (v. 1) and became a member of the covenant community: secure protection and a new relationship (v. 1), source of nourishment (v. 2), counsel and advice (v. 12). By family/tribal membership one received a portion (v. 2) of the land allotted by God to one's tribe. The psalm verses are a fitting response to Paul's paternal relationship to Timothy; they describe the blessings of family bonds.

First Reading (Year II)

1 Corinthians 9:16-19, 22b-27

I have become all things to all, to save at least some.

Preacher as Believer

Anyone who bears the obligation to preach knows the sense of duty to be faithful to the message proclaimed; Paul preaches the very good news in which he hopes to share personally (v. 23). Sometimes that fidelity is also an occasion for tension as the preacher inevitably reveals personal failings and struggles in the process. Every preacher is both a "before" and "after" illustration of grace at work. Even though the focus should be on the message and not on embarrassing self-revelations, the medium does also become the message. To acknowledge that is itself a humbling grace.

All Things to All

The proper focus of this Pauline principle "all for all" (see v. 22) should be the needs of those served. That duty presumes two further considerations: (1) an inner principle of conviction regarding the message (no wishy-washy pandering to everyone without guiding principles or foundational truth of the Gospel), and (2) a knowledge of the true needs of people beyond their wants at the moment. Our faith and our personal experience enable us to see what people need for their spiritual growth.

Urgency

Paul insists that a preacher grounded in God's Spirit and Christ's mission will have a certain focus and urgency about the task (v. 27); for that reason he writes, "woe to me if I do not preach" (v. 16). Most people possess an inner "canon within a canon," a preferred viewpoint or truth that somehow governs and unifies everything else. Both believers and preachers need to know their own hearts, to make adjustments accordingly, and to remain open to the fuller grace of God who calls everyone, even teachers of the faith, to ongoing conversion and growth. The urgency should not blind us to constant spiritual development.

ANTIPHON (YEAR II)

Psalm 84:2

How lovely is your dwelling place, Lord, mighty God!

The Beauty of the Temple

The first temple under Solomon was crafted by the best artists available to capture the attention of visitors and to give honor to God. It was truly "lovely" (v. 2). Physical beauty, however, is not an end in itself. One should never allow familiarity with a place to blind a person to its inherent beauty or to forget its ultimate purpose. The Catholic tradition, based for example, on the values of Israel and the historical work of Solomon, prizes artistic beauty and the use of sacred art in the construction of our places of worship. This is honor, not idolatry. Without the best of religious art, a building is somehow not yet fully Catholic! It is important to periodically resurvey the beauty of our sacred places.

Transcendence of God

No matter how artfully crafted a structure nor how impressive its decoration, the reality of God is infinitely beyond all material religious objects, howsoever gorgeous. God always remains "mighty" in every way (v. 2). The psalm refrain suggests that we look again at our own church architecture in order to see the space as if for the first time, and to remember its true purpose! God must remain completely above and beyond anything human beings may do to offer the witness of material and spiritual beauty.

GOSPEL

Luke 6:39-42

Can a blind person guide a blind person?

Literary Link

In these verses the literary logic of the sermon on the plain presents a curious contrast. Having just condemned the act of judging others (vv. 37-38), the gospel balances that command and turns to the need for sight and discernment in anyone entrusted with leadership. If they are blind (v. 39), they are not able to serve others.

Careful analysis is not the same as judgment. The ministry of discernment and sorting out options is the positive side of the coin, but definitively judging the ultimate inner motives of others is forbidden.

Friday of the Twenty-Third Week in Ordinary Time

Prejudice and Bias

The gospel presents the contrasting images of the log versus the splinter (v. 41). Any truly wise teacher or preacher must beware of personal prejudices, namely, the log in his or her own eye that can limit or even twist the message. Sometimes catechists and preachers simply expound their own prejudices rather than the truth of the Gospel or the authentic teaching of the church. Sometimes scholars teach what is in their eyelashes rather than what is in the text! Anytime we find ourselves surprised in a new situation, we should look inward because the very fact of surprise may indicate a prejudice or at least a presumption in the face of something unexpected. The "expected" could be the prejudice.

The Growth of the Hearer

Every true teacher of the gospel or instructor in any branch of human knowledge should live with a constant focus on the personal, ongoing development of the student listener (v. 40). A good teacher overcomes any self-centered or arrogant sense of self-importance. When trained, the learner equals or surpasses the teacher. A good teacher cares greatly about the truth and about the maturing faith of the one to whom that truth is passed on.

Saturday of the Twenty-Third Week in Ordinary Time

First Reading (Year I)

1 Timothy 1:15-17

Christ Jesus came into the world to save sinners.

Salvation of Sinners

The fundamental truth, which Paul claims is trustworthy and deserving of full acceptance, is the simple fact that Christ Jesus came to save sinners (v. 15). Wealth of knowledge and the various ministerial gifts of leadership may also be side products, or even the construction of beautiful churches and temples, but the basic purpose of Christ's coming is to save sinners. Continuing the theme of spiritual candor between Paul and Timothy, Paul admits that he is the foremost of sinners (v. 15). Perhaps it is out of a great sense of gratitude for God's mercy that the reading ends with a doxology (v. 17).

The Patience of Christ

I suspect a twinkle in Paul's eyes when he notes that his own case was a test of Christ's patience (v. 16), especially given the enormous task required to move him from his determination to persecute Christians to his decision to become one. It was a moment of great grace. God must undoubtedly also have a great deal of patience in regard to each and all of us. When we are tempted to be short and impatient with the faults of others, we might best remember how much of that same patience God needs to expend when dealing with us. We have much to learn.

Antiphon (Year I)

Psalm 113:2

Blessed be the name of the Lord for ever.

Praise for the Name

It was out of growing reverence for God that Jewish leaders were inclined to refrain from using the actual name of God. They simply praised "the name," as is done three times (vv. 1-3) throughout the course of this responsorial psalm. The refrain repeats the phrase. Many Orthodox Jews even today object to the printing of "in God we trust" on currency because the name of God is thus so open to disrespect and misuse. Our American culture has no qualms about using the Lord's name in so many casual or even disrespectful ways. This psalm's reticence could serve as a reminder and a remedy. "Oh, God!" is a prayer, not an expression of surprise.

One Who Raises Up the Poor

The characteristic action of God that immediately comes to mind when praising his name, as the psalm indicates, is the fact that he raises up the poor from the dust and dunghill (v. 7). The verse may have been chosen by the Lectionary in acknowledgment of Paul's humble admission of himself as foremost among sinners (v. 15), and therefore as one who was himself symbolically raised from the dust and the dunghill.

First Reading (Year II)

1 Corinthians 10:14-22

We, though many, are one Body,
for we all partake of the one bread.

Avoidance of All Idolatry

Paul's admonition to avoid all idolatry (v. 14) made eminent sense to the ancient Corinthians whose public places were filled with temples of all sorts. For centuries the city's great forum was dominated by a magnificent temple to Apollo the sun god. The city's meat markets were filled with portions of animals that had been first sacrificed, and then offered for sale to the public (v. 18). It was not easy to avoid contact with that pagan world, especially for occupational guilds that had their own religious ceremonies. A member of the profession was expected to participate in the ritual. Our own more modern society is also filled with the "worship" of mere human values that are often contrary to the gospel. Anything that assumes ultimate value in life, such as money, social prestige, or popularity, is a virtual god or an idol; subservience to that value is a sort of idolatry! This is not merely a quaint bit of antiquity.

Participation in the Eucharist

To share in the Eucharist is to become part of the Body of Christ (v. 16). It also implies becoming part of an entire world in which the death and resurrection of Jesus himself is paramount. Sharing the cup and the loaf is sharing in Christ himself. The ritual thus presumes the assumption of the mind of Jesus, namely, self-sacrificing love of neighbor and full submission to the will of the Father for the transformation of the entire world. This encompasses all of creation and history. Sharing the prayer is not a matter of an isolated ritual or a single hour. It is the work of a lifetime!

Saturday of the Twenty-Third Week in Ordinary Time

ANTIPHON (YEAR II)

Psalm 116:17

To you, Lord, I offer a sacrifice of praise.

Praise as Sacrifice

Every song of praise presumes the assumption of a humble stance before the person praised (v. 17). Every word of praise, therefore, is like an offering, verbal in this instance, which acknowledges that relationship. The words of the praise take something of human value, perhaps artful phrases and lilting cadences, and then offer them humbly and place them at the disposition of the one so honored. The song itself is a form of verbal sacrifice. It should never be casually uttered or distractedly pronounced! Psalm 116 also presumes the ritual action of offering a "cup of salvation" (v. 13). These verses have many eucharistic overtones and form a fitting echo of Paul's words regarding the Eucharist.

The Relationship of the Song to Life

Psalm 116 suggests that praise is related to all the blessings of the life of the singer (v. 12). Precisely because of blessings received and benefits experienced in any single experience, the praise is uttered to God who is the source of all blessings and all life. One blessing cannot be separated, therefore, from all the other experiences of one's life. To divorce the song from the rest of life is to cut it off from the ground from which it should spring, and from the motive that inspires the praise. Moreover, everything focuses back on God.

GOSPEL

Luke 6:43-49

Why do you call me, "Lord, Lord," but do not do what I command?

Literary Link

After dealing with the impossibility of seeing well if one has a log in his or her eye (v. 41), the gospel now moves to the necessity of action in life beyond mere words. Both impaired vision and lack of action are obstacles to doing God's will.

Good Fruit

Many familiar proverbs presume a moral relationship and continuity between generations. "Apples don't fall far from the tree" and "like father like son" are two examples. Rotten trees bear rotten fruit (v. 43). In families we generally presume good from good and bad from bad. Often attitudes toward life and toward neighbors are intergenerational, that is, they are learned from our ancestors and shared with those who come after us. Actions flow from one's heart; good and noble actions from a good heart. Anyone can make mistakes, but the general principle remains: each generation influences its successor, and intentions influence behavior.

Action beyond Words

Both Matthew's Sermon on the Mount and Luke's Sermon on the Plain conclude with the same set of contrasting imagery, namely, the foundation upon which a person builds a home. Those who build on solid rock are those who put their words to work and live the talk. Words alone are light and airy, easily moved and without solid roots or foundations. The "Lord, Lord" of praise (v. 46) or petition is easily spoken, but remains incomplete without the follow-up of action or the proof of commitment. One might say that the purpose of the church is to praise God by transforming the world. Without the latter, the initial praise is insincere and empty.

Monday of the Twenty-Fourth Week in Ordinary Time

First Reading (Year I)

1 Timothy 2:1-8

I ask that prayers be offered for everyone to God who wills everyone to be saved.

Prayers for Kings

At the time that the letter was written, probably toward the end of the first century AD, Christians were already being persecuted. Peter and Paul had been martyred in Rome. Accused of atheism because they refused to offer sacrifices to Roman gods, Christians were viewed as a people who undermined social order. In ordering prayers for those in various levels of authority (v. 2), church leaders like Timothy were instructed to pray for their enemies and to respect the very authority that was often used against them. Those who received the letter must have said, "Oh, really?" In presenting themselves as an orderly people (v. 2), Christians attempted to remove the basis for accusations, but also to exercise a missionary effort for the salvation of those in authority. Our contemporary prayers must go beyond political divisions and partisan factions with an eye toward everyone's growth in truth (v. 4). Do our contemporary prayers ever surprise anyone?

Christ for All

Faith in Christ, the one mediator and ransom for all (vv. 5-6), should lead to a deeper respect for the fundamental unity of all people, no matter what function they may have in society or what nationality they may share. The prejudices and difficulties of each generation produce their own boundaries between the "us and them"; all delineations should be put aside because humanity is one, and all people are the objects of concern and salvation for Christ. Do our prayers ever exclude anyone? What does that say about our God? or about us?

Antiphon (Year I)

Psalm 28:6

Blessed be the Lord, for he has heard my prayer.

Psalm 28: A Prayer for Rescue

The psalm verses chosen by the Lectionary offer an abbreviated version of the traditional lament: first a plea to be heard (v. 2), then a prayer of praise on the assumption that God had already put their rescue into motion (v. 7). Because the verses are all about prayer, they form a suitable liturgical response to the reading that commands prayers, even for the pagan king. The verses offer an example of how to obey that request.

The Motive for Blessing

The refrain (v. 6, not repeated in the response itself) seems restricted to the fact that God has responded to our own individual prayers. It sounds as if we only bless God because of individual personal benefit. A fuller expression of praise and gratitude should also include everyone in those words of blessing. Thus, for example, a petition at Mass for a friend undergoing surgery should be expanded to include everyone in that situation. Any prayer that is too focused only on our personal needs and wants should be viewed with caution. Such a prayer does not really reflect the universal love of Christ for all people!

First Reading (Year II)

1 Corinthians 11:17-26, 33

If there are divisions among you, then you do not eat the Lord's supper.

Christian Meetings

To say, as Paul does in the very first verse, that the meetings of Corinthians do more harm than good (v. 17) is very damning. Although Paul's concern was primarily about eucharistic gatherings, his criticism could be far more general. This admonition to the Corinthians could become an occasion for Christians in every land and in all time to simply pause for an evaluation of the actual effect of any meeting. Do the sessions promote the common good, deepen the bonds of charity and justice within the community, or merely serve the whims of individual participants? A US Midwestern diocese once asked that the last question on every parish committee agenda be the following: "Have the poor been assisted by this meeting?" What makes a meeting "Christian"? The motive for the meeting, as well as its results, remains crucial.

Divisions

Paul acknowledges that differences of opinion, and even factions, can in fact be helpful at times (v. 19). This is true, especially if they contribute to mutual understanding, or allow for individuals to surface as clear spokespersons for an opinion or perspective. Disagreements could even ultimately result in the development of leadership within a community. Differences can in fact promote the larger truth and deepen unity if each opinion is heard respectfully and accorded the best interpretation possible (as Ignatius of Loyola suggests).

Eucharist as Model of Self-Sacrifice

The primacy of the Eucharist in the early communities founded by Paul is acknowledged by the very fact that it was a tradition already received by Paul some twenty years after the resurrection (v. 23). The fact that Christ gave himself away and poured himself out is the measure of the entire meeting/gathering of every Eucharist, namely, concern for the welfare of others, not selfish preoccupation with our own individual wants and needs. That same spirit should be the measure of every other noneucharistic gathering in a truly Christian community.

ANTIPHON (YEAR II)

1 Corinthians 11:26b

Proclaim the death of the Lord until he comes again.

Psalm 40: Obedience, Not Sacrifice

The psalm chosen by the Lectionary is an expression of gratitude for a saving intervention of God whose justice is announced to all (v. 10). Going beyond the mere external ritual of sacrificial offering, the psalm's verses acknowledge the need for the deeper attitude of humble obedience (v. 8). This same psalm is cited by the Letter to the Hebrews as a fundamental attitude attributed to Jesus (10:5).

Proclaiming the Lord's Death

Contrary to the usual practice of the Lectionary, the refrain is not selected from the psalm but from the text of the reading. There Paul insists that the meaning of sharing the bread and cup (v. 23) is to give witness to the Lord's death. At the center of all Christian worship is the perennial proclamation of Christ's death for the forgiveness of sins. It is not the fact of his death that stands at the center of our faith, but its loving purpose. The daily insistence on that historical event, even into our day, keeps our world in focus amid the rest of life's activities and concerns. The death of Christ is not endlessly repeated (as if it were not sufficient once and for all), but rather extended into our day so that we might share its transforming power.

Final Return

The final glorious return of Christ, as noted in the refrain (v. 26), needs to be kept in mind as we await the full future revelation of the victory of Christ. Only then will the meaning and final effect of Christ's death become crystal clear to everyone. For both Jews and Christians, history has a purpose and a conclusion. That reality is very much part of our faith.

GOSPEL

Luke 7:1-10

Not even in Israel have I found such faith.

Literary Link

After Christ's teachings about a tree revealed through its fruits (6:43), and the importance of a house built of rock (v. 48), the sermon on the plain is concluded. Luke now provides concrete examples of that goodness and of words flowing into actions. The gospel's examples describe two healings, one for men in the centurion's servant (7:1-10) and another for women in the raising of the widow's son (vv. 11-17). Luke is a model for inclusivity. The fruits of Christ's ministry are universal.

The Roman Centurion

It may be helpful to pause for a moment to consider the qualities of the centurion described in the gospel. He is (1) a paragon of concern for his servants and social inferiors, (2) generous to the local Jewish population by building the synagogue (v. 5), (3) possibly a "God-fearer" who found Jewish morality and monotheism very attractive, and (4) clearly humble in his exercise of authority. He modeled in his own life what he expected of others (v. 6). Moreover, this is an officer in the army of the generally detested occupational Roman army! Luke praises the centurion and unexpectedly makes him a model of foreign presence and leadership. Luke's gospel was concerned about demonstrating that Christians were not subversive members of the society of his day.

Ritual Formula for Holy Communion

The fact that the church's liturgy has chosen the words of this Roman soldier (v. 6) as the humble prayer of each Catholic prior to the reception of Communion suggests that we ought to ponder these words and all their implications thoroughly. We should never allow them to become thoughtless rote phrases. The new translation of the Missal makes this biblical allusion clearer and more fruitful for authentic devotion. The centurion refers to Jesus entering his home and his world. The larger reference should not be lost at the moment of individual consumption of the Consecrated Bread. The Catholic ritual phrase unites the centurion and the healed servant with the recipient of Communion.

Tuesday of the Twenty-Fourth Week in Ordinary Time

FIRST READING (YEAR I)

1 Timothy 3:1-13

The bishop must be irreproachable; similarly, deacons must hold fast to the mystery of the faith with a clear conscience.

Bishops

The qualities expected in the life and demeanor of anyone summoned to serve as a bishop/overseer in the local church are listed in this reading (vv. 2-7). The presumption of the letter is that the Christian community is now more settled and developed as a group of residents. This gives some reason for thinking that the letter was in fact written toward the end of the first century by someone with the spirit of Paul. Both personality and practice are reflected in this "job description." Notice that issues of authentic faith are presumed, and that "style" seems to be of primary concern here. The qualities are the same as those expected in any family leader (v. 4). Wisdom in dealing with children and managing a household are expected of both bishop (vv. 4-5) and deacon (v. 12). In some way the bishop should belong to the entire community and be "ordained/reordered" to the service of the entire community. Reputation in the wider community is expected (v. 7). It is always good to be reminded of the ideal, and helpful to pray for those so called.

Deacons

Deacons are mentioned only in Paul's Letter to the Philippians (1:1). Although Acts 6 is often cited as the occasion for the institution of this ministry, most contemporary scholarship thinks otherwise. The men and women (v. 11) involved in this ministry as partners or spouses are also expected to be skilled household managers (v. 12) and persons of solid faith (v. 9). The fact that they must not be seen as greedy (v. 8) may be related to their duty of dispensing the community's charity to those in need. The same qualities are in fact expected of all members of the community.

ANTIPHON (YEAR I)

Psalm 101:2

I will walk with blameless heart.

Psalm 101: Servant Leadership

From ancient times this psalm was understood as the prayer of the prince because it speaks so clearly of the personal attitudes and duties of a faithful leader: integrity (vv. 2, 6), blamelessness (v. 2), as well as public honesty and humility (v. 5). It is a very fitting profession of ministerial responsibility that could be renewed before the community regularly.

Refrain

In particular, because the verse from which the refrain is taken concludes with the words "within my house" (v. 2), it fits the first reading's requirements for both bishop and deacon well. Immediately after that passage, First Timothy speaks of the "household of God," which is equated with "the church of the living God" (1 Tim 3:15). The verb "walk" is used biblically to describe one's entire moral life. The psalm also speaks twice of the "way/path" of integrity (vv. 2, 6), namely, a clean seamless unity of inner attitudes and external actions. The ideal is clear.

FIRST READING (YEAR II)

1 Corinthians 12:12-14, 27-31a

Now you are Christ's Body, and individually parts of it.

Body as Image for the Church

Every image used for spiritual reality merits careful study in order to determine precisely what truths it may contribute to our understanding. Among the insights of the metaphor of "body" (v. 12) we might list aspects such as diversity of functions, vitality, and organic (not mechanical) unity for a special purpose or task at any time. Though equal in value, not every part does the same thing, yet all work for the common good. Every image also has a limitation because of the aspects of truth not addressed by the description. In this case the "salvation" of those not formally united to the organism remains to be addressed by another metaphor. For that reason "people of God" was stressed during the Second Vatican Council. It provided a complementary and useful perspective to include the entire human race, called by God and moving forward together in pilgrimage toward the fullness of truth and justice.

Christ and the Uniting Vital Spirit

The resulting "one Body" is that of Christ (v. 12), not, however, restricted to the uniquely individual person active in Judea during his earthly ministry, but *Christus Totus*. This "Total Christ," comprised of all people united to Christ through the gift of the Holy Spirit at baptism (v. 13), extends through history and is present in all parts of the world. This "Total Christ" continues the work of giving glory to God by the redemption and transformation of the world. His person, mission, and message have become ours through baptism. Each of the individual "parts" is listed (v. 28), apostles, prophets, teachers, healers, administrators, and so forth. Paul hopes that the Corinthians will understand the respective contribution of every ministry to the spiritual health and well-being of the whole living "Body" that is the church. Can similar labels be given to those who gather for daily Eucharist?

Tuesday of the Twenty-Fourth Week in Ordinary Time

ANTIPHON (YEAR II)

Psalm 100:3

We are his people: the sheep of his flock.

Psalm 100: Prayer at the Doorway

The invitation to enter temple gates and courtyards with praise (v. 4) is a clear indication of the psalm's use as an entrance procession hymn. This demonstrates continuity with the theme of the Corinthian reading because Paul lists the many different social functions needed for a healthy spiritual body, now imagined as entering the temple, united for the worship and praise of God.

God's People

The verse chosen for this antiphon (v. 3) is able to add other images besides "the body" for the church, that is, a pilgrim people in transition and a flock under the guidance of a shepherd. Each makes its own contribution to understanding the church. Each metaphor has its own limitations, however, which in turn require yet other images for completeness. The nature of God's people remains a profound mystery, rooted in the life of the Trinity! No single image exhausts its reality.

GOSPEL

Luke 7:11-17

Young man, I tell you, arise!

Literary Link

Luke joins several events within this section devoted to the Galilean ministry (7:1–8:3). After healing the Gentile centurion's slave (vv. 1-10), the gospel now turns toward the widow's son. Both are minors. After a mention of the disciples of John the Baptist (vv. 18-35) and the pardon offered to the sinful woman (vv. 36-50), the section will conclude with a recognition of the generous women who traveled with the disciples and helped support them financially (8:1-3). These are favorite themes of Luke.

The Widow's Son

Throughout the history of Israel widows and orphans were considered among the most vulnerable in society. Having lost their immediate vital connection with a family, they often became desperately dependent on the kindness of others. Because widows were often ignored or exploited, they were regularly commended to the care of covenant members (Deut 24:20). The prophet Elijah was remembered for caring for a widow and her son during a terrible famine (1 Kgs 17:7ff.) and for raising that woman's deceased son (v. 23). Elisha also raised a woman's son from the dead (2 Kgs 4:20). Jesus is portrayed by Luke after the model of the great prophets. This gospel text can also become an occasion for activism on behalf of these people in society. How is our contemporary American society caring for widows and orphans?

Jesus as Prophet

Not only does the story of the raising of the widow's son remind us of prophets, but the praise from the people makes the relationship of Jesus and the great prophets explicit because they recognize Jesus as a great prophet in their midst (v. 16). Prophets spoke in the name of God, but they also did mighty deeds. Their actions served as illustrations for the messages they proclaimed and lived. Jesus, like the great prophets of Israel, was a religious reformer, and his actions illustrated the range of blessings available for those who renewed their lives in service to the people of the covenant.

Wednesday of the Twenty-Fourth Week in Ordinary Time

FIRST READING (YEAR I)

1 Timothy 3:14-16

Undeniably great is the mystery of devotion.

Metaphors for the Church

In the Scriptures we are repeatedly confronted by new and different images for the church, whole and entire as well as partial and local. Two are presented side by side in this passage. First, the church is the "household of God" (v. 15), an interrelated group of people, each sharing different functions and tasks but all working together for the common good. The community is also called the "pillar and foundation of truth" (v. 15). The later metaphor comes from the world of architecture. It would suggest in a slightly more abstract fashion that the community itself is founded upon truth and uses that same truth of God to shore up the roof of protection and shelter in difficult times. In Semitic categories of thought, "truth" is not the correspondence between idea and external reality, but rather something strong enough to lean against with security and confidence. That latter type of truth provides safety and security for the community, which in turn provides the same for the larger world.

Mystery of "Devotion"

The second section of this reading offers the words to an ancient hymn celebrating *eusebeia*, a very difficult Greek word to translate. Diversely rendered as "devotion" (NAB) or "religion" (NRSV), the word itself means piety and the type of practical reverence given to the gods in the ancient world. The mystery of the incarnation is described and celebrated (v. 16), and the reverence owing to a deity is requested as the proper respectful response to the truth of God made flesh. Eusebeus was a common name in early Christian circles, perhaps similar to "Pio" in Italian today.

ANTIPHON (YEAR I)

Psalm 111:2

How great are the works of the Lord!

Psalm 111: God Is Great

Psalm 111 is a ringing confession of the greatness of God with propositions placed side by side in an alphabetic acrostic pattern. With a series of abstractions God is celebrated in the assembly of the just (v. 1) as King of creation and Lord of history. Deeply liturgical in character, the psalm reflects the reading from First Timothy and its notions of the church. This psalm is similar to the *Tekbir* ("*Allāhu Akbar*," meaning "God is great"), a phrase common to Islam but by no means alien to Judeo-Christian beliefs.

Food to the Hungry

The ancient kings of the Near East were expected to feed the poor. The reference to giving food (v. 5), therefore, links God to royalty. The psalm also celebrates the way in which God feeds the poor, similar to the manner in which food was distributed to the participants of a sacrifice on Zion or at a Eucharist in the early church. The washing of the presider's hands at Mass, though now expressing sorrow for personal unworthiness, stems historically from the collection of produce for the poor at every Eucharist.

FIRST READING (YEAR II)

1 Corinthians 12:31–13:13

So faith, hope, love remain, these three;
but the greatest of these is love.

The Basic Nature of Love

The long litany of characteristics of true "love/*agape*" reveals the profound fact that mature Christian love always has the other person, not oneself, as the primary point of reference. This distinguishes Christian love from romantic infatuation or sentimentalism. One could translate this word "love" (13:1), therefore, as "concern." This would underscore its origin in the human will, and its expression of covenantal obligation to others. Dorothy Day wrote that true love is "a harsh and dreadful thing" because of the demands it can make on us in times of difficulty.* This text is a very familiar passage of Scripture and is often used for weddings. Because of its profundity, it can help turn the wedding into a marriage!

Eternal Quality of This Love

Because *agape* shapes the inner person of the believer, it will last forever (v. 13). This notion contrasts with faith dissolved by vision and hope fulfilled by possession. Beyond the vicissitudes of life and all the ups and downs of life's journey, a fundamental attitude of concern for the well-being of others becomes a perennial and defining character for the disciple of Jesus who was that love incarnate. Everything else is partial, temporary, and transitional.

ANTIPHON (YEAR II)

Psalm 33:12

Blessed the people the Lord has chosen
to be his own.

The Nature of God's Actions

The world as understood by the entire Jewish-Christian tradition is not an automatic creation of God's mind like some sort of spiritual emanation. The cosmos is the result of a deliberate free choice of God. God freely and deliberately chooses to create, to redeem, to love, and to save. We are the object of divine free will (v. 12), not simply a casual thought over which God has no control! To recognize our origin in God's free will is to allow ourselves to be clothed in a unique dignity. Any truly pro-life attitude is founded in this reality. It extends to every creature.

Divine Possession

Imagine for a moment the implication of being God's own precious possession (v. 12), belonging to God who fiercely preserves and protects yet respects human freedom. An early creed (Exod 19:5) speaks of the people as God's *segullah*, a personal possession in ancient Semitic (and modern Bedouin) culture that a woman wears as jewelry on her forehead as her own forever. It was a part of her dowry and remained hers for life.

GOSPEL

Luke 7:31-35

We played the flute for you, but you did not dance.
We sang a dirge, but you did not weep.

Literary Link

After giving testimony to the importance of the ministry of John the Baptizer (vv. 24-30), Jesus turns his attention on his audience, and he accuses them of being like petulant and moody children who expect the world to obey their quickly passing whims. This passage returns to the crowd's reaction to the figure of John (v. 33). It completes a subtheme, namely, references to John, in the literary circle (vv. 18-35).

Children

Although often proposed as models of dependence, helpfulness, and openness to learning, children can also be more negative examples of attitudes or behaviors not so endearing. When children become moody, emotionally fickle, and even irritable (v. 32), they can offer less praiseworthy models! Perhaps the speed with which children can go from tears to laughter is the background to the gospel's contrasting comparison. They can be so invested in the moment as to forget the past and ignore the future. Immediate gratification is problematic.

John the Baptist

The eating and drinking was apparently rejected by John out of his own sense of asceticism. The gospels show Jesus, however, as enjoying meals as occasions for conversation and conversion (v. 34). These differences are contrasted in this brief passage as yet another example of the utter inconsistency and fickleness of the generation to which Jesus spoke. As disciples of Jesus we are asked to be steady in our choices, consistent in our practice, and faithful in our relationships with others.

* Quoting Fr. Zossima in *The Brothers Karamazov*; chap. 7 (p. 136) in *House of Hospitality, The Catholic Worker Movement*, http://www.catholicworker.org/dorothyday/Reprint2.cfm?TextID=442.

Thursday of the Twenty-Fourth Week in Ordinary Time

First Reading (Year I)

1 Timothy 4:12-16

Attend to yourself and to your teaching; you will save both yourself and those who listen to you.

Youth

In the early church youth was not only measured by chronology of years but also by immaturity of faith as a result of being a recent convert. It is precisely Timothy's mature faith (v. 12), however, in spite of his few years, that is praised. This includes Timothy's understanding of the power of the paschal mystery of the Lord's death and resurrection, his appreciation of the bond between Christ and the church, and his embrace of the need for personal transformation. Paul exhorts Timothy to stand firm should anyone tend to dismiss his lack of years. Paul asks Timothy to demonstrate the spiritual leadership that is his by God's gift and grace (v. 14). Does a contemporary parish ever single out young people for praise and genuine respect?

Imposition of Hands

In first-century Judaism and in early Christianity the gesture of imposition of hands was a common ritual action. Rather than a centrifugal action that conveyed and extended authority outwards, it was a centripetal gesture inwards, welcoming and associating the individual into the person and ministry of the one imposing hands (v. 14). Forgiveness of sins conveyed by the imposition of hands signaled renewed membership in a forgiven community. The gift of the spirit was signified by this same gesture because it brought a person into relationship with a "spirited community." The imposition of hands over the bread and wine associates the eucharistic elements with the Body of Christ and transforms them.

Antiphon (Year I)

Psalm 111:2

How great are the works of the Lord!

Praise for a Good Person

The verses selected by the Lectionary as a response to the description of Timothy's personal gifts serve to place his individual personality among all the great works of God in history. The psalm summarizes the works of God and describes them as "faithful," "just," and "sure" (v. 7), "wrought in truth and equity" (v. 8). Human works are wise and prudent when rooted in "fear of the Lord" (v. 10). This becomes a remarkable tribute to God, but also to Timothy! Every single human being can be listed among the "works" of God.

Refrain

The refrain, recited four times, concentrates on God's works (v. 2). This properly reflects the contents of Psalm 111, which focuses on God as contrasted with its companion, Psalm 112, which places the spotlight on the human person. It would seem that they were composed as a pair. When using one, we should keep the other in mind.

First Reading (Year II)

1 Corinthians 15:1-11

So we preach and so you believed.

A Place to Stand

Paul insists that the gospel he preached is the place where Corinthians stand (v. 1), that is, the fundamental solid foundation from which they view the entire world and within which they live and work. Legend has it that when called to recant his confession of justification by faith through grace, Martin Luther insisted, "Here I stand. I cannot do otherwise!" We are all called to stand firmly on our fundamental convictions.

Source of Salvation

When Paul states that the Corinthians are being saved (v. 2) through the Gospel, he indicates that this is a matter of words, but also much more. The Good News announced by Paul to the Corinthians, and to each community he founded, is an entire new creation, established by the Lord's death and resurrection into which people are welcomed by baptism. Talk is cheap, but there is a profound reality beneath the words. It is the deeper truth to which Paul points as the ultimate reality of the world.

The Fourfold Proclamation

Hardly twenty years after the death of Christ, Paul already summarizes the four essentials of the Christian kerygma: Christ's death for sin according to the Scriptures, his burial, his resurrection according to the Scriptures, and his appearances to many (vv. 3-8). This fourfold announcement of the historical events and their biblical meaning is the nucleus of the gospels. The summary became the measurement by which all other "gospels" in the early church were judged and either accepted or discarded.

Apparition Groups

Jesus is remembered for having appeared to the various groups after his resurrection, namely, Cephas/Peter, the Twelve, the five hundred, James, the apostles, and finally Paul (vv. 4-8). The list clearly indicates that the early Christian community was already differentiated into various groups of individuals with diverse charisms and functions. It is a hierarchy in the basic sense of the word, a sacred order of interrelated individuals, each blessed with spiritual gifts for others, not merely for themselves. This network of interrelated functions is the true notion of "hierarchy," not any upper versus lower existence, status, or activity.

ANTIPHON (YEAR II)

Psalm 118:1

Give thanks to the Lord, for he is good.

The Goodness of God

A favorite dessert is good (tasty), a well-behaved child is good (well-mannered), a skilled cook or carpenter is good (skillful). The word has many meanings within the wide spectrum of human life: skill, effectiveness, admiration, or moral value. Goodness is material, instrumental, and moral. To apply all those attributes to God, as done in this refrain (v. 1), is in itself remarkable and worthy of reflection and prayer. So often we summarize our grateful reaction to events with a simple confession, "God is good!" Exploring the meaning of the phrases is helpful for spiritual insight and growth.

Mercy

The rest of the verse from which the psalm's refrain (v. 1) is taken is also important, that is, the celebrated fact that God's goodness is demonstrated in divine mercy, which does indeed "endure forever." The Hebrew word behind the translation of "mercy" is crucial, namely, *hesed*. This is faithful covenantal kindness, a mutual concern for each other and a bond that can require intervention for the well-being, freedom, and prosperity of those to whom we are bound. This type of mercy is praised as the primary evidence of God's eternally enduring goodness. The Hebrew phrase translated as "forever" is *ʿolam*, meaning the world as it historically unfolds and develops. It is precisely in our very real world that God's mercy flourishes from one generation to another.

GOSPEL

Luke 7:36-50

Her many sins have been forgiven; hence, she has shown great love.

Literary Link

Luke regularly includes references to women as both partners and objects of compassion. Within his Galilean ministry, Jesus made reference to the Baptist as "greatest among those born to women" (see v. 28). Today's passage about the woman pardoned is now reported (vv. 36-50), followed by a brief account of the wealthy women who traveled with Jesus (8:1-3).

Hospitality

That the Pharisee would have so uncharacteristically omitted the basic ancient hospitality of washing the dust of the road from the traveler, offering a welcoming sign/kiss of peace, and providing ointment for face and hands (v. 44) seems very strange to anyone familiar with the ancient world. Such an omission would have been very uncharacteristic of Pharisaic spirituality. Whether by ignorance on the part of Luke the Gentile or oversight or deliberate snub, it can serve as a springboard for recommending contemporary courtesy to all guests at a Christian home.

Thursday of the Twenty-Fourth Week in Ordinary Time

"Teacher"

The fact that Jesus is addressed by the Pharisee as "teacher" (v. 40) indicates a sign of formal respect for him (making the omission of hospitality even harder to understand). The title also suggests that Jesus has something to teach. In spite of the rebuke given by Jesus to this host, the use of the name (v. 4) indicates deference rather than hostility on the part of the host. Whatever our situation in life and wherever we may happen to be at any given moment of activity, we can also apply the title to those around us, and implicitly ask what we can learn from the experience. Jesus always has something to say to us, and some point to make for us. Among the many titles and attributes given to Jesus, that of "teacher" should never be far from our minds! The morning's proclamation could be an occasion to pray for all the teachers who have influenced us over the years of our formal and informal education.

Forgiveness and Love

This gospel story offers a puzzle: Did the woman's great love precede the forgiveness, or did the forgiveness produce the love (v. 47)? The NAB version suggests the latter. The story is not so clear, but it does serve to encourage both possibilities in the concrete dynamics of our relationships with God and each other. One cannot exist without the other. The love that we bring to our relationship with God can also deepen into ever greater gratitude, just as gratitude deepens love.

Friday of the Twenty-Fourth Week in Ordinary Time

FIRST READING (YEAR I)

1 Timothy 6:2c-12

But you, man of God, pursue righteousness.

These Things

The "these things" that the apostle urges to be taught (v. 2) pertain to the respectful relationship required between Christian slaves and owners (vv. 1-2) just discussed in the prior verses. That preceding concern is the background for this passage and should be reviewed to understand this text adequately. In the ancient world false teachers were revealed by the wrangling and rivalry among their disciples (v. 3). This explains the passage's logical flow of apostolic concern for social harmony. The tuition paid to teachers could also have inspired the letter's comments about contentment (v. 6) with one's material possessions, however extensive or minimal they may be. We certainly do not condone the abuse of human dignity embodied in the institution of slavery, but we acknowledge that all human relationships ought to be marked by righteousness (v. 11), as the Lectionary's summary insists. Employers and elected officials serve employees as well as clients. For that reason the admonition about righteousness, patience, and gentleness addresses everyone.

Money

Greed was also an issue among false teachers. It is worth pointing out that this text does not condemn money as such, but rather the inordinate "love of money" (v. 10). To value monetary wealth more than human beings is indeed the root of sin and evil because such an attitude slips easily into virtually every possible violation of neighbor. Unfettered desire for money, as the apostle points out, not only produces many of life's pains, but can even lead people to stray from the community of faith. We rarely preach about money/wealth except to ask for it.

ANTIPHON (YEAR I)

Matthew 5:3

Blessed the poor in spirit; the Kingdom of heaven is theirs!

Psalm 49: Wealth Saves No One

Psalm 49 was selected by the Lectionary as a response because it is a remarkable "wisdom song" aimed at the believer who is surrounded by affluent opponents (v. 7). The wicked possess the material means to assure their success in whatever they may put their minds to. The psalm contains a reminder that money cannot redeem a person before God (v. 8). Wealth disappears at death (v. 18). The value of coinage or accumulated wealth is transitory at best, as Qoheleth points out so patiently (1:2-11; 2:4-12).

The Refrain

The refrain is borrowed from the Beatitudes of Matthew's Sermon on the Mount (see Matt 5:3). It offers a fitting response to the apostle's teaching about money. Those who are poor in spirit, whether materially rich or poor, are those who understand that everything is gift. Even when one has labored hard for one's possessions, they still remain pure gift from God who both gives freely and expects an accounting.

FIRST READING (YEAR II)

1 Corinthians 15:12-20

If Christ has not been raised, your faith is in vain.

The Logic of Faith

There is a clear interrelationship between the faith we profess, our sense of personal identity, and our future destiny. Everything is somehow logically connected, as Paul pointed out in his comments about resurrection (vv. 12-13). This is sometimes called the "hierarchy of truth," not so much that there are primary central truths and other realities more marginal and less important, but rather that everything exists in a holy and interrelated unity. Intellectual and spiritual "beliefs" or convictions are often also very practical. They shape our decisions and guide our lives. If in fact our beliefs are opposed to God, they can easily turn into idolatries.

The Parade of "Ifs"

Six times in this passage we hear the conjunction "if." Everything is somehow based upon the reality of the resurrection. Having recited the four fundamental components of our faith (vv. 3-8), Paul now focuses on the importance of resurrection because of specific problems among the Corinthian Christians. Although we may not know all the precise particulars regarding the how and when of resurrection (and we ought to be much more modest in our descriptions of the mysteries of God's future plans), we are clear about the central reality of resurrection. Paul makes that point (v. 20). This conviction may be of special importance today when the lack of knowledge about the details can be understood as a lack of personal conviction regarding this fundamental truth and teaching of our faith.

Friday of the Twenty-Fourth Week in Ordinary Time

ANTIPHON (YEAR II)

Psalm 17:15b

Lord, when your glory appears, my joy will be full.

Glory

The very word "glory" is a multifaceted reality. Each term used by the classical languages of our faith adds its own nuance. The Hebrew word "*kabod*/glory" suggests something weighty and shining, and therefore very valuable. The Greek word "*doxa*/glory" emphasizes the person's judgment and her conviction that something is important. *Gloria* in Latin might tend to stress an inner brilliance that shines forth and elicits honor and praise. In any case there is something bright that catches one's attention and occasions a second look!

Appearance of Glory

We should never forget that there is, buried within the dynamics of human history, a final revelation of how God has been wonderfully at work throughout all ages. There is an inner surge or current of divine power within everything, almost like electricity, which is only visible in its effects of illumination or heat. The account of the Lord's transfiguration (Luke 9:28-36) reminds us of that reality. The final public revelation of God at work will be visible to everyone. The refrain (v. 15) is a slightly reworked expression from the final verse of this psalm response. The refrain expresses the certain conviction that in good time and in God's time, God will reveal his presence.

GOSPEL

Luke 8:1-3

Accompanying them were some women, who provided for them out of their resources.

Literary Link

Still within the portion of the gospel devoted to the Galilean ministry (4:14–9:50), Luke follows the account of the forgiveness lavishly extended to the penitent woman (vv. 36-50) by today's account of the affluent women who traveled in the company of Jesus. The gospel will then move to Saturday's parable of the sower whose seeds will inevitably have a rich and abundant harvest (8:4-8). Their travel was also a sowing of seed that is "the word of God" in the added moral allegory (v. 11).

Towns and Villages

Like the apostle Paul in the next generation, Jesus seems to gravitate to the centers of human habitation and community cooperation (v. 1). Although he often draws images from agriculture for his teachings, as seen in his parables of the kingdom, he seems to settle into these small communities, perhaps because they offer the best example of the kingdom of God, namely, the sovereign action of God at work among people. Different social functions cooperate for the common good. The communities are cross-pollinated by political, economic, and social currents of thought and exchange. The manner in which people interrelate through forgiveness, compassion, justice, or truth can offer the ultimate sign of the new creation and of a world restored to its primal goodness.

Women Disciples

The casual mention of the fact that women of influence and means were part of the inner circle of Jesus as he traveled reveals the importance of those women during the early ministry of Jesus and throughout the early centuries of Christianity. Their presence as friends and colleagues of Jesus was a sign of what God had in mind as a pattern for human relationships in the new creation proclaimed by Jesus. They were also generous in providing material support (v. 3). By the very fact of this mention by name, their memory is recognized as important for shaping the message they proclaimed. We sometimes forget that the gospel's generic references to "disciples" referred to groups that included both genders. Moreover, we should not forget women like Evodia and Syntyche (Phil 4:2) who subsequently became heads of prominent household churches.

Seven Demons

To be cured of evil spirits (v. 2), as apparently was Mary Magdalene, is to be relieved of multiple emotional burdens. Depression and lack of self-confidence could well have been among Mary's troubles addressed and cured by Jesus. To presume issues of sexuality reflects the false exegetical interpretation of past centuries that merged the "three Marys" into a single figure. We should also recall that this is the woman who became "the apostle to the apostles" after the resurrection (see John 20:17).

Saturday of the Twenty-Fourth Week in Ordinary Time

First Reading (Year I)

1 Timothy 6:13-16

Keep the commandment without stain or reproach until the appearance of our Lord Jesus Christ.

Pastoral Accountability

The apostle reminds young Timothy of the fundamental "commandment" (NB: singular!) he has received (v. 14): the call to live as both disciple of the Lord and witness to his teachings. To be a witness before Christ is to be a servant to the entire community, and to live with the realization that the final appearance of Christ will entail accountability for all the gifts received from God. Community leaders and members alike will be asked to give an accounting of their entire lives. In a later final verse (v. 20) Timothy is reminded to guard what has been entrusted to him. Each person has one's own gifts, but they are only leased for the duration of our earthly pilgrimage.

Praise at the Parousia

The letter concludes with this final expression of praise for Christ and of eager expectation of his return in glory. The titles and phrases (v. 15) seem to echo the text of Handel's famous "Hallelujah Chorus" so familiar at Christmastime. The immediate and urgent sense of the Lord's return was beginning to fade into a larger and more distant perspective when this letter was written. Nevertheless, that final definitive event remains the context and measure of everything we are and do throughout our entire life, even amid the most mundane and ordinary of activities.

Antiphon (Year I)

Psalm 100:2

Come with joy into the presence of the Lord.

Psalm 100: Praise at the Temple Gate

This brief hymn was apparently written and used to accompany a liturgical entrance procession for temple worship. The verses describe joyful songs of gratitude and physical movement through the temple gates (v. 4) with blessings for God's holy name. It is a very fitting community response to the letter's expression of praise for Christ's return in glory.

The Refrain

The emphasis of the refrain (v. 2) on joy sets the tone for the response. This choice ensures that the thought of the Lord's return as expressed in the reading does not evoke fear at judgment, but jubilation at victory for all God's faithful. It is also a suitable expression of the community's joy at Christ's final victory over all evil, sin, and death. This psalm is a marching song of triumph for all of God's people. It should not be muttered quietly, but sung enthusiastically!

First Reading (Year II)

1 Corinthians 15:35-37, 42-49

It is sown corruptible; it is raised incorruptible.

Metaphor of a Seed

Paul used the image of a kernel of wheat (v. 37) because it is buried in the ground like a body at death, changes dramatically as it sprouts and grows, yet exhibits some continuity of person like the individual raised to the new creation. In dealing with such a great mystery it is useful to seek elements from within our own personal experience for instruction and understanding. These examples and metaphors are useful for teaching. They explain the rationality of our faith, even when dealing with mysteries and promises that stretch our minds. A natural body and a spiritual body are still both bodies, open to radical transformation. By using the example of a seed, Paul was able to contrast the before and after of corruptibility (v. 42), something we know all too well from human experience on this side of the great divide!

Adam as Fresh Start

Paul also returns frequently to the figure of Adam (v. 42) to show similarity and continuity between the first creation and its new counterpart. The first "earthly" Adam (v. 47) was living, namely, breathing and moving, whereas the New Christ/Adam not only possesses life but also gives it to others spiritually and brings an entirely new world into being. All who are reborn in Christ are invited to share Christ's mission to bring the life of the new creation into the world. They become instruments of biblical justice, being in right relationship with all of creation and capable of exhibiting compassion for those who die and rise in a new way. This is another manner of describing the people who gather for morning Mass at any parish in the world.

ANTIPHON (YEAR II)

Psalm 56:14

I will walk in the presence of God, in the light of the living.

Psalm 56: Trusting God at One's Side

Psalm 56 is a short prayer (fourteen verses) of confidence in the protective presence of God even though one is surrounded by hostile enemies of all sorts. Trusting in God's promises (v. 11), a faithful person enters the mystery of death (as described by Paul in the first reading) and returns transformed, still walking in the light of the living (v. 14). Both the reading and its psalm response deal with the same mystery of life after death.

Walking as "the Moral Life"

To walk, as the refrain suggests (v. 14), is to use one's physical ability to move from one place to another. It implies intention, energy, and change. Thus there is in the image itself something totally comprehensive for all the levels of movement, activity, growth, and change throughout life. In this verse the Hebrew verb form is reflexive, suggesting that we walk "as far as we ourselves are concerned." The refrain insists that our entire moral life is lived in God's transforming presence. As the popular hymn states, "We walk by faith, and not by sight."

Presence of God

The refrain literally speaks about walking/living /working, as far as we are concerned, before the very face of God (v. 14). This implies a literal and personal presence of God to everything we think, say, and do. The creative act of God is not limited to a once-and-for-all intervention at the beginning of each creature, but includes God's deliberate sustaining us and keeping us in existence at every second of our lives. This is how we understand the mystery of the divine presence in our world throughout history. Philosophers tell us that we would disappear if God stopped thinking about us, even for an instant!

Saturday of the Twenty-Fourth Week in Ordinary Time

GOSPEL

Luke 8:4-15

As for the seed that fell on rich soil, they are the ones who embrace the word and bear much fruit through perseverance.

Literary Link

After describing the women of affluence who traveled with Jesus (vv. 1-3), Luke presents some parables that explain his Galilean ministry. This passage presents the basic parable of the sower (vv. 4-8), followed by the questions of the disciples for interpretation (vv. 9-10) and then the further allegorical application (vv. 11-15). All three Synoptic Gospels offer the same pattern.

The God of Abundant Harvest

It is very easy and tempting to move quickly to moralizing the parable, and to turn it into an allegory so that each aspect indicates a specific reality. We ought to remember, however, that for the most part parables have one primary point; they are about God. Thus one can make a case for the fact that the parable's original teaching as Jesus first expressed it was different from the allegory. The parable itself was intended as one of encouragement: no matter what obstacles may come along in the form of birds (v. 5), stones (v. 6), or thorns (v. 7), God's word will produce a rich harvest with and for all of us! No matter how limited we may feel, God's strength will prevail. No matter what our difficulties in life, and they are always many, God will produce a rich harvest if we allow God to do so in God's way and in God's time.

Later Allegory

Scholars suggest that the application to the various categories of hearers is a later, though logical, development of the parable. Rabbinic methods sought to find meaning in every portion of every sentence, and thus in every category of human receptivity. This interpretation personalizes the original parable, and moves from the wider range of history to the fruitfulness of grace in each individual. Distractions, lack of depth (v. 13), and thorny anxieties (v. 14) inevitably interfere with any harvest. The word of God as seed can only produce fruitful harvest if received by a generous and good heart (v. 15). It is also helpful to remember that the "heart" of a person is the core of human existence that makes decisions and plans. Curiously, the explanation has moved from a focus on an active God to one on the receptor human being. One is logically prior, but both are useful.

Monday of the Twenty-Fifth Week in Ordinary Time

First Reading (Year I)

Ezra 1:1-6

Those who are any part of God's people, let them go up and build the house of the Lord in Jerusalem.

The Book of Ezra

Although the Christian order of inspired books places the prophets as a culminating voice of the first covenant, the Hebrew canon ends with a final series of historical works: Ezra and Nehemiah, then First and Second Chronicles. The text of Ezra and Nehemiah is chronologically disrupted and difficult to reconstruct for a clear historical sequence; therefore the dating, whether fifth or fourth century BC, is highly debated. Ezra as priest and scribe attempted to assist the returned exiles as they reestablished their life of faith back in Israel after the Babylonian exile. Israelite identity as illumined by the Torah was his primary pastoral concern because the will of God mattered more than anything else!

Return and Restoration

The way by which history unfolds is often mysterious and surprising. The authority of King Cyrus of Persia (v. 1) is invoked as the initial force behind Israel's return to Jerusalem after the Babylonian exile. It was the beginning of the second temple period. Acknowledging the decree of Cyrus (vv. 2-4) gives political legitimacy to this new era without necessarily presuming any conversion of the king to the worship of Israel's God. God is the First Cause and Prime Mover of everything. God uses human authorities, however, great and small alike, to accomplish his ultimate divine purposes. Similarly, our own age is ultimately ruled by a Divine Providence far beyond anything we can control or even fully understand. God continues to do what God has always done: bring people home!

Exodus Repeated: Laden with Gifts

Persian generosity to the returning exiles, even if by royal command, is deliberately described so as to suggest a repetition of the way Israel left Egypt so many centuries earlier, laden with gifts from their former Egyptian neighbors (Exod 12:36). That prior event had been described theologically as a fulfillment of the command that emancipated slaves were to be freed and laden with gifts from their former masters (Deut 15:13-14). This is "accumulated compensation." To use the same elements in describing the departure of Israel from Babylon is to suggest that their time of indentured service was completed, and their guilt expiated (Isa 40:2). God's generosity will not be outdone.

Antiphon (Year I)

Psalm 126:3

The Lord has done marvels for us.

Psalm 126

The Lectionary's selection of this pilgrimage psalm "of ascents" (v. 1) provides the perfect response to the reading from Ezra. It speaks of the sheer delight and joyful surprise of the people, a fitting response to the deliverance from captivity suddenly offered by God. The song almost imagines the people pinching themselves into wakefulness (v. 1) in sheer disbelief at the sudden reversal of their situation. The psalm reflects a common New Testament theme, the great reversal of the lowly lifted up and the powerful cast down.

Marvels

Our Catholic theology has developed a narrow definition of "miracles," namely, those events completely without explanation by human factors or natural causes. The refrain's use of the word "marvels" (v. 3), however, is much broader. The refrain desires to evoke the memory of anything that surprises, delights, and inspires thanks and praise on our part. Listing some of those events in our own lives can make the psalm come alive for us anew.

First Reading (Year II)

Proverbs 3:27-34

The curse of the Lord is on the house of the wicked.

Recognizing Claims

This reading is a list of four distinct proverbs, each worthy of reflection in itself. The first seems eminently practical, namely, the admonition not to delay responding to those who have a right to assistance or justice (vv. 27-28). The saying among canonists that "justice delayed is justice denied" can be rooted in this very proverb. Our response is not automatic, however, but presumes some further discernment regarding what will truly benefit the claimant. There are times, for example, when it is an act of genuine charity to say "no" or "not today." The rationale for such a response, however, would be rooted in the good of the other, not merely in one's own convenience. A further proverb, still considering the claims of others and relationships to one's neighbors, would forbid plotting evil or quarreling without cause (vv. 29-30). The initial introductory summary to this reading in the Lectionary regarding cursing (v. 34) seems odd, if not misguiding, because the passage itself is wider and much more positive.

Monday of the Twenty-Fifth Week in Ordinary Time

God's Friends

The wisdom garnered from observations about life indicates that material prosperity is not necessarily a sign of God's friendship! Someone who is lawless (v. 31) should never be envied no matter how affluent or socially prominent. God's true favor is granted to the "upright" and to the "humble"; to them he offers friendship (v. 32). These are people who live in right relationship with God and neighbor. Once again the double commandment of love of God and neighbor lies behind this ancient litany of proverbs, as does the reminder of eventual accountability and judgment.

The Book of Proverbs

This collection of didactic poetry and ancient sayings comes from a wide range of centuries, and is generally ascribed to Solomon as the patron of Hebrew wisdom, even though briefer sections of the book are attributed to other figures. Virtually every aspect of social life is considered among these sayings, and advice is offered to all who desired to move gracefully and successfully through life's challenges. Purely secular concerns are addressed as well as the recognition of God's ultimate power, providence, and goodness in directing history and requiring eventual accountability from all human beings.

Antiphon (Year II)

Psalm 15:1

The just one shall live on your holy mountain, O Lord.

Torah/Instruction

Psalm 15 is an example of an examination of conscience presumably proclaimed by a temple guardian to would-be worshipers. The verses detail the moral qualities expected of anyone who would be acceptable in the presence of God: justice (v. 2) and truthfulness (v. 3). These would be the marks of anyone who lives in true humbleness before God. Not everyone is welcome, therefore, but only those who recognize the conduct required of a faithful covenant member, and who humbly acknowledge their adherence to the commandments as well as their faults before God.

Walking

The classic general word for moral behavior in the ancient Semitic world of the first covenant is "walking" (v. 2). This action encompasses one's entire day of activities, and the goals toward which we move as well as the journey along the way. This is why many New Testament miracles of Jesus depict the cure of the lame and the paralyzed. The object is spiritual as well as physical.

Truth, Justice, and Reverence

A review of all the various activities listed in these psalm verses indicates how comprehensive they are: internal attitude and external actions, speech and activity, works of justice (being in right relations with the world as well as paying debts), and full respect for others who in turn demonstrate a respectful and reverential fear of God in their lives.

GOSPEL

Luke 8:16-18

A lamp is placed on a lampstand so that those who enter may see the light.

Literary Link

After the explanation of Jesus regarding the various types of people who either receive or reject the Word sown in their lives (vv. 11-15), he proceeds to speak of the light that reveals all hidden attitudes (vv. 16-18). This teaching will in turn lay the ground for tomorrow's gospel reading about the true family of Jesus (vv. 19-21).

Lampstands

By definition a lampstand is utilized to lift up the light (v. 16) and to make it visible and useful for maneuvering in the dark. After all, light is to be used, not put in a closet! The darkened houses of the ancient world may have required some assistance for nighttime movement because they were often without windows and certainly without the electricity that we now take for granted. Light lifted for visibility is a metaphor related to the guidance needed for correct moral "walking" and moral decisions. Though not stated explicitly in this image, the early church understood the example of Jesus as Light for their lives. Early patristic writers even imagined that God's command at creation, "Let there be light" (Gen 1:3), already included the intent to bring forth the Christ, "light from light" (Creed).

Judgment

The image of light readily leads to Luke's decision to proceed with a further reference, to the ultimate visibility of all our secrets. Light enables us to see and to be judged. We are led to the recognition of inevitable accounting (v. 17) when all will be seen by God and judged accordingly. It may be helpful to remember that this type of revelation is not simply the exposition of our secret and hidden selves to those around us. Perhaps the final judgment will primarily reveal an understanding of our own motives and actions to ourselves! Absolutely everything will be made manifest.

Tuesday of the Twenty-Fifth Week in Ordinary Time

First Reading (Year I)

Ezra 6:7-8, 12b, 14-20

They completed the temple of God, and ate the Passover.

Rebuilding the Temple

The actual historical sequence of events as reported in this work of Ezra/Nehemiah is confusing and debated among scholars. Apparently, after some interference and delay ascribed to the Samaritans who had remained in the land (possibly out of sheer prejudice against them on the part of the returnees), King Darius in 520 BC reconfirmed the original decree of Cyrus (538 BC). Darius is remembered for supporting the restored city and temple (v. 12). The prophecies of Haggai and Zechariah (v. 14) also offered encouragement in the name of the Lord. All building projects, even our own today, somehow seem inevitably more complicated than expected. Unfortunately they can also be the occasion for disagreements and enduring resentments. That was in fact the origin of the animosity between Jews and Samaritans who then built their own temple on Mount Gerizim. The antagonism lasted for centuries, even into the time of Jesus. Both the construction of the physical building of the temple and the restoration of Israel's religious identity under Ezra were interwoven in this effort (as in all contemporary parish building projects).

Dedication Ceremonies

According to historians the actual date for the dedication was either on Sabbath, March 12, 515 BC, or Friday, April 1, 515 BC. The abundance of sacrifices (v. 17) signaled the importance of the event for the returnees. At the same time the event was much more modest than the 22,000 oxen and 120,000 sheep allegedly sacrificed by Solomon at the first temple's dedication over four centuries earlier (1 Kgs 8:63)! What makes a place "holy"? It would seem that ritual alone is not sufficient unless accompanied by the significant religious experience of the participants.

Antiphon (Year I)

Psalm 122:1

Let us go rejoicing to the house of the Lord.

Psalm 122: A Pilgrim's Joy

This psalm is another of the classical pilgrimage songs "of ascents" (v. 1). It was presumably sung at the end of a visit to the Holy City and its temple. Having stood within the gates of the city (v. 2), and now filled with joyful memories, the pilgrims prepare to return to their homes. The words are a fitting response placed on the lips of the departing pilgrims. They are suitably sung as a response to Ezra's account of the dedication of the restored second temple. The same words could well provide the verses of a hymn after the morning celebration of the Eucharist as the participants prepare to return home or to the work of the day. Each morning Mass is a pilgrimage of sorts to a place made holy by experiences of the holiness of God.

First Reading (Year II)

Proverbs 21:1-6, 10-13

Various proverbs.

Ten Proverbs

The simple liturgical summary of introduction above seems to acknowledge the diversity of these maxims, which are only united by the themes of inner integrity known to God, the value of ethical behavior, and the superior value of justice over wicked arrogance. Each proverb is worthy of homiletic commentary as moral measurement for the thoughts and actions of those who gather for prayer.

Israelite Wisdom

It seems as if Wisdom literature flourished in Israel during times of great social change when familiar patterns of religious thought seemed uncertain and unhelpful. In such a lacuna, the religious leadership of Israel tended to revert to human experience when seeking guidance from their traditions. In the time of David and Solomon the new court introduced Wisdom themes, sometimes borrowed from Egypt or other neighboring nations, into the education of the youth. Again, at the time of the exile, books of wisdom became popular among the people while the religious leaders sought new expressions for their ancient faith. Proverbs, whether ancient or modern, are clever ways of expressing perennial truths.

ANTIPHON (YEAR II)

Psalm 119:35

Guide me, Lord, in the way of your commands.

Psalm 119: Life-Giving Commands

The repeated generic encouragement of this psalm to human obedience before God seems a suitable response to the diversity of proverbs collected in the first reading. By recognizing the fundamental value of all of God's commands, and the guidance they can provide for anyone genuinely desiring to lead a moral life, the psalm points a direction and offers lights for the path forward. The commands are "guidance" as described in the refrain (v. 35) because they require the compliance of free will in order to be effective.

GOSPEL

Luke 8:19-21

My mother and my brothers are those who hear the word of God and act on it.

Literary Link

Perhaps it is merely the repetition of the Lord's admonition to "[t]ake care, then, how you hear" (v. 18) that explains and justifies Luke's editorial placement of the story of the true family of Jesus in this brief text. His family is comprised of those who listen and follow through in actions (v. 21).

Hearing

A special quality of the Hebrew language and the Semitic mentality is the fact that there is no simple word in Hebrew for "obey." The word invariably used for that reality, especially in the expanse of prophetic literature, is simply "to hear." The presumption is that if one truly hears, one will comply and act accordingly! In the books of Kings, leaders are roundly condemned for not hearing the prophets who spoke to them. The *Shema*, the great prayer of Israel, simply begins, "Hear, O Israel! The LORD is our God" (Deut 6:4).

The True Family of Jesus

We are told that the true family of Jesus is comprised of those who listen to the Word and follow through in their lives (v. 21). This image could—and perhaps should—be a description of the church as family in the new creation! Listening and obeying creates a profound and permanent bond with God and with others. Any experience of mutual concern deepens one's motivation to constitute a family worthy of the name.

Wednesday of the Twenty-Fifth Week in Ordinary Time

FIRST READING (YEAR I)

Ezra 9:5-9

In our servitude our God has not abandoned us.

A Prayer of Repentance

The moving words of Ezra provide a response to the fact that, contrary to the stipulation of Deuteronomy 7:3, priests have intermarried with the pagan populations of the land. The basic issue is loss of religious identity. The prayer is both an effusive acknowledgment of Israel's sin and a recognition of God's mercy in offering once more that land of ancient promises. The people of God have been again freed from Babylonian bondage (v. 8) just as they had been so many centuries earlier when they were liberated from Egyptian slavery.

New Beginnings

Ezra acknowledges a new exodus of mercy. Although Ezra's specific motive for his prayer of repentance dealt with intermarriage (v. 1; not included in the liturgical passage itself), the deeper error was a loss of Jewish identity and the primacy of faith for their lives. One should not forget that the Scriptures also bear witness to outsiders like Ruth, the Moabite daughter-in-law of Naomi, who were welcomed into the land of Israel at an earlier age and then entered the genealogy of David himself. Our God is always willing to offer a fresh start to those who humbly acknowledge their sins. Ezra's demand for divorce may seem harsh in an ecumenical age such as our own, but it does recognize the value of marrying within one's faith tradition for mutual support in fidelity to God. Even today contemporary rabbis lament the numbers of Jewish young adults marrying outside the community. A new beginning and a fresh start may be a simple return to the basics.

ANTIPHON (YEAR I)

Tobit 13:1b

Blessed be God, who lives for ever.

The Prayer of Tobit

In an unexpected turn of events, the Lectionary has chosen verses from the final hymn of praise uttered by Tobit after the return of his son Tobiah with his new daughter-in-law and after the healing from blindness accomplished by the ministrations of the archangel Raphael "the healer." That prayer was originally placed on the lips of someone still living under religious persecution in Babylon. The prayer acknowledges in moving words the way in which God punishes and raises up (v. 2), offering abundant blessings to those who had been sent into exile for their sins (v. 3). Whether in Babylon or back in the land of Judah, God's concern for his people is always medicinal and aimed at healing their spiritual wounds.

The Refrain

If one recalls that the refrain (v. 1) was also used by Job after losing his entire family and possessions, its poignancy is deepened. Job refused to curse God, even after all the tragedies in his life and after the encouragement of his wife to do so, but simply and humbly acknowledged, "The LORD gave and the LORD has taken away; / blessed be the name of the LORD!" (Job 1:21). Tobit's prayer in exile echoes the same sentiments.

FIRST READING (YEAR II)

Proverbs 30:5-9

Give me neither poverty nor riches; provide me only with the food I need.

Adding to God's Word

This brief reading is taken from a collection of wise numbered proverbs ascribed, not to Solomon, but to the otherwise unknown sage Agur (v. 1) from a family of north Arabia. Like the book of Deuteronomy, the sage insists that nothing should be added to the word of the Lord (v. 6), either by way of additional harshness or undue levity. Anything proclaimed should be God's words, not our own! That also is wisdom. We may interpret or rephrase for a different culture, but the message remains God's, not ours.

The Danger of Extremes

Both excessive poverty and significant affluence are dangers (v. 8), as this proverb from the unknown Agur points out, the one becoming the occasion for theft and the other a temptation to presume that abundance is due to one's own ability and skill alone. This advice also reflects the warning of Deuteronomy 8:11-14, a reading often chosen for the annual celebration of Thanksgiving, that one should never become haughty or unmindful of the source of all blessings, namely, God alone. It was the wisdom of Agur to note his desire should focus on "needs," not "wants" (v. 8).

ANTIPHON (YEAR II)

Psalm 119:105

Your word, O Lord, is a lamp for my feet.

Psalm 119: Commands That Illuminate

Because of its great length and generic repetitions, this psalm is often selected to serve as a response to a reading, in this case possibly because of its initial admonition to protect the individual from any falsehood (v. 29), such as adding or subtracting from God's word. As the refrain (v. 105) insists, it is the word of God alone that serves as a lamp and guide for moral behavior, not human sophistry.

GOSPEL

Luke 9:1-6

He sent them to proclaim the Kingdom of God and to heal the sick.

Literary Link

Curiously, the Lectionary chooses to omit several events reported in Luke's gospel after Jesus' acknowledgment of his true family: the calming of the storm at sea (8:22-25), the healings of the Gerasene demoniac (vv. 26-39), and the cures of the daughter of Jairus and the woman with the hemorrhage (vv. 40-56). The Lectionary moves immediately from the description of his true family (vv. 19-21) to the mission of the Twelve (9:1-6). This new liturgical pairing may suggest that the Twelve are members of such a family or imply that only those who hear the Word and truly obey it can be sent as instruments and agents of the kingdom!

Power and Authority

Heralding the kingdom (v. 2) is more than words. It presumes the possession of God's authority because the kingdom is all about the transformation of the world by God's sovereign action. No real change can occur unless demonic evil is confronted and the sick are healed (v. 1); for this reason these two actions seem to be inherent in the transforming power of God at work in our world. Anyone sent to proclaim the kingdom must demonstrate its power and give evidence of personal legitimacy by making a difference in the lives of those to whom they are sent.

Without Supplies or Extra Resources

The mission mandate given by Jesus to the Twelve who now represent a renewed Israel includes the admonition not to depend on extra food, clothing, supplies, or even a stick for protection (v. 3). Rather, they are to depend upon the kindness and generosity of others (v. 4). In this way it becomes very clear that the effectiveness of their words and works is the result of God alone, not human initiative or skill.

Thursday of the Twenty-Fifth Week in Ordinary Time

First Reading (Year I)

Haggai 1:1-8

Build the house that I may take pleasure in it.

The Book of Haggai

The prophet Haggai rose in 520 BC to speak words of encouragement for those newly returned exiles who seemed overwhelmed by the task of rebuilding the nation's temple. He remains a voice for all involved in fresh starts and new beginnings.

A Time of Discouragement

Meager crops, insufficiently nourishing food, ineffective clothing, and disappearing savings (v. 6) converged to leave the newly returned exiles feeling as if they had accomplished nothing. This text is most appropriate for hard economic times or for people on the economic fringes of society who feel that they simply can't make headway no matter how hard they try. Anyone can face such difficulties at some point in life, and Haggai continues to speak his message of encouragement to every generation.

Priorities

Haggai's strong words attempt to remind the people that the rebuilding of the temple should be a priority in their efforts because it was the Lord alone who was the source of any sustenance they might receive or any prosperity they might experience. The repeated invitation, "Consider your ways!" (vv. 5, 7), asks for a careful examination of conscience by the entire nation. The command to initiate the second temple (v. 8) was important because it recognized that the Lord alone was the true foundation of the newly restored people. Like Hosea before him (2:10), Haggai saw the Lord as the One who alone blessed the land and made it productive.

Antiphon (Year I)

Psalm 149:4a

The Lord takes delight in his people.

Psalm 149: Praise and Worship

Unfortunately, this psalm has a long history of use during religious wars between Christian groups because of its reference to praise on their mouths and two-edged swords in their hands (v. 6b, omitted in the response). Thus purified, the psalm has become a festive liturgical expression of gratitude and praise for the builders of the temple and for the God whom they praise by their efforts.

The Refrain

The refrain (v. 4) was probably chosen because it repeats the word "pleasure/delight" (v. 8) from the prophetic exhortation of Haggai. The same God who promised to take delight in the new temple also takes delight in the people who build it! The human delight of, for example, (grand) parents in their (grand)children or workers in their accomplishments is now applied to God himself as he takes pleasure in the life of his people. God's delight, however, is infinitely beyond anything human beings know or experience. Apophatic theology uses an image, but then quickly admits its complete inadequacy before the reality of God.

First Reading (Year II)

Ecclesiastes 1:2-11

Nothing is new under the sun.

Vanity

The Hebrew word used here, *hebel*, means something that might appear real and substantial but, like smoke or misty cloud, is revealed to be ultimately without substance. It has been traditionally translated as "vanity" (v. 2). Thus the preacher claims that in the last analysis, labor, wealth, time, and change are only apparently positive but ultimately valueless. The author's attitude might be depressing, but his doctrine serves to counterbalance the presumption of Deuteronomy, that obedience always brings prosperity and satisfaction. Wise and mature believers know that life is a bit more nuanced than that!

The Book of Ecclesiastes (Qoheleth)

Probably written almost three centuries before Christ, the book is attributed to a wisdom teacher with the generic personal name of Qoheleth, meaning "one who convokes the assembly." The doctrine has a pessimistic tone because every human effort or accomplishment is presented as very transitory and only very momentarily satisfying. The wise person is therefore invited to enjoy whatever passing pleasure can be found in human life.

The Cycle of Seasons

The passage's description of the endless rotation of days and seasons (vv. 5-6) may be inspired by the promise of God to Noah after the flood (Gen 8:22). God offered a fresh start and promised that the pattern of seedtime and harvest, cold and heat will last forever. Nature's endless rotation of seasons leads the author to his conclusion that there is nothing new under the sun (v. 9). We need to be cautious, however, lest we take the natural world for granted and forget to be grateful stewards. Each new season is a fresh start for everyone. God calls us to be "green" partners in caring for the world around us.

ANTIPHON (YEAR II)

Psalm 90:1

In every age, O Lord, you have been our refuge.

Psalm 90: Human Dust and Divine Glory

Psalm 90 is a perfect response to the reading from Qoheleth because it celebrates the eternal nature of God as contrasted with transient human existence. Human beings return to their original dust (v. 3) like the grass (v. 5) of the fields. They are therefore invited to count their days in order to become wise (v. 12). True wisdom will thus recognize the fact that it is God who grants the gift of "*hesed*/covenantal kindness" each morning anew. Every day the covenant community is re-created and renewed!

The Refrain

The word translated as "age" is *dor*, a circle, a turnaround, or a generation. For each generation that rises and then returns to its dust, God remains its origin and its refuge for protection and assistance (v. 1). God's love supports every generation and unites them across time and space.

GOSPEL

Luke 9:7-9

John I beheaded. Who then is this about whom I hear such things?

Literary Link

The final section of Luke's report on the Galilean ministry (4:14–9:50) concludes with a subsection dealing with the kingdom in a focused fashion. The Twelve are sent to proclaim the kingdom (9:2). They are implicitly contrasted with John the Baptizer (vv. 7-9). This also serves literarily to prepare for the tentative responses of Peter to the question of Jesus regarding his identity (v. 19).

Herod as Model for Believers?

Although this Herod (son of Herod the Great) does not have the best reputation in the gospels, especially because of his spineless acceding to the wishes of young Salome (Mark 6:27) and his role in the Lord's passion (23:6-16), he is presented here as someone very curious about Jesus. Curiosity can be a gift of the Spirit. In this spiritual journey curiosity marks a person always eager to know more about Jesus, and hoping to see and speak with him. To be perplexed is to recognize that one doesn't have all the answers. Herod's question about the identity of Jesus (v. 9) is answered by the subsequent accounts: Feeder of the hungry (v. 16), Messiah of God (v. 20), suffering Son of Man (v. 22), Master (v. 23), and chosen Son (v. 35). Each title makes its own contribution to the full mosaic.

Luke's Portrait of Rulers

As we know from the gospel's introduction, the work was dedicated to the "most excellent Theophilus" (1:3), presumably someone educated, affluent, and prominent. It may be for that reason that rulers are not usually presented as venal or villainous in this gospel, and that the followers of Jesus are generally described as not posing a threat to orderly society. Although Christians do offer a countercultural critique to their world, it is a cultural "revolution" of values from within, not by violence from without. Luke's community was wealthy for the most part, and therefore Luke is repeatedly concerned about the dangers of greed in all forms (12:15) and the duty to care for the needy (18:22).

Thursday of the Twenty-Fifth Week in Ordinary Time

Friday of the Twenty-Fifth Week in Ordinary Time

First Reading (Year I)

Haggai 2:1-9

One moment yet and I will fill this house with glory.

Sad Memories

The temple had been destroyed by the Babylonians in 587/86 BC and the city's leaders sent into exile shortly thereafter. The decree of Cyrus allowing their return to Jerusalem was dated about fifty years later. Undoubtedly some of the returnees were old enough to remember the magnificent glory of that holy place; their memories may have been enhanced by the passing of time. By comparison the new structure must have seemed very modest and simple (v. 3). Something similar happens when people who left Europe as children for a new life in America return to home villages and discover that everything is smaller and much less spectacular than they had "remembered"! The "it used to be better/bigger" syndrome can touch anyone's heart because our memories are influenced by our wants. Minds and memories conspired to change reality for the returning Judeans. Membership in a community, however, can help keep the memories real by recalling both the blessings and the burdens of the past. How can we help each other remember things accurately?

Future Glory

In the name of God, Haggai promises that in due time the treasures and wealth of the nations will be given to enhance the temple's beauty beyond all of their wildest dreams (v. 7). When God is at work, even the most modest beginnings can hold the promise of future grandeur and glory (v. 9). God is not afraid to start small. Some of the parables of the kingdom, such as the mustard seed (Matt 13:31-32), make the same promise and offer the same assurance.

Antiphon (Year I)

Psalm 43:5

Hope in God; I will praise him, my savior and my God.

Psalm 43: A Plea for Divine Justice

Because of the triple repetition of the same refrain, almost as an exhortation to hope (42:6 and 12; 43:5), the two psalms (42 and 43) are considered to be a single song of personal lament and an assurance of God's saving intervention. The verses selected by the Lectionary represent an appeal for justice against faithless and deceitful people (v. 1), a lament that God seems so distant (v. 2), and a plea for God's assistance in returning to the temple (v. 4). These seem to be perennial prayers for all generations.

The Refrain

The words of the psalmist are chosen from the thrice repeated invitation (v. 5). They echo the very encouragement expressed by Haggai to those who lived in sadness because of their modest circumstances. For Christians hope is a theological virtue and a grace given by God to those who rest their trust in a God who is ever faithful and true. Pope Benedict XVI's encyclical *Spe Salvi* (2010) was addressed to all those struggling for hope amid the pressures and heartaches of our age. To hope is to both acknowledge the absence of something desired and to live in confidence that God will be generous in God's time.

First Reading (Year II)

Ecclesiastes 3:1-11

There is a time for everything under the sun.

Time as *Kairos*

There are two Greek words for "time." One is *chronos*, namely, what a watch or calendar may tell in terms of the sequences of hours, days, and months, but the other is "*kairos*/appointed time," that is, the right time for decision or action in light of converging circumstances and needs. This magnificent and consoling passage from Ecclesiastes/Qoheleth uses the latter some thirty times. Each case lists a contrasting situation that may require respectively different responses from a truly wise person. Life has its own rhythm, and we learn best by responding to the challenges of the moment and by allowing the individual events of a day to lift us up and carry us along!

God Behind the Times

Throughout that entire series listed in this reading, and indeed under the surface of every human situation, remains a God at work for the good of those who love him (Rom 8:28). To suggest that God is "behind the times" is not to imply that God is quaintly outmoded, but rather to insist that, as a matter of faith, God is at work in each of those "times/*kairoi*." Qoheleth does not use a great deal of religious language in his reflections on the transient quality of human life, but he does acknowledge that it is God who assigns a "task" to be performed by human beings (v. 10) in each of the "times" as described in this truly wonderful reading.

Friday of the Twenty-Fifth Week in Ordinary Time

Antiphon (Year II)

Psalm 144:1

Blessed be the Lord, my Rock!

Psalm 144: A Trusting Leader

Psalm 144 is understood as an expression of trust on the part of a royal figure. At the time of the Greek Septuagint translation the psalm was interpreted as the song of David before Goliath. Only the two initial sections of the psalm have been selected by the Lectionary for this response, the first (vv. 1-2) expressing confidence in the Lord's protection, and the second (vv. 3-4) acknowledging the insignificance of any human being. The latter feels like an echo of Psalm 8. In this particular liturgical context the verses underscore the frail human reality amid the changing "times" as described in the reading from Ecclesiastes/Qoheleth.

The Refrain

The refrain (v. 1) praises God as a Rock of security and protection, almost like a high and protected cave to which one could retreat in times of danger. In all circumstances and in every contradictory situation a person who is truly faithful, like David in danger or Job in distress, should simply bless (v. 1) and praise God.

Gospel

Luke 9:18-22

You are the Christ of God. The Son of Man must suffer greatly.

Literary Link

The Lectionary chooses to omit the report of the returning Twelve (v. 10) and the feeding of the five thousand (vv. 11-17). The result is that this brief passage about the confession of Peter represents yet another answer to the question of Herod (v. 9). In this episode Jesus is named by Peter as "[t]he Christ of God" (v. 20). Jesus felt the need to clarify that confession with his first passion prediction (v. 22).

The Question of Jesus

Almost out of the depth of his personal prayer (v. 18) Jesus is moved to inquire about the people's opinions and reactions to his Galilean ministry. Luke consistently paints the portrait of Jesus in prophetic imagery and allusions, and therefore it is consistent for the initial response to be cast in similar terms, namely, the Baptizer, Elijah, or some other ancient prophet (v. 19). Note that major events in Luke's account of the life of Jesus are often described as occurring within prayer. Even beyond that pattern, however, it would seem reasonable for any question regarding one's personal identity and mission to be framed within prayer before God and then to be refined within the context of a believing community such as the disciples. The church community always aids us in the gradual discovery of our identity.

The Answer of Peter

For reasons not immediately evident the Lectionary version of the New American Bible has decided to change the translation's original rendering of "Messiah" into "Christ." Although the terms, one Hebrew and the other Greek, mean the same, the resulting liturgical translation risks obscuring the fundamental Jewishness of the gospel. In both cases the word refers to an initial anointing for a mission that retains a certain Davidic royal character. It is maybe surprising that Peter is rebuked (v. 21) for his response, probably because Jesus wishes to stress the suffering nature of his mission, not simply the glory and ultimate victory usually associated with that term. Apparently Peter's initial human answer was not big enough for God's purposes.

Saturday of the Twenty-Fifth Week in Ordinary Time

First Reading (Year I)

Zechariah 2:5-9, 14-15a

See, I am coming to dwell among you.

The Book of Zechariah

The prophetic call of Zechariah occurred in 520 BC, the very same year as that of his contemporary colleague Haggai. Both were inspired to offer words of strong encouragement for the rebuilding of the temple. Zechariah does so with eight symbolic night visions. The latter portion of the inspired book (chaps. 9–14) is not included in this section of the Lectionary, and was probably written by another person, reflecting a more apocalyptic "end-time" style.

The Surveyor

The focus of this third vision seems to be on city planning (v. 6). Ancient Near Eastern cities were invariably placed on hills for protection in siege. Therefore, they were often crowded and often filled with a tangle of crooked streets and alleyways. The prophet's vision would suggest a renewed city grid that would be refreshingly more spacious and open to the use of both families and flocks alike (v. 8). Grazing areas, almost like modern parks, would be incorporated into this rebuilt city as envisioned by Zechariah. Modern urban renewal can often provide the opportunity for redesigning blighted neighborhoods. Zechariah was a man with a dream.

God at the Center

The prophetic imagery of this text moves from architecture to social relations, and insists that God remains at the center of this urban renewal project. As an encircling wall of fire (v. 9) God will provide the only protection needed by the returned exiles. Moreover, God promises to actually dwell in their midst, not as a guest, but as the principal member of a renewed covenantal community whose formal formula of establishment is cited at the end of the reading (v. 15). The new city is built with God at the center of everything, closely related to everyone and once again always responsible for their prosperity and well-being.

Antiphon (Year I)

Jeremiah 31:10d

The Lord will guard us as a shepherd guards his flock.

The Song of Return

Departing from the usual practice of the Lectionary, this response is taken from a poem of Jeremiah rather than from a psalm. Its four verses invite distant nations (v. 10) to witness to the fact that God is redeeming Israel from indentured service (v. 11) and bringing them home to prosperous gardens (v. 12) amid great jubilation (v. 13). The utter jubilation of "homecoming" is the spirit of this text, not of an annual high school athletic event, but of those finally returned from residence, foreign military deployment, or labor in a distant land.

God as Shepherd

Jeremiah invoked the image of watchful shepherd for God's new role in the rebuilt city of Jerusalem (v. 10). Once the space between buildings is sufficiently open for the purpose of grazing, the Lord could easily become responsible for uniting, protecting, and caring for the newly returned exiles. The image as repeated in the hymn's refrain reflected the fact that "shepherd" was a royal title as well as an agricultural profession. Ezekiel invoked the same metaphor (34:11-16).

First Reading (Year II)

Ecclesiastes 11:9–12:8

Remember your Creator in the days of your youth, before the dust returns to the earth, and the life breath returns to God.

Wisdom for the Young

The advice offered to the young by Ecclesiastes/Qoheleth includes an admonition to enjoy the blessings and opportunities of that initial energetic stage in life: the ways of the heart and clear physical vision (v. 9) as well as freedom from grief (v. 10), while still being conscious of the inevitable advance of old age and the judgment of God. Each age in life has its own blessings, and its own lessons to be learned. Gratitude to God is a constant duty, no matter what stage in life we may enjoy. The young would also be wise to refrain from unwarranted arrogance as if youthfulness had all the answers to life's persistent questions.

Wisdom for Elders

The final portion of this passage represents an extraordinary and truly exquisite poetic reflection on the reality of old age: diminished vision, palsy, loss of teeth, deafness, physical uncertainty, and eventual death. The latter is evoked by the image of the shattered pitcher and broken pulley (v. 6). Although the understanding of this imagery may be melancholic, its realistic inevitability is described as an occasion for remembering one's Creator (v. 1) throughout all of life. The God who has called each person into being remains constantly present throughout each stage of our life, consistently molding us into the figure envisioned by divine plan from the beginning.

Antiphon (Year II)

Psalm 90:1

In every age, O Lord, you have been our refuge.

Psalm 90: Trust from the Dust

In a departure from the usual pattern of the Lectionary, this response and its antiphon is an exact repetition of the material from the prior Thursday of this same week (Year II). Perhaps the sardonic attitude of Ecclesiastes/Qoheleth suggested refuge in God's care as a remedy for the human spirit. In this case, however, the refrain's word "age/*dor*" (v. 1) does not refer to different generations within history, but rather to the different stages of life's maturation and decline, all of which are placed under the protection of the Lord. The refrain is a very fitting mantra for each age group in any family or parish community.

Gospel

Luke 9:43-45

The Son of Man is to be handed over to men. They were afraid to ask him about this saying.

Literary Link

In an unexpected fashion the Lectionary has chosen in rapid succession Luke's first passion prediction (9:22) as the gospel for yesterday, and then his second passion prediction (vv. 43-45) today. Between the two the fuller gospel text offers further reports of the wondrous deeds of Jesus, each illustrating some title of Jesus and his identity and spelling out further considerations after Herod's puzzlement. Luke's third prediction (18:31-34) is not found in the Lectionary. In Semitic culture, the triple repetition indicates its great importance. A triplet is the equivalent of a superlative, as in "Holy, holy, holy" (Isa 6:3).

Lack of Understanding

With the double repetition of the lack of understanding on the part of the apostles, even within the same verse (v. 45), Luke's gospel is able to stress their bewilderment. They had been accustomed to anticipate a grand and glorious restoration of Israel by God, but not through suffering and rejection. What was so inevitably clear to Jesus, perhaps because of the death of John the Baptizer, remained, at least for the time, beyond their comprehension. Jesus had to insist that they pay attention (v. 44) because death and resurrection is a key element in his life and teaching.

Being "Handed Over"

In this second prediction Jesus does not speak of a necessity, namely, that he must "be handed over," but rather of a future certainty. At the end of the gospel Jesus will speak of this reality to the pilgrims to Emmaus as a paschal imperative, that he "had to suffer . . . " (see 24:26). In this text, however, the gospel begins to create a subtle preparation for the Eucharist in which Jesus willingly hands himself over to others (22:19, 21). The same Greek noun for "handing over/*paradosis*" means both tradition and betrayal.

Saturday of the Twenty-Fifth Week in Ordinary Time

Monday of the Twenty-Sixth Week in Ordinary Time

First Reading (Year I)

Zechariah 8:1-8

I will rescue my people from the land of the rising sun, and from the land of the setting sun.

The Jealousy of God

One of the more ancient titles for the Lord is simply "jealous God" (Exod 20:5; 34:14)—namely, one who brooks no opposition or rivalry from any other god, and who is determined to protect and preserve his own people! That may sound strange to us who think of jealousy as a flaw, if not a sin. The jealousy of God for Zion (v. 1), however, can only exist as a result of God's intense protective love for the city and its inhabitants. Because of that special and unique relationship, God is determined to return again (v. 2) to the place of ruin and devastation by Babylonian oppressors. God's plan was to bring them all home, and to take up residence once more with them on Zion. The devastation was only remedial. Our God is a God of second chances and new beginnings.

Young and Elders

The image of peace and prosperity is evoked by Zechariah in his description of elderly sitting with their canes in the sunshine (v. 4) and children playing in the streets (v. 5). All ages, especially those most dependent on others, are encompassed in this image of social and neighborhood renewal. The prophet asks if such a dream seems impossible (v. 6) to the newly returned exiles who were still so overwhelmed by the daunting tasks of rebuilding a ruined city. Of interest may be the fact that the most advanced modern care for the elderly has found ways to bring children into their environment for serenity and interaction. Both benefit.

Antiphon (Year I)

Psalm 102:17

The Lord will build up Zion again, and appear in all his glory.

Psalm 102: Praise for Urban Renewal

This is the fifth penitential psalm of the early church, but the portion selected to serve as a response to the promises of Zechariah is the hymn's final section of pure praise for the rebuilding of Jerusalem (v. 17). In typical biblical mentality, individual laments and sorrows can never be separated from the larger picture of the entire community, and in this case, a community restored to wholeness and health. The psalm's reference to children (v. 22) echoes the prophet's vision.

Rebuilding Zion

The refrain (v. 17) properly attributes to God the ultimate power in the reestablishment of the holy city. Even though the human effort is arduous and exhausting, especially given the huge stones to be cleared and the buildings to be restored by newly quarried blocks, it is God alone who is the ultimate source of unflagging energy for that restoration! Human laborers may be tired at the end of the day, but for people of faith it is God who is the primary agent in this new beginning. The response echoes Zechariah's vision.

First Reading (Year II)

Job 1:6-22

The Lord gave and the Lord has taken away; blessed be the name of the Lord!

Satan the Tester

The book of Job begins with a description of a conversation between God and Satan in his earliest profile, that of a servant of God whose task it is to test and prove the inner motives and genuine goodness of human beings (vv. 9-11), hence the Hebrew name "*satan*/stumbling block." In the most

The Book of Job

This majestic work takes an ancient moral tale of the initial testing of Job and his final restoration, and inserts some forty chapters of sheer poetic reflection on human sinfulness and divine justice. Bad things do sometimes happen to good and innocent people. Different portions of this book will find their way into the readings of the Lectionary throughout the week.

ancient Israelite traditions, Satan is not an evil opponent of God but rather an operator on special assignment. It is very helpful to know the historical development of the religious traditions reflected in the Bible. Similarly the Greek word *diabolos* originally meant a "false accuser." The terms and ideas gradually coalesced into an enemy of God.

The Tale of Job

The ancient saga of Job is told in a set of literary repetitions that make the tale easy to memorize and to repeat. Job loses his most prized family members and possessions in rapid sequence, but even amid the experience of one disaster after another, he refuses to give open reign to his emotions. Like an ever just and humble servant, he simply blesses the name of the Lord (v. 21). His prayer, repeated in the introductory rubrical summary for the reading noted above, is one that should be said by all of us, no matter what disaster or heartache we may encounter in life.

Monday of the Twenty-Sixth Week in Ordinary Time

Antiphon (Year II)

Psalm 17:6

Incline your ear to me and hear my word.

Psalm 17: Fidelity in Tough Times

Picking up on Job's final refusal to say anything disrespectful of God (v. 22), the response pictures a person burdened by sorrow who refuses to fall into deceit (v. 1) but rather insists on opening his heart to the probing of God (v. 3). The psalm is a plea for God's righteous judgment, vindication (v. 2), and mercy (v. 7). The verses could well be the prayer of Job himself, or that of any person burdened with serious heartaches.

The Refrain

Repeated four times in this response to the woes of Job is this poignant plea for God's ear. "Just hear me out," says the congregation at prayer (see v. 6). It is almost as if each person brings her own sorrows to God's attention, supported by the prayer of the community. In a sense this refrain brings the heartaches of each worshiper into the liturgical context of the Eucharist, where they are associated with the saving death and resurrection of the Lord.

Gospel

Luke 9:46-50

The one who is least among all of you is the one who is the greatest.

Literary Link

Immediately after the second passion prediction (vv. 43-45), Luke feels it appropriate to insert the teaching of Jesus regarding precisely who is the greatest (v. 46). If Jesus is one who is "handed over" for the service of others, then the most important of community leaders must similarly be servants of others.

Children as Models

Throughout the gospel children are constantly held up by Jesus as models and paragons of discipleship because they are the least of community members (v. 47). They are models of "learning" because they are curious to question and learn, eager to offer assistance (even when their efforts are messy at times and make the work more challenging), and humbly willing to admit their need for help and assistance. It is valuable to reflect on those characteristics regularly during our adult efforts to be disciples after the heart of Christ. There may also be a deeper level in the proposed model for early Christian communities. Newly initiated were often referred to as children and the more spiritually mature as elders in the faith. Receiving a child in this sense can therefore include welcoming newcomers or "converts" into the community and viewing them as the representatives of Christ himself. The newcomers also possess the curiosity, eagerness, and humility of children. They teach us not to allow our faith to become routine or taken for granted.

Insiders and Outsiders

The apostle John seems to have been inclined to draw strict boundaries between those who were intimate members of the inner circle and outsiders. Those who do not "follow in our company" (v. 49) were apparently challenged if they acted as exorcists and confronted evil in the name of Jesus. In this text (also in Mark 9:40), however, Jesus shows himself willing to recognize good in people who did good works even if they were not immediately associated with the Christian community. Luke insists that petty rivalry and intolerance are not compatible with being disciples of Jesus.

Tuesday of the Twenty-Sixth Week in Ordinary Time

First Reading (Year I)

Zechariah 8:20-23

Many peoples shall come to seek the Lord in Jerusalem.

Universalism

The prophet's vision, and therefore God's hope for the future, includes the cooperation of cities and nations (v. 20). Beyond the conversion of individuals Zechariah envisions larger and more numerous groups of people uniting for pilgrimage to the temple in Jerusalem (v. 22). Each of the Major Prophets spoke oracles of condemnation against the nations, especially those that had mistreated and oppressed Israel over the years. Even though the call of Abraham (Gen 12:3) promised that he would be a blessing to all nations, it was only gradually that Israel came to see the nations as existing within the ambit of God's salvific plans for the world. Similarly our minds and hearts expand as we mature in God's grace. God always has a bigger world in mind.

Pilgrimages

The specific purpose of the nations' journey to Jerusalem is their recognition of the importance of God's favor (v. 21). It is the experience of God's presence that makes certain places "holy." It is the grace of God that deepens human relationships and transforms people into attractive creatures. Like Isaiah 2 before him, Zechariah's postexilic perspective envisions the nations coming to Zion to "seek the Lord" (v. 21). Such seeking is often an expression for consulting God's will in making decisions.

Minyan

The mere fact that they come in groups of ten (v. 23) could remind someone familiar with the early tales of Abraham and Sarah of the minimum number of ten faithful needed to avert the destruction of a city (Gen 18:32). According to Jewish piety these are small groups, at least ten in number, who form a community of powerful prayer for the welfare of the larger community. Such a group is called a minyan. As Paul noted often, salvation comes through the Jews, the original olive tree into which all others have been grafted (Rom 11:17).

Antiphon (Year I)

Zechariah 8:23

God is with us.

Psalm 87: Tourism Promotion

Although the refrain (v. 23) is taken from the end of the reading itself, the fuller response comes from the initial verses of Psalm 87, which delight in God's presence. By the choice of this response, the wider journeys of distant cities and nations are presented imaginatively as extended processions to Zion from every nation. Even ancient enemies such as Egypt and Babylon (v. 4) are now considered among the faithful devotees of the God of Israel. They claim some type of residential citizenship (v. 6) in Zion. Psalms like this were part of the religious motivation for the establishment of the nation of Israel in 1948.

First Reading (Year II)

Job 3:1-3, 11-17, 20-23

Why is light given to the toilers?

The Curse of Job

Job opened his mouth for a curse (v. 1), not of God the ultimate source of all reality, which he resolutely refused to do throughout all his sufferings, but rather of the specific time frame of life within which all his pain and sorrow had been received. To curse is to condemn to total ruin and permanent destruction. It was considered a sin punishable by death to curse or condemn God (Lev 24:16). Job focused his anger and frustration on the times within which he lived and the burdens that he was forced to suffer. The dramatic and bitter lament of Job only concludes with his repentant silence (40:3-5) and his recognition of the great mystery of God. At the end of the story Job would be confronted by the immensity of God and his own meager human understanding.

Depression

This extraordinary lament of utter sorrow and paralyzing grief before the overwhelming hardships of Job's life is a powerful description of the kinds of depression that can overtake a person at desperate moments. Feeling "bitter in spirit" (v. 20), utterly hemmed in and without a clue as to which path to take, is an emotional state that can overtake anyone. Light is offered day after day, however, to those who labor with difficulty and who might prefer not to see another day of such misery. The antidote is the psalm response's acknowledgment of God as source of release and help. This reading could become an occasion for the parish to pray for all those who might be trapped in such emotional darkness.

ANTIPHON (YEAR II)

Psalm 88:3

Let my prayer come before you, Lord.

Prayer

This antiphon suggests prayer as petition (v. 3). As a call for help such a request can give helpful expression to the profound personal needs of a person in distress. At the same time, prayer can also fall into other categories such as an action to atone for one's mistakes, a remedy for the situations caused by sin and selfish preoccupation, or even praise for the utter mystery of God's wisdom. It can ultimately include the simple state of assuming a contemplative presence before the incomprehensible mystery of God. Early Christian writers suggested a sequence of praise, thanksgiving, sorrow, petition, and final summary praise.

Psalm of Lament

The verses of this response are taken from the lament Psalm 88, and can easily be seen as a continuation of the sentiments of Job expressed in the reading from Job. The verses, like a cry in the night (v. 2), seem almost unrelieved by any joy or hope. Rather than a mere description of the depression, however, the verses recognize the existence of God (v. 3). They offer words for the use of someone seeking deliverance and healing. They "say it like it is." These verses can be recommended for all the sadnesses and hurts of life. Scripture offers God's words for every human emotion.

GOSPEL

Luke 9:51-56

He resolutely determined to journey to Jerusalem.

Literary Link

Luke's account of the Galilean ministry of Jesus extends over six chapters (4:14–9:50) and concludes with the teaching that "whoever is not against you is for you" (v. 50). Luke now turns to begin his famous travel narrative toward Jerusalem and the destiny that awaits Jesus there (9:51–19:27).

Resolute Determination

The phrase translated here by "resolutely determined" (v. 51) is literally, "he turned his face toward." The gospel wishes to convey a sense of decisive determination, which is made all the more poignant by the hostility immediately encountered from the Samaritans (v. 53). That final journey will be difficult for Jesus from the very beginning, not simply because of the opposition and betrayal that would await him in the Eternal City! The decision to obey the will of the Father may be costly. Change is never easy. Even love, as Dorothy Day once noted, can be "a harsh and dreadful thing."*

Samaritan Hostility

In ironic contrast with the prophetic hope expressed in the day's first reading from Zechariah in Year I, we find in this gospel passage a case of ethnic hostility and resistance to any group going to Jerusalem (v. 53)! That friction had begun some four hundred years earlier when the Samaritans resisted the rebuilding of the temple in Jerusalem under Ezra and Nehemiah, and established their own temple on Mount Gerizim. National differences and ethnic hostilities can be obstacles to God's will as well as instruments of God's purpose. Our own age has witnessed countless examples of ethnic hatred and the horror of ethnic cleansing. Christians have a distinctive vocation to purify ourselves and our world from any ethnic prejudices.

Impetuous Disciples

The brothers James and John seem to have possessed fiery temperaments, as evidenced by their desire to summon God's punishing fire upon such hostile and inhospitable people (v. 54). Jesus, however, repeatedly rejected any suggestion of invoking divine punishment on anyone who resisted his mission. As John's gospel noted, Jesus came to save the world, not to condemn it (3:17). For that reason he rebuked those disciples who sought revenge upon their opponents and rivals. Like the parable of the weeds and the wheat (Matt 13:24-30), Jesus is more inclined to allow things to mature in the hope of conversation and eventual blessings.

Tuesday of the Twenty-Sixth Week in Ordinary Time

* Quoting Fr. Zossima in *The Brothers Karamazov*; chap. 7 (p. 136) in *House of Hospitality, The Catholic Worker Movement*, http://www.catholicworker.org/dorothyday/Reprint2.cfm?TextID=442.

Wednesday of the Twenty-Sixth Week in Ordinary Time

First Reading (Year I)

Nehemiah 2:1-8

If it please the king, send me to the city of my ancestors and I will rebuild it.

The Book of Nehemiah

Originally the books of Ezra and Nehemiah were treated as a single work under the title of "Ezra." They were probably written by the same person who wrote the two books of Chronicles as well. Everything is told in the light of the history and the importance of the temple and its worship of the Lord. There seem to be some genuine autobiographical sections from the life of Governor Nehemiah scattered throughout this work.

Homesickness

Nehemiah's personal story began with a random conversation with the king of Persia while serving wine at table. One never knows what casual events might have extraordinary consequences! This inquiry changed the history of the world because it led to the naming of Nehemiah as governor of Judea and laid the foundation for the rebuilding of the temple in Jerusalem. Moreover, it really started with Nehemiah's sadness (v. 2) over the destruction of Jerusalem and his homesickness for the land of his ancestors. Homesickness reveals the existence of values no longer experienced, and demonstrates an appreciation for the blessings of an earlier age in life. One can only feel pity for anyone who has never experienced those sentiments. They are gifts from God. The story could be an occasion to pray for all who suffer the sorrow of being far from home, whether for college, military service, or work.

Practicalities as Vocation

The final portion of this reading gives ample evidence of the fact that Nehemiah with his sense of practicality was the right person for the task of rebuilding the city and the temple (vv. 7-8). He knew that letters of safe conduct would be needed for the journey and that royal orders were necessary to obtain the requisite building materials for the construction. Every person is created by God for a task and equipped with abilities needed for that work. Moreover, the wise person and effective leader knows how to work together with others for the common good.

Antiphon (Year I)

Psalm 137:6ab

Let my tongue be silenced if I ever forget you!

Psalm 137: Angry Tears Shed in Exile

There is a sense of an authentic sentiment of sorrow in the verses selected for this response. They support the scholarly conviction that the psalm was written by one who personally experienced the terrible pain of Jerusalem's destruction and knew the burden of exile. Weeping in a foreign land (v. 1) and resentment over being asked to provide entertainment for captors (v. 3) brings the vivid poignancy of that experience to our attention even after two and a half millennia!

The Refrain

There are times when utter silence is the only suitable response to such tragedy and grief as articulated by this lament. The refrain recasts the idea from "remember you not" (v. 6) to "forget" as spoken in the refrain. This change aptly describes the sorrow and intensifies the conviction. Survivors of the Holocaust/*Shoah* like Elie Wiesel are determined never to forget that horror lest it be repeated.

First Reading (Year II)

Job 9:1-12, 14-16

How can one be justified before God?

The Utter Majesty of God

With remarkable skill the poet author of Job attempts to describe the power of God who moves mountains (v. 5) and shakes the entire earth (v. 6), establishes the heavenly constellations (v. 9), and remains utterly immaterial and invisible (v. 11). The best sequence of prayer, as taught by the early fathers of the church, was praise, then thanksgiving, penitence, petition, and finally praise. It best begins with praise!

Human Frailty

Repeatedly throughout this poem the author insists on the impossibility of any human being to be justified before God (v. 1). Beset by moral, intellectual, and physical limitations, a human being always stands guilty before God, even when seemingly innocent. Who dares to argue (v. 14) with God? Throughout Christian tradition, the holier the person, the more conscious he is of his moral weakness and failures. When one comes closer to a mirror in bright light, the lines and wrinkles of one's face become glaringly evident.

Wednesday of the Twenty-Sixth Week in Ordinary Time

ANTIPHON (YEAR II)

Psalm 88:3

Let my prayer come before you, Lord.

Psalm 88: Prayers from the Dead?

Although the refrain is exactly the same as the prior day, the verses selected today from Psalm 88 come from the later portion of the psalm. With words that express a primitive understanding of life after death (v. 11), the psalmist wonders if those who have died can truly praise God (v. 14). All the more reason, then, for the psalmist to offer praise now, even in the midst of human sorrow or troubles.

The Refrain

The refrain (v. 3) simply asks that the psalmist's prayer find access to God. The prayer uttered each morning (v. 14) can only await God's attentive response, but the waiting is accompanied by an implicit sense of confident hope that God will respond in God's time and in God's way. Although we may know our wants, we are not always conscious of our real needs.

GOSPEL

Luke 9:57-62

I will follow you wherever you go.

Literary Link

With precise editorial logic Luke moves from acknowledging that Jesus turned his face toward Jerusalem (v. 51) and that his journey passed through a hostile Samaritan village on the way (v. 56), to considering those who express a willingness to follow him (v. 57). He does not travel alone to Jerusalem.

Without Home Base

In response to someone willing to join the journey to Jerusalem (v. 57), Jesus points out that it is a lifelong trip, without a base to which they would return (v. 58). Thus the "following" and the journey itself is more about a close relationship of learning than about geography. The rabbis point out that only we can choose a teacher for ourselves, someone from whom we will learn. Once we do so, we are reminded to watch everything carefully, even the way he ties his shoes. This "following" is one of apprenticeship.

Burying the Dead

Although the responses of Jesus to the two family concerns may seem sharp and even harsh, the teaching is expressed in classic Semitic terms. The apparent denial and dismissal of family was their way of indicating the greater relative importance of one's relationship to Jesus as much more significant than even burying a parent (v. 59) or kissing one's own family in farewell (v. 61). Sometimes looking back (v. 62) may be important, but looking and moving forward "on the Way" is more so. This is neither command nor permission to ignore parents and family.

Thursday of the Twenty-Sixth Week in Ordinary Time

First Reading (Year I)

Nehemiah 8:1-4a, 5-6, 7b-12

Ezra opened the book of the law, blessed the Lord, and all the people answered, Amen! Amen!

The "Torah/Law/Instruction"

There is great uncertainty about the precise dating of this historic assembly, the chronological interrelationship of Ezra the priest (very active in this book that bears the name of Nehemiah) and the governor Nehemiah, and even about the content of what was read to the people that day. The tale has the feel of a covenant renewal ceremony with the people giving the assent of "amen" (v. 6). The account also represents a biblical witness to good liturgy with full participation of the people (v. 8), because the text of Hebrew is explained (possibly in the Aramaic spoken by most folks of the time). From the very beginning the Word plus interpretation and application was considered crucial for the lives of God's people. Classic Israelite liturgy always included some portion of reading from the Torah that the gathered assembly was expected to hear, understand, and integrate into their lives.

Weeping and Rejoicing

Scholars sometimes suggest that the weeping experienced by the people upon hearing the words of this instruction (v. 9) refers to their chagrin over the sudden realization of how far their daily customs had departed from the will of God. Rejoicing becomes their "strength" (v. 10) when they realize that the instruction is a gift from God. Rejoicing is also part of their renewed motivation to wrap their lives around this expression of the will of God for his people! In our contemporary culture we may be less emotionally demonstrative, but our personal inner response is not necessarily less profound.

Antiphon (Year I)

Psalm 19:9ab

The precepts of the Lord give joy to the heart.

The Refrain

This expression (v. 9) is a remarkably apt combination of both the ideas of obedience and joy as expressed in the text of the reading. Listening to Orthodox Jews who continue to practice the stipulations of a kosher kitchen, for example, we learn that they never see it as a burden. Rather they welcome the prescriptions as an opportunity to fulfill God's will in their daily lives. Just as humanly we are eager to anticipate the wishes of those we love, so the spiritually mature find joy when they can embrace a command of God.

Many Forms of Instruction

The vast extent of the ways in which God's will for us is expressed can be seen in the many words used in these verses from Psalm 19 for that reality: laws and decrees (v. 8), precepts and commands (v. 9), and even ordinances (v. 10). The rabbis deduced many directives for daily life from every type of story in the Scriptures. It was always their attempt to keep the lives of their people holy and at times to "build a fence around the Torah" by adding customs to make sure that the will of God was respected in all ways. We know that we can learn from personal experience, and from the example of others as well as from directives.

First Reading (Year II)

Job 19:21-27

I know that my Vindicator lives.

False "Good" Friends

Earlier in the book, Job's three so-called "friends" (Eliphaz in 4:1; Bildad in 8:1; and Zophar in 11:1) approach him with feigned sympathy but insisting that Job must be guilty of some secret sin, and wanting to know what it may have been. Job accepts their pity (v. 21) but complains that they are "hounding" him with their subtle accusations (v. 22). Scripture always cautions us against presuming to judge the inner motivation and guilt of others, such as these friends did of Job (v. 20), even when we feel impelled to label their external actions as wrong. More to this point, however, the "friends" had an erroneous notion of God. They were not friends of Job or of God!

Vindicator

The word in Hebrew is *goʾel*/redeemer/"Vindicator" (v. 25), namely, a family member with the obligation to restore an indentured servant relative to his or her rightful place within the family. This text is a clear statement of conviction that Job will see his vindicator with his own eyes (v. 26) even after having been reduced to the dust, which is everyone's destiny. Even after death this remarkable relative will restore Job to his place within the family. No wonder that it is a favorite text for Christian funerals.

Thursday of the Twenty-Sixth Week in Ordinary Time

ANTIPHON (YEAR II)

Psalm 27:13

I believe that I shall see the good things of the Lord in the land of the living.

Psalm 27: Begging for Pity

The verses of Psalm 27 were chosen by the Lectionary because they reflect the same themes of the text from Job: the plea for pity (v. 7), the hiddenness of God in the midst of human suffering (v. 8), confidence in God's helping presence (v. 13), and a basic encouragement to wait for God's intervention with patient courage (v. 14).

The Refrain

This refrain (v. 13) masterfully picks up Job's conviction that his own eyes of flesh will see God. By its very repetition this refrain deepens the conviction of the psalmist that he will yet see God's many good gifts in the land of the living. As we gather for daily eucharistic prayer, we acknowledge that we are met by God in this life and that our response to God must be given in this life.

GOSPEL

Luke 10:1-12

Your peace will rest on him.

Literary Link

Having just acknowledged three different disciples and their respective excuses for not responding immediately and fully to the call of Jesus (vv. 57-62), Luke turns immediately to his description of the mission of the seventy-two disciples (vv. 1-12). Note that for some curious reason the Lectionary has chosen to omit Luke's earlier account of the mission of the Twelve (9:1-6). Perhaps this is because the proclamations of the Lectionary are addressed to the larger church membership of the baptized, not to leaders alone. The omission may also be explained by the fact that the Lectionary had already cited Matthew's version of this mission on Wednesday of the fourteenth week in Ordinary Time.

Sent before His Face

The "seventy-two" are sent "ahead" of Jesus (v. 1), literally, "before his face." This provides an exact literary echo of the phrase used earlier, namely, that Jesus had resolutely turned his face (9:51) to Jerusalem. Because of our understanding of the church as the "Mystical Body of Christ," those forerunners are in some limited yet profound fashion the face of Jesus: truthful, faithful, loving, and wise. The number is symbolically large, six times twelve; three is the superlative and four the universal. The faces are proposed as many. What does Jesus look like? Study the faces of his friends, the saints.

A Peaceful Person

Without any extra burdensome possessions and therefore utterly dependent upon God and others for their sustenance and basic needs, the disciples are encouraged to greet others with the Jewish greeting of *Shalom* (v. 5). The deeper meaning, of course, is that of reunited reality, like pieces of a puzzle put back together or members of a family reunited after distance or disagreement. Only a "peaceful person" (v. 6; literally, "a son of peace"), one open to reconciliation with God and neighbor, will truly receive and welcome them. This creates a community base out of which the kingdom can be lived and proclaimed.

Eat and Drink What Is Offered

The twice repeated admonition to eat and drink whatever is offered (vv. 7, 8) is much more than an encouragement to basic human politeness. One must remember that the great controversy in the early church was whether Gentile converts to "the Way" were obliged by the dietary rules of kosher. This mission mandate commands that such considerations not be a matter of concern to the early missionaries. The gospel was written after the matter had been resolved by what we call the Council of Jerusalem (Acts 15). These verses, therefore, also ask that we contemporary Christians not be concerned with any such trivialities that might divide us today! Our contemporary ecumenical dialogues continue to explore whether existing differences between churches are necessarily "church-dividing."

Friday of the Twenty-Sixth Week in Ordinary Time

First Reading (Year I)

Baruch 1:15-22

We have sinned in the Lord's sight and disobeyed him.

The Book of Baruch

The order of books as found in our Christian canon of Scriptures lists the book of Lamentations immediately after the book of Jeremiah because that book contained the dirges sung over the ruins of the Holy City and temple destroyed by the Babylonians. Immediately after Lamentations come the six chapters ascribed to Baruch, the well-known secretary to Jeremiah (36:4). Though written at a later date, these passages project back to the exiles the very sentiments of penitence that later led God to call them home.

Word of Authentic Penance

Often the Scriptures propose precise wording for our penitence, even so many centuries later. In particular the words placed on the lips of the Babylonian exiles (v. 15) accept the blame for the tragedy as their own (v. 16). They do not deflect it off to other people or situations, as did Adam and Eve in the story of the sin in Eden (Gen 3:12-13). Their prayer acknowledges personal sin and communal refusal to listen to/obey the voices of the prophets (v. 21). Moreover, the prayer recognizes a long history (v. 19) of such misbehavior: following the wickedness of their hearts (where plans and decisions are made), serving other gods, and doing evil (v. 22).

God's Justice

The prayer begins with a humble recognition of God's justice (v. 15) in meting out the punishment of exile. Even in the narrow sense of justice, they recognized that they had deserved the punishment of life in Babylon. The deeper sense of biblical justice, however, is larger, namely, God's right relationship with every creature. Israel's sins offended that as well. These words present yet another fine model of prayer for a modern Christian penance service!

Antiphon (Year I)

Psalm 79:9

For the glory of your name, O Lord, deliver us.

Psalm 79: The Horror of Desecration

Psalm 79 is a very fitting response to the passage from Baruch because it continues the description of the terrible violation of the temple's holiness by the Babylonians (v. 1), the dreadful memory of corpses strewn in the streets (v. 2), and the scorn of neighboring nations (v. 4). The prayer does not dodge the bitter truth of it all. The response is a plea for the cessation of divine anger and for the arrival of God's healing compassion (v. 8).

The Refrain

The prayer's refrain (v. 9) does not dare to presume a right to compassion and forgiveness but only begs that such be offered by way of testimony to God's own inherent goodness. To forgive makes God himself ever more glorious and adds to God's glory (v. 9) rather than minimizing it. Mercy is never a sign of weakness.

First Reading (Year II)

Job 38:1, 12-21; 40:3-5

Have you ever in your lifetime commanded the morning and entered into the sources of the sea?

Mysteries of Creation

God speaks out of the storm (v. 1) to list some of the wonders of the universe with exquisite poetry. In this reading we listen to God describing aspects of life on our planet that should continue to astound us in their power and utter beauty: earthquakes that make the ground shake (v. 13), the deepest springs whence come the seas and oceans (v. 16), the daily magic of light that comes and then recedes in almost choreographed precision (vv. 19-20)! We do well to ponder these experiences often, even so many centuries later, because of what they continue to teach us about God the Creator. We should never take them for granted!

Final Silence of Job

After all the complaints and expressions of human sorrow over the apparent unfairness of life when the good suffer while the evil prosper, Job's littleness is confronted by the power and majesty of God—and he is reduced to silence (v. 4). His complaints and sorrows suddenly appear overwhelmingly trivial and insignificant. There are times when complete silence is the only legitimate response to things simply too big for human comprehension. Job places his hand over his mouth (v. 4) and says no more because there is nothing more to say.

Antiphon (Year II)

Psalm 139:24b

Guide me, Lord, along the everlasting way.

A Wisdom Psalm

From its very first verses, Psalm 139 provides wording for a magnificent confession of the completeness of God's knowledge of our entire life, both our inward thoughts and our outward behavior. This is yet another aspect of God's almighty power. The psalm offers a useful complement to the poetry of the passage from Job. In the moments of our sitting and standing (v. 1), our traveling and resting (v. 3), God knows us thoroughly and by that very fact (since in biblical parlance "knowing" includes "caring") we are the object of God's affection—almost like children of vigilant and doting parents. There is no escape or hiding from the divine presence!

"The Everlasting Way"

Biblical imagery uses the phrase "walking a path" for one's entire moral behavior, which is why the New Testament finds special significance in the occasions when Jesus heals the lame and enables them (metaphorically) to live upright and just lives. The psalm refrain's reference to an "everlasting way"/path (v. 24) adds to this a confession of belief in God's presence throughout our entire history. The word translated here as "everlasting" is really *ʿolam*, namely, the world as it unfolds through the ages. This is a world that is gradually revealed, with God's mysteries and secrets yet to be seen. God's guidance accompanies us as we walk into new situations and are confronted by still new wonders of creation within and around us.

Gospel

Luke 10:13-16

Whoever rejects me rejects the one who sent me.

Literary Link

After acknowledging the possibility that the disciples on mission may not be well received (v. 10) and suggesting that the very dust from their streets may have to be shaken off of the disciples' feet in judgment (v. 11), Luke moves to the denunciation of Jesus against three specific towns: Chorazin, Bethsaida, and Capernaum.

Judgment on Unreceptive Communities

A modern pilgrim today finds nothing at the site of ancient Chorazin but a few large black basalt boulders amid fields of grain. That view presents a dramatic illustration for this condemnation (v. 13). The towns had often been invited to repent, that is, to change their thinking about how God works, but unfortunately they apparently had other more pressing things to do. As a result, sadly and permanently, they were bypassed by history. God's patience does not last forever. The same fundamental judgment was made later in Luke, though perhaps more gently, when Jesus wept over Jerusalem because it had not "recognize[d] the time of [its] visitation" (19:44).

Identification of Jesus and His Disciples

Jesus widens the horizon of conversation by noting that rejection such as that displayed by the towns is not focused on the individual itinerant speaker alone. If communities reject the disciples, they are in fact rejecting him who sent them, and ultimately the Heavenly Father who is the source of all mission (v. 16). The disciples' proclamation of the kingdom is therefore an encounter with the living God. With astonishing insistence the bond between the disciples and the Lord is so intense, in first-century times as well as in our own, that the human voice is somehow the voice of God, and the human face, then and now, is the face of Christ to the world. This is a humbling and even terrifying responsibility for those who speak in the name of Jesus. This reality explains yet another tragic dimension of the sin of the sexual abuse crisis of our day.

Friday of the Twenty-Sixth Week in Ordinary Time

Saturday of the Twenty-Sixth Week in Ordinary Time

First Reading (Year I)

Baruch 4:5-12, 27-29

He who brought disaster upon you will bring you back enduring joy.

Medicinal Punishment

Baruch recognized that the handing of Jerusalem over for punishment was not intended for their destruction (v. 6), but for their healing. Like his master Jeremiah, Baruch did not shrink from speaking clearly about the terrible events that fell upon Jerusalem as a result of God's anger (vv. 6, 9). God remains like the punishing parent who says honestly, "This hurts me more than it hurts you!" The city is left like an abandoned mother who watched her children go off into exile (v. 11).

Restoration

The ruins of the destroyed city, however, are not to remain desolate forever. The widowed city encouraged the exiles to call upon God who would remember them (v. 27) and bring them back (v. 29). When all is said and done, even after bitter prophetic condemnations and subsequent historical disasters, God remained in love with his people and was determined to save them, even from themselves!

Antiphon (Year I)

Psalm 69:34

The Lord listens to the poor.

Psalm 69: A Poor Person's Gratitude

Psalm 69 begins with a vivid description of an individual's sorrow, suffering, and shame, together with a description of his penance in sackcloth (v. 12). The specific portion selected as a response to the reading, however, is taken from the psalm's final verses, which voice a prayer of gratitude for kindness to the poor (v. 34). The heavens and the earth, which once joined in the condemnation of Job, now praise the person who remained faithful during times of distress (v. 35).

The Refrain

The Hebrew word behind "poor" in this refrain (v. 34) is *ʾebyon*, meaning someone truly without resources. The first word for lowly (v. 33) found in the psalm response itself (not the refrain), however, is *ʾanawim*, meaning those who have learned and lived a spiritual dependence on God. For that reason, God listened carefully to their pleas. As Israel reflected on the mystery of poverty over the centuries, it became clear that these poor are especially beloved by God. It was a remarkable development in spiritual meaning from the days of Deuteronomy when the poor were presumed by that very fact punished by God.

First Reading (Year II)

Job 42:1-3, 5-6, 12-17

But now my eye has seen you and I disown what I have said.

The Final Silence of Job

After promising to be silent (40:5) in the face of all his former futile complaints and accusations against God's injustice, Job cannot resist adding another comment because he finally clearly sees the big picture of divine power (v. 1) and utter transcendence (v. 2). He is ashamed of his outbursts, no matter how poetic and refined in elegant prose, and disowns his own words (v. 6) and repents in dust and ashes. Similarly the final attitude and mindset of the very best among contemporary scientists is not so much knowledge but awe and wonder at the beauty of everything! The more one knows about the mighty forces of the macrogalaxies of the universe or the microworlds in a single cell, the more silent one must become in utter wonderment.

Blessings Renewed

At the end of the tale (which began in the first two chapters of the book and included the successive destruction of Job's possessions and beloved family), everything is now restored in even greater abundance (v. 12). The entire book has dismantled the traditional assumption that goodness is always blessed; bad things do indeed sometimes happen to good people, as the story so vividly describes. Yet, when all is said and done, God does bless and reward his faithful ones. Good eventually triumphs, but in God's way and in God's time!

ANTIPHON (YEAR II)

Psalm 119:135

Lord, let your face shine upon me.

The Shining Face of God

The word for "face/*panim*," as found in the refrain (v. 135), is really in the plural, because it often signifies the changing moods of God, or the actual presence of God in our lives in so many different ways. This divine presence illumines us because it enables us to appreciate God's personal if mysterious action in our lives: sometimes challenging, sometimes encouraging, sometimes judging—but always illuminating.

Saturday
of the Twenty-Sixth Week
in Ordinary Time

Knowledge and Understanding

Psalm 119 is an alphabetic acrostic poem based on the twenty-two letters of the Hebrew alphabet. Each stanza of eight verses begins with the same letter. Here we have a selection of different verses (vv. 66, 71, 75, 91, 125, 130), all stressing the psalmist's prayer for wisdom and understanding of God's mysterious and often inscrutable will. Because we know so little about God, we must simply stand in humble trust, even when sorely afflicted, as was Job.

GOSPEL

Luke 10:17-24

Rejoice because your names are written in heaven.

Literary Link

After acknowledging the possibility of destruction and ruin for communities that refused to accept the message of the kingdom (vv. 13-16), Luke now logically considers the returning disciples themselves. Jesus contrasted any less than successful proclamation on the earthly level with victory over heavenly powers (vv. 18-19).

Accountability

Every mission and every task inevitably includes the need for a final report before God (v. 17) on the experience and on the results of the commission. Jesus sees the victory over the evil that accompanies all our efforts to be faithful and he links that result to the final destruction of evil at the end of the world, "fall[ing] like lightning" (v. 17). The seventy-two are wise enough to know that any success they experienced was not due to their own efforts or skill but to "the name of Jesus" who is the true ultimate source of all healing and conversion.

The Prayer of Jesus

The Gospel of Luke regularly depicts Jesus as praying at key moments in his earthly ministry, even when dying on the cross. Here we are given the privilege of eavesdropping, as it were, and overhearing his prayer. This is a prayer of praise to his heavenly Father (v. 21) who reveals the most important things in life to children and to those whose childlike relationship to God makes them docile to the big mysteries. Jesus gives thanks for the way God reshapes our world into humble dependence on God and prompt generosity toward our neighbors, just like little children. They are consistently presented as Gospel models for adults who have entered the kingdom.

Monday of the Twenty-Seventh Week in Ordinary Time

First Reading (Year I)

Jonah 1:1–2:1-2, 11

But Jonah made ready to flee away from the Lord.

The Book of Jonah
By using the figure of a very reluctant prophet, this tale from the fifth century BC depicts a God who will not be confined to any narrow or vindictive stance against Israel's ancient Assyrian enemies, no matter how evil their earlier deeds. This is a story of God's magnificent mercy and the total repentance of an improbable people, much to the chagrin of Jonah!

The Runaway Prophet

Upon receiving God's command to preach repentance "against" Nineveh (v. 2), Jonah was so stubbornly shocked as to flee immediately in precisely the opposite direction, to Tarshish (v. 3). The name was a generic reference meaning "refinery" somewhere to the west. Thus Jonah becomes the classic figure for everyone and anyone who flees from doing the will of God, either out of personal fear of the obstacles or prejudiced reluctance or religious intolerance. In some manner this is a story about each of us.

The Inevitable Triumph of God's Will

As the tale unfolds, it becomes very clear that God will not be circumvented by human willfulness or disobedience. The dreadful storm that rises at the Lord's command (v. 4) to foil Jonah's plans is a sign that God will not be deterred. When the sailors discover Jonah as the cause and source of their danger, and reluctantly throw him overboard at Jonah's own request (v. 12), it was God who saved him through the actions of the giant fish sent by God (2:1). No one can escape the will of God because, even though God respects free will, he will not cease from his efforts to save the world. Even the most unlikely and unworthy remain objects of God's perennial concern.

Antiphon (Year I)

Jonah 2:7

You will rescue my life from the pit, O Lord.

The Prayer of Jonah

The response chosen by the Lectionary is not a psalm but rather the prayer of Jonah from the fish's belly (2:3-10). Jonah prays from the depth of his rebellion and is heard by God who even saves those who flee his will. The imagery describes the watery depths (v. 4), which are the occasions of death but also an ancient image for new life through baptism. Even from such a moral distance Jonah thinks of the temple and turns toward it (vv. 5, 8).

The Refrain

In general terms the refrain (see v. 7) simply celebrates God as the one who rescues from impossible situations over which the individual, like Jonah, has no control and no means for self-deliverance. The "pit" is a classical reference to the grave and the afterlife of the dead. The use of the future tense "will" expresses trusting confidence that God will do what only God can do.

First Reading (Year II)

Galatians 1:6-12

The Gospel preached by me is not of human origin but through a revelation of Jesus Christ.

A Passionate Paul

Paul is so carried away by his passionate denunciation of those who were teaching contrary to him, that he is willing to place them under a curse. Indeed he felt so vehemently about the matter as to repeat it twice (vv. 8, 9). He probably apologized afterwards, but the passion of his conviction demonstrated that every human sentiment can be an effective argument for truth. Paul's sense of conviction could never be accused of being halfhearted or wishy-washy.

The Letter to the Galatians

Written to recent converts from paganism who were being urged by new missionaries to adapt the obligations of Judaism, including circumcision, Paul passionately defended his version of the Gospel by insisting on the power of Christ's sacrifice. Paul would not tolerate the undermining of his authority in this matter. Later he would send the Romans a more carefully reasoned defense of those teachings, but the urgency of the situation compelled him to this immediate intervention.

Human Respect

Because Paul was charged by the risen Lord with the task of preaching to the Gentiles, and shaping his instruction about how their newly baptized life was to be led—even with the elimination of many of the specific Jewish prescriptions of the law—he was accused of modifying his teaching to the whims and likes of his audience. He denies currying favor from his audience or weakening the message for petty human approval (v. 10). Paul insists, and indeed passionately, that his teaching is based on revelation, not mere human pandering (v. 12). In defending his Gospel message, he was defending the will of God for the entire non-Jewish world. How does one distinguish accommodation from weakness, or divine kindness from diffidence? The principle at stake is what makes the difference.

ANTIPHON (YEAR II)

Psalm 111:5

The Lord will remember his covenant for ever.

Remembrance

To remember something (v. 5) is to keep it alive and real. If God "remembers" his covenant, he continues to extend his promise of an enduring relationship. It is the covenant that unites and transforms Israel, and keeps it in existence for all generations. God's perspective always includes the big picture. In choosing Psalm 111, the Lectionary seems to acknowledge the enduring reality of the covenant for Jews. The reference to the "just" (v. 1) without reference to Israel or Jerusalem could also rejoice in the order of salvation offered to non-Jews.

"For Ever"

Once again the Hebrew phrase, which is translated as "for ever" in this refrain (v. 5), is "*ʿolam*" (v. 5), the unfolding of the world's history from one age to another. There is in this word, therefore, the notion of something still unseen, but gradually being revealed to the watchful eye. The reality of God's covenantal relationship is disclosed to each successive generation. To the Romans Paul insisted that God's gifts and the calling given to Jews remained "irrevocable" (11:29). There is also a mysterious plan of salvation for the Gentiles, who are revealed as coheirs (Eph 3:6). The double plan of salvation is the form of God's everlasting care for the world.

GOSPEL

Luke 10:25-37

Who is my neighbor?

Literary Link

After reporting the success of the returning disciples (vv. 17-20) and citing the prayer of Jesus for the little ones (v. 21), Luke now turns to the question of the great commandments. The use of the parable in this literary context might suggest that even innocent victims of violence can be numbered among the vulnerable "little ones" in need of care. Rarely do commentators link the two ideas.

Love of God and Neighbor

It is important to note that this teaching about love of God (Deut 6:5) and neighbor (Lev 19:18) was cited by a scholar of the law

(v. 27). It was not unique to Jesus. Already at the end of the first century AD, Rabbi Akiba was also remembered for teaching the importance of the double commandment of love as part of the Pharisaic tradition. Even today little children in Israel are taught a song that recalls the name of the revered rabbi and his association with this teaching. The double teaching is an insight that holds Judaism and Christianity together. It illustrates the Jewish wellsprings of our Christian faith.

Neighbor

The scholar requested a description of "neighbor" (v. 29). Curiously, the parable's definition of "neighbor" goes both ways. Going far beyond mere like-mindedness or neighborhood residence, the parable indicates that a neighbor includes both whomever we encounter in need of assistance (no matter what their faith or ethnic identification) and whoever might happen to help us in our need. Both helper and helped are neighbors to each other. The roadside victim and the Good Samaritan could be anyone. The gospel's notion of neighbor, at least in this famous parable, brings need and caring response into the circle of love, not romantic or sentimental, but practical and effective.

Tuesday of the Twenty-Seventh Week in Ordinary Time

First Reading (Year I)

Jonah 3:1-10

The Ninevites turned from their evil way and God repented of the evil he had threatened.

God of Second Chances

After Jonah's disastrous effort to flee from God's will and his prayer of thanksgiving (2:3-11) and after his deliverance from drowning by the huge fish, God tries again. This time Jonah is more receptive, at least externally, and goes off to obey the Lord's command. The Ninevites also received their second chance through Jonah's warning (v. 4). In biblical symbolism, "forty" is a period of preparation for grace or revelation (v. 4). We are all the beneficiaries of God's repeated invitations. God's mercy endures as long as our free wills are able to respond. Like the "Hound of Heaven" in the famous poem of Francis Thompson, God seeks us constantly and relentlessly. God loves us more than we love ourselves, and knows our needs even when we don't.

Astonishing Conversion

The results of Jonah's preaching were intended to be stunning to any devout Israelite. Even the long-hated Assyrians respond positively and completely. King and cattle alike do penance (v. 7). The king, once legendary for cruelty but now in sackcloth and ashes, humbly acknowledges the possibility of God's renewed mercy. Conversion is possible for anyone, including those whom we (like Jonah, as we shall see) think unworthy of such grace. How often we are obviously smaller than the God we worship, and much less generous.

Antiphon (Year I)

Psalm 130:3

If you, O Lord, mark iniquities, who can stand?

Psalm 130: An Act of Contrition

This brief psalm introduces the assembly to the "book of Pilgrim psalms" (Pss 120–34). It was considered the sixth penitential psalm of the ancient church. Its sentiments of tender contrition and confidence provide the perfect response of a nation such as the repentant Assyrians to God's mercy. The Lectionary, however, delays until tomorrow the report that Jonah was not happy about the extent of God's mercy. We might wryly note that Psalm 130 is one that Jonah would probably be unwilling to recite even though he was in need of penance himself.

The Refrain

By selecting this verse for the congregation's repeated response (v. 3), the church underscores the universal human need for personal penance. Indeed, "all have sinned," as Paul insisted when writing to the Romans (3:12). That same universal lack of human justice before God was acknowledged by Job as well. It is not sufficient to point to the ancient Assyrians or any other sinful group as "them" without recognizing that we merit the same condemnation as well. God does truthfully "mark iniquities" but does not allow the truth to stand unparalleled by mercy.

First Reading (Year II)

Galatians 1:13-24

God was pleased to reveal his Son to me, so that I might proclaim him to the Gentiles.

Apostolic Zeal

It is interesting to note that Paul brought the passionate convictions of his personality to everything he did (v. 13). If he was perhaps excessive in his denunciations and fulminations against his opponents (v. 14), it is because everything he did was with passion! His personality was placed at the total service of the subsequent Christian communities that he founded; it remains a gift to all of us even to this day. God uses what we are (by God's very creative grace), and every aspect of our distinctive personalities, for the benefit of the larger world. All personalities are good when refined and perfected. They are also enhanced when complemented by others in the community.

Pauline Conversion

Looking back, Paul recognized that his prior zeal (v. 14) was good but not sufficiently matured. He was always passionate about doing God's will, completely and wholeheartedly. It was the overwhelming grace of God that caught Paul up short and redirected his enthusiasm toward Jesus the Christ (v. 15). Eventually that same new devotion to Christ led him to Jerusalem in order to touch base with Simon Peter "Cephas," who had been a companion with Jesus during his earthly ministry (v. 18). Checking with the faith of the leadership of the larger community for both support and verification is necessary, no matter what century we may live in! Our calling is personal, but not merely individual, because in Catholic teaching the church/community is the perennial instrument of God's grace to us. The church is the means of grace, not only the occasion.

ANTIPHON (YEAR II)

Psalm 139:24b

Guide me, Lord, along the everlasting way.

Psalm 139: The All-Knowing God

Curiously and almost without precedent the Lectionary uses the same antiphon (v. 24) and portions from the same psalm as a response to Paul's personal confession of excessive passion in today's reading as in last Friday's confession of Job's prideful arrogance. Very differing personal flaws can each use the same words of Scripture in penance before God. The specific guidance may vary according to need, but the Guiding Lord remains the same.

Paul's Prayer

In making this antiphon (v. 24) our own prayer today, we stand beside the apostle Paul who recognized the way in which God had been guiding him throughout all of life. The revelation of the risen Lord on Paul's journey to Damascus (Acts 9:3-6) was a concrete example of the divine guidance he experienced throughout all the missionary travels of his entire life. Even today we should look backwards to the subtle and ultimately providential way of grace in our lives, and then forward with confidence in God's continual guidance in the future.

GOSPEL

Luke 10:38-42

Martha welcomed him into her house.
Mary has chosen the better part.

Literary Link

Immediately after the parable of the Good Samaritan (vv. 25-37) in which the traveler extended care and hospitality to the robbers' victim, Luke moves to give the example of Martha and Mary's mutual hospitality to Jesus, who in turn welcomed them into his teachings. The hostesses and their guest served each other.

Discipleship of Women

One of the characteristics of Luke's gospel is his constant concern to report the way in which Jesus was remembered for his positive regard for women in the ancient world, and for the way in which he welcomed them into the circle of his disciples. We often read the word "disciple" and erroneously presume "men," possibly because of the existence of the Twelve. This story, however, serves as a reminder of a different reality. That Mary/Miriam sat at his feet and listened was important (v. 39), especially since Hebrew has no special word for "obey." Whoever truly heard changed her behavior and carried out the message. Miriam is remembered as friend, disciple, partner in the Gospel, and servant in the work of the kingdom.

Martha's Hospitality

The most significant virtue of the ancient Near East was hospitality, and Martha was completely engaged in that sign of respect for a friend and guest (v. 40). In the ancient world of desert existence, one's life could depend upon help from a casual passerby if caught in a desperate situation. On this occasion Mary's effort to listen serves as a reminder that we not only welcome and serve others but we must make an effort to learn from them as well. Hospitality and discipleship turn out to be two sides of the same coin. They remain beacons of moral behavior even in contemporary discussions of issues such as immigration reform or racial integration. Those whom we welcome have much to teach.

Tuesday of the Twenty-Seventh Week in Ordinary Time

Wednesday of the Twenty-Seventh Week in Ordinary Time

First Reading (Year I)

Jonah 4:1-11

You are concerned over a plant. And should I not be concerned over Nineveh, the great city?

Religious Bitterness

Jonah's angry bitterness over God's mercy toward the Ninevites (Assyrians) showed that he had not been able or willing to understand the God he worshiped. The text includes Jonah's citation of an ancient creed about God being rich in mercy and slow to anger (v. 2; see Exod 34:6-7), whose radical implications Jonah wanted no part of. Mature spirituality understands that such bitterness risks harming the person who bears it more than anyone or anything else. In the last analysis such bitterness can be lethal. Jonah is admittedly a very angry person (v. 9). Some people live with such burning anger as to be destructive to themselves as well as others. Zeal against evil is very different from zeal against good. This is a day to pray for angry people. This is also a day to pray for people who are more Catholic than the church.

Bad Priorities

God's final judgment reveals the sad fact that Jonah cares more about a gourd plant that might have provided temporary shelter from the sun (v. 10) than a major city and a great nation against whom he had harbored anger contrary to the will of God (v. 11). The contrast is deliberately ludicrous. It illustrates the danger of harboring prejudices against those to whom God is willing to extend mercy. Anger can be righteous, but it can also lead to twisted priorities. The moral tale teaches that national and ethnic hatreds are wrong. Earlier prophetic condemnations against the Assyrians like those of Nahum are time conditioned and do not stand forever. Every biblical text is balanced by another. To base one's entire spirituality or theology upon a single verse risks serious "heresy" contrary to the full truth of God.

Antiphon (Year I)

Psalm 86:15

Lord, you are merciful and gracious.

Psalm 86: Endless Divine Mercy

Psalm 86 is an individual lament, but the sections chosen by the Lectionary focus exclusively upon God's mercy to those in need. They thus echo and reflect the reading's theme of God's mercy (v. 5), even toward the Ninevites.

The Refrain

This antiphon (v. 15) recognizes the divine characteristic of mercy (v. 3), even though Jonah himself chooses not to share that attitude. The Hebrew words behind the refrain are "mercy/*rehem*" in the sense of maternal compassion and "favorable/*hanan*" in the sense of a gift that makes people attractive. It can be a profession of faith for the members of a liturgical congregation. The refrain can also be a challenge to faith if applied to other groups of people not easy to forgive. Like Jonah, we who assume and desire God's mercy for ourselves can be loath to see that same mercy extended to others.

First Reading (Year II)

Galatians 2:1-2, 7-14

They recognized the grace bestowed upon me.

The Right Hand of Partnership

A crucial decision of the early church was to recognize Paul's God-given mission to the Gentiles (v. 2) as complementary to the welcome extended to Jews who desired to become disciples of Jesus. Those who were not called to the full expression of the covenant as Jews through the compliance of dietary laws and the acceptance of circumcision were still welcomed into fellowship. The symbol of the right handshake (v. 9) acknowledged the deeper bond between both groups. Note that the right hand was for social interactions, while the left was reserved for personal hygiene.

The Peter/Cephas and Paul Debate

Table fellowship was an important issue in the early church as they attempted to sort out the respective obligations of Jewish and Gentile members of the community. We hear Paul's side of the debate, that is, his denunciation of Peter for suddenly separating himself from table fellowship with Gentiles (who did not follow strict kosher dietary rules) in order to eat with Jewish visitors (v. 12). It might have been interesting, however, to hear Peter's side of the story. Peter may have decided on a different pastoral strategy, beginning where the Jews were in order to lead them to a more open understanding of the deeper implications of table fellowship. Judging the actions of people without knowing their motivation is always dangerous. Although Christian history has rejoiced in Paul's words of forthright condemnation, Peter deserves his day in court too!

Wednesday of the Twenty-Seventh Week in Ordinary Time

Antiphon (Year II)

Psalm 19:5 (revised)

Go out to all the world, and tell the Good News.

Psalm 117: Global Praise

This brief psalm of only two verses represents an invitation to all nations to praise God. It is most appropriate that the psalm be used here because it can express the very sentiments of the nations to whom Paul was sent, as his Letter to the Galatians demonstrates.

The Refrain

Curiously and contrary to the practice of those who compiled this Lectionary, the refrain is not taken from the psalm response. It seems to be a revision of Psalm 19:5, which expresses the joyous element in Paul's work with the Galatians. The refrain celebrates the universalism inherent in Paul's mission.

Gospel

Luke 11:1-4

Lord, teach us how to pray.

Literary Link

After Jesus praised Mary for her willingness to abide in quiet at his feet in order to listen to his teaching (10:39), Luke moves to the petition of the disciples for instruction in how to pray. This enables them to listen to God in prayer and to be instructed accordingly. Both Mary and the other disciples learn from Jesus.

Jesus, a Man of Prayer

Throughout the entire Gospel of Luke, Jesus is repeatedly remembered as a person of regular and constant prayer. It was his example as witnessed by the disciples (v. 1) that inspired them to seek instruction in how to pray with similar benefits to their own lives and their work. Prayer is more often a humble stance before God, not merely petition. A fundamental relationship with God should remain as the basis for everything we do and are. The entire Christian life is a witness to fundamental values and core beliefs that shape our lives and in turn can inspire others. The best means of evangelization is through personal example, not through any imposition by force or coercion, whether it be moral or physical.

Luke's Version of the Our Father

As contrasted with the formulation of Matthew's Sermon on the Mount (6:9-13), Luke's version is briefer, possibly the older and more original of the two forms, and less influenced by ancient liturgical usage. Absent from Luke's version are three elements: the specification of Father as heavenly, the petition to fulfill God's will on earth as in heaven, and any reference to our own practice of forgiveness as a measure for the forgiveness that we receive from God. This is called a perfect prayer because it contains everything that should be part of our prayer: relationship, origin of life, respect for the title of Father as a name for God, desire for the success of God's sovereign action in the world, dependence, forgiveness, and the need for God's grace in order to be saved from the final test.

Thursday of the Twenty-Seventh Week in Ordinary Time

FIRST READING (YEAR I)

Malachi 3:13-20b

The day is coming, blazing like an oven.

The Book of Malachi

This collection of the prophetic oracles of Malachi, a generic Hebrew word simply meaning "my messenger," is the last book of the Old Testament canon as Christians have received their form of the Scriptures. Presumably composed shortly before Nehemiah's arrival in Jerusalem as the new governor (455 BC), the work spoke of the purification of the temple and of the priests who served therein. It also promised the return of a figure like Elijah to reunite parents and children in a radically new fashion.

Judgment

This reading begins with a strong word of condemnation for those who casually dismiss faithful service to God as without profit for their lives. They discard the benefit of reverential penance (v. 14) as utterly useless and they extol the motive of profit as a supreme good in life (v. 15). Obviously this challenge is perennial and can afflict every age in human history when the possession of wealth is considered life's single goal and only worthwhile achievement. This utterly secular and material existence is judged by the prophet as misguided and terribly superficial. It is worth nothing more than stubble to be burned after the harvest (v. 19). The struggle to rebuild Jerusalem and its society after the return from exile, like any age of economic recovery, easily led to such narrow but dangerously lethal ambition.

Fear of the Lord

The second half of the passage (v. 16), however, by way of contrast, celebrates those who live in a spirit of reverential fear before the transcendent reality of God. Echoing Psalm 1's comparison between those who follow the counsel of the wicked and those who thoughtfully ponder God's law (v. 18), Malachi leaves no doubt about which group is truly blessed. They have the Lord's attention when they speak and they are considered God's special possession (v. 17). In the day of fiery judgment they will experience the healing rays of the sun of justice (v. 20). Though not easy to sort out with the human eye alone, the same groups stand before God's judgment in every generation, including our own!

ANTIPHON (YEAR I)

Psalm 40:5a

Blessed are they who hope in the Lord.

Psalm 1: Two Groups

This initial poem in the Psalter provides an overture for the entire book of Psalms. Much to our surprise, it was chosen by the Lectionary to serve as a response to this Malachi reading because the psalm expresses the very same message of differentiation between the shallow wicked and the stable just. There is a difference between these groups, and that difference matters, regardless of what the powers of the world may think. One can't help but also think of Matthew's parable of the sheep and the goats (25:31-46).

The Refrain of Hope

The response provided for the psalm, however, is taken from the majestic ode (Ps 40) to those who live in trusting confidence before God's will as it unfolds in their world. The gift of hope is a marvelous treasure, enabling an individual person to be confident about the future even if it isn't fully understood or seen as yet. Hope is a blessing (v. 5) given by God. The root of true hope is not in oneself but in the power and fidelity of another, in this instance, God. Hope celebrates what is not yet possessed, as well as the confidence that the gift will be ours in God's good time.

Thursday
of the Twenty-Seventh Week
in Ordinary Time

FIRST READING (YEAR II)

Galatians 3:1-5

Did you receive the Spirit from works of the law, or from faith in what you heard?

Experience of the Spirit

Paul's triple reference to the Spirit (vv. 2, 3, 5) as a source of faith and a powerful element in the initial experience of the Galatian Christian community suggests a strong charismatic flavor to their religious life. It can be assumed, therefore, that the basic theological gifts of faith, hope, and charity were supplemented by joyful enthusiastic song, powerful preaching, and generous response ("mighty deeds," v. 5) to the needs of others. All of this was a community response to the proclamation of Christ crucified as the first flashpoint of faith, not simple obedience to the law of Moses. Even their observance of the law, however, is a response to the gift of the Spirit. Human obedience is not the initial action that "merits" this gift.

Stupidity

Twice Paul's heated argument leads him to use the word *anoetoi* in addressing the Galatians (vv. 1, 3). Translated as "stupid" in our passage, as if to illustrate Paul's exasperation with his former converts and disciples, the word itself means "without knowledge, thoughtless, and without consideration for consequences." Every decision to accept Christ's teaching should be made with clear understanding and due appreciation for the implications of that decision in our lives. In what circumstances would we have to recognize that we stand beside those hapless Galatians and acknowledge our own stupidity as well? Would Paul be forced to say the same things about us at times? Faith has consequences for life. Though freely given by God without being the result of our good works (v. 5), it has a price in terms of social implications of generosity and courageous commitment to the truth.

ANTIPHON (YEAR II)

Luke 1:68

Blessed be the Lord, the God of Israel; he has come to his people.

The Benedictus

The Lectionary curiously offers the Benedictus of Zechariah (Luke 1:68-79) as the liturgical response to this portion of Paul's Letter to the Galatians. Focusing on the future, the prayer is offered every morning by those who recite the church's Liturgy of the Hours. In response to the Galatians who were tempted to refocus their lives on compliance to the law (v. 5), this prayer of Zechariah pauses in wonder at God's gracious gift of a "mighty savior" (v. 69), as the entry point for God's favor into our lives. The song of Zechariah celebrates the arrival of a Savior, as did the song of the angels at Bethlehem. That Savior is God's grand personal intervention in human history, which makes all the difference in the world.

The Coming of God

The refrain (v. 68) blesses God for "com[ing] to his people." In fact, the entire history of Israel had been comprised of a long series of divine "visits." In a variety of ways God had become flesh amid his people—in the experiences of their journey out of Egypt, in the daily life of families around sanctuaries, and in repeated protection and delivery from danger and harm. In the birth of Jesus of Nazareth, God came in a new and more sharply focused personal way. God has come from without, namely, external currents of history, and from within, namely, the spiritual energy of the people sparked by grace and flourishing in lives of faithful service. For us God comes again each day in the Eucharist as well.

GOSPEL

Luke 11:5-13

Ask and you will receive.

Literary Link

After providing the Lukan version of the "Our Father" (vv. 2-4), which includes a petition for daily bread, the gospel logically moves to a story about a neighbor who comes seeking bread for a guest at midnight (v. 5). The desperate neighbor at the locked door leads in turn to the teaching of Jesus concerning praying, seeking, and knocking (vv. 9-13).

Bread

The bread of the ancient Near East was in loaves like "pita" bread, baked each morning. It served as the staple of daily nourishment, sopping up lentil gravy or yogurt. It is easily understood that a midnight visitor (v. 5) would find nothing readily available because the baking began at dawn each day and was limited to the needs of that day. A surprised host could logically seek assistance from a neighbor in order to exercise hospitality in a suitable fashion (v. 6). The parable contains a subtle allusion to the petition of the Our Father for "daily bread."

Persistence

The verbs "ask," "seek," and "knock" are in the present tense (v. 9), thus suggesting a repeated action, not simply something done once and for all (which would be expressed in the Greek aorist tense). God encourages persistence in our petitions, not because of a divine hearing impairment or any tendency to ignore human requests, but rather because every prayer is itself somehow transformative. When we ask humbly with frequency, we come to understand our utter dependence and we learn of our limitations. We are changed in the process.

The Goodness of God

The reminder that God, like any good parent caring for a child, will not give snakes (v. 11) or scorpions (v. 12) to those who beg for fish or bread (subtle eucharistic allusion?) serves as a reminder that our God is never malicious or capricious. Moreover, our God is able to distinguish needs from wants when responding to our requests. The gospel wisely extends the spectrum of our human needs beyond the material to even include the spiritual by referring to the ultimate gift of the Holy Spirit (v. 13). The Gospel of Luke often refers to the gifts and the work of the Holy Spirit in many different passages, perhaps because Jesus is portrayed in the mantle of Elijah or one of the great prophets to whom the Spirit was generously given.

Friday of the Twenty-Seventh Week in Ordinary Time

FIRST READING (YEAR I)

Joel 1:13-15; 2:1-2

The day of the Lord is coming, a day of darkness and of gloom.

The Book of Joel

Composed about the year 400 BC, this book was occasioned by a devastating horde of locusts that consumed everything in their path, and that became a symbol for the final judgment of God. Summoned by the prophet to an assembly of liturgical repentance before the great and terrifying "Day of the Lord," the people of Israel were promised a time of peace and prosperity together with a final gift of the Spirit poured out on all people. God is praised as the liberator of his people and the source of all their future blessings. This book became important for understanding Pentecost.

Communal Existence

Although Ezekiel had insisted on individual responsibility some two hundred years earlier, the constant assumption of the biblical witness was that people were first and foremost members of a community from which they took their identity, and within which they lived. Penance was experienced by fasting within an assembly (v. 14). Elders and inhabitants alike were summoned to the temple for laments and desperate prayers. It is God who calls his people into existence, and God who listens to their combined voices. The passage will seem familiar because it also serves as the first reading for Ash Wednesday each year. It is primarily through the community that God's truth, grace, and forgiveness can be mediated. As a matter of fact, communal mediation is both biblical and Catholic.

The Day of the Lord

In autumn as the days grow shorter in North America and the end of the year gradually approaches, the prophetic imagery of judgment looms in dark clouds and trembling (v. 2). Joel's apocalyptic message threatens full and final accountability from the people, just as the harvest of the fields reveals the results of the year's work. The phrase "Day of the Lord," which originally described major interventions of salvation by God as in the ancient defeat of Midian (Num 31; Ps 83:9), came to mean general judgment, against God's people as well as on their behalf.

ANTIPHON (YEAR I)

Psalm 9:9

The Lord will judge the world with justice.

Psalm 9: Evil Condemned

The Greek Septuagint has transmitted Psalms 9 and 10 as a single unit, combining praise for God's powerful judgment in justice and equity with a strong denunciation of all evil enemies of God. It is the initial verses that are chosen by the Lectionary as a communal response to Joel's prophecy. The people exult in offering praise (v. 3) for the way in which God has and will punish evil nations (v. 6). This response positions Israel (and contemporary eucharistic congregations) as objects of God's salvation, not condemnation!

The Refrain

To "judge" in the Hebrew mentality is more than to make a decision about some situation. The biblical notion of "judging" assumes actual physical intervention in order to make sure that the decision is carried out effectively and that things are changed in the process. The ancient Judges of Israel were military leaders who both saved their people in times of distress and convened law courts to assure that justice was done on behalf of God's people. This refrain (v. 9) celebrates the conviction that God will continue to exercise that power in every age.

First Reading (Year II)

Galatians 3:7-14

Those who have faith are blessed along with Abraham who had faith.

Faith

Paul's notion of faith is more than trust and confidence in God's goodness and promises. It is not merely propositional either, as if our faith is nothing more than agreeing to truths that are accepted and collected into a creedal litany to be recited. By faith we personally encounter the spirit of the living God (v. 14). We open ourselves to an existence shaped by God as a new creation and we agree to enter into that world. We accept the truth of our dignity and the reality of our calling to be partners with God in the transformation of the world. This transforming invitation to faith is far more than simple trust. The invitation already embodies and grants the reality that it promises.

Children of Abraham

Having that type of faith makes us children of Abraham and Sarah (v. 7). They accepted the call of divine friendship and partnership in bringing blessings to the nations (Gen 12:1-3). By sharing Abraham's faith we become like him and are joined to his family (v. 9). Such spiritual DNA is the mark of kinship in God's family. The Letter to the Galatians goes on to insist that it is the specific type of faith found in Christ, the Son of Abraham, that sharply characterizes the group of Galatians whom Paul had catechized. The dying and rising, together with the gift of forgiveness, mark the unique faith of Christ's disciples (v. 14).

Antiphon (Year II)

Psalm 111:5

The Lord will remember his covenant for ever.

Psalm 111: The Greatness of God

The Lectionary has chosen to use the same psalm as a response to today's reading as for last Monday when the readings from Galatians began. Although the psalm verses may differ slightly, each response celebrates God's enduring goodness and grace by offering salvation through faith in Christ, not through obedience to the law. Jews and Gentiles alike are beneficiaries of that grace and belong to the "assembly of the just" (v. 1). Similarly, the same refrain is repeated on both occasions, almost like bookends to the prayer and work of the week. In this response the works of the Lord include works of justice (v. 4) and giving food to those who fear him (v. 5).

Gospel

Luke 11:15-26

If it is by the finger of God that I drive out demons, then the Kingdom of God has come upon you.

Literary Link

After yesterday's teaching regarding the importance of perseverance in asking God for the gifts that are needed, the Lectionary omits a brief account of casting out a spirit that made a man mute (v. 14) and proceeds immediately to describe one of the controversies about the source of the power of Jesus. Perhaps it was the reference to the fact that even wicked humans give good gifts to their children (v. 13) that led to the allegation of some opponents that Jesus did good works through the power of Beelzebul, prince of demons (v. 15).

The Power of Jesus

An old human subterfuge when one is unwilling to accept the implications of someone's power or authority is to dismiss it or explain it away as evil or self-serving in origin. Having done so, one no longer needs to take it seriously. Saying that Jesus cast out demons by the power of demons (v. 15) is a perfect example of such an evasive technique. This should not mean, however, that we accept every assertion uncritically. A reasonable human response to grace does require that the motive for our initial response should be a deep desire to do the will of God, not an effort to finds ways of weaseling out of compliance or obedience!

Preventing Recidivism

The powerful example of a spirit returning with renewed determination to its prior "residence" in a person's heart and mind (v. 25) could be an occasion for acknowledging the reality of addiction in our world. Shifting the focus for a moment from the evil spirit to our personal receptivity can be helpful in our contemporary world. Everyone has some inclination to repeat bad habits, especially if their prior frequency makes them easy guests in our lives. Cleansing our attitudes, not merely cleaning out the house, but rearranging the rooms of our hearts so that evil no longer fits in, is the requirement for this type of "sobriety."

Friday of the Twenty-Seventh Week in Ordinary Time

Saturday of the Twenty-Seventh Week in Ordinary Time

First Reading (Year I)

Joel 4:12-21

Apply the sickle, for the harvest is ripe.

Prophetic Imagery

When Jesus taught by parables, he was consistent with the entire prophetic tradition of Israel. Prophets used images to convey the specific message of God for any given generation. The imagery became part of God's word, inviting people to unpack the poetry for greater understanding of the truth. Doing so is a personal exercise of *lectio divina*. That practice enables people to receive the communication, ponder its meaning, and assimilate the message. The church's teaching about biblical inspiration recognizes the need to balance both God's initiating grace of revelation and the human writer's personal contribution to the expression of the truth about salvation that God wishes to communicate. Prophets speak in the name of God, but the words used to clothe the truth come from their human experience. Revelation is the word of God in human speech.

Harvest Imagery

The Valley of Jehoshaphat (v. 2) is the name given to the broad deep ravine between the Temple Mount in Jerusalem and the Mount of Olives. Hebrew and later Jewish tradition assigned the final judgment to that site, which explains why it has been a special place for burial cherished by countless generations. All the metaphorical elements of harvest seem very appropriate as a description of divine judgment: the end of the growing time when the fruits of life become apparent, divine intervention to end the season and judge the results, discarding the chaff, as well as welcoming the grain into storage for the great messianic banquet. It is the *kairos* for cutting, sifting, evaluating, gathering, celebrating, and honoring. It is God's action, not ours. We give thanks for the harvest, of which we ourselves are a portion.

Antiphon (Year I)

Psalm 97:12a

Rejoice in the Lord, you just!

Psalm 97: A Truly Royal God

Like Psalms 47, 93, 96, and 98, this is an enthronement psalm that celebrates the kingship of God. Psalm 97 was probably used in the annual covenant renewal festival in the Jerusalem temple. The majesty of God reigns, seated upon a throne surrounded by mysterious clouds and darkness, justice and judgment (v. 2), not caprice or malice. Even the most solid and mighty of mountains melt away before the burning divine presence (v. 5). Everything that human beings might ascribe to an ancient oriental throne room is magnified in these poetic images, and applied to the majesty of the Lord.

The Joy of the Just

Even though evildoers may cringe and burn into ashes at the time of judgment, it is the just and upright of heart (v. 11) who look forward to God's final judgment without fear. They rejoice in its unfolding when the intentions of their hearts will be revealed once and for all. For God's faithful people, gladness and joy are the dominant sentiments both at harvesttime and at the time of God's final intervention at the consummation of the world. The French poet Léon Bloy is remembered for observing that "joy is the infallible sign of God's presence."

First Reading (Year II)

Galatians 3:22-29

Through faith you are all children of God.

The Law as Pedagogue

The liturgical reading from Galatians describes the Torah, namely, God's instruction, as a "disciplinarian" (vv. 24 and 25). The idea for Paul is that the law trains us in the way God expects us to live, somewhat like a teacher might instruct youngsters in proper etiquette or a boot camp sergeant might train new recruits in proper soldiering. Paul always demonstrated respect for the law but insisted that obedience to it was not the fundamental source of our salvation (which would make us our own saviors!). It is faith in Christ expressed in baptism that makes us children of God (v. 26). Only the transforming love of Christ saves us, and provides the grace we require in order to obey. The obedience is a sign of salvation received, not a means to merit that gift. Obedience to the instructions of God is a consequence of justification, not a preliminary requirement on our part. The subtle refinements of this question were the issues of much-heated debate at the time of the sixteenth-century Reformation.

Neither Jew nor Greek

The famous passage that dismisses the difference between Jew or Gentile, slave or free person, male or female (v. 28) may well be part of an ancient baptismal formula that insisted on the fundamental equal dignity of all who are baptized in Christ. The phrase does not deny the obvious distinctions in our social world, however, but insists that they matter little before God. Paul would still insist, therefore, that the Gospel for the Jews relegated to the ministry of Peter and the Gospel to the Gentiles given to himself was a distinction not to be dismissed. In the larger context of Pauline teaching, this statement cannot be invoked in one hermeneutical leap when discussing qualifications for ministry. Different functions in the life of the church for teaching or prophesying or presiding or consoling or healing are all needed; each has its own requirements.

Saturday of the Twenty-Seventh Week in Ordinary Time

ANTIPHON (YEAR II)

Psalm 105:8a

The Lord remembers his covenant for ever.

The Refrain

For a third time this week the Lectionary chooses to repeat the same antiphonal response to a reading from Paul's Letter to the Galatians, even though the psalm used for the full response differs from day to day. In each case it would seem that the Pauline teachings to the Galatians merit the reminder of God's promise of enduring relationship and mutual care no matter what the specific historical circumstances of God's people may be in any given age. What are the individual situations that would find this reminder so helpful and consoling for us today? When is it pastorally helpful to recall the way God "remembers his covenant for ever"?

Psalm 105: The Lord of History

This psalm is quoted in 1 Chronicles 16 as part of the solemn celebrations when David brought the ark of the covenant to Mount Zion. Its liturgical usage in song and its generic joyous acclamation in response to God's "wondrous deeds" (v. 5) make it most appropriate for any occasion of communal worship and praise for universal divine power. Add your own verses of personal events to the list.

GOSPEL

Luke 11:27-28

Blessed is the womb that carried you. Rather, blessed are those who hear the word of God and observe it.

Literary Link

Perhaps Luke, who regularly emphasizes the role of women in the public ministry of Jesus, moves to the blessing voiced by the woman because he wishes to pose a sharp contrast between those opponents who accused him of consorting with Beelzebul's demons (v. 15) and this woman who praises his mother's nourishing care (vv. 27-28). These are the eighth and ninth beatitudes of Luke's gospel.

Praise for the Mother of Jesus

The voice of the anonymous woman from the crowd raises a tribute to the mother of Jesus (v. 27) and reminds us of how much of our attitudes in fact stem from our initial home training. In Semitic culture one's ethnic heritage was primarily passed from nursing mother to infant (hence the importance of Moses being nursed by a Hebrew woman in Exod 3:7). If Jesus became like us in all things except sin (Heb 2:17), we would assume that the same type of parental influence existed in his human life. A gospel passage such as this offers a useful springboard to personal exploration of the attitudes we have instinctively assimilated from our parents, consciously or unconsciously. We can all recognize the subtle tapes that often continue to play in our lives over the course of time. What would Mary have passed on to her Son, especially given the tone and content of her song, the *Magnificat* (Luke 1:46-55)?

Mary as Model Disciple

Jesus chooses to describe and define his mother as first and foremost one who "hear[s] the word of God and observe[s] it" (v. 28). There is a large group of people among whom she stands as exemplar. This reference also serves to underscore the biblical notion of "hear," which always includes some form of response as a sign that the message has truly been heard. Mary as Mother of the church and Model Disciple were Marian titles that became especially popular after the Second Vatican Council. The titles could well serve as rich sources for our own prayer and contemplation. That this reading occurs on a Saturday, the day traditionally associated among Catholics with special Marian devotion, is fortuitous.

Monday of the Twenty-Eighth Week in Ordinary Time

First Reading (Year I)

Romans 1:1-7

Through Christ Jesus we have received the grace of apostleship, to bring about the obedience of faith among the Gentiles.

The Letter to the Romans
This is one of Paul's major writings, presenting a thoughtful and systematic treatment of his apostolic service to the Gospel of salvation, his understanding of the relationship of faith and works, and the profound bond between Christianity and the Judaism from which it sprang. Probably written from Corinth, the letter was intended to be a personal introduction to the community in Rome (founded by someone else) in preparation for a possible future visit to Spain.

Introductory Self-Description

In accordance with the prescribed format for ancient letters, Paul begins with a description of himself as he understands his life and mission, a slave/servant of Christ and an apostle (v. 1), namely, one officially sent from one Christian community to another. He acknowledged that he has become someone completely dedicated to the proclamation of the good news of Christ, son of David and son of God, risen from the dead (v. 4). He lived with total certitude that his mission was to bring that news to the Gentile world of his day (v. 5). His self-identity was sharply focused and passionately zealous. If we were following that ancient pattern in our correspondence, how would we best describe ourselves spiritually? Into which category of ministry would we place our lives?

Greetings

As in all his letters, Paul proceeds to offer a brief formal greeting of "grace" and "peace" (v. 7). The statement is classic and profoundly rich in meaning. He wishes the Romans "grace/*charis*," the favor of God that makes them attractive and appealing to God and to others. He wishes them "peace/*irene*/*shalom*," which signifies the bond that reunites them to God and to each other. Paul acknowledges that both those gifts come from God and from Jesus the Christ whom he calls "Lord/*Kurios*," the title that Greek Jews reserved as the personal name of the Divinity. This is indeed a rich and densely theological greeting. Protestant preachers often use such a phrase as an introduction to their preaching, a custom that Catholics could well consider imitating.

Antiphon (Year I)

Psalm 98:2a

The Lord has made known his salvation.

Psalm 98: Creation at Praise

As has been suggested for Psalm 96, this hymn with all its joyous musical accompaniment (v. 6) may well have been used for the annual celebration of an enthronement festival in the temple. The final portion of the psalm, though not used in this response, adds references to the seas, streams, and even the entire mountains of creation shouting for joy! The song of creation joins the chorus.

The Refrain

The deliverance and salvation (v. 2) of God's people is not merely celebrated internally within the nation but should be made known to all the nations of the world. This is news proclaimed to the very ends of the earth (v. 3), a reality so wonderful that the beneficiaries simply can't repress their joy or stop talking about it to everyone! It is a fitting response to Paul's mission to the Gentiles (v. 7). This public tribute among the nations is but one of the many ways in which the family of Abraham becomes a blessing for all nations (Gen 12:3). That same type of joyful communication is at the heart of what we call evangelization.

First Reading (Year II)

Galatians 4:22-24, 26-27, 31–5:1

We are children not of the slave woman but of the freeborn woman.

Children and Heirs

Because Hagar was the slave servant of Sarah (Gen 16:3), her children were presumed to share that same social status. In selecting an image that could explain the fact that the children of Abraham were heirs to the promises of God given to Abraham, it was necessary that Paul distinguish between the two children of Abraham, Ishmael the son of Hagar, and Isaac the son of Sarah (v. 22). Paul knew the ancient rules of inheritance, and used them in his teaching to the Galatians. Worthy of our reflection are the implications of being heirs: pure gift, relationship, moral obligation to use the gift well, and recognition of the larger family circle within which we receive the gift.

Spiritual Freedom

Paul admonishes the Galatians to stand firm in their freedom, and to know that they have been endowed with that precious gift from God himself (5:1). Little children sometimes think freedom is the ability to say emphatically, "No!" but mature freedom is the capacity to say, "Yes!" True freedom is not the chance to choose any response from a wide range of possibilities but the opportunity to freely select what is in our best interest without compulsion. Real freedom is always both freedom "from" and freedom "for." The issue behind this teaching is Paul's effort to counteract missionaries who arrived in Galatia, insisting that they could not be Christians without accepting all the requirements of the Jewish response to the Torah. It was the ancient debate of law versus grace.

Antiphon (Year II)

Psalm 113:2

Blessed be the name of the Lord forever.

The Name

In the ancient world, and often in our own, a name signified the person who bore the name (v. 2). The use of the word "*Shem*/name" among the Jews in the centuries of the second temple period (520 BC to AD 69) became spiritually fashionable as an expression of respect for God whose personal name, YHWH, could not be pronounced publicly by people with unclean tongues. This explains why contemporary Orthodox Jewish communities often protest the American motto "In God we trust" on our stamps and coins—because they are convinced that the name of God should not be so carelessly bandied around and so open to desecration by the less than noble uses for such items.

Blessings

The notion of "blessing/*berachah*" suggests a certain life-giving quality. First of all, God is the source of all blessings. To bless a created object, therefore, underscores the power of God to grant or to enhance some life-giving quality in and through that creature. More than procreative fertility, this invocation of blessing associated with "the name" can also be an expression of praise and good wishes for someone's prosperity. We have traditionally distinguished between *invocative* blessings, which call down God's gifts upon some creature, and *constitutive* blessings, which render the object holy and set apart from profane use.

Gospel

Monday of the Twenty-Eighth Week in Ordinary Time

Luke 11:29-32

This generation seeks a sign, but no sign will be given it, except the sign of Jonah.

Literary Link

Perhaps it was the reference to the generation of those who heard and obeyed the Word (v. 28) that led to the gospel's subsequent contrast with the "evil generation" that heard but still demanded signs. By contrast both the queen of the south (v. 31) and the Ninevites heard and obeyed (v. 32).

"Evil Generation"

The fact that a person looks for signs is not necessarily evil or wrong. We are created by God and endowed with the gift of reason and the need to make judgments. We are expected to be healthily critical in assessing the value of things and the decisions to be made as we move through life. We look for evidence of a person's truthfulness, credibility, and trustworthiness. If, however, we keep looking for more and more signs simply because we selfishly intend to avoid making a positive commitment or because we wish to dismiss the request and to defer a response, then our reasons are wrong—and we become members of an "evil generation" (v. 29). The evil is not in seeking a sign but in using that request as means of rejection.

Jonah

The book of the "prophet" Jonah is a short story, intended to teach a moral about human response to the will of God and about the true universalism of God. Somewhere along the way, the figure of Jonah caught the attention of Jesus and the early community of his disciples (v. 29). The two most significant factors that justified the comparison were, first of all, the dramatic positive response of the Ninevites (ancient enemies of God and Israel) to Jonah's message of repentance (v. 3), much to the surprise of even Jonah himself, and, secondly, freedom after the three days during which Jonah was held captive in the whale's belly. The latter was interpreted as a pattern for the days of Jesus in the tomb prior to his resurrection, after which he empowered his disciples to preach the Good News to all the nations.

Monday of the Twenty-Eighth Week in Ordinary Time

Tuesday of the Twenty-Eighth Week in Ordinary Time

First Reading (Year I)

Romans 1:16-25

Although they knew God they did not accord him glory as God.

The Power of the Gospel

With a profound sense of human psychology, Paul understood that the truth of the Gospel, once heard and assimilated into the mind of the one who heard it, became a power at work in that individual (v. 16). A person's acceptance of that message by faith enabled the beginning of the process of one's inner transformation. Salvation, therefore, is not a single once-and-for-all event, but rather a dynamic process by which one's attitudes and one's entire world is being changed. The purpose of the individual's transformation is so that God's glory might become ever more apparent, and even radiant, in that individual's actions and words. Conversely, any rejection of that Good News leaves human minds darkened (v. 21).

Proofs for the Existence of God

Over the centuries it has been traditional to speak of the way in which human reason can deduce the existence of God. The astonishing order of the universe, its utter beauty and terrifying power, and the chain of causality that eventually requires an uncaused cause at the beginning of everything are examples of natural proofs for the existence of a Supreme Being (v. 20). Paul laments the fact that sinfulness has prevented people from attaining the truth (v. 18) and has darkened their minds (v. 21). Because pagan humanity did not conclude to the existence of God, they gave neither honor nor respect (v. 25). For that reason Paul concluded that they easily fell into actions of human degradation and idolatry (v. 24).

Antiphon (Year I)

Psalm 19:2a

The heavens proclaim the glory of God.

Natural Revelation

The verses from Psalm 19 are used in the Lectionary's response to reinforce Paul's conviction, as stated in his Letter to the Romans, that the natural world itself reveals the power and majesty of God. The psalm insists that the constellations of stars and the movements of planets, the rhythm of day and night (v. 2), and the entire pattern of the universe silently proclaim to each other (v. 3) the glory of God. The verses should provoke an extended meditation on the beauty of the material universe. Composing a litany could be homework for the travel back home after Mass.

First Reading (Year II)

Galatians 5:1-6

Neither circumcision nor uncircumcision counts for anything, but only faith working through love.

"Faith Working through Love"

The ancient battle between faith and works marked the most contentious debates of the sixteenth-century Lutheran Reformation, just as they had in Paul's day. At issue was the initial moment of becoming justified or restored to friendship with God. This, as Paul insisted, was only through God's transforming grace, not by our own initial human efforts (good works) to obey God's commands. In Paul's mind mere obedience without grace was a sort of slavery (v. 1). As a result of ecumenical dialogue over the past forty-five years, there is agreement that works are needed, not as the first means of being justified before God, however, but as the sign that a person has truly received and already accepted that gift of grace. Faith consequently is expressed in the wide spectrum of acts of charity toward our neighbors, namely, "faith working through love" (v. 6).

Circumcision

The topic is a bit awkward for contemporary conversation, certainly in mixed company, even though, at least in our modern Western culture, that surgery is now primarily seen as hygienic and not religious. For Judaism (and later for Islam as well) the purpose was religious, and signified total personal obedience to the God of Abraham and membership in the Abrahamic family of faith. The apostle Paul understands the action, however, as the concrete sign of submission to the Torah/law; therefore he sees the ritual as an indication that a person seeks salvation through obedience to the law (v. 3). Paul insists that the true focal point of membership into a saved people is the free gift of the new creation by grace and the life it inaugurates.

ANTIPHON (YEAR II)

Psalm 119:41a

Let your mercy come to me, O Lord.

Mercy

This psalm refrain (v. 41) translates as "mercy" the word *hesed*, which primarily signifies the mutual concern that members of a covenant owe to each other. It represents a "covenantal kindness" that is expected in times of need. Such mercy is the mark of the bond created in community by a covenant. The translations are many, but at heart there is a reciprocal and almost obligatory character to this type of mercy. Moreover, as a matter of fact, one might say that by his own gift of covenant, God "owes" such mercy to us, as astonishing as that might be! That may even be the subtle message of the refrain. The selection of the antiphon may have been suggested by the final verse of the reading from Galatians (v. 6), namely, that faith works through love.

Comes from Without

Because God is the other partner in this extraordinary covenant, his "mercy" comes to us from outside ourselves and from beyond our mere human ability. It is received, not generated, by our own desires or efforts. This antiphonal request that it "come" (v. 41) suggests human receptivity and willingness to cooperate; nevertheless such "mercy" always remains a gift.

GOSPEL

Luke 11:37-41

Give alms and behold, everything will be clean for you.

Literary Link

The Lectionary chooses to omit the teaching of Jesus regarding the need to place a light where it will be seen, and his teaching about one's inner light of understanding (vv. 33-36). This decision results in the story of the Pharisee's complaint about the fact that Jesus did not perform the customary ritual of washing of hands before a holy meal (vv. 37-41) immediately following the day after the reading of the complaint of Jesus about the evil generation. Unfortunately, such editorial decisions can contribute to a Christian's unduly negative assessment of the Pharisaic movement.

The Prescribed Washing

One of the remarkable developments in Pharisaic spirituality was the insight (and practice) of transferring the rituals of the temple to domestic life. Thus, just as animal sacrifices were washed prior to the temple ritual, so everything done in preparation for a family meal was also cleansed, thus giving a distinctly religious character to those meals. To invite a guest, as did the Pharisee in this passage (v. 37), is a gesture of welcome into a religious relationship, not only a social gathering. Since the teachings of Jesus were usually within the general Pharisaic tradition, his omission of the ritual may have understandably occasioned surprise (v. 38). This Pharisaic practice should never be ridiculed in Christian circles, but rather respected —just as we tend to replicate the waters of baptism and the use of the holy water font at church, in our own homes, and places of residence.

Alms

There was a common conviction in early centuries of Christianity that paid special attention to the giving of alms to the needy. They even saw that practice as one that forgave sins and purified the donor (v. 41). Jesus, always concerned with inner attitude and personal intention, insists that any purification must be internal as well as external. Because alms come from the goodwill of a person's mind and heart, they purify more than does external rinsing. It would be a very interesting development to bring that mindset to every check we write in response to the appeals that flood our mail at times. Our charity cleanses us as well as assists the needy. We might even say that writing a check or giving a gift to the needy "washes our hands," not in the dismissal of an obligation, but in the sharing of a holy action.

Wednesday of the Twenty-Eighth Week in Ordinary Time

First Reading (Year I)

Romans 2:1-11

God will repay each according to his works,
Jew first and then Greek.

The Danger of Human Judging

The Christian community at Rome was comprised of Torah observant Jews and Gentiles (often called simply "Greeks"). It is easy to imagine that the Jewish members were critical of the religious and cultural laxity exhibited by the Greeks (vv. 1-2), and that the Greeks in turn found the religious customs of their Jewish neighbors quaint, outdated, and unnecessary. After condemning idolatry and sexual misconduct among the pagan population of Rome (1:23-24), Paul felt the need to make sure that the Jewish Christians did not consider themselves beyond criticism. All who pass judgment on others while having subtle traces of the same sins in their own lives, he insists, will be subject to the same standard of judgment (v. 1).

Jew First, then Greek

God's election of the family of Abraham (Gen 12:2) gave them a historical priority in the salvation promised by God to the world. Paul's mission to the Gentile nations helped him to remember that others were also included in that initial call because all nations were promised blessings through Abraham as well. The historical priority of the Jewish people makes them models for the rest of the world but did not establish any exclusive claim on God's goodness. Paul insists that judgment and punishment (v. 9) as well as blessing and honor (v. 10) will come upon all. God is not partial (v. 11)!

Antiphon (Year I)

Psalm 62:13b

Lord, you give back to everyone according
to his works.

God as Rock and Stronghold

This psalm repeats twice the sentiment of trust in God who is rock and stronghold (vv. 3, 7), security and protection. Similarly, the hymn describes the type of trust and confidence that enables us to live at rest in God (vv. 2, 6). Many other images could be devised for the confidence that the psalm celebrates: a cellar in a tornado, a rooftop in a flood, or a clinic in illness. God, however, is the true reality that the metaphors merely suggest.

Return and Reward

Although God's gifts are not tightly conditioned, God does presume that all gifts will be used gratefully, wisely, and generously. Moreover, as the refrain insists (v. 13), there is some accountability woven into our lives, for our God is also just and will not be outdone in generosity. The refrain (v. 13) is a repetition of a verse from the reading itself (v. 6). As the refrain notes, our actions set the standard for God's assessment of our lives and his level of mercy toward us.

First Reading (Year II)

Galatians 5:18-25

Those who belong to Christ Jesus have crucified
their flesh with its passions and desires.

Works of the Flesh

For Paul the category of "flesh" suggests anything that is marked by human weakness, limitations, and the inclination to self-serving sin (v. 19). The litany of such works provided by Paul as an examination of conscience is very inclusive and extensive (vv. 19-21). Because none of these can in any way illustrate how God works in our world, they cannot be part of his kingdom (v. 21). In fact, these actions and attitudes completely separate us from God and neighbor, and therefore indicate the antithesis of love. This first reading could easily serve as an examination of conscience or a penitential rite for a contemporary Christian community.

Works of the Spirit

Almost all the gifts of the Spirit (v. 22) are in fact gifts that operate between individuals and among them rather than exclusively within the heart and mind of any single individual. God's Spirit vivifies and unites a person to the Body of Christ and is therefore intensely social in effect. The same Spirit operative at Genesis as well as the Spirit poured out at Pentecost brought a world and its people into being and created new life.

ANTIPHON (YEAR II)

John 8:12

Those who follow you, Lord, will have the light of life.

Citation from John's Gospel

In an unusual departure from the Lectionary's practice, this antiphon is taken from the very verse of John's gospel in which Jesus proclaims himself the "Light of the World" and promises the light of life to those who follow him. As a communal response to the passage from Galatians that speaks of the works of the Spirit, this liturgical combination suggests that all the works of the Spirit, in fact, bring light and hope to a world darkened by sin and evil.

Psalm One

The first psalm serves as an introduction to the entire Psalter, and sets up two fundamental categories of human beings: the just who keep themselves separated from the wicked and become like fruitful flourishing trees (v. 3), and the utterly dry and totally lifeless wicked who are not rooted in God's Torah (v. 4). The metaphor for the just unfolds fruitfully into a great harvest. The unjust, however, experience a slippery slope of lifelessly following, walking, and then finally dwelling with the insolent (v. 1). This psalm offers the same fundamental options in life as the reading from Galatians—namely, flesh or spirit.

GOSPEL

Luke 11:42-46

Woe to Pharisees! Woe also to you scholars of the law!

Literary Link

Immediately after some strong language addressed to his supper host who had been critical of the lack of a cleansing ritual by Jesus, and who had been criticized in turn for being overly concerned about mere external washing (v. 39), Luke adds two other condemnations of his fellow Pharisee guests: unbalanced priorities (v. 42) and the quest for public recognition (v. 43). Finally, Jesus includes the scholars of the law as well (vv. 45-46). That judgment will be repeated again in tomorrow's gospel reading (v. 52).

Pharisees

Since Jesus was himself a member of the Pharisaic tradition, he does not really set himself apart from them, but rather points out the dangers of any and every type of spirituality, even the most worthy and legitimate. Leaders of popular spirituality must be exemplary in the witness they give. It is not a matter of "us" and "them," but always about "us."

Tithes on Mint

The condemnation of Jesus falls upon everyone who becomes so intensely preoccupied with the minutiae of religious practice (for example, a tithe on herbs; v. 42) as to ignore the basics, such as justice and love of God. There is a relationship between the fundamentals and the smaller expressions of piety, but the basics come first. The tithes on mint, small as they may be, do express a sense of obedience and submission to the supremacy of God. The more fundamental questions, however, flow from and are based upon justice and charity (v. 42), which include one's neighbor and embrace an entire community with God as its centerpiece. Without the basics, the less significant cannot retain meaning very long.

Seats of Honor

Every human community shows signs of respect to those who offer the service of leadership. Children are trained to be deferential to elders. Seats of honor (v. 43) of themselves, therefore, are never forbidden. The problem arises when leaders see such signs as entitlements, and as directed to themselves as persons rather than to the office they hold. Religious leaders should be especially deferential to family elders when entering a home as a guest.

Wednesday of the Twenty-Eighth Week in Ordinary Time

Thursday of the Twenty-Eighth Week in Ordinary Time

First Reading (Year I)

Romans 3:21-30

A person is justified by faith apart from works of the law.

The Universality of Sin

Whether Paul looked around in the marketplace or within the Christian community (Jewish and Gentile), he was convinced that all had sinned and are deprived of God's glory (v. 23). That, however, is not the end of the story, for all have equally been brought back into a share of God's righteousness by God's grace (v. 24). Centuries earlier Jeremiah had condemned his entire people for their universal deceitfulness (Jer 9:2-4).

The Grace of Justification

Although the theological language is dense, Paul knows that the gift of justifying friendship with God comes through "grace/*charis*" (v. 24). It is a free gift that makes people attractive to God once again. Again and again throughout this Letter to the Romans, just as he did more passionately in his Letter to the Galatians, Paul insists that mere human obedience to the law is not the occasion or the means for receiving the gift of renewed divine friendship. Such friendship is gift and remains gift; for that reason people are justified by grace and not by faithful performance of the works of the law (v. 28). Moreover, to make the point even more specifically, Paul states that God belongs to the Gentiles as well as to the Jews (v. 29). This ought to be very good news for us so many centuries later, especially since most Christian congregations today are completely Gentile.

Antiphon (Year I)

Psalm 130:7

With the Lord there is mercy, and fullness of redemption.

Psalm 130: Penitent Pilgrims

Psalm 130, the sixth among the "penitential psalms" of the ancient church, is also a song of pilgrimage (v. 1), composed to be sung by pilgrims on their way to the temple. Like the reading from Romans to which it responds, these verses recognize that no one can stand sinless before God (v. 3). For that reason, therefore, all pray from the depths of their sin and sorrow (v. 1). Moreover, all are called to live in trusting confidence before God (v. 5).

The Refrain

If all the pilgrims began their journey consciously immersed in the depth of their sins (v. 1), they do not remain stuck in that pit of mire, because with God there is pardon and covenantal "mercy/*hesed*" as well as an abundance of redemption (v. 7). The God to whose temple the pilgrims travel is not simply characterized by the truth of his judgment, but also by the mercy of his forgiveness. If asked to imagine what God looks like and what expression might be found on God's face, it is that of mercy, and that is the song they sing as they journey. The liturgy repeats the refrain as if to offer confidence and assurance to the pilgrims. Those who travel each day to the weekday Eucharist are also pilgrims.

First Reading (Year II)

Ephesians 1:1-10

God chose us in Christ before the foundation of the world.

Grace and Peace

The letter extends the very same greetings and good wishes (v. 2) as had been sent to the Galatians (1:3)! These words may have been favorites of Paul, who recognized grace, the divine gift that made people attractive, and peace, the gift that binds them together, in the lives of those to whom he spoke or wrote. Both gifts are understood as having a divine origin from God through Christ. The two notions complement each other as a pair. That greeting should never be quickly spoken without grasping its true import, meaning, and wish.

The Letter to the Ephesians

This message to the Ephesians is a great work filled with Paul's ideas about the church. The letter is immensely rich in its teachings for the life of Christians in community with Christ and each other. Although traditionally ascribed to Paul in one of his final imprisonments, most scholars over the past century have been convinced that the differences in style and vocabulary would suggest rather that it was written either by a secretary of Paul or by a very talented (and inspired) disciple in the latter part of the first century.

The Sweep of History

Letters from Paul and his associates did not envision the recipients as communities isolated in time. They insist that every group was already known by God from the very foundations of the universe (v. 4) and specially chosen for adoption into God's own family (v. 5). They shared a destiny from the beginning and an eternal existence through time and beyond. The dignity conveyed by such a divine choice and the importance conferred by such a mission made each community of Christians distinctive and immensely valuable. There had been none like them in the history of the world, and there never would be—ever! Throughout all of history they were bearers of God's grace/favor (v. 9). Their mission was to sum up all things in Christ (v. 10), that is, by the grace of God's transforming love to pull everything together in origin and destiny.

Thursday of the Twenty-Eighth Week in Ordinary Time

Antiphon (Year II)

Psalm 98:2a

God has made known his salvation.

God's Salvation

It may be helpful to note that the refrain of Psalm 98 speaks of a particular kind of salvation (v. 2), one that reflects God's nature and purpose. Other types of salvation might be merely financial when a big bill is paid much to our relief, or perhaps social when we are somehow extricated from a very awkward and potentially damaging family situation or even military if we are freed from attack and regain peace. God's salvation, however, has to do with the forgiveness of our sins and the restoration of all relationships, human and divine. Psalm 98 connects God's salvation with justice (v. 2), kindness/*hesed*, and faithfulness (v. 3).

Revelation

The instruments chosen by God to make known his intentions are his special friends who speak in his name and reveal his plans. God also makes his salvation known to the ends of the earth (v. 3) through the forces of history that bring people together in new and unexpected ways. Just as we reveal ourselves in the choices we make, the friends we cherish, and possessions that we hold dear, God's revelation of his type of salvation is found in the community he gathers and sustains. They sing gratefully and celebrate with music, song, and dance (vv. 5-6).

Gospel

Luke 11:47-54

The blood of the prophets is required, from the blood of Abel to the blood of Zechariah.

Literary Link

Today's gospel passage continues the woes and condemnations of yesterday's reading (vv. 42-44). Although the explicit words of the gospel direct them to the Pharisees, we should not forget that Jesus considered many as his friends and often dined as a welcome guest in their homes (v. 37). The teachings therefore are directed to all religious leaders of every age, among whom the Pharisees were the primary examples of that time.

Building Memorials to the Prophets

At first blush it would seem good and devout to build a monument to the great prophetic figures of the past (v. 47), but Jesus saw it differently. Surprisingly enough, precisely because the prophets were killed for speaking unwelcome messages in the name of God, Jesus sees the monument as dedicated, not to their memory or message, but to the historical fact of their murder! The very stones sealed their fate and silenced their voices permanently. Sometimes our own national monuments accomplish the same effect. It was easier to build a monument to Dr. Martin Luther King when his unsettling voice of accusation had been stilled. Most of the great prophets of Israel were opposed during their lifetimes and only venerated after their death. This morning's gospel passage becomes an opportunity to ponder precisely what our own historical monuments really point to. Do they celebrate victorious war or peace? How many monuments commemorate narrow national victorious expansion and the submission of others? We are asked to look at monuments through the keen fresh eyes of the Christ.

Knowledge of God's Torah

Scholars of the Torah/law (v. 52), namely, those who possess the religious knowledge of God's will in any community, are also singled out for Christ's judgment. They have a responsibility both to preserve that knowledge with faithfulness and integrity and to share it with loving clarity. Jeremiah's promise of a new covenant (31:31-34) included the dream that human beings would experience knowledge of God without intermediaries. Jesus promised the gift of the Spirit who would teach all things and remind everyone of what Jesus had said (John 14:25). All gifts, including that of knowing God's nature and will, are given to individuals for the entire community, not merely for themselves alone. This is also the purpose for all genuine religious education and adult faith formation in any parish.

Friday of the Twenty-Eighth Week in Ordinary Time

First Reading (Year I)

Romans 4:1-8

Abraham believed God, and it was credited to him as righteousness.

The Boast of Abraham

Most people can point to a human accomplishment or a special achievement of which they are proud. Paul insists that Abraham's primary action in his life was that of believing in God's promise and accepting the gift of a covenant with God. Because it is God's gift, it was not the object of a boast (v. 2) but an occasion for gratitude. Abraham's faith justified him before God and made him righteous in God's sight (Gen 15:6). His boast was about God, not himself!

The Blessing of Forgiveness

Paul's praise for the grace of friendship with God concludes with two beatitudes (vv. 1-2) from the beginning of Psalm 32, the second of the great penitential psalms of the ancient church. The blessings offered in Romans are for those whose sins are forgiven and not recorded (v. 7). If friendship with God does not come from Abraham's good works, then it is appropriate to celebrate the forgiveness that God grants so graciously to those who believe and accept God's goodness. From our own experience we know something of the sense of personal freedom and liberation that occurs when giving or receiving forgiveness. All the more when the issue is personal sin and the gift is from God.

Antiphon (Year I)

Psalm 32:7

I turn to you, Lord, in time of trouble, and you fill me with the joy of salvation.

Psalm Response

The first verses of this response (vv. 1-2) are precisely the same as the two beatitudes quoted by Paul (Rom 4:7-8). They form an echo from the reading itself. They celebrate the utter joy of forgiveness. When placed at the beginning of the Liturgy of the Word immediately after the penitential rites, these verses continue to celebrate the reality of forgiveness celebrated anew at the beginning of each Mass. This should never be treated casually or taken for granted by the congregation.

Utter Honesty

The verses chosen for this response include a candid acknowledgment of one's sins (v. 5), preceded by the refrain's (v. 7) expression of confidence in God's gift of salvation. Integrity requires an honest recognition of the specific sins that have blemished us before God and neighbor and placed us in the stance of the need for forgiveness. Only then can we truly appreciate the joy of forgiveness (v. 11). Mercy can only build on truth.

First Reading (Year II)

Ephesians 1:11-14

We first hoped in Christ, and you were sealed in the Holy Spirit.

Chosen and Sealed

The Letter to the Ephesians always approaches the mystery of Christ with the big picture, and with a large sweep of history. God's choice and call of Christians is for a grand and majestic purpose. The author highlights the call to be a genuine partner in God's plan of salvation and ultimately to be part of the universal chorus of praise for God (vv. 11, 14). Every person so chosen is "sealed" with the Holy Spirit (v. 13), and thus made a permanent possession of God. Slaves were branded and sealed as a sign of ownership. Through the invisible imprint of his grace God remains with those whom he calls. The spiritual seal endures throughout the entire process of receiving and assimilating the word of truth (v. 13). God's seal is experienced sacramentally through anointing.

First Installment

The big picture of Ephesians includes the final destination, that is, the fullest of joy in the company of friends and relatives, and even God himself. Being "redeemed" (v. 14) literally means that one is bought back and restored to one's rightful place. A new image is suddenly offered, the first installment of that gift. To have a first installment of an inheritance (v. 14) in one's possession is to share already in some initial fashion the final full gift. In this case it is God who makes the "down payment," thus showing his goodwill and guaranteeing us a "time-share" in eternity when Christ will be all in all. Only the serious sin of full and final rejection of God's love can lead us to forfeit the inheritance and foreclose our mortgage on eternity.

Antiphon (Year II)

Psalm 33:12

Blessed the people the Lord has chosen to be his own.

Chosen

To appreciate the richness of this single word, it may help to think of all the inner mental steps we take before actually buying a new car, home, or furniture. To choose is to consider the options, clarify the purpose for which the object will be used, determine its value in the grand scheme of things, and decide what cost one is willing to pay for its availability and use. If God chooses us (v. 12), it is with his full knowledge and understanding; God's choices are never casual or arbitrary. Stepping back for a moment to see the larger picture, we acknowledge that our God is a God who freely chooses to create, redeem, love, and save the world.

Inheritance

The psalm specifies that the object chosen is not merely "his own" as the refrain states it, but his own "inheritance" as the actual psalm phrases it (v. 12). The people had a prior history of somehow belonging to someone else, and now are handed over as a newly prized gift to be cherished and protected by God. Worthy of thought throughout the day is the invitation to consider our human experience of receiving and possessing an inheritance. By analogy we leap from the limits of our lives to the reality of God's dealings with us. To think that God actually prizes us as his inheritance is to be filled with joy (v. 1)!

Gospel

Luke 12:1-7

Even the hairs of your head have all been counted.

Literary Link

Luke's gospel moves from the harsh condemnation of religious leadership gone awry (11:39-52) and the note of their initial organized hostility to Jesus (vv. 53-54) to a warning about their inner motivation (12:1). His encouragement to trust Divine Providence is the proper attitude of a disciple when faced with opposition or persecution.

Leaven

There is something initially mysterious and hidden about leaven. The yeast is mixed into the dough, and then brought into the warmth of the sun in order to begin the fermentation process. In one sense the yeast disappears. In another sense it is transformed, thoroughly permeating the dough into the makings of bread when heated in the oven. What is initially secret eventually becomes visible in the rising of the dough (v. 2). There is an inner logic to this section of Christ's teaching. He uses an image that would be very familiar to the women who rose each day to bake enough for the household's daily needs. All eventually becomes public (v. 3). Likewise our inner values and decisions, our own "leaven" like that of some of the Pharisees, are eventually revealed in our lives and actions.

Living without Fear

First-century disciples of Jesus knew something about fear. They were confronted by the ruthless power of the Roman occupying forces. They saw the bodies of rebels periodically crucified and abandoned just outside the city walls to inspire terror and submission. Jesus himself had been the victim of such cruelty and injustice. Nevertheless, Jesus insists that God knows all and sees all because nothing escapes God's notice. "Fear not" was a frequent admonition from the prophets. The same phrase was addressed to Mary at the annunciation when she was welcomed into God's plan of salvation for the entire world (Luke 1:30).

Friday of the Twenty-Eighth Week in Ordinary Time

Saturday of the Twenty-Eighth Week in Ordinary Time

FIRST READING (YEAR I)

Romans 4:13, 16-18

Abraham believed, hoping against hope.

Righteousness

The word "righteousness" (v. 13) might have a legal ring to it and may possibly have conveyed a distinctly negative tone to Paul's Roman audience. It could introduce the subtle suggestion of "self-righteousness" in its wake. The word itself, however, actually means being in a right relationship with all of creation and sharing a friendship with God. Paul insists that such righteousness comes from God's gift (v. 16) of faith (v. 13). That should keep us humble and grateful, rather than arrogantly proud of ourselves and our accomplishments.

Authentic Genealogy

Tracing a family tree has become a popular avocation, especially for those curious about their family history and familiar with the vast resources of the internet. God gave the promise of a covenant with Abraham and his descendants (Gen 18:18), but Paul clarifies that the family tree in question is not simply a lineage of blood relationships. For Paul the family includes all those who share Abraham's faith (v. 16). The characteristic profile is not hair color, the shape of chin or nose, or racial identity, but the spiritual DNA evident in having the same faith.

ANTIPHON (YEAR I)

Psalm 105:8a

The Lord remembers his covenant for ever.

The Refrain

Curiously, this is precisely the same refrain used by the Lectionary as a response to the prior Saturday's reading from Galatians where Paul insisted that the former pagan members of that community were now to be considered among the descendants of Abraham because of their faith. The same logic makes the refrain (v. 8) also most appropriate for today's reading from Romans. All generations of believers fall into a relationship with the family of Abraham (v. 6). They become members of God's covenant with Abraham.

The Exodus

The verses chosen from Psalm 105 include Isaac (v. 9) who received a promise of blessing (Gen 26:4) and perhaps even the people led forth from Egypt so joyously (v. 43). The history is obscure, and scholars are not able to determine the number of generations or centuries between the times of the patriarchs and the exodus. All of that expanse of time, however, even up to our own age, is included in that "for ever" noted in this refrain (v. 8).

FIRST READING (YEAR II)

Ephesians 1:15-23

He gave Christ as head over all things
to the Church, which is his Body.

Paul's Prayers

The typical pattern for Pauline letters includes an expression of gratitude, in this case for the faith of the Ephesians and for their love of the "holy ones" (v. 15), the baptized members of their own community. With that prayer of thanksgiving (which should be a key element in all our prayers) also comes a prayer of petition for an abundance of God's wisdom and insight (v. 17). A very poetic phrase is used in the prayer, namely, the plea that the "eyes of [their] hearts be enlightened" (v. 18) so that they may understand the hope of their call. Given the fact that the heart is the place for planning and deciding, its "eyes" enable the person's heart to plan wisely and well, taking all things into consideration. Note that the author's petition is for spiritual blessings, not merely material things like food or shelter! How often do we take time to pray for spiritual blessings?

Supreme Centrality of Christ

Again and again the Letter to the Ephesians places Christ at the center of the world's origin, development, and destiny. This includes the fullness of the apostolic teaching on resurrection. By being raised from the dead with Christ and seated at the right hand of God (v. 20), all of creation has been placed under Christ's feet (v. 22). The latter phrase is certainly influenced by the psalm response (v. 7).

ANTIPHON (YEAR II)

Psalm 8:7

You have given your Son rule over the works of your hands.

Psalm 8: The Jewel of Humanity in Context

Psalm 8 is a masterpiece of literary creation. It celebrates the wondrous decision of God to place human beings over all of creation and to make the "son of man" the special object of divine care (v. 5). The poetic description of human beings became a title for the "One to come," and laid the foundation for interpreting Psalm 8 as christological. In this sense it echoes the affirmations of Ephesians.

Sensus Plenior

Once again we have a phrase, "son of man" (v. 5), that was later revealed to have a fuller meaning that might have never been understood or intended by the first human author. Certain phrases deepen and develop over the centuries to convey new meaning for later believers.

Saturday of the Twenty-Eighth Week in Ordinary Time

GOSPEL

Luke 12:8-12

The Holy Spirit will teach you at the moment what you should say.

Literary Link

Perhaps it was the Lord's promise that all things would be revealed (v. 2) and its implicit reference to the final judgment that led Luke to move immediately to the fact that those who acknowledge the Son of Man will be acknowledged in turn before the angels (v. 8). The earlier reference to hostility and plotting (11:53-54) logically led Luke's Jesus to promise the assistance of the Holy Spirit when brought before the authorities (v. 12).

Blasphemy against the Holy Spirit

This is one of the more difficult passages of the New Testament, and many attempts have been made to offer an explanation. Perhaps easiest is to recognize that the forgiveness of sins was often linked with the gift of the Holy Spirit (John 20:2-23). If the Holy Spirit is understood as the source of forgiveness, blasphemy against that same Holy Spirit could remove openness to forgiveness, as well as its possibility. Such blasphemy would, therefore, be seen as unforgivable (v. 10). We know that God's deepest desire is the fullness of life for each of his human creatures, and that God's mercy is infinitely beyond human understanding. God respects human freedom, however, including the bad choices we may make. Nevertheless, like the Hound of Heaven God devotes earnest attention and zeal throughout our entire lifetime, trying to bring human good out of human evil.

Confident Witness

The more timorous among us usually want to rehearse and practice anything we say publicly. Classes in public speaking always encourage careful preparation. At the same time, this gospel passage encourages us to live and think so closely to the mind of God that we will be able to speak spontaneously and confidently in defending our faith and in explaining our lives (v. 12). That type of remote preparation finds its best roots in daily prayer. It is the abiding relationship with God that will enable a word of defense to be given when needed (1 Pet 3:15).

Monday of the Twenty-Ninth Week in Ordinary Time

First Reading (Year I)

Romans 4:20-25

It was written for us when it says that our faith in God would be counted.

Abraham's Lack of Doubt

It is part of our human reason to test things out and to make sure that our actions are reasonable. Critical testing, however, does not mean that we doubt. It does mean that we take time to go through the normal process of reflection. Then we can come to the conclusion that God can be trusted because God is trustworthy. Paul insisted in writing to the Romans that Abraham did not doubt (v. 20) because he knew that God could do what God had promised (v. 21)! Moreover, belief that God will fulfill all promises is the first step toward biblical righteousness (v. 23). Elizabeth praised Mary for that same type of confident assurance (Luke 1:45). Such righteousness entails being in right relationship to the entire world and all creatures within it.

Gift, Not Wages

Paul continues to insist that being in proper relationship to the world is not something we can achieve on our own. It is always a gift from God (v. 5). The promises of God find their focus in the Lord's death and resurrection (v. 24). They are rooted in the history of our salvation, not in mere mindless human speculation. Our acceptance of the fact that God can do what he promised, together with our belief that we can share in Christ's death and resurrection through baptism, is the doorway to all God's promises. Belief is a gift as is the final share in the resurrection.

Antiphon (Year I)

Luke 1:68

Blessed be the Lord, the God of Israel;
he has come to his people.

The Benedictus

Perhaps because of its reference to God's oath to Abraham (v. 73), the Lectionary has chosen as a response some verses from the hymn uttered by Zechariah on the occasion of the birth of his son, John the Baptist. The *Benedictus* also refers to God's promises through the prophets (v. 71). The response's references to being saved from enemies (vv. 71, 73) nicely picks up the manner in which the Lord's resurrection saves from death, the great enemy.

God's Coming

God "came" to the people of Israel in countless ways over the centuries: in salvation from slavery in Egypt, in the gift of the land and the consecration of the temple, in liberation from captivity in Babylon, in the messages of judgment and forgiveness through the prophets, and finally in the coming of John and the birth of Jesus. The simple reference of the refrain to the coming of God (v. 68) opens up all of history because it is a process, not a single event. A further note of reminder for another time: the various traditional aspects of Advent include God's coming in history, in the flesh, in grace, and finally in glory.

First Reading (Year II)

Ephesians 2:1-10

God brought us to life with Christ and seated us with him in the heavens.

Rich in Mercy

Even though we were once dead in sin (v. 1), and totally absorbed by existence in a dying world, God who is "rich in mercy" (v. 4) loved us into forgiveness and new life. The phrase is taken from a self-revelation of God to Moses after the tragedy of the golden calf. This affirmation of divine mercy accompanied God's gift of a second set of commandments. In that original context the phrase was part of a more expanded ancient creed of belief, revealed by God and taken to heart by Israel: "a merciful and gracious God, slow to anger and rich in kindness [mercy] and fidelity" (Exod 34:6). This same phrase (v. 4) provided the title (*Dives in Misericordia*) for one of John Paul II's more famous encyclical letters (1980).

By Grace Saved through Faith

One of the great debates of the sixteenth-century Reformation was the relationship of faith and good works to God's initial gift of justification. The finer points of truth in these questions were argued bitterly for five hundred years. They finally found fundamental resolution in 1999 when representatives of the Holy See and the Lutheran World Federation signed the Joint Declaration on the Doctrine of Justification (JDDJ). The phrase that best captures the truth, which both groups affirmed together, is rooted in this biblical passage and expressed in the traditional formula "by grace through faith, not from works" (see v. 8). Good works are important, but only subsequent to our justification and as a sign that we have accepted the gift of friendship with God (v. 10).

ANTIPHON (YEAR II)

Psalm 100:3b

The Lord made us, we belong to him.

Psalm 100: Joyful Service

This brief hymn was used to accompany joyous processions into the temple (v. 4). It was most fitting to use the song year after year, because of its reference to "forever . . . all generations" (v. 5). References to "joyful song" (v. 2) and "enter[ing] his gates" (v. 4) demonstrate why its use in processions was frequent.

Monday of the Twenty-Ninth Week in Ordinary Time

Creation and Ownership

The refrain (v. 3) underscores the fundamental relationship between an object and its maker. It also picks up its theme from the final verse of the reading from Ephesians, which declares that we are God's "handiwork" (2:10). By the very fact of our creation by God, he holds "the patent," giving him full rights to our lives and our working. The "deed" is written and preserved at the very center of our existence. Though independent by the gracious gift of God, we are not our own.

GOSPEL

Luke 12:13-21

And the things you have prepared, to whom will they belong?

Literary Link

Yesterday's gospel spoke of being acknowledged by the Son of Man at the final judgment (vv. 8-9). The theme of ultimate accountability running through the last few sections of the gospel moves easily and logically to the parable of the foolish rich man who is so concerned with his possessions and the life they afford that he forgets the inevitability of death and God's final review of his life (vv. 14-21).

Greed

There is general agreement among scholars that the community for which Luke's gospel was written was to a large extent affluent, hence the admonition to avoid greed in all its forms (v. 15). Similarly the concern of Jesus for the poor throughout the gospel, and the beatitude of blessing for the poor (6:20, not merely the "poor in spirit" as in Matthew) and of condemnation of the rich (6:24), underscores the targeted audience for this version of Christ's good news. The amassing of possessions simply for the sake of having them is the sin of greed, especially if accompanied by actions to remove them from availability to the poor and needy!

The Foolish Farmer

The parable about the wealthy but foolish farmer, totally preoccupied with keeping his harvest for his own pleasure (vv. 14-21), serves to remind the audience of Christ's day as well as ourselves of the few possessions that remain into eternity.

The multiplicity of barns might signal large flocks to be fed, or personal prosperity, but they could also indicate greed. It might be important to spend time in the calculation of the precise nature of "what matters to God" (v. 21): forgiveness, compassion, generosity, and charity. These are the qualities that best reflect God's true nature, and that we are invited to imitate and to store up, even into the next age!

Tuesday of the Twenty-Ninth Week in Ordinary Time

First Reading (Year I)

Romans 5:12, 15b, 17-19, 20b-21

If by the transgressions of one person death came to reign, how much more will those who receive grace come to reign in life.

Adam and Christ

The Lectionary omits a few verses from this complicated passage in order to simplify the argument and to sharpen the contrast between the first and second Adams (v. 12). The first one disobeys and everyone else is negatively affected, as the rabbinic Paul points out, and the second obeys and all are restored to friendship with God. From this comparison the early patristic writers proceeded to extend the contrast to Eve, the mother of all human beings, and Mary the mother of the new creation. Each term is a corporate personality, including all subsequent generations. Sometimes a similar concept is found in the use of the word "I" in lament psalms where the singular in fact represents the entire nation of Israel, not only an individual person in distress.

The Many

When Paul uses the term "the many" (v. 15), he reflects the wording in the writings of Isaiah regarding the mysterious Servant of Yahweh whose shameful death justified "many" (53:11). The Semitic phrase carries a truly universal sense; this is the original significance of the term that was recently restored to the English account of the institutional narrative of the Eucharist in its revised liturgical translation.

Antiphon (Year I)

Psalm 40:8a, 9a

Here I am, Lord; I come to do your will.

Psalm 40: Humble Submission over Ritual

Psalm 40 has the surprising format in which thanksgiving (vv. 2-4; not used in the response) seems to precede the actual petition. This may well be an expression of utter confidence in God who knows human needs and grants their resolution. It may also be a sign of trust that once God has spoken, even if through a prophet in the temple, the deed is accomplished and the effect has in some fashion already occurred! The word is spoken; the deed is done.

Obedience

The verses actually chosen for the response insist that obedience to the will of God is more important than sacrifice (vv. 7-8). This was stated as part of Samuel's rejection of King Saul (1 Sam 15:22), who offered sacrifices rather than obeying God. The prophet Hosea also insists on the primary value of covenantal mercy over sacrifice (6:6; as cited in Matthew 9:13). These verses of the psalm offer an echo to Paul's praise for the obedience of the New Adam (v. 19). The same verses were applied to the obedience of Christ (Heb 10:9). All of these references demonstrate a consistent use of Psalm 40 among the early church's favorite insights into the person, message, and mission of Jesus. It may also be of interest that Islam (literally, "submission") takes all the biblical figures known for their obedience, including Mary, as major examples for their faith in God.

First Reading (Year II)

Ephesians 2:12-22

He is our peace; he made both one.

Christ Jesus Our Peace

In the mind and experience of ancient Israel, the world was sharply divided between the people of Israel and the Gentiles (the nations). Recognition of these two groups dominated the religious consciousness and practice of devout Jews. Biblical peace (*shalom*) is the reconciliation of separated groups, not tranquility or quiet. Christ is proclaimed as "peace"/Greek *irene*/Hebrew *shalom* (v. 14), namely, the one who has healed that ancient dichotomy, broken down walls of separation, and united those near and far (v. 17). By divine call Paul was commissioned to proclaim this peace to the Gentiles as a life's work. Jesus is acknowledged as the divine Power who alone can truly heal all the divisions of our contemporary world and of the church within it.

Jesus Christ the Capstone

Images for our relationship to Christ and each other seem to melt from one to another, first in terms of fellow citizens and members of God's own household (v. 19), then parts of a building (v. 20). The architectural reference to a divided wall (v. 14) prepared for the image of "capstone." To speak of a "capstone" is to invoke the power of the stone at the apex of an arch, pressing down and holding the lower stones in place by the power of its presence and pressure. The moral authority of Christ's person and message keeps people bonded in unity. That solidarity then becomes a holy place where God can dwell in charity, justice, and peace. It is helpful to explore any and every image used in the Scriptures so that the richness of its teaching can be understood and assimilated by those who hear, study, and pray out of the Word.

ANTIPHON (YEAR II)

Psalm 85:9

The Lord speaks of peace to his people.

Divine Proclamation of Peace

When God speaks of "peace," as is reported in the refrain (v. 9), the effect is immediately realized in human history; this is the God who spoke the word at creation (Gen 1:3) and the entire world came into being. The revelation offered by our God can be described as one of "peace," that is, the fundamental and deeply desired reconciliation of people. The very characteristics mentioned in the psalm verses, namely, kindness and truth, justice and peace (v. 11), are social qualities that bind people together.

God's People

The refrain (v. 9) refers to the fact that God speaks to "his people." What identifying marks of a people can be described as also belonging to their God? Would they not be precisely the qualities that bind people together with God and each other? The uniting force would not be material prosperity, military power, or economic clout, but rather the very qualities of reconciled unity and mutual respect as mentioned above. Popular maxims such as "Like priest, like people" and "Like people, like God" illustrate the desired mutuality between the two groups.

GOSPEL

Luke 12:35-38

Blessed are those servants whom the master finds vigilant on his arrival.

Literary Link

From the parable of the foolish, greedy farmer (vv. 16-21) and the report of God's final judgment upon his self-centered existence, Luke's gospel presented the teaching of Jesus regarding Divine Providence and our need for complete dependence upon it (vv. 22-34). The Lectionary, however, has chosen to omit that passage, and has turned to the disciples' need for attentive vigilance (vv. 35-38) in preparation for the final Day of the Lord.

Expectant Vigilance

In an ancient society without illumination at night except for modest lamps of oil or occasional torches, the importance of welcoming lights at a late homecoming cannot be exaggerated. It was a matter of safety as well as convenience. This passage moves easily and logically from vigilance on the part of the servants to the somewhat improbable reward of reciprocal kindness from a humble master who waits on them in turn (v. 37). The ways of God are not our ways, as Isaiah reminded his contemporaries (55:8-9). The image, however, stresses God's complete delight in finding his servants watchful (v. 37). Good servants are attentive servants.

Reward

The unexpected exaggeration captured in the image of the master now serving his servants illustrates the point of divine pleasure over such servants (v. 37). This is the same Lord who described himself at the Last Supper as one who stands and waits (Luke 22:25) when disciples were arguing over which was the greatest. Careful attention to one's duty brings reward. Curiously, the reward in this instance is not to one who works, but to the one who is simply vigilant, ready to do so whenever needed. Availability and inner disposition is what matters most of all. As the poet John Milton once noted, "They also serve who only stand and wait."* Reward comes to those whose heads, hearts, and hands are available.

Tuesday of the Twenty-Ninth Week in Ordinary Time

* "On His Blindness," *Minor Poems* (New York: Allyn and Bacon, 1901).

Wednesday of the Twenty-Ninth Week in Ordinary Time

First Reading (Year I)

Romans 6:12-18

Present yourselves to God as raised from the dead to life.

The Human Body as an Instrument of Goodness

One of Paul's foundational images is that of the Body of Christ, which includes Christ himself plus all those joined to Christ through baptism (1 Cor 12:12). That insight began with the revelation on the way to Damascus (Acts 9:5). Here Paul uses the same metaphor for the individual person and points out that one's individual members (eyes, ears, tongue, hands, etc.) can be used either for sin (v. 13) or as weapons/instruments for righteousness. We are invited to use our bodies for the establishment of proper relationships among all of creation. In this new creation, for example, hands can be dedicated to generosity, compassion, forgiveness, and justice. This vision of human dignity should animate all our efforts for justice and human rights.

Slaves and Servants

Paul's letters often introduce himself as a servant/"slave"/*doulos* of Jesus Christ (Rom 1:1). The image of servant slavery can be traced all the way back to the existence of Israel in Egypt and their liberation from "the house of slaves" for the pharaoh's work (Deut 5:6) into service to the Lord as his people. Here again Paul applies the metaphor to the individual person. Each baptized individual is no longer a slave to sin, which leads to death (v. 16), but a servant to obedience (v. 17), which leads to righteousness before God. Elsewhere the idea is expanded remarkably from servants to family members and heirs (Gal 4:7). The title can even become honorific as government officials are called "ministers." Formal letters in Spanish often conclude with the phrase *su servidor*.

Antiphon (Year I)

Psalm 124:8a

Our help is in the name of the Lord.

Psalm 124: A Journey of Pilgrimage

This psalm is inscribed as one of the pilgrimage songs (v. 1). It could easily have been a popular hymn used by groups traveling up to the temple in Jerusalem. It acknowledges danger and deliverance with metaphors understandable from the experience of ancient travel, namely, hostile robbers (v. 3) or flash floods (v. 4). The same images for danger from enemies or natural disasters could also easily be applied generically to any time of national threat or disaster. All of life is a pilgrimage to the full and final embrace of God.

The Refrain

The refrain (v. 8) is the final verse of this pilgrimage hymn. It acknowledges the protection provided for travelers through space and time by the invocation of the sacred name of God, YHWH, which might be translated as "he who will be whatever he will be" (see Exod 3:14). Disasters would have occurred "had not the LORD been with us" (vv. 1, 2). The most effective help is not weapons or resources, but confidence in a God who travels with his people and who provides the protection needed in every age. God does not free us from all pain, but travels with us through it.

First Reading (Year II)

Ephesians 3:2-12

The mystery of Christ has now been revealed and the Gentiles are coheirs in the promise.

Stewardship of Grace

The grace entrusted to Paul as a faithful steward (v. 2) and treasured by him was the knowledge that the Gentiles are coheirs, members of the same body and partners in the Gospel's promises (v. 6). No matter what grace we contemporary believers may have received from God by gift or calling, it must also be preciously cherished by us. A steward, however, doesn't own whatever is confided to his or her care. The gift of God's grace should be treasured without hoarding because it is always destined for sharing with others. Any knowledge of how God works is not a private treasure but a public "commodity" for distribution. Everything we have is merely on loan.

Boldness and Confidence

As a result of the knowledge given to all of Christ's disciples regarding how God works in our world, Paul feels a sense of profound confidence and boldness (v. 12). Speaking with "confidence/boldness/*parresia*" is an apostolic virtue given by the Holy Spirit to the Twelve and to the entire church at Pentecost (see Acts 2:29; 4:29). There is nothing tentative or waffling about Paul or his convictions! That same gift of the Spirit remains the motivating energy for our personal efforts at evangelization. By words and actions we give witness to God at work in our world. Our faith can give us confident assurance.

Antiphon (Year II)

Isaiah 12:3

You will draw water joyfully from the springs of salvation.

The Song of Salvation

The Lectionary chooses to use Isaiah 12 as the response to the great news described by Paul (or his associate). Scholars note that this hymn concludes Isaiah's collection of Immanuel prophecies (6:1–12:6). The hymn's final form may even have been influenced by the experience of the Babylonian exile and Israel's return to rebuild the temple. The Lord is celebrated as Savior (vv. 2, 3) whose mighty deeds are now known to the nations (v. 4). This chapter is a song often heard at funerals and during the liturgical season of Advent.

Wednesday of the Twenty-Ninth Week in Ordinary Time

The Joyous Refrain

We Western moderns take for granted the immediate availability of running water in our homes. For that reason we find it hard to appreciate the utter joy of fresh water, even if a walk to a nearby spring is required. The social gathering of neighbors around the community spring/well at sunrise or sunset is the joyful community event echoed in the refrain (v. 3). The same social joy can easily be applied poetically to the refreshing blessing of salvation and rescue from oppressors. God's people are joyful, even in tough times.

Gospel

Luke 12:39-48

Much will be required of the person entrusted with much.

Literary Link

The same thread of concern for the end time carries from the prior admonition to be vigilant for the master's return (v. 35) to the similar vigilance needed lest a robber break into the house (v. 39). Scholars are quick to point out that this image must have come from Jesus himself since the early church would certainly not have made any reference to their Lord as somehow similar to a thief. The question asked by Peter expands the teaching to community servant leadership (v. 42) during the time of waiting for the Lord's return.

The Distribution of Food

Luke's decision to use food distribution at the "proper time/*kairos*" (v. 42) as an example of faithful stewardship may reflect the practice of at least one community in Jerusalem described by him as having all things in common (Acts 2:44). It may also refer to the regular common meals of Pharisees or to the weekly celebration of the Eucharist after the Lord's resurrection. The servant leader in a Christian community, ancient or modern, is expected to provide spiritual nourishment as well as material food for the needy. The leader is also responsible to offer solid teaching for the growth of the community according to its level of maturity in faith. Every Christian community is in some sense a *Bethlehem*, namely, a "house of bread."

Accountability for Leadership

The image provides an opportunity for condemnation of any Christian leadership that mistreats other community members, undernourishes them, or gives bad example of personal misuse of resources (v. 45). Exemplary conduct is expected, even demanded, from those chosen for leadership. Full and final accountability is promised at the time of the master's return, always in accord with what the servant may have known about his responsibilities, the wishes of the master, and the specific circumstances of misconduct (v. 47). More is required of those to whom more is given (v. 48). Given the circumstances of our lives, that probably includes most of us!

Thursday of the Twenty-Ninth Week in Ordinary Time

First Reading (Year I)

Romans 6:19-23

Now you have been freed from sin and have become slaves of God.

Corporeal Instruments

Paul continues his treatment of the parts of one's body as potential instruments for impurity and lawlessness (v. 19). Violations of any or all of the instructions of the Torah fall into this category if hands, feet, tongue, or genitals are used against God's will for our salvation. If used as shameful slavery to sin (v. 20), they earn the wages of death (vv. 21, 23). Wages, namely, earned recompense or consequences, come in many forms. They can be monetary or "in kind."

Sanctification for Eternal Life

Paul the teacher loves to present contrasts, as when earlier comparing the first and the second Adam, or now describing the different uses of the body for either death or eternal life. Ancient Israel's "Holiness Code" (Lev 17:1–26:46) emphasized the fact that many different acts of human immorality violated the holiness of the temple. Those actions excluded an individual from temple worship. That code of proper conduct was based on the nature of God who asked that his people be holy for he was holy (19:2). Paul the rabbi seems to use this same broad category of moral behavior when encouraging the Roman Christians to live lives that reflect "sanctification" and lead to a share in eternal life (v. 22). This is the life of the next age, already present in our midst because of baptism into the new creation of Christ.

Antiphon (Year I)

Psalm 40:5

Blessed are they who hope in the Lord.

Responsorial Psalm

Once again the Lectionary has chosen Psalm 1 as a communal response to Paul's comments regarding the contrast between being slaves of sin for death and servants of God for eternal life. This is fitting because the initial psalm also contrasts those who follow the path of the wicked (v. 1) described as chaff before the wind (v. 4) with those who ponder the law of God (v. 2) who are like a tree planted near running waters (v. 3).

The Refrain

Perhaps because the final verse of the reading from Romans speaks of eternal life as a gift from God (v. 23), the Lectionary has chosen a refrain from Psalm 40 that blesses those who live in hope (v. 5). Those who hope in the Lord live with the confident expectation that what is promised, but not yet received, will yet be theirs as a gift from God who is ever faithful! The ability and willingness to live in hope merits a special blessing. Pope Benedict XVI's encyclical *Spe Salvi* (2007) pondered the great theological gift of hope.

First Reading (Year II)

Ephesians 3:14-21

Rooted and grounded in love, you may be filled with the fullness of God.

Invocation of the Trinity

It took decades, perhaps even centuries, for the early church to find a manner of speaking about the Trinity in a way that was both fully faithful to the truth and intelligible to contemporaries. Nevertheless, in obscure ways the Three Persons are occasionally mentioned in passages from the New Testament. In this reading we have the invocation of the Father from whom all families flow (v. 14), his Spirit who strengthens people with power (v. 16), and Christ who dwells in human hearts through faith (v. 17). The letter prays that the Ephesians be filled with the "fullness [*pleroma*] of God" (v. 19), a concept already used in this letter (1:10, 23). Just imagine the dignity that gift conveys. Only when a person is truly rooted in Christ's love (v. 17) can we begin to understand the breadth and depth (v. 18) of Christ's transforming love for us!

The Doxology

Paul often pauses in the midst of a teaching or exhortation to burst into praise of God. In this reading he recognizes that God's transforming power is at work in each believer (v. 20), and is moved to express praise. Early Christian writers insisted that the best prayer always began with praise, thanksgiving, and repentance before any petition or plea. Mature Christians pause often for praise and thanksgiving. That attitude finds special communal focus in the final doxology of the eucharistic prayer.

Antiphon (Year II)

Psalm 33:5b

The earth is full of the goodness of the Lord.

Joyous Praise

Psalm 33 begins with an invitation to join our human voices to the music of harp and lyre in praising God. Like so many other psalms, this seems to be a hymn for a festive occasion in the temple, possibly a covenant renewal celebration because of the refrain as explained below. The psalm insists that God's word is faithful and that his works are trustworthy (v. 4). Divine promises of blessing to those who are faithful to the covenant support the theory that this psalm was used in such a ceremony. Moreover, all the saving deeds of God, which are usually recited at the beginning of a covenant by way of historical background for the covenant's stipulations, also suggest the use of this hymn in covenant renewals. Both salvation history and God's promised blessings evoke our joyous praise every day of our lives.

The Fullness of Goodness

The refrain's reference to "full[ness]" (v. 5) easily picks up the prior use of the word *pleroma* (v. 19) in the reading from Ephesians. Moreover, the word of the refrain (v. 5) translated as "goodness" is in fact *hesed*, the mutual concern that marks the relationship of covenant members with each other. Imagine a world completely filled with such mutual care and concern! That relationship would certainly result in goodness beyond measure, whether in the family, the neighborhood, or the larger community.

Gospel

Luke 12:49-53

I have not come to establish peace but division.

Literary Link

In contrast with yesterday's reading, which stressed the harmony within the community when the leadership takes care of its members and feeds them in due time (v. 42), Luke now turns to the disharmony and division caused at times by the gospel itself. The community of faithful disciples is often separated from the larger world, which cannot accept Christ's teaching.

The Passion of Jesus

Even though we often restrict the word "passion" to the sufferings of Jesus at the time of his brutal execution, the word also refers to his urgent and compelling determination to fulfill his mission. One can become very passionate about a major cause or project. Burning with love for all people, especially those who need love most, Jesus was driven with a blazing fire of love and zeal (v. 49).

Family Division

Later in this gospel Luke will report on the insistence of Jesus that a true disciple must "hate" his family, that is, in Semitic idiom, consider them of lesser importance than Jesus himself (14:26). This was radically countercultural and even scandalous to the ancient world, which prized family/tribal relationships so highly. Perhaps saying the same thing here from a different perspective, Jesus acknowledges that entering the kingdom that he heralded could at times divide families bitterly (vv. 52-53). Undoubtedly the inclusion of this warning reflected the actual experience of early disciples, especially where the line of demarcation between Jews and Gentiles was sharp and vigorously observed! Those who chose to ignore the difference in the light of the Gospel suffered for their decision.

Thursday
of the Twenty-Ninth Week
in Ordinary Time

Friday of the Twenty-Ninth Week in Ordinary Time

First Reading (Year I)

Romans 7:18-25a

Who will deliver me from this mortal body?

Inner Personal Struggle

With humble candor Paul admits the great inner struggle he experiences between the desire and the doing of good (v. 18). The all too human gap between proposal and performance is something well known to all of us. We find consolation in learning that the great apostle Paul himself was no stranger to such an inner dichotomy between the members of his personality! He explained the struggle by reference to the power of sin (not "the devil") deep within his being. Unfortunately, initial motive and meaning sometimes never reach maturity of action. We need inner transformation, not just external healing.

Resolution through Grace

After posing a rhetorical question about deliverance (v. 24) and expressing a plea for inner healing and personal perseverance into decision, Paul reports his answer to the dilemma of inner conflict. The Greek word translated as "thanks" by all modern versions is "grace/*charis*" (v. 25). Although the verse does not explicitly say that the resolution is by grace, it does recognize that the solution to Paul's inert conflict (and ours) comes from outside himself, specifically from God through Jesus the Christ. That is another manner of referring to the gift of transforming grace.

Antiphon (Year I)

Psalm 119:68b

Lord, teach me your statutes.

Psalm 119: God's Guidance

As noted elsewhere Psalm 119 is arranged with eight verses for each of the twenty-two letters of the Hebrew alphabet. This results in considerable stretching of creative imagination and sometimes tedious repetition of words simply to fill out the artificial structure of the poem. The psalm, however, fits the reading from Romans because the verses chosen as response offer a list of God's commands, statutes, promises, and precepts, which Paul's inner spirit finds so difficult to obey without God's grace.

The Refrain

The Lectionary selects a verse that serves as the community's prayer of request to be taught by God (v. 68). Those who accept and assimilate God's teaching find it easier to overcome the inner resistance of the flesh. A faithful disciple begs to be taught and venerates the one who can teach well. A true Christian is a lifelong learner. We are called "disciples." Because the notion as used by Christians is both practical and academic, we might better call ourselves "apprentices."

First Reading (Year II)

Ephesians 4:1-6

There is one Body, one Lord, one faith, one baptism.

A Life Worthy of "the Call"

Every profession has built-in ethics for its respective responsibilities. Physicians, for example, are responsible for accurate diagnosis, best treatment, and confidentiality. Butchers are expected to sell fresh meat, maintain hygienic conditions, and label their merchandise accurately. The call of the Christian as such, however, is deeper and more comprehensive. The reading specifies that the call should be exercised with "humility and gentleness, with patience," mutual forbearance (v. 2), and seeking unity in peace (v. 3) as qualifying attitudes. The passage, however, does not state precisely what that call (v. 1) essentially entails! It is a call to enter the community of those who are immersed in the paschal mystery of the Lord's death and resurrection, to receive and share the grace of forgiveness, and to be God's partner in the work of the kingdom, which is a new creation. The Christian community becomes the place where the implications of that call are spelled out, practiced, and lived. Our willingness to change the habits of our lives demonstrates the level of our worthiness.

Seven Signs of Unity

The letter spells out seven different bonds of unity within which the call (v. 1) is experienced and deepened: one Body (of Christ), one Spirit, one hope (for future glory) (v. 4), one Lord, one faith, one baptism (v. 5), and one God and Father over, in, and through all (v. 6). Note that among other aspects of "the call" we find the invitation to shared divine life, future orientation, sacramental experience, and a comprehensive trinitarian context. This represents a description of the entire Christian community as well as the life of each individual member of that church assembly. Also note that the shared reality of this call does not eliminate the fact that there remain different functions for individuals within each community (as spelled out in tomorrow's reading).

Antiphon (Year II)

Psalm 24:6

Lord, this is the people that longs to see your face.

Psalm 24: Instruction at the Doorway

This psalm is a good example of what scholars call a "Torah liturgy," one that poses a question regarding qualifications for entrance into a temple precinct (v. 3). The psalm then responds with a brief list of general moral requirements: sinless hands, clean heart, and lack of vain and foolish aspirations (v. 4). The verses provide liturgical instruction. The Lectionary has chosen wisely in order to assist further reflection on the meaning of "a life worthy of [one's] call" (see Eph 4:1). Even though not quantifiable, the response can be measured.

Friday of the Twenty-Ninth Week in Ordinary Time

The Refrain

The fact that the refrain (v. 6) specifies "this is the people" presumes the context of both the reading from Ephesians and the rest of the psalm response. Any community that really longs to see God's face, both in its worship and at the end of time, will be characterized by these attitudes and actions. These two portions of Scripture, namely, the reading and the response, offer an ideal profile as well as criteria for judgment on the authenticity of Christian life in community. A person or community unwilling to change doesn't really "long" for God.

Gospel

Luke 12:54-59

You know how to interpret the appearance of the earth and sky; why do you not know how to interpret the present time?

Literary Link

In the prior passage Jesus expressed his zeal for his mission (v. 50) and the unfortunate family divisions it may sometimes occasion. In this following passage, Luke goes on to speak of the urgent imperative to judge weather conditions or to settle with opponents when the opportunity presents itself before any court appearance (v. 58). In the context of consequences for our relationships, timely decisions are always crucial.

The "Right Time"

The reference to the common human experience of checking the weather for impending rain (v. 54) or heat (v. 55) is an excellent way of pointing out the need for making practical decisions. In view of those realities, one decides what to wear or how to arrange the work of the day. The primary focus of this gospel teaching is the need to make timely decisions. The two Greek words for time are *chronos*, time in the sense of past and future, and *kairos*, the right time for decision and action. It is the latter term that is found in this text (v. 56), translated as "present time." Jesus expects his disciples to make decisions about the kingdom and to live their lives accordingly. Some circumstances require action. A good disciple worthy of the name is timely and decisive, courageous and forthright about what should be done—and does it! It was this very gospel passage that was proclaimed at daily liturgy when a human being first walked on the face of the moon (October).

Reconciliation and Resolution

Once again this passage reflects the gospel's recurring current of thought about accountability in view of the impending final judgment. The Lord's Prayer begs for forgiveness as we forgive others (Luke 11:4). This teaching of Jesus encourages prompt and timely resolution of human conflicts between community members (v. 58) lest they be left for divine judgment, much to our dismay and discredit. True disciples are not afraid to make decisions, especially about how to reconcile differences and resolve disagreements. Dithering can be very costly.

Saturday of the Twenty-Ninth Week in Ordinary Time

First Reading (Year I)

Romans 8:1-11

The Spirit of the one who raised Jesus from the dead dwells in you.

The Transforming Gift of the Spirit

In response to the plaintive plea expressed in 7:24, "Who will deliver me from this mortal body?" Paul offers the solution. He proclaims that the gift of membership in the Body of Christ (v. 1) through the revitalizing gift of the Spirit (v. 2) removes condemnation and death. The same Holy Spirit that raised Jesus from the dead (v. 11) also gives new life to us by living at the very core of our being. The indwelling Spirit is not merely a Spirit of faith, hope, and charity, but one who constantly raises us from the dead. This profound teaching of Paul explains the inner renewal of everyone baptized into Christ and the bond that the baptized have with each other as members of Christ's Body, the church. Every day of our lives, we are being raised!

The Flesh and the Spirit

In our daily lives as disciples of Jesus we all experience something of the struggle between flesh and spirit. Paul attempts to describe the characteristic signs of "those who live according to the flesh" (v. 5): preoccupation with self-centered, weak and fallible matters as well as hostile resistance toward God (v. 7). In Paul's Letter to the Galatians, moreover, he offers more concrete examples: "immorality, impurity, licentiousness, idolatry, sorcery, hatreds, rivalry, jealousy, outbursts of fury, acts of selfishness, dissensions, factions, occasions of envy, drinking bouts, orgies, and the like" (5:19-21). To the Romans Paul now states that those who live in the Spirit are freed from sin and death (v. 2) and are concerned with life and peace (v. 6), righteousness (v. 10), and can look forward to sharing the Lord's resurrection (v. 11). Back to Galatians for a moment in order to learn of more concrete signs of life in the Spirit, we read, "love, joy, peace, patience, kindness, generosity, faithfulness, gentleness, self-control" (5:22-23). These lists would be excellent examinations of conscience, both negative and positive! First readings can often function as extended penitential rites of the Eucharist.

Antiphon (Year I)

Psalm 24:6

Lord, this is the people that longs to see your face.

Psalm Response

Remember that Psalm 24 is a "Torah liturgy." The temple priest guardian is exercising his responsibility for only admitting those qualified to approach God. In Paul's First Letter to the Corinthians, he warns early Christians against eating or drinking unworthily (11:27).

The Refrain

Note, curiously enough, that this is the very same psalm response and refrain as was selected the previous day for Year II's response to the Lectionary's first reading from Ephesians 4:1-6. The point is that both readings seem to require the same comment by way of response. Each text describes the type of community desired by God as sign and instrument of the new creation. An appropriate response, therefore, is found in the refrain, an acknowledgment that the same sort of community could be characterized as above all longing to see God's face (v. 6).

First Reading (Year II)

Ephesians 4:7-16

Christ is the head from whom the whole Body grows and builds itself up in love.

Various Ministries

After listing the seven ways in which a profound unity is established among members of Christ's Body (vv. 4-6), the letter proceeds to add another list of some varying functions that individuals can exercise within their respective community, each ultimately ordered to "equip the holy ones for the work of ministry" (v. 11). Prophets, evangelists, pastors, and teachers (v. 11) each have distinctive roles to play within the community, but all are designed to help the entire church community perform its fundamental mission, that is, praising God in Christ by transforming the world. Gifts are never for the individual recipient alone. The church as the body of Christ continues the mission of Christ in this world. Every person at a weekday liturgy could be invited to discover and label one's own contributing function toward that goal. No one is insignificant.

Living the Truth in Love

Jesus proclaimed himself as "the truth" (John 14:6). As his disciples we are committed to speaking the deepest and fullest truth about God and about ourselves. Sometimes, however, the truth can be told harshly to hurt others, or deviously for self-interest or personal gain. This passage insists that any truth-speaking should be done in the context of love (v. 15) and out of genuine care for others. The foundational commandment of love for God and neighbor even governs what and how we speak God's truth. Its purpose is to build up the Body of Christ in healthy interaction and maturity (v. 16).

ANTIPHON (YEAR II)

Psalm 122:1

Let us go rejoicing to the house of the Lord.

Psalm 122: Joy

This psalm is found among the pilgrimage songs (v. 1) of Israel. It was most probably used when departing from Jerusalem after one of the great festivals celebrated each year in the temple. The refrain (v. 1) recalls that first invitation to leave home for the Holy City. Other verses of this brief hymn make mention of the purposes of the pilgrimage, namely, thanks and praise to the sacred name of God (v. 4) and seeking justice and judgment (v. 5) to resolve disputes and achieve reconciliation. Joy (v. 1) marks a true pilgrimage because of the bond of mutual respect and cheerfulness, which binds the pilgrims together, and because of the effect of the journey on the lives of those who make it. Those who continue to make the famous medieval pilgrimage to Santiago de Compostela in Spain learn something about this type of joy.

GOSPEL

Luke 13:1-9

If you do not repent, you will all perish as they did!

Literary Link

The prior mention of harsh judgment and possible imprisonment for those who do not reconcile with others in a timely fashion (vv. 58-59) leads logically to this passage with Christ's renewed call for repentance for all (13:3). True reconciliation is not only for others. Everyone must change and be changed in the process.

Political Massacres and Fallen Towers

Tragedies of all sorts seem inevitably to raise questions about the culpability of the victims who suffered in them. Even today natural disasters are the occasion for foolish assertions of God's punishment for sins of lifestyle or bad decisions. Jesus rejects such simplistic and false conclusions (vv. 3, 5). All human beings are somehow guilty before God (not merely those caught in disasters) and, in fact, bad things do happen to good people! Any quick link of pain and culpability does not automatically reflect God's will or God's manner of governing our world. Laws of physics collide and innocent people sometimes tragically get caught in the crush of it all. God demands repentance from everyone (v. 5).

Nurturing the Fruitless Fig Tree

The delightful parable of the fig tree illustrates God's patience with human beings and God's eager willingness as the gardener to work extra hard in order to achieve our conversion, growth, and a fruitful harvest (vv. 6-9). It is God who seeks us, as pointed out by the poet Francis Thompson in his "Hound of Heaven." Nevertheless, God's desire respects our free will, and that patience does not preclude eventual accountability at the time of the Day of the Lord and Last Judgment. Elsewhere we do encounter a puzzling reference to Jesus cursing a fig tree without fruit (Mark 11:12-14). As a parable this teaching is primarily about God's patient persistence by the gifts of grace, the encouragement of friends, the instruction of the Word, and the nourishment provided by sacraments. The same God who requires repentance (v. 5) is willing at times to offer some slack for slow human response.

Saturday of the Twenty-Ninth Week in Ordinary Time

Monday of the Thirtieth Week in Ordinary Time

First Reading (Year I)

Romans 8:12-17

You have received a spirit of adoption through which we cry, Abba, Father!

Children of God

Family membership on the natural level is often demonstrated by similar physical characteristics such as facial features, skin or hair color, body profile, or even DNA. Relatives claim that a baby "looks just like her mother!" Paul suggests that a fundamental trait of God's children is that they are led by the Spirit (v. 14) just as Jesus was constantly led by that Spirit during his earthly ministry: in the desert of testing (Luke 4:1) and into his Galilean ministry (Luke 4:14) and into announcing glad tidings to the poor (Luke 4:18), and so forth. Intimate knowledge of God's will and an inclination to obey are signs of family relationship with Christ because they demonstrate kinship (Luke 8:21). Sometimes a translation of this text resists a more inclusive rendering as "children" rather than "sons" (v. 14), precisely in order to underscore one's identification with Jesus as part of that new creation "in and through Christ" to which the Spirit bears witness (v. 16). It may help to understand the translators' theological rationale as more than mere stubbornness or insensitivity.

If Children, Then Heirs

The relationship to God in Christ includes a historical dimension, and also establishes a trajectory toward the future as heirs of eternal glory (v. 17). The bond is not simply static "here and now" but also dynamic, and, therefore, aimed toward the future. The bond actually entitles such a person to full future participation in eternal life. To be an heir is to have some sort of right to future gifts. The First Letter of John teaches the same reality: "we are God's children now; what we shall be has not yet been revealed . . . for we shall see him as he is" (3:2). Imagine the surprise when the family gathers for the "reading of the will" and discovers us sitting there too!

Antiphon (Year I)

Psalm 68:21a

Our God is the God of salvation.

The God of Salvation

Psalm 68 responds to Paul's promise to the Romans by describing the way enemies flee when God shows up (v. 2) as father of orphans, defender of widows (v. 6), refuge of the forsaken, and liberator of prisoners (v. 7). These are all concrete examples of salvation in specific situations of need. An extension of that same prayer would be the addition of a reference to whatever tight spot we may be in as we seek divine intervention and assistance. When a presider asks, "For what else shall we pray?" add what needs "salvation," namely, freedom from a tight spot in life.

Bearing Our Burdens

Pope John XXIII often autographed pictures of himself with a citation from this psalm: "*Benedictus Dominus qui portat onera nostra*/Blessed be the Lord who shares our burdens" (see v. 20). The quotation is an expression of childlike gratitude to God, and a prayer of confident trust in God's enduring presence, even amid the burdens of life. God knows and understands our burdens even better than we do.

First Reading (Year II)

Ephesians 4:32–5:8

Walk in love, just as Christ.

Walking in Love

Each of Paul's letters includes a section of moral exhortation (*paranesis*). Ephesians is no exception (4:25–6:20). In each case these verses unpack the specific demands of mutual charity. Most of us know the experience of "falling in love" with its initial infatuation that can see no wrong in the object of our affection. "Being in love" deepens that reality with the honest recognition of the person's flaws and limitations, but still holds that person in the deepest affection. "Walking in love" puts it all in practice day after day. Such loving care includes ample measures of kindness, compassion, and forgiveness (v. 32)—always extended toward the other person as he or she really is, not as an idealized figure. Real love demands sacrifice at times (v. 2), includes truth (v. 25), and does not "enable" unacceptable behavior in those we love.

Fitness for the Kingdom

Immorality, impurity, and greed are mentioned twice (vv. 3, 5) as the very things that would militate against a life of "walking in love" with someone. They are precisely the qualities that would exclude a person from full and active participation in God's kingdom (v. 5). There are certain types of behavior, as we know from family experiences, that could so offend as to result in a person's name being excluded from the will. The Letter to the Ephesians requires that we "[l]ive as children of light" (v. 8).

ANTIPHON (YEAR II)

Ephesians 5:1

Behave like God as his very dear children.

Psalm 1: Two Kinds of People

Once again the Lectionary chooses to use Psalm 1 as a response to the passage from Ephesians because it adds its own illustration of the difference between children of darkness and children of the light. That psalm offers a blessing to those who avoid the wicked, and promises that they will bring forth fruit in due season (v. 3) while the wicked are chaff that blows away (v. 4). One is stable through the seasons; the other quickly becomes invisible and forgotten.

Imitation of God

Note that the refrain (v. 1) provided by the Lectionary is a verse from the reading, not a selection from the psalm. There are times when we are moved by admiration for someone, and say by way of complement and encouragement, "You are just like God!" In that comment we refer to the fact that we see something extraordinarily "godlike" in that person's attitude or action. This refrain could inspire further reflection about precisely the types of behavior that are characteristically godlike. The reading from Ephesians would suggest kindness, compassion, and forgiveness. There are other expressions and activities that would also fit the category of reflecting and imitating God, such as cleaning up the mess people make or helping people see the bigger picture.

GOSPEL

Luke 13:10-17

This daughter of Abraham, ought she not to have been set free on the sabbath day?

Literary Link

It may have been that the parable of God's patient care for the fruitless tree (vv. 6-9) led Luke to move to the story of the long-suffering woman with the eighteen-year affliction of spinal deformity (v. 11). Both God and the human images of God are sometimes called to be patient. Even infirmity has lessons to teach.

Divine Compassion

Almost as if to provide a direct example of the compassion described as godlike in the reading from Ephesians (4:32), Jesus reaches out to the woman crippled with some type of arthritis (v. 12). She didn't even have to express a plea or request for healing! The action was an instinctive gesture of outreach on the part of Jesus. Luke's gospel consistently includes examples of ministry to, for, and by women; this is an example of that evangelical concern on his part. Scholars suggest that Luke's community was comprised of leadership by women. Syntyche and Evodia (Phil 4:2) may be examples of that leadership at the level of house churches. The example and the conjecture merit our contemporary concern for a greater role of women in the church and in greater society.

Sabbath Healing

The leader of the synagogue who was responsible for good order and proper teaching responded negatively and indignantly to this healing (v. 14). (Note that there is no suggestion that he was of the Pharisaic religious tradition.) The law of Sabbath rest was intended to avoid, sometimes even scrupulously, anything that smacked of the type of labor that filled the rest of the week. The religious leaders sometimes exaggerated and extended the boundaries of prohibition as if to build "a fence of protection" around the law and prevent its violation. At the same time, authentic Judaism always placed the safety of human life above and beyond that prohibition of labor. Jesus characteristically responded by reframing the question from the work of healing to that of liberation from bondage (v. 16) and thus resolved the question to the delight of the crowd (v. 17).

Tuesday of the Thirtieth Week in Ordinary Time

First Reading (Year I)

Romans 8:18-25

Creation awaits with eager expectation the revelation of the children of God.

The Sufferings of the Present

The contrast between the present situation of being children of God (v. 19) and the future reality of being heir of a promise led Paul to further realistic reflection about the sufferings of life. Whatever those sufferings may entail, and they are sometimes terribly painful and profoundly burdensome as people care for ailing relatives or live with afflictions of all kinds, Paul insists that they are nothing compared with future glory (v. 18). Over the years such teaching has sometimes been dismissed as "opium" for the poor and oppressed portions of our society. That would be true if it were not linked to a passionate effort for justice as well! Paul notes that the entire world of material creation struggles with seeming futility (v. 20). He also insists, however, that this situation comes from a God also committed to freedom from injustice, slavery, and corruption (v. 21).

Hope for the Future

Paul understands our present share in divine life through baptism as the "firstfruits of the Spirit" (v. 23), a sort of down payment or installment of future glory already partially possessed. This passage concludes with a mention of "hope" five times. The text explains that for Paul the precise meaning of true hope implies present lack of possession but confidence in the eventual reality of that gift of full adoption and redemption. Patient endurance is the sign of hope (v. 25). Benedict XVI's encyclical *Spe Salvi* (2007) takes its title from this passage (v. 24).

Antiphon (Year I)

Psalm 126:3a

The Lord has done marvels for us.

Psalm 126: Joyful Return from Exile

This psalm is found within the collection of pilgrim songs (Pss 120–34) offered for use when traveling (usually on foot) to and from the temple. The recollection of the return of captives back to Zion, possibly after exile in Assyria or Babylon, is celebrated with great joy and laughter (v. 2). Faithful Jews, still living in exile "among the nations" (v. 2), witnessed that event from a distance with praise for God. Perhaps, note the commentators, it was even the nations themselves who saw the facts of history and joined in praise for God. The going forth with tears and the return with harvest (v. 6) is another possible reference to the exile. There are lessons to be learned in exile too. This sentiment offers a fitting response to Paul's conviction of hope (Rom 8:25) for the future, for God will not disappoint, even if God insists on working in God's time!

Marvels

The psalm repeats twice its reference to "great things"/mighty deeds (vv. 2, 3). The Hebrew phrase is literally "[God] made great for the working," that is, personally intervened to do something great by way of divine involvement. The events are visible. They inspire awe because God is at the heart of it all, and the events are beyond mere human accomplishment. The refrain, when placed on the lips of a weekday morning congregation, should inspire personal reflection on the events in their own lives that were clear signs of God's presence and his saving power at work.

First Reading (Year II)

Ephesians 5:21-33

This is a great mystery, but I speak in reference to Christ and the Church.

Husband's Love

The biggest original challenge of this reading (especially because it comes off very differently to our contemporary culture, which is justly concerned about the rights of women and the elimination of gender "submission") is in fact the command that husbands should love their wives (v. 25)!

In first-century Roman times, marriages were arranged by families for economic, political, and social advantage, but with little concern for mutual love and concern. Insisting that a husband should truly love his wife was countercultural for them and often heard with incredulous ears. Each age hears the living word of God in its own cultural context, and is challenged accordingly. Modern mores of casual sexual freedom might do equally well to hear the command of genuine love. This does not mean to imply that the contemporary concerns of feminism should be lightly dismissed or ignored! The relationship is called a "*musterion*/mystery" (v. 32), namely, that which reveals the deeper reality of God's grace. This is the word that was later translated as *sacramentum* and developed into our Catholic Christian sacramental tradition.

"Just As"

Often we are so eager to proceed to the "heart" of the biblical text that we ignore the adverbs and conjunctions. To admonish husbands to love their wives "just as" (v. 23) Christ loved the church is to encourage our contemporary curiosity and further reflection regarding precisely *how* did Christ love the church? The response would include self-sacrifice (v. 25), concern for mutual purification in baptism, doing everything to avoid blemish (v. 27), and holding them in physical affection (not merely in an intellectual relationship). If that is how Christ loves the church, says the author Ephesians, then precisely that is how every husband should truly love his wife. This is love in action.

Antiphon (Year II)

Psalm 128:1a

Blessed are those who fear the Lord.

Psalm 128: A Blessing

This pilgrim psalm (v. 1) would seem to be an extended blessing given to those who completed their visit to the temple and were preparing for the journey home. A blessing is pronounced at the psalm's beginning (v. 1) upon the person who has reverence for the Lord and at its ending (v. 5). The same verb of blessing is also stated twice in the body of the hymn. No one can miss the point that it is a psalm of blessings requested and granted.

Fruits of the Blessing

The responsorial psalm specifies the effects of the blessing: fruitful labor (v. 2), domestic peace and happiness (v. 3), and even the prosperity of Jerusalem (v. 5) as a communal consequence from the prosperity of the individual family. It is easy to understand why the Lectionary has chosen this psalm as a response to the teaching of Ephesians regarding mutual respect and love between husband and wife. The blessings of the larger community are presumed to flow from those of the nuclear family that lives in reverential fear of God (vv. 1, 4). The psalm suggests that there is something "contagious" about the blessings given to those who travel on pilgrimage to the Holy City. Truly effective pilgrimages bring benefits to more than those who participate physically.

Gospel

Luke 13:18-21

Where it was fully grown, it became a large bush.

Literary Link

Luke follows the story of the Sabbath cure of the crippled woman (vv. 10-16) by two brief parables of how the kingdom of God works in our world (vv. 18-21). Perhaps his intent was to link her cure with the kingdom and to indicate that such cures (especially on the Sabbath, which in some manner shares and anticipates the new creation) are also evidence of the kingdom at work.

The Images as Offered

We are first told that the work of God is something small

(mustard seed) that grows greatly in order to be of service to others (v. 19) and then also something (yeast) that permeates, enlarges, and disappears into a new and different reality (v. 21). The queries of the disciples that inspired these teachings may have stemmed from a worry about their own insignificance (mustard seed) and their inability to see any initial effect from their lives (yeast).

The Questions of Jesus

In our haste to explore the images, we forget that each of the parables is introduced with the question, "To what can I compare . . . ?" This could be the equivalent of "Well, what do you think?" We are invited, therefore, to consider the examples and to offer some of our own imagination. The two images of insignificance and subtle transformation might elicit similar examples from contemporary life: the work of God could be like the bellboy in the hotel who cleans the glass doors every morning to erase the smudges of thoughtless guests and visitors (cleansing). Or could the work of God be like the woman who rises early six days a week to work unseen and virtually ignored while making breakfast at the local college campus diner (nourishing)? Or like the heating/air conditioning expert in the basement who makes the atmosphere enjoyable for everyone (permeation)?

God at Work

The kingdom of God is not territorial, but dynamically active. The metaphors are intended to teach how God really works subtly in our world. The work is personal. Parables are so frequently mentioned in the gospels that a true disciple of Jesus should feel obligated to get a good grasp on their teaching, their significance, and their import.

Tuesday of the Thirtieth Week in Ordinary Time

Wednesday of the Thirtieth Week in Ordinary Time

First Reading (Year I)

Romans 8:26-30

All things work to the good for those who love God.

The Spirit's Help for Our Weakness

In the larger context of this letter, Paul lists three testimonies to Christian identity: the glory to be revealed (v. 18), the hope of Christians (v. 23), and the help given to us by God's Spirit (v. 26). It is consoling that only the grace of God and the guidance of the Spirit enable us to pray "as we ought" (v. 26). We can't do it by our own efforts alone. It is only God who can thoroughly search our hearts (v. 27) and who is able to distinguish the true prayers of the Spirit from the more selfish wants and wishes of the human heart. God loves us enough to sort out what we need (in accord with God's will) from what we may want (in accord with our own). A moment of silence at morning Mass allows space for God's Spirit to move us gently and properly.

All Things Work for Good

Our lives are filled with easy days and more difficult ones. Only in retrospect can we look back to see that the tough times were often, in fact, filled with grace and growth. No matter what happens by way of headache or heartache, Paul insists that everything works for the ultimate good of those who love God (v. 28). We need to keep that truth in mind always, conscious that there is in our lives an unfolding dynamic of God's foreknowledge, God's decision to aim our lives into conformity with Christ (called "predestination"), our subsequent justification into friendship with God, and finally our glorified destiny (v. 30). John Calvin of Geneva seems to have falsely concluded from these verses that God actually determined in advance who would be destined for heaven or hell. More accurately, it would seem, Paul simply recognizes that God's eternal knowledge knows and respects our choices from the beginning of creation.

Antiphon (Year I)

Psalm 13:6a

My hope, O Lord, is in your mercy.

Psalm 13: A Desperate Plea for Help

The Lectionary offers this lament psalm as a response to Paul's grateful recognition of the Spirit's help in praying. The chosen text ignores the psalm's first two verses' desperate cry of "How long?" in order to concentrate on the psalm's actual prayer for understanding and salvation (vv. 4-5) and its final expression of confidence (v. 6). This very psalm is an example of a prayer inspired and aided by the Spirit that Paul assured the Romans (v. 26) would be given by a loving God.

Hope for Mercy

Once again, it may be helpful to point out that the "mercy" for which the psalmist hopes (v. 6) is *hesed*, the mutual covenantal care of members for each other. In this case, consequently, human beings hope with confidence for God's "mercy" as promised to all those who have been embraced by God's covenant with them. By invoking *hesed* the refrain acknowledges the presence of a mutual "debt" of duty and obligation on the part of God beyond mere compassion for those in need.

First Reading (Year II)

Ephesians 6:1-9

Willingly serving the Lord and not human beings.

Parents and Children

The letter logically turns from its extended treatment of the respectful and loving care of husbands and wives (5:21-33) to the consideration of children in a Christian family (vv. 1-4). Paul doesn't seem to differentiate between children who are still minors and those already matured into young adulthood, even though Jewish tradition would assume that only those over the age of twelve or thirteen (namely, after their *bar mitzvah* when they became children of the law) were obligated to obey the Torah, and therefore were fully obliged by God's teaching regarding obedience toward parents. Paul also noted that the command to obey parents was the first commandment that carried a special blessing, that is, a long life (Exod 20:12). As a wise Pharisee, Paul added the corresponding obligation of parents to give good instruction and to "not provoke your children to anger"/resentment (v. 4). The obligation of obedience, therefore, is two-sided, like the responsibilities of spouses mentioned earlier.

Slaves and Masters

The letter concludes the instruction by adding the third major social dichotomy of the ancient world, namely, slaves and masters (v. 5-9). Although the division was promised to be eliminated in the new creation (Gal 3:28), this letter simply assumes the existence of the social institution of slavery. Servants, and by extension all hired employees in our contemporary society, are asked to see Christ in their owners/employers, and to act accordingly (v. 5). Masters are commanded to act in the same manner, seeing their servants as Christ (v. 9), and treating them respectfully without bullying or harassment. While there won't be slaves in any contemporary congregation, there may be plenty of employees, and many employed in service industries who see customers as bosses.

Antiphon (Year II)

Psalm 145:13c

The Lord is faithful in all his words.

Mutual Fidelity

The Lectionary chooses to omit Psalm 145's initial repeated references to God's mighty works (vv. 1-7). By moving toward the second portion of Psalm 145, the response focuses on the relationship of faithful people (v. 10; literally, *hasidim*, those bound together by covenantal mercy/*hesed*) to God who is himself also faithful. (Note, however, that the refrain [v. 13c] is a reading from the Latin Vulgate, even though the Dead Sea Scrolls, the Greek Septuagint, and most Hebrew manuscripts do not have that last portion of v. 13.) The mutual divine/human fidelity in this version of the psalm reflects the mutuality of husbands and wives and children and parents as well as that of slaves and masters.

Wednesday of the Thirtieth Week in Ordinary Time

Lifting Up the Fallen

God's fidelity toward his faithful people goes beyond merely sustaining his covenanted human partners in their success. God's care is not limited to those who are strong, steady, and physically upright. The God of this covenant also lifts up and raises those bent by burdens (v. 14).

Gospel

Luke 13:22-30

And people will come from the east and the west and will recline at the table in the Kingdom of God.

Literary Link

After the two brief parables of the kingdom (vv. 18-21), Luke reverts to themes related to the final age of judgment that had been literarily submerged like an underground river since the reproaches of Chorazin, Bethsaida, and Capernaum (9:13-16). Luke resumes that eschatological concern by reporting the teachings of Jesus regarding the narrow door (v. 24), those left outside (vv. 25-27), and others welcomed from the farthest corners of the world (v. 29).

Narrow Gate

The gospel notes the discrepancy between the large numbers called and those fewer in number finally admitted into the final celebration (v. 24). By way of example, not everyone who shared the community meals or listened to the teachings of Jesus (v. 26) would be automatically welcomed into the kingdom! Perhaps the "entrance ticket" is only given to those who hear the word and do it (Luke 11:28). The image of the narrow gate never fails to recall memories of the surging crowds that converged upon Paul VI, John Paul II, and Benedict XVI when they visited Jerusalem and walked through the gates of the Holy City! A more secular world would imagine crowded entrance gates at sports arenas and busy ticket scalpers for those left outside.

Final Insiders

As Jesus and his disciples moved on their great journey toward Jerusalem (v. 22), he surprised the crowds by stating that some of them would be excluded from the kingdom, much to their proverbial wailing and gnashing of teeth (v. 28). By contrast, he envisioned that others from far distant places would join the patriarchs Abraham, Isaac, and Jacob at the table of the heavenly banquet (v. 29). Luke's gospel emphasizes a universalism that reflected the gospel's initial dedication to the affluent patron Theophilus (1:3) and anticipated the new universalism served by Peter and Paul in Acts. The geographical and ethnic plurality of contemporary parish congregations reflects that same universalism if the worshipers not only listen and eat but also actually obey the Word they celebrate! Looking at any Catholic gathering comprised by a single race leads to the conclusion that "all of God's children aren't here yet."

Thursday of the Thirtieth Week in Ordinary Time

FIRST READING (YEAR I)

Romans 8:31b-39

Nor any other creature will be able to separate us from the love of God in Christ Jesus our Lord.

God's Generosity and Justice

Paul begins with an implicit allusion to a court of law in which God takes our side as a defender against whom no one can argue (v. 31). Most commentators see this section as a series of emotional rhetorical questions within the context of a mock trial, ending with a definitive acquittal by God (v. 33) who handed over his own son (v. 32) as the one who intercedes for us (v. 34). In spite of our human culpability, God simply will not allow us to be condemned because of Christ's great love for us (v. 35). When placed as a scriptural proclamation within the eucharistic celebration, the passage should logically lead to and evoke a great hymn of gratitude in the form of Christ's prayer for us to the Father.

Impotent Obstacles

Three lists of obstacles are cited by Paul as potential but powerless forces that are unable to separate us from God's love. First mentioned are any possible challengers in court (vv. 33 and 34) who are left virtually speechless. Secondly, Paul mentions seven difficult experiences in the course of life that could cause us pain and suffering: anguish, distress, persecution, famine, nakedness, peril, or physical violence (v. 35). None of these, no matter how stressful, can render Christ disinterested in our plight! Finally, Paul lists another seven quasi mythical and superhuman forces beyond the range of human power: death/life, angels, principalities, present/future, powers, heights or depths (vv. 38-39). None of these is strong enough to separate us from the surpassing love that God in Christ Jesus has for us (v. 39). By the grace of God we are ultimately invincible, and nothing can get in the way!

ANTIPHON (YEAR I)

Psalm 109:26b

Save me, O Lord, in your mercy.

Psalm 109: A Plea in Court

As if in stark contrast to Paul's impassioned plea on our behalf, Psalm 109 begins with a different request, that is, an equally impassioned petition for a verdict of court condemnation against a deceitful and cursing enemy. The psalmist begs that all his enemies' lies and curses come back thundering against their own wicked heads (v. 17) with endless punishments. The Lectionary omits those first twenty verses from the text of this psalm response, possibly in conformity with the decision of Pope Paul VI to eliminate the cursing psalms from the church's Liturgy of the Hours or sacramental rituals. Instead the responsorial psalm begins with ardent prayers from a wretchedly poor person (vv. 22, 30) for salvation, mercy, and help (v. 26). The staccato of imperatives suggests urgency on the part of the desperate petitioner. Paul's confidence in his words to the Romans now finds a psalm prayer to express the desperate human cry when confidence wanes under duress.

The Refrain

The Hebrew verb in this petition (v. 26) is slightly more complicated from a grammatical standpoint than it would seem. The literal refrain begs God to become intensely and intentionally active and "to make me safe" as a result of divine *hesed*, that covenantal kindness to which God has bound himself.

FIRST READING (YEAR II)

Ephesians 6:10-20

Put on the armor of God, that you may be able, having done everything, to hold your ground.

The Armor of God

In the Letter to the Colossians they are told to put on a series of virtues as if they were articles of clothing for dressing each morning: compassion, kindness, humility, gentleness, patience, mutual forbearance, and forgiveness (3:12-13). Here in Ephesians the outfit is the armor (vv. 11, 13) of God's warfare against superhuman powers: truth and righteousness (v. 14), readiness for the gospel of peace as shoes (v. 15), faith as a shield (v. 16), the helmet of salvation and the sword of the Spirit that is the word of God (v. 17). No matter what we may wear when attending weekday Mass or going about the work of the day, we are in fact part of an invisible but very real spiritual fashion show. We wear much more than skirt or shirt!

Apostolic Boldness

The passage ends with a prayer for *parresia*/confident "boldness" (v. 19) on Paul's part as he exercises his mission to the larger world. This quality is an apostolic virtue that was a gift of the Holy Spirit and that marked the lives and speeches of the apostles after Pentecost (Acts 4:13). It takes a certain amount of courage to wear the clothing, and even more to put the outfit to good use. These are work clothes, not just a party costume.

ANTIPHON (YEAR II)

Psalm 144:1b

Blessed be the Lord, my Rock!

Psalm 144: God the Source of Strength

In some of the manuscripts this psalm has been linked with David's fight against Goliath (1 Sam 17:32-51), and therefore seems to offer consistency with the military armor themes of the reading from Ephesians. The psalm is focused, not on the human combatant as such, however, but on God as the source of physical prowess and strength (v. 1b), whose enduring stable protection is a fortress (v. 2) for his faithful servants. Perhaps the association with Goliath arose because of the deliverance given to David (v. 10). In this psalm there is some similarity with the royal Davidic themes of Psalm 18.

The Refrain

The refrain (v. 1), which offers a beatitude of praise and blessing for God the Rock of Refuge, is said four times in this response. The cumulative result emphasizes the protection desired and experienced by the congregation assembled for worship, both in the ancient temple of Israel and in the contemporary parish community.

GOSPEL

Luke 13:31-35

It is impossible that a prophet should die outside of Jerusalem.

Literary Link

Jesus stated the necessity of his eventual prophetic death in Jerusalem (v. 33), thus reminding the gospel readers that he is on a continuing journey since he turned his face toward that city (9:51). Looking forward, the same citation (v. 35; Ps 118:26) will be repeated by the multitude in his solemn entrance into Jerusalem at the beginning of Holy Week (19:38).

The Warning of the Pharisees

The fact that it was Pharisees who came forward to warn Jesus about the lethal plans of Herod (v. 31) may indicate (in spite of the narrator's more negative judgment in 11:53) that some members of that group were supporters of Jesus and his message. Pharisaic opposition was not universal, and many of them were his friends. It is valuable to note these positive references to counteract the popular assumption (simplistically fanned at times by negative preaching) that they were all hostile. The reality of first-century Judaism was very complex, and most groups were divided by their inner differences of Torah interpretation and their strategy for the preparation and participation in God's kingdom.

Lament over Jerusalem

In this passage Jesus is described as experiencing great

sorrow over the negative reaction of the leadership in Jerusalem to his message and person (v. 34). In words very similar to those recorded by Matthew (23:37), Jesus anticipates the tragedy of the city's destruction by the Romans in AD 69/70. The final text may even reflect the historical pain of that event for those forced to witness the utter heartache of it all. Conversely, the lament presumes a great love for the Holy City, which should be a mark of all Christians, and by extension for every city within which they live and work. Jeremiah once ordered the exiles of his day to pray for the city of Babylon (Jer 29:1-9), where they had been relocated. The mission of the church is to praise God in Christ by the transformation of the world. How often we lament over our communities without praying for their salvation!

Thursday of the Thirtieth Week in Ordinary Time

Friday of the Thirtieth Week in Ordinary Time

First Reading (Year I)

Romans 9:1-5

I could wish that I were accused for the sake of my own people.

"In Christ"

This phrase (v. 1) occurs constantly in the letters of Paul and serves to provide a bigger picture for virtually everything about which Paul writes. Sometimes the preposition expresses not geographic location but rather relationship to Christ, as in this passage where Paul claims to speak "the truth in Christ." In other contexts the phrase may reflect a Hebrew background and may connote instrumentality. Perhaps because of his initial dramatic experience of the risen Lord on the way to Damascus (Acts 9), when Paul learned that Christ was completely identified with the persecuted early Christian community, Paul saw everything in that glorious context. Here it is the truth of his relationship with his fellow Jews (v. 3) that the apostle places in the larger picture of his risen Savior. Our task is to do the same with all our relationships and blessings!

Paul's Love for Israel

Sometimes a translation will erroneously place this list of God's blessings and graces to the Jews (vv. 4-5) in the past tense (as if to say "theirs [was] the adoption," etc.), thus giving a supposed reason for thinking that they have been replaced by Christianity. A more accurate version, however, sees these as enduring perennial blessings that Paul recognizes and celebrates in this famous passage. The list invites us, therefore, to express our own respect for contemporary Judaism as an ongoing object of God's love, and as an instrument of salvation for the world. This section of the letter will find a remarkable conclusion in Paul's conviction that Israel's gifts and calling are "irrevocable" (11:29).

Antiphon (Year I)

Psalm 147

Praise the Lord, Jerusalem.

Psalm 147: God's Special Love for Israel

The Lectionary selects the final portion of this psalm as a response, possibly because, after recounting all the blessings conferred upon the city of David, the psalm acknowledges that "God has not done this for other nations" (v. 20). This aptly echoes Paul's list of spiritual gifts given irrevocably to Israel (Rom 9:4-5).

The City of Praise

The verses chosen by the Lectionary stress the security of the city's gates (v. 13), the blessings of peace and abundant food (v. 14) given to its children, as well as the gift of the Torah with its statutes (v. 19). The earlier portion of this psalm acknowledges God as the city's builder (v. 2) and praises God for all the actions performed for its people: gathering outcasts (v. 2), healing the brokenhearted and binding wounds (v. 3), lifting up the downtrodden (v. 6), and even feeding its animals and birds (v. 9). Because of all these divine actions, the city as an integral unit is encouraged to praise God (v. 12). Forgetting for a moment the way in which Deuteronomy complains about the rejection of the prophets, the psalm exalts the entire city of Jerusalem, with its history and its geographical context as well as its political and economic structures. Everyone and everything is encouraged to praise God. The same should be done for each of our own contemporary towns and cities!

First Reading (Year II)

Philippians 1:1-11

The one who began a good work in you will continue to complete it until the day of Christ Jesus.

Paul's Prayer of Thanksgiving

Following the same format used in other letters, Paul begins with a prayer of gratitude for the Philippians' partnership in the work of the gospel (v. 5), their openness to the grace of God at work in their midst (v. 6), and the genuine affection that he has for all of them (v. 8). His friendship with them began with Lydia the purple cloth merchant (Acts 16:14) and grew to include the overseer/"bishops and deacons" whom he greeted in a special fashion (v. 1). This is the first time we find a New Testament reference to those ministries. Scholars note that the titles may have possibly been borrowed from the civil structures of the city. Any prayer for a community should include all their ministries of leadership and service as well as the members within the group.

The Letter to the Philippians

The small community at Philippi was Paul's first Christian foundation after crossing over into Europe (Acts 16:13). That group of believers remained dearly beloved throughout the rest of his missionary activity. Even though there were divisions and rivalries (4:2), Paul held this community up as an example for all other foundations! Only under judicial order did he leave that town for Thessalonica (Acts 16:40).

Paul's Prayer of Petition

The general intercessions at weekday celebrations of the Eucharist often include an invitational question from the presider: "And for what else should we pray?" Paul's initial prayer for the Philippians included a desire for their increase of love (v. 9), their greater knowledge and discernment regarding what was of real value (v. 10) so that they may be pure and blameless by God's grace, filled with righteousness when the Lord returns (v. 11). These could well become standing petitions in every contemporary congregation as well.

Friday of the Thirtieth Week in Ordinary Time

ANTIPHON (YEAR II)

Psalm 111:2

How great are the works of the Lord!

Psalm 111: The Greatness of God

Perhaps because this psalm begins with thanks and praise from the midst of the assembly (v. 1), it offers an appropriate response to Paul's expression of delight with the church of Philippi. The psalm goes on to praise God for giving food to those who fear him and for being ever mindful of the covenant that binds them together (v. 5). God feeds every faithful community, often raising up generous individuals who act as instruments of divine generosity.

Great Works

The psalms of praise often focus on the wonders of nature as specific signs of divine power. Majestic mountains and mighty seas easily reflect back to the power of the One who created such wonders of beauty and strength. Here, however, it is the goodness of the community at Philippi that evokes the evidence of God's "great works" (see v. 2). Perhaps we take for granted the works of justice, generosity, mutual kindness, and the courageous witness to truth found in the Christian communities within which we live. It would be "right and just" to consider all those actions among God's "great works"!

GOSPEL

Luke 14:1-6

Who among you, if your son or ox falls into a cistern, would not immediately pull him out on the sabbath day?

Literary Link

The Pharisee at whose house Jesus was a guest for dinner (v. 1) may have been among those who had just cautioned him against the evil intent of Herod (13:31). Luke often pairs men and women in his examples and messianic mission, so this Sabbath cure of the man with dropsy completes the dyad with the Sabbath cure of the crippled woman (13:11).

Sabbath Dinner

The Friday evening *Sabbath* meal (v. 1) was the high point of Jewish family life. Guests were especially welcomed and celebrated on those occasions. The invitation was a sign of honor. It was also an occasion for serious discussion of the important religious realities of the day, especially the gift of knowing God's will and the duty to explore its implications during the rest of the week. For the devotional life of the Jewish people, the Sabbath observance was a serious matter and considered both obligation and blessing. During the persecutions of the Hellenist King Antiochus Epiphanes IV (175–163 BC), celebrating the Sabbath, circumcision of children, and keeping a scroll of the Torah were crimes punishable by death! Faithful Jews, however, were willing to die for their beliefs (2 Macc 7).

Careful Observation

If the people were "observing him [Jesus] carefully" (v. 1), it was not necessarily with hostile intent. Devout Jews were encouraged to pick a teacher and to learn something from every single gesture and action of that individual. The issue of healing on a Sabbath was in fact controverted among Jewish scholars of that time because care for life took precedence over lesser values. Their silence (v. 4) in response to the question of Jesus regarding healing the man with dropsy may have been hostile, but not necessarily so. It could have been the reaction of students simply unsure of what the teacher was looking for.

Saturday of the Thirtieth Week in Ordinary Time

First Reading (Year I)

Romans 11:1-2a, 11-12, 25-29

If their transgression is enrichment for the world, how much more their full number.

Jews and Gentiles

Paul's writings to the church in Rome needed to address the perplexing and sometimes painful question of the relationship between God's ancient promises to Israel and this new sense of justification by faith in Christ. The presence of Gentiles within the Roman community required further instruction on this issue and Paul devoted much thought to the question (9:1–11:36). Having warned against the clay foolishly complaining about the Divine Potter's mysterious plan (9:21), and having reminded his Gentile readers that they were the wild olive branch lately grafted into the original (Jewish) tree (11:17, 24), Paul insists that God has not rejected his people (v. 2). This is directly contrary to the teaching of some early Christians to the effect that the Jews were replaced by Christianity in God's scheme of salvation (radical supersessionism). Paul's "take on this matter" concluded that the Jewish leaders had been temporarily set aside so that Gentiles could be incorporated into the full and final people of God (vv. 25-26). Quoting Isaiah 59:20 and Jeremiah 31:31, Paul insists that all Israel will be saved (v. 26).

Contemporary Interreligious Relationships

In the decades since the Second Vatican Council, especially with the strong example and encouragement of Blessed Pope John Paul II, a new beginning in Catholic relationships with our Jewish neighbors has slowly been forged. Catholics have been encouraged to study Judaism in order to understand our own Christian heritage and mission. Given the painful history of centuries of warm cooperation suddenly followed by bitter persecution, Jewish leaders are appropriately wary and quick to point out signs of the former prejudice as well as inconsistent teachings or actions by the church. That Catholicism should be thus carefully scrutinized shows the importance of the relationship for all parties concerned. The comments of the epistle to the Hebrews regarding the new and the old covenants have not as yet been fully probed (8:7-13). The two Catholic teachings that still require much Christian reflection are (1) the ongoing bond of God and the Jewish people (11:29), and (2) the universal redemption by Christ's death and resurrection. Precisely how to reconcile those two truths remains a challenge for us Christians. Patience, prayer, and study are our companions in this journey toward a new partnership. The final verse of this reading (v. 29) is very important.

Antiphon (Year I)

Psalm 94:14a

The Lord will not abandon his people.

Psalm 94: Gratitude for God's Fidelity

This has been called a psalm of "vengeance" because the first eleven verses are a prayer to God for vengeance upon enemy evildoers. Note that they are not included in this response! The remainder of the psalm, however, from which our Lectionary's responsorial verses do come, is an expression of thanks for instruction (v. 12), rest from one's enemies (v. 13), divine help (v. 17), and enduring "mercy/*hesed*" (v. 18).

The Refrain

The repeated refrain to the effect that God will not forsake or abandon his people (v. 14) is a perfect echo for Paul's insistence that God's call remains "irrevocable" (11:29). The acknowledgment that God's covenantal care remains a reality throughout all of Israel's history even to the present recognizes divine fidelity, especially in times of their weakness or sin. It is God who saves, in spite of human failing, and perhaps especially in moments when we clearly cannot save ourselves!

First Reading (Year II)

Philippians 1:18b-26

For me life is Christ, and death is gain.

Blessings from Imprisonment

The Lectionary omits the verses that would explain the beginning of this passage, namely, Paul's indifference to the circumstances of life as long as Christ is proclaimed (v. 18). In the section not included Paul had noted that his imprisonment and its inherent witness to Christ had become widely known (v. 13). Moreover he had stated, even if mere envy or rivalry (v. 17) had been the ultimate cause for contrary teaching and thus for his punishment, Christ had still been proclaimed! In our liturgical reading Paul feels the prayers of the Philippians and the support of the Spirit (v. 19), and therefore knows that he will not be put to shame (v. 20). Christ, he proclaims, will be magnified whether by his life or his death (v. 20).

Boldness

Paul shared with his beloved Philippians the fact that all the circumstances surrounding his imprisonment have only contributed to the proclamation of Christ with boldness (v. 20). That type of confident candor remained an apostolic virtue in the early church, even if sustained by persecution and hardship. Consequently Paul truly remains undecided whether to prefer life or death because both are "gain" (v. 22). Nevertheless he was completely confident in his love for the Philippians and in their faith in Christ. Therefore, even his imprisonment was for everyone a "win/win" situation.

Antiphon (Year II)

Psalm 42:1-2 (revised)

My soul is thirsting for the living God.

Thirsting for God

The Lectionary intuits that Psalm 42 could be the perfect prayer for the prisoner Paul. Caught in the cruel and often degrading conditions of primitive prison life, and possibly destined for beating or even death given the circumstances, Paul was "thirsting for God" (see v. 3). The image is particularly strong when one remembers that the Hebrew word *nephesh*, which is often translated as "soul/vital principle," also means "throat" or the place in the upper chest of human anatomy that experiences vitality and life. Using the psalm refrain as a prayer, Paul was probably thirsting in prison for water, but certainly also thirsting for God with every fiber of his being.

Joy and Thanksgiving

Psalm 42 refers to religious processions to the house of God (v. 5) within which an entire crowd of people eagerly approach the place of God's presence. Even from the darkness and indignity of his prison, Paul easily recalled times of joyful community prayer in the temple at Jerusalem or with the Philippians. The psalm fitted his situation very well. It can now be used as a prayer for all who are incarcerated and yearn for justice, freedom, and God's consolations.

Gospel

Luke 14:1, 7-11

Everyone who exalts himself will be humbled,
but the one who humbles himself will be exalted.

Literary Link

This gospel reading repeats an earlier reference to the careful observation that fellow guests at the dinner hosted by the Pharisee directed toward Jesus (v. 1). Today's reading omits the story of the Sabbath cure of the man with dropsy (vv. 2-6), which had been proclaimed yesterday in order to emphasize the fact that Jesus in turn had been watching them!

Etiquette for the Wise

The familiar parables of the kingdom are always about God and how God really works in the world. Their aim is *metanoia* or conversion, namely, invitations to help people think differently about their God. This parable is a sly teaching on the part of Jesus to think less about one's own stature in the community and to seek a lower place at table (v. 10). Not only would that avoid social embarrassment but it could also provide an opportunity for special honor and recognition should one be invited higher (v. 10). This instruction seems to be very similar to the wisdom offered by Ben Sirach regarding table manners (31:12-31). The advice represents shrewd etiquette as well as spiritual humility.

Self-Exaltation

The passage concludes with a final perennial principle for living life wisely, that is, the necessity of avoiding self-exaltation (v. 11). The advice fits well with one of the themes that characterizes the repeated eschatological teachings of Jesus: in the end the lowly will be lifted up and the mighty cast down from their thrones. The Great Reversal to be achieved by the final judgment is even demonstrated by banquet etiquette! Mary's *Magnificat* said as much (Luke 1:52).

Saturday of the Thirtieth Week in Ordinary Time

Monday of the Thirty-First Week in Ordinary Time

First Reading (Year I)

Romans 11:29-36

God delivered all to disobedience, that he might have mercy upon all.

Reciprocal Mercy

As if to insist on the importance of God's perennial love for the Jewish people, the Lectionary has decided to repeat Paul's teaching from Saturday regarding the irrevocability of their calling (v. 29). This verse had formed the climax of the prior day's reading from Paul's Letter to the Romans. It is now repeated to establish a launching pad for his further reflections. In Paul's experience the Gentiles received mercy because of the initial disobedience by Jewish leadership (v. 30), which in turn will become the occasion for extending renewed mercy back to the Jewish people (v. 31). As Paul saw it, the historical exchange was a way for God to show mercy to everyone (v. 32). As noted in the Letter to the Ephesians (2:4) and long before that to the Israelites on Mount Sinai (Exod 34:6; Ps 145:8), God is indeed "rich in mercy" (Eph 2:4).

The Inscrutable Will of God

Paul concludes his extended reflection on the relationship between Jews and Gentiles with an ode of praise for the utterly mysterious ways of God (v. 33) borrowed from the prophet Isaiah (40:13-14). It is a common human experience to look back over life and to marvel at the way in which things have fallen into place in a completely unexpected and very favorable manner. Our experience, sometimes initially painful, becomes an opportunity for growth and provides wisdom for something later in life. Old friends become partners and colleagues in new endeavors. Every day one can exclaim about the wonders of Divine Providence and its workings in our world.

Antiphon (Year I)

Psalm 69:14c

Lord, in your great love, answer me.

Psalm 69: A Plea from Someone in Pain

This lament is the psalm most frequently quoted in the New Testament after Psalm 22. The repeated initial expressions of physical pain and of the suffering resulting in social rejection and mockery quickly became a favorite prism in the early church for viewing the sufferings and rejection of Jesus of Nazareth. It is a classic example of what scholars call the *sensus plenior*, namely, a statement originally said about a different historical situation that later found deeper meaning when applied to the life and ministry of the Christ. The verses chosen by the Lectionary acknowledge pain and beg for protection, confident that God hears the cry of the poor (v. 34). In its new liturgical context the poor are the Gentiles who suddenly receive unexpected mercy even as God promises to save Zion and rebuild the cities of Judah (v. 36).

God's Love

As one might suspect, the Hebrew word translated in the refrain as "love" (v. 14) is in fact *hesed*, the reciprocal mercy of a covenantal God who remains faithful to his people. In this context it is the Jewish people who are reminded of God's enduring love, especially because his gifts are "irrevocable" (Rom 11:29). God's love precedes our existence and journeys with us to our final destination.

First Reading (Year II)

Philippians 2:1-4

Complete my joy by being of the same mind.

Apostolic Joy

Like any pastor passionately in love with his flock, Paul finds the true source of joy in the spiritual health and maturity of his congregation. This is the type of en-

Monday of the Thirty-First Week in Ordinary Time

couragement that Christ gives (v. 1) to his followers. Such joy is evidence of participating in God's Spirit; it is marked by compassion for the welfare of others. One of the repeated sentiments in this fond expression of Paul's affection for the Philippians is that of "joy," which is mentioned five times in this brief letter. He even calls them his "joy and crown" (4:1). Paul's invitation to "rejoice" became the annual theme for Advent's third "Gaudete" Sunday (4:4).

Rivalry

The one pastoral problem that Paul addresses in this letter of fond affection is some type of rivalry, possibly between leaders of the household churches in Philippi. In this passage Paul exhorts them to be of "the same mind, with the same love, united in heart, thinking one thing" (v. 2). Elsewhere he encourages Evodia and Syntyche to "come to a mutual understanding in the Lord" (4:2). Repeatedly from the beginning of his letter he insists that he loves "all of them" (see 1:4, 7, etc.). The call to unity is a perennial challenge. Differing approaches to common problems and diverse personalities are not always easy to weave together. As a new year of activity begins each fall, every parish community would do well to choose this letter of Paul for an autumn day of reflection for staff and lay leadership!

Antiphon

(Various)

In you, O Lord, I have found my peace.

The Refrain

The antiphon of response to Paul's exhortation seems to be a composition from the various sentiments of Psalm 131 rather than a specific citation from any of its verses. Perhaps rooted in the serene confidence of a newly weaned child in its mother's arms (v. 2), the refrain echoes Paul's confidence in the friendship that he feels for his beloved Philippians. It is this same sense that every member should share when participating in the daily life of a community that is truly united in mind, heart, and action. Then there will be peace in the biblical sense of reconciled diversity.

Psalm 131: The Prayer of Hope

This brief psalm "of ascents" (v. 1) celebrates the humility of the pilgrim when journeying through Judean hills toward the temple. Without any personal preoccupation over honors or foolish ambitions (v. 1), the pilgrim simply has "hope in the Lord, / both now and forever" (v. 3). Whatever the headaches or heartaches left at home may be, the person who journeys toward God does so with serenity and confidence.

Gospel

Luke 14:12-14

Do not invite your friends, but those who are poor and crippled.

Literary Link

After curing the man with dropsy under the watchful eyes of fellow guests (14:1-6), and after offering some advice to them about unwisely choosing the head table much to their possible embarrassment (vv. 7-12), Jesus next offers some advice as well to the host about guest lists (vv. 13-14). This in turn will prepare for his next teaching regarding God's invitations to the great messianic banquet (vv. 15-24). The persistent Lukan theme of the end time shows its head once more!

The Danger of Reciprocity

Jesus cautions against any way of life that measures actions according to what others "did or might do" in turn for us (see v. 12). We know that Christmas cards, wedding invitations, and even the sending of flowers at the time of a friend's death are often determined in just that way! In the mind of the Great Rabbi from Nazareth, invitations to dinner should have a higher standard of motivation. "If we invite only those who invite us, what merit is that?"

Jesus would ask, just as he was cited elsewhere as expressing disapproval for only loving or greeting those who love or greet you (Matt 5:46-48). In that latter context he pointed out that even pagans and tax collectors act that way. His disciples are called to a different and higher standard. As learned in the parable about the workers hired at different hours of the day (Matt 20:1-16), God isn't constrained to mechanical reciprocity!

Kingdom Ethics

The advice of Jesus to the host concluded with the suggestion that he make sure to invite people who couldn't possibly reciprocate in this world (v. 13), namely, the poor, crippled, lame, and blind. Elsewhere, in speaking to the disciples of John the Baptist, these were precisely the groups cited as evidence of his true messianic mission. When asked if he was "the One to Come" (Luke 7:22), Jesus cited the prophet Isaiah (29:18-19; 35:5-6; and 61:1). God's norms are so different from normal human values. God judges and rewards accordingly (v. 14).

Tuesday of the Thirty-First Week in Ordinary Time

First Reading (Year I)

Romans 12:5-16ab

We are individually parts of one another.

One Body, Many Parts

As we know, a favorite Pauline image for the church is that of the human body with its profound vital unity but diversity of functions. Apparently Paul returned to that metaphor often, as evidenced in his similar comments to the Corinthians (1 Cor 12:12-31). When gathered for a contemporary weekday Eucharist, that means that each of us has a specific function within the community, and each is expected to take that work seriously and do it well. Beyond and beneath the different functions, however, is the unity we have through baptism into Christ's paschal mystery. How "connected" do we feel to others who join us at worship?

Ethical Measurements

As a sample menu of different ministries Paul lists activities such as prophecy, ministry of service, teaching, and financial generosity (vv. 6-8). Each has its own standard of excellence and its occupational hazards. Does prophecy come from faith or partisan ideology? Does service meet the needs of others or only our own? Does teaching tell the truth? Are donations without strings or personal advantage? The question of motivation is crucial. Question: What do you do, and how do you know if you are doing it as well as possible? The reading concludes with about twenty brief "commandments" or admonitions (vv. 9-18). They could provide a very practical examination of conscience!

Antiphon

(Various)

In you, O Lord, I have found my peace.

Antiphon and Psalm Response

The Lectionary has chosen to use the same Psalm 131 and its nonbiblical antiphon as the response to this reading from Romans 12 (Year I) as was suggested for yesterday's reading from Philippians 2 (Year II). Both readings stress mutual charity and both recommend that each person consider others as more important than ourselves. In both cases the image proposed by the psalm is that of a young recently weaned child, confidently resting in her mother's arms (v. 2).

Children as Models

The reading draws attention to unity and diversity within the community. Maintaining the balance requires the humility of little children (v. 2) who seem to instinctively respect the abilities of others. The psalm, therefore, serves to reinforce the notion of children as models for life in the kingdom (Luke 18:16).

First Reading (Year II)

Philippians 2:5-11

He emptied himself and because of this,
God exalted him.

The Service of Voluntary Subordination

We are so accustomed to the liturgical use of this famous christological hymn during Holy Week each year that we assume it is a statement about the movement of suffering into exaltation. The earlier verses, however, show that Paul intends a different point. A background issue is Paul's admonition elsewhere that Evodia and Syntyche need to find a new mutual understanding (4:2). Toward that end Paul asks that all people consider "others as more important than [them]selves" and that they look out for the interests of others rather than merely their own (2:3-4). He proposes that all Christians share the same attitude as Jesus himself (v. 5). The great hymn, then, gives the example of Christ who even gave up the prerogatives of divinity (v. 6) and humbly emptied himself (vv. 7-8). In this hymn as used in its proper context it is the self-emptying, not the suffering, that receives final praise and glory from God (v. 9). This perspective is very important in the context of Paul's Letter to the Philippians.

The Form of a Slave/Servant

Since Jesus did indeed become a servant to all others (v. 7), we can legitimately ask what that service might look like in the course of our daily life. Among possible answers we might easily list primary concern for the needs (not wants) of others, a willingness to be patient in sorting out those needs with and for others (not deciding arbitrarily in advance), the ability to maintain our own dignity while being attentive and subordinate to others (not become servile in the process), the ability to develop a genuine love for others (not merely toleration), and an enduring blindness to the social or economic status of those we try to serve. Inner attitude must match external demeanor.

ANTIPHON (YEAR II)

Psalm 22:26a

I will praise you, Lord, in the assembly of your people.

Psalm 22: Deliverance and Promises Fulfilled

Psalm 22 is arguably the most frequently cited psalm in the New Testament. Its initial twenty-two verses contain a soulful individual lament from the depths of suffering. Its first statement (v. 2: "My God, my God, why have you abandoned me?") was reported as spoken by Jesus from his cross (Mark 15:34 and Matt 27:46). It is only the second portion of the psalm, however, that the Lectionary has chosen as a response to the reading from Philippians, namely, the song of thanksgiving (vv. 26-32). These verses speak of praise in the assembly (applied to the risen Lord's apparitions in the Upper Room), praise from the ends of the earth (v. 27), divine dominion, and praise from those who sleep in the earth (v. 30).

Praise in the Eucharistic Assembly

True spiritual maturity assumes that we can eventually even give thanks for the sufferings and hard times of life, especially if we can come to recognize them as moments of grace and growth for us and for those whom we love and serve. Every human experience is also somehow for the benefit of others. Every personal event merits being recognized as somehow communal when we gather in the liturgical assembly for prayer (v. 26). That same maturity assumes that we will exercise prudence in what we choose to share in the prayers of the faithful, for example, but every experience is somehow ecclesial in nature, and should be an occasion for gratitude at Mass.

GOSPEL

Luke 14:15-24

Go out quickly into highways and hedgerows and make people come in that my home may be filled.

Literary Link

It was eminently logical for Luke's gospel to move from the Sabbath cure at dinner (vv. 1-6) and the admonitions of Jesus to guests (vv. 7-11) and host (vv. 12-14) alike, to this parable of the great wedding feast (vv. 15-24). The Lord's instructions on kingdom etiquette will then conclude with some general admonitions on kingdom apprenticeship (vv. 25-33) and a comment about salt (vv. 34-35).

Universalism

The beatitude voiced by one of the guests regarding those who "dine in the kingdom" (v. 15) served as an introduction to the sharply pointed parable of the great feast (vv. 16-24). Since the community leaders who had been initially invited casually dismissed the invitation and chose to do other things, the offended and angered host turned to the streets and byways of

Tuesday of the Thirty-First Week in Ordinary Time

the town (v. 21). Echoing the very advice given to the host in yesterday's gospel, the man's servant is ordered to bring in "the poor and the crippled, the blind and the lame" (v. 21). Note that Luke's version of the parable (as contrasted with Matt 22:1-14) has no reference to violent treatment of servants or to the absence of a proper wedding garment. Luke's emphasis is clearly on the fact that absolutely everyone, socially acceptable or not, is welcomed in (God's) feast. Without judging those who may not be at any given weekday Mass, we are invited to look around as to see if the morning's congregation reflects the larger community, poor and rich alike.

Priorities

Buying a new field (v. 18) or some oxen (v. 19) or even getting married (v. 20) are surely worthy activities and important in the daily lives of those invited to the great feast (v. 17). The point of the parable is that God wants everyone present, and the universal will of God takes priority over our individual needs and wants. Some things are more important than others. God's universal plan of salvation is one of them and excuses of personal business or relationships are not sufficient excuses for self-centered activities. What takes preeminence in our own lives whenever we line up the works of any given day?

Wednesday of the Thirty-First Week in Ordinary Time

First Reading (Year I)

Romans 13:8-10

Love is the fulfillment of the law.

Preeminence of Charity

The Lectionary chooses to omit Paul's admonitions to obey civil authorities in the city of Rome (vv. 1-5) and to pay the taxes they impose (vv. 6-7). Amid all the contemporary financial burdens in a time of economic downturn, such as mortgage and car payments, huge credit card bills and large debts, it is a reality check to learn that the largest debt we have, as Paul points out to the Romans and to each and all of us today, is the debt of love to one another (v. 8). No other debt or social duty compares to that obligation! When listing the priorities at the beginning of each day, therefore, or reviewing the key elements in one's monthly budget, love/*agape* is in first place at the top of the list. The issue is not romantic sentimentality of affection, but consistent deep concern for the welfare of others. Early patristic writers would even claim that our excess money belongs to the poor. For that reason we sometimes prefer the word "charity" over "love," which has so many other levels of human meaning.

Love of Neighbor

Note that the commandments cited here by Paul are not those from the beginning of the Decalogue that relate to God, but those that refer to other human beings: adultery, murder, theft, or covetousness (v. 9). Paul's list concludes, as if to make the point very clear, with the second great commandment (Lev 19:17). These areas of human relationship reflect love for one's neighbor as for one's self. They encompass the entire debt of charity we have toward each other. Paul states that this love is the fullness/*pleroma* of the law (v. 10). In using that word, the reading is linked to the way in which the very "fullness" of God dwelt in Christ (Col 1:19). We might conclude that God's "fullness" is the "fullness" of love.

Antiphon (Year I)

Psalm 112:5a

Blessed the man who is gracious and lends to those in need.

Psalm 112: The Faithful and Just Person

Like two matching bookends, Psalm 112 with its comments on the blessings given to others by one who fears the Lord seems to match the earlier praise of God in Psalm 111. There is an echo of parallelism between these two psalms and the matching commandments of love of God and love of neighbor. For that reason, Psalm 112 is well chosen by the Lectionary as a response to Paul's comments regarding love of neighbor to the Romans. Graciously lending to those in need, as noted in the refrain (v. 5), is one way in which we imitate God who graciously lends so much to each of us throughout life.

The Whole "Package" Included in "Fear of the Lord"

Psalm 112 states that the person who reverently fears the Lord (v. 1) will delight in the commandments and enjoy posterity (v. 2). Such an individual is described as "gracious and merciful and just" (v. 4), doing the acts of justice (v. 5) and lavishly giving to the poor (v. 9). These actions also reflect the reality of God who is ever "slow to anger and rich in kindness and fidelity" (Exod 34:6). These actions and attitudes are the positive side of the same coin that forbids the deeds mentioned in the Decalogue (Rom 13:9). The church's social justice teachings are rooted in the Scriptures. Once again, the litany would make a great examination of conscience at the end of a day or at a parish communal penance service.

First Reading (Year II)

Philippians 2:12-18

Work out your salvation. For God is the one who works in you both to desire and to work.

The Desire and the Deed

One of the fundamental truths about our Catholic teaching on grace is that God is the

Wednesday of the Thirty-First Week in Ordinary Time

source of both the initial desire to do good and its actual accomplishment (v. 13). We cooperate, and indeed freely, but God starts the engine moving by charging the human battery and providing the key. God's inspirations to do good have often been named "actual grace." They fill our days with thoughts of noble possibilities. We should explore those divine suggestions for their feasibility, label them as the graces they are, respond generously, and then celebrate them with joy.

Grumbling

Paul's admonition to do things without grumbling (v. 14) follows his insistence that God is the ultimate source of all good inspirations, and therefore we should not go through the day grumbling about the things that fill our life. Paul suggested that such grumbling could in fact be a sign of human resistance to God's grace, and might well be ungracious if not sinful. Questioning (v. 14), however, in the sense of testing the idea to see if it is "of God," may be an obligation at times for a wise person. We are called to be children of God, blameless, innocent, and without blemish (v. 15). A wise mentor once said with a smile, "You don't have to like it; you just have to do it!" The ancient monastic tradition, thinking back to the grumbling of Israel in the desert (Num 14:2), sometimes considered grumbling in the monastery a sign of lack of faith in God's providence. Elsewhere Paul encouraged his converts to "[t]est everything" (1 Thess 5:21).

Joy

Contrasted with the grumbling and indeed permeating this entire Letter to the Philippians is Paul's invitation to live in joy (vv. 17-18). The fact that Paul's life is poured out as a libation (v. 17) does not remove his profound sense of joy. This is not superficial giddiness, therefore, but a deep sense of confidence in God's goodness, no matter what may be the surface circumstances of our lives. Paul also reveals a pervasive sense of gratitude for everything. True gratitude always makes us joyful.

Antiphon (Year II)

Psalm 27:1a

The Lord is my light and my salvation.

Psalm 27: Total Confidence

Scholars often divide Psalm 27 into two very distinct units: verses 1-6, which seem to be a song of unshakable trust in God, and verses 7-14, which express a lament from the midst of great distress. The Lectionary has chosen the psalm's initial expression of joyful confidence as the liturgical response to Paul's belief in the transforming power of God, and has added the note of hope from the end of the psalm's urgent petition (vv. 13-14). The reference to pain has been eliminated from the liturgical prayer. We also have the ability to pick and choose from the many emotions of life, concentrating either on the positive or the negative as circumstances demand. At a deeper level as we age, one might say that we are what we choose to remember.

The Refrain

To someone we love dearly, we might say in admiration and gratitude, "You are the light of my life!" This refrain (v. 1), repeated four times in the response, echoes Paul's delight over the Philippians and turns that same sentiment toward God as well.

Gospel

Luke 14:25-33

Everyone of you who does not renounce all his possessions cannot be my disciple.

Literary Link

The parable of the great feast is followed by these sayings about discipleship/apprenticeship (vv. 25-27) and then by an admonition to calculate the costs before making the decision to accompany Jesus on the journey, presumably to Jerusalem (vv. 28-33).

Accepting the Cross

Jesus is unwilling to hide the full costs of being his disciple in the fine print at the bottom of the contract. Up front and very clearly the Teacher insists that a relationship to him takes precedence over family bonds (v. 26). Another cost will be the willingness to accept whatever difficult burdens may come one's way because of one's faith. Calling it a "cross," possibly in light of his final terrible execution (v. 27), Jesus insists that the hardships of life must be accepted if not welcomed. Perhaps we could call the "cross" whatever might be the one thing we would change in life if we could—but we can't, so it must be accepted. We can understand this reality best if we think for a moment about the demands of studying for a career under any great musician, artist, athlete, or tradesperson. The years of preparation can be grueling and demanding; the basic practice may be tedious. Only practice makes the perfected professional! This is all the more true when speaking about life in the kingdom.

Calculating the Full Expense

At issue in this concluding comment is making absolutely sure that one takes the time to calculate the full cost of moving forward, whether it be for building a tower addition to one's house (vv. 28-30) or for marching off to battle (vv. 31-32). Jesus provides a few examples for thought, hoping that his disciples will understand how foolish they would look if they left the job half done. The final verse of this instruction is the bottom line (v. 33): no matter what one's profession, all one's possessions need to be on the table for negotiation when signing up as an apprentice of Jesus. Great saints such as Anthony the Hermit or Francis of Assisi have understood the command physically and radically; others understood the admonition in terms of their attitude toward the wide range of human possessions in life.

Thursday of the Thirty-First Week in Ordinary Time

First Reading (Year I)

Romans 14:7-12

Whether we live or die, we are the Lord's.

Short- and Long-Term Goals

Most meetings begin with an agenda. We wake up in the morning with a mental list of things "to-do" that day. Some goals in life are slightly more distant, such as providing for one's family, preparing for a career and getting a job, saving for a new house or paying off the mortgage. Other goals are ultimate, and in that light Paul insists that everything we do in life and death belongs to the Lord (v. 7). That basic understanding provides the big picture for our daily lives and keeps life from becoming needlessly fragmented or disappointing. Ultimately it is the Lord alone who has proprietary rights on our lives (v. 8). We are created by God as absolutely unique individuals, destined for some particular task and ultimately responsible to God for everything (v. 12).

Christ's Death and Resurrection

In his life as well as in his death and rising to new life, Jesus experienced everything. Therefore he became, as Paul insisted, the Lord of the living and the dead (v. 9). Jesus claims authority over all the stages and the unfolding phases of our lives. As children, mature adults, or elders we belong to Christ with everything we have and are. Moreover, there is an accounting to be given (v. 12) to God. The ancient patristic adage stated, "What is not assumed is not redeemed." Christ, therefore, knows everything human except sin. He also understands everything human from its possible blessings or its potentially disastrous consequences in our world.

Antiphon (Year I)

Psalm 27:13

I believe that I shall see the good things of the Lord in the land of the living.

Psalm 27: Confidence

In an unexpected coincidence, the psalm chosen by the Lectionary for today's response to the reading from Romans (Year I) is the same as that suggested for yesterday's response to Philippians (Year II). Even the verses are the same; the refrain is different. The sentiments of trust and lack of fear (v. 1) are also appropriate after acknowledging that we belong to Christ, both in life and in death! Sometimes it is not death we fear so much as the dying. The grace of trust is therefore something for which we should pray with sincere confidence.

The Refrain

If, whether alive or dead, we belong completely to Christ, it is fitting to add a liturgical expression of Christian faith in the resurrection (v. 13). Life and death without the addition of "life again" is incomplete. The refrain supplies a further reference to that reality from the final section of the psalm response. Moreover, the reality of resurrection is an important element in Paul's teachings for the Romans. Belief in the resurrection was a conviction that Paul shared with his Pharisee colleagues (Acts 23:6).

First Reading (Year II)

Philippians 3:3-8a

But whatever gains I had, I even consider as a loss, because of Christ.

Friendship with God through Faith, Not Obedience or Entitlement

Paul lists all his autobiographical accomplishments as a devout religious Jew: circumcision, tribal affiliation, Pharisaic observance, and even persecution of any group seen as inimical to Judaism (vv. 5-6).

He proceeds to warn, however, that mere complacency or even obedience to the law does not guarantee the right to preferential treatment before God (v. 6). Such compliance could be all about the human person himself rather than the true ultimate object of devotion—namely, God! Only by centering one's life on Christ can we feel confident in God's loving mercy (v. 7).

Loss as Gain

Only by putting all human achievements aside and treating them almost as misspent time and energy, that is, utter "loss" written in red ink (v. 7) because of a new discovery of the mystery of Christ, can a person bring real value into life. Paul's accounting methods and his life's ledger might make a CPA scratch her head, but it makes total sense with God. The ultimate question is, what really matters before God? To say it differently, when taking an inventory or counting one's "treasures," what is on the short list?

Antiphon (Year II)

Psalm 105:3b

Let hearts rejoice who search for the Lord.

Psalm 105: Joyful Pilgrims

The first fifteen verses of this psalm are quoted as a festal hymn in 1 Chronicles 16:8-22 in connection with David's bringing the ark of the covenant to Zion. The six verses from the psalm used by the Lectionary today as a response to Paul's comments to the Philippians speak of those who seek the Lord, both as joyful pilgrims and as people amid their daily lives at home. By extension we ought to bring God wherever we go, and introduce the divine presence to all aspects of our lives. The curious reality is the fact that we already possess (v. 7) what we seek.

Seekers for God

Perhaps the refrain (v. 3) was chosen because it fits with Paul's insight about loss as gain (v. 7). We need to spend time and energy seeking to find the gain in each of life's "losses." We are all seekers of God, even though it is God who is even more zealously seeking us, as noted by Thompson's "Hound of Heaven." Should every parish acknowledge itself as a support group of "Seekers Anonymous"? First-century Judaism recognized Gentiles who obeyed many commandments without full membership in the covenant, and called them "God seekers." The monastic ideal of Saint Benedict welcomed all "God seekers."

Gospel

Luke 15:1-10

There will be more joy in heaven over one sinner who repents.

Literary Link

Luke continues his theme of issues related to meals. The advice to guests and hosts (14:7-14), followed by the parable of the great feast (vv. 15-24), resurfaces with the complaint from Pharisees that Jesus eats with sinners (15:2). Jesus replies with the parable of the lost sheep (vv. 4-10). Implicit is the suggestion that sharing meals with sinners is yet another way of seeking out the lost sheep of Israel because most of the meal stories in the gospels are occasions for conversion, accepted or rejected.

The Lost Sheep

The quest for the single lost sheep reveals God's care for each individual of creation. The parable highlights the importance of every person for the full and final redemption of the world in all its history and its final destiny. Even one among so many (v. 4) is worthy of God's full attention and personal energy. In light of this teaching, we should not easily overlook the presence of the sheep at the manger scene each Christmas. They are more than artistic embellishment. They also remind us of Jesus as the eventual Paschal Lamb of God.

Thursday of the Thirty-First Week in Ordinary Time

The Process of Repentance

It is the person "in the process of repenting" (the Greek verb is in the present tense), engaged in thinking freshly (*metanoein*) about God and God's ways, who makes the angels of heaven rejoice (v. 7). Such a person is prized more, no matter what the past, than the ninety-nine who don't think they need to change their minds about anything. Self-righteous complacency is the most effective barrier to God's grace. "Repent" is the first command of Jesus in the Gospel of Matthew (4:17). In a sense, everything else follows, and nothing else matters! When was the last time we revised our thinking or changed our minds about how God works?

Lost Coin

Luke often parallels men and women in the examples; today's passage presents a clear example. God is like both the man with a lost sheep and the woman with the lost coin (vv. 8-10). The parables insist that God is diligently searching and even more active than the person struggling to return. While it may not be a frequent reason for a party, it is a common motive for housecleaning. If heaven has a party, it is because in God's sight every coin, not merely the rare and valuable, is important (v. 10), even a penny! To party for a penny may seem desperate for festivity, but the point is made about God.

Friday of the Thirty-First Week in Ordinary Time

First Reading (Year I)

Romans 15:14-21

A minister of Christ Jesus to the Gentiles, so that the offering up of the Gentiles may be acceptable.

Praise for a Community as Yet Unseen

Because Paul has a reputation of saying what he means, without flattery or human respect, we can presume that the praise for an unknown community (Rome) is not merely buttering his bread in preparation for a warm welcome. The reputation of the church at Rome must have included the fact that they truly were full of goodness and knowledge, willing to admonish each other into further growth (v. 14). It is a remarkable tribute to the church at Rome, and a worthy set of criteria for measuring the quality of any parish community that gathers for prayer each morning. Could an outsider say that about us? Note that Paul wanted to go still further, possibly all the way to Spain after his stop in Rome (v. 20). The fact that the entire known world at the time spoke the same language (Latin) made his missionary dreams possible.

The Priestly Service of the Gospel

Paul speaks of his own work of evangelizing the Gentiles as a "priestly service" (v. 16). Bringing the Gospel to others and establishing a new relationship between God and an unbelieving world is mediation. It is teaching God's will to others and enabling them to become part of the new creation—it is priestly! It may be of interest to realize that the ministry of the Word, namely, teaching and announcing God's will (not sacrifice, which all family heads could perform), was the primary task of priests in the first covenant (Jer 18:18).

Antiphon (Year I)

Psalm 98:2b

The Lord has revealed to the nations his saving power.

Psalm 98: The Nations

Psalm 98 is the perfect echo and extension of Paul's teachings regarding ministry to the Gentiles in the first reading. He revealed God's salvation to the nations (v. 2), and probably hoped to extend that knowledge to the very "ends of the earth," namely, Spain (v. 3). Because of the work of Paul and so many subsequent men and women missionaries over the years, one of the blessings of being Catholic is the fact that we live locally but belong to a worldwide church of many languages and cultures. The global reality, however, can also make development and change slower and more tedious since not all groups think alike. Each makes its own contribution to the worldwide community, and in its own time.

A New Song

The lived proclamation of the Gospel in new languages and often in new musical instruments is a new song (v. 1). In a real sense, every new witness of faith and every new invitation is a hymn of praise to God never heard before. Each human being is absolutely unique; each moment is fresh and unrepeatable in the historical unfolding of the universe.

First Reading (Year II)

Philippians 3:17–4:1

We await a savior who will change our lowly body to conform with his glorified Body.

Modeling

With humble candor Paul dares to offer his own life as a model to the Philippians (v. 17). He also recommends the example of others who have in turn patterned themselves after his own life and work. This is similar to the basic proposition of Jesus when he says, "The kingdom of God is at hand"/present right here (Mark 1:15). His reference is not only to the historical circumstances and currents of thought about to break in upon the people of his age but also to the way in which God's kingdom was at work in his own person. He also said, "learn from me, for I am meek and humble of heart" (Matt 11:29). What person

Friday of the Thirty-First Week in Ordinary Time

can say this? What Christian/parish community dares to invite such imitation?

Heavenly Citizenship

Not only are we called to be good examples of Christian life as individuals and as communities but we are expected to clearly demonstrate the future perfection already anticipated in the here and now. Paul claims to have citizen papers for heaven, from whence will come the Savior (v. 20) in final glory. Like the first model home or the first demo for the next year's automobile model, Paul wants everyone to look at the Philippian community and to get an idea of the future. Sacraments anticipate and already share the next age.

ANTIPHON (YEAR II)

Psalm 122:1

Let us go rejoicing to the house of the Lord.

Psalm 122: Judgment and Reconciliation

This is a pilgrimage psalm, possibly used at the end of a stay in Jerusalem by way of final blessing for those returning home. Because the reading from Paul had condemned those whose Gods are their bellies (Phil 3:19; possibly a reference to those who were preoccupied with issues of kosher diet), the psalm's reference to seats of judgment (v. 5) was logical. Paul felt competent to judge actions not in conformity with the Gospel that he preached. In any case pilgrimages to Jerusalem were always occasions to resolve disputes and seek reconciliation between aggrieved parties. The seats of judgment were for the reconciliation and peace of pilgrims.

The Refrain

Pilgrimages were always occasions for song, especially when entering the temple (v. 1). The same attitude should accompany every entrance into the parish church because of a deep delight among God's people over the fact that God has chosen to dwell in their midst. Entrance into God's presence should never be casual or nonchalant. Authentic Pharisaic spirituality also made the home a holy place, so similar songs should accompany us whenever we enter the door.

GOSPEL

Luke 16:1-8

For the children of this world are more prudent in dealing with their own generation than are the children of light.

Literary Link

The Lectionary chooses to omit the parable of the Prodigal Son, or the Prodigal "Father" as some commentators would suggest (15:11-32), and moves immediately from yesterday's parables of the lost sheep and the lost coin to the parable of the dishonest steward (16:1-8). The logic may be the similarity between the woman who invites neighbors for rejoicing (v. 9) and the steward in today's gospel who was seeking a home after his dismissal.

Rash Judgment?

The steward is denounced as unjust (v. 2) and treated as if he were indeed guilty, but no evidence is provided for that judgment other than a presumed accusation from others. Although the parable is targeted at praise for his decisiveness and his quickly improvised strategy for economic survival (v. 4), the tale could also be used as a caution against rash judgment in dealing with others. Even our legal system presumes one's innocence until proven guilty.

Theft or Forgoing Commission?

The steward quickly changes the terms of the loan agreements from a hundred to fifty (v. 6) or eighty (v. 7). Commentators have opined that the action taken by the steward might not be actual theft from his master, but rather the elimination of the percentage that would normally have been his "agent's fee" in the course of legitimate loans of his master's property. In that case the steward may have voluntarily forfeited a sort of "service fee" for the transaction. Were that the situation, the master's praise would be for the servant's self-sacrifice as well as for his quick cleverness.

Saturday of the Thirty-First Week in Ordinary Time

First Reading (Year I)

Romans 16:3-9, 16, 22-27

Greet one another with a holy kiss.

Friends and Colleagues

The lengthy list of Paul's friends and partners, both those to whom he sends greetings in Rome (vv. 3-9) and those working with him in Ephesus (vv. 21-23), is a testimony to the fact that the apostle is not a lone ranger. Paul works as a member of a team. This is even the case in the writing of this famous letter as noted by the special greeting from Tertius (v. 22), who claims to be the writer of the epistle. There are many individuals in Rome whom the Lectionary has chosen not to mention, including Paul's relative Herodion (v. 11). Paul may be acknowledging everyone as part of his strategy to obtain a ready and warm welcome when he might finally arrive in Rome on his way to Spain. Unfortunately those latter plans never materialized because he was arrested in Judea and felt compelled to appeal to Caesar (Acts 25:11). When he finally did meet the folks in Rome, he was a prisoner on his way to eventual martyrdom. The potential hosts must have then become in turn his visitors in his confinement. Paul was a team player to the end!

Apostles

Andronicus and Junia, presumably a husband and wife team (though the question of gender is debated among scholars), are acknowledged as prominent among the apostles (v. 7). The note of a woman among the early apostles of Christianity should be an occasion to review our presumptions about the makeup of the early church leadership. The liturgical calendar of saints in the Eastern Catholic and Orthodox churches is filled with many names of people called "apostles." This would be consistent with the distinction made in Paul's First Letter to the Corinthians when he described the different groups that had witnessed the risen Lord. He listed both the "Twelve" (15:5) and "all the apostles" (15:7). So often we forget that many gospel references to the "disciples of Jesus" include men and women alike.

The Final Doxology

The Letter to the Romans ends with an extended expression of praise to God for all the graces and events mentioned in the correspondence, and for Paul's own life and ministry. It contains a prayer for strength (v. 25) among the Roman Christians, Jewish and Gentile alike. The footnote to the New American Bible acknowledges the fact that the doxology is found in different places in this letter according to the various manuscript traditions, and may not even have been written by Paul himself. In any case, it is inspired by God's Spirit, and makes a very fitting and charming conclusion for this extraordinary apostolic letter. Everything we do should end in praise.

Antiphon (Year I)

Psalm 145:1b

I will praise your name for ever, Lord.

Psalm 145: Generations of Praise

The Lectionary has chosen this psalm as a response to Paul's long list of friends, possibly because of its reference to the many generations who praise God's works (v. 4). The psalm's reference to God's unsearchable greatness (v. 3) echoes the revelation of the great long-hidden but now revealed mystery that is celebrated in the doxology (v. 25).

The Refrain

When all is said and done, we, like Paul before us, can do nothing but praise God (v. 1) for the history of salvation, which includes so many heroes of faith. That long chain of witnesses even allows us to join the group so many centuries later! The history of our own salvation has been woven into that of the entire world. Therefore, we have an obligation and duty to add our

Saturday of the Thirty-First Week in Ordinary Time

praise. "It is right and just," as the preface dialogue introducing the eucharistic prayer suggests.

First Reading (Year II)

Philippians 4:10-19

I have the strength for everything through him who empowers me.

Paul's Gratitude for Assistance

With a sense of gratitude Paul acknowledged that the Philippians had "revived" their concern for him (v. 10), and had more than once sent something for his needs (v. 16). As a result, he now considered himself well supplied (v. 18). Although those who had been sent on mission by the Lord had been urged to eat whatever was set before them (Luke 10:7), which was probably a reference to the debate over kosher food laws, Paul made it clear that such assistance was a gift, never an entitlement. Paul's comments offer an opportunity to ask ourselves what we feel we have a right to receive from others. By what reason?

Philippians Enriched for Their Generosity

Paul insists that the gift from the community at Philippi in turn actually accrued to their own account before God (v. 17). The paradox is that whatever is given away shows up in one's own ledger as "receivable." Paul calls their gift "a fragrant aroma" (v. 18) because it creates an atmosphere in which both giver and recipient find pleasure. What we give away somehow makes us richer! This is the unique bookkeeping of the kingdom.

Antiphon (Year II)

Psalm 112:1 (revision)

Blessed the man who fears the Lord.

Psalm 112: Enduring Generosity

The Lectionary had chosen these same psalm verses and refrain as the responsorial hymn on Wednesday of the Thirty-First Week Year I (in response to Romans 13:8-11). Remember that Psalm 111 is devoted to praise of God, while its counterpart, Psalm 112, praises the faithful servant of that same God. Psalm 112 praises the just person who is held in everlasting remembrance because he graciously lends to others (v. 5).

Reverential Fear

The repeated generosity of the Philippians is the result of their grateful reverence for God's many blessings. The refrain (see v. 1) introduces this type of "fear" into the prayer of any contemporary community that hears this passage and praises the God of such generosity. Only because of God's grace are people moved to be generous; it is also grace at work that evokes this sense of reverence. We extend the same reverence to all those whom we love and respect.

Gospel

Luke 16:9-15

If, therefore, you are not trustworthy with dishonest wealth, who will trust you with true wealth?

Literary Link

Luke has collected sayings and teachings about wealth into this section of the gospel. Following the parable of the allegedly dishonest steward (vv. 1-7), we have a series of statements about trustworthiness and dishonesty. Even though people caught in material poverty can also be dishonest and untrustworthy, this collection of ethical instructions would be most appropriate for an affluent community such as Luke's.

Being Trustworthy

Trustworthiness is something that one must earn. It is found in matters large and small with a certain consistency (v. 10), springing from a person's fundamental integrity demonstrated on a daily basis. Among the many signs of such a virtue is one's ability to admit a mistake whenever it occurs, one's practice of keeping one's word, and one's pattern of personal care for details. These qualities are what make a person trustworthy. Are there individuals in the parish who have a special reputation for being trustworthy? Do we take that quality for granted when it is in our midst?

Lovers of Money

The gospel's condemnation of Pharisees as those who love money (v. 14) seems unduly harsh and overly generic. One of the qualities outlined for a worthy bishop was that he not be a "lover of money" (1 Tim 3:3). That same letter admits that it is not money as such, but the love of money that is the root of all evil (6:10). Luke's statement about the Pharisees, however, may have stemmed from a particular incident or a specific problem in his community. This is not the way in which Pharisees were usually described in other ancient sources. They were primarily respected for their deep devotion to the will of God in every detail of life. Nevertheless, unhealthy care for money can become a problem in any community; it undercuts trust in God's providence.

Monday of the Thirty-Second Week in Ordinary Time

First Reading (Year I)

Wisdom 1:1-7

Wisdom is a kindly spirit, the Spirit of the Lord fills the world.

The Book of Wisdom

About a hundred years before the coming of Christ this work was written by an unknown author from the Jewish community of Alexandria who spoke as if he were Solomon. Gathering ancient wisdom as a consolation for those who were suffering, this book recalls major lessons from the history of God's people, and speaks of the folly of idolatry as well as the blessings of divine mercy and justice. The first ten chapters exalt divine wisdom and are often used in the church's liturgy.

The Quest for God

In the worldly cosmopolitan atmosphere of Alexandria with countless new popular philosophies and religions, the faithful people of Israel are encouraged to seek a true understanding of God. To do so requires integrity of heart (v. 1), basic faith (v. 2), and the avoidance of evil (v. 4), especially injustice (v. 5). Without these requirements a person can never be truly wise. In contrast to the newest intellectual fads of the day, the traditions of Israel's faith are recommended as the best way of being truly successful in life.

God's Spirit

In a modern world constantly excited by discoveries in fundamental physics, the faithful person is encouraged to understand God's wisdom as filling the world and holding all its elements together (v. 7). Ancient cosmology could explain the way the physical world operates by pointing to God's spirit as somehow providing that benefit for the universe. The movement of the stars, the annual flooding of the Nile, and the way the inner body functions could be explained by God's Spirit at work. Modern science may have different principles, but we still see God at work in everything as the Primary Cause of all that exists.

Antiphon (Year I)

Psalm 139:24b

Guide me, Lord, along the everlasting way.

Psalm 139: Divine Omnipresence

In a very concrete fashion this poem responds to the teachings of Wisdom by describing the universal knowledge and presence of God who knows absolutely everything about each person: thoughts (v. 4) and actions (v. 1) alike. There is nothing in our lives that remains hidden or secret from God, and nowhere we can go to hide from God (vv. 7-9). The entire congregation at Mass is a library of open books before the God of All Knowing.

The Refrain

Divine knowledge is very personal, intensely practical, and intimately involved in every aspect of our lives. The refrain (v. 24) insists that the purpose of God's knowledge is to guide us through life (v. 10), something that is stated at the very conclusion of the response. God's knowledge is not remotely abstract, but at the very heart of all our decisions and actions. Who are our most trusted guides and mentors when we make decisions and choices?

First Reading (Year II)

Titus 1:1-9

Appoint presbyters in every town, as I directed you.

Slave of God

Whether translated as "servant" or "slave," the term that the author applies to himself (v. 1) suggests constant attention to the needs and wants of another; it may signal voluntary lack of personal freedom and the willing status of being merely a possession of someone else. The title can also allude to the famous Servant Songs of the prophet Isaiah (42:1), which were readily applied to the Christ figure in the early Christian communities. If Paul assumed the title, should not contemporary Christians do so as well? What would the title and its assumed attitude mean in practice for daily life? A traditional title for the Holy Father has been "servant of the servants of God."

The Letter to Titus

This letter is addressed to the leader of the early Christian community at Crete. It describes the type of organization needed for sustaining good conduct in a world of alien ideas and competing religious movements. Probably written in the spirit of Paul's teaching by a later disciple, it offers guidance for new communities and for the servant leadership that is authorized to shape authentic Christian life.

Appointing Presbyters

This letter is normally judged to be written by a disciple of Paul, fully imbued by Pauline views and concerned about the stability of the next generation of faithful disciples. Presbyters, or elders, as the word is often translated, signified maturity of faith, especially a readiness to understand the paschal mystery at work in the lives of Christians. They were to be appointed in every town (v. 5) so that unity, cohesion of purpose, and quality of Christian life would be maintained. The selection, however it occurred, required some discernment and decision among the leadership of the Christian community. Historians see slightly different patterns of leadership in the earliest Christian communities, and the roles of the *presbuteros*/elder or *episkopos*/bishop were not clearly delineated (Phil 1:1). This letter seems to suggest overlapping ministries. The moral qualities of probity and stable family life are lifted up as characteristics required for leadership. Titus is instructed by "Paul" to choose the best and the brightest in his task of stabilizing the community and selecting its leadership. If a congregation today had to write a job description, what would it contain? Which qualities would they desire most of all?

ANTIPHON
(YEAR II)

Psalm 24:6

Lord, this is the people that longs to see your face.

Searching for God

Something deep within the human heart keeps urging us to look for more. This psalm acknowledges that dynamic and searching quality in every stable Christian community. As human beings, whatever we have never seems to be enough, whether the issue is possessions, money, relationships, or personal skills. The impetus can turn a human being into a miserly hoarder, an addict of one kind or another, a compulsive shopper, or a mystic. The quest for God (v. 6) also takes many forms according to our individual personalities. Saint Ignatius of Loyola turned that longing into the principle of "*magis*/more" in the spiritual life, namely, the desire to do ever more in obedience to the will of God. Even showing up for a weekday morning Mass is an exercise in that longing to be nourished by God's presence (v. 6).

The Mountain of the Lord

High places have often been viewed as special sites where God's presence abides. The psalm gives a list of requirements for anyone wishing to enter the sanctuary of God's holy high place (v. 3). Simply by the fact of physical elevation it can seem closer to heaven, transcendent in some fashion and able to provide a view of the rest of the world. Mount Sinai, or Horeb, as it is sometimes called, was the sacred place of the great covenant with Moses. Every local sanctuary contained an elevation for the altar, and could be called the "mountain of the LORD" (v. 3). Even the steps in a parish church's sanctuary are patterned after this biblical metaphor. Simply physical visibility isn't the only issue.

Monday of the Thirty-Second Week in Ordinary Time

Gospel

Luke 17:1-6

If your brother wrongs you seven times in one day, and returns to you seven times saying, "I am sorry," you should forgive him.

Literary Link

The Lectionary omits the parable of the rich man and Lazarus (16:19-31) in order to move from the teachings of trustworthiness and dishonesty to the punishment given to any bad example that leads another to sin (v. 2). Our actions affect others as well as ourselves.

Little Ones

Although we often think of the "little ones" (v. 2) as young children, innocent and proposed as models of the true disciple of Jesus, the term was also applied to recent converts and novices in the life of Christian discipleship. Thus the term may mean someone recently baptized rather than merely someone chronologically young and immature. To somehow lead a new convert into sin is condemned as a serious sin by Jesus and subject to grave punishments. The caution can be a reminder to be especially respectful of those recently welcomed into the church through the RCIA and baptism during Holy Week.

The Mystery of Forgiveness

As noted in the "Our Father," the obligation to extend to others the same forgiveness received from God is a fundamental Christian obligation (v. 3), no matter how often it may be sincerely requested (v. 4). Even this obligation, however, requires discernment lest it fudge the truth of the offense or slip into some type of enablement for addiction. Nevertheless, others have a right to claim forgiveness from us, and we have an obligation to comply. No wonder the response of the apostles is an amazed and astonished request for "increase [of] faith" (v. 5).

Faith

The faith demanded by Jesus (v. 6) is not only something that illustrates power over nature, such as moving a tree by the sheer force of one's mind (v. 6). More appropriately, our faith is an attitude that envisions a radically changed world, one in which a tree can flourish in the sea as well as on land! Genuine faith envisions a new creation, and includes both confidence in God's power and the intellectual acceptance of a new and very different order of reality. By our faith we enter that new world and freely choose to live there. The Catholic notion of faith is more than mere trusting confidence. It includes the full acceptance of the truth as proposed by a living and loving God.

Tuesday of the Thirty-Second Week in Ordinary Time

First Reading (Year I)

Wisdom 2:23–3:9

In the view of the foolish they seemed to be dead, but they are in peace.

Liturgical Use at Funerals

Because this passage is frequently chosen for funeral liturgies, the reading becomes an opportunity to pray for all our beloved deceased friends and relatives. Parish communities often keep an annual "Book of the Dead" with the names of those members who have recently died inscribed therein. This practice encourages their remembrance and our ongoing prayer for them. Inevitably individual names come to mind as we hear the words of this reading.

Christian Death

The book of Wisdom explains our human experience of death by reminding readers that God originally intended human beings to be imperishable (v. 23). The teaching explains that death is the result of the envy of the evil one (v. 24). For people of faith, however, the loss in death is only temporary, as the Lectionary reminds us, because of God's gift of life beyond this life.

Peace

Great consolation is extended by the conviction that the dead remain in the hand of God forever (v. 1) at peace (v. 3), because they are the object of God's everlasting care (v. 9). Biblical peace is more than quiet and tranquility, which the reading could suggest; it includes one's restoration to a rightful place where we best belong, in God's heart forever.

Antiphon (Year I)

Psalm 34:2a

I will bless the Lord at all times.

Divine Attention to the Lowly

As a prayerful response of care for the deceased, the psalm acknowledges all the just who cry for God's attention (v. 16) in distress (v. 18) or when brokenhearted (v. 19). We are assured that God pays attention and listens to their cry (which was one of the words of ancient Israel for a legal petition for justice). These are the ones who will shine like sparks and judge nations, as the book of Wisdom promises (3:7).

The Refrain

To bless God at all times (v. 2) is more than offering words of praise while following the sequence of hours through the day. Although the church's use of this expression could refer to the liturgical hours of the Breviary, it also acknowledges the "times" that are comprised of sadness and joy, of justice and oppression, of health and sickness, as well as of life and death. There is a "time for everything under the sun," as Qoheleth reminds us (see 3:1), and every such "time" is an opportunity to praise God!

First Reading (Year II)

Titus 2:1-8, 11-14

We live devoutly in this age, as we await the blessed hope, the appearance of our savior Jesus Christ.

Sound Community Order

In the face of severe criticism from pagan neighbors who feared that Christians would upend proper decorum, the leaders of Christian communities insisted on the proper behavior of each of the significant groups within the local church: older men (v. 2) and women (vv. 3-5) as well as young men (vv. 6-8). The general acceptance of Christianity was largely dependent upon their good example, and their ability to reflect the best of human behavior. The qualities listed for each group are presented as a type of evangelization, rendering opponents unable to say anything bad about the assembly. The larger local community should be able to say similar things about every Catholic Christian parish today as well.

The Appearance of the Grace of God

From the earliest years, Jesus of Nazareth was venerated as the physical appearance of God in the flesh (v. 11). Christians simply say, "This is how God looks." This passage has long been a favorite text. It enjoys the special status of proclamation at Christmas Midnight Mass each year. The section introducing this great mystery of God's appearance includes the description of an exemplary and orderly community of believers (vv. 1-10). This sequence of ideas suggests that God's appearance also occurs in the life of the community that in some sense is the physical and social appearance of God too. God is totally transcendent, and yet the community can also be said to be "what God looks like in action." This passage moves smoothly into the anticipation of Christ's final appearance at the end of time (v. 13). What already is, will become more so!

Tuesday
of the Thirty-Second Week
in Ordinary Time

ANTIPHON (YEAR II)

Psalm 37:39a

The salvation of the just comes from the Lord.

Salvation

The basic meaning of this word (v. 39), as noted before, suggests a liberation from a tight spot, whether that be understood in physical, emotional, or financial terms. Jesus spoke of this great act of God as even including liberation from the ultimate "tight spots" of sin and death. Curiously Jewish members in our contemporary interreligious dialogues tend to shy away from the term "salvation" when Christians speak of the Jewish people as a "community saved by God" for fear of subtle proselytism. The psalms and the prophets, however, use the term readily and they seek this gift of salvation from God (alone).

The Just

When the psalm speaks of the "just/*tzediqim*" (v. 39), it envisions all those people who live in right relationship with God. This relationship includes their neighbors and all of material creation. The utter and total comprehensiveness of the word "just," therefore, and its popularity in Old Testament literature, suggests people who offer exemplary models of a life well lived. The refrain insists that such are the ones whom God is eager to save (v. 39). Christians tend to call the same group "saints." Each can be heroic and worthy of imitation.

GOSPEL

Luke 17:7-10

We are unprofitable servants; we have done what we were obliged to do.

Literary Link

Yesterday's discussion of the mystery of forgiveness (vv. 3-4) and the necessity of faith in Christian life (vv. 5-6) led Luke to speak about the attitude of a Christian as servant of God (vv. 7-10). Believers are forgivers and servants.

The Good Servant

The gospel often teaches lessons based on the relationship of master and servant, sometimes overturning conventional practice, as when a pleased master serves a meal to a hardworking servant (v. 7). At other times gospel teaching will simply reaffirm common practice, as in this case when the master simply presumes that a good servant will move from one task of field work to the expectation of domestic service at table (v. 8). The typical modern job description often ends with the summary catchall, "and all other tasks as assigned." The activities are many and often varied. The basic willingness to accept them all marks a genuinely "good" servant, both in the sense of moral behavior as well as one who is skillfully capable. Who are good servants in any parish? How do we recognize them?

Merely "Unprofitable"

The final statement remains a perfect summary of all human activity before God, not boasting of labor accomplished but simply acknowledging that whatever we may do is simply our duty (v. 10) and the result of God's grace. One may take pride in doing one's duty well, and be grateful for praise, but when all is said and done, it still remains our "duty." The traditional Japanese culture is offended by tips "for good service," because they consider it a mark of courtesy to always give "good service"! "Do we not always give good service?" they say, slightly offended by the thought of a special gratuity. For the gospel to speak of generous service as "unprofitable" is to be countercultural to the secular economic world of radical Western capitalism.

Wednesday of the Thirty-Second Week in Ordinary Time

FIRST READING (YEAR I)

Wisdom 6:1-11

Hear, kings, that you may learn wisdom.

Political Accountability

This passage contains a very stern, almost harsh, threat of punishment for the misuse of all human authority. Kings and magistrates alike are reminded that their authority was given by God (v. 3) who shows no partiality toward the mighty (v. 7). Judgment is promised and will come "*[t]erribly and swiftly*" (v. 5; emphasis added). In a democratic society this somehow includes every citizen who exercises the right and duty to vote. This text could well serve as a penitential rite during election time of the year. The Egyptian origin of this book may reflect situations of tyrannical authority experienced so frequently in the ancient (and modern) world. Pharaohs are not always kind or just.

Judgment according to Responsibility

In the very uneven distribution of social responsibility across the levels of society, those with more authority can expect stricter scrutiny from God (v. 6). Again and again, whether in the traditions of wisdom or in the judgments of prophets, God consistently brings a renewed leveling of human beings in every generation. More will be asked of those to whom more is given (Luke 12:48).

ANTIPHON (YEAR I)

Psalm 82:8a

Rise up, O God, bring judgment to the earth.

Psalm 82: The Judgment

This brief hymn imagines God convening the heavenly court (v. 1) in order to bring the gods of the nations to accountability. They are condemned for their lack of justice to the lowly and the fatherless as well as to the afflicted and destitute (v. 3). God promises to rescue the lowly and the poor (v. 4). The same criteria are invoked in judging all human authorities. Therefore these verses form a fitting communal response to the teachings of the book of Wisdom.

The Refrain

This invocation (v. 8) insists that the judgments from the heavenly throne will be extended to earth and to all who exercise authority here below. All human beings and their gods/idols will stand before the scrutiny of God. The refrain is a petition for the justice of heaven. The verse offers an echo to a portion of the Lord's Prayer: "thy will be done on earth as it is in heaven" (see Matt 6:10). We pray for divine/human consistency every time we invoke the words of that ancient and treasured prayer at Mass.

FIRST READING (YEAR II)

Titus 3:1-7

For we ourselves were deluded, but because of his mercy, he saved us.

Civil Obedience

The reading begins with an encouragement to remind "them" (v. 1; namely, the community of Titus) to live under human authority. Given the content of prior verses, it would seem that the reference is to all people, young and elderly, slaves and masters alike! Once again it is an effort to demonstrate that Christians were not subversive elements in an otherwise orderly society (even though they refused to participate in the customary pagan worship taken for granted in that ancient world and were therefore called "atheists"). In this letter Christians were encouraged to obey all lawful civil authority. It was important for them to be seen as law-abiding residents in all public actions and events. At the same time this basic Christian attitude does not preclude legitimate "civil disobedience" when issues of morality are at stake.

Bath of Rebirth

The appearance of God's kindness and generous love (v. 4) in the person of Christ Jesus is a text that appears in the liturgy of the Christmas Mass at dawn. These verses would seem to be a song sung at ancient Christian gatherings, celebrating both the incarnation and the spiritual share in that mystery given to each newly baptized follower of Jesus. The ritual of baptism changes individuals from deluded people pursuing their individual pleasures and destructive behavior (v. 3) into a people newly filled with hope for eternal life in the world to come (v. 7). The reading celebrates the wonder of baptism. To use the text at Christmas acknowledges the fact that the incarnation is social as well as individual. The Mystical Body of Christ is celebrated at Christmas too.

ANTIPHON (YEAR II)

Psalm 23:1

The Lord is my shepherd; there is nothing I shall want.

Royal Shepherd

This delightful psalm is the perfect response to the Pauline encouragement's respect for authority. Although we normally think of a shepherd in the fundamental sense of a guardian of sheep in an agrarian and pastoral setting, the word also referred to royal authority in the Ancient Near East (Ezek 34). All nations presumed that a good ruler would exercise care for everyone, especially the poor. King David was a primary exemplar of both meanings, beginning as one delegated to care for the family herds (1 Sam 16:11), and then rising to be anointed king of both Judah and Israel. This reading also presents an opportunity to pray for all civil authority everywhere.

The Lord as Shepherd

What does it mean to be a "shepherd"? To speak of God in this metaphor is to see the Lord as the source of nourishment, health, protection, and safety for the entire people, not merely for individuals. Modern contemporary culture tends to dismiss the image of "sheep" as by definition overly docile and unworthy of application to mature adults. There is, however, an important social and communitarian aspect to the title and the reality it proclaims. When Jesus claims himself to be "the good shepherd" (John 10:11), he uses the Greek term for good in the sense of competent, skilled, and effective (*kalos*)—like a "good" cook. This reading provides an opportunity for all with responsibilities to examine the exercise of their service and the degree to which they imitate Christ.

GOSPEL

Luke 17:11-19

Has none but this foreigner returned to give thanks to God?

Literary Link

It may be that the parable of the servant who humbly did his job (v. 10) logically led to the story of the nine cured lepers who simply did as instructed after their cure, that is, go to the priests (v. 14) without pausing to offer thanks. In both situations, obedience is requested/expected.

Jewish/Samaritan Rivalry

The traditional animosity between Jews and Samaritans in the ancient world of the first century forms an ironic background to the passage, for the Samaritan is surprised that a Jew should care for him and cure him (v. 15), and Jesus is surprised that a Samaritan should stand out by expressing gratitude and praise (v. 18). The praise for the Samaritan is consistent with the inclusive Gospel of Luke, which embraces everyone and prepares for the spread of the church to all nations in Acts. Our contemporary welcome for strangers should be equally universal, even including anyone viewed negatively in the culture of our contemporary communities. Ethnic antipathies have no place in the kingdom of God.

Obedience Rather Than Discourtesy?

Wednesday of the Thirty-Second Week in Ordinary Time

It may strike the reader that the nine lepers who did not return were simply obeying the command of Jesus, going off to show their newly cleansed health to the priests for the customary/required judgment of worthiness for reinstatement into temple worship (v. 14). The Samaritan had a different temple (Mount Gerizim, not Mount Sion), so he came back to do what he could in order to follow the command of Jesus and the expected ritual. We are accustomed to give a negative judgment to the nine who didn't express gratitude, but the parable may also be an occasion for the reminder to presume the best about the actions of others whenever possible! We inevitably bring some prejudices to familiar Scripture passages; for that reason a fresh look at what the text itself says can help us distinguish between the words on the page and the eyelashes of the reader.

Thursday of the Thirty-Second Week in Ordinary Time

First Reading (Year I)

Wisdom 7:22b–8:1

For wisdom is the refulgence of eternal light,
the spotless mirror of the power of God.

Personified Wisdom

In the ancient world, which did not have our modern knowledge of physics and chemistry, it was the spirit that was imagined as the "glue of the universe." In this remarkable passage we find God's ability to do everything wonderfully well described as "Wisdom," defined with twenty-one characteristics, mostly immaterial and virtually all of them in some way divine. Omnipotence (v. 23) and mobility (v. 24) are singled out in various ways. The amazing rhythm of the material universe led to the conviction that there must be some subtle but universal spirit of divine wisdom permeating all material creation. Later Christian speculation quickly applied all these attributes to the Word and to Jesus the Christ. This, therefore, is the Christ we worship as we gather for prayer, holding the entire universe in the palm of his hand. He is the Almighty "Pantocrator" of the ancient Byzantine mosaic icons.

Friendship with God

The same Power when present in an individual human person transforms him or her into a friend of God (v. 27) and perhaps even into a prophet. We are reminded that, more than anything else, God loves the person who lives with wisdom (v. 28) because that individual also always does what is good and just. The greatest of saints are wise people because they know how to live life wisely and well. Which members of the parish community with whom we pray also stand out as "friends of God," wise and holy in their daily life?

Antiphon (Year I)

Psalm 119:89a

Your word is for ever, O Lord.

Eternal Word

The Lectionary has chosen to return to the lengthy Psalm 119 for a response to this hymn in praise for God's Wisdom, which assumes so many forms in our society: truth, ordinances, revelation, and statutes. God's communication with us remains forever, even when it dresses differently according to the specific human situation to which it is addressed. Each form is wise in its own way, and all are necessary for a well-ordered human society. God speaks and the entire world, with all its complex interrelationships, comes into being. God's created world is the cosmos (cosmetic), beautifully and attractively arranged.

The Refrain

The liturgy repeats seven times its conviction that God's speech to us remains forever (v. 89), no matter what the form. The repetition is an important part of the message. We may change, but God does not; we may need different types of address, but God remains the one who speaks and seeks an answer.

First Reading (Year II)

Philemon 7-20

Have him back, no longer as a slave but more than a slave, a brother, beloved especially to me.

Philemon's Dilemma

This single example of an authentic personal letter from Paul to an individual (the letters to Timothy and Titus would seem to have been written slightly later by a disciple well-schooled in the mind and theology of Paul) contains a powerful moral challenge. If Philemon simply accepts Onesimus (literally, "useful"), the runaway slave (v. 15), he risks stirring unrest among other slaves. If he punishes the slave for his crime of flight, does he recognize the effects of the slave's conversion and baptism, "no longer as a slave but . . . a brother" (v. 16)? What does baptism do to any existing social order of unequals? When Paul sent Onesimus back home, he, perhaps mischievously, provoked a moral quandary and set up a situation best solved at that moment in history by simply sending the slave back to Paul! Because we all face moral dilemmas so often in life, Philemon becomes a patron saint of discernment, moral choices, and puzzling options.

Thursday of the Thirty-Second Week in Ordinary Time

The Letter to Philemon

By this letter and the events that occasioned it, Paul seems to have placed poor Philemon in an impossible situation. A runaway slave was befriended and then converted by Paul in prison before being sent back to his original owner. If not punished, other servants would contemplate a similar escape. Onesimus, the runaway slave, however, was now a fellow Christian. The moral dilemmas of crime and punishment, baptism and fellowship, justice and charity are unfolded in this challenging micrositulation of social morality.

The Gift of Friendship

It would seem that Paul and Philemon had been friends for a long time (v. 7). Suddenly added to the relationship by the unusual circumstance of flight, Onesimus enters the scene as a new friend of Paul (v. 16) and as someone now proposed for friendship with Philemon (v. 17). Recall all the curious ways in which friendship has flourished in our own lives over the years. It is a gift from God to be cherished and carefully cultivated out of a sense of stewardship; it should never simply be taken for granted. NB: For some reason, the Byzantine liturgical traditions consider Saint Philemon as one of the apostles with a feast on the 22nd of November. An annual novena of prayer to him might become a helpful Catholic devotion.

ANTIPHON (YEAR II)

Psalm 146:5a

Blessed is he whose help is the God of Jacob.

Blessed

The Hebrew word "*ʾasher*/blessed" that describes the beatitude (v. 5) includes both the recognition of a gift given by another and the positive joyous response of the recipient. Thus to say merely "blessed" is to stress the gift, but not the concomitant happiness; to say merely "happy," however, as some translations would suggest, overlooks the fact that the cause for the person's joy is a gift from outside one's control or ownership. Perhaps "fortunate," or even "lucky," is the best and most comprehensive term for this reality and this expression of divine generosity.

Divine Help

The refrain from Psalm 146 states that the mere offer of help from God, whatever the human situation may have needed, is in itself a blessing (v. 5). The psalm may be saying in so many words, "Are you ever lucky, you have help from God," or possibly expressing a more profoundly spiritual truth, "Are you ever lucky because you are in a state of dependence and need help!" This refrain comes very close to the famous beatitude that proclaims as truly blessed those who are "poor in spirit" (Matt 5:3), namely, those who recognize that everything is gift, even the troubles of life.

GOSPEL

Luke 17:20-25

The Kingdom of God is among you.

Literary Link

As Luke moves closer to the destination of the great journey from Galilee to Jerusalem, where the Lord God is worshiped as King of Israel, the Pharisees raise the question of the solemn inauguration of the kingdom (v. 20), which was thought to be imminent. This in turn provoked a discussion of the "Day of the Lord," when all things would be brought to conclusion and judgment.

The Kingdom of God

A shorthand explanation for the phrase "Kingdom of God" (v. 20) is God's "sovereign action in the world." It is clearly not a geographical space with delineated borders, but rather signifies some sort of dynamic activity of God, as might also be conveyed by the phrase "the reign/rule of God." This divine force is invisibly active within all the currents of human history and thought. In a profound sense the popular secular salutation from *Star Wars*, "May the Force be with you," may not be far from the religious reality! This sovereign action is not outside of human existence, but rather at the heart of everything. Our task as disciples is to become mature instruments of God, not obstacles to his work.

Cautions against Novel Revelations

At a later time Luke will also repeat the caution (v. 23) against running from one distant location to another in order to find God at work (21:8). Perhaps there was a special concern regarding this issue in Luke's local community. The truth is that any and every age seems to find people willing to rush off in zealous fervor for any report of apparitions or so-called spiritual phenomena. Given the fact of multiple possible natural explanations, and possible personal illusion, the Catholic Church prefers to judge such things cautiously through a prudent study by the local bishop and not to rush headlong into false credulity. The ordinary rhythm of prayer, worship, and almsgiving within one's own local community is the best place to encounter God at work! It is the Gospel and the Creed formed by it that express the important elements in our lives as believers.

Friday of the Thirty-Second Week in Ordinary Time

First Reading (Year I)

Wisdom 13:1-9

For if they so far succeeded in knowledge that they could speculate about the world, how did they not more quickly find its Lord?

Proof for the Existence of God

Already in the ancient world we are confronted by this classic argument for the existence of God from the beauty and order of the material universe (vv. 4-5). The very order of the *cosmos*, a Greek word that itself refers to orderly beauty (as in "cosmetic"), forces any truly wise person to acknowledge the orderly Divine Mind behind everything. This reading is an invitation to praise the God of material creation in each of its seasons of beauty. The stunning pictures of each season, which often illustrate the months of a calendar year, are the created realities that point to the power of God.

Idolatry

The reading from the book of Wisdom laments that many people were so taken by the beauty of this material world as to erroneously claim the creatures themselves "gods" (v. 2). Those willing to seek God are praised, however, even if they do not discover the full nature of God (vv. 6-7); even they, however, are chided for their inability to follow the search to its full and final conclusion (v. 9). The sin is stopping too short of the goal to enjoy the beauty without praising the artist. At the same time we ought to acknowledge that some of the ancients were sophisticated enough to see the idols as mere symbols for the power of the Great God. An example of this deeper wisdom may be found in the worship of the sun god by the ancient Egyptian Pharaoh Tutankhamen in the fourteenth century BC.

Antiphon (Year I)

Psalm 19:2a

The heavens proclaim the glory of God.

The Heavenly Chorus

The refrain (v. 2) echoes and reaffirms the whole point of the reading, namely, the fact that the wonders of creation themselves sing praise to their Maker. Modern astronomers sometimes speak of the ethereal humming of outer space. Ancient pagans and modern Wiccans may personify and even deify the forces of heaven, but we confess the One God with whom there is no other (Isa 40:18-26).

Psalm 19: Ode to Creation

This psalm combines two sections, the first of which deals with the way material creation reveals the wonder of God's power. This is the portion chosen by the Lectionary to serve as a response to the reading from the book of Wisdom. The rest of the psalm, though not used here by the church's liturgy, goes on to praise the way God has given guidance and instruction to his faithful people. Both forms of revelation merit our obedient thanks and praise.

First Reading (Year II)

2 John 4-9

Whoever remains in the teaching has the Father and the Son.

The Second Letter of John

This brief note from an unknown individual serving as "presbyter" in his own community is written to "Lady," probably a personified community, possibly under the house church leadership of an affluent early Christian woman. Their challenge seems to be the influence of some Christians so "progressive" as to question the basic teachings of Jesus and his life-giving death and resurrection.

Love of God

This letter insists that true love of God includes "walking/living" in the truth revealed by God in the gospels (see v. 6). The requested human response is not a mere intellectual embrace of God's truth, but one that is to be translated into our entire lives, including everything we say and do and are. Even on a purely human level, an affirmation of love means little unless backed up with daily signs of that affection and care.

Docetism

One of the earliest Christian heresies taught that the Word only "appeared" to take on human flesh in the incarnation (v. 7). Human nature was judged unworthy of contact with the divine. The error was called "Docetism," the belief that the Word only seemed to be human. That was an example of the "progressive" thought against which the letter warns (v. 9) because it does not accept the Gospel of Jesus who was tested like us and accepted everything human except sin (Heb 4:15). The early Christian writers insisted that "whatever was not assumed was not redeemed." Each age, it seems, develops its own group of teachers who attempt to go beyond the teachings of the gospels in order to present something more "modern" and up to date. They fashion a Christ according to our desires, rather than allowing themselves to be fashioned by God's revelation and truth.

ANTIPHON (YEAR II)

Psalm 119:1b

Blessed are they who follow the law of the Lord!

Psalm 119: Full Compliance

The Lectionary has chosen the first few verses of an extended meditation on obedience as the response to the letter's admonition of "walking in the truth" (2 John 4). It is God's laws (v. 1), decrees (v. 2), commands (v. 10), promises (v. 11), words (v. 17), and wonders (v. 18) that enable a person to walk/live in that truth. Like advice given by a mentor or master artist, all these directives enable each faithful member of God's people to live a life that is wise, loving, generous, and compassionate. Guidance is offered by God, and accepted by good and faithful people.

The Refrain

People are "blessed" (v. 1) if they have received a gift that delights them. All of these words that describe instructions and advice in various forms are gifts from God, not burdensome impositions to personal freedom. They delight a truly faithful member of God's family. Obedience to God's law is not something that human beings can do without grace. That makes them "blessed." The beatitude is pronounced on those who comply with God's wishes.

GOSPEL

Luke 17:26-37

So it will be on the day the Son of Man is revealed.

Literary Link

After discouraging his followers from rushing from one place to another in eager anticipation of the final coming of the Son of Man (vv. 22-25), the gospel turns to further emphasizing the suddenness of that event without warning (vv. 25-37).

The Days of Noah

The gospels, reflecting the rabbinic teaching methods of Jesus himself, constantly turn toward the Scriptures of Israel, combing them for clues and patterns of God's favored ways of dealing with human beings. Like the story of Jonah, early Christians found self-understanding in the story of Noah (v. 26). Amid all the normal daily preoccupations with the enjoyment of food and drink and the festivities of marriage around him, Noah entered the ark with his family and his menagerie of animals as commanded by God (Gen 7:13); he left everything behind and the rest of the world was suddenly washed away! Terrible natural disasters, such as tornadoes, earthquakes, and tsunamis, come quickly and devastate lives. We see them not as punishments but as natural forces in collision even when they create devastation. God's people pay attention to even the slightest signs of material disruption around them. God remains in our midst for new beginnings and offers instruction about rebuilding our world.

Friday of the Thirty-Second Week in Ordinary Time

Lot's Wife

Scripture tells us that Lot's wife was turned into a pillar of salt (Gen 19:26). The tale, however, was probably an ancient popular local legend based on a crude pillar that somehow resembled a human figure (v. 32). Luke's point is that, when the final call comes into our lives, we must resist looking back fondly on material possessions and human activities as if that were our only option. The new creation offers something better for those who enter the kingdom preached by Jesus. That kingdom is wrapped in the mystery of God's will. Neither "when" nor "where" are questions to be asked, because the focal point is a new relationship to God, not merely human history or material geography!

Saturday of the Thirty-Second Week in Ordinary Time

First Reading (Year I)

Wisdom 18:14-16; 19:6-9

Out of the Red Sea an unimpeded road appeared and they bounded about like lambs.

The All-Powerful Word

Although this reference to the powerful word leaping down from heaven in the course of the stillness of night (v. 14) is often used liturgically for celebrations of Christmas Eve, the original intent of the image was more ominous. Its actual reference was to the final plague in Egypt when the children of the Egyptians were struck down and killed during the night (v. 16) to force the pharaoh's permission for Israel's flight from Egypt. The original biblical issue in the image is divine power, not divine compassion related to the incarnation. The very same intervention by God brought sorrow to Egypt and freedom to Israel. Sometimes a similar double effect is experienced, not simultaneously as in the exodus, but sequentially, when people first experience sadness, but then later in retrospect understand the deeper blessing that had been granted to them.

Poetic Reimagination

With remarkable creativity this portion of the book of Wisdom retells the story of the crossing of the Re(e)d Sea. Once a story of desperate but divinely protected escape through the waters, all creation is now described as remade anew (19:6) with dry land and grassy plains emerging from the waters almost like the first days of creation (Gen 1:9). Thus the exodus is presented here as if it were a new creation in which all natural laws are transformed. One telling invites us to stand with the freed slaves in gratitude; the other version looks forward to joyful participation like bounding lambs (v. 9) in a new world of God's remaking. We always need a big picture for our daily lives.

Antiphon (Year I)

Psalm 105:5a

Remember the marvels the Lord has done.

Psalm 105: Salvation History

This psalm is a summary of salvation history from the time of God's promises to Abraham to the day of Israel's entrance into the Promised Land. We are implicitly invited to add our own personal experience of God's grace to that epic. In particular, the first fifteen verses of Psalm 105 are cited in 1 Chronicles 16:8-22 as a festal hymn, celebrating David's victorious transfer of the ark of the covenant to Mount Zion. Historical memories, poems, and songs are woven together into worship.

The Lord's Marvels

The witness of the Scriptures is filled with marvels done by God for nations and individuals, as the refrain reminds us (v. 5). Depending on whether the events are recounted by Egyptians or Israelites, the mood is changed from lament to thanksgiving. Each parish community has its own history of God's marvels for their behalf! Because these verses express a communal response to the Word, they implicitly invite us to add the marvels of our lives to their litany of praise!

First Reading (Year II)

3 John 5-8

We ought to support such persons, so that we may be co-workers in the truth.

The Third Letter of John

This brief letter addressed the practical challenge of a community's welcome to traveling missionaries as well as some obscure problem of serious disagreement among its leaders over how to best support the efforts of the itinerant evangelists. As in all subsequent centuries, those who offer support become coworkers for the Gospel.

Love for Strangers

The letter was apparently triggered by a dispute between Gaius, the leader of the community, who encouraged support for missionaries (vv. 5-6), and Diotrephes, a prominent member of that same community who opposed doing so and ignored instructions from the writer of the letter (vv. 9-10). At issue are two major concerns for every Christian community: our duty to deepen a sense of inner cohesion and unity within the community, on the one hand, and the duty to remain in communion with other communities of shared faith, on the other. Maintaining a sense of support for missionaries expresses the outward motion to which we are also called by God. The Lord sent his disciples on mission, and urged us to maintain the same dynamic sense of mission in everything we do. How do we show our unity with congregations located elsewhere? How do we reach out to others? How do we deal with visiting missionaries? At times religious leadership may differ in strategy or short-range goals, but mutual respect should govern all their communications and activities.

Saturday of the Thirty-Second Week in Ordinary Time

"Co-Workers in the Truth"

We support the church's missionary efforts by our interest in learning about the challenges and successes of missionary work around the world, by our regular prayer for those engaged, and by our financial support (v. 8). Missionary work is not merely a marginal or arbitrary interest on the part of individuals; it emerges from our very identity as Christians. Christ is the primary Missionary, sent by the Father to save the world. As the familiar adage expresses it, "It is not the church that has a mission, but the mission that has a church!"

Antiphon (Year II)

Psalm 112:1 (revision)

Blessed the man who fears the Lord.

Psalm 112: The Ideal Israelite

The two "bookend" psalms are mutually complementary, with Psalm 111 praising God and Psalm 112 praising the blessedness of the truly good and faithful person. This response depicts the full profile of an ideal Israelite who reverences God and welcomes the commandments (v. 1), gives generously to the needy (v. 3), and is known for his justice (v. 5).

The Refrain

Reverence for the Lord (see v. 1) can never be separated from one's relationship to one's neighbor. Love for both God and neighbor are ancient interrelated obligations that must mark the life of anyone called to covenantal membership. This psalm makes it very clear that "fear" of the Lord may be blessed by prosperity (vv. 2-3), but must also be expressed by one's generosity (v. 3), mercy (v. 4), and willingness to lend to others in need (v. 5).

Gospel

Luke 18:1-8

Will not God then secure the rights of his chosen ones who call out to him day and night?

Literary Link

After the teachings about the sudden and unexpected nature of the final "Day of the Son of Man/Day of the Lord" (see 17:26-37), the gospel immediately turns to the need for a life of consistent prayer (18:1-8). A habit of prayerfulness is the single most important preparation one can maintain in the face of the suddenness of the Lord's return. Prayer equips us to see the full picture, and to see it clearly.

Persistence

The parable of the persistent widow and the unjust judge contains many important truths: acknowledgment of our dependence on others for the resolution of matters beyond our control (v. 3), the importance of repetition for matters of real significance in life (v. 5), and the need to see our entire life and all its contents as gift (not earned possessions). The persistence of the widow is praised because she is an example of praying without becoming weary (v. 1), and is vindicated with success by her perseverance. When one applies the metaphor to God, it is our acknowledgment of utter dependence on God that achieves our success, rather than the suggestion that God changes his mind!

The Silence of God

We must come to terms with the disparity between the promise of this gospel passage that God will act speedily for the just (v. 7) and the reality of our own human experience of God's apparent silence before utter tragedy and so many terrible evils in our world. These cannot be easily explained away—and yet we are asked to trust in a God who loves us more than we love ourselves! Sometimes it helps to remember that God will be God. It is also useful to recognize that sometimes we ourselves can find benefit from living with our heartaches. Doing so enables us to sort out the differences between our wants and our needs. Often only in retrospect do we realize that painful experiences have become moments of grace and growth for us. Physical pain can demonstrate what is important in life, and what is not working well. The waiting can produce spiritual maturity.

Few or Many?

The final question about the number of faithful people at the time of the Lord's return (v. 8) is a haunting one, especially for those who hunger and thirst for justice, but find no relief from the oppression and injustice of our world. Woven into the long history of the world's salvation is the reality of human sin, the respect that God has for our human freedom, God's patience with the wayward in the hope of conversion, and, finally, the ultimate mystery of God. We hope for universal salvation, and we understand that such a grand finale will only come into being as a pure gift from God. At the same time our Scriptures recognize the reality of moments of human puzzlement before the mystery of God's mind.

Monday of the Thirty-Third Week in Ordinary Time

First Reading (Year I)

1 Maccabees 1:10-15, 41-43, 54-57, 62-63

Terrible affliction was upon Israel.

The First Book of Maccabees
Written by an unknown Hebrew author in about 100 BC, this book describes the successful efforts of the family of Mattathias to resist evil authority and to revolt against the religious oppression of Hellenistic Seleucid kings. God's fidelity to the chosen people is reaffirmed and celebrated.

The Bitter Cultural/Religious Clash

After the death of Alexander the Great (323 BC), his kingdom was divided among three major generals. One of these, Antiochus Epiphanes IV (v. 10), became king of Syria and, with cooperation from some of the Hellenized Jewish leaders in Jerusalem, attempted to impose radical Greek culture upon the Jewish people: gymnasiums (v. 14), pagan sacrifices, discarding of the Sabbath (v. 42), and the placement of an idol in the temple (v. 54). They decreed the penalty of death for anyone possessing a copy of the Torah and found observing its laws (v. 57). Therein began a terrible persecution against all things Jewish in order to force a common culture and religion upon the entire region (v. 63). It became a time of heroic witness by those who were still determined to be faithful to the covenant of God (v. 63). The memory of those saints and martyrs also provided encouragement to all successive generations who profess faithfulness in time of persecution from their larger world. Though more modest and mitigated, our own time knows the often contemptuous disregard of religion by the secularism of our world. Courageous fidelity is the badge of those who love the Lord in every age.

Gymnasiums

Gymnasiums (v. 14), fitness clubs, and other common amenities of contemporary culture around us may be innocent enough, and often even healthy. A faithful believer in the God of the covenant, however, constantly seeks the underlying values of one's culture to judge its true compatibility with the faith we have professed at baptism. The human body is a gift, and care for good health is part of faithful stewardship. Spiritual values, however, are even more important for the fullness of life in this world as preparation for the next! The body beautiful is only a relative value in the larger spectrum of concerns.

Antiphon (Year I)

Psalm 119:88

Give me life, O Lord, and I will do your commands.

Psalm 119: God's Will

The portions of Psalm 119 selected to serve as a response to the biblical account of second-century BC persecution highlight the suffering of those who attempted to follow God's will in spite of the malice of truly wicked countrymen (vv. 53, 150). These verses describe contempt for the wicked (v. 158) and offer words of desperate prayer to God from the victim of such persecution.

The Refrain

Knowing the background to the reading from First Maccabees, one can immediately see how the refrain's request for life, as expressed by one who is determined to be obedient to God's laws (v. 88), reflects perfectly the sentiments of a persecuted Jewish person under Antiochus Epiphanes IV. In times of serious opposition and religious persecution the refrain becomes the perfect prayer! Human life and commandments are both gifts.

First Reading (Year II)

Revelation 1:1-4; 2:1-5

Realize how far you have fallen and repent.

John the Visionary

John, the recipient of the visions, is called "the Theologian" in the Greek Orthodox tradition. Although the ancient world presumed that the apostle, the writer of the gospel, and the visionary were the same identical person, more contemporary scholarship distinguishes the three as separate figures. The individual mentioned in the beginning of the book of Revelation (v. 1) was probably a leader of a Christian community at Ephesus, uncompromisingly opposed to the idolatry of the Roman culture of that city and punished by exile to the penal colony of Patmos (v. 9) for his rejection of the temple built to honor the "divine" Emperor Domitian (AD 94). The author of these visions called himself a "partner" in the distress, the kingdom, and patient endurance (v. 9). Anyone suffering hostility because of one's faith can identify with the experiences of John. In the Acts of the Apostles we are told that, even after being flogged by Sanhedrin authorities, they "rejoic[ed] that they had been found worthy to suffer dishonor for the sake of the name" (5:41).

The Book of Revelation

In richly symbolic language, perhaps deliberately obscure to all but the inner members of John's Christian community, this book offers a series of letters of encouragement and visions of explanation for the events that will accompany God's final resolution of human history in favor of his faithful people. Uncompromisingly opposed to idolatry in all forms, this work embodies the paschal imperative for the church and insists on the need for patient endurance by the truly faithful followers of Christ. Portions from this final book of the New Testament provide the readings for the last two weeks of Year II.

Letter to Ephesus

The reading selected by the Lectionary as an introduction to the book of Revelation gives some personal background to the visions (vv. 1-4), and then offers a major portion (2:1-5) from the seer's first of seven letters, namely, the message addressed to the Christian community at Ephesus. The "star" is the "angel" leader of that community, and the "lampstands" represent the community itself in the presence of the victoriously glorified Christ (2:1). The community is commended for maintaining true leadership among the faulty apostolic imitations called "impostors" (2:2). The Ephesians are praised for their endurance under suffering (2:3). The summons to repentance comes because of the community's loss of first fervor as its daily life absorbs the reality of faithful obedience to Christ's teachings. Like the Ephesians, every community can and should be summoned to a permanent attitude of repentance (*metanoia*) before God (2:5). Every person and every community can easily take its faith for granted.

ANTIPHON (YEAR II)

Revelation 2:17

Those who are victorious I will feed from the tree of life.

Psalm 1: The Perennial Contrast

The Lectionary has chosen Psalm 1 as a response to this first reading from the book of Revelation, perhaps because the psalm contrasts the faithful Israelite described as a fruitful tree planted near running water (vv. 1-2 and 3) with the wicked who are like rootless chaff in the wind (v. 4). The former are the members of John's community in Ephesus who remain faithful to God's law night and day (v. 2). The latter are flawed and fake Christians overly influenced by the paganism of their age.

The Refrain

The Lectionary has taken a verse from John's second letter, to the church of Pergamum (v. 17), where the faithful are in battle with false teachers over eating meat from pagan sacrifices. To those who remain steadfast in their convictions John promises the reward of nourishment from the tree of life, a symbol for eternal life in the next age. To the faithful person described as a well-planted tree is promised nourishment from the tree of life.

GOSPEL

Luke 18:35-43

What do you want me to do for you? Lord, please let me see.

Monday of the Thirty-Third Week in Ordinary Time

Literary Link

After the parable of the persistent widow and her unjust judge (vv. 1-8), the Lectionary omits the parable of the Pharisee and the tax collector (vv. 9-14), the welcome of Jesus to children (vv. 15-17), the inquiry of the rich official regarding eternal life (vv. 18-23), the difficulty of the wealthy regarding entrance into the kingdom (vv. 24-30), and the third passion prediction (vv. 31-34) in order to move to the story of the blind beggar (vv. 35-43). Perhaps a certain level of continuity is thereby created between the persistent prayers of the widow on Saturday and the similar persistence of today's blind beggar for restored sight from Jesus.

Luke's Blind Beggar and the Crowds

In one's prayer over a gospel story, it is helpful to see what is not said as well as what is affirmed. To make that contrast a comparison with the other Synoptic accounts can shed light on Luke's purposes. The way the Gospel of Luke tells this story is different than the accounts in Mark or Matthew. The others place the miracle as Jesus was leaving Jericho, but Luke makes this an entrance event (v. 35) because he has another story to tell in the same context of entering Jericho, that of the tax collector Zacchaeus up in the sycamore tree (19:1-10). Although Mark remarks that the blind beggar casts aside his cloak (his way of life since it is the place where coins are tossed; see Mark 10:46-52), the gesture receives no mention in Luke, who is eager to insist that the crowds (vv. 35, 43), which are constantly present in his gospel, should glorify God and take up the hymn of praise. A modern parish congregation that sings God's praises becomes associated with all similar groups described in Luke's gospel!

Cure and Consequences

The triple prayer of the blind beggar in spite of resistance from the crowd and his request to see receives a cure from Jesus (v. 42). Immediately upon receiving his sight, he joins the journey with Jesus to Jerusalem and follows Jesus (v. 43). It might be helpful to recall that the name given to early Christianity was "the Way," and that those whom Jesus cured became his faithful travel companions in the kingdom. Not only is the sight of the beggar restored but his entire person is welcomed and integrated into the Way of Life prescribed by the gospel! The blind beggar is miraculously cured and the crowd is miraculously changed from being a voice of rebuke (v. 39) to one of praise (v. 43).

Tuesday of the Thirty-Third Week in Ordinary Time

First Reading (Year I)

2 Maccabees 6:18-31

I will leave to the young a noble example of how to die willingly and generously for the revered and holy laws.

The Second Book of Maccabees

The contents of this book deal with a briefer time span (180–161 BC) than its companion volume of First Maccabees. It offers accounts of overlapping events treated from different perspectives. This book is an abridgment of a lost earlier five-volume work by a Jason the Cyrene, and contains tales of many moralizing events for catechetical instruction and encouragement during a time of bitter persecution.

The Martyrdom of Eleazar

The story of Eleazar, a much respected elderly man who was noble and completely devoted to God's will (v. 18), is a moral tale for the elderly of every community. He was determined to die rather than compromise the example he had always given to the youth of the community throughout his entire lifetime (v. 28). The account highlights the importance of the example by elderly in every community of faith. Eleazar refused to compromise for the sake of transitory convenience or a few years of extended mortal life (v. 24). The passage describes his courageous execution (v. 30). The perseverance of our own contemporary beloved elderly in good times and more difficult ones offers us a fine example for living a life of total integrity and faithfulness (v. 31). We praise ancient and modern elders alike. Wise grandparents are important parts of every family. Unfortunately for the children in our mobile American society, the elderly are often distant and absent.

Just a Pork Chop "For God's Sake"

In one sense the action proposed to Eleazar is only a pork chop, and our use of the phrase "for God's sake" could indicate the inherent insignificance of that action. There are times, however, when even a pork chop can become bigger than life, and can serve as a symbol for right living in the face of public hostility or mockery of God's law. In the fullest sense, it truly became a pork chop "for God's sake." Real heroes and saintly martyrs understand which symbolic gestures are religiously crucial in any given age. Are there any such significant symbols in our day? Where would/should we draw the proverbial line in the sand of social values that we will not ignore? The early Japanese martyrs were asked to step on a cross. Which ultimately unacceptable compromise is offered casually in our day?

Antiphon (Year I)

Psalm 3:6b

The Lord upholds me.

God's Enemies

Once again with remarkable fittingness the Lectionary has chosen Psalm 3 as a response to the story of Eleazar's courageous resistance to the temptation and compromise offered by God's enemies and adversaries (vv. 2, 7). Whether the enemies are the newly paganized Jewish Hellenists of the second century BC or the mocking secularists and new pagans of our age, the pressures can be severe and the penalties for refusing to compromise can be grave. In our contemporary world the demands of society for unethical prescriptions or procedures can seriously challenge the conscience of pharmacists and medical personnel. Religious freedom is a value to be prized and defended in every age.

The Refrain

Amid all the pressures marshaled against a person of ethical morality the refrain is a clear expression of trusting confidence in God's protection (v. 6). The Lord is a shield (v. 4) ever present, even when a weary human being rests at night (v. 6). In the face of similar hostility from fellow citizens in Jerusalem centuries earlier, Jeremiah confidently entrusted his cause to the Lord (11:20).

First Reading (Year II)

Revelation 3:1-6, 14-22

If anyone hears my voice and opens the door, I will enter his house and dine with him.

Tuesday of the Thirty-Third Week in Ordinary Time

More Letters to the Churches

The Lectionary has chosen two more letters from the collection offered by the book of Revelation, the fifth to the community at Sardis (vv. 1-6) and the seventh to the church at Laodicea (vv. 14-22). They are once again directed to the "angel leaders" of those respective churches. John concludes that only a few Christians at Sardis have retained their baptismal repentance (v. 3) and innocence (v. 4); he reminds them of the Lord's imminent sudden return (v. 3) lest they be found wanting. To those at Laodicea John warns of their affluent tepidity/"lukewarm[ness]" (v. 16); he reveals their deep inner spiritual blindness and shameful poverty (v. 18). Should these letters be written to us? Each of John's messages are perennially relevant. They could be directed toward any contemporary parish congregation with spiritual benefit for everyone.

Knocking and Dining

To the affluent community of Laodicea with its presumed custom of fine dining, the Lord poses as someone desiring to join them at supper (v. 20). It is an image for Christ's eagerness to be closely associated with his disciples, but also a sign of his respect for their freedom. A famous popular religious painting portrays Jesus standing outside a wooden door without an exterior handle, clearly illustrating the fact that the door can only be opened from within. In the early Christian communities, just as in our day, that relationship between Christ and his disciples is celebrated at the eucharistic banquet. Christ comes when invited. In the gospels the stories of dinners are almost inevitably occasions for conversion, accepted or rejected.

Antiphon (Year II)

Revelation 3:21

I will seat the victor beside me on my throne.

Psalm 15: Entrance Requirements

Psalm 15 is a portion of a classic "Torah liturgy," that is, the ritual by which a person seeks entrance to the sanctuary, and is instructed regarding the moral requirements expected of any worshiper: justice (v. 2), truth (v. 3), respect for neighbors (v. 3), generosity (v. 4), and rejection of bribes (v. 5). The sequence is a valuable description of moral uprightness and possibly useful for an examination of conscience!

The Refrain

The Lectionary has chosen the blessing given to those from the church of Laodicea who rekindle their fervor, welcome their visiting Lord, and live a life of fidelity to the Lord. The offer of a throne in the final victorious banquet (v. 21) is the fulfillment of the promise of Jesus to his disciples at the Last Supper, namely, that they will sit on thrones to judge the twelve tribes of Israel (Luke 22:30). Even church pews and table chairs might be changed into thrones!

Gospel

Luke 19:1-10

The Son of Man has come to seek and to save what was lost.

Literary Link

Both the roadside beggar who calls out from his blindness (18:35-43) and Zacchaeus the tree-climbing tax collector are examples and models for those who seek out Jesus, whatever their situation or physical abilities may be. The deeper issue of both stories is the person's desire that God rewards.

Short in Stature

First of all, a playful comment: although we generally presume that it is Zacchaeus who is short of stature and therefore must climb the tree (v. 4), this is not in the text, which only reads "he" (v. 3). In fact, it could be Jesus himself who is not seen because of the crowd! This small observation can serve as a warning against whatever assumptions and prejudices we carry through life and bring to our reading of Scripture. Every physical stature brings its blessings as well as its need for assistance in dealing with respective limitations.

Conversion or Alternate Calling?

The story of Zacchaeus is usually presented as a tale of conversion because he climbs down from the tree, stands his ground, and promises to give half his possessions to the poor, and to return fourfold what he has defrauded anyone (v. 8). The actual Greek text, however, puts those verbs in the present, and could well be a tale recognizing alternative forms of Jewish piety other than that of the Pharisees. Zacchaeus states (in Greek) that he *does* give half his possessions to the poor, and fourfold to anyone defrauded. In this alternate reading of the text, therefore, Jesus would be insisting that the tax collector is also a descendant of Abraham (v. 9) and worthy of a visit from Jesus in order to become an instrument of grace and conversion for his fellow tax collectors (lost sheep) at table (v. 10). Jesus, like John the Baptist before him (Luke 3:12-13), does not demand that one stop working as a tax collector, but only asked that the occupation be exercised with justice and integrity.

Wednesday of the Thirty-Third Week in Ordinary Time

First Reading (Year I)

2 Maccabees 7:1, 20-31

The creator of the universe will give you back both breath and life.

A Mother's Love

This is a powerful tale of the heroic faith of a mother willing to see the death of her seven sons rather than have them deny their faith in the God of Israel (v. 20), even under persecution. As the story unfolds, it demonstrates the concern we need to have for the spiritual as well as the material well-being of those who form our circle of family and friends. The account states that she spoke her exhortation in the language of their ancestors (v. 21). That may have been the Aramaic (v. 27) spoken by the people of that day (thus giving grounds for the fear of insult felt by Antiochus in v. 24) or in the words of the ancient religious traditions of Israel so familiar to them all.

The Gift of Life

The mother's prayer includes her testimony about the mysterious origins of human life in the womb (vv. 22-23). This expression of her belief is a powerful statement about the value of human life from its very first stirrings (v. 27). The woman becomes a biblical witness for the full dignity of prenatal human life in our own day as well when negative cultural forces seem to dismiss its inherent importance. She also gives witness to her belief in the destiny of human life in the fullness of resurrection (vv. 23, 29).

True and False Friendship

Note that Antiochus promised to make the youngest his "Friend" (v. 24), a title of royal honor usually accompanied by wealth and social prominence. The title will come back into mind when we hear the threat of the crowds surging around Pontius Pilate in the passion: "If you release him, you are not a Friend of Caesar" (John 19:12). Political honors at the price of one's integrity are hollow and ultimately poisonous. The title also reminds us of Abraham who was a friend of God (Exod 33:12) and of the Last Supper when Jesus called his disciples no longer servants but friends (John 15:15). Whom do we claim as our friends today, and by what criteria?

Antiphon (Year I)

Psalm 17:15b

Lord, when your glory appears, my joy will be full.

Psalm 17: Trusting Confidence

The Lectionary chooses this hymn of trusting confidence as a fitting response to the story of the family's faithful resistance to royal torture and persecution. The faithful claim a place of preferred divine favor as the "apple of your eye" and protection under God's wings (v. 8). A person's true character is revealed in times of persecution or hardship.

The Refrain

Those who trust in God and resist false religious practices are assured of reward. The "fullness of joy" at the final appearance of God's glory (v. 15) has always been the hope of God's holy ones. There has been a long history of scholarly debate regarding whether the psalms express any belief in the resurrection, but verses such as this refrain give hints in that direction. Moreover, the belief of the family of Maccabean martyrs expresses their clear convictions about their future share in God's glory forever. This refrain could be the prayer of anyone experiencing hardship or trouble in life.

First Reading (Year II)

Revelation 4:1-11

Holy is the Lord God almighty, who was, and who is, and who is to come.

God in Glory

After selections from letters to the churches, the book of Revelation moves to an initial description of the overwhelming glory and majesty of God's heavenly court. Influenced by the poetry of Isaiah 6 and Ezekiel 1, the throne is described as brilliant like precious jewels (v. 3), surrounded by twenty-four elders (v. 4), seven flaming spirits (v. 5), and four mysterious living creatures (v. 6). Images of mystery, radiance, power, opulence, and splendor are heaped up in an effort to suggest the utter transcendence of God. The seer almost makes it impossible to reduce all the images into any logical order in his effort to present the utter supremacy of God. What images might we add from modern life? Would we also invoke nuclear explosions, the phenomena of cosmic splendor, or the buried riches of Central America? How can one describe the Indescribable? The proper human response is humble awe, and sorrow for sin.

What "Must Happen"

The book repeatedly makes reference to the things that "must happen" (v. 1) as history unfolds toward its inexorable destiny. Allowing evil to reveal the fullness of its inherent wickedness, enabling the faithful to be tested and proven, and offering assurance of God's final triumph in glory are all parts of "what must happen" for the final perfecting of the world. This is the "paschal imperative" that described the destiny of the Son of Man, the entire church of God, and each member therein. The necessity is "moral," not physical, because human freedom remains an enduring gift of God to human beings.

ANTIPHON (YEAR II)

Psalm 150:1b

Holy, holy, holy Lord, mighty God!

Psalm 150: Praise Music

The Lectionary chooses the final "Alleluia Chorus" of the Psalter as a fitting response to the description of the glory of the victorious heavenly court of God. Musical instruments of virtually all known types are described (vv. 3-5) as if adding to the grandeur of that divine triumph. The magnificence of the royal Egyptian, Assyrian, Babylonian, and Persian courts of the Ancient Near East have supplied the patterns for this vivid and imaginative picture. The psalmist, like all poets, can steal images from every possible source!

The Refrain

The refrain seems improperly ascribed to Psalm 150 itself (v. 1), but in fact echoes the cry of the heavenly seraphim in Isaiah's inaugural vision (6:3). The triple acclamation reflects the Hebrew superlative in praising God's "holiness," namely, the manner in which God is absolutely and completely different from everything human! Bumping our flawed and faltering language against the utter transcendence of God, we can only sing "holy/*qadosh*" in praise. We repeat that same acclamation of Isaiah whenever we pause at the opening edge of our daily eucharistic prayer.

GOSPEL

Luke 19:11-28

Why did you not put my money in a bank?

Literary Link

Perhaps it was the tale of Zacchaeus the tax collector (19:1) that logically led to today's parable of the distribution of gold coins. It may have been Luke's recollection of the wealth of pilgrims approaching Jerusalem with Jesus and his disciples (v. 11), well supplied with coins for the required distribution of alms to the poor by all pilgrims. Those who envisioned Jesus as a messianic figure destined for the redemption and freeing of Jerusalem from Roman oppression began to sense a new enthusiasm and excitement among fellow Jews. Jesus needed to teach about accountability, not merely victory.

The Reward for Diligence

In this version of the parable of the gold coins (literally, *minas*, each equivalent to a hundred drachmas/denarii or a hundred day's wages), each servant receives a single precious gold coin (vv. 16, 18, 20), as contrasted with Matthew's parable of the more valuable money called "talents" where the distribution is five, two, and one (25:15). The increase obtained by the first servant is dramatic when one makes ten more (v. 16). Hard work and creativity are richly rewarded while the fearful one who is unwilling to take a risk is condemned (v. 22). Cowards are never praised in the gospel (Rev 21:8)! The parable is one of accountability as well as reward. Industrious diligence marks a partner with God in the work of the kingdom. Nevertheless, it begins with God's gift; all we do is cooperate!

Wednesday of the Thirty-Third Week in Ordinary Time

Accountability and Judgment

The main point of the parable is the distribution of the gifts to be used wisely and the rewards given to those who do so (v. 16). Even though the story may reflect Herod's actual travel to Rome to seek the emperor's patronage and his subsequent brutality with potential rivals or enemies, the allegorical details are less important, that is, the departure for a distant country, the opposition of some countrymen (and eventual punishment), and the final rewards or punishments. As eschatological hopes rose after the resurrection and the imminent return of Christ occupied the minds of early Christians, the parable became a mirror for the final phases of Christ's victory over sin and death. God is generous and we must be both grateful and industrious.

Thursday of the Thirty-Third Week in Ordinary Time

First Reading (Year I)

1 Maccabees 2:15-29

We will keep to the covenant of our ancestors.

The Zeal of Mattathias

The courageous faith of Mattathias, head of the entire family of Maccabees, in killing the Jewish fellow who was willing to offer pagan sacrifice (v. 24) as well as the royal messenger (v. 25), mirrored the zeal of the priest Phinehas (v. 26; see Num 25:8), who had also once killed someone in the act of grievously violating the covenant with God. In the prior case it was fornication and involvement in the fertility cults of Canaan, here more blatant idolatry. It is not murder that is recommended by these stories, but rather the willingness to place one's own life on the line for one's faith. One must be very careful in praising these biblical figures from another age lest so doing offers encouragement to any modern Christian who resorts to violence in expressing opposition to those who break the moral law. The murder of abortionists, for example, in our age must be thoroughly condemned because it arbitrarily takes God's judgment into human hands.

The Call to Resistance

The invitation of Mattathias to all who shared his zeal for the Lord (v. 29) met with surprising success. Many others were inspired to join him in the desert. Part of the rationale for their flight to the desert was an effort to reclaim the simple fervor of an earlier age in the wilderness. The importance of courageous example and personal witness has always been a significant element in religious communities. We follow the inspiration of religious leadership and often are willing to follow and imitate those who take clear stands against the culture of their days. In a very different context Francis of Assisi was a stellar model of peace and simplicity who has attracted others for centuries. Sometimes we are surprised by those who follow because we simply never know from mere externals the depth of the faith of others. That is also true of those around us at work, in the Christian assembly, or in the neighborhood. Hidden heroism can flourish from unexpected sources!

Antiphon (Year I)

Psalm 50:23b

To the upright I will show the saving power of God.

Psalm 50: The Faithful Assembly

The Lectionary has chosen this psalm because of its reference to God's call (v. 1) gathering faithful members of the covenant (v. 5) to fulfill their vows to the Most High (v. 14). This is precisely the summons of Mattathias in his response to the paganizing commands of the Hellenistic king. One's fidelity needs to be expressed externally at times by the witness of one's life, especially when confronted by the forces that oppose and reject our convictions. The witness of an entire community is more powerful than that of individuals.

The Refrain

The final verse of the psalm from which the refrain is taken offers a more extended description of the actions that are praised, namely, those who offer their praise as a sacrifice and work in the right way (v. 23). These are called "upright." To them is promised an experience of God's saving power that will extricate them from any oppression or persecution they encounter. How might we describe the "upright" today? Who from within our community stands tall in their witness to truth, justice, and compassion?

First Reading (Year II)

Revelation 5:1-10

The Lamb that was slain purchased us with his Blood from every nation.

The Scroll

The scroll with the seven seals (v. 1) would seem to be the heavenly book in which the destiny of the world and all parts thereof are written. The assumption is that all of history has a purpose and a final point of conclusion according to the will of God. The person found worthy to break the seals (v. 2) and open the scroll (v. 3) is the one who can initiate the events that will happen. The scroll is opened, not merely to share secret information, but to initiate what must still come to pass. Codices, that is, bound volumes of pages, only replaced scrolls after the beginning of the Christian era. We have a past, and we know it from our experiences. We believe that we have a future as well, and we look forward to its unfolding, but nothing can happen unless the scroll is opened! Imagine the distress of being frozen in this moment, especially if it were a period of persecution.

Thursday of the Thirty-Third Week in Ordinary Time

The Lamb

Many pieces of Israelite faith and history converge to create and explain this figure, including Israel's practice of offering "communion sacrifices" for reconciliation, the paschal lamb of Exodus (12:3), and the sacrifice of the Suffering Servant (Isa 53:7, 12). Multihorned (v. 6) for great power sufficient to become victorious over all the great beasts of creation, the gentle Lamb is paradoxically recognized as powerful enough to initiate the final victorious events of history. By being slain the Lamb has become the sacrifice that establishes atonement and reconciliation with God forever. This symbol of the lamb and the book of seven seals, often carved into the front altar panel of parish churches or depicted in stained glass, represent the sacrificial death and resurrection of Jesus, which alone brings human history to its final destiny.

Antiphon (Year II)

Revelation 5:10

The Lamb has made us a kingdom of priests to serve our God.

Psalm 149: Song of Victory

The hymn chosen as a response to the Lectionary's reading from the book of Revelation is Psalm 149, a song of exultation celebrating God's victory over all enemies. Because of its reference to vengeance (note that v. 7 is not included in the response), it was often the battle cry of various parties involved in the terrible religious wars of the sixteenth and seventeenth centuries. Its use in liturgy should caution and humble us, however, lest we falsely and foolishly presume to be the favored beneficiaries rather than the potential enemy objects of that final action of God.

The Refrain

The refrain is the last verse (v. 10) of the heavenly hymn of the twenty-four elders. They sing of God's salvation for those representatives from all tribes, languages, and nations (v. 9) that have become consecrated by the Lamb's blood into service as priests of the eternal heavenly liturgy. The refrain transforms this Israelite hymn into a song of Christian exultation. It is thus intended as consolation for all Christians suffering persecution by the evil forces of this world.

Gospel

Luke 19:41-44

If you only knew what makes for peace.

Literary Link

Luke's gospel follows the parable of the ten coins (vv. 11-27) with his account of the triumphant entrance into the city of Jerusalem (vv. 28-40, which is omitted from the daily readings of the Lectionary). That in turn is followed in Luke by the lament of Jesus over the resistance of the leadership of Jerusalem to his mission and message. This reference to the personal sorrow of Jesus is only found in Luke's gospel.

The Lament of Jesus

Like the prophet Elisha before him who wept over the evil actions and atrocities that the king of Damascus would inflict on the Israelites (2 Kgs 8:11-12), Jesus lamented the inability and the blindness of the city leaders who simply could not see or accept his summons to become part of God's kingdom (v. 41). The Jesus of Luke's gospel is not afraid to cry over ignorance and sin. It is important to universalize that action, for it includes Christ's sorrow over all sinners, not merely those of the Judea of his day. Unfortunately this passage has been misused in anti-Jewish rhetoric of the past, perhaps because its universal character was not recognized. Jesus cried over stubborn and rebellious humanity, not merely over Jerusalem.

The Roman Attack on Jerusalem

Once again the specific details of palisades, siege walls, destruction, and the murder of little children (vv. 43-44) could have been added to this gospel passage in retrospect after the terrible destruction of the city by the Romans in AD 69/70. The construction of the siege wall and the full range of terrors devised by the Romans at their conquest of Judea haunted Jews and Christians for years. The gospel seems eager to associate the death of Jesus with that massacre and annihilation. The futile rebellion of the political leaders of that time should never be presented as the end of Judaism. It is Paul who insisted, by way of contrast, that God's call and gifts to the Jewish people were irrevocable and eternal (Rom 11:29).

Friday of the Thirty-Third Week in Ordinary Time

First Reading (Year I)

1 Maccabees 4:36-37, 52-59

They celebrated the dedication of the altar and joyfully offered burnt offerings.

Hanukkah

This is the account of the origin of the Jewish feast of "Hanukkah/Dedication," which marked the occasion of the rededication of the temple in Jerusalem in December of 165/64 BC, the very date of Antiochus's earlier desecration of the temple by the erection of the detested idol (v. 54). The military victories of Judas Maccabeus thus achieved Jewish independence and provided the opportunity for the reestablishment of the sacrificial system (v. 56) and the redecoration of the temple (v. 57). This is the origin of the annual Jewish eight-day festival of Hanukkah each December (v. 59). Even in the Diaspora when Jews are scattered throughout the world, it is an occasion for their celebration of God's liberating presence in their midst. The feast is also an opportunity for Christians to offer greetings and good wishes to them and their families today. Our God is a God who always liberates his people from oppression on every level.

Reverence for God's Name

The people are described as having "praised Heaven, who had given them success" (v. 55). For the Jewish people of that day, this was a traditional manner of speaking that avoided the casual use of God's personal name. The reference illustrates their growing and deepening reverence for God's name over the years. By the last centuries before Christ, they preferred to say "Heaven" rather than "God," a practice even found in Matthew's gospel, which repeatedly speaks of "the kingdom of heaven." This insignificant and almost casual reference to the object of the festival's praise is a good moment to caution against our own contemporary American invocation of the divine name, often so casually and sometimes even flippantly! In the not too distant past, the men's Holy Name Society in parishes took an annual promise to avoid the misuse of God's name in profanity. In the face of reality, the ritual was a helpful reminder.

Antiphon (Year I)

1 Chronicles 29:13b

We praise your glorious name, O mighty God.

Response

The Lectionary has chosen to use as a response to the reading the magnificent hymn of praise attributed to King David (1 Chr 29:11-13) on the occasion of his great collection of wealth for the building of the temple. Having handed over to Solomon the detailed plans for this great temple (28:11-19), the First Book of Chronicles was clear in ascribing the existence of the temple to David's genius and piety. It is fitting, therefore, to reuse his words of praise in this liturgical account of the temple's rededication under Judas Maccabeus. Although not mentioned in the Lectionary's reading, the casual reference to the Persian coin "daric" (29:7) just prior to the words of David's prayer gives a hint as to the later date (fifth century BC) of the writing of this account in First Chronicles. Each age adds its own contribution to praise and thanksgiving. What do our age and our culture add?

The Refrain

The use of the word "God" in this refrain (v. 13) illustrates the earlier practice of Israelite prayer, which had less caution about referring to the divine name in prayer. Because of the repetition of the refrain, the congregation praises God five times in this liturgical acclamation of divine power. In the early church's pattern of prayer, they made sure that praise, thanksgiving, and humble sorrow for sin preceded any petitions for God's assistance. Praise should precede begging. One should reestablish friendship before asking for help.

First Reading (Year II)

Revelation 10:8-11

I took the small scroll and swallowed it.

The Second Open Scroll

This reading is taken from an experience of John that introduces the book's second series of visions. In contrast to the sealed scroll (5:1), which could only be opened by the Lamb, this smaller scroll is already open (v. 8) and reveals in greater detail the events that would constitute the last age. The endless duplications and repeated descriptions of the book militate against any easy application of the symbols to specific events in human history. Images are heaped one upon another to create a mood and to communicate a profound truth. This type of sacred literature is not a documentary but a foretaste of things yet to come as part of the paschal imperative of history. God has much to say about the dying and rising of our world.

Consuming the Revelation

Like the prophet Ezekiel so many centuries earlier (3:1-3), John the seer is commanded to eat the scroll offered to him by the angel (v. 9). The action is a primary image for integration and personal assimilation of the message. Eating the scroll is a way of affirming that we have made God's will our own. The message becomes the person and the person becomes the message! Initially sweet as a gift from God, but then sour and bitter as a difficult task to be performed in warning God's people (v. 10), the scroll changes its flavor. One could see a relationship between these verses in the book of Revelation and the sixth chapter of the Gospel of John where the Bread from heaven is both revelation (6:35) and the Eucharist (6:51). They both nourish the individual recipient. In a similar sense we modern worshipers at a parish Eucharist consume both the word of God and the Bread of Life as we listen and approach the altar table. Some messages console, but others disconcert. Some messages are bitter medicine that eventually heals and cures.

Antiphon (Year II)

Psalm 119:103a

How sweet to my taste is your promise!

Psalm 119: God's Word: A Delight to Receive

Once again the Lectionary reverts to a portion of Psalm 119 for a response to this account of eating the message of God. The verses from the psalm list a litany of the many types of divine commands and instructions. They also describe the sheer delight (v. 14) of the faithful in accepting them and taking them to heart. Some commands are easier to accept than others. If we agree with a command, do we really ever "obey" it? Would we not become partners and colleagues in the action rather than servants or subordinates?

The Refrain

The promises of God are sweeter than honey (v. 103) to the first taste, even if they become burdensome later as a person attempts to put them into practice against the current of peer pressure, cultural opposition, or the personal cost of discipleship. Our own contemporary language speaks of "sweet/bitter words" and of being "sweet-talked" into doing something. "Sweet" is often falsely considered less substantial/nourishing.

Gospel

Luke 19:45-48

You have made it a den of thieves.

Literary Link

The triumphant entrance of Jesus into Jerusalem (vv. 28-40) is immediately followed by his weeping over the city (vv. 41-44) and his courageous witness in cleansing the temple of all the merchants (vv. 45-48). The combination of human sorrow and prophetic action mark this transition from the teaching ministry of Jesus to his passion.

Friday of the Thirty-Third Week in Ordinary Time

Cleansing the Temple for Prayer

Luke's description of the final act of Jesus in purifying the temple at the very beginning of Holy Week does not mention the violent actions described in Matthew (21:12-13) and Mark (11:15-17): the use of the rope as a whip or his overturning the tables of sellers and money changers. Prayer continues to be a major theme in this Gospel of Luke, and the issue of prayer even appears during his dramatic confrontation with the merchants in the temple, whatever they may have been selling. Authentic prayer is not some sort of crass exchange of goods with God in a *do ut des* ("I give so that you may give") proposition. Prayer, rather, is a humble stance before God who knows what we need even before we do. The posture already is the prayer, long before any petition can be articulated. The great masters of Christian prayer insist on removing the chatter of inner distractions and on quieting our minds before beginning true prayer. As one pastor used to quip, "Silent prayer begins when the coughing stops!"

Temple Presence

The daily presence of Jesus in the temple for the purpose of teaching (v. 47) is correlated to the hunger of God's people for the Word and for divine instruction. In a striking image the people are described as "hanging on his words" (v. 48). Within Luke's gospel, the crowds seem to gather wherever Jesus appears or travels. Like the nourishing honey of John's scroll in the reading from the book of Revelation (10:10), the words of Jesus meet the spiritual needs of his people. One might easily deduce some thoughts about the obligation of contemporary preachers to offer nourishment of Word and sacrament for those who come to the daily parish Eucharist. Devotional sweet talk alone is not a healthy diet. The essential task of the ancient Israelite priest was to teach the will of God (Jer 18:18). In this activity Jesus demonstrates the priestly character of his ministry.

Saturday of the Thirty-Third Week in Ordinary Time

First Reading (Year I)

1 Maccabees 6:1-13

On account of the evils I did in Jerusalem,
I am dying in bitter grief.

Reaping the Fruits

The Lectionary concludes a week of readings from First Maccabees with the death of King Antiochus Epiphanes IV, scourge of the Jewish people of God, humiliated by defeat in Persia (v. 4), and overcome by sorrow at the success of the Maccabees. The king learns that his armies had been rebuffed everywhere (v. 6) and that the temple had been rebuilt and purified for worship of the Lord (v. 7). To remain merely on the level of human history, choices have consequences; harsh decisions evoke similar harshness from those negatively impacted by our acts of oppression or persecution. It is a fact of human relations that we reap as we sow. This axiom is true within family relations as well as in commerce and industry. A wise person knows this truth and acts accordingly.

Punishment for Sin

Surrounded by his circle of "Friends" (v. 10), namely, those granted that royal title of honor, Antiochus recognized that he was reaping the fruit of his sinful determination to destroy the inhabitants of Judah (v. 12). He died in bitter grief in the foreign land of Persia. The author of First Maccabees was a teacher of morality and used the life of the king to demonstrate the sorrow that eventually comes to those who dare defy the Living God and his chosen people. Thus on the moral level as well as the historical, God works within the currents of human events and punishes sin. Actions are wrong, not simply because God says so, but because they eventually harm and hurt those who choose them. We thus return to the ancient covenant morality embraced by the Deuteronomic school: fidelity is eventually blessed and sin is ultimately cursed (Deut 5:9-10).

Antiphon (Year I)

Psalm 9:16a

I will rejoice in your salvation, O Lord.

Psalm 9: Promises Come to Fulfillment

Although this psalm is often designated as a song of praise for victories achieved, the future tense of the initial verses chosen by the Lectionary (vv. 2-3) suggests that the psalm describes a vow at the beginning of battle, with complete confidence that one's action would be victorious. The destruction of wicked enemies (vv. 4 and 6) might be seen as a forgone conclusion once God promises to protect and defend his people. This sequence illustrates the power of temple prophets who speak in the name of God and offer assurance to God's faithful people. One is reminded of the visitation and of the blessing spoken by Elizabeth to Mary for believing that "what was spoken to you by the Lord would be fulfilled" (Luke 1:45). This psalm, therefore, would seem to be the perfect response to the announcement of the death of King Antiochus as reported in the reading from First Maccabees.

Salvation

The Hebrew word for salvation, and also therefore the Hebrew meaning of the name of Jesus, refers literally to deliverance from some "tight spot" historically or emotionally. Freedom from the king's harsh penalties for obedience to the Torah would have constituted just such a deliverance from the humanly impossible situation faced by the people of Israel at that time. The actual word "salvation" is found in verse 15, rather than in verse 16 as noted in the Lectionary's citation. The refrain links today's congregation to all those who, like the Israelites of the second century BC, courageously face discrimination or persecution for their faith. We, like those before us, know that God will prevail.

FIRST READING (YEAR II)

Revelation 11:4-12

These two prophets tormented the inhabitants of the earth.

Two Witnesses

This vision of the two mysterious figures called olive trees, lamp stands (v. 4), witnesses/martyrs (v. 3), and prophets (v. 10) is inserted between the sixth and seventh trumpets. Some scholars claim that they represent the royal figure of Zerubbabel and the priestly figure of Joshua at the time of the rebuilding of the temple after the Babylonian exile. A more likely interpretation, however, would simply have them as two mutually confirming persons who testify to God's works, are killed by enemies (v. 7), and rise again by God's power after three and a half days (v. 11). Thus they prefigured and, at least in the minds of Christians, shared the death and resurrection of the Great Witness, Jesus the Christ. The word "*martur*/witness" had not as yet become the technical "martyr" put to death for his or her faith. It still served as a symbol for all who testify to their faith amid scorn and persecution. This is the call of every Christian in every age. We support each other, two by two, in this vocation that is rooted in our baptism.

The Beast

The visions of John refer to the "beast . . . from the abyss" (v. 7). The description is very generic and seems to refer to the final adversary of the end time, whoever that may turn out to be. That such a figure will rise from the pit of evil to engage in definitive battle with the forces of God was assumed by the early Christians who eagerly awaited Christ's return. The people of John's day were convinced of the ultimate victory of the God who summoned the two witnesses to heaven in a cloud of glory (v. 12). The hostile adversaries of faithful people today may or may not be the final figures in God's war with evil. That information remains known to God alone (Mark 13:32). At all times, however, evil should be resisted, says John, with all the vigor of truth, holiness, and justice!

ANTIPHON (YEAR II)

Psalm 144:1b

Blessed be the Lord, my Rock!

Psalm 144: Divine Victory

As noted elsewhere, this psalm has been associated with David's victory over Goliath. The reference to hands and fingers trained for war (v. 1), the ten-stringed lyre (v. 9), and royal victory over the sword (v. 10) may have suggested the attribution. The verses quoted are primarily an expression of praise for the protection given to those who fight successfully against great odds because of God's victorious presence. So often in history, God has chosen the weak and improbable in order to make it perfectly clear that victory is ultimately God's alone.

God as Rock

Perhaps it was indeed the poetic genius of David that first associated the Lord with the mighty rocks and mountains of Judah (v. 1), but the reference is logical, especially when one has been privileged to visit the land and to see the actual terrain surrounding Jerusalem and Zion, the City of David. High, impregnable, and associated with the mysterious heavenly dwelling of God, any mountain became a ready symbol for the mighty God, who was in fact called "*Shaddai*/mountain" by early Israelites (Gen 17:1). The power of God is beyond all human description, but we still stretch for images from our limited experience to convey the ultimate divine reality.

GOSPEL

Luke 20:27-40

He is not God of the dead, but of the living.

Literary Link

The Lectionary chooses to omit the controversy over the authority of Jesus (20:1-

8), the parable of the tenant farmers (vv. 9-19), and the question of taxes to Caesar (vv. 20-26), thus moving directly from the cleansing of the temple (19:45-48) to the controversy with the Sadducees over resurrection (20:27-40). Perhaps the Lectionary simply wished to link the cleansing of the dwelling of the Living God with the conclusion suggested by Jesus (v. 39)—namely, that the God of Abraham is the God of the living!

Resurrection and the Sadducees

The membership of this affluent political and religious group was formed from the elitist priestly class in Jerusalem. They were committed to belief in the written text of the Scriptures, but refused to believe anything not found in the *Torah*/Pentateuch (first five books of the Bible attributed to Moses). Their rivals and opponents, the Pharisees, however, accepted oral tradition and did not feel bound to the letter of Scriptures alone. Because the Torah does not explicitly mention resurrection, the Sadducees were opposed to that teaching as held by the Pharisees. Our day and age seems to have an abundance of modern Christians who share similar doubts. The text provides an opportunity to address that fundamental tenet of Christianity.

The Argument

When the Sadducees posed the question of resurrection in its most absurd terms, that is, the marriage of one woman to a succession of seven brothers without children (vv. 28-31; based on the teaching of Deut 25:5-10), Jesus promptly reframed the question as he did so often. Jesus spoke out of his own personal relationship and referred to the God of the living and the dead (v. 38). In his reference to the words of God at the burning bush (v. 37; referring to Exod 3:6), Jesus thus found a subtle instruction about resurrection among the teachings of the Pentateuch itself. He won the day and as a result the Sadducees no longer dared to ask him anything (v. 40). The praise of the scribes (v. 39), a group often associated with the Pharisees, was an important victory for Jesus in his final debates with the religious leadership of Jerusalem. Not every member of those groups was hostile to Jesus.

Monday of the Thirty-Fourth, or Last Week in Ordinary Time

First Reading (Year I)

Daniel 1:1-6, 8-20

None were found equal to Daniel, Hananiah, Mishael, and Azariah.

The Book of Daniel

Written by an unknown author, the book is attributed to a young Jewish hero who lived in Babylon during the exile. The tales, crafted to catechize the Jewish practice of faith and the visions describing the end time, were intended to provide encouragement and consolation for faithful Jews living under the terrible persecutions of Antiochus Epiphanes IV. Thus a second-century-BC apocalyptic writing about contemporaneous events was retrojected back some four centuries to make it seem like prophecy.

Vegetables

Beside the terrifying visions in the book of Daniel (7:1–12:13), we also find some delightful tales almost certainly shaped for young children or for relatively uninstructed adults (possibly an early Jewish equivalent of RCIA). In this reading the young men chosen for royal court service are described as attractive, "intelligent and wise, quick to learn, and prudent" (v. 4). They chose not to eat the unclean/unkosher diet of the royal table, but only vegetables and water (v. 12). Much to everyone's surprise, they flourished so well that they not only stood out above the rest (v. 15) but also were far wiser than their pagan colleagues (v. 20). The point is that total obedience to God's will brings natural and spiritual rewards! The story might even be useful for encouraging youngsters to eat their spinach!

Fidelity under Persecution

At a deeper level the tale offers encouragement to be faithful to one's religious practices, even in the most hostile social settings where religious rituals or regulations are mocked and dismissed. The fidelity of these young men, especially at an age when peer pressure is so strong, was richly blessed by God's abundant natural gifts (v. 20). These four young men become heroes of faith and models of Jewish wisdom, richly rewarded by the king because of their outstanding abilities. Compliance with the instruction of God brings wisdom tenfold and gives evidence of God's wisdom (Deut 4:6). Our contemporary Western secularism easily dismisses certain religious practices as foolish and an utter waste of time. These four young fellows claim otherwise.

Antiphon (Year I)

Daniel 3:52b

Glory and praise for ever!

The Responsorial Hymn

The Lectionary has chosen as a response to the vegetable story the canticle of the three young men from a different catechetical tale. These three (called Shadrach, Meshach, and Abednego) had been condemned by King Nebuchadnezzar to a fiery furnace for refusing to worship the king's royal idols (Dan 3:1-97). They were completely untouched by the flames, however, and from the midst of the fire blessed the God of Israel forever. Still a tale for children, the chapter ends by noting that even the king himself was transformed by the miracle (v. 95). Remember that Nebuchadnezzar was the king of Babylon who had ordered the destruction of Jerusalem in 586 BC. History is changed in these stories for the purposes of religious instruction.

Praise

The repeated sixfold reference to praise for God, even from the difficult situation of severe punishment, suggested that praise for God should be on our lips in every human circumstance, joyful or painful! Like Job from the depth of his misery, we also can say, "The Lord gave and the Lord has taken away; / blessed be the name of the Lord!" (Job 1:21). Note in previewing the rest of the week's liturgies that different creatures will be chosen to praise God in subsequent days of this week. Today's response concentrates on heavenly realities associated with God's eternal throne of glory.

First Reading (Year II)

Revelation 14:1-3, 4b-5

His name and his Father's name are written on their foreheads.

Names on Foreheads

One of the ancient ways to label slaves was to brand the names of their owners on their foreheads (v. 1). It was intended to be a public and irremovable indication of ownership, possession, and correspondingly human service and devotion. Curiously contemporary society seems to have no qualms about accepting a permanent tattoo of the word "Mother" or the initials of a loved one on an arm or shoulder. Accepting and proudly displaying the name of the Lamb (v. 1) and his heavenly Father was understood as a permanent public expression of personal commitment to God. It was also a profession of one's participation in the new creation. At a modern baptism the cross is traced on the forehead of each infant or adult candidate. At confirmation we are anointed with chrism in that same sign. Every time that we trace the sign of the cross on our foreheads at the beginning of the proclamation of the gospel at Mass, therefore, we renew that allegiance and acknowledge that "ownership."

Symbolic Mystery of Numbers

Sometimes numbers mean more than they mean. One and one, for example, mean two, but when combined into "two by two" they also suggest cooperation and even mutual verification in witness (Deut 17:6) as the gospels indicate (Matt 18:16). The 144,000 (v. 1) is clearly a symbolic number: three (the Hebrew superlative as in "holy, holy, holy") times four (universality as in the four directions) times a thousand (symbolic for a large number) squared conveys a very large number of people who now praise God in a new and previously unheard fashion. Twelve evokes the memory of the twelve chosen tribes of Israel, greatly increased in the last age. Even that is only the firstfruits of all those human beings who are close to God. Elsewhere in the book a "great multitude, which no one could count" (Rev 7:9), also gathers before the throne of God. One should be very cautious about interpreting any of these numbers as if they were intended to restrict the numbers of those chosen by God. The explanatory notes required for any Bible translation approved for Catholics (indicated by the mention of the *imprimatur* behind the book's title page) help the modern reader to understand the ancient world, its practices and its method of speech.

Spiritual Training for Sacred Music

Those sealed are able to sing the new song because they have not been tarnished by deceit (v. 5) or by the all too human (and in fact sinful) fudging of truth in their lives. The fuller original text also makes reference to chastity (v. 4), but the liturgical text focuses on deceit. The ultimate choir practice for the hymns of heaven is moral as well as vocal. Rarely, it would seem, do contemporary preachers speak about the sin of deceit in business, educational testing, or family life. One can't sing praise for God, however, if one's tongue is accustomed to untruth.

The Music of the Next Age

The music of heaven is beyond mere human description or comparison. Here harp music is cleverly described as rushing waters or distant rolling thunder across the skies (v. 2). The special cadences of a harp were often chosen as background for the festive banquets of the wealthy. That sound with its cultural backdrop became the music of preference for the final heavenly supper of the Lamb. One wonders if this bit of historical trivia might be the origin for the popular notion of harps in heaven. Perhaps more to the point, however, the book of Revelation indulges in the richness of poetry, heaping up image upon image to suggest an existence far beyond our limited earthly human experience.

ANTIPHON (YEAR II)

Psalm 24:6

Lord, this is the people that longs to see your face.

Torah Liturgy

As noted elsewhere, Psalm 24 was originally used as an examination of conscience at the entrance to a sanctuary (v. 3). It describes people eagerly desiring an encounter with God in worship and praise (v. 6). That very desire, deep and heartfelt, marks people who recognize a need for God in their lives and who know the blessings of friendship with the Living God. The same phrase, "longing to see God's face," can be fittingly applied to those who regularly attend weekday Eucharists at the parish.

Monday of the Thirty-Fourth, or Last Week in Ordinary Time

Community at Prayer

The fact that the antiphon speaks of a "people"/race (v. 6) rather than the individual reminds us that we are primarily united with others when we pray. In the eyes of the ancient biblical world (and the Catholic tradition) the social bond and membership in a family or tribe surfaces as the primary characteristic of everyone who enters the celebration of the church's worship by baptism. Each individual person is always and everywhere a member of the One Body of Christ.

GOSPEL

Luke 21:1-4

He noticed a poor widow putting in two small coins.

Literary Link

The Lectionary chooses to omit the debate regarding the title "son of David" (20:41-44) and the following warning against the leaven/attitude of some of the Pharisees (vv. 45-47). We move immediately, therefore, to the story of the poor but generous widow (21:1-4). Perhaps the intent is to offer a liturgical contrast between the widow bereft of seven husbands (20:30) and the generous widow at the entrance to the temple. The Lectionary has chosen to tell two widow stories in sequence, one on Saturday and one on Monday.

Relativity of All Gifts

"More" is a very relative term (v. 3), both in terms of its numerical "less" and in terms of its relationship to the person about whom it is said. In this case it signifies an enormous gift for the poor widow, namely, her entire livelihood (v. 4). Many gifts, such as a crudely drawn card from a youngster, may be without value on the market, but precious and worthy of keeping as a treasured heirloom by a doting parent or grandparent. Price tags often say very little about an object's ultimate value, which is rooted in the love of the donor, not the object itself. We also know of lavish gifts given thoughtlessly and without any forethought. God knows us to the core of our being and therefore appreciates the real value (to ourselves) of anything we give.

The "Poor" Box

Today when approaching the ruins of the Western Wall of the temple in Jerusalem to pray, as is the custom of Jewish residents or pilgrims, one encounters a "poor box" for donations. There the label is not "charity," however, as we might expect, but simply "*tzedeqah*/justice." This gift is not aimed at our narrow Western notion of justice understood as the repayment of debts, but rather reflects the larger biblical concept of the restoration of right relationships throughout the entire world. Any pilgrimage or visit to a holy place, even if familiar and merely around the corner at the parish church, should always have that larger picture of God's purpose in mind.

Tuesday of the Thirty-Fourth, or Last Week in Ordinary Time

First Reading (Year I)

Daniel 2:31-45

The God of heaven will set up a kingdom that shall never be destroyed and shall put an end to all these kingdoms.

Dreams

Because of Daniel's faith and faithfulness to God, he was given the power to interpret the mysterious realm of dreams (v. 36). In the ancient world dreams were presumed to be ways in which God communicated with human beings (v. 45). Some daydreams may simply be our hopes for the future. Today we may understand night dreams as "revelations" in a different sense, not from God so much as from our inner subconscious hopes and fears. There exist areas of life beyond the mere physical that only the greater insight of wisdom and faith can see. At the same time, because we believe in the incarnation, God can use our sentiments to reveal us to ourselves!

History in Retrospect

Classical apocalyptic prophets like Daniel love to recount and judge the sequence of historical kingdoms. They use secret symbols to convey negative judgments lest grievous punishment be meted out for political treason or insurrection. That type of "prophet" also retrojected present reality into the minds and mouths of past heroes in order to present it as if in prophecy. In today's reading the various successive world empires are described as parts of a single statue comprised of differing elements, namely, gold, silver, bronze, iron, and clay tile, each having less value and declining inner chemical cohesion. This is the origin of the phrase "feet of clay" (see v. 41) to describe an empire inherently weak and unstable. The stone that shatters (v. 34) is the power of God choosing a simple nation like Israel under the Maccabees to destroy all the great empires. God uses history for his purposes. These verbal pictures might be equivalent to modern political cartoons in which certain characteristics become the defining mark of prominent figures such as presidents, senators, or more local political figures. To those who recognize the caricature, the communication and its judgments are very clear. This is challenging to modern readers, however, who may not share the explanatory code of the ancient world. Once again, for Catholics the footnotes are often essential. Because historical figures are also representative, the Word is also about us!

Antiphon (Year I)

Daniel 3:59b

Give glory and eternal praise to him.

The Canticle of Daniel

The Lectionary has chosen to use the hymn of praise attributed to Daniel as the responsorial psalm for each of the readings from Daniel selected for the entire final week of Year I. Yesterday's theme for the responsorial song was the many places worthy of praise, such as the heavens, temple, throne, or firmament, because they were made holy by God's presence. Today the elements invited to praise God are heavenly creatures such as angels (v. 58), heavens (v. 59), heavenly waters (v. 60), and "hosts," the starry angelic armies (v. 61).

Heavenly Hymns

It may be helpful to note that the portion of Scriptures chosen for the final week of Year II is the book of Revelation, which contains over a dozen different hymns of praise for the power and majesty of God. Usually some type of heavenly power is associated with those hymns in order to suggest their supranatural character and their origin from beyond human history. In choosing the extended hymn of praise from the book of Daniel as the responsorial for Year I, the

Lectionary thus ends both liturgical years with hymns of praise. Subtly, therefore, the liturgy also associates the mysterious purpose of these two books (Daniel and Revelation), and unites all expressions of praise, whether in heaven or on earth, with our eucharistic worship.

Tuesday of the Thirty-Fourth, or Last Week in Ordinary Time

First Reading (Year II)

Revelation 14:14-19

The time to reap has come, because the earth's harvest is fully ripe.

The Son of Man

The central actor in this passage is someone associated with divinity (white cloud), in a distinctively human shape and form, with royal crown (*stephanos*), and the agricultural tool/weapon of a person reaping a harvest (v. 14). The ancient pharaohs of Egypt were often pictured with the harvesting flail in hand as a symbol of their ultimate authority and ownership. The use of the title "son of man" here (v. 14) could be assumed to refer to Jesus, since he is remembered as having often used that title in the gospels (Mark 2:10; etc.). The reference is unclear, however, because the next verse refers to "another angel"/messenger (v. 15). Heavenly messengers of God regularly assumed human form for communication with our world. As a matter of fact God uses every human method of communication except deceit. Nevertheless, for early Christians Jesus was the paragon and full expression of God's word by which all other messengers were measured. In this type of literature there remains some deliberate obscurity to convey the ultimately mysterious nature of God and God's dealings with our world.

Reaping the Harvest

As experienced farmers know, fields usually come to readiness for harvest one at a time. Many factors need to be taken into consideration in making a judgment to reap: the ripeness of the grain, the dryness of the crop (lest mildew ruin everything in the barn), and the day's weather. These are some of the issues that determine whether it is the hour/right time (v. 15) for harvesting. God's considerations, however, are moral, not meteorological. If the son of man is commanded (v. 15) to begin reaping the entire universal harvest of "wheat," the whole world has come to its "time," literally its "hour," of productivity, judgment, and accountability. Imagine the utter finality and import of the phrase "the earth was harvested." This is divinely accomplished with one single, majestic divine swing of the sickle (v. 16). The issue of accountability is inherent in viewing the final age of the world as a great harvest. There is a God, and he is not of our making. There is an end time, and it is not under our control.

Antiphon (Year II)

Psalm 96:13b

The Lord comes to judge the earth.

Judging the Earth

Curiously, the verb "judge" is found in the antiphon but not in the translation of the psalm verses selected by the Lectionary for this day. The verb "*shaphat*/judge" is in fact used twice in the psalm's final verse (v. 13). In our contemporary notion of judging, we have separated the legislative, executive, and judicial functions of government. For us judging, therefore, primarily refers to making decisions about legality, culpability, or the rightness of competing claims. The ancient world of Israel, however, assumed that one takes action when judging, intervenes to save the oppressed, and moves to establish right relationships once more. That was the role of the ancient judges of Israel. For the people of Israel God is always one who steps into the fray of human conflict to resolve the issues by his decisive divine action.

Joyful Response

Rather than reacting with fear or anxiety, all of creation is described as sharing festive delight in the arrival of the God of mercy and justice. Heavens are glad and earth rejoices (v. 11). All material creatures are delighted by God's interventions. In almost Disney-like happiness, the very seas, plains, and trees (v. 12) sing out their joy. All of creation is imagined as fully involved in a common canticle of praise.

GOSPEL

Luke 21:5-11

There will not be left a stone upon another stone.

Literary Link

The gospel editor has decided to move from the story of the generous widow at the temple gate's poor box (v. 1) to a consideration of the temple's physical beauty (v. 5) especially after the lavish renovation by Herod. That in turn was also logically connected to the realization of the temple's imminent destruction by the Romans (v. 6). The final expression of that sad prophecy may have been colored by the reality that had already occurred before Luke's gospel was written.

Stone upon Stone

In densely populated urban areas most buildings were built of hand-sized mud bricks or rough fieldstones of which Israel and Judah had plenty. The temples built by Solomon and later modestly rebuilt after the exile before being grandly expanded by Herod, however, were built of massive blocks of dressed stone, carefully cut and trimmed from nearby limestone quarries in the Judean hills. Herod's work was beautiful and costly (v. 5). Those immense blocks had been thrown down by the Babylonians in 586 BC. They would be treated similarly by the Romans in AD 69 (v. 6). At the time Luke's gospel was written and read, the Roman destruction had already occurred, and its evidence strewn across the devastated temple mound. What had seemed preposterously impossible, had happened. What could such a disaster mean? Generations of Jewish scholars and rabbis pondered that terrible catastrophe in subsequent centuries. Tragedy, individual or communal, always seeks meaning.

Not Immediately the End

Virtually every conceivable natural and political disaster is listed, including wars, revolutions, earthquakes, famines, and plagues (v. 11). These catastrophes inevitably signal the end of the world as its victims had known it. In an ancient world filled with anxiety over the impending end of the entire universe, each disaster seemed to be the final musical coda for the world. Jesus insisted, however, that such were not necessarily the immediate signals of the end, but merely part of the world's rhythm of collapsing natural order. Those biblical literalists who check off famines in China or earthquakes in Pakistan as sure signs of the immediate end seem to ignore the caution of Jesus to the effect that "it will not immediately be the end" (v. 9). Such alarmists become themselves counter to the Bible they cite so ominously because they do not understand the difference between different types of biblical literature. It was the Jesus of both the gospels of Mark (13:32) and Matthew (24:36) who reminded his disciples that only the Father knows "the day or the hour"!

Wednesday of the Thirty-Fourth, or Last Week in Ordinary Time

First Reading (Year I)

Daniel 5:1-6, 13-14, 16-17, 23-28

The fingers of a human hand appeared, writing on the plaster of the wall.

The Emperor's Idolatrous Feast

This tale of Belshazzar's feast contains the type of repetition often characteristic of children's literature, as, for example, in the phrases describing the groups present (vv. 2, 3, 23) and the contemptuous types of gods praised by the banqueters (vv. 4, 24). The exotic lavishness of the scene is heightened by the repetition in order to prepare for the drama of the mysterious message. For children's instruction, the tale insists that everyone, even the greatest of kings, is called to task and punished for disobedience to the will of God. The worship of false gods is not acceptable, no matter what the context or who the instigator!

Writing on the Wall

Because of the king's drunken irreverence in using the stolen sacred vessels of the temple (v. 2), he is judged harshly. This is the origin of another familiar and common phrase, "the writing on the wall," which some can read, and others cannot. The three mysterious verbs *mene*, *tekel*, and *peres* (v. 25) are known from other languages related to Hebrew or Aramaic. In particular, for example, *mene* means to count, and *tekel* means to weigh. The latter is the same Semitic root word from which comes the word "shekel," a weight of metal worth a certain value and therefore a coin. Similarly *peres* is related to the root word from which comes the title Pharisee, the group separated from the common folks by their piety and devotion to God's will. The full meaning of the message would therefore refer to the king and his reign being counted, weighed, and separated off (see vv. 25-28)! Although initially applied to the Babylonian king, the mysterious message could also sum up the final judgment given by God to each individual evildoer throughout all of human history.

Antiphon (Year I)

Daniel 3:59b

Give glory and eternal praise to him.

The Canticle of Daniel

In today's responsorial hymn we move into a list of those created realities that come from the heavenly spheres to affect our lives: sun and moon (v. 62), stars (v. 63), showers and dew (v. 64), winds (v. 65), fire and heat (v. 66), and cold and chill (v. 67). Perhaps this litany was the biblical source behind the "Canticle of Saint Francis of Assisi." In any case it is good to remember that all these realities, whether welcome or received with disappointments, are creatures that praise God by being precisely what they are.

Harvest Powers

Each of the creatures mentioned in this portion of Daniel's hymn makes its contribution to the fertility of the earth and the fruitfulness of its annual harvest. Each element praises and exults God forever because God had promised Noah that the cycle of "seedtime and harvest, / cold and heat, / Summer and winter, / and day and night" would last forever (Gen 8:22).

First Reading (Year II)

Revelation 15:1-4

They sang the song of Moses and the song of the Lamb.

Signs

The book of Revelation is filled with descriptions of "signs." The word itself signals something visible that gives evidence of something far greater and more profound—such as popular expressions referring to the "signs" of spring or the "signs" of anger or the "signs" of love. Here the seven bowls of plague (v. 1) are the evidence of God's anger at the evilness in the world. The ancient world knew only too well the sudden deadly devastation of the bubonic or black plague that could wipe out an entire city virtually overnight. Still, the fact that the signs of Revelation are seen in heaven suggests a divine origin and a consoling assurance that God remains in control, no matter what happens! We should be very careful, however, not to assume or suggest, as a few recent TV evangelists have foolishly done, that any contemporary outbreak of disease is automatically divine punishment. The author has chosen this symbol for the end time because of its sense of individual finality.

The Fiery Sea of Glass

The waters of the sea were frightening to nomads from the desert, wildly turbulent at times, and often with a very dangerous undertow. They easily became a symbol for seductive and destructive evil. Like all evil, the frozen fiery glass sea is an inner contradiction. This final sea is permeated by the fire of divine purification, solidified and permanently stilled to allow the holy ones to stand upon its surface as a sign of their victory over evil (v. 2). Does the way in which Jesus walked on waters (Matt 14:25) indicate some anticipated reference to the last age and his victory over evil?

ANTIPHON (YEAR II)

Revelation 15:3b

Great and wonderful are all your works,
Lord, mighty God!

Psalm 98: Waters of Praise

Among the verses chosen from Psalm 98's hymn of praise for God's victory (v. 1) are those that celebrate the way in which the sea and the rivers (vv. 7-8) clap and rejoice. The same waters described as sufficiently solid enough for people to stand upon them in the passage from Revelation (15:2) are now melted in the psalm and transformed into choruses of praise. The sheer poetry of the reading from the book of Revelation and the psalm is used here to celebrate the joy of a creation finally freed from the effects of evil. The world is finally able to enter the cosmic hymn of praise when the Lord's kingly rule is established forever.

The Refrain

The refrain is chosen not from the psalm but from the first line of the heavenly hymn (15:3). If all of God's works are indeed wonderful (v. 3), how much more wonderful is their Creator? Again and again the book of Revelation gives evidence of offering comfort and hope to those who may be suffering persecution and oppression. Such difficult events are not the last word; God will achieve and assert the final victory of his justice and peace.

GOSPEL

Luke 21:12-19

You will be hated by all because of my name, but
not a hair on your head will be destroyed.

Literary Link

Among the roles ascribed to Jesus of Nazareth was that of an eschatological prophet, namely, one who announced the final age in the unfolding history of the world. The themes of such an announcement were traditional, and included the end of each level of existence. The natural disasters and international upheavals described in yesterday's portion of the final days of Jesus' teaching in Jerusalem (vv. 10-11) now logically lead to more local disruptions within families when members hand each other over to civil authorities for punishment.

Persecution

Persecutions and opposition seem inevitable, even in response to the Good News of the gospel (v. 12). Paul reminds us that it is "only through tribulations that one enters the kingdom of God" (see Acts 14:22). Often the opposition comes from the fact that a new Christian must sever social bonds with colleagues in his or her occupation who were accustomed to participation in various pagan temple rituals. This social separation resulted in marginalization and distancing of former friends. The rejection of the new Christian from society, and the related charge of atheism, especially from members of one's own family (v. 16), was unfounded, unfair, and isolating. The heartache of broken families was acknowledged by Jesus when he spoke of his coming, not for initial peace, but for division (Luke 12:51). A wise disciple of Jesus counts the consequences of his or her action beforehand (Luke 14:28-33). Nevertheless, sometimes all we can do is hand the sorrow over to the God who cares even more than we do.

Witness

One of the unexpected blessings of persecution is its opportunity to give witness/*marturion* (v. 13) to God's work in the world and to divine goodness. God can bring good, even out of pain and difficulty, for those who love the Lord (Rom 8:28). We are invited to give witness with utter confidence. There's a grace to allowing God's Spirit to do the talking rather than worrying about mere human defense of our actions or beliefs (v. 14). To qualify for the grace of speaking without preparation or forethought, however, one must be so attuned to the will of God as to be truly God's Friend. One of the great apostolic virtues was "*parresia*/boldness," which enabled early believers to speak clearly and forthrightly about their faith in Christ as did Peter at Pentecost (Acts 2:29).

Death and Salvation

There's an obvious paradox in the mysterious contrast between being put to physical death, but without a hair of one's head destroyed (v. 18). Faith makes the difference and enables one to move from life to Life. In continuity with the Lord's own death and resurrection, the faithful disciple endures even physical death with a spirit of enduring confidence that he or she will receive a share in the life of the next age. At the turning of the millennium in AD 2000, ecumenical lists of modern martyrs were compiled throughout the world in acknowledgment of those who suffered for God's peace and justice.

Thursday of the Thirty-Fourth, or Last Week in Ordinary Time

First Reading (Year I)

Daniel 6:12-28

My God has sent his angel and closed the lions' mouths.

Divine Protection

This tale of Daniel in the lion's den describes a royal punishment reluctantly meted out for Daniel's refusal to obey the royal edict and to offer idolatrous worship only to the king (vv. 15-17). The penalty was occasioned by the denunciation made by jealous officials who sought to bring Daniel down in power and to destroy him. The story was told to offer encouragement to Jewish people persecuted for their fidelity to God's law under the persecutions of Antiochus Epiphanes IV. Daniel was miraculously preserved by God, however, and remained "unhurt because he trusted in his God" (v. 24). In ironic justice the accusers themselves paid the price for what they had sought to pour out on Daniel's head when they were devoured by the same beasts (v. 25). It is divine justice that sees beyond the surface, knows all things, and eventually punishes the hidden designs of the hearts of the wicked.

Evangelization

Daniel's fidelity, even in the face of possible death, became the occasion of a sort of "evangelization," when King Darius of Persia proclaimed the God of Daniel and ordered reverence from the entire kingdom (vv. 27-28). We never know what action of ours, whether heroic or seemingly insignificant, may catch the attention of others, elicit a positive response, and increase the numbers of the faithful. True evangelization encompasses our entire lives, not merely the words we may speak. The root meaning of the word "martyr" is to give witness. That includes every baptized follower of Jesus the Christ, the great witness (Rev 1:5).

Antiphon (Year I)

Daniel 3:59b

Give glory and eternal praise to him.

The Canticle of Daniel

Continuing the long litany of created creatures invited to join the eternal hymn of praise are still other elements from the weather each season: dew and rain (v. 68), frost and chill (v. 69), ice and snow (v. 70), days and nights (v. 71), light and darkness (v. 72), and lightning and clouds (v. 73). This is the sort of prayer that a person could recite every time he or she happens to look out a window and notices the weather of the moment. We notice reality around us, as did Saint Francis of Assisi, and we invite everything to sing God's praises. By its very existence, each element praises and glorifies the God who called it into existence for his purposes!

First Reading (Year II)

Revelation 18:1-2, 21-23; 19:1-3, 9a

Fallen is Babylon the great.

The Destruction of Pagan Rome

John, the visionary of the book of Revelation, and his entire community in Ephesus held the city of Rome and its powerful culture in contempt because of their pervasive idolatry. John's visions chose the ancient name of "Babylon" as a code word for the true object of their opposition (Rome) and predicted its total and final demise (v. 2). The stone-tossing angel (v. 21) had biblical precedent because centuries earlier Jeremiah had ordered that his final written condemnations of Babylon should be tied to a stone and thrown into the Euphrates River with the chant, "Thus shall Babylon sink. Never shall she rise" (Jer 51:64). Prophetic actions were understood to be the actual beginning of what they foretold. By this condemnation, every arrogantly evil political power is also promised eventual final judgment by God. In the past century alone we have witnessed the crumbling of Bolshevist Communism as well as countless totalitarian fascist governments. Similarly, America would not be immune from God's judgment if it traveled that idolatrous path.

Culture under Judgment

The verses chosen for proclamation in the day's liturgy include a list of cultural elements that are perceived as embodying a country's values. They all face judgment together with the nation's political and military leadership: musicians, craftspeople, agriculture and food producers (v. 22), artificial lighting, and even marriage festivities (v. 23). This announcement of condemned activities, all somehow tainted by idolatry, receives a hymn of praise and thanksgiving from the heavenly multitude (19:1-3). Christian faith is not intended to remain merely personal and private, but must enter the public forum to provide witness and to offer judgment on its surrounding culture. Parents and teachers should help young people and the entire general population to critique the world in which they live and work. The final goal, however, is not merely negative because God's victory is described as a joyous wedding of the Lamb with the new and heavenly Jerusalem (v. 9).

Thursday of the Thirty-Fourth, or Last Week in Ordinary Time

ANTIPHON (YEAR II)

Revelation 19:9a

Blessed are they who are called to the wedding feast of the Lamb.

Psalm 100: Pilgrimages and Processions

Psalm 100 provides the verses of the responsorial hymn, even though the refrain is taken from the text of Revelation (v. 9). The psalm seems to give clear evidence of its frequent and familiar use in temple processions. References to entering the gates (v. 4) and singing in the sacred courtyards make that plain. The psalm explicitly celebrates God's covenantal fidelity/*hesed* (v. 5). This responsorial hymn, therefore, could be understood as an extension of the heavenly song of praise that confirms God's judgment over Babylon and all its subsequent evil political reincarnations. It is almost as if the customary American "ticker tape parade" of victory has been recast into a liturgical procession into the temple.

Wedding Feast of the Lamb

The parables of Jesus often referred to the final messianic banquet as a wedding feast to which all are invited (Matt 22:1-14). That theme has been employed in these apocalyptic visions as a wedding of the victorious risen Lamb with the church to which faithfully persevering disciples are invited (19:9). The "wedding feast" phrase has become the antiphon of blessing for the final destruction of Babylon (Rome). Every Eucharist, even the most humble, is an anticipation of that final wedding and its celebration of divine victory! Every Eucharist looks backward to Christ's once-and-for-all victory on the cross, and forward to its final cosmic celebration.

GOSPEL

Luke 21:20-28

Jerusalem will be trampled underfoot by the Gentiles until the times of the Gentiles are fulfilled.

Literary Link

Luke's final eschatological discourse was probably written when the destruction of Jerusalem by the Romans in AD 70 had already occurred. The Lord's speech is described as logically concluding with attention to the city of Jerusalem itself (vv. 20-24). Evidence of the terror and tragedy of that exercise of Roman brutality (v. 23) was all around. The fall of the Holy City seemed a bitter echo of the destruction of Babylon predicted by Jeremiah and celebrated in the book of Revelation.

End-Time Prophecies

These apocalyptic sections that mark the conclusion of each of the Synoptic Gospels are important. They are the "Gospel for hard times," when the entire world seems oppressed by an evil storm of enormous magnitude, devastating and destructive. They signal, however, not the end of time in the last minutes of an athletic match, but the crucial play that determines without doubt the outcome of the match. Clarity about the different meanings of "end time" may be helpful to those at morning Mass. The discourse of Jesus promises the end of the evil empire, namely, a "time of punishment" (v. 22) for whatever evil political form may be assumed for our human government.

Encouragement

It may be helpful to remember that this discourse is primarily intended as an assurance of God's final victory over everything that has shown hostility of any kind to God's kingdom. The very force of the storm should encourage confident hope because the believer knows that God is even in the storm itself. The list of terrors is intended to communicate divine encouragement, not to inspire terror. God wins.

Friday of the Thirty-Fourth, or Last Week in Ordinary Time

First Reading (Year I)

Daniel 7:2-14

I saw one like a son of man coming,
on the clouds of heaven.

The Four Beasts

The fearful animals under the names of lion (v. 4), bear (v. 5), leopard (v. 6), and terrifying dragon (v. 7), each frightful in its appearance almost like a science fiction extravaganza and arising from the evil sea (v. 2), represent the successive major evil kingdoms of human history just prior to the Maccabean revolt (167 BC). Although the empires and their symbols have historical foundations, they are not presented in historically accurate portraits, but rather in poetic depictions. As the vision unfolds, each and all of the beasts are finally defeated by the appearance of someone in human form (v. 13) and of human origin (though under the providence of God). Beasts, horns, teeth, and claws, combined with arrogance, described the powers of the various earthly kingdoms opposed to God's sovereign authority. Initially terrifying, they are eventually revealed as pathetic figures of papier-mâché.

The Son of Man

There are two figures in this passage. First, the descriptive image of God is intended to suggest "One who is truly ancient," crowned with the white hair of the elderly (see v. 9), and therefore wise beyond all telling, brilliant and luminous, seated on the throne of divine fire. If we spend time in prayer with the image of fire, we soon understand its divine symbolism: immaterial though very real, possessing power to consume as well as to comfort, mysterious in origin and intense. The vision also includes the figure of someone in human form "like a son of man" (v. 13). Perhaps as a consequence of the truth of our belief in the incarnation, we understand that our God uses human instruments, even in his final victory over evil. Christians have understood this mysterious figure to be enfleshed in Jesus of Nazareth who on occasion used the title and image to refer to himself. The phrase signaled both profound humanity and final agent of divine victory. His messianic mission, however, was not merely one of political or military triumph, but a complete and definitive embrace of humanity to redeem and transform us. His sovereign victory is eternal (v. 14).

Antiphon (Year I)

Daniel 3

Give glory and eternal praise to him!

The Canticle of Daniel

The responsorial hymn (Dan 3) now moves to include yet another group of creatures of our earth whose voices are invited to join the chorus of praise to God: mountains and hills (v. 75), growing plants (v. 76), springs of water (v. 77), seas and rivers (v. 78), dolphins and water creatures (v. 79), birds of the air (v. 80), and beasts of the field (v. 81). Each is somehow personalized and included in Daniel's cosmic hymn of praise to the majesty of God's glory!

The Refrain

Throughout the entire last week of the liturgical year virtually the same refrain has been used by the Lectionary as a response to the sections of Daniel's hymn. The first four days have used specific verses from the hymn as the refrain (vv. 52, 59), but the final two days offer a combination of words without explicit citation. The liturgical year ends, therefore, with a word of praise that is stretched out beyond human time into eternity.

FIRST READING (YEAR II)

Revelation 20:1-4, 11–21:2

The dead were judged according to their deeds.
I saw a new Jerusalem, coming down out of heaven from God.

Reality of Evil

No matter which may be our symbol of preference, dragon, ancient serpent, devil, or Satan (v. 2), the fact is that evil is real. It is Catholic to know the history of things. Although originally Satan was a watchful spirit and servant of God appointed to patrol the earth in search of wrongdoing (Job 1:6-12), he quickly became considered an opponent in the evolving biblical witness to God's work. From exposing evil, perhaps because of his role in testing Job, somehow he became an individual who was thought to promote evil. This text from Revelation describes evil as tied up and locked in the deepest of prisons (vv. 2-3). This is a clear indication that God is superior and eventually victorious. A reader misunderstands apocalyptic spirituality if he or she merely counts years and seeks a correlation to actual events of human history. The actual historical events surrounding the year AD 1000 gave ample evidence of that mistake! The point is that evil is real, always subordinate to God, even if briefly allowed to enter a final battle against divine forces. The battle serves to reveal the true inner reality of evil, and to demonstrate that evil is vanquished forever. Whatever the heartache or headache in human history, God wins.

Judgment

The final victory of God over all evil includes a review of every human life, executed with fairness, justice, and truth (vv. 4, 12, and 13). Mercy and compassion will find a place in the universal and final judgment because the fullness of truth will demand recognition of the weakness of the human heart and the complexity of all human choices. There is no truth without compassion, and no compassion without truth! God's judgment will include both.

New Jerusalem

This final series of visions, which provide an explanation for the dynamic undercurrent of human history, ends with a new Jerusalem (21:2), a gift not of our own merely human making but from heaven. The dream of God is an entire community of interrelated persons, each serving the common good. Human beings are social by design and destiny. In spite of the radical individualism of our contemporary Western culture (itself eventually to be judged by God), God's plans for us are essentially communal. We are called by baptism to be members of the Mystical Body of Christ and productive citizens in that final future glorious Holy City. Every parish Eucharist is essentially a community, not a gathering of individuals who happen to have decided to show up at the same time! Moreover, the church is the social instrument of God's grace, not simply the occasion for grace. We are communal by origin and destiny.

ANTIPHON (YEAR I)

Revelation 21:3b

Here God lives among his people.

Here God Lives

Curiously, the very next verse (v. 3) from Revelation is used as the antiphon for Psalm 84, which describes the ancient city of Jerusalem with the temple as its center as well as the individual's ardent desire to participate in the worship of that temple (v. 3). God is proclaimed as a stable presence, living at the heart of all ritual activity and prayer, the object of attention and joy for all visitors to the temple and the perennial focus point of life for the resident citizens of the Holy City. God is at the core and center of every current of history, human thought, and ongoing activity!

His People

The refrain reminds us that a city is not the sum total of its buildings nor is it simply defined by its geographical location or climate. It is the people (v. 3) who comprise and define a city, and in this case they belong exclusively to God both by their very created existence and by their subsequent election as God's own people. Once again, the image is fundamentally communal (and ecclesial). We may begin existence as individuals, but we reach our final destiny as members of God's people. As Archbishop Tutu observed, "The totally self-sufficient person is sub-human."*

Friday of the Thirty-Fourth, or Last Week in Ordinary Time

GOSPEL

Luke 21:29-33

When you see these things happening, know that the Kingdom of God is near.

Literary Link

Luke's gospel concludes the eschatological discourse of Jesus (21:5-28) with a teaching from the fig tree (vv. 29-33). The point seems to be the timeliness of his death and the consummation of the world's history. It is a moment of *kairos* when all things converge to require a decisive response!

The Buds of the Fig Tree

The springtime buds of the fig tree or any other plant represent yet another image for the way God works: rising mysterious out of the depth of the plant, unfolding slowly yet purposefully to mark the year's new season, and promising a harvest in due time (v. 29). In the land of Israel olive trees never shed their leaves, but favorite and familiar plants like the fig tree do. Consequently their early springtime buds serve as a perfect illustration for the initial eager springtime anticipation by inhabitants (v. 30). In other climates it may be the magnolia, the lilac, or the maple tree; each serves as the harbinger of spring and the promise of a future harvest. Each budding season signals a new age and looks forward to the purpose of creation, a harvest of righteousness for the common good. In the northern hemisphere the reading occurs not in spring but in the autumn of the year with its beauty and fruitfulness. A different *kairos* may be the experience of those who gather for the morning parish Eucharist this week.

This Generation

The generation alive at the time of Jesus did indeed pass away in its time, but they witnessed the decisive action of God during their lives, that is, the victory of God over sin, evil, ignorance, and death in Christ's death and resurrection. In this sense they were witnesses to everything (v. 32). We summarize that event as "the paschal mystery." It remains the certain signal that the last age has been introduced into human history, that the game was over and that God had won, even if centuries were needed to bring things to their inevitable and clearly visible conclusion. The "this generation" (v. 32) therefore includes all subsequent centuries of human history.

Not Pass Away!

For all believers the eternal nature of Christ's words remains forever (v. 32). Once spoken along the shores of the Sea of Galilee or in the temple courtyards of Jerusalem, his words continue to be effective and life-giving. The spoken human phrases of Christ and the message they communicated were ultimately rooted in the very heart of the mystery of the Trinity. His words were at the very center of the mission of the Word to our frail and fragile human race. They stand at the turning point of human history. Nothing can ever be the same again!

* "The Truth and Reconciliation Process—Restorative Justice" (Third Longford Lecture, Church House, Westminster, February 16, 2004).

Saturday of the Thirty-Fourth, or Last Week in Ordinary Time

First Reading (Year I)

Daniel 7:15-27

Kingship and domain will be given to the holy people of the Most High.

The Fourth Terrible Beast

The explanation of the vision of the last and dreadful beast serves as the Lectionary's dramatic conclusion of the church's liturgical year. The contrast is very clear and strong, namely, between the powerful empire of the Antiochus Epiphanes IV, persecuting Judaism to the death and armed with terrifying military and political strength (vv. 23-25), on the one hand, and the "holy ones of the Most High" (v. 25) who will triumph over all opposition because of the ultimate power of God alone. That king attempted to impose a Hellenistic calendar on the Jews, abolishing their Sabbath under pain of death. He was given three and a half years (v. 25), half of the perfect number of seven, for his evil actions so that the full intent of his designs might be apparent. Then the heavenly court was convened, and the beast of consummate evil was condemned forever. This final vision is written as a message of perennial hope for people who feel completely overpowered by evil forces beyond their control. Even the most desperate of negative circumstances in the lives of God's people cannot and will not be successful!

The Holy Ones

The "holy ones [*qadishim*] of the Most High" (v. 21) are mentioned six times in this passage, and thus become the targeted audience for this message. Though brutally attacked and almost thoroughly beaten, the holy ones are vindicated when the heavenly court convenes and renders final judgment on the world (v. 27). This passage provides a perfect opportunity for further reflection on the true notion of holiness. One might, for example, recall the teaching of the prophet Micah who described what God requires of his people as living with covenantal faithfulness (*hesed*), loving justice, and walking humbly before God (6:8). These are the people beloved by God, whether in the second century BC or in the contemporary world of Catholic parish life. They are holy in the profoundest sense of the word. Although not always primly pious, they remain most beloved. These are the people celebrated by the Catholic Church's annual feast of All Saints (November 1st).

Antiphon (Year I)

Daniel 3

Give glory and eternal praise to him.

The Canticle of Daniel

Today concludes the use of the canticle (Dan 3) as a response to the week's first reading from the book of Daniel. The responsorial hymn ends with a series of different human beings who are invited to join the cosmic hymn of praise for the God of history and creation: human beings (v. 82), Israel (v. 83), priests of the Lord (v. 84), servants of the Lord (v. 85), spirits and souls of the just (v. 86), and holy men/people of humble heart (v. 87). This final litany brings the list of chorus members to an end and completes the full range of those invited to praise God. Praise should ultimately be communal, and only secondarily the work of any individuals.

The Glory of God

One cannot resist concluding with the famous citation from Saint Irenaeus of Lyons: "The glory of God is the human being fully alive!'"* Once again, we need to understand the social character of God's creation and the communal nature of God's plans for the world. The two great commandments of love of God and neighbor find their perfection in this paradigm. The

* *Against Heresies*, 4, 20, 7.

Trinity is both divine Source and divine Destiny for all of creation. It even embraces any future galaxies of existence we may yet discover.

Saturday of the Thirty-Fourth, or Last Week in Ordinary Time

FIRST READING (YEAR II)

Revelation 22:1-7

Night will be no more, for the Lord God shall give them light.

A Final Vision of the Future

The Semitic sense of history presumed a resonance between origin and destiny. For that reason the final state of human society is envisioned as a reprisal of Eden. Based upon the story of the tree of life in Genesis (2:9) and the hope of a wonderfully restored Israel as envisioned by Ezekiel (47:12), the book of Revelation paints a verbal picture of the final joy to which all human beings are invited. Included in God's dream would be life-giving waters (v. 1), abundantly fruitful orchards (v. 2), a personal friendship with God face-to-face (v. 4), and constant light (v. 5). Both material and social creation will be brought into full harmony and perfection! We conclude the church's liturgical year with that picture of God's peace. Everything once again fits together perfectly in *shalom*.

The Throne of God and of the Lamb

At the center of that renewed and complete happiness is the throne shared by God and the Lamb (v. 3) that is the source of unity and the fullness of joy! The holy ones gathered around the throne will see God face-to-face "as he is" (1 John 3:2). The divine name will be written on their foreheads (v. 4) because they belong to God and to God alone. When all is said and done, the eternal presence of God will give life and unity to everything. It is helpful for people at a local parish Eucharist to keep that vision and goal in mind. God's plan is larger than any local community. The reading concludes with a blessing upon those who keep the prophetic message of the book in mind, heart, and action (v. 7).

ANTIPHON (YEAR II)

1 Corinthians 16:22b (Revelation 22:20c)

Marana tha! Come, Lord Jesus!

Psalm 95: A Covenant Renewed

The Jewish Mishnah considered Psalm 95 as an ancient New Year hymn, that is, one recited on the annual festivities that acclaimed the kingship of the Lord (v. 3) and renewed God's covenant relationship with his people (v. 7). It seems most appropriate, therefore, to conclude the liturgical year with a proclamation of God's kingship, which includes all of material creation (v. 4) and which lasts forever.

The Refrain

Among the most popular prayers and liturgical hymns of the early Christian church was the ancient Aramaic acclamation "*Marana tha.*" It is found in its original Aramaic form at the end of Paul's First Letter to the Corinthians (16:22) and in its translated version at the end of the book of Revelation (22:20). As a matter of fact it can mean two different things depending upon how it is transcribed. *Mara natha* means "the Lord has come," and *Marana tha* would be the imperative, "O Lord, come." Its invocation at the very end of the book of Revelation signaled the urgent and ardent desire of that community for the Lord's second coming in glory. Contemporary Christianity has virtually lost the sense of urgent desire for the Lord's return. Forgetting that aspect of our faith, however, is done at our peril. Every daily Eucharist could well conclude with that prayer from the fullness of our hearts and deepest longings of our spirits. With this day's celebration, we now stand at the edge of Advent, which each year celebrates God's coming in history, grace, flesh, and glory.

GOSPEL

Luke 21:34-36

Be vigilant that you may have the strength to escape the tribulations that are imminent.

Literary Link

The Lectionary has chosen to conclude the annual liturgical year with this passage from the end of the Lord's eschatological discourse dealing with vigilance (vv. 33-36). In Luke's gospel this is the last message of Jesus before the beginning of the passion narrative.

Vigilance

The gospel's admonition to attentiveness and vigilance (v. 36; *gregoreite* in Greek, like the Christian name Gregory) comes remarkably close to the Buddhist notion of mindfulness, the virtue of being conscious of all the realities of life around us. We are instructed, however, to be ever focused on the work of God rather than becoming absorbed by our own worries or preoccupied by ourselves. Attentiveness to the God who is at work in every detail of the world's existence is the heart of holiness. We do so not out of fear but out of joyful eagerness for the signs of God working out our salvation and freedom from sin. Only Luke's gospel includes a final expression of hopeful jubilation associated with the end time, namely, the admonition to stand tall and lift up our heads because our redemption is at hand (see 22:28).

The Dangers of Darkness

One of the negative consequences of drunkenness (v. 34) is the dulling of our awareness before the needs of others or the duties that fall upon us as adults in our world. Being alert to the earliest signs of the dawn and to the Lord who comes each day on that first ray of morning light is a mark of Christians, especially those who gathered each weekend in the early church to await the dawn and to celebrate the resurrection anew.

Drunkenness (v. 34) remains a serious matter in our own contemporary society, which struggles over how to deal with this addiction. Its tragedy extends beyond the individual because drunkenness can also claim lives on the highways and destroy families through domestic abuse. Alcohol is a blessing as one of the fruits of the earth and the joyous works of human hands except when it is abused. It can also, however, bring darkness and despair. Hence vigilance in all forms is the Lord's concluding admonition!

Marana tha! Come, Lord Jesus!

Appendix: Sparks for the Preacher*

Prayer before reading Scripture: *Come, Holy Spirit, fill the hearts of your faithful and enkindle in them the fire of your love.*

[S]o you might know that it is not by bread alone that people live, but by all that comes forth from the mouth of the LORD. (*Deuteronomy 8:3*)

But if a prophet presumes to speak a word in my name that I have not commanded, or speaks in the name of other gods, that prophet shall die. (*Deuteronomy 18:20*)

In your statutes I take delight;
I will never forget your word.
(*Psalm 119:16*)

My soul longs for your salvation;
I put my hope in your word.
(*Psalm 119:81*)

Your word is a lamp for my feet,
a light for my path. (*Psalm 119:105*)

"Whoever despises the word must pay for it,
but whoever reveres the command
will be rewarded." (*Proverbs 13:13*)

"Their root shall rot
and their blossom scatter like dust;
For they have rejected the instruction of the LORD of hosts,
and scorned the word of the Holy One of Israel." (*Isaiah 5:24*)

"All flesh is grass,
and all their loyalty like the flower of the field.
The grass withers, the flower wilts,
when the breath of the LORD blows upon it.
Yes, the people is grass!
The grass withers, the flower wilts,
but the word of our God stands forever."
(*Isaiah 40:6-8*)

The Lord GOD has given me
a well-trained tongue,
That I might know how to answer the weary
a word that will waken them. (*Isaiah 50:4*)

Then the LORD said to me: "You have seen well, for I am watching over my word to carry it out." (*Jeremiah 1:12*)

I say I will not mention him,
I will no longer speak in his name.
But then it is as if fire is burning in my heart,
imprisoned in my bones;
I grow weary holding back,
I cannot! (*Jeremiah 20:9*)

Is not my word like fire—oracle of the LORD—
like a hammer shattering rock?
(*Jeremiah 23:29*)

[W]hatever word I speak shall happen without delay. In your days, rebellious house, whatever I speak I will bring about—oracle of the Lord GOD. (*Ezekiel 12:25*)

[T]he word of the LORD came to me:

Son of man, I have appointed you a sentinel for the house of Israel. When you hear a word from my mouth, you shall warn them for me.

If I say to the wicked, You shall surely die—and you do not warn them or speak out to dissuade the wicked from their evil conduct in order to save their lives—then they shall die for their sin, but I will hold you responsible for their blood. (*Ezekiel 3:16-18*)

[W]hoever breaks one of the least of these commandments and teaches others to do so will be called least in the kingdom of heaven. But whoever obeys and teaches these commandments will be called greatest in the kingdom of heaven. (*Matthew 5:19*)

* The following Scripture quotations are taken from the New American Bible, Revised Edition.

Everyone who listens to these words of mine and acts on them will be like a wise man who built his house on rock. (*Matthew 7:24*)

I tell you, on the day of judgment people will render an account for every careless word they speak. (*Matthew 12:36*)

But the seed sown on rich soil is the one who hears the word and understands it, who indeed bears fruit and yields a hundred or sixty or thirtyfold. (*Matthew 13:23*)

Then every scribe who has been instructed in the kingdom of heaven is like the head of a household who brings from his storeroom both the new and the old. (*Matthew 13:52*)

This is the meaning of the parable. The seed is the word of God. (*Luke 8:11*)

In the beginning was the Word,
and the Word was with God,
and the Word was God. (*John 1:1*)

And the Word became flesh
and made his dwelling among us.
(*John 1:14*)

Amen, amen, I say to you, whoever hears my word and believes in the one who sent me has eternal life and will not come to condemnation, but has passed from death to life. (*John 5:24*)

Whoever loves me will keep my word, and my Father will love him, and we will come to him and make our dwelling with him. (*John 14:23*)

Now they know that everything you gave me is from you, because the words you gave to me I have given to them, and they accepted them and truly understood that I came from you, and they have believed that you sent me. (*John 17:7-8*)

I did not at all shrink from telling you what was for your benefit, or from teaching you in public or in your homes. I earnestly bore witness for both Jews and Greeks to repentance before God and to faith in our Lord Jesus. (*Paul's farewell to the elders of Ephesus at Miletus, Acts 20:20-21*)

One who is being instructed in the word should share all good things with his instructor. (*Galatians 6:6*)

[H]aving taken encouragement in the Lord from my imprisonment, dare more than ever to proclaim the word fearlessly. (*Philippians 1:14*)

[A]s you hold on to the word of life, so that my boast for the day of Christ may be that I did not run in vain or labor in vain. (*Philippians 2:16*)

Indeed, the word of God is living and effective, sharper than any two-edged sword, penetrating even between soul and spirit, joints and marrow, and able to discern reflections and thoughts of the heart. (*Hebrews 4:12*)

Be doers of the word and not hearers only, deluding yourselves. For if anyone is a hearer of the word and not a doer, he is like a man who looks at his own face in a mirror. He sees himself, then goes off and promptly forgets what he looked like. (*James 1:22-24*)

The servant of God should listen to the Word of God and salutary doctrine with a ready mind, thirsting for spiritual light; and this disposition he should have without reference to the person of him who may be preaching, or to the simple nature of the things he may utter. In this way he will secure lasting fruit from what he hears, even if he should forget the actual things that were said. And if he has felt weary in listening to pious things, it would be better humbling to blame himself rather than the preacher. Nor should he much care if he perceive certain defects in the preacher's style, provided the truth be spoken. Let him attend to the truth itself, looking on it as coming from its origin and fountain, God, without curiously discussing the nature of the channel through which it has run its course. The mind should be ready to put into practice all useful advice that may be heard or read, as far as is practicable . . .

And indeed if he only reads such things humbly, piously, simply, diligently, and reverently, he will derive immense benefit from them, even if he does not thoroughly understand them. After reading he should give thanks to God, and those things which he has heard or read he should offer to the eternal praise of God in union with the divine love he bears himself. He should reflect on the things he has read, as far as he has an opportunity, and he should beseech God to enable him to guide his life by the things he has read, and through them to make progress in the love of God. (*Venerable Blosius, Abbot of Liessies, France [+1566]*)*

Let no man . . . think or maintain that a man can search too far or be too well studied in the book of God's word, or in the book of God's works . . . but rather let men endeavour an endless progress or proficiency in both. (*Francis Bacon [+1626]; chosen by Charles Darwin as the introductory quotation for the flyleaf of his* Origin of Species *[1859]*)

* Cited in *A Book of Spiritual Instruction*, ed. a Benedictine Nun of Stanbrook Abbey, trans. Bertrand A. Wilberforce, OC (Westminster, MD: Newman Press, 1955).

Index of Readings

Index of Antiphons

FIRE STARTERS

FIRE STARTERS

Igniting the Holy in the Weekday Homily

Richard J. Sklba

LITURGICAL PRESS
Collegeville, Minnesota

www.litpress.org

Cover design by Stefan Killen Design. Cover photo © Thinkstock 2013.

Printed in the United States of America.

1 2 3 4 5 6 7 8 9

Library of Congress Cataloging-in-Publication Data

Sklba, Richard J.
Fire starters : igniting the Holy in the weekday Homily / Richard J. Sklba.
p. cm.
Includes index.
ISBN 978-0-8146-3415-8 — ISBN 978-0-8146-3416-5 (ebook)
1. Catholic Church—Prayers and devotions. 2. Catholic Church. Lectionary for Mass (U.S.) I. Title.

BX2149.2.S55 2012
242'.38—dc23 2012028608